THE ENCYCLOPEDIA OF
PLANTING
COMBINATIONS

THE ULTIMATE VISUAL GUIDE TO SUCCESSFUL PLANT HARMONY

THE ENCYCLOPEDIA OF

PLANTING
COMBINATIONS

TONY LORD   PHOTOGRAPHY BY ANDREW LAWSON

FIREFLY BOOKS

A FIREFLY BOOK

Published by Firefly Books Ltd., 2002

First published in 2003 by Mitchell Beazley, an imprint
of Octopus Publishing Group Ltd, 2–4 Heron Quays, London E14 4JP

First Printing

National Library of Canada Cataloguing in Publication Data
Lord, Tony
      The encyclopedia of planting combinations
Includes index.
ISBN 1–55209–623–8
   1. Plants, Ornamental. 2. Gardens–Design. 3. Color in gardening. 4.
Companion planting. I. Lawson, Andrew II. Title.
SB454.3C64L67 2002   635.9   C2002–900766–6

Publisher Cataloging-in-Publication Data (U.S.)
Lord, Tony
   The encyclopedia of planting combinations: the ultimate visual guide to
successful plant harmony/Tony Lord; photographs by Andrew Lawson. – 1st
ed.
[416]p. : col. ill. : photos. ; cm.
Includes index.
Summary: Guide to 4,000 color and planting schemes including shrubs and
small trees, climbers, roses, perennials, bulbs and annuals.
ISBN 1–55209–623–8
1. Perennials. 2. Planting design. 3. Gardens – Design. I. Title.
635.9/ 32 21   CIP   SB434.L67   2002

Published in Canada in 2002 by
Firefly Books Ltd.
3680 Victoria Park Avenue
Toronto, Ontario M2H 3K1

Published in the United States in 2002 by
Firefly Books (U.S.) Inc.
P.O. Box 1338, Ellicott Station
Buffalo, New York 14205

Art Director **Vivienne Brar**
Project Editors **Michèle Byam, Selina Mumford**
Design **Terry Hirst**
Contributing Editors **Andi Clevely, Polly Boyd,
Lesley Riley, Jo Weeks, Mary Loebig Giles**
North American Consultant **Jennifer Bennett**
Production Controllers **Rachel Stavely, Alix McCulloch**
Picture Researchers **Emily Hedges, Guilia Hetherington**
Indexer **Valerie Chandler, Sue Farr**

Set in Plantin and Frutiger

Printed and bound in China by
Toppan Printing Company Limited

CONTENTS

HOW TO USE THIS BOOK	6
HARDINESS ZONES	8
THE ART OF COMBINING PLANTS	10
Assessing the site	12
Choosing plants	13
Form and texture	14
Color in the garden	16
Planting borders	18
SHRUBS AND SMALL TREES	22
Rhododendrons	80
CLIMBERS	100
Clematis	106
ROSES	132
Climbers & Ramblers	138
Old shrub roses	146
Larger species and larger modern Shrub roses	152
Hybrid Teas & Floribundas	162
Smaller species & smaller modern Shrub roses	168
Ground Cover roses	170
PERENNIALS	172
Geraniums	224
Hostas	242
Irises	248
BULBS	294
Tulips	342
ANNUALS	358
Dahlias	370
COMMON PLANT NAMES	408
INDEX	410
ACKNOWLEDGMENTS	416

How to use this book

This book is not meant to be a series of recipes for perfect planting but rather a menu of suggestions from which readers can choose or reject, revise or augment combinations to suit their own tastes and conditions. Some combinations here are bright to the point of garishness, others delicate to the point of blandness, depending on one's own viewpoint. As the book does not discuss the culture, propagation, or a wide range of plant varieties in the detail found in a planting encyclopedia, such a work would be invaluable used in conjunction with this book, both to supply such detail, and to show similar but different varieties that could be used to refine combinations suggested here, or to rework them in different colors.

FEATURE SPREADS

Seven genera from chapters throughout the book are selected as feature spreads because of their importance and usefulness in creating plant combinations. Each embraces many species and cultivars, giving variety of color and/or form, and thus versatility. Introductory text discusses aspects of culture and garden use common to the whole genus.

CAPTIONS

Captions give detailed information on the color and form of the plants shown in combination, with prominence given to the featured plant. They also give suggestions for varying the planting schemes.

RUNNING HEADS

On the left, the page number, chapter title, and name of the first plant covered are given; opposite, the plant named in the running head is the last entry on that page.

PLANT PORTRAITS

These are chosen to show the featured plant in an effective combination, whether a harmony or a contrast, with one or more other plants. A second photograph is sometimes used, for instance, if there is more than one season of interest, or to show both a harmony and a contrast.

PLANT COMBINATIONS

At the end of each plant entry this symbol indicates further suggestions for effective planting partners. A plant name, followed by a page number and a letter (A, B, etc.), denotes an illustrated entry elsewhere in the book, showing the featured plant in a successful combination. Where only a page number and a letter are given, following the symbol ⨆, this denotes a photograph in which the featured plant appears but not as one of the main players of the planting scheme.

PLANT ENTRY HEADINGS

The full botanical name of the featured plant is given for each plant. The genus is followed by the species and, where appropriate, the variety.

INDIVIDUAL PLANT ENTRY

An analysis of the characteristics of the featured plant, mentioning also any unusual cultural requirements, leads to discussion of combinations that could be created with plants suited to the same conditions and, in the case of floral effects, having the same flowering season.

---

64 SHRUBS AND SMALL TREES – *Lavandula angustifolia* 'Hidcote'

Lavandula angustifolia 'Hidcote' makes a telling contrast with gold-variegated sage (*Salvia officinalis* 'Icterina'), a popular combination both visually and for its fragrance. The partnership is useful equally in a herb garden, at the front of a border, or alongside a path, where passers-by will brush against the plants, releasing their aromatic scent.

The silvery foliage of *Lavandula lanata* is perhaps never more effective than when set against rich blue *Ceanothus* 'Puget Blue', which grows with branches down to ground level, is a perfect companion in a sunny border backed by a wall.

Lavandula angustifolia 'Hidcote' ♀

L. angustifolia, an evergreen Mediterranean sub-shrub 15–90cm (6–36in) tall, has greyish leaves and flowers in pale to deep lavender, occasionally white or mauve-pink. 'Hidcote' is a richly colored dwarf cultivar, suitable for use at the front of a border, or for edging or a dwarf hedge. The true cultivar is difficult to obtain and is propagated by cuttings; seed-raised plants are more common, but tend to be variable and often lack the rich color of 'Hidcote'. It associates with mauve, pink, purple, or blue, and with purple or silver foliage, and contrasts well with yellow-green foliage and flowers. Like all lavenders, it can become leggy and die in patches unless pruned annually in early to mid-spring, although some gardeners prefer to prune as the blooms fade. Plants can be sheared over, removing most of the previous year's growth and maintaining a natural mounded form.

⚬ *Anthemis* Susanna Mitchell, *A. tinctoria* 'E.C. Buxton', *Cistus* 'Grayswood Pink', *Convolvulus cneorum*, *Dianthus* 'Haytor White', *Sedum* 'Vera Jameson'

H: 60cm (24in) **S: 75cm** (30in)
❋ Mid- to late summer
▭▭▭ ◌-◌◌ ▭-▭ **Z6 pH5.5–7.5**

Lavandula lanata ♀

The appeal of this lavender lies both in its purple flowers and in the broad, intensely silver foliage, which looks attractive at any time of year. A little more demanding than *L. angustifolia* cultivars (above), it requires good drainage, full sun, and freedom from winter damp. It is a superlative shrub for the front of a border, especially with grey-leaved plants or cool-colored flowers, and an asset in rock or gravel gardens, where it may be combined with other Mediterranean plants such as cistus, helianthemums, halimiums, and phlomis. It harmonizes well with yellow-green foliage and flowers, and contrasts with yellow flowers. Mid-spring is the best time to prune, to avoid fungal disease.

⚬ *Anthemis punctata* subsp. *cupaniana*, *Artemisia schmidtiana*, *Halimium* 'Susan', *Phlomis chrysophylla*, *Salvia chamaedryoides*, *S. officinalis* 'Purpurascens'

H: 75cm (30in) **S: 90cm** (36in) ❋ Late summer
▭▭▭ ◌ ▭ **Z7 pH5.5–7.5**

Lavandula stoechas subsp. *pedunculata* combines agreeably with many alliums, whose round flower heads provide a contrast of form, while their colors are usually harmonious. In this informal patchwork of plants that are suited to Mediterranean conditions, the dying leaves of *Allium cristophii* are hidden by young shoots of gypsophila, with chives (*Allium schoenoprasum*) in the foreground.

Lavandula stoechas subsp. *pedunculata* ♀

The flowers of this deep purple lavender, almost black and scarcely visible except at close range, sport a showy topknot of mauve bracts. The flower heads are born on long stems and are held well above the greyish evergreen foliage, unlike those of French lavender (*L. stoechas*), which have short stalks and less conspicuous bracts. The mauve coloring, useful for echoing similar tints in plants such as alliums, pinks, and cranesbills, combines well with cool shades such as lilac or lavender and with carmine, crimson, or rich purple. Attractive when partnered with silver or glaucous foliage, or with plants such as cistus and other lavenders, it is excellent for the front of a border or in gravel. 'James Compton' has particularly showy bracts.

⚬ *Cistus* 'Grayswood Pink', *Crambe cordifolia*, *Dianthus* 'Becky Robinson', *D.* 'Musgrave's Pink', *Helianthemum* 'Wisley White', *Rosa* Pink Flower Carpet

H & S: 60cm (24in)
❋ Late spring to early summer
▭▭▭ ◌ ▭ **Z8 pH5.5–7.5**

Lavatera 'Barnsley' ♀

This floriferous, long-flowering, deciduous sub-shrub produces long annual stems from a woody base. It rapidly develops into a medium to large shrub, valuable for quickly filling gaps in a border, where it blends with cool colors and purple, silver, or glaucous foliage, and makes an excellent partner for old roses or a backdrop of clematis. Its slightly amorphous habit is best combined with architectural plants, or those with flower spikes or plates or other equally contrasting floral forms. 'Barnsley' may be pruned back to a basal framework of branches in mid-spring, but in cold climates, frost can cut growth to below ground level. As long as they are not severely frosted, plants will regenerate

LIGHT LEVELS

This symbol indicates the full range of light levels and the featured plant's preferred part of this range. See Key to Symbols.

SOIL WATER CONTENT

This symbol shows the plant's preferred soil water content. See Key to Symbols.

FLOWERING SEASON

This symbol indicates the plant's typical flowering season. Where the season appears in parentheses, the flowers are insignificant, or not the plant's main feature. See Key to Symbols.

PHOTOGRAPHIC CROSS-REFERENCES

The letter here will be found in cross-references from plant combinations given under featured plants elsewhere in the book.

Clematis

THE GENUS *CLEMATIS* is immensely diverse, with flowers, from large to tiny, of almost every color except pure blue, always presented with poise and elegance. Most are moderately vigorous and easy to keep in balance with other plants, producing slender stems that can drape themselves over or through their neighbors without suppressing them. Along with roses, they are the most useful climbers in association with other plants. Yet clematis are often grown in isolation, without any attempt to allow them to interact with their companions. It is true that the most vigorous sorts – like *Clematis montana* var. *rubens* – create such large areas of color that any interaction is apparent only around the fringes of the plant; and on pillar or obelisk, a single clematis of

Above: Summer-flowering Jackmanii and Viticella clematis (purple: C. Jackmanii Superba; crimson 'Ville de Lyon', and pink 'Comtesse de Bouchaud') mingle harmoniously here against a dry stone wall.

Left: Combining clematis of different flower sizes and distinct colors can add sparkle, as here with red Texensis 'Gravetye Beauty', soft lavender Jackmanii 'Perle d'Azur', and white Viticella 'Huldine'.

Alpina Group cultivars and *C. montana*) are pruned after flowering, while large- or later small-flowered cultivars are pruned in late winter or early spring. Regularly tying in new shoots, ideally at least once every two weeks, helps to spread out the stems for maximum floral display and prevents kinking and clematis wilt disease. If the rootball is set 8cm (3in) or so below the soil surface, the plant will usually regrow after an attack by wilt. Mildew can be a problem for groups such as Jackmanii, Texensis, and some Viticellas, particularly if grown on a wall. Bare stems at the base of the clematis are best hidden by other plants, casting the roots into the shade they prefer.

Clematis 'Alba Luxurians' ♀

From mid-summer onwards, C. 'Alba Luxurians' produces flowers of the purest white, its sepals often having a leafy green tip and/or central section. These are not shed as the flowers age but wither and turn brown, although this does not usually disfigure the plant. As with its parent *C. viticella*, some of its flowers nod gracefully downwards: the reverse of the flower is not such a pure white, but the plant is still attractive if grown across the ground. A vigorous grower, the plant can smother smaller shrubs and ground covers; if used with these, some thinning of its shoots might be needed. It combines well with pink, mauve, blue, or soft yellow flowers and looks pleasing when grown through gold foliage. Gentle harmonies with silver-leaved shrubs are also possible, although the overall color tones of clematis and shrubs are often so similar that such combinations are best seen at close range. It flowers well in areas where summers are hot, but in cooler regions it may not be so floriferous unless given the sunniest position. Like all other members of the Viticella Group, this clematis should be pruned hard in early spring.

● *Buddleja* 'Lochinch', *R.* 'Pink Delight', *Ceanothus × delileanus* 'Gloire de Versailles', *Clematis* 'Prince Charles', *Hippophae rhamnoides* p.58 **A**, *Prunus spinosa* 'Purpurea', *Salix elaeagnos* subsp. *angustifolia*

H: 4m (13ft) ☀ **Mid-summer to early autumn**
◊◊ ▣ Z5 pH5–8

Clematis 'Alba Luxurians' scrambles among pretty blue periwinkle (*Vinca major*) and arching white *Lysimachia clethroides*, with spiky-leaved *Astelia chathamica* behind.

Clematis alpina ♀

C. *alpina* and the other species and hybrids of the Alpina Group, including *C. macropetala* (p.113), usually have nodding blue flowers, with white petal-like staminodes at the center, although many mauve-pink, light purplish red, purple, and white variants also occur. The single, bell-shaped blooms of *C. alpina* have a charming simplicity, while those of *C. macropetala* variants and hybrids are more showy, with numerous sepals making them appear double, and staminodes extending beyond these. All clematis alpina produce their flowers in spring, and tend to carry a few more later in the year.

The best blue cultivars are bright enough to stand up to combinations with yellow flowers or foliage, particularly soft, light lemons such as in *Forsythia suspensa* f. *atrocaulis*. However, clematis alpina do not usually bloom profusely enough for really showy display. Nor are pinkish, purplish, or most white cultivars sufficiently pure for shining color combinations – although the best whites, *C.a.* 'White Columbine' ♀ and subsp. *sibirica* 'White Moth', are excellent with the blue of early ceanothus or the rich

The soft, light purplish red of *Clematis alpina* 'Ruby' creates a subdued harmony with the unfurling leaves of weeping silver willow-leaf (*Pyrus salicifolia* 'Pendula'). A combination with any strong color would have overwhelmed the delicate tints of the clematis.

pink of the better *Ribes sanguineum* cultivars. The repeat-flowering white subsp. *sibirica* 'Riga' is sweetly scented, as are other Alpina cultivars, such as 'Columella' and 'Propertius'.

Alpina Group clematis do not need regular pruning unless intertwined with another plant, when pruning will help keep the two in balance, and prevent the buildup of a "nest" of dead clematis stems, which may cause the death of sections of the supporting shrub. Stems that have bloomed should be cut out immediately after flowering.

● **Blue:** *Amelanchier lamarckii*, *Chaenomeles × superba* 'Issai White', *Philadelphus coronarius* 'Aureus', *Prunus glandulosa* 'Alba Plena', *Ribes sanguineum* 'Tydeman's White', *Rosa primula*, *Viburnum opulus* 'Roseum'. **Pink/Ruby:** *Berberis thunbergii* 'Rose Glow', *Exochorda × macrantha* 'The Bride', *Malus × zumi* 'Golden Hornet' p.68 **C**. **White:** *Chaenomeles × superba* 'Pink Lady', *Ribes sanguineum* p.86 **B**, *R.s.* 'Porky Pink', *Rosa xanthina*

H: 3m (10ft) ☀ **Mid- to late spring**
◊◊ ▣ Z5 pH5–8

---

s, although they do then tend ... e original clone, the deeper ... a'. Protecting the base of the ... e winter usually averts this ... pare plants can very easily be ... uttings.

... *mmarum* 'Bicolor', *Buddleja davidii* ... *istus × argenteus* 'Blushing Peggy ... *ha* 'Gerrie Hoek' p.372 **B**, *Hebe* ... auty', *Romneya californica*, *Rosa* Iceberg, ... ray 'Hewitt's Double' ... J p.178 **A**

☀ **Early to late summer**
◊◊ ▣ Z8 pH5.5–7.5

... ch as *C.* 'Perle d'Azur' make an ideal ... *atera* 'Barnsley'. Planted nearby, the odd ... perhaps a Jackmanii, Viticella, or Texensis ... ue, crimson, or sumptuous burgundy, can ... ve itself through the lavatera

With identically shaped foliage in dramatically contrasting colors, *Ligustrum ovalifolium* 'Aureum' and *Prunus × cistena* make a striking combination. Pruning will keep both at comparable size, even to below 1m (3½ft), allowing this partnership to be used in the smallest gardens.

Ligustrum ovalifolium 'Aureum' ♀

GOLDEN CALIFORNIA PRIVET

The foliage of this bright deciduous shrub can vary between uniform yellow-green and green with a yellow-green margin. If left unpruned, it makes a rather shapeless bush, whereas pruning in late winter or early spring to a framework of branches or a column stimulates long sprays of more definite form. In full sun its color approaches yellow, which is especially useful for mixing with hot yellows or oranges and red foliage or flowers, and with blue flowers such as delphiniums. The foliage is less markedly yellow in shade, but very attractive with sulfur-yellow or cream flowers. Plants can be used as specimens or as a repeated accent along a border, and make excellent hedges, both on their own and with other colored-foliage shrubs. They are valuable hosts for climbers whose flowers contrast or harmonize with the creamy white panicles of the privet – a blue clematis or cream honeysuckle, for example.

● *Achillea* 'Lucky Break', *Clematis macropetala* p.113 **A**, *Delphinium* 'Butterball', *D.* 'Fenella', *Hemerocallis* 'Golden Chimes', *Kniphofia* 'Sunningdale Yellow', *Miscanthus sinensis* 'Strictus', *Phlomis russeliana*, *Rosa* Graham Thomas, *Tithonia rotundifolia*

H & S: 3m (10ft) ☀ **Mid-summer**
◊◊ ▣ Z6 pH5–7.5

AWARD OF GARDEN MERIT

This symbol is for those plants that have the Royal Horticultural Society's Award of Garden Merit because of their outstanding excellence and easy culture.

HEIGHT AND SPREAD

This symbol indicates the approximate height and spread of each feature plant. See Key to Symbols.

SOIL CONDITIONS

These symbols indicate the plant's preferred soil conditions. In this example, the preferred soil is either light, well-drained conditions or medium conditions. See Key to Symbols.

HARDINESS ZONES

This symbol shows the hardiness zone for each featured plant, while the pH indicates the level of soil acidity or alkalinity the plant will tolerate. See Key to Symbols.

COMMON NAME

The plant's common name, if it has one, follows the botanical name and is given in small capitals, with large capitals for those letters that are conventionally always capitalized, e.g. MADONNA LILY, SIBERIAN SQUILL.

KEY TO SYMBOLS

These indicate the main characteristics of the plant and its cultural requirements.

H&S	✿	▣	◊◊◊	▢▢	Z3 pH

| These are given at reasonable maturity, although shrubs and small trees can exceed stated figures in old age or hot climates. For tender perennials used for summer bedding or containers, they represent the dimensions reached by a plant over-wintered from cuttings taken the previous year. | The flower symbol indicates the typical flowering season, and can vary a little from that stated, especially in extreme climates. Accurate matching of flowering season is essential for successful combined floral effect, and can be judged from plants that flower together in your own locality. | The colored bar represents the full range of light levels from full, day-long sun on the left, via partial-shade to dense leaf-canopy shade on the right. The white and black bar beneath represents the featured plant's preferred part of this range (black) and the part of the range it will tolerate (white). | The raindrop symbols show the plant's preferred soil water content. One raindrop indicates dry conditions; two raindrops, soil that is always moist, never waterlogged, or dry; while three indicates plenty of moisture throughout the year, suited, for example, to marginal (waterside) plants. | The colored squares show the plant's preferred soil conditions. From left to right, these are: light, well-drained, e.g. chalky or sandy; medium with adequate drainage, e.g. silty loam; heavy soil, usually based on clay; humus-rich, for instance, peaty soils or leaf mold, preferred by e.g. ericaceous plants. | The hardiness zone on the left is explained on pp.8–9. The pH range shows the soil acidity or alkalinity the plant will tolerate, pH7 being neutral, lower values acidic, and higher ones alkaline. Acid-loving species, such as rhododendrons, generally prefer pH6.5 or below. |

Hardiness zones

The hardiness zone for each plant according to the system devised by the United States Department of Agriculture (USDA) is given towards the end of each entry. The letter 'Z' is followed by a number relating to the minimum winter temperature a plant will tolerate according to the chart below. Comparing this with a zoned map of average winter minimum temperatures gives a helpful indication of where the plant should survive the winter without protection. However, zones can only be a rough guide. The hardiness of a plant depends on a great many factors, including the depth of its roots, its water content at the onset of frost, the duration of cold weather, and, especially for evergreens, the force of the wind. For woody plants, hardiness can depend on light- and heat-induced summer ripening of the wood; where

ZONES AND TEMPERATURE RANGES
FOR NORTH AMERICA AND EUROPE

ZONE 1	below −50°F (−46°C)
ZONE 2	−50° to −40°F (−46 to −40°C)
ZONE 3	−40° to −30°F (−40.0 to −34.5°C)
ZONE 4	−30° to −20°F (−34 to −29°C)
ZONE 5	−20° to −10°F (−29 to −23°C)
ZONE 6	−10° to 0°F (−23 to −18°C)
ZONE 7	0° to 10°F (−18 to −12°C)
ZONE 8	10° to 20°F (−12 to −7°C)
ZONE 9	20° to 30°F (−7 to −1°C)
ZONE 10	30° to 40°F (−1 to 4°C)
ZONE 11	above 40°F (above 4°C)

summers are hot and long, trees and shrubs can often withstand colder winter temperatures. The zone ratings also assume that the plants have no winter protection; a blanket of snow could insulate them, allowing them to grow in colder climates than their hardiness ratings suggest. In addition, it is not uncommon for, say, a Zone 8 area, such as northern Florida, to experience a Zone 7 winter, and Zone 6 winters occur perhaps every 10–30 years. Inevitably, severe winters kill some plants but this then gives opportunities for new combinations.

Within each zone and even within every garden, there are likely to be areas that are especially sheltered or unusually exposed, where the effective zone rating is one more or less than the maps suggest. Using sheltered areas, such as sunny walls or slopes, for plants that need one zone warmer than the local norm can extend the range of plants that will survive and hence increase the possible combinations.

Zone ratings are allocated to plants according to their tolerance of winter cold in cool temperate areas (latitudes 50–60°). In climates with hotter and/or drier summers, as in Australia, central America, and North Island, New Zealand, some plants will survive colder temperatures: their hardiness in these countries will occasionally be one or, rarely, two zones lower than that quoted. Because Australasia is, on average, hotter than North America, an alternative system, shown below, is used there, with seven zones covering the range of average winter minimum temperatures experienced throughout the continent.

ZONES AND TEMPERATURE RANGES
FOR AUSTRALIA AND NEW ZEALAND

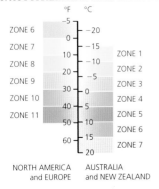

	°F	°C	
ZONE 6	-5	-20	
ZONE 7	0	-15	ZONE 1
ZONE 8	10	-10	ZONE 2
ZONE 9	20	-5	ZONE 3
ZONE 10	30	0	ZONE 4
ZONE 11	40	5	ZONE 5
	50	10	ZONE 6
	60	15	ZONE 7
		20	

NORTH AMERICA   AUSTRALIA
and EUROPE   and NEW ZEALAND

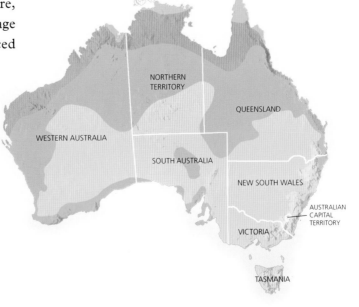

THE ART OF COMBINING PLANTS

FOR MOST PEOPLE a garden's beauty comes from the plants that it contains, the way they work together, and the overall effect they produce. A successful garden also fits comfortably in its surroundings but has its own distinctive character.

Assessing the site

MAKING A SUCCESSFUL GARDEN is a question of balancing what is already there with what is required of the plot. Most gardens take several years to create and there are bound to be mistakes along the way; however, careful planning can greatly accelerate the emergence of something satisfying.

In the first place, analysis of the site – its structures, existing planting, soil, and climate – is important. Taking aspect and microclimates into consideration will ensure that suitable plants are selected for each part of the garden. Where buildings cast shade for most of the day, the growing conditions will be cool and damp, while walls or fences that face the sun will have dry, warm soil at their feet. Even on a small scale, high ground will be drier than its surroundings, and hollows wetter. Under trees the soil will be shaded and full of roots, making it dry and low in nutrients. Aspect can be important in unexpected ways: many flowers, especially daisy-like ones, face towards the sun, so they should be planted with care, otherwise only their backs will be visible.

Many gardeners start with a simple framework. Here, it is a lawn that stretches the length of the plot and has straight edges and flanking borders which, although planted with a variety of shrubs and herbaceous perennials, look uniform and uninteresting. Only the bench at the far end invites the viewer to enter the garden and explore.

This is the same garden as above, in early summer five years later. Reshaped so that plants spill onto the lawn or hide in discrete bays, the borders have also been filled generously with evergreen and deciduous shrubs and herbaceous plants that offer a livelier structure and more interesting contrasts in shape, the planting exploiting foliage form and texture as well as using flower color.

It is vital to take time before making any lasting decisions. For example, the first impression of an old apple tree may be that it fills valuable space with useless branches. With careful pruning, however, it could frame a view, provide welcome shade, and retain the garden's sense of maturity, as well as yield apples again. Alternatively, a suitable companion plant, such as a clematis or Rambler rose, might revive its beauty in a different way. Time will also give seasonal plants a chance to show and may reveal patches of invasive weeds that need to be dealt with.

It is useful to look beyond the garden's boundaries. This will indicate what plants thrive in local conditions (a soil-testing kit will confirm the nature of the soil) and may reveal views that could be emphasized through structures such as paths, trellis, or pergolas, or by careful positioning of trees and shrubs.

Right: Seasonal planting can be used to augment the main display that will be provided later by permanent herbaceous perennials. Their promise is heralded here by the brilliant color of tulips such as 'Black Swan' and 'Gold Medal'.

Below: In this hard-working and highly effective combination of perennials, in which *Achillea* 'Moonshine', *Sisyrinchium striatum*, *Santolina pinnata* subsp. *neapolitana*, and *Lavandula angustifolia* 'Hidcote' contribute harmonious variations in form to produce a satisfying composition of slender foliage and light airy flowers.

Choosing plants

Once any hard landscaping is in place, selection of the plants can begin. An important first consideration is the overall effect required: bright and cheerful or cool and restrained, neat and tidy or informal and naturalistic are just some options. It also makes sense to match the

selection to the energy of the person who is to tend it: a keen gardener may enjoy some more challenging plants, whereas someone who likes to relax outdoors would probably prefer low-maintenance varieties.

To ensure a wide and effective choice, it is helpful to make lists of plants that look good together and are suitable for the various sites around the garden. This book provides plenty of ideas for plant associations; gardens – whether open to the public or privately owned – are also a good source of inspiration. It is worth noting information such as height, season, color, and other useful characteristics, so when a particular combination of features is required, a selection of suitable candidates is readily accessible.

When planning an entire garden, structural plants – trees, major shrubs, and hedges – and those required for specific purposes – screens or windbreaks – should be decided on first. These will establish the overall character of the site and provide its basic structure. For an individual border, it is the taller plants, the chief focal points, and any major tone-setters that should top the agenda.

Flowers are important, but foliage, with its variations in form and texture, makes an invaluable contribution and should always be taken into account. Planting lists should include a reasonable proportion of evergreens of all

types and sizes according to climate; even in predominantly herbaceous borders, strategically sited groups of bergenias and liriopes, winter-green plants such as arums and cyclamens, and small shrubs such as daphnes might provide color during the winter months. In addition, it makes sense to combine plants of different growth habits. Carpeting the ground beneath a deciduous shrub with bulbs, for example, will produce at least two seasons of interest, and the permanence of the shrub will accentuate the fleeting charm of the bulb flowers. Similar long-lasting displays can be achieved with climbers grown through shrubs, or roses planted with herbaceous perennials.

Scale is also an important consideration. A huge shrub in a small garden can be oppressive, while numerous small plants in a large area will make it seem flat and desolate. However, in any garden it is necessary to have changes in size to provide excitement. A tiny plot filled with miniatures will serve only to emphasize the garden's smallness. The inclusion of a towering bamboo, a tall grass, or a giant gunnera will draw attention away from the tight confines.

Form and texture

In making successful plant combinations, it is vital to consider the plant as a whole – its form and texture – taking into account the stems and foliage, as well as the flowers. With most plants, the form and texture are the most durable attributes, so a planting arrangement that makes good use of these qualities will be much more satisfying than one based solely on flowers.

Plants of softly rounded form are gentle in their effect and make excellent companions for extravagant focal points or other visually demanding specimens. Whether they are billowing conifers, lax Shrub roses, or spherical hebes, rounded plants are ideal for associating with each other and for blending into masses for shelter or as a solid backdrop.

Vertical plants are often used as focal points. One tall and thin plant, such as a spiky yucca, draws the eye to it, perhaps emphasizing a long vista; two upright plants draw attention to the space between them, and are invaluable for framing a view. Combinations of upright plants and spreading or rounded ones can be very appealing, especially where color and texture is also taken into account. For example, a group of foxgloves would be perfectly complemented by mound-forming cranesbills beneath.

Shrubs and trees of strongly horizontal growth, such as *Cornus controversa* 'Variegata', require space to display their beauty. However, herbaceous perennials with horizontal forms provide useful architectural weight in a crowded setting. For example, the flattened flower heads of some of the achilleas are very effective among less formal shapes in mixed borders.

Grasses have outstanding design potential, whether as focal points and in intimate contrasting partnerships or, as here in the Royal Botanical Gardens, Kew, as a lively and extended community of species and cultivars – all of similar form and growth habit but with infinite subtle variations in color and texture.

In Christopher Lloyd's garden at Great Dixter, England, the Long Border is planted with visually arresting plants such as heleniums, crocosmias, nicotianas, and Lacecap hydrangeas, demonstrating that bold flourishes and extravagant combinations can be very effective on a large scale.

upright yew, their colors as well as their forms creating an attractive contrast.

A plant's texture is determined by the scale of its parts, usually its leaves and flowers. A large entire glossy yellow-green leaf is coarser in effect than a small matt blue-green one. For example, an ash tree has a fine appearance because of its small grey-green leaflets while, with its large glossy leaves, a low-growing bergenia seems much tougher. The same principle applies to flowers, but the form of the inflorescence also plays a part. Although the individual flowers of a kniphofia are small, the spiky flower head has a strong presence, as does the rounded globe of tiny allium flowers.

Many planting displays can be lifted out of the ordinary by careful positioning of textures. For example, *Lonicera nitida* 'Baggesen's Gold' has tiny bright leaves that provide a gentle but contrasting background for a large-flowered clematis; a small-flowered climber or shrub would simply appear fussy with the lonicera.

Like those with a rounded habit, weeping or arching plants are useful for softening strong foliage shapes or rigidly upright habits. Grasses with fountain-like leaves make good partners for hostas or rodgersias, while the flowing branches of a Japanese maple can be stunning beside an

In the old rose garden at Great Dixter, England, the roses have been replaced with more striking plants. Here, foliage and flowers including bananas, cannas, *Verbena bonariensis*, and dahlias are juxtaposed with apparent disregard for compatability, producing a dramatic landscape of extremes in exotic, almost tropical profusion.

Color in the garden

As with all other aspects of garden design, color choice is very personal. A riot of different shades, a serene scene of white or blue, or simply a variety of greens – all these are acceptable if the gardener likes them. It is worth remembering that harmonious color combinations will be more permanently satisfying than contrasting ones, which quickly lose their impact. However, too much harmony would become bland, so some points of contrasting color in any planting are useful to enliven the scene.

The relationship between colors is often described using the color wheel. This is divided into six main segments in which the primary colors (red, yellow, and blue) alternate with the secondary colors (orange, green, and purple). Orange is a combination of red and yellow so is positioned between them. For the same reason, green is between yellow and blue, and purple between red and blue. The spectrum is increased by variations in the amounts of each primary color in each secondary color. For example, brick-red contains more red than yellow, and lime green contains more yellow than blue.

The color wheel is helpful in garden design in that it indicates the effect a combination of colors might produce. For example, unrelated colors, such as yellow and purple or orange and blue, contrast most strongly with each other, while related colors, such as yellow and orange or red and purple, are more harmonious. However, in gardens the fact that colors are never seen in isolation complicates the theory: flowers, which are rarely a single color themselves, invariably have a background of foliage, which can be various shades of green, grey, bronze, purple, yellow, or a combination. Despite this, it is still possible to predict that some color mixtures will be gentle and unchallenging, while others will be exciting or dazzling. Pinks, lavender-blues, and similar soft colors are relaxing. Blue with pink, particularly soft tones of both, is normally a safe choice, producing gentle, cool combinations – roses in

Cool shades such as pink, mauve, and lilac combine here to give a relaxed and informal effect that has sufficient variety to avoid blandness.

warm pink with mauve clematis, for instance. Reds, oranges, and strong yellows (the "hot" colors) are exciting, so when they are combined the effect is exhilarating – red roses paired with orange crocosmias or scarlet tulips paired with orange wallflowers, for example. The majority of reds have impact when grouped with most other colors, but particularly with deep greens, bronze, and blues – scarlet poppies with blue

In the famous White Garden in Vita Sackville-West's Sissinghurst, the background of green or silver foliage enhances rather than challenges the predominantly white or near-white display.

delphiniums, for example, can be quite startling. Although invigorating, this type of contrast should be used with care. If the required effect is of a woodland glade, then the choice of shrubs such as rhododendrons should be restricted mainly to those in cooler colors, with just a few brighter hues interspersed; many of the azaleas are best left out of such an arrangement as they cover themselves too thickly with flowers, making strong, solid blankets of color, which do not suit such naturalistic planting.

The strength of the colors involved will influence the effect of a grouping. For example, soft yellow with almost any shade of blue, such as wild primroses with muscaris or hyacinths, will be soothing, but if the yellow is stronger, a golden yellow goldenrod with a blue or purple heliotrope, for instance, the overall result is much more demanding.

Most colors containing some white – soft silvers or creamy shades – or those with warming tones – blood-red, salmon, apricot, or peach – can be used to tone down a number of stronger colors, although the flowers or foliage concerned need a pronounced form to avoid losing their identity. A butter-yellow rose can hold its own against red valerian because the rose has a more defined flower than the valerian, while the loose beige-brown flower heads of a tall grass will mitigate any heavy effect created by, say, orange-red gallardias, but its stature ensures it is in no danger of being overwhelmed.

White is interesting in gardens. In carefully chosen situations, flowers and foliage in chalky white and grey – silvery elaeagnus, variegated grasses, or white-flowered campion – create Mediterranean warmth, while translucent greenish white blooms among light or bright green foliage will provide a sense of a cool woodland area – pale hellebores or white foxgloves with ferns and hostas, for instance. In a "white garden" the effect of the many tones of white can be magical, but in mixed plantings it needs to be used in moderation to avoid overpowering any more subdued or softer colors. Conversely, white should not be

peppered about in small groups as it draws too much attention to itself. In combination with hot colors, white is useful in emphasizing the richness of red, and brightening yellows and oranges. It is also good for injecting sparkle into combinations of more muted shades. For example, two clematis in rich red and lavender-blue benefit from the addition of a white companion to brighten their luxurious effect. Without the white, they would be in danger of receding into the background.

Once the garden is planted, it is beneficial to watch the varying distribution of color throughout the year – the best effects are achieved where plants that flower over a similar period are grouped together, rather than sprinkled all over the garden. This ensures that the strong areas of color and interesting combinations will draw the eye to them, while non-flowering areas will merge into a fine green backdrop. When flowers are scattered, the surrounding non-performers dilute their effect.

Right: Hot colors such as red, orange, and bright yellow light up a border when used in isolation or can be assembled with stimulating results in a color-themed planting. Here, the fiery shades of crocosmias are combined with a glowing background of purple foliage and rich red clematis in an incandescent display.

Planting borders

Before putting any plants into the garden, it is a good idea to make some sort of planting plan. This can be detailed or just an overall aim, and it can be adapted as ideas change or plants different from those originally envisaged are chosen, but it will provide a sound basis from which to lay out a border. It is much easier to alter planting plans than to move plants around once they are in the soil.

Thorough preparation of the ground is necessary for a successful and healthy display. All plants will make a better start if the soil is deeply dug, and plenty of manure, compost, or other organic material is incorporated. Where shrubs or trees are to be planted at wide intervals, it is more sensible and less time-consuming to prepare individual planting holes; whole beds or sections of beds for replanting are best fully dug over. Existing plants that are to be retained in the new design can be left in place, or dug up and divided before replanting to give

them a new lease of life. The main aim of such cultivation is to enable new plants, fresh from luxurious conditions in the nursery, to adapt quickly to the hard life in the garden. The addition of organic material will enrich the soil without providing too many nutrients; it will also improve its moisture-retaining properties as well as the drainage of water, and help to ensure that air reaches plant roots, which will avoid stagnation and encourage growth.

Although expert advice stresses the importance of eradicating perennial weeds before planting, no one admits that this is virtually impossible. Nettles, docks, and many other tough weeds may be dug out without too much difficulty. Dandelions and thistles are more persistent but can be eliminated in time. The great villains are couch grass, bindweed, and goutweed. The easiest way to deal with them is to spray with a suitable herbicide. The area then needs to be left for two weeks so that the herbicide acts on the roots, then the soil should be cultivated and resprayed as regrowth

A spring border plan

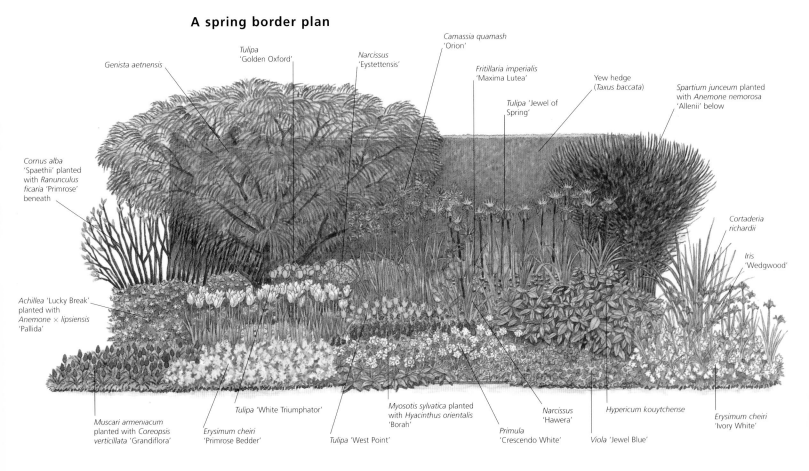

Genista aetnensis

Tulipa 'Golden Oxford'

Narcissus 'Eystettensis'

Camassia quamash 'Orion'

Fritillaria imperialis 'Maxima Lutea'

Yew hedge (Taxus baccata)

Spartium junceum planted with Anemone nemorosa 'Allenii' below

Tulipa 'Jewel of Spring'

Cornus alba 'Spaethii' planted with Ranunculus ficaria 'Primrose' beneath

Cortaderia richardii

Iris 'Wedgwood'

Achillea 'Lucky Break' planted with Anemone × lipsiensis 'Pallida'

Muscari armeniacum planted with Coreopsis verticillata 'Grandiflora'

Erysimum cheiri 'Primrose Bedder'

Tulipa 'White Triumphator'

Tulipa 'West Point'

Myosotis sylvatica planted with Hyacinthus orientalis 'Borah'

Primula 'Crescendo White'

Narcissus 'Hawera'

Viola 'Jewel Blue'

Hypericum kouytchense

Erysimum cheiri 'Ivory White'

appears; after a further wait of two weeks, it can be cultivated again, and is then ready for planting. Where weed infestation was very heavy, planting annuals in the first summer will allow any weed fragments still remaining to emerge and they can be treated again when the annuals have died off at the end of the growing season. There is always a risk of reinfection from deep in the soil or from beneath nearby shrubs, hedges, or paving, so it is wise to avoid planting ground covers or clump-forming perennials for a year or two. Spot treatment of isolated weeds is not difficult if it is done regularly, but ground ivy and bindweed can easily regain a foothold among ground-covering plants, meaning the whole border will need to be cleaned and replanted once more.

Deciding on the best way to fill a complete border at once can be difficult. While it is possible to buy plants in sufficient quantities, it is cheaper, and perhaps more satisfying to purchase a few and propagate them, or lift and divide plants that are already in the garden.

Where large areas are to be planted, a combination of the two options is probably most sensible. If speed is important, it is worth remembering that many mail order nurseries will sell plants in fives and tens, as well as hundreds, if the total order is of a reasonable size. Buying in this way can be up to 75 percent cheaper than going to the local garden center, especially with herbaceous perennials. Small plants are very much cheaper than larger ones, too, and will usually adapt more quickly to their new situation, soon catching up with larger pot-raised neighbors.

Once the soil is prepared and the plants obtained, or earmarked to be moved from other parts of the garden, the next step is to transfer the planting plan to the ground. The easiest way to do this is to divide the area into sections and then to use silver sand to indicate the position of each group of plants. If there is a general planting strategy but no specific plan, it is advisable to start by positioning key elements and then the secondary groups before filling in

A mid-summer/autumn border plan

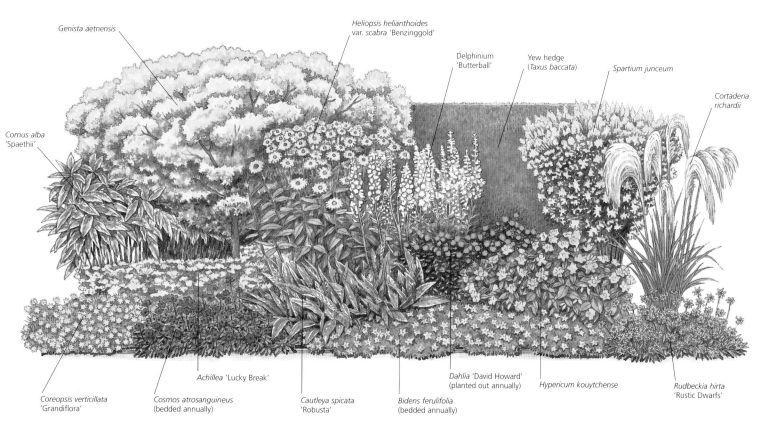

Genista aetnensis

Heliopsis helianthoides var. scabra 'Benzinggold'

Delphinium 'Butterball'

Yew hedge (Taxus baccata)

Spartium junceum

Cortaderia richardii

Cornus alba 'Spaethii'

Coreopsis verticillata 'Grandiflora'

Cosmos atrosanguineus (bedded annually)

Achillea 'Lucky Break'

Cautleya spicata 'Robusta'

Bidens ferulifolia (bedded annually)

Dahlia 'David Howard' (planted out annually)

Hypericum kouytchense

Rudbeckia hirta 'Rustic Dwarfs'

with the rest. Trying out ideas with the still potted plants, branches or stems cut from shrubs and plants that are to be moved into the area, and with canes and other objects, will ensure that everything works before anything is installed.

Planting systematically, from the middle to the edge of an island border or from one end to another of a long border, will ensure there is no chance of treading on new plants. Generous holes make it easy to position plants without damaging the roots, some of which will benefit from being worked out of the main root ball if the specimen has been grown in a pot. Perfect planting conditions are cool, and into a moist, but not wet soil, followed by a gentle downfall of rain. However, where this cannot be arranged, planting can be carried out successfully as long as exposed roots are protected from drying out and all newly planted specimens are watered well immediately afterwards.

Mulches should be applied after planting to retain moisture, suppress weeds, and reduce the work required to establish the plants. Whether the mulch is shredded bark or other materials such as grass clippings, garden compost, or gravel, it is important to ensure that it does not smother the crowns of dormant or emerging herbaceous perennials, but otherwise it should be spread thickly and evenly over the whole area.

After-care

As the plants grow and flower, it is almost inevitable that unexpected associations will reveal themselves and these might be pleasant or they may mar the overall effect. It is best to remove or resite any plants that are unattractive as soon as possible. There is no point in spoiling the border for any longer than is necessary. Photographs taken of the garden through the seasons will serve as reminders of any other necessary alterations, and will enable plans to be made for sowing seed or taking cuttings in readiness for the following year. Routine tasks such as pruning of shrubs and trees and dividing perennials should be done as necessary, before the balance of the planting becomes affected.

Facing page: The most successful borders often depend on plenty of flair and some daring, as here where unlikely companions such as grasses, thistles, tufted monardas, spiky persicarias, and the airy flower heads of umbellifers are allowed to jostle together in a rewarding and exhilarating composition.

Left: With its variation in color, shape, and texture, foliage is an important ingredient in any planting arrangement. It can even be the major component where complementary or contrasting plants such as variegated hostas and brunneras, delicate ferns, and round-leaved saxifrages are deliberately combined.

SHRUBS &
SMALL TREES

*AS THE GARDEN'S building blocks,
shrubs and small trees should be chosen
with care to ensure interesting shapes
and attractive foliage and flowers all
year, as well as to provide shelter,
vistas, and focal points. Even small
gardens need one or two trees and a
few shrubs to create a basic structure.*

IN MOST garden plantings a proportion of shrubs and a small selection of trees are essential to provide height, bulk, structure and, with the inclusion of some evergreens, year-round interest.

There is a wide choice of shrubs, varying from low ground-covering potentillas to towering abutilons, from fine-textured genistas to giant-leaved rhododendrons, from those shrubs with fleeting flowers such as amelanchiers to those that are non-stop performers such as hydrangeas, their dried flower heads persisting through the winter months. Some shrubs are deciduous, perhaps with colorful autumn foliage, others are evergreen.

The boundary between shrubs and small trees is a blurred one. Pittosporums, lilacs, philadelphus, and many others start their life as shrubs and if pruned to a single stem, can eventually make picturesque small trees. Trees display all the attributes of shrubs, but higher above ground level, often on trunks that have their own merits of elegant outline or attractive bark.

Making a selection

Trees and shrubs contribute to both the structure and the decoration of the garden, and it is important to bear these two aspects in mind when selecting and arranging them. In most situations, it is best to avoid thinking in terms of the "shrub border" and to plan instead to use trees and shrubs to enhance the whole garden. Selecting only those species that will grow well in the particular soil and situation will ensure that they thrive with minimum effort and will also create a strong sense of unity in the garden.

Small trees and the taller shrubs can be used to create height and as focal points. Birches with their pale trunks, lilacs with their spring blossom, or the very elegant paperbark maple, in groups or as single specimens, will draw the eye, frame views, and create a canopy to capture views of the sky. In large enough groups – even a well-placed trio in a small garden – the atmosphere of a wood or wild garden can be created: viewed from the rest of the garden, the trees form attractive masses, while under their canopy is a scene of vertical trunks and cool green shade with a rich woodland ground flora.

Once the high points have been decided on, the major shrubs can be distributed to form bold accents at a lower level: witch hazels for their spidery winter flowers, magnolias and rhododendrons for their blooms in spring and early summer, along with bright green-yellow or gold-leaved specimens such as euphorbias and *Philadelphus coronarius* 'Aureus'. Hydrangeas are ideal for autumn interest. Mahonias and

In this intimate partnership between neighboring shrubs the solid yellow-green spikes of *Pinus mugo* 'Winter Gold' are enlivened by the airy soft yellow flower sprays of broom (*Cytisus praecox*). The reddish purple foliage of purple sage (*Salvia officinalis* 'Purpurascens') introduces a note of restraint and is linked to the main display by a ribbon of vivid blue *Lithodora diffusa* 'Grace Ward'.

many of the conifers are good for texture and greenery all year round, playing an especially important role in maintaining structure and interest through the winter. The shrubs at this level should not be crowded together to grow into shapeless masses but, instead, are best placed where they will display themselves most effectively: those with autumn color where the sun will shine through them; those with bright winter stems where the low winter light falls; fragrant plants near enough to the edge of the planting to be smelled and in sheltered situations so the scent will be concentrated.

When the star cast of trees and specimen shrubs has been assembled, attention can be turned to the chorus, the less dramatic but no less important plants that will enclose and shelter the garden, guide people through it, subdivide larger plots into smaller and more comfortable spaces, and conceal any undesirable views. For these purposes there is a great army of well-behaved but less exciting (and usually much less expensive) shrubs.

Finally, having established the structure of the garden with shrubs growing from waist height (where they will obstruct physical movement) to eye level and above (as visual barriers), attention can be turned to the ground plane. Here low plants can be woven together: lavenders, cistus, and rosemaries do well on dry soils, while the heathers, leucothoes, smaller rhododendrons, and many others are ideal for moist, acid situations. Knee-high shrubs will cover the ground to reduce the necessity for weeding; they will also soften the transition between lawns and paving and fences, walls, and trees, and will create their own tapestry of foliage, flowers, and form.

Designing shrub borders

Where a shrub border is what is required, it should not be thought of as a form of herbaceous border – a series of more-or-less equally sized blocks or drifts with a different plant in each. While occasionally helpful in a herbaceous border, in a shrub border this

approach can be disastrous because the basic building unit, the shrub, is much larger and usually less colorful than the individual herbaceous plant. Therefore, each shrub group will be too large to relate effectively to its neighbors. What is needed in shrub planting is much greater variation in grouping, from individual specimen plants to substantial masses of ten, twenty, or more lower ground covers. The outlines of the larger groups should be irregular, like pieces in a jigsaw, so that they are linked together more firmly. The spacing between specimens in a group should also be varied, unless formality is intended. Lessons can be learned from natural groupings of trees, rocks, or even animals in a field, and it is worth spending time playing with circles on paper to achieve the right effect.

Shrubs can act as highlights in a complex composition, as above, where yellow robinia and philadelphus are framed by the reds and blues of anchusas, alliums, and cranesbills, or they can blend into a monochrome canvas like the yellow azaleas and laburnum below.

Finishing touches and after-care

Woody plants usually start off much too small for their situation but then grow inexorably, often eventually becoming much too large. Thinness in the early stages can be compensated for by interplanting the permanent selection with short-lived and quick-growing shrubs (brooms and lavateras, for example), herbaceous perennials, or annuals. Care must be taken to avoid smothering the long-term plants with their temporary companions, but this type of planting is much better than crowding together the permanent plants for instant effect, and paying the penalties of overcrowding forever after.

In fact, useful though trees and shrubs are in a garden, it is neither necessary nor desirable to grow them to the exclusion of other plants. Spring bulbs provide an intensity of color and freshness of new life unrivaled by any shrub, and they will clothe the ground beneath deciduous shrubs and trees with an early and beautiful carpet. Lilies will push through the lower shrubs to flower in late summer. Herbaceous plants extend the flowering season and break the monotony of an over-reliance on shrubs. Stout clumps of peonies, arching sheaves of daylilies, and tall branching heads of Japanese anemones will all create a greater sense of seasonal change and welcome lightness among the woody permanence of the shrubs. For an even lighter effect, proportions can be shifted from a mainly shrubby border, relieved by occasional marginal groups of other plants, to a thoroughly "mixed" border in which shrubs, herbaceous plants, annuals, bulbs, and climbers are assembled in a balanced community.

Once the permanent shrubs and trees have reached the desired size, it may be necessary to restrict their growth to prevent the garden deteriorating into a tangle of the most aggressive species. If time is available, rule-book pruning can be adopted. This is an art in itself and very satisfying. On a larger scale it is often simpler to prune plants periodically, cutting one in five – or perhaps one group in five – to ground level and allowing them to regrow.

Facing page: In a mid-spring display of foliage in green and yellow-green, the bulky forms of evergreens such as euonymus and *Ozothamnus ledifolius* perfectly balance a foreground of smaller shrubs and lush herbaceous plants such as salvias and euphorbias.

Below: The star of this border is a young *Cornus controversa* 'Variegata', whose fresh spring foliage shines in a lively but not overcrowded scheme that includes Exbury azaleas and varied herbaceous plants.

The gold-variegated foliage of *Abelia* × *grandiflora* 'Francis Mason' contrasts effectively with the blue flowers of *Caryopteris* × *clandonensis* 'Ferndown'. This partnership is perhaps seen at its best before the abelia's pink flowers and bronze calyces appear.

Abelia × *grandiflora* 'Francis Mason' ♛

Most often grown as a foliage plant, this vigorous semi-evergreen shrub has bright gold-edged leaves, which overwhelm its pale blush-pink flowers and reddish bronze stems, calyces, and young shoots. It contrasts well with blue flowers and glaucous foliage, but it is most effective with warm and hot colors, gold-variegated foliage, red- or orange-leaved shrubs like photinias, and yellow-green foliage and flowers. Its slightly amorphous form benefits from association with plants of contrasting growth habit, such as bamboos, grasses, Japanese maples, and pyracanthas pruned to produce long, arching shoots. 'Sunrise' is similar, less than 1m (3¼ft) high and wide, and makes an excellent ground cover – as do 'Prostrata' and cream-variegated **Confetti** ('Conti'), both 50cm (20in) by 1.5m (5ft). *A.* × *grandiflora* is more vigorous than the cultivars with unmarked leaves, and is useful for its late flowers.

⬤ *Aralia elata* 'Aureovariegata', *Berberis temolaica*, *B. thunbergii* 'Red Chief', *Delphinium* Belladonna Group, *Fargesia murielae* 'Bimbo', *Pyracantha* 'Golden Dome'

H: 1.5m (5ft) S: 2m (6½ft) ❀ Mid- to late summer
◊◊ ▢-◼ Z6 pH6–8

Abies koreana 'Silberlocke' ♛

A slow-growing fir with glaucous silver-backed needles and deep purplish blue upright cones, 'Silberlocke' produces its best colors in full sun and relatively poor soil. It deserves prominence as a single specimen in a heather garden, island bed, or large rock garden, surrounded by shorter carpeting plants such as heaths and heathers, shorter-growing ericaceous plants including dwarf rhododendrons, prostrate vacciniums and cassiopes, and smaller grasses like fescues. This ground cover may be planted with smaller spring bulbs, especially blue-flowered kinds such as scillas and muscaris, and soft yellow or white narcissi. 'Silberlocke' is not suitable for borders, where neighboring plants can suppress growth on one or both sides of the fir, spoiling its attractive symmetry.

⬤ *Calluna vulgaris* 'Gold Haze', *Cassiope* 'Edinburgh', *Narcissus* 'April Tears', *N.* 'Ice Wings', *Rhododendron* 'Sarled', *Scilla siberica*, *Vaccinium vitis-idaea* 'Koralle'

H: 1.8m (6ft) S: 1.2m (4ft) ❀ (Spring)
◊◊ ▢-◼ Z5 pH5–6.5

The bold form of *Abies koreana* 'Silberlocke', its glaucous leaves twisted to reveal their showy white undersides, presents a telling focus in a mixed bed of winter heaths, including the rich pink *Erica carnea* 'Myretoun Ruby' (bottom) and the slightly paler *E.c.* 'R.B. Cooke' (top). Planting small grasses such as stipas and blue fescues around the abies would provide interest in summer.

Crowded spikes of white foxgloves (*Digitalis purpurea* f. *albiflora*) lift themselves high enough to offer a contrast of floral form with *Abutilon vitifolium* var. *album*, while providing a quiet color harmony.

Abutilon vitifolium var. *album*

This large, upright deciduous shrub, quick-growing but short-lived, has grey-white woolly stems, vine-shaped leaves, and large, translucent white flowers with a central golden disk. It benefits from a sunny site, particularly in areas with cool summers, and looks effective against a dark evergreen background, or in a shrub border if isolated to emphasize its vase shape. It mixes well with tall herbaceous plants, such as white foxgloves or delphiniums and silvery Scotch thistles, while its flowering season suits combinations with larger Shrub roses and early-flowering buddlejas. Although blending successfully with almost any color, it is outstanding with pale flowers and silver or glaucous foliage, and may be used to support clematis or honeysuckles flowering in late spring or early summer. 'Tennant's White' ♛ is a particularly choice selection.

⬤ *Buddleja alternifolia* 'Argentea', *Clematis* 'Bees' Jubilee', *Delphinium* Galahad Group, *Eremurus robustus*, *Onopordum nervosum*, *Rosa* 'Fantin-Latour'

H: 5m (16ft) S: 2.5m (8ft)
❀ Late spring to mid-summer
◊◊ ▢-◼ Z8 pH5.5–7

The rich brown bark of the paperbark maple (*Acer griseum*) glows orange where lit from behind by the sun, allowing it to harmonize with *Crocosmia* 'Lucifer'. Bold rodgersia leaves provide a foil without masking the maple's stem.

Acer griseum ♔

PAPERBARK MAPLE

The trifoliate leaves of this small deciduous tree turn an appealing orange-yellow in autumn, but its most attractive feature is its orange-brown peeling bark, especially striking when lit by the sun in a prominent position in front of other plants of similar height. As with silver-barked birches, a single plant can look unsatisfactory unless made to fork into three to five branches, with a length of exposed stem below its canopy of leaves; where there is room, a small, loosely spaced grove, perhaps with a path winding between the trees, is enchanting. This maple blends well with bronze and red-flushed foliage plants, including some Japanese maples, and also with other autumn-coloring shrubs, small trees, herbaceous plants, and some of the deciduous azaleas. Surplus shoots arising from main stems should be removed to reveal as much of the bark as possible.

◖ *Berberis thunbergii* 'Atropurpurea Nana', *B. wilsoniae, Ceratostigma plumbaginoides, Euphorbia amygdaloides* 'Purpurea', *Stephanandra tanakae*

H: 10m (33ft) S: 7m (23ft) ✿ (Mid-spring)
◊◊ ▢-▇ Z5 pH5.5–7

Acer palmatum

This elegant deciduous shrub or small tree is the most common Japanese maple, with several hundred cultivars notable for their growth habit and autumn tints. The species is suitable for a woodland garden, with azaleas and rhododendrons planted underneath. Vigorous cultivars include 'Aoyagi', which turns from bright green to golden yellow in autumn; 'Arakawa', with red autumn tints; and the tall 'Asahi-zuru', with leaves splashed pinkish white. *A.p.* f. *atropurpureum* and 'Atropurpureum Superbum' are purplish red, turning bright red; deep blackish purple 'Bloodgood' ♔ is crimson in autumn. 'Linearilobum' ♔ is tall, with narrow-lobed leaves that are bright yellow in autumn. Cultivars of var. *dissectum* ♔ are the smallest, with deeply cut leaves, and include the reddish purple 'Crimson Queen' ♔. Traditionally planted with Japanese plants such as bamboos, they look great near water, with Japanese irises in warm or hot colors.

◖ **Green-leaved:** *Fothergilla major* Monticola Group p.52 **C**, *Hosta fortunei* var. *hyacinthina* p.245 **A** ⏋p.81 **A** **Purple-leaved:** *Erysimum cheiri* (red-flowered), *Fuchsia* 'Checkerboard' p.53 **A**, *Nandina domestica* p.69 **B**, *Rhododendron* Blinklicht Group p.81 **B**, *R.* 'Fandango' p.82 **C**, *Sambucus nigra* f. *laciniata* p.91 **A** ⏋p.315 **B**

H: 1–10m (3¼–33ft) S: 1.5–8m (5–26ft)
✿ (Mid-spring)
◊◊ ▢-▇ Z6 pH5.5–7

The delicate, feathery leaves of *Acer palmatum* Dissectum Atropurpureum Group contrast subtly with those of mondo grass (*Ophiopogon planiscapus* 'Nigrescens') while dusky purple, before turning a dramatic scarlet in autumn.

Grown through a carpet of *Gaultheria mucronata*, the fiery coral stems of *Acer pensylvanicum* 'Erythrocladum' clash agreeably with rich pink *Camellia* × *williamsii* 'E.T.R. Carlyon'. A scarlet or blood-red camellia would be a harmonious alternative to flatter the maple.

Acer pensylvanicum 'Erythrocladum' ♛

This cultivar – a deciduous large shrub or small tree, smaller than the species itself – has twigs that are bright coral when young, turning golden yellow in autumn. They lose this yellow coloration in their second season, but the branches and trunk remain attractively striped and marked, most effectively in winter if lit by the low rays of the sun against a dark evergreen background. It can be used as a specimen or planted in a border with dogwoods, witch hazels, and other shrubs with warm winter colors, or surrounded by herbaceous perennials or ground-cover plants that do not compete with its regular, upright shape. Good companions include scarlet camellias, gold-variegated evergreens, stephanandras, and rubus, or pruned willows with colored stems.

◑ *Camellia japonica* 'Bob Hope', *Cornus sanguinea* 'Winter Beauty', *Hamamelis* × *intermedia* 'Jelena', *Ilex aquifolium* 'Pyramidalis', *Rubus thibetanus*

H: **12m** (40ft) S: **10m** (33ft) ❀ (Mid-spring)
◊◊ ▢-▨ Z5 pH5.5–7

Acer shirasawanum 'Aureum' ♛

Long misidentified as an *Acer japonicum* cultivar, this deciduous Japanese maple has the brightest yellow-green foliage of its genus. Slow-growing, it makes a dense, upright shrub that, except in areas with cool summers, benefits from some shade (it can scorch in full sun). It is best planted within a carpet of shorter companions, so that its elegant vase shape is not impaired. In autumn the leaves may take on scarlet tints, or change through butter-yellow to golden brown. It can be combined with yellow, cream, or white deciduous azaleas, lilies, hostas, gold-variegated hollies, bamboos, and other autumn-coloring shrubs such as linderas and witch hazels. It looks attractive with glaucous foliage plants, and contrasts with blue flowers such as blue poppies.

◑ *Brunnera macrophylla*, *Hosta* 'Blue Vision', *Iris* 'Cambridge', *Lilium martagon* var. *album*, *Lindera obtusiloba*, *Meconopsis grandis*, *Miscanthus sinensis* 'Zebrinus', *Pleioblastus auricomus*, *Rhododendron* 'Persil'

H: **6m** (20ft) S: **5m** (16ft) ❀ (Mid-spring)
◊◊ ▢-▨ Z5 pH5.5–7

The fan-shaped leaves of *Acer shirasawanum* 'Aureum', almost pure yellow on unfurling, contrast with the bold glaucous foliage of *Hosta* 'Krossa Regal'. White, blue, or pale yellow flowers could be added to extend the planting.

Showy leaves of *Amelanchier lamarckii* and bright berries of *Cotoneaster frigidus* 'Cornubia', grown at the same height, make a classic autumn combination that could be topped by a sorbus and interwoven by a colorful vine.

Amelanchier lamarckii ♔

LAMARCK SERVICEBERRY

This is perhaps the most satisfactory amelanchier for a sunny garden, where it offers two seasons of interest, first when the bronze foliage emerges with the white spring flowers, and again in autumn, when its leaves turn fiery red. It is a dainty tree, suited to a wild garden among flowers such as cow parsley, or a sunny woodland glade with spring bulbs like Poeticus narcissi. Trees such as ornamental cherries and crab apples are attractive partners, as are magnolias, early roses, kolkwitzias, flowering dogwoods, hawthorns, whitebeams, and more delicately colored deciduous azaleas. Larger plants can support a spring climber, such as a soft pink *Clematis montana* cultivar, or a purple vine. White and pale-colored lilacs combine well in spring, while Japanese maples, aronias, and cotoneasters add autumn harmonies.

⊕ *Anthriscus sylvestris* 'Ravenswing', *Clematis montana* 'Gothenburg', *Exochorda giraldii* var. *wilsonii*, *Magnolia* × *loebneri* 'Merrill', *Malus hupehensis*, *Narcissus* 'Geranium', *N. poeticus* var. *recurvus*, *Pieris* 'Forest Flame', *Prunus* 'Shirotae', *Pyrus communis* 'Beech Hill'

H: 10m (33ft) S: 7m (23ft) ❀ **Mid-spring**
◊◊ ⬜-◼ **Z5 pH5–7**

Aralia elata 'Aureovariegata'

In late summer this deciduous shrub produces attractive clouds of creamy white flowers on branching panicles, but the foliage is its most eye-catching feature. The large leaves, up to 1.5m (5ft) long and almost as wide, are edged with yellow when young, fading to cream by summer. With its bright color and complexity, it makes a magnificent specimen plant, or striking focal points along a grand or sophisticated border, planted among shorter subjects that tolerate partial shade, so that the aralias ultimately provide a canopy of leaves above the other plants. It combines well with warm or hot colors, cream flowers, glaucous foliage, and yellow-green foliage and flowers, and can be contrasted with blue, most dramatically while its foliage is still young. The white-marked 'Variegata' ♔ is equally impressive.

⊕ *Agapanthus* 'Loch Hope', *Crocosmia* 'Vulcan', *Dahlia* 'Autumn Lustre', *D.* 'Glorie van Heemstede', *Hibiscus syriacus* 'Oiseau Bleu', *Ipomoea tricolor* 'Heavenly Blue', *Miscanthus sinensis* 'Strictus', *Nepeta sibirica*, *Philadelphus coronarius* 'Aureus'

H & S: 5m (16ft) ❀ **Late summer**
◊◊-◊◊◊ ⬜-◼ **Z5 pH5.5–7.5**

The dramatic foliage of *Aralia elata* 'Aureovariegata' harmonizes with the warm apricot-yellow of *Crocosmia* × *crocosmiiflora* 'Lady Hamilton'. Agapanthus would give a similar foliage effect with a contrasting flower color.

A filigree cushion of *Artemisia* 'Powis Castle' nestles beneath gracefully arching stems of *Fuchsia magellanica* 'Versicolor', with its elegant, pendant flowers and greyish leaves flushed red and edged with white – an association that is especially charming at close range. The slender fuchsia flowers set off the silvery artemisia, while the foliage colors blend agreeably.

Artemisia 'Powis Castle' ♔

This relatively hardy, semi-evergreen sub-shrub is an outstanding foliage plant, its filigree silver-grey leaves developing into dense, mounded clumps that look impressive at the front of a border or in containers. It tolerates poor soils and dry conditions, helping it to thrive in a gravel garden with Mediterranean plants such as lavenders and cistus. It is very effective with other silver-leaved plants, glaucous foliage, and plants with contrasting leaf form and texture, especially grasses such as fescues, and it is an essential component of a white garden. It combines well with flowers in cool colors and looks satisfying grown in front of roses, including old Shrub roses. The bush can break apart if left to grow indefinitely, particularly after heavy snow, and so benefits from cutting back each year in mid-spring.

⊕ *Ballota pseudodictamnus* p.196 **C**, *Cistus* × *argentus* 'Silver Pink', *Convolvulus cneorum*, *Cosmos bipinnatus* 'Sonata White', *Euphorbia dulcis* 'Chameleon' p.219 **A**, *Lavandula* 'Sawyers', *Rosa* Surrey p.171 **C** ⌑ p.376 **A**

H: 60cm (24in) S: 90cm (36in) ❀ **Summer**
◊-◊◊ ⬜-◼ **Z6 pH5.5–7.5**

Evergreen *Berberis darwinii* supplies a pleasant backdrop for the bright spring flowers of *Forsythia × intermedia*, its stems yet to be furnished by foliage. The soft orange flowers of the berberis, here just starting to open, will also dazzle before the forsythia fades.

Berberis darwinii ♔

One of the best evergreen, spring-flowering shrubs, this is valuable for contributing structure and solidity to the garden early in the year, before deciduous plants come into leaf. Like the holly, the lobes and prickles on its leaves add sparkle to the shiny surfaces. Plants may be grown as specimen shrubs or as a hedge, combined with white or hot-colored flowers or with gold-variegated, evergreen foliage. They also associate well with bamboos, forsythias, camellias with white or deepest red flowers, winter jasmine, narcissi, and gold-variegated hollies or elaeagnus. Any surplus growth should be cut back immediately after flowering. Very large specimens may be cut hard back to 10–15cm (4–6in) above ground to maintain the elegant, arching growth habit of the stems.

◉ *Chaenomeles × superba* 'Rowallane', *Euphorbia griffithii* 'Dixter', *Narcissus* 'Ambergate', *Rosa* 'Helen Knight', *Syringa vulgaris* 'Primrose'

H & S: 3m (10ft) ❋ Mid- to late spring
◇-◇◇ ☐-■ Z7 pH5–7.5

Berberis thunbergii ♔

The most striking feature of this deciduous shrub is its autumn display of fiery orange and red tints and red, elliptical fruits. Its modest green leaves for the rest of the year suit a wild garden and other subdued displays. Useful cultivars with variegated, purple-flushed, or golden leaves include *f. atropurpurea*, often rich deep purple turning rich red in autumn; 'Atropurpurea Nana' ♔ (60cm/24in) and 'Bagatelle' ♔ (30cm/12in), both ideal for the front of a border or as edging; and the columnar 'Helmond Pillar' (1.5m/5ft), which is suitable for emphatic accents. The leaves of 'Golden Ring' have narrow yellow-green edges, while those of 'Harlequin' and 'Rose Glow' ♔ are splashed with pale pink. The yellow-green 'Aurea' makes an eye-catching contrast with pure blue flowers.

◉ **Purple-leaved:** *Agastache* 'Firebird' p.181 **B**, *Clematis* 'Prince Charles' p.117 **A**, *Euphorbia myrsinites* p.220 **A**, *Phalaris arundinacea* var. *picta* 'Picta' p.272 **B**, *Phygelius × rectus* p.73 **C**, *Rosa* Evelyn Fison p.164 **A**, *R.* 'Madame Pierre Oger' p.149 **A** ❑ pp.46 **B**, 58 **C**, 99 **A**, 99 **C**, 184 **C**, 193 **C**, 194 **C**, 216 **B**, 307 **C**
Yellow-green leaved: *Eryngium giganteum* p.378 **A**

H: 1.5m (5ft) S: 2m (6½ft) ❋ Late spring
◇-◇◇ ☐-■ Z5 pH5–7.5

Above: *Berberis thunbergii* 'Atropurpurea Nana' is the key player in this combination of smoky purple foliage and flowers. The other purples, of dark-leaved *Rosa* 'Rosemary Rose' and *Tulipa* 'Queen of Night', are joined by gently contrasting hybrid bluebells and the soft yellow berberis flowers. Adding another taller berberis further back in the border would provide a unifying theme.

Below: Nodding wands of dark-leaved *Berberis thunbergii* f. *atropurpurea*, carrying pale yellow flowers tinged with red, contrast dramatically with the yellow-green foliage of *Philadelphus coronarius* 'Aureus'. Although the outer flowers of the berberis are camouflaged by the philadelphus, most show well against the dusky berberis leaves.

A carpet of low foliage provides a soft foil for a multi-stemmed *Betula utilis* var. *jacquemontii*, grown in moist semi-shade. In the foreground, the bronze-flushed leaves of Japanese shield fern (*Dryopteris erythrosora*) tone with the beige-tinted white stems of the birch and its brown twigs, while the creamy white flowers of *Astilbe* 'Deutschland' harmonize with the birch's base.

Betula utilis var. jacquemontii

Birches are elegant, fast-growing trees that cast dappled shade and offer good deciduous ground covers for woodland plants, including rhododendrons, in medium-sized to large gardens. This variety is a form of Himalayan birch with strikingly white-barked stems, dramatic when placed where the tree catches the winter sun against a dark background of evergreens such as yew and holly. Cultivars with particularly white bark include 'Doorenbos' ♀, 'Jermyns' ♀, and 'Silver Shadow' ♀. In smaller gardens, a multi-branched birch is a space-saving option. This is created by cutting back a young tree or (if inexpensive seedlings are used) by planting several in one hole. The ground beneath the birch can be carpeted by ferns, dicentras, epimediums, spring bulbs such as cyclamens and snowdrops, or other woodland plants.

◉ *Dicentra* 'Pearl Drops', *Epimedium* × *versicolor* 'Sulphureum', *Fatsia japonica*, *Ilex aquifolium* 'Pyramidalis', *Narcissus* 'Actaea', *Polystichum setiferum*, *Rubus cockburnianus*, *Stephanandra tanakae*

H: 18m (60ft) **S: 10m** (33ft) ✿ **(Mid-spring)**
◌◌ ■-■ **Z6 pH4.5–7**

The broad panicles of *Buddleja davidii* 'Dartmoor' form a magnificent lilac backdrop for a planting in which the curious sunflower *Helianthus salicifolius*, grown principally for its bold bottle-brush columns of foliage, is the other main attraction, partnered by the bamboo *Phyllostachys nigra* f. *punctata*. A pretty pale blue covering of *Clematis* × *jouiniana* 'Praecox' fills the foreground.

Buddleja alternifolia ♀

This deciduous large shrub or small tree bears long, drooping wands of attractive lilac blooms. The silver-leaved cultivar 'Argentea' is even prettier and slightly less vigorous than the species, but not as free-flowering in areas with cool summers. Both are superb when combined with purple, white, blue, mauve, carmine, or lime green flowers, and with purple or silver foliage. Good companions include old roses, delphiniums, lupines, purple sloe, and purple smoke bush. These buddlejas need pruning annually straight after flowering. Unpruned plants develop short, tangled flowering stems, so it is best to limit the number of stems to about five or six, stopping these 1m (40in) below the height ultimately required, or to train a single main stem to form a standard, several of which may be planted at intervals along a border to provide rhythm.

◉ *Allium* 'Gladiator', *Campanula lactiflora*, *Delphinium* 'Bruce', *Elaeagnus* 'Quicksilver', *Geranium psilostemon*, *Philadelphus* 'Belle Etoile', *Rosa* 'Cerise Bouquet'

H & S: 4m (13ft) ✿ **Early summer**
◌-◌◌ ■-■ **Z6 pH5.5–7.5**

The slightly unruly growth habit of *Buddleja alternifolia* turns exuberant as its lilac pompons of flowers appear, strung together to make continuous garlands. Purple sage (*Salvia officinalis* 'Purpurascens') grows beneath, while in front matching pompons of chives and *Allium hollandicum* 'Purple Sensation' chime in close harmony.

Buddleja davidii 'Dartmoor' ♀

Perhaps the most dramatic cultivar of the common buddleja or butterfly bush, this is distinguished by its immensely wide panicles of lilac flowers. It forms a broad, spreading deciduous bush at first, becoming narrower and more upright. Each arching stem flowers for several months, even longer if panicles are cut out as their blooms fade, to encourage flowering sideshoots. It is superb planted behind old roses or harmonizing in a mixed or shrub border with mauve, purple, lilac, and blue flowers, or with silver, purple, or glaucous foliage. It contrasts well with soft yellow flowers, and with yellow-green foliage or flowers. Most *Buddleja davidii* cultivars are pruned like *B. alternifolia* (left), as a standard or a bush with a handful of main growing points, but if they originate close together the annual stems of 'Dartmoor' fall apart after heavy rain, so the bush should be hard pruned to encourage new basal growth.

◉ *Cotinus coggygria* 'Royal Purple', *Elaeagnus commutata*, *Euphorbia schillingii*, *Lilium* 'Casa Blanca', *L.* Imperial Gold Group, *Rosa* 'Felicia', *R. glauca*

H & S: 3m (10ft) ✿ **Mid-summer to early autumn**
◌-◌◌ ■-■ **Z5 pH5–7.5**

Buxus sempervirens ♔
COMMON BOXWOOD

The great virtue of this versatile evergreen is its fine-textured, fairly amorphous foliage, which provides a superb background for plants of more definite form or leaf color. It is a handsome shrub for a woodland garden, and can help to define a space, screen a boundary, or give a backbone to a mixed border. Cultivars such as cream-splashed 'Elegantissima' ♔ and yellow-variegated 'Latifolia Maculata' ♔ are attractive supports for flowering climbers. Boxwood is excellent as a hedge or topiary subject, as it accepts a crisp, architectural shape; the best cultivar for this is 'Suffruticosa' ♔, dwarf boxwood, traditionally used for low hedges in knot gardens. (In cold climates, a hardier plant such as *B.* 'Green Mountain' or a cultivar of *B. sinica* var. *insularis* is more successful.) Foliage color varies between blue- and grey-green and yellow-green, and it is often worth choosing the most appropriate clone for a particular color scheme. For informal plantings in a woodland garden, seedling boxwood has a pleasant, natural-looking variation in color and growth habit. Upright cultivars can be less effective as taller hedges, because their branches do not knit together and so cannot withstand a heavy fall of snow.

🌑 *Aruncus dioicus* p.191 **A**, *Aucuba japonica*, *Camellia japonica* 'Lovelight', *Euonymus japonicus* 'Ovatus Aureus', *Fatsia japonica* p.51 **C**, *Hedera colchica*, *Helleborus* × *hybridus*, *Ilex* × *altaclerensis* 'Golden King', *Polystichum setiferum*, *Rhododendron* 'Dora Amateis', *Sarcococca confusa*, *Taxus baccata* 'Fastigiata'

H & S: 5m (16ft) ❀ **(Spring)**
⬛⬜ ◊◊ ⬜-⬛ **Z6 pH5.5–8**

Right: Boxwood does not have to be clipped to be attractive, but its size may have to be limited by pruning, taking care not to impair its natural growth habit. Here, the tiny, neatly cream-edged leaves of *Buxus sempervirens* 'Marginata' lend themselves to close inspection, partnered by a Lenten rose (*Helleborus* × *hybridus*) and spring bulbs.

Below: Dwarf boxwood (*Buxus sempervirens* 'Suffruticosa') is an ideal parterre plant, clipped into bold patterns of crisp compartments and filled with more informal planting. Its fine texture and geometric shape can provide a perfect foil for a froth of spring flowers followed by summer annuals. Here, each compartment is simply planted with herbs – common and purple sage (*Salvia officinalis* and *S.o.* 'Purpurascens') and curry plant (*Helichrysum italicum*).

Calluna vulgaris
SCOTCH HEATHER

The foliage of these acid-loving evergreens can be green, grey, gold, orange, bronze, or brick-red, sometimes tipped gold or cream, and often changing with the seasons; the flowers are pink, mauve, crimson, burgundy, magenta, or white. Heathers make an excellent ground cover in open, sunny sites, associated with other heathland plants such as smaller rhododendrons, gaultherias, and vacciniums. Varieties with orange or reddish foliage are good for winter displays, combined with colored dogwoods or willows and early bulbs. Among the most useful are 'Allegro' ♀,

Colored-leaved heathers are immensely valuable ground-cover plants for the winter garden. Combining *Calluna vulgaris* 'Ariadne', whose leaves are tipped with orange and cream, with the Darley Dale heath *Erica × darleyensis* 'White Perfection' avoids the often seen clash between orange-, gold- or bronze-leaved types and those with mauve-pink flowers.

in burgundy; the double pink 'Annemarie' ♀; 'Anthony Davis' ♀, in white with grey-green leaves; 'Dark Star' ♀, in crimson; 'Gold Haze' ♀, with yellow-green foliage and white flowers; 'Mair's Variety' ♀, in white; 'Spring Cream' ♀, with white flowers and spring foliage tipped cream; the double magenta 'Tib' ♀; and the prostrate 'White Lawn' ♀.

Abies koreana 'Silberlocke', *Cornus alba* 'Sibirica', *Gaultheria mucronata*, *Juniperus horizontalis* 'Wiltonii', *Molinia caerulea* 'Variegata', *Pinus mugo* 'Ophir', *Salix daphnoides* 'Aglaia', *Vaccinium vitis-idaea* 'Koralle' ⌐pp.110 **C**, 170 **A**

H: 10–60cm (4–24in) **S: 30–75cm** (12–30in)
✿ **Mid-summer to late autumn**

 ◊◊ ▣ ■ **Z4 pH4–6**

Camellias (here, *Camellia japonica* 'Latifolia' and mixed daffodils) and early narcissi are well suited to informal displays in deciduous woodland. Scarlet camellias could equally be paired with white narcissi, perhaps with a red-rimmed cup or salmon trumpet, or where a jazzier effect is wanted, with a rich orange sort such as *N.* 'Ambergate'.

Camellia 'Cornish Snow' ♀

This evergreen hybrid between *C. cuspidata* and *C. saluenensis* has masses of small, single white flowers, delicately flushed with pink. Although a fairly hardy plant, the blooms are sometimes damaged in cold weather, so it is best grown in areas that seldom experience frost. Its graceful, open growth habit and simple flowers give an air of unsophisticated charm to wilder parts of a woodland garden. It looks best in subtly colored arrangements, especially with shrubs of similar natural grace, such as other camellias and early rhododendrons with soft coloring and loose growth habit. Other companions include winter honeysuckles, evergreen shrubs such as osmanthus, and early bulbs – snowdrops and pale crocuses or cyclamens for example.

Camellia 'Winton', *Galanthus* 'Straffan', *Lonicera × purpusii*, *Osmanthus delavayi*, *Prunus pendula* 'Pendula Rosea', *Rhododendron lutescens* 'Bagshot Sands'

H: 3m (10ft) **S: 1.5m** (5ft)
✿ **Mid-winter to late spring**

◊◊ ▣ ■ **Z8 pH4.5–6.5**

Camellia 'Cornish Snow' with one of several valuable early rhododendrons, *R.* Cilpinense Group. An intervening evergreen with contrasting foliage, for instance a bamboo, and a carpet of early bulbs could enhance the planting.

Camellia japonica
COMMON CAMELLIA

Cultivars of this superlative evergreen shrub vary in flower color from white to deep red, and in floral form from single to very formal double; some blooms are anemone-centered or have prominent anthers. Plants need a partially shaded position, ideally facing west in frost-prone regions so that there is less chance of the flowers being damaged by early morning sun when frosted; in areas where they are not hardy, they make excellent greenhouse plants. Cultivars with formal double flowers and rich colors have a sophistication that may seem unnatural in outer parts of the garden, but they are excellent near the house, perhaps combined with early rhododendrons and spring bulbs such as narcissi. Their solid form benefits from association with shrubs of lighter, more open growth habit, such as bamboos, *Prunus mume* cultivars, and early-flowering deciduous trees that provide beneficial overhead shade.

Fargesia murielae, *Fatsia japonica*, *Galanthus elwesii*, *Magnolia × loebneri*, *Narcissus* 'Mount Hood', *N.* 'Thalia', *Prunus* 'Accolade', *P. mume* 'Omoi-no-mama', *P. pendula* 'Pendula Rubra', *Rhododendron augustinii*, *R.* 'Christmas Cheer', *R. schlippenbachii*

H: 9m (30ft) **S: 8m** (26ft) ✿ **Early to late spring**

◊◊ ▣ ■ **Z7 pH4.5–6.5**

The rich blue flowers of *Ceanothus* 'Cascade' contrast strikingly with the acid yellow-green foliage of *Hedera helix* 'Buttercup'. Although here the ivy is in its shrubby phase, this combination would more normally be seen with the ivy clinging to a wall and the ceanothus loosely trained in front of it.

Usually a sprawling shrub, *Ceanothus foliosus* can be trained upwards, for instance against a wall, allowing it to achieve double its usual height. This means it can be combined with a range of different plants, among them the broom *Cytisus nigricans*, with its graceful, arching sprays of yellow flowers.

Ceanothus 'Cascade' ♔

Evergreen Californian lilacs or ceanothus are quick-growing shrubs that tend to be relatively short-lived, particularly in frosty gardens, where they prefer a sheltered sunny wall. 'Cascade' is one of the larger cultivars, with an open, arching growth habit and rich blue flowers in long, airy clusters. It is tall enough to interact with large shrubs and small trees, especially laburnums, brooms, and early-flowering Climbing and Shrub roses. Its color combines well with yellow, white, yellow-green, or pale blue flowers, and with silver, glaucous, or yellow-green foliage – a wall clothed with yellow-green or gold-variegated ivies makes a stunning backdrop. It should not be allowed to grow too large, since it will not respond to heavy pruning; size can be limited by pruning slender branches back into the center of the bush.

◯ *Cytisus* × *praecox* 'Warminster', *Euphorbia characias* subsp. *wulfenii* 'John Tomlinson', *Laburnum* × *watereri* 'Vossii', *Rosa banksiae* 'Lutea', *R.* × *fortuneana*, *R. xanthina* f. *hugonis*, *Syringa vulgaris* 'Madame Lemoine', *S.v.* 'Primrose', *Viburnum opulus* 'Roseum'

H & S: 4m (13ft) ✿ **Late spring to early summer**
◐ ◌-◌◌ ◻-◼ **Z8 pH5.5–7**

Ceanothus × *delileanus* 'Gloire de Versailles' ♔

This deciduous ceanothus with airy clusters of powder-blue flowers is hardier than the evergreen kinds, and thrives in an open site as well as against a wall. Its soft texture and subtle coloring make it suitable for combinations with bold foliage and plants of more definite floral form. The flower color complements cool shades such as deep blue, lavender, or mauve, and looks effective with white, cream, or very pale yellow, but it is too delicate for strong yellow. It associates well with silver or glaucous foliage, especially glaucous grasses. On a wall it can be combined with Viticella clematis or repeat-flowering Climbing roses, while in a border it looks charming planted with repeat-flowering bush roses and hydrangeas, such as *H. paniculata* cultivars and Lacecap cultivars.

◯ *Aconitum* 'Spark's Variety', *Clematis* 'Huldine', *Elaeagnus* 'Quicksilver', *Euphorbia schillingii*, *Hydrangea macrophylla* Libelle, *H. paniculata* 'Grandiflora', *Lilium* Imperial Gold Group, *Miscanthus sinensis* 'Morning Light', *Rosa* 'Climbing Iceberg', *R.* 'Mermaid'

H & S: 1.5m (5ft) ✿ **Mid-summer to mid-autumn**
◐ ◌-◌◌ ◻-◼ **Z7 pH5.5–7**

The powder-blue flowers of *Ceanothus* × *delileanus* 'Gloire de Versailles' provide a delicate haze of blooms alongside the bold flower heads and handsome foliage of *Hydrangea quercifolia*. The height of the ceanothus is usually kept to 1.5m (5ft) by annual pruning to a low framework, but by building up a taller framework of perennial branches, the ceanothus can be made to rise above the hydrangea.

Ceanothus foliosus

One of the more tender species of ceanothus, this is a spreading, semi-prostrate evergreen shrub producing numerous long-stalked, round clusters of dark blue flowers, with paler filaments, that give it an airy appearance. It is best placed towards the front of a border because its foliage grows down to the ground, although low carpeting plants can be used effectively beneath its fringes. It looks particularly attractive with silver or glaucous foliage; with white, cream, yellow, and pale blue flowers; and with yellow-green foliage and flowers. Suitable companions include smaller Shrub or bush roses, early-flowering annuals or biennials, white-flowered cistus, and any halimiocistus or halimiums.

◯ *Camassia leichtlinii*, *Choisya ternata* Sundance, *Cytisus* 'Moonlight', *Euonymus fortunei* 'Silver Queen', *Exochorda* × *macrantha* 'The Bride', *Rosa* × *harisonii* 'Harison's Yellow', *R.* 'Madame Alfred Carrière', *Spiraea* 'Arguta', *Tulipa* 'Spring Green', *T.* 'White Triumphator'

H: 90cm (3ft) S: 1.2m (4ft)
✿ **Late spring to early summer**

◐ ◌-◌◌ ◻-◼ **Z8 pH5.5–7**

Ceanothus impressus

This is one of the hardier evergreen ceanothus species, which may be grown as a free-standing bush or trained against a wall, where it will reach a height of about 3m (10ft). It produces billowing masses of solid blue flowers that look most impressive contrasted with yellow, white, and the very palest or deepest pure blue flowers, silver or glaucous foliage, and yellow-green foliage or flowers. Early yellow roses are satisfying companions, as are laburnums, although these need to branch fairly low if their flowers are to interact successfully with the ceanothus. Other fine deep blue ceanothus include *C.* 'Concha', 'Dark Star', and 'Puget Blue' ♡, which has sumptuous coloring but is not so conspicuous seen from a distance.

◉ *Clematis* 'Moonlight' p.116 **A**, *Cytisus × praecox* 'Warminster', *Euphorbia characias*, *Fritillaria imperialis* 'Maxima Lutea', *Rosa pimpinellifolia* 'Grandiflora', *R. × xanthina* f. *hugonis*, *Sambucus nigra* 'Aurea', *Tulipa* 'Maja', *T.* 'Sweet Harmony'

H: 1.5m (5ft) S: 2.5m (8ft) ✿ **Mid- to late spring**
▬▭ ◌-◌◌ ▢-▉ **Z8 pH5.5–7**

Laburnum anagyroides is here made to branch, and thus produce blooms, lower than usual, allowing it to contrast spectacularly with the much lower-growing *Ceanothus impressus*. *L. × watereri* 'Vossii' has longer racemes and might be even more dramatic, while a little shade would subdue flowering for a more subtle effect.

Trained low across a wall, flowering quinces such as *Chaenomeles × superba* 'Knap Hill Scarlet' will produce plentiful bloom at a height that allows them to combine effectively with spring bulbs such as narcissi, as well as with relatively short plants such as wallflowers, euphorbias, and geums.

Chaenomeles × superba 'Knap Hill Scarlet' ♡

The rounded vermilion blooms of this deciduous flowering quince are followed in autumn by amber-yellow fruits. It can be grown as a sprawling shrub near the front of a border, but it is even more effective trained on a wall or trellis and pruned in mid-summer like an apple or pear. Its brilliant coloring is good with slightly lighter hot colors, such as orange, or warm shades like salmon-pink; it also contrasts well with light apple-green and yellow-green flowers or foliage. The flowers coincide with most of the spring bulbs and look outstanding with tulips, crown imperials, and narcissi, especially those with orange trumpets, while their season lasts long enough to interact with the red-flushed growth of shrubs such as photinias, spiraeas, and bush roses. Hellebores make equally congenial partners.

◉ *Cytisus* 'Lena', *Fritillaria imperialis* 'Aurora', *Helleborus × sternii*, *Narcissus* 'Ambergate', *Spiraea japonica* 'Goldflame', *Tulipa* 'Orange Favourite'

H: 1.5m (5ft) S: 2m (6½ft) ✿ **Mid- to late spring**
▬▭ ◌-◌◌ ▢-▉ **Z5 pH5–6.5**

Chamaecyparis lawsoniana 'Winston Churchill'

The Lawson cypress (*C. lawsoniana*) is a fairly hardy, evergreen conifer, useful as a specimen tree or for hedges. 'Winston Churchill', one of its brightest yellow cultivars, grows fairly slowly to produce a small to medium-sized tree. As a hedging plant, its brightness may be a disadvantage, distracting attention from the plants growing in front, but it makes a superb specimen tree of regular conical habit, useful both in isolation and as a punctuation mark among other planting. It combines easily with other conifers, contrasting particularly well with the darkest kinds and those with glaucous foliage, and it looks appropriate planted among ericaceous shrubs such as pieris, rhododendrons, and kalmias, especially cultivars with yellow, white, or contrasting lavender-blue flowers.

C.l. 'Lutea' ♡, up to 15m (50ft) high, is another fine yellow cultivar for specimen planting, broadly columnar but less formal in growth habit, with large, flattened feathery sprays of foliage and a slim, drooping top.

Although *Chamaecyparis lawsoniana* 'Winston Churchill' and *Picea pungens* Glauca Group are usually grown as free-standing plants, here they are juxtaposed for the dramatic foliage contrast of the feathery cypress with the layered branches of silvery blue-green spruce.

◉ *Abies concolor* Violacea Group, *Rhododendron* 'Albatross Townhill White', *R. macabeanum*, *Sequoia sempervirens* 'Cantab', *Thuja plicata* 'Atrovirens'

H: 10m (33ft) S: 4m (13ft) ✿ **(Spring)**
▬▭ ◌◌ ▢ ▉ **Z6 pH5.5–6.5**

Choisya ternata ℣

MEXICAN ORANGE

With its solid shape, glistening foliage, and fragrant, white spring blooms, this evergreen shrub is a valuable plant for the front of a shrub or mixed border, as foundation planting, or as a hedge. Some shade is acceptable, especially where summers are hot, but in areas with cool summers it needs full sun and protection from cold winds. It makes an excellent background for winter and spring flowers, or it can be combined with more open plants and lighter foliage, such as ceanothus, ozothamnus, pyracanthas, or cistus. Larger specimens can be draped with a spring-flowering climber such as a small clematis. *C. ternata* Sundance ('Lich') ℣ has

Swags of a pale pink *Clematis montana* var. *rubens* here drape themselves prettily across *Choisya ternata*. The vigor of the clematis makes this an effect most easily achieved if the choisya is large and planted toward the limit of the spread of the clematis, although a less rampant Alpina clematis could be substituted. A cultivar with flowers of a more definite pink might be even more effective.

bright yellow-green foliage, approaching pure gold in full sun, and makes a spectacular contrast with blue flowers. Like the species, in areas with hot summers it tends to scorch, and may benefit from some shade.

◉ *Camassia cusickii* 'Zwanenburg', *Ceanothus* 'Blue Jeans', *Cistus* × *hybridus*, *Cytisus* × *praecox* 'Albus', *Pyracantha* 'Navaho', *Rosa* 'Maigold' ⌐ pp.89 **C**, 109 **A**

H & S: 2.5m (8ft) ❈ Late spring
◊◊ ☐-■ Z8 pH5–7

Cistus × *cyprius* ℣

One of the hardiest of the rock roses (a mainly Mediterranean evergreen genus), this upright, fairly open shrub usually has white flowers, with a central disk of golden anthers and a deep maroon blotch at the base of each petal. With its preference for hot, sunny sites and good drainage, it is well suited to a gravel garden or sunny border or a shrubbery, especially with other Mediterranean shrubs such as helianthemums, lavenders, and sages. Its color allows associations with almost any other, and it combines well with shrubby helichrysums, artemisias, catmints, phlomis, alstroemerias, and summer-flowering bulbs such as smaller species gladioli. The commonly grown, plain white 'Albiflorus' looks very handsome with blue flowers, including nigellas, glaucous or silver foliage, and yellow-green foliage and flowers.

◉ *Ceanothus* 'Blue Mound', *Dianthus* 'Paisley Gem', *Euphorbia seguieriana* subsp. *niciciana*, *Lavandula stoechas* subsp. *pedunculata*, *Salvia lavandulifolia*

H & S: 1.5m (5ft) ❈ Early to late summer
◊-◊◊ ☐-■ Z8 pH6–7.5

The stark white blooms of *Cistus* × *cyprius* are tempered by *Alstroemeria ligtu* hybrids in warm shades of salmon. The yellow in the center of the cistus flowers is echoed by golden flashes on the alstroemeria's upper petals.

The large crinkled blooms of *Cistus × purpureus* are perfectly complemented by the small crimson flowers and loosely branched growth habit of *Leptospermum scoparium*. Both plants are suited to sunny, well-drained conditions.

Cistus × purpureus ♛

This is a rounded evergreen shrub with dark green leaves and carmine flowers enlivened with a central disk of golden anthers and a maroon blotch at the base of each petal. Thriving in well-drained sunny sites, it is a choice plant for combining with helianthemums, lavenders, phlomis, and sages in a gravel garden, scree bed, large rock garden, or sunny border, where it looks best in the second row, surrounded by shorter plants. Its vivid pink coloring suits associations with other cool colors, crimsons, and reddish purples, and with silver- or glaucous-leaved plants. Good companions include leptospermums, pinks, eryngiums, earlier gypsophilas, summer-flowering alliums, smaller gladioli and convolvulus, and annuals such as alyssums, nigellas, or annual lupine species.

◉ *Allium* 'Globemaster', *Convolvulus cneorum*, *Dianthus* 'Haytor White', *D.* 'Old Velvet', *Eryngium bourgatii* 'Picos Blue', *Gypsophila* 'Rosenschleier'

H & S: 1m (40in) ✿ **Early to late summer**
⬛▬▬▬▬ ◊-◊◊ ◻-▬ **Z9 pH6–7.5**

Clerodendrum bungei ♛

The heart-shaped leaves of this deciduous suckering shrub are bold and handsome, but its chief glory is the tightly bunched, domed heads of vivid pink blooms, born from late summer into autumn, when few other shrubs are in flower. Its upright growth habit makes a strong impact in large borders, where its flower color combines successfully with cool tints and purple, silver, or grey foliage, using late partners such as Japanese anemones, large fuchsias, hydrangeas, *Hibiscus syriacus* cultivars, indigoferas, lespedezas, Rugosa roses and late-flowering hostas. Seasonal companions include *Cosmos bipinnatus* cultivars, cleomes, chrysanthemums, and asters. A larger specimen can be draped with a late-flowering climber such as a Viticella clematis or an autumn-coloring vine to contrast with its own strong green foliage.

◉ *Anemone × hybrida* 'Elegans', *Clematis* 'Minuet', *Cotinus* 'Grace', *Fuchsia* 'Riccartonii', *Hibiscus syriacus* 'Red Heart', *Hydrangea macrophylla* 'Veitchii'

H & S: 2m (6½ft) ✿ **Late summer to mid-autumn**
⬛▬▬▬▬ ◊◊ ◻-▬ **Z8 pH5.5–7**

Clerodendrum bungei (glory tree), grown against a sunny wall for protection and to encourage production of its vibrant pink blooms, mingles easily with the sumptuous purple foliage of the wine grape (*Vitis vinifera* 'Purpurea').

Convolvulus cneorum ♛

This enchanting small evergreen shrub forms a mound of silky silver leaves, with funnel-shaped white flowers, yellow at their base and pink on the reverse, appearing mainly in late spring, although some later flowers are often produced. In areas with cool summers it needs a warm, sunny, sheltered site with good drainage, and will then thrive in a gravel garden, rock garden, or scree bed, at the front of a border, and even in walls that do not become bone-dry for long. Its flower color allows combinations with any other, while its foliage works well with other silver- or glaucous-leaved plants, and with contrasting foliage such as that of fescues. It associates naturally with Mediterranean plants like cistus, lavenders, sages, and phlomis, and can also be partnered with perennial wallflowers, ceanothus, daphnes, and hebes.

Growing through the outer branches of the soft blue *Ceanothus thyrsiflorus* var. *repens*, the white flowers and silvery foliage of *Convolvulus cneorum* combine charmingly, enhanced by other plants that thrive in Mediterranean climates, including the perennial wallflower *Erysimum* 'Bowles' Mauve'. Both the convolvulus and the wallflower will continue to bloom long after the ceanothus.

◉ *Ceanothus* 'Southmead', *Cistus* 'Silver Pink', *Dianthus* 'Inchmery', *Festuca glauca* 'Blaufuchs', *Lavandula stoechas*, *Nigella damascena* 'Miss Jekyll'

H: 60cm (24in) S: 90cm (36in)
✿ **Late spring to late summer**
⬛▬▬▬▬ ◊-◊◊ ◻-▬ **Z8 pH5.5–7.5**

Cornus alba and *Cornus sericea*

These deciduous dogwoods, with winter stems in red, yellow, or black, look best when sited to catch the low rays of the sun and given contrasting plants beneath. Some also have gold or variegated leaves and color well in autumn. *C. alba*, the red-barked dogwood, is a vigorous species, quickly developing into a thicket of upright stems with conspicuous red bark, especially when young, and foliage that assumes glowing orange and red tints in autumn. Older stems bear flattened heads of white flowers, sometimes followed by creamy white or light blue berries. *C. sericea* (syn. *C. stolonifera*), the red osier dogwood, is even more vigorous, suckering freely, especially in moist soils, to produce dense thickets of tall stems with deep red bark. It flowers, fruits, and colors in autumn like *C. alba*. Both species are taller and more rampant than their many cultivars, most of which have been selected for improved stem color or variegated foliage.

All these dogwoods grow well near water, where reflections can double the display of their stems, although such sites are often in more natural areas where bold variegation seems out of place. Regular pruning gives the brightest stem color. Pruning the clumps to 10–15cm (4–6in) each year in late winter or early spring results in stems about 1m (3¼ft) tall the following season, although the slower-growing *C. alba* 'Kesselringii' is best pruned every two to three years. Pruning leaves the clumps bare for a time and can result in an effect that is too even for semi-wild parts of the garden. Pruning on a two-year cycle, cutting half the stems to the base each year, gives a looser, more natural appearance, although a little brightness is sacrificed. If grown as foliage plants in a mixed border, pruning will be determined by the size of companion plants, which might include Tall Bearded irises, dieramas, red or green smoke bush, and purple *Cercis canadensis*. In wilder situations, they combine well with wild roses, elderberries, willows, and viburnums. For winter display, the bright red stems look spectacular rising from a green and gold bed of foliage, such as variegated euonymus, or partnering the parchment seedheads of grasses like pennisetums or pampas grass.

C.a. 'Sibirica' ♀, the Westonbirt dogwood, is perhaps the best for rich red stems. Among those with white-edged leaves, the compact 'Sibirica Variegata' is held to be superior to the more common 'Elegantissima' ♀ and to the taller and coarser 'Variegata'. Gold-variegated 'Spaethii' ♀ has the showiest foliage of all the cultivars; 'Gouchaultii' has leaves that are edged with soft yellow and tinged pink; and 'Aurea' ♀ has golden leaves; all have good autumn color. 'Buds Yellow' has probably the yellowest stems, and the black-stemmed 'Kesselringii' has red and purple autumn leaf color. The shoots of *C. sericea* 'Flaviramea' ♀ have a yellowish green tinge, not quite as buttery as 'Buds Yellow', while *C.s.* 'White Gold' has stems like 'Flaviramea' and white-edged leaves.

A

B

Above: The creamy variegation and bold leaf shape of *Cornus alba* 'Elegantissima' set off the dissected foliage and blue, early summer flowers of *Geranium × magnificum*.

Left:. The apple-green flowers of hellebore (*Helleborus foetidus*) contrast with the bright stems of *Cornus alba* 'Sibirica'. White-flowered heaths or golden heathers could be used instead of the mauve heaths *Erica carnea* 'King George' and *E. × darleyensis* 'Darley Dale'.

Below: With its yellow-green stems, *Cornus sericea* 'Flaviramea' makes a subtle partner for the white-variegated *Euonymus fortunei* 'Variegatus'. This is a combination that works effectively when viewed at close range.

C

⬤ **Black-stemmed:** *Carex oshimensis* 'Evergold'
Red-stemmed: *Rubus thibetanus* ⬌ p.47 **B**
Yellow-stemmed: *Phyllostachys nigra* ⬌ p.45 **B**
Yellow-green/yellow-edged foliage: *Alchemilla mollis* p.182 **C**, *Astilbe* 'Red Sentinel' p.194 **B**, *Eryngium bourgatii* 'Picos Blue' p.216 **C**, *Helianthus* 'Monarch' p.235 **A**, *Rudbeckia* 'Herbstsonne' p.282 **A**
White-edged foliage: *Dahlia* 'Grenadier' p.373 **B**, *Zinnia* 'Chippendale' p.407 **B**
Autumn color: *Deschampsia cespitosa* , *Juniperus virginiana* 'Grey Owl', *Miscanthus sinensis* 'Silberturm'

H: 2–3m (6½–10ft) S: 3–4m (10–13ft)
✿ **Late spring to early summer**

 ◌◌-◌◌◌ ■-■ Z2 pH4.5–7.5

Cornus controversa 'Variegata' ♔

This large, upright, deciduous shrub or small tree has spreading side-branches arranged in table-like layers, giving it a dramatic horizontal structure. This makes a particularly telling contrast to columnar shrubs and small trees and to herbaceous plants with flowers born in tall spikes. The bold leaves are emphasized by neat white margins, giving the whole plant a pale tone that contrasts with dark foliage and harmonizes with silver leaves or white flowers. Its creamy white blooms are largely camouflaged by the young leaves and, although charming at close range, contribute little to its effect.

The plant can be used as a focal point, perhaps with a carpet of woodland flowers in white or blue beneath, but is difficult to use in quantity without the risk of overstatement. Sited in a border, it needs space to display its structure and should not be hemmed in: other shrubs or tall herbaceous plants of comparable size should be kept at a distance, although shorter plants can provide a foil beneath its spread. *C. alternifolia* 'Argentea' ♔ is similar but has smaller leaves, suiting it to arrangements on a smaller scale.

◐ *Fatsia japonica, Hedera colchica, Hesperis matronalis, Hosta ventricosa, Lilium martagon* var. *album, Phlox divaricata, Stephanandra tanakae* ⌐p.255 **C**

H & S: 8m (26ft) ❀ **Early summer**
◊◊ ■-■ **Z6 pH5–7**

The layered growth habit and cream-edged leaves of *Cornus controversa* 'Variegata' combine well with the looser form and colored leaves of *Philadelphus coronarius* 'Aureus'.

Cornus florida

FLOWERING DOGWOOD

Flowering dogwoods are deciduous large shrubs or small trees of conical habit with clusters of tiny green florets surrounded by showy, white or pink bracts. Their leaves turn rich red or purple in autumn. There are many cultivars selected for their large bracts (such as 'Cherokee Princess' and 'Cloud Nine', both white), rich bract color (deep carmine 'Cherokee Chief' ♔), plentiful flowers ('White Cloud'), or variegated foliage ('Hohmann's Gold' and 'Welchii'). Their growth habit is less striking than that of *C. controversa* 'Variegata' (left) and so they are less suited to use as a focal point, but more amenable to grouping; however, they still need space and good light to flower evenly and profusely. Although fairly hardy, they can be damaged by late spring frosts and do not flower well in areas with cool summers. Attractive plants for a sunny glade in a woodland garden, where they thrive in the slightly acid soil, they go well with kalmias and deciduous azaleas, and with late spring flowers such as violets, sweet rocket, and cranesbills.

◐ *Dicentra* 'Bacchanal', *Hesperis matronalis* var. *albiflora, Hyacinthoides hispanica, Lunaria annua, Rhododendron austrinum, Tiarella wherryi*

H & S: 6m (20ft) ❀ **Late spring**
◊◊ ■ **Z6 pH5–6.5**

This charmingly simple combination of *Cornus florida* with *Phlox divaricata* beneath is made more pleasant by the pervasive fragrance of the phlox.

In a subtle grouping, the glaucous cream-edged leaves and yellow flowers of *Coronilla valentina* subsp. *glauca* 'Variegata' are joined by silver-leaved *Teucrium fruticans*, backed by golden hops (*Humulus lupulus* 'Aureus'). The coronilla and the hops both have compound leaves, while those of the teucrium are simple and lance-shaped; the teucrium's small blue flowers present a delicate contrast.

Coronilla valentina subsp. *glauca* 'Variegata'

With its tiny cream-edged glaucous leaflets and small fragrant yellow flowers, this pretty semi-evergreen shrub is best appreciated at close range. Its main flowering is from late winter into spring, but it produces some bloom all year round, with a significant second flush from late summer. A charming plant for the front of a border, a sunny bank, or a gravel garden, it associates well with yellow, white, or blue flowers, yellow-green foliage and flowers, and glaucous foliage. It mixes well with smaller ceanothus, brooms, choisyas, helianthemums, genistas, *Aurinia saxatilis* cultivars, smaller narcissi, and white, yellow, or yellow-green daphnes, and benefits from association with plants of more definite form – celmisias, for example. Where summers are cool, it needs a sunny sheltered site.

◉ *Brunnera macrophylla*, *Ceanothus × delileanus* 'Gloire de Versailles', *Choisya* Goldfingers, *Narcissus* 'Charity May', *Rosmarinus officinalis*, *Scilla siberica*

H & S: 80cm (31in) ❀ **Late winter to mid-spring**
◊-◊◊ ▢-▨ **Z9 pH5.5–7**

Cotinus coggygria 'Royal Purple' ♛

The reddish purple leaves of this smoke bush have a fiery red glow when backlit by the sun and before they are shed in autumn. A shrub with great poise, it forms rosettes of leaves towards the shoot tips and flowers profusely when mature, covering the foliage with cloud-like inflorescences. Its ultimate size may be too large for many situations, but it can be pruned to 2–3m (6½–10ft) high, when it will support herbaceous or annual climbers such as morning glories or perennial peas; larger plants can be draped with climbers such as Viticella or Texensis clematis. Its coloring blends well with purple, blue, crimson, and carmine-pink flowers, or with scarlet, coral, orange, or flame. Specimen plants achieve an attractive framework of branches, which can be planted beneath with harmonious flowers such as dark-leaved heucheras laced with *Lilium speciosum* cultivars. Other variants include 'Notcutt's Variety', slightly less rich in color; Purpureus Group, with green leaves and purplish flowers; and Rubrifolius Group, plum-purple, aging to purple-flushed green and turning fiery red in autumn.

◉ *Agastache* 'Firebird', *Alonsoa warscewiczii* p.362 **C**, *Dahlia* 'David Howard', *Hemerocallis* 'Stafford' p.239 **B**, *Ipomoea lobata*, *Knautia macedonica* p.254 **A**, *Ligularia dentata* 'Desdemona' p.258 **A**, *Lilium* 'Journey's End', *Lonicera caprifolium* p.126 **B** ⌷ pp. 72 **C**, 95 **C**, 230 **B**

H & S: 5m (16ft) ❀ **Mid-summer**
◊◊ ▢-▨ **Z5 pH5.5–7.5**

By allowing this purple smoke bush (*Cotinus coggygria* 'Royal Purple') to grow branches to ground level, sprawling and scrambling plants can be encouraged to weave themselves through its stems, creating an attractive tapestry of foliage and flowers. The vigorous cranesbill *Geranium × oxonianum* 'Claridge Druce' here provides contrasting leaves and harmonious mauve-pink flowers.

A subdued combination of the grey-green leaves of *Cotoneaster conspicuus* 'Decorus' and silvery *Brachyglottis* (Dunedin Group) 'Sunshine' is saved from monotony by the elegantly arching sprays of the cotoneaster's pink-tinged blooms. The brachyglottis flowers will be bright yellow when they open and might upstage the quiet charm of the cotoneaster; they can be pruned away before they develop fully.

Cotoneaster conspicuus 'Decorus' ♀

Pinkish white, early summer flowers and scarlet autumn fruits emphasize the attractive arching branches of this low evergreen shrub. It is useful for the front of a shrub border or for a ground cover, and it blends well in wild and woodland gardens, where it tolerates dappled shade. For maximum flower and fruit production, it is best in a sunny site, where it combines easily with deutzias, philadelphus, small-flowered roses, kerrias, kolkwitzias, later-flowering rhododendrons and lilacs, spiraeas, potentillas, and plants like columbines, cranesbills, foxgloves, and geums. It is good with martagon lilies, and with foliage of more definite form – bergenias or hostas, for example. Draping its dusty grey-green foliage with a scrambling plant, such as a small-flowered clematis, can enhance its appearance in summer.

⬤ *Bergenia* 'Sunningdale', *Philadelphus* 'Natchez', *Rosa elegantula* 'Persetosa', *R.* 'Manning's Blush', *Syringa meyeri* var. *spontanea* 'Palibin'

H: 1.5m (5ft) **S: 2.5m** (8ft) ⚘ **Early summer**
◌◌ ☐ - ▓ **Z6 pH5–7.5**

Herringbone sprays of *Cotoneaster horizontalis* laden with scarlet fruits and the amber leaves of *Aronia arbutifolia* about to be shed supply satisfyingly warm autumnal tints. The ground beneath is carpeted with the fan-shaped leaves of lady's mantle (*Alchemilla mollis*).

Cotoneaster horizontalis ♀

A versatile semi-evergreen fruiting shrub, this makes an excellent ground or wall cover, each branch forming a flat spray of branchlets arranged like a fishbone. Its tiny glistening leaves often remain until late winter, turning vivid scarlet before they fall and making a colorful combination with the dusky red fruits; even when bare, its branchlets form a pleasant pattern, especially when emphasized by frost. It bears fruit best in sun, but will tolerate a shady wall, behind plants of contrasting form, including hostas, ferns, willow gentians, and smaller scrambling plants like some wispier cranesbills and codonopsis. On a bank or at the front of a border, it works well with smaller scramblers and plants of contrasting foliage; it may be backed by taller perennials and small shrubs, especially those grown for autumn color, such as aronias, berberis, and smaller maples.

⬤ *Codonopsis grey-wilsonii*, *Geranium kishtvariense*, *G.* × *riversleaianum*, *Hosta* 'Buckshaw Blue', *Nandina domestica* 'Fire Power', *Polystichum setiferum*, *Schizostylis coccinea* 'Major' p.284 **C**

H: 1m (40in) **S: 3m** (10ft) ⚘ **Late spring**
◌◌ ☐ - ▓ **Z5 pH5–7.5**

Cotoneaster frigidus 'Cornubia' ♀

This tall, elegant deciduous shrub produces long, arching stems, weighed down through autumn and winter with glistening red fruits. It can be used to provide a light canopy over other shrubs and plants, especially those coloring well in autumn and winter. The fairly open branch structure casts little shade, allowing a wide range of plants to be grown beneath its spread. These include Japanese maples, aronias, deciduous azaleas and euonymus, miscanthus cultivars, nandinas, Chinese lanterns, berrying or variegated hollies, dogwoods, and berberis. Bamboos, fruit-bearing crab apples, and amelanchiers make good companions, while the strong stems will happily support a wispy vine, such as less vigorous parthenocissus species.

⬤ *Acer palmatum* 'Crimson Queen', *Amelanchier lamarckii* p.31 **A**, *Euonymus alatus*, *Miscanthus sinensis* 'Zebrinus', *Nandina domestica* 'Umpqua Chief', *Parthenocissus tricuspidata* 'Lowii'

H & S: 6m (20ft) ⚘ **Early summer**
◌◌ ☐ - ▓ **Z6 pH5–7.5**

The tiny yellow-green leaves of *Lonicera nitida* 'Baggesen's Gold' contrast in size with those of *Cotoneaster frigidus* 'Cornubia' while harmonizing with those cotoneaster leaves that have turned yellow before being shed; they also act as a foil for the cotoneaster's bright scarlet fruits.

The tiny flowers and warm tints of *Cytisus* 'Zeelandia' perfectly complement the boldly shaped, orange and vermilion tulip 'Queen of Sheba', although the broom would normally rise over the tulip. Both are set off effectively by the immature yellowish green flower heads of the snowball bush (*Viburnum opulus* 'Roseum').

Cytisus hybrid cultivars

The numerous broom hybrids raised by crossing *C. multiflorus* with *C. scoparius* and *C. purgans* are among the most useful of late spring flowers. They vary from yellow to red, white, pink, or peach, including bicolors, which gives them the potential to mix attractively with spring bulbs and biennial bedding plants, while their diffuse structure provides a foil for plants of more definite form. Cultivars include 'Hollandia' ♔, whose flowers combine cream and pink and deep pink; and 'Zeelandia' ♔, which has blooms in pale creamy yellow and pink. They are outstanding companions for late narcissi, tulips, and wallflowers; yellow cultivars contrast well with forget-me-nots, and rich scarlet ones with euphorbias. The shrubs, which are deciduous, may be short-lived, but they will last longer and flower more lavishly if most of the flowered wood is pruned off once the blooms have faded, taking care not to cut back into old wood.

⊕ *Aquilegia formosa*, *Euphorbia characias*, *E. griffithii* 'Dixter', *Exochorda × macrantha* 'The Bride', *Geranium phaeum* 'Album', *Narcissus poeticus* 'Plenus', *Rosa* 'Roseriae de l'Haÿ' p.160 **A**, *Tulipa* 'Spring Green'

H & S: 1.5m (5ft) ❀ **Late spring to early summer**
◇-◇◇ ☐-■ **Z6 pH5–7**

Cytisus nigricans

Unlike the more familiar spring cultivars, this late summer broom produces its flowers in a solid spike, creating a structured, less nebulous effect. An erect, deciduous shrub, it is attractive with hot colors, cream or yellow-green foliage or flowers, and glaucous or yellow-variegated foliage, and makes an effective partner for grasses, cranesbills, and *Buddleja × weyeriana* cultivars. It contrasts memorably with blue flowers such as late aconitums and *Ceanothus × delileanus* cultivars, and purple-leaved shrubs such as *Prunus × cistena* and smoke bush. 'Cyni' is a compact cultivar, 1m (40in) tall and wide, and better suited to the front of a border. Since plants flower on the current season's wood, they must be pruned in early spring.

⊕ *Aconitum* 'Spark's Variety', *Ceanothus × delileanus* 'Gloire de Versailles', *Crocosmia* 'Vulcan', *Dahlia* 'Moonfire', *Hemerocallis* 'Marion Vaughn', *Lilium* Imperial Gold Group, *Miscanthus sinensis* 'Pünktchen', *Nicotiana* 'Lime Green'

H: 1.5m (5ft) S: 1m (40in)
❀ **Late summer to early autumn**
◇-◇◇ ☐-■ **Z6 pH5–7.5**

The sharp yellow flowers of *Cytisus nigricans* harmonize with the yellow-green leaves of *Geranium* 'Ann Folkard' while contrasting strikingly with its magenta flowers.

Delicate sprays of *Cytisus × praecox* 'Warminster', its flowers sulfur-yellow on dark green stems, are set against the acid yellow-green leaves of *Philadelphus coronarius* 'Aureus'. This bright combination will have an impact in any border, but the philadelphus may scorch in hot areas.

Cytisus × praecox 'Warminster' ♔

WARMINSTER BROOM

This is an attractive, airy deciduous shrub, particularly useful for combining with late spring flowers such as tulips, narcissi, forget-me-nots, wallflowers, brunneras, crown imperials, and euphorbias, as well as with yellow-green foliage. Its soft yellow coloring mixes well with warm colors such as peach and apricot, but is also strong enough to contrast with blues. In the second or third row of a border, its gently arching shoots can be used to show off the contrasting growth habit of *C. × kewensis* ♔, a prostrate broom that merits planting towards the front. 'Allgold' ♔ is another cultivar of *C. × praecox*, producing flowers in a richer shade of gold, that can be used in the same ways.

⊕ *Aquilegia canadensis*, *Brunnera macrophylla*, *Choisya ternata* Sundance, *Euphorbia polychroma* 'Major', *Geranium sylvaticum* 'Mayflower', *Narcissus poeticus* 'Plenus', *Rosa primula*, *Syringa × persica* 'Alba', *Tulipa* 'Golden Artist', *T.* 'Queen of Sheba'

H: 1.2m (4ft) S: 1.5m (5ft) ❀ **Mid- to late spring**
◇-◇◇ ☐-■ **Z6 pH5–7**

Daphne cneorum 'Eximia' and the perennial candytuft *Iberis sempervirens* are of similar height and growth habit, allowing them to interweave to create a harmonious late spring carpet of pink and white flowers.

Daphne cneorum 'Eximia'

This particularly showy, large-flowered daphne, with evergreen foliage and heavily fragrant rose-pink blooms opening from crimson buds, requires good soil, with efficient drainage and enough moisture to never become dry at the roots. As long as it is given these exacting conditions, the shrub will create an enchanting carpet of bloom in a rock garden or at the front of a border. It is an excellent choice for a prominent position near a sitting area or alongside a path, where its remarkable beauty and fragrance can be fully appreciated. It blends well with cool colors, especially white or apple-green flowers, and purple-flushed or glaucous foliage. Good partners include other daphnes, aubrietas, rock cress, saxifrages, and smaller spring bulbs, even tulips if larger cultivars in overwhelmingly hot colors are avoided.

⬤ *Arabis alpina* subsp. *caucasica* 'Schneehaube', *Dicentra* 'Stuart Boothman', *Helleborus* × *sternii*, *Omphalodes cappadocica* 'Lilac Mist', *Ornithogalum nutans*, *Tulipa saxatilis*

H: 20cm (8in) S: 1.5m (5ft) ❄ **Late spring**
▪▪▫▫ ◊◊ ▪ ▪ **Z5 pH6–7.5**

Daphne mezereum

FEBRUARY DAPHNE

This valuable early-flowering deciduous shrub has flowers varying in color from mauve-pink to burgundy, followed by scarlet fruits in summer. The white form, f. *alba*, has yellow fruits. Both enjoy limy soils and cool positions, and prefer an open area rather than one against a wall; they can also be used near the front of a border, although they may become misshapen if hemmed in by herbaceous plants. They are successful with winter heaths and flowers in cool colors,

Daphne mezereum, here growing through a carpet of white Darley Dale heath (*Erica* × *darleyensis* 'Silberschmelze'), harmonizes in growth habit with the stems of *Cornus alba* 'Flaviramea' while contrasting effectively with their yellow-green color. Heaths with pale mauve or rich ruby flowers could be added to the carpet, avoiding colors too close to that of the daphne.

including bulbs such as crocuses, snowdrops, white or palest yellow early narcissi, and *Cyclamen coum* variants, as well as pale green hellebores. Container-grown plants can become root-bound, so it is important to use generously potted plants and to unwind the roots before planting.

⬤ *Bergenia cordifolia* 'Purpurea', *Galanthus* 'S. Arnott', *Helleborus* × *nigercors*, *H.* × *sternii*, *Heuchera* 'Purple Petticoats', *Narcissus* 'Dove Wings'

H: 1.2m (4ft) S: 1m (3¼ft)
❄ **Late winter to early spring**
▪▪▫▫ ◊◊ ▪ ▪ **Z5 pH6–8**

Deutzia longifolia 'Vilmoriniae'

In full sun this deciduous shrub makes a billowing mass of growth almost completely smothered by a froth of white blooms. It is a superlative plant for a white garden or a mixed or shrub border, especially partnered by old roses. It combines successfully with almost any other color, and can be used as a host for late-flowering clematis such as Viticella cultivars, which will wreathe the deutzia with late summer and autumn flowers. Immediately after flowering, its stems need to be pruned back to a framework of branches, which will stimulate production of the next year's flowering wood. 'Veitchii' ♥ is another fine cultivar of *D. longifolia*, producing mauve-pink blooms that have white margins to the petals.

⬤ *Campanula lactiflora*, *Hebe* 'Midsummer Beauty', *Iris* 'Cambridge', *I. orientalis*, *Lupinus arboreus*, *Potentilla fruticosa* 'Vilmoriniana', *Rosa* 'Fantin-Latour'

H: 2m (6½ft) S: 3m (10ft)
❄ **Early to mid-summer**
▪▪▫▫ ◊◊ ▫-▪ **Z6 pH5–7.5**

Contrasting red valerian (*Centranthus ruber*) and yellow-green *Euphorbia polychroma* provide a foil for *Deutzia longifolia* 'Vilmoriniae'. The deutzia lightens the color scheme and adds height, while occasional foxgloves supply punctuation and help unify the scheme, white harmonizing with the deutzia and magenta with the valerian.

Brightly variegated *Elaeagnus* × *ebbingei* 'Gilt Edge' harmonizes with *Rubus cockburnianus* 'Goldenvale'. In winter the bramble's white stems make a striking contrast.

In a colorful foliage display *Elaeagnus pungens* 'Maculata' combines with harmonious *Lonicera nitida* 'Baggesen's Gold' and contrasting *Berberis thunbergii* f. *atropurpurea*.

Elaeagnus pungens 'Maculata' ♛

A robust cultivar, this large, variegated evergreen elaeagnus (syn. 'Aureovariegata') makes a fine spreading bush for the middle of a border or the front of a shrubbery. It is less upright than *E.* × *ebbingei* 'Gilt Edge' (left) but the foliage is of similar coloring – large splashes of golden yellow with rich green leaf margins. It is striking as a partner for blue ceanothus cultivars or as a support for climbers such as white perennial peas, or a restrained clematis or honeysuckle. Other *E. pungens* cultivars for these roles include 'Frederici', which has narrow creamy yellow leaves margined with green; 'Variegata', with narrow white leaf edges; and the fairly slow-growing 'Dicksonii', with broad gold leaf margins. Stems that revert to green should be cut out while still small.

◐ *Ceanothus arboreus*, *Cytisus* × *praecox*, *Dahlia* 'Klankstad Kerkrade', *Euphorbia characias*, *Iris* 'Cambridge', *Lilium* Imperial Gold Group, *Mahonia* × *media*, *Miscanthus sinensis* 'Strictus', *Rosa* Elina

H: 3m (10ft) S: 5m (16ft) ☼ **Mid-autumn**
◐◐ ▪ **Z7 pH5–7.5**

Elaeagnus × *ebbingei* 'Gilt Edge' ♛

Variegated cultivars of evergreen *E.* × *ebbingei* are dependable foliage plants for mixed borders and shrubberies on most soils except chalk. 'Gilt Edge' is one of the most colorful, with brilliant yellow leaf margins and, as a bonus, fragrant, creamy white flowers in autumn. Plants harmonize successfully in yellow and cream color schemes, and make a lively contrast to pure blue flowers; they also blend with other evergreens in hedges and screens. The coloration is vivid in sun or light shade. 'Limelight' is less strident, with yellow-green splashes on its green-edged leaves. As with all variegated elaeagnus, any stems that revert to green should be pruned out. Grafted plants (identified by an obvious graft union near the base) are best avoided since they usually have shorter lives than plants on their own roots.

◐ *Aconitum* 'Ivorine', *Berberis julianae*, *Euphorbia sikkimensis*, *Forsythia ovata* 'Tetragold', *Kerria japonica* 'Golden Guinea', *Physocarpus opulifolius* 'Dart's Gold', *Rosa* 'Chinatown', *Syringa vulgaris* 'Primrose'

H & S: 4m (13ft) ☼ **Mid-autumn**
◐◐ ▪ **Z7 pH5–7.5**

Elaeagnus 'Quicksilver' ♛

The middle of a border is the best place for this outstanding, fairly tall deciduous shrub (syn. *E. angustifolia* Caspica Group). Grown mainly for its dainty silvery foliage, it also has small, sweet-scented creamy flowers in early summer. Its soft coloring, especially when young, mixes wonderfully with old-fashioned roses, blue-flowered shrubs, and Viticella or Texensis clematis (but not early clematis cultivars, which flower before 'Quicksilver' is in full leaf). Annual climbers such as morning glories are also excellent partners. If pruned low to encourage production of basal sideshoots, 'Quicksilver' may be grown among herbaceous plants, which then mingle with the lower branches. This shrub enjoys plenty of sun and a well-drained sandy site, but will tolerate most soils and drier conditions than other elaeagnus.

◐ *Aconitum hemsleyanum*, *Clematis* 'Huldine', *C.* 'Prince Charles', *Delphinium* Summer Skies Group, *Ipomoea tricolor* 'Heavenly Blue', *Rosa* 'Sander's White Rambler' ⌐ pp.51 **B**, 79 **B**, 105 **B**, 265 **C**

H & S: 4m (13ft) ☼ **Early summer**
◐-◐◐ ▫-▪ **Z3 pH5–7.5**

Leaving the lower stems on *Elaeagnus* 'Quicksilver' allows its softly silver foliage to blend attractively with herbaceous plants such as *Symphytum caucasicum*.

Erica carnea
WINTER HEATH

Among the hundreds of heath and heather cultivars some of the most popular and valuable are those of *E. carnea*, a low-growing, shrubby heath that flowers in late winter and early spring, when there is often a dearth of color elsewhere in the garden. The wiry, branching plants spread to form clumps of evergreen ground cover on most well-drained soils. The flowers, tiny and tightly packed in long, slender spikes, have a wide range of colors, from white and lilac-pink to purplish red. There are also richly colored gold- and bronze-leaved forms, many with deeper red and orange foliar tints in very cold weather.

Winter heaths are effective when massed in beds, although care should be taken to avoid any color clash between flowers and foliage, which is sometimes a problem with colored-leaved forms. They look especially fine when planted with late winter and early spring bulbs beneath, such as snowdrops, hardy cyclamens, and *Crocus tommasinianus,* and are very much at home with other ericaceous shrubs such as dwarf rhododendrons, gaultherias, vacciniums, or the prostrate *Leiophyllum buxifolium*. Daphnes and prostrate brooms are also congenial partners; bergenias offer dramatic contrasts of leaf shape and texture; and dwarf junipers make natural heathland associations. In more extensive heath gardens, taller forms of *Juniperus communis* can provide startling accents that relieve the uniform appearance of the heaths.

All heaths benefit from an overall trim after flowering to prevent straggly growth. However, since plants are naturally rounded, each one should be clipped individually to avoid producing a flat carpet. Hot, impoverished sites may lead to fungal ailments; plants will tolerate some shade but not the deep shade beneath trees.

⊙ **Bronze-leaved:** *Cornus alba* 'Sibirica', *Crocus* 'Gypsy Girl', *Heuchera* 'Amber Waves', *H.* 'Sashay' **Mauve/purple-flowered:** *Bergenia stracheyi*, *Cyclamen coum*, *Pulmonaria* 'Lewis Palmer' p.279 **B** ❏ p.40 **B** **White-flowered:** *Bergenia ciliata*, *Galanthus* 'S. Arnott', *Heuchera* 'Green Spice', *Ipheion uniflorum* **Yellow-green leaved:** *Cornus sericea* 'Flaviramea', *Narcissus* 'Little Witch', *Scilla siberica*

H: 20–25cm (8–10in) S: 50cm (20in)
❀ **Late winter to early spring**
◌◌ ▨-▨ ■ **Z5 pH4.5–7**

A

Winter heaths such as *Erica carnea* 'Springwood White' are delightful partners for early bulbs such as *Narcissus* 'Tête-à-tête' and the persistently perennial *Tulipa turkestanica*. Even fairly small bulbs such as these are vigorous enough to grow beneath the spread of the heaths.

Erica × darleyensis
DARLEY DALE HEATH

This is a natural hybrid between *E. carnea* (above) and the tree heath *E. erigena* (syn. *E. mediterranea*). It is a little larger than *E. carnea*, forming a vigorous, bushy shrub with textured plumes of young growth, and it likes similar sites in sun or light shade with moist but well-drained soil. The cultivars include the original hybrid 'Darley Dale', which produces pale pink flowers over many weeks. Flower color ranges from the purity of 'White Perfection' ♀ and the other well-known white cultivar 'Silberschmelze', through pink to the deep rose-red of 'Jack H. Brummage'. This neat form has yellow foliage darkening to reddish gold in winter, and cream and pink young growth in spring.

E. × darleyensis cultivars are natural companions for *E. carnea*, their greater height and bulk making them most effective as a backdrop to their more compact relatives. They combine equally well with the associates recommended for *E. carnea*, together with smaller gorses and dwarf spruces.

⊙ *Calluna vulgaris* p.35 **A**, *Crocus sieberi*, *Daphne mezereum* p.45 **B**, *Galanthus elwesii*, *Hedera colchica* p.121 **A**, *Heuchera* 'Can-can', *Picea pungens* Pendula Group p.74 **C**, *Rhododendron* 'Praecox' ❏ pp.40 **B**, 90 **A**

H: 30–60cm (12–24in) S: 30–75cm (12–30in)
❀ **Late winter to early spring**
◌◌ ▨-▨ ■ **Z6 pH4.5–7**

Pink *Erica × darleyensis* 'Darley Dale' and *Euonymus fortunei* 'Variegatus' provide a carpet for bright-stemmed dogwoods *Cornus alba* 'Sibirica' and *C. sericea* 'Flaviramea'. *E. × d.* 'White Perfection' would also be effective here.

B

Subdued mauves, purples, and pinks, together with grey-green foliage, make up this carpet of late spring flowers in which *Erysimum* 'Bowles' Mauve' is the prominent plant, with *E. cheiri* 'Purple Queen' and *Skimmia japonica* 'Rubella'. *Allium hollandicum* and tulips will follow shortly.

Erysimum 'Bowles' Mauve' ♀

This wallflower is a short-lived sub-shrub that forms a domed bush with slightly greyish leaves. Its purplish mauve flowers appear continually through much of the year, most profusely in late spring and early summer. An excellent candidate for the front of a border, especially surrounded by low carpeting plants, it also thrives in rock gardens and gravel gardens, and even grows well in walls. The distinctive flower color can be combined with cool shades and with purple, silver, or glaucous foliage, and contrasts effectively with yellow-green foliage and flowers. It associates well with euphorbias, pinks, catmints, artemisias, and alliums, and looks particularly attractive when grown in front of old roses. Plants must be propagated from cuttings, which should not be allowed to become pot-bound because they are then susceptible to uprooting and are difficult to establish. As a general rule, windy sites are unsuitable for this plant.

⬤ *Artemisia alba* 'Canescens', *Convolvulus cneorum* p.39 **C**, *Dianthus* 'Musgrave's Pink', *Euphorbia characias*, *Tulipa* 'Angélique' p.343 **B** ❏ pp.125 **B**, 260 **B**

H & S: 60cm (24in) ❀ **Late winter to late summer**
◊-◊◊ ☐-■ **Z7 pH5.5–8**

Erysimum 'Wenlock Beauty' ♀

A charming plant for the front of a border or for a rock garden, this perennial wallflower has a more prostrate growth habit than 'Bowles' Mauve' (left) and is less prone to wind damage. The florets open buff and then develop shadings of tawny-red before aging to dusky mauve-purple, a slightly subdued color scheme that is flattered by dusky pink, deep crimson, wine-purple, and dusky mauve. Plants combine well with cream flowers and purple foliage, and make satisfying blends with apple-green and yellow-green. Seeds are rarely set and do not come true to type, so plants must be propagated from cuttings. Another perennial wallflower for similar planting schemes is *E. mutabile*, a spreading plant with flowers in a blend of rose-red and purple, which echo dusky shades, including those of 'Wenlock Beauty'.

⬤ *Artemisia caucasica*, *Aubrieta* 'Joy', *Euphorbia polychroma* 'Major', *Helleborus* × *sternii*, *Heuchera* 'Purple Petticoats', *Narcissus* 'Hawera'

H & S: 45cm (18in) ❀ **Early to late spring**
◊-◊◊ ☐-■ **Z7 pH5.5–8**

Erysimum 'Wenlock Beauty' mixes with soft yellow, double-flowered *Narcissus* 'Yellow Cheerfulness' – the wallflower's amber young florets harmonize while its purple mature florets contrast. Both plants are topped by the sharp yellow-green heads of *Euphorbia characias* subsp. *wulfenii*.

The weeping crab apple *Malus* 'Butterball', its abundant yellow fruits flushed with warm orange, cascades in a curtain, forming a backdrop for the dazzling autumn tints of *Euonymus alatus* var. *apterus* as it changes color from warm mahogany to blazing red.

Euonymus alatus var. *apterus*

The prime attraction of this deciduous euonymus is its fine display of brilliant tints in autumn, especially in full sun, when the leaves assume shades of pink, crimson, and scarlet, making a flamboyant accompaniment to the purplish fruits as they split open to reveal scarlet seeds. The flowers are relatively insignificant, and neither foliage nor growth habit offers great interest during spring and summer, although the shrub can be draped with a flowering climber. It is an outstanding companion for large grasses such as pampas grass and miscanthus, Japanese maples, sorbus, deciduous hollies, and other autumn-coloring plants. The typical species, *E. alatus* ♔, has corky wings growing from its stems, adding curiosity if not decorative value to the overall effect. *E.a.* 'Compactus' ♔ is smaller, no more than 1m (3¼ft) high, with very dense foliage that withstands clipping, making it suitable for plants to use as a dwarf hedge.

◉ *Acer palmatum* f. *atropurpureum*, *Berberis wilsoniae*, *Cotoneaster selloana* 'Pink Feather', *Cotinus* 'Grace', *Ilex verticillata* 'Winter Red', *Miscanthus sinensis* 'China', *Rhododendron quinquefolium*, *Rhus typhina*

H: 2m (6½ft) S: 3m (10ft) ☼ (Early summer)
◊◊ ▢-▪ Z5 pH5.5–8

Euonymus fortunei 'Silver Queen' ♔

The dark green leaves of this bushy evergreen euonymus have butter-yellow margins in spring, turning white by summer. This cheerful variegation, particularly welcome in winter, is attractive at close range, although at a distance the foliage has a paler tone useful for contrasts with darker-leaved plants or for illuminating a shady corner. The yellow spring coloring harmonizes with other yellows, yellow-greens, and cream, and contrasts with pure blue flowers such as forget-me-nots and omphalodes. Other good variegated cultivars are 'Emerald Gaiety' ♔, with white leaf margins that assume pink tints in winter, and 'Emerald 'n' Gold' ♔, with bright gold leaf margins flushed red in winter. All three tolerate sun or shade, grow in fairly poor soil, and if planted against a wall may be trained up to about 3m (10ft). They are useful for edging beds and as a ground cover.

◉ *Brunnera macrophylla*, *Helleborus argutifolius*, *H.* × *hybridus*, *Meconopsis grandis*, *Milium effusum* 'Aureum', *Muscari armeniacum*, *Narcissus* 'Pipit', *Omphalodes cappadocica*, *Tulipa* 'Monte Carlo'

H: 2.5m (8ft) S: 1.5m (5ft) ☼ (Early summer)
◊◊ ▢-▪ Z5 pH5.5–7.5

The yellowish cream variegation of *Euonymus fortunei* 'Silver Queen' contrasts effectively with the sky-blue flowers of Spanish bluebells (*Hyacinthoides hispanica*). Other spring bulbs with blue, soft yellow, or white flowers could be added to enhance the color scheme.

The curious rose-pink fruits of *Euonymus hamiltonianus* subsp. *sieboldianus*, opening to reveal clashing orange seeds, are born on a spreading and unstructured bush that benefits from companion plants of more definite form, such as dwarf pampas grass (*Cortaderia selloana* 'Pumila').

Euonymus hamiltonianus subsp. *sieboldianus*

This deciduous euonymus makes a spreading bush, considerably larger than *E. alatus* var. *apterus* (left) and suited to planting on a larger scale. Its most appealing feature is the autumn coloring of its foliage, the leaves turning various shades of peach, pink, and red, and providing a warm background for the ripening fruit capsules that display orange seeds upon splitting. The autumn leaf tints may vary according to climate, situation, and the particular clone. Like *E. alatus* var. *apterus*, it has few notable charms during spring and summer, but makes an excellent host for flowering climbers, and succeeds in the same plant combinations.

◉ *Celastrus orbiculatus*, *Clematis* 'Abundance', *C. rehderiana*, *Miscanthus sinensis* 'China', *Sorbus* 'Eastern Promise', *Xanthorhiza simplicissima*

H & S: 6m (20ft) ☼ (Early summer)
◊◊ ▢-▪ Z5 pH5.5–7.5

Euphorbia characias subsp. *wulfenii* ♔

This upright, evergreen sub-shrub differs from the typical *E. characias* in having yellow-green rather than brown or blackish nectaries at the center of each floret. Its flower stems are formed in summer and start to bloom the following spring, when they look very effective with late bulbs such as narcissi and the daintier tulips. Plants sometimes appear a little stalky at the base, and benefit from screening with shorter, cushion-forming plants. Impressive harmonies can be made with yellow-green or cream flowers and hot colors like orange, while bronze foliage and blue flowers such as brunneras and omphalodes contrast well. Good companions include crown imperials and Mediterranean shrubs such as white-flowered cistus and phlomis. There are some striking variegated cultivars, but these tend to be weaker-growing and less hardy. Plants enjoy well-drained soil and tolerate some drought, although the foliage can lose its handsome appearance in prolonged dry spells. Once the flowers fade, the stems should be cut back near their base to allow next year's stems to ripen.

◐ *Aquilegia* 'Hensol Harebell', *Camassia leichtlinii*, *Ceanothus* 'Cascade', *Erysimum cheiri* 'Primrose Bedder', *Euphorbia griffithii* 'Dixter', *Fritillaria imperialis* 'The Premier', × *Halimiocistus wintonensis*, *Lupinus* 'Thundercloud' p.260 **B**, *Phlomis chrysophylla*, *Rosa pimpinellifolia* 'Grandiflora' ⌷ pp.48 **B**, 380 **C**

H: 1m (40in) S: 1.2m (4ft)
❋ **Early spring to early summer**

◌◌◌ ◇-◇◇ ■-■ **Z8 pH5.5–7.5**

Right: *Euphorbia characias* subsp. *wulfenii* 'Lambrook Gold' and *E. polychroma* 'Major' match exactly in color but differ sufficiently in form to make an attractive combination.

Below: A large-scale planting of *Euphorbia characias* subsp. *wulfenii* 'Lambrook Gold' and *E. polychroma* 'Major' with *Physocarpus opulifolius* 'Luteus', *Smilacina racemosa*, and *Kirengeshoma palmata*, creates a symphony in chartreuse.

Euphorbia × *martini* ♛

A hybrid derived from *Euphorbia characias* crossed with wood spurge (*E. amygdaloides*), this evergreen sub-shrub has yellowish green flowers with reddish nectaries, together with red stems and dark green leaves. From the wood spurge it inherits greater hardiness than *E. characias* and more tolerance of shade, and it makes an altogether more impressive clump for a woodland garden or a sunny or lightly shaded border. The flowers lose some of their yellow coloring as they age, turning a dull green that is lighter than the foliage and very effective as a contrast with rich deep red flowers, which will harmonize with the euphorbia's stem and nectary coloring. It works well with bronze or yellow-green foliage, and looks pleasant with flowers in shades of yellow, light yellow-green, cream, and orange.

◐ *Epimedium* × *youngianum* 'Niveum' p.215 **B**, *Geum* 'Beech House Apricot', *Helleborus argutifolius*, *H. hybridus*, *Primula* Cowichan Venetian Group

H & S: 1m (40in) ❀ **Mid-spring to mid-summer**
◊-◊◊ ■-■ **Z7 pH5–7.5**

The sumptuously colored, shade-tolerant *Primula* 'Tawny Port' has flowers that harmonize with the stems of *Euphorbia* × *martini* but contrast with its blooms.

The dwarf weeping beech *Fagus sylvatica* 'Purpurea Pendula' acts as a focal point in this deep border, where it is combined with other purple-leaved plants, such as *Berberis* × *ottawensis* f. *purpurea*, and contrasting *Elaeagnus* 'Quicksilver' and yellow asphodel (*Asphodeline lutea*). The beech will need careful pruning to keep it contained but without impairing its natural growth habit.

Fagus sylvatica 'Purpurea Pendula'

This deciduous, dwarf weeping beech makes an excellent specimen but is also small enough to include in large borders. It is usually top-grafted as a standard onto a 1.5–2m (5–6½ft) stock, and grows slowly into a mushroom-shaped mound of foliage, spreading as it ages. As a border plant it needs to be planted in front of neighbors that might obscure its round, even shape. It tends to form a visual block to views along the length of a border, which can be an advantage if the contents are not to be seen in their entirety from the path, but it will not compromise distant views from an angle. It suits dusky schemes with dark foliage and blue, purple, or dark red flowers, and makes effective contrasts with silver or yellow-green foliage, or as a background for pale flowers such as white or apricot foxgloves.

◐ *Angelica gigas*, *Digitalis purpurea* 'Sutton's Apricot', *Lilium* 'Ariadne', *Lonicera sempervirens* 'Cedar Lane', *Phormium tenax* Purpureum Group

H: 25m (80ft) S: 15m (50ft) ❀ **(Mid-spring)**
◊-◊◊ □-■ **Z5 pH5–8**

Fatsia japonica ♛

Both sun and shade are acceptable to this immensely handsome evergreen shrub, which is an excellent plant for shady city courtyard gardens. It bears imposing panicles of spherical, creamy white flower heads in autumn, and broad, glossy, dark green leaves whose size can be increased by keeping plants moist and removing the clusters of black fruits that form after flowering. This results in an almost tropical luxuriance, which qualifies it for inclusion in plantings with exotic foliage such as that of tetrapanax, stooled paulownias or catalpas, bananas, hedychiums, and cannas, with the exception of canna cultivars whose brash colors might be discordant in groupings based emphatically on foliage. It is also a superb candidate for Japanese themes, combined for example with bamboos, hostas, and Japanese maples.

◐ *Hedychium coccineum* 'Tara', *Hosta* 'Sum and Substance', *Lilium auratum*, *Musa basjoo* 'Sakhalin', *Nandina domestica*, *Pleioblastus auricomus* ❑ p.123 **C**

H & S: 2m (6½ft) ❀ **Mid- to late autumn**
◊◊ □-■ **Z6 pH5–7.5**

Used in a relatively narrow border, this pairing of *Fatsia japonica* with contrasting *Phormium tenax* 'Variegatum' has an almost tropical air. The fatsia's dramatic white-stemmed inflorescences add to the effect above a carpet of fine-textured dwarf boxwood (*Buxus sempervirens* 'Suffruticosa').

Forsythia × intermedia

Renowned for its yellow spring display, this deciduous shrub mixes well with white flowers, hot-colored tulips (Fosteriana and Darwinhybrid Groups), and yellow-green foliage and flowers, and contrasts effectively with blue flowers such as forget-me-nots. Companion plants need to compete with the forsythia's brilliance and form; good ones include white flowering currants, early-flowering euphorbias, white and pale yellow narcissi, blue hyacinths, and plants with gold-variegated foliage, such as evergreen elaeagnus cultivars. *F. × i.* 'Spectabilis' has a slightly messy appearance, improved in 'Lynwood' ♡; Week-End ('Courtalyn') ♡ is shorter, at 2m (6½ft), with neater, erect stems, while 'Minigold', at 1.5m (5ft), is a useful size for combining with spring bulbs without overwhelming them. Most of these tend to be amorphous and uninteresting in summer unless draped with summer-flowering climbers; larger forsythia, especially grouped together, look impressive supporting an early-flowering white clematis.

◉ *Aucuba japonica*, *Berberis darwinii* p.32 **A**, *Corylopsis pauciflora*, *Daphne mezereum* f. *alba*, *Helleborus hybridus*, *Ilex aquifolium* 'Silver Queen', *Narcissus* 'February Silver', *Ribes sanguineum* 'Tydeman's White', *Salix aegyptiaca*, *Tulipa* Fosteriana Group

H & S: 1.5–2.5m (5–8ft) ❀ **Early spring**
◊◊ ☐ - ■ **Z5 pH5.5–7.5**

Left: The handsome foliage of tender evergreen *Mahonia napaulensis* provides a foil for the bright flowers of *Forsythia × intermedia*, decorated in front with *Symphytum* 'Goldsmith', its leaves bordered by a yellowish cream.

Below: When grown large, perhaps trained against a wall, *Forsythia × intermedia* may be draped lightly with an early-flowering clematis such as *C. armandii*, preferably in its white-flowered form rather than pale pink.

The gold, orange, and red autumn tints of *Fothergilla major* Monticola Group perfectly complement the seasonal colors of Japanese maples such as *Acer palmatum* 'Ôsakazuki' while providing a contrast of leaf shape.

Fothergilla major Monticola Group

Fothergilla major ♡ is a deciduous 3m (10ft) relative of witch hazel, bearing creamy white bottle-brush flowers before the leaves unfurl, and with yellow, orange, or scarlet leaf tints in autumn. Monticola Group is smaller, with brilliant orange or scarlet autumn color, and a good choice for sunny glades in a woodland garden. Its spring flowers are effective with bluebells, yellow or warm-tinted deciduous azaleas, and the yellow-green of smyrniums. Later in the year it associates well with other autumn-coloring shrubs, such as linderas, berberis, dogwoods, deciduous euonymus, vacciniums, sumacs, maples, and clethras. In a less wild setting, plants can be combined with Chinese lanterns, and Rubellum or Korean chrysanthemums in autumn colors.

◉ *Acer palmatum* f. *atropurpureum*, *Berberis wilsoniae*, *Lindera obtusiloba*, *Physalis alkekengi*, *Rhododendron luteum*, *R.* 'May Day' p.84 **B**, *Rhus typhina*

H: 2.5m (8ft) S: 2m (6½ft) ❀ **Late spring**
◊◊-◊◊◊ ☐ - ■ ■ **Z5 pH4.5–6.5**

The nodding flowers of *Fuchsia* 'Checkerboard', their red tubes and corollas harmonizing with the reddish purple foliage of *Acer palmatum* Dissectum Atropurpureum Group, are enlivened by their white sepals. The male fern cultivar *Dryopteris affinis* 'Cristata' provides a pleasant contrast of foliage form.

Fuchsia 'Checkerboard' ♔

The dramatic red and white flowers help this relatively hardy, deciduous fuchsia show up in situations where cultivars with purple and red flowers might be less visible. It is most successful with cooler colors and with the purple or red foliage of plants like Japanese maples and dark-leaved dahlias or berberis. Plants need full sun where summers are cool, but tolerate partial shade in hotter climates. In frost-free areas, growth survives winter without injury, allowing earlier flowering and taller stems to combine with old shrub roses and other large neighbors. A splendid choice for the second row of a border and for light woodland, it mixes well with contrasting foliage – that of watsonias, ferns, grasses, and bronze sedges, for example – or with tender perennials planted out for summer, such as argyranthemums and osteospermums.

⬤ *Anemone × hybrida* 'Elegans', *Berberis thunbergii* 'Red Chief', *Rosa* 'Mevrouw Nathalie Nypels', *Schizostylis* 'Sunrise', *Watsonia* 'Stanford Scarlet'

H: 90cm (36in) S: 75cm (30in)
✷ **Early summer to mid-autumn**
▰▰▰▱▱ △△ ▢-▉ **Z8 pH5–7.5**

Fuchsia magellanica var. *gracilis* ♔

This fairly hardy fuchsia is particularly showy from mid-summer to fall frosts, with small, dainty, red and deep violet-purple flowers. It has a spreading growth habit, and slender arching growth that suits positions near the front of a border, behind a low wall, or within a carpet of short, shade-tolerant ground-cover plants such as ivies or bugleweeds, together with spring bulbs or early-flowering annuals or biennials. Its flowers, best at close range, blend equally well with salmons, carmines, or mauves, and with red or purple-flushed foliage, and red, deep pink, or purple flowers; yellow-green foliage or flowers make pleasant contrasts. Good companions include late-flowering heucheras, smaller Japanese anemones, nicotianas, prostrate verbenas, nerines, asters, and Korean, Rubellum, or Charm chrysanthemums. It prefers partial shade in hot climates, but in cooler regions needs full sun to flower well. A deciduous shrub, its spreading stems are cut back to the ground in winter in frost-prone areas.

Charming at close quarters, the dainty flowers of *Fuchsia magellanica* var. *gracilis* give the shrub a diffuse covering of red. The grey-green, cream-edged leaves of the ivy *Hedera canariensis* 'Gloire de Marengo' provide an effective foil.

⬤ *Aster amellus* 'Jacqueline Genebrier', *Chrysanthemum* 'Emperor of China', *Heuchera* 'Purple Petticoats', *Nerine* 'Zeal Giant', *Pennisetum setaceum* 'Rubrum'

H & S: 2m (6½ft) ✷ **Mid-summer to late autumn**
▰▰▰▱▱ △△ ▢-▉ **Z8 pH5–7.5**

Fuchsia 'Tom Thumb' ♔

More dwarf than many hardy fuchsias, 'Tom Thumb', which is deciduous, is suitable for the front of a border, and can be used as an edging or to fill a parterre. Its light red and lilac flowers mix prettily with most of the companions recommended for *F. magellanica* var. *gracilis* (above), and with short, dark-leaved dahlias, *Begonia* Semperflorens Cultorum Group, impatiens, pelargoniums, and petunias. Although effective with softer yellow-green foliage and with lime green flowers, it does not contrast well with stronger yellow-green shades. Used en masse to cover an area, it can be planted under with spring flowers such as scillas, muscaris, and blue or pink wood anemones, and with bronze foliage. It is rather amorphous in growth habit, and is best combined with plants of more definite structure and form.

The flowers of *Fuchsia* 'Tom Thumb', born on a plant short enough for the very front of a border, are on the blue side of primary red in color, making them clash gently but not disagreeably with the orange-red berries of *Arum italicum* 'Marmoratum', whose marbled leaves occupy the fuchsia's space before it emerges in late spring. A polypody fern provides foliage contrast.

⬤ *Artemisia alba* 'Canescens', *Brassica oleracea* (Acephala Group) 'Redbor', *Festuca glauca* 'Blaufuchs', *Geranium* 'Chocolate Candy', *Nerine bowdenii*, *Nicotiana* Domino Series, *Sedum* 'Bertram Anderson'

H & S: 20cm (8in) ✷ **Mid-summer to late autumn**
▰▰▰▱▱ △△ ▢-▉ **Z8 pH5–7.5**

The small, evenly spaced flower heads of *Genista hispanica* create a fine-textured effect, contrasting with the large heads and layered growth of *Viburnum plicatum* 'Mariesii'.

Genista hispanica

SPANISH BROOM

This cheerful, robust, Mediterranean shrub forms a dense mound of evergreen twigs and spines, with tiny, deciduous leaves only on the flowering stems. Yellow pea-shaped flowers smother the neat bush, making a strong block of color that illuminates a dry border or gravel bed. The even mounds look more natural in irregular groups, with neighboring plants infiltrating their fringes.

Good companions include other Mediterranean plants such as sages, cistus, and halimiums, and most other drought-tolerant plants from hot, dry regions such as Australia, South Africa, and California. The dense habit and bright coloring complement silver-leaved plants and those with a looser, more open form, and make striking contrasts with purple and blue shades.

Convolvulus cneorum, C. sabatius, × Halimiocistus wintonensis, Phlomis chrysophylla, Rosmarinus officinalis 'Aureus', *Salvia officinalis* 'Icterina'

H: 75cm (30in) S: 1.5m (5ft) Early summer
Z7 pH5.5–7.5

Halimium ocymoides

A shapely shrub from Spain and Portugal, this slightly lax, spreading bush is evergreen, with small greyish leaves. These make a perfect background for the delicate-looking, purple-centered, golden yellow blooms that appear in summer. The flowers resemble those of helianthemums and cistus, to which the halimium is closely related; like them, it prefers hot, dry, well-drained sites. Here it associates well with more formal shrubs such as lavenders and sages, combining pleasantly with white and mid-blue flowers. Plants are short-lived, but can be renewed every few years from cuttings before the shrubs age.

Cistus × hybridus, Helianthemum 'Boughton Double Primrose', *Lavandula angustifolia* 'Nana Alba', *Phlomis fruticosa, Potentilla fruticosa* 'Maanelys', *Rosa* 'Golden Wings', *Spartium junceum, Stachys citrina*

H: 60cm (24in) S: 1m (40in)
Early to mid-summer
Z8 pH6–7.5

Hamamelis × intermedia

Witch hazels are an indispensable genus of moisture-loving, deciduous shrubs and small trees. They are appreciated for their attractive vase-like shape and, above all, for their spidery flowers with curiously strap-shaped petals, born prolifically on leafless stems in winter. Cultivars of this popular hybrid range from the pale yellow of 'Moonlight', through gold and orange, to the rich tawny brown of 'Jelena' and 'Ruby Glow'; lemon-yellow

In this combination of plants favoring a Mediterranean climate, all of them of comparable stature and growth rate, *Halimium ocymoides* provides plentiful golden flowers, matched by the yellow-edged foliage of *Salvia officinalis* 'Icterina'. The grey leaves of *Lotus hirsutus* and its near-white flowers harmonize with the arrangement.

The silvery leaves of *Brachyglottis* (Dunedin Group) 'Sunshine' provide an effective foil for the mahogany-red flowers of a young witch hazel, *Hamamelis × intermedia* 'Diane'. When mature, the witch hazel flowers will bloom too high to interact with such a companion, and its shade will prevent the brachyglottis from growing.

'Pallida' has the largest flowers. In autumn, cultivars such as 'Diane' and 'Arnold Promise' assume opulent red leaf tints. Some cultivars, such as 'Moonlight' and 'Vesna', are also spicily fragrant, making them welcome cut flowers for winter vases.

The elegant shape of these shrubs should not be hidden in a mixed shrubbery. Each needs its own personal space, ideally where it will be lit by the low rays of the winter sun and set against a dark background, perhaps of evergreen hollies or yew, to emphasize the fragile beauty of the flowers. They can be combined with colored-stemmed dogwoods for maximum winter effect, and carpeted with spring bulbs and bergenias, with hardy cranesbills for summer interest.

Camellia 'Cornish Snow', *Eranthis hyemalis, Erica × darleyensis* 'White Perfection', *Galanthus* 'Atkinsii', *Hedera colchica* 'Sulphur Heart', *Mahonia japonica*

H & S: 4m (13ft) Mid- to late winter
Z5 pH5.5–7.5

Hebe 'Midsummer Beauty' ♛

Taller hebes are outstandingly showy evergreen shrubs, although some of the most eye-catching are the least hardy. 'Midsummer Beauty' is a reliable cultivar for gardens with fairly mild winters and cool summers, where its flowers are less likely to be bleached by bright sunlight; it is an ideal choice for windy, exposed sites near the sea.

The flowering season is spectacular, lasting for much of the summer and autumn, and sometimes even into winter. In full bloom the rounded bush has a two-tone effect, varying from the rich lilac of the younger flowers and buds to the much paler lilac of older blooms – all are often covered in foraging butterflies. 'Midsummer Beauty' is effective in the middle of a mixed border, among pink, purple, red, or white flowers, although strong yellow can overwhelm its subtle coloring. It is good, too, with purple and silver foliage, and can be combined with restrained climbers such as clematis or perennial peas that will not smother the neat, domed bush.

◉ *Buddleja* 'Pink Delight', *Lavandula stoechas* subsp. *pedunculata*, *Lavatera* 'Barnsley', *Penstemon* 'Burgundy', *P.* 'Evelyn', *Perovskia* 'Blue Spire', *Rosa* Iceberg

H & S: 2m (6½ft) ❀ **Mid-summer to late autumn**
◌◌ Z8 pH5–7.5

A mature plant of *Hebe* 'Midsummer Beauty' is large enough to be draped with a late-flowering Texensis or Viticella clematis. Here, the harmonious but much deeper color of Viticella 'Etoile Violette' and its contrasting floral shape make a successful combination.

This combination of *Hebe* 'Nicola's Blush' and *Euonymus fortunei* 'Emerald 'n' Gold' would work equally well with a rich lavender-blue hebe or a white-variegated euonymus.

Hebe 'Nicola's Blush'

This is one of the most popular smaller hebes, hardier than larger cultivars and easy to grow in an open site. The younger blooms are a clear soft pink, fading to white with age. It makes an effective ground cover or a slightly formal edging to a border, on its own or combined with pinks, carnations, dwarf lavenders, and grasses of similar stature. Its quiet coloring blends charmingly with blue, mauve, crimson, and white flowers, and with silver foliage plants. Like all hebes, it prefers a well-drained but not too dry position, and in severe winters benefits from protection to prevent the shallow roots from drying out. Other fine small hebes include the white-flowered *H.* 'Pewter Dome' ♛, 'Red Edge' ♛, with red edged grey-green leaves, and the prostrate, glaucous *H. pinguifolia* 'Pagei' ♛.

◉ *Artemisia* 'Powis Castle', *Festuca glauca* 'Blaufuchs', *Lavandula angustifolia* 'Hidcote', *Salvia officinalis* 'Purpurascens', *Sedum* 'Vera Jameson', *Senecio viravira*

H & S: 75cm (30in)
❀ **Late summer to late autumn**
◌◌ Z8 pH5–7.5

Hebe ochracea combines with other clump-forming plants that have leaves of contrasting shapes and sizes to create a subtle patchwork at the front of a border. The white flowers of the hebe echo the pale-edged leaves of *Astrantia major* 'Sunningdale Variegated', while purple sage (*Salvia officinalis* 'Purpurascens') and heucheras add to the display.

Hebe ochracea

This is one of the whipcord hebes, with tiny evergreen leaves carried on sprays of arching branchlets that slowly form a domed shrub, and white flowers when five or six years old. Its perfect shape needs space to develop – it might be overcrowded in a border, but will star in an island bed or larger rock garden, with good drainage, full sun, and surrounded by shorter plants such as heaths, heathers with colored leaves, and prostrate junipers. The foliage combines ochre and green, good with bronze or yellow-green foliage, with warm-colored flowers such as heleniums, helianthemums, and smaller hypericums, and with white flowers like celmisias and smaller cistus. 'James Stirling' ♥, brighter and more compact, is useful for smaller-scale plantings.

◐ *Celmisia semicordata*, *Euphorbia rigida*, *Helianthemum* 'Wisley White', *Hypericum cerastioides*, *Juniperus communis* 'Depressa Aurea', *Salvia officinalis* 'Icterina'

H: 1m (40in) **S: 75cm** (30in)
✻ **Late spring to early summer**
◌◌ ▨-▨ **Z7 pH5–7.5**

The success of this pretty combination with *Hebe* 'Watson's Pink' depends on a contrast of foliage, rather than of flower form or color. The silvery, slightly invasive *Artemisia ludoviciana* lingers at the outer fringes of the hebe rather than scrambling into it.

Hebe stenophylla ♥

One of the hardier broad-leaved hebes, this bushy evergreen (syn. *H. parviflora* var. *angustifolia*) forms a loose dome of light green upright shoots that look effective in borders and can support a scrambling plant such as codonopsis, *Helichrysum petiolare*, or a cranesbill. Its spikes of lilac-tinted white flowers combine with almost any other color, but excel with mauve, lilac, pink, and white flowers, and with silver foliage. Good companions are larger lavenders, olearias, penstemons, tree poppies, silver-leaved alstroemerias, and carmine phygelius, as well as philadelphus, early-flowering hydrangeas, and smaller deutzias, buddleias, and weigelas. Its second flowering in autumn coincides with late asters and nerines, abelias, fuchsias, lespedezas, and early-flowering winter heaths.

◐ *Artemisia ludoviciana*, *Buddleja davidii* 'Nanho Petite Indigo' *Geranium* 'Brookside', *Lavandula lanata*, *Penstemon* 'Sour Grapes', *Phygelius aequalis* Sensation

H & S: 1m (40in) ✻ **Mid- to late summer**
▨▨▨ ◌◌ ▨-▨ **Z8 pH5–7.5**

Hebe stenophylla, like other hebes that are not too dense and grow to the ground, is an attractive host for plants of contrasting floral form or color. Here, *Geranium × oxonianum* scrambles through its lower branches.

Hebe 'Watson's Pink'

This broad-leaved evergreen shrub, one of the showiest pink hebes, prefers mild winters and relatively cool summers, in a border where the soil does not dry out. It works well with silver or purple foliage, and with flowers in white, deep pink, crimson, mauve, lilac, or campanula-blue. It mixes congenially with lavenders, veronicas, campanulas, smaller old-fashioned roses, and scrambling convolvulus, together with feathery silver-leaved plants like artemisias and grasses such as blue fescues. Tender perennials such as penstemons, argyranthemums, and osteospermums, and early-flowering annuals such as nigellas are other good partners. It has a second flush of flowers in mid- to late autumn, when it can be combined with asters, Japanese anemones, and later-flowering annuals such as cosmos.

◐ *Argyranthemum* 'Summer Melody', *Campanula* 'Van-Houttei', *Helictotrichon sempervirens*, *Lavandula angustifolia* 'Bowles' Early', *Penstemon* 'Cherry'

H & S: 1m (40in) ✻ **Early to mid-summer**
▨▨▨ ◌◌ ▨-▨ **Z8 pH5–7.5**

Above: Helianthemums are spreading plants that can scramble into other open and low-growing shrubs. Here, 'Mrs C.W. Earle' pushes its way through *Juniperus communis* 'Depressa Aurea', resulting in a striking contrast of scarlet flowers and yellow-green plumes of foliage.

Below: Two helianthemums, coral 'Fire Dragon' and scarlet 'Ben Hope', interplanted with dramatically contrasting and gently invasive *Euphorbia cyparissias*, combine to create a tapestry of flowers in varied colors. Seedling *Eryngium giganteum* is poised to continue the display.

Helianthemum cultivars

SUN ROSES

These are low, spreading, evergreen or semi-evergreen shrubs, with flowers of yellow through orange to scarlet, or pale yellow through apricot to rose-pink, and mid- to deep green or silvery foliage. They like full sun and well-drained soil, at the front of a border or in a rock, scree, or gravel garden. Some are single-flowered, opening fully only in sunlight and lasting through the morning, with a charming simplicity enlivened by a central disk of golden anthers. Double forms stay open even in dull weather, and last longer into the afternoon. The strong yellows, oranges, and scarlets can be combined with other hot colors, and with bronze, red, or yellow-green foliage, and associate well with smaller poppies, *Rosa persica* hybrids, bronze sedges, halimiums and halimiocistus, Bearded irises, hot-colored anthemis, euphorbias, and yellow-green prostrate junipers. Paler colors such as peaches, apricots, and pale yellows look outstanding with bronze foliage and white flowers, while rose, salmon-pink, scarlet, and white cultivars blend with alpine pinks and glaucous foliage. Yellow cultivars make good contrasts with blue – prostrate ceanothus and flaxes, for example.

Acaena caesiiglauca, *Anthemis* 'Beauty of Grallagh', *Briza maxima* p.366 **B**, *Carex comans* (bronze), *Euphorbia seguieriana* subsp. *niciciana* p.221 **B**

H: 30cm (12in) **S: 45cm** (18in) ❀ **Early summer**
🌢-🌢🌢 ☐-☐ **Z6 pH6–7.5**

The soft lavender flowers of *Hibiscus syriacus* 'Oiseau Bleu', enlivened by their red markings and white stamens, are valuable for late-blooming cool color schemes.

Hibiscus syriacus

This late-flowering deciduous shrub, equally at home in shrub and mixed borders, has upright growth useful for training into a standard, either as a specimen plant or for repeated accents. There are white, pink, mauve, and lavender-blue kinds, some with double flowers, others with a crimson blotch near the petal base. Single flowers open more readily than double ones in damp, cool weather. The delicate shading harmonizes with cool-colored flowers such as actaeas, agapanthus, penstemons, and asters, and with silver, glaucous, or purple foliage, especially purple sloe, berberis, and smoke bush, and silver elaeagnus and artemisias. Contrasting foliage such as that of taller grasses (including *Miscanthus sinensis*) adds a dramatic flourish. Good companions include cultivars of *Hydrangea paniculata* and *H. macrophylla*, late-flowering lilies, ceanothus, lespedezas, elsholtzias, and fuchsias. Larger hibiscus can be draped with slight, late-flowering climbers such as Viticella or Texensis clematis.

Aconitum 'Blue Sceptre', *Agapanthus* 'Loch Hope', *Anemone* × *hybrida* 'Honorine Jobert', *Aster* 'Little Carlow', *A. turbinellus* hort., *Elaeagnus* 'Quicksilver'

H: 3m (10ft) **S: 2m** (6½ft)
❀ **Late summer to mid-autumn**
🌢🌢 ☐-☐ **Z6 pH6–8**

Hippophae rhamnoides ♛
SEA BUCKTHORN

With its remarkable tolerance of poor, dry, or wet soils and salt spray, this upright, suckering deciduous shrub is valuable for seaside situations, gravelly soils, and roadside plantings. It has long, slender, silvery grey-green leaves and, in drier sites, it is a good alternative to willows as a foliage plant for mixed or shrub borders, combined with cool colors and white flowers or draped with climbers such as clematis and morning glories. It is also effective in wilder parts of the garden. The flowers are inconspicuous, but if pollinated by a male, female plants produce a crop of eye-catching orange fruits, which can last through autumn into spring. Only one male – such as 'Pollmix' – is needed for every five or six female clones – 'Leikora', for example – to ensure a good display. Their impact is enhanced in combinations with fruit-bearing or autumn-coloring shrubs, such as berberis, pyracanthas, amelanchiers, deciduous euonymus, and smoke bush.

◐ *Clematis* 'Blekitny Aniol', *Ipomoea tricolor* 'Heavenly Blue', *Lavatera* 'Barnsley', *Miscanthus sinensis* 'Morning Light', *Pittosporum* 'Garnettii', *Rosa* 'Prosperity'

H & S: 6m (20ft) ❀ **(Mid-spring)**
◊·◊◊ ▢·▨ **Z4 pH6–7.5**

A useful component of a white garden, a large plant or group of sea buckthorn (*Hippophae rhamnoides*) can readily be draped with a Viticella clematis such as *C.* 'Alba Luxurians'. Beneath, a white Shasta daisy (*Leucanthemum* × *superbum* 'Wirral Pride') continues the color theme. An extra row of herbaceous plants or shrubs of intermediate height could be added between daisy and buckthorn.

Hydrangea arborescens

Lacy white heads of small fertile flowers, with an irregular margin of large sterile flowers, make this deciduous shrub a bold plant for a woodland garden or a mixed or shrub border in light shade (full sun in cooler areas). The showiest cultivars are those with mainly sterile florets, especially 'Annabelle' ♛, with its 30cm (12in) heads, 'Grandiflora' ♛, and subsp. *discolor* 'Sterilis'. All have pale green blooms, maturing to creamy white and aging to light green once more. They combine with hostas, lilies, day lilies, larger cranesbills, herbaceous phlox such as *P. paniculata*

cultivars, Japanese anemones, holodiscus, *Potentilla fruticosa* cultivars, and Rugosa roses. Other hydrangeas associate well with them, as do larger grasses such as miscanthus. They are good shrubs for containers, edged with trailing plants like ivy, and for the front of a border, surrounded by low carpeting plants; they will also suit positions further back in a border if only lightly pruned.

◐ *Aconitum* 'Ivorine', *Cortaderia richardii*, *Hemerocallis* 'Marion Vaughn', *Hosta plantaginea*, *Lilium regale* p.329 **A**, *Phlox maculata* 'Omega' ↵ p.183 **B**

H & S: 2.5m (8ft) ❀ **Mid- to late summer**
◊◊·◊◊◊ ▢·▨ ■ **Z5 pH5.5–7.5**

Hydrangea aspera
Villosa Group ♛

A very variable deciduous shrub that may be spreading or upright, this has downy leaves and delicate lacecap heads of flowers, with pink fertile florets aging to lilac within a ring of sterile lilac or lavender florets. It benefits from the shade of a high canopy of deciduous trees or a wall, ideally facing west, where the soil is moister and there is less risk of rapid thawing after frost. It is useful for late color in woodland gardens and shrub or mixed borders, combined with pink, mauve, lilac, lavender, blue, and crimson flowers, including aconitums, lilies, Japanese anemones, and smaller hydrangeas. Other good companions include holodiscus, late-flowering deutzias, paler *Potentilla fruticosa* cultivars, fuchsias, and plants of contrasting form, such as tree ferns. Larger plants in light shade can be draped with a Texensis, Viticella, or other wispy clematis. 'Macrophylla' ♛ is another attractive variant of *H. aspera*, with larger leaves and flower heads.

Lacy flower heads of *Hydrangea aspera* Villosa Group contrast with the more solid inflorescences of a *Phlox paniculata* cultivar, accompanied by *Berberis thunbergii* 'Rose Glow', its purple-red leaves splashed with pink.

◐ *Aconitum* 'Newry Blue', *Clematis* 'Madame Julia Correvon', *C.* 'Prince Charles', *Fargesia nitida*, *Fuchsia* 'Riccartonii', *Lilium* 'Marie North', *Phlox maculata*

H & S: 3m (10ft) ❀ **Mid- to late summer**
◊◊ ▢·▨ ■ **Z7 pH4.5–7.5**

The solid outline of *Hydrangea arborescens* and its bold flower heads act as punctuation at the end of a pair of white borders. Beyond, not part of the white-flowered theme, the emphatically vertical variegated yellow iris (*Iris pseudacorus* 'Variegata') terminates the vista, acting equally as a punctuation but of contrasting form, flanked by the deep peach-pink plumes of *Filipendula rubra*.

Hydrangea macrophylla

The most popular of all hydrangeas, this is a late-flowering deciduous shrub for mixed or shrub borders, particularly in maritime climates. Flower colors range from red to blue, with white. Cultivars that are blue in acid soils often turn pink or red in alkaline ones, but can be changed back to blue with soil amendments. There are two basic types: Hortensias (Mopheads), with large sterile florets, and Lacecaps, with heads of tiny fertile florets ringed by showy sterile ones. Hortensias can look incongruously bright in wilder gardens, but succeed in formal settings, whereas the Lacecaps are more attractive in a semi-natural situation. The colors blend with other cool tints such as mauve, crimson, lavender, blue, and pink; blue cultivars combine with yellow-green foliage and flowers and make telling contrasts with yellow. Their solid outline can be contrasted with softer, looser plants – grasses, ferns, and bamboos, for example, maples, late-flowering lilies, and Japanese anemones.

Above: *Hydrangea macrophylla* 'Générale Vicomtesse de Vibraye', one of the most reliably floriferous Hortensia hydrangeas, contrasts with the Lacecap hydrangea *H. serrata* 'Rosalba'. The boldly striped *Hosta undulata* var. *univittata* decorates the front of the planting arrangement.

Below: *Hydrangea macrophylla* 'Mariesii Perfecta', perhaps the most popular of the Lacecap Group, combines attractively with cool colors and silver foliage, such as *Artemisia absinthium* 'Lambrook Silver'.

⬤ *Aconitum × cammarum* 'Bicolor', *Astilbe chinensis* var. *taquetii*, *Miscanthus sinensis* 'Gracillimus', *Monarda* 'Beauty of Cobham', *Potentilla fruticosa* 'Maanelys'

H: 1–2m (40in–6½ft) S: 1.2–3m (4–10ft)
✿ **Mid- to late summer**

 ◊◊-◊◊◊ ▢-▣ ■ Z6 pH4.5–7.5

The conical flower heads of *Hydrangea paniculata* make a boldly emphatic statement here, with the glaucous foliage of the giant reed (*Arundo donax*) providing contrast behind.

Hydrangea paniculata

This elegant, fairly upright deciduous shrub has conical, creamy white, attractively lacy flower heads of mainly fertile flowers, studded with larger sterile ones. Its color mixes agreeably with almost any other, particularly pale green, blue, or white, and with glaucous or white- or gold-variegated foliage. Good companions are hypericums, agapanthus, Japanese anemones, later-flowering lilies, larger grasses such as miscanthus, buddlejas, *Hibiscus syriacus* cultivars, and holodiscus; larger plants can be draped with climbers like perennial peas and morning glories. Cultivars with a pronounced lacy appearance include 'Floribunda' ♀, creamy white with a pink flush, and 'Kyushu' ♀, white with green tints later. 'Praecox' ♀, with leaves emerging yellow in mid-spring, flowers early with domes of pure white sterile florets scattered around a flower head of greenish white fertile florets.

⬤ *Agapanthus caulescens* subsp. *caulescens*, *Ipomoea tricolor* 'Heavenly Blue', *Lathyrus latifolius* 'Blushing Bride', *Lilium* 'Casa Blanca', *Nicotiana* 'Lime Green'

H: 3–5m (10–16ft) S: 2–4m (6½–13ft)
✿ **Mid- to late summer**

 ◊◊ ▢-▣ ■ Z5 pH5–7.5

This contrast in flower head shapes, conical *Hydrangea paniculata* 'Grandiflora' set against round agapanthus, is striking and perhaps most appealing when the hydrangea blooms are young, before they assume their eventual pink shading.

Hydrangea paniculata 'Grandiflora' ♚

PEEGEE HYDRANGEA

Perhaps the most remarkable *H. paniculata* cultivar, this deciduous shrub produces conical flower heads, packed with large sterile florets that hide the smaller fertile flowers. Initially white tinged with pink, the panicles develop a pronounced pink flush as they age. This hydrangea's bold shape is useful for providing accents along a border, and it looks particularly attractive grouped with pink, crimson, or white flowers, or with glaucous, purple-flushed, silver, or white-variegated foliage. It combines well with hostas, Japanese anemones, nicotianas, larger grasses, and late-flowering lilies; in autumn its reddish pink tints complement Korean, Rubellum, and Charm chrysanthemums.

◉ *Actaea racemosa*, *Buddleja* 'Lochinch', *Ceanothus × delileanus* 'Gloire de Versailles', *Lilium regale*, *L.* 'Sterling Star', *Potentilla fruticosa* 'Tilford Cream'

H: 3m (10ft) S: 2m (6½ft) ❀ **Mid- to late summer**
◌◌ ▢-▢ ▮ **Z5 pH5–7.5**

Hydrangea paniculata 'Greenspire'

This is a lax deciduous shrub, eventually reaching 4m (13ft) across unless pruned annually to keep it more compact. Its conical panicles are entirely green before the flowers mature, but later the numerous large sterile florets near the base of the panicle become creamy white, with a froth of white fertile flowers higher up; fertile florets towards the tip remain green and often do not open, and the whole panicle ages to green once more, without the pink flush of some cultivars. This coloring provides restful combinations with green, blue, or white flowers, yellow-green foliage and flowers, and glaucous foliage. Plants are especially effective with white agapanthus, green nicotianas, white or cream lilies, hostas, and miscanthus.

◉ *Fuchsia magellanica* 'Versicolor', *Hosta* 'Sum and Substance', *Ilex × altaclerensis* 'Golden King', *Rosa* 'Ballerina', *R.* Iceberg

H: 2m (6½ft) S: 4m (13ft) ❀ **Mid- to late summer**
◌◌ ▢-▢ ▮ **Z5 pH5–7.5**

Combining one plant with large inflorescences and another with small individual flowers often succeeds, as here with *Hydrangea paniculata* 'Greenspire' and *Nicotiana langsdorffii*, both in subtle shades of green.

Hydrangea serrata 'Rosalba', its relatively small lacecap flower heads assuming shadings of red as they age, are gracefully draped with the flame nasturtium (*Tropaeolum speciosum*) and studded with its scarlet blooms.

Hydrangea serrata 'Rosalba' ♚

Sometimes called the mountain hydrangea, *H. serrata* (syn. *H. macrophylla* subsp. *serrata*) is a compact deciduous shrub, with lacecap flowers consisting of tiny fertile florets surrounded by a ring of showier sterile ones. Small in stature, it suits the front rows of a sunny or lightly shaded border, where it starts to flower quite early and continues until the frosts. 'Rosalba' has pink fertile florets and white sterile ones, aging to deep pink in the center (lilac on acid soils), with a pink-edged border. It is excellent for large-scale plantings and lighter parts of a woodland garden, especially with late summer flowers in cool colors (such as Hortensia hydrangeas, lilies, and Japanese anemones), hostas, smaller bamboos, grasses, and Japanese maples.

◉ *Buddleja* 'Pink Delight', *Deutzia setchuenensis* var. *corymbiflora*, *Hydrangea macrophylla* p.59 **A**, *Perovskia* 'Blue Spire', *Rosa* Bonica, *R.* 'Yesterday'

H & S: 1.2m (4ft) ❀ **Mid- to late summer**
◌◌-◌◌◌ ▢-▢ ▮ **Z6 pH4.5–7.5**

Hypericum forrestii ♔

This deciduous shrub (semi-deciduous to evergreen in warm climates) has an elegant, arching growth habit and large golden yellow flowers. Although naturally shapely, it can be tall and spreading for general use in shrub and mixed borders, unless limited to about half its height by annual spring pruning. It combines well with hot colors, yellow-green, yellow-variegated, and glaucous foliage, and yellow flowers, and contrasts with blue. Suitable partners include agapanthus, hostas, crocosmias, and variegated grasses such as hakonechloas and miscanthus. In autumn it is embellished with reddish brown seed capsules and red leaf tints. *H.* 'Hidcote' ♔ is similar, if not so graceful, and flowers into mid-autumn.

⬤ *Agapanthus* 'Blue Moon', *Crocosmia* × *crocosmiiflora* 'Lady Hamilton', *Hosta* 'August Moon', *Miscanthus sinensis* 'Strictus', *Rosa* Elina, *R.* Graham Thomas

H: 1.2m (4ft) **S: 1.5m** (5ft) ✷ **Late summer**
◌◌ ☐-■ **Z6 pH5.5–7**

Hard annual pruning restricts the height of *Hypericum forrestii* to about 60cm (24in), allowing it to be combined with herbaceous plants of similar height – as with the contrasting foliage and flowers of *Crocosmia* × *crocosmiiflora*.

Ilex aquifolium ♔

EUROPEAN HOLLY

One of the most useful evergreen shrubs, European holly is available in hundreds of cultivars, some variegated and others with different leaf shapes or growth habits. Shade tolerant and leafy to its base, it is invaluable in woodland gardens and shady shrub or mixed borders, adding bulk to the winter landscape. If male and female clones are grown together, the females produce bright red, occasionally gold berries that color in mid-autumn and remain until spring – one male plant is needed for every six or so females. Green-leaved hollies provide a marvellous foil for swags of pale flowers such as small-flowered clematis and scrambling forsythias. Among variegated kinds, those with paler marginal coloring are the most effective.

⬤ *Clematis potaninii*, *Forsythia suspensa* 'Nymans', *Holodiscus discolor*, *Miscanthus sinensis* 'Strictus', *Parthenocissus tricuspidata* 'Lowii', *Rosa* 'Climbing Paul Lédé' p.140 **B**

H: 2–20m (6½–65ft) **S: 1.5–8m** (5–26ft)
✷ (**Late spring to early summer**)
◌◌ ☐-■ **Z6 pH4.5–7.5**

Right: The narrow, neat gold edging to the leaves of *Ilex aquifolium* 'Pyramidalis Aureomarginata' emphasizes the shape of its foliage and harmonizes with a hybrid of *Mahonia aquifolium* in spring. This upright, fruit-bearing, red-berried holly eventually reaches 6m (20ft) high with a spread of 5m (16ft).

Below: Compact *Ilex aquifolium* 'Myrtifolia Aurea Maculata', its relatively small leaves generously splashed with yellow on a bush leafy to ground level, provides a support for scrambling *Potentilla* 'Flamenco' in fiery scarlet. This is a non-fruit-bearing holly that ultimately achieves a height of 2m (6½ft) and a spread of 1.5m (5ft).

Above: The feathery foliage of *Juniperus squamata* 'Filborna', a vigorous, upright cultivar, harmonizes with the blue flowers of *Brunnera macrophylla* in spring.

Left: Glaucous sprays of *Juniperus squamata* 'Blue Carpet' contrast boldly with the fiery autumn foliage of Virginia creeper (*Parthenocissus quinquefolia*). Removing some parthenocissus shoots helps to stop it engulfing the juniper.

Juniperus squamata
SINGLESEED JUNIPER

This evergreen conifer varies between a spreading prostrate shrub and a small tree. All singleseed junipers are characterized by drooping shoot tips, which give a pleasantly feathery appearance. Many have glaucous foliage that looks attractive with other heathland plants such as dwarf conifers, heaths, and heathers. They are suitable for inclusion in large rock gardens or, in the case of the more prostrate cultivars, towards the front of a border. Useful cultivars include the spreading, glaucous 'Blue Carpet' ♀; 'Blue Star' ♀, which makes a low-growing bush; 'Holger' ♀, with yellowish green foliage that turns sulfur-yellow in summer; and 'Hunnetorp', with glaucous foliage. 'Meyeri' is a semi-erect, large shrub with ascending angular branches and glaucous foliage.

ⓘ *Abies koreana* 'Silberlocke', *Calluna vulgaris* 'Beoley Gold', *Erica × darleyensis* 'Silberschmelze', *Rhododendron* 'Blue Diamond', *R.* 'Yellow Hammer'

H: 4–6m (13–20ft) S: 1–6m (40in–20ft)
✿ **(Late summer)**

 ◊-◊◊ ☐-■ **Z4 pH4.5–7**

Juniperus virginiana 'Grey Owl' ♀

The evergreen Eastern red cedar (*Juniperus virginiana*) has produced many cultivars, varying in shape from conical or bushy to prostrate. Possibly the most useful is 'Grey Owl', a low, spreading shrub with glaucous, slightly arching branches, capable of forming an excellent ground cover. It can be combined with the same heathland plants as *J. squamata* (above), or grouped to make a dense ground cover, perhaps draped with a wispy climber such as a perennial pea or slender clematis. It also works well in a large shrub or mixed border, but tends to spread if planted at the front – this may be countered by leaving space in front for another group of herbaceous plants or a low shrub.

ⓘ *Clematis × cartmanii* 'Avalanche', *C.* 'Edward Prichard', *Daboecia cantabrica* f. *alba*, *Erica arborea* 'Albert's Gold', *Lathyrus latifolius* 'Albus'

H: 2m (6½ft) S: 3m (10ft) ✿ **(Late spring)**
◊-◊◊ ☐-■ **Z3 pH4.5–6.5**

A carpet of *Juniperus virginiana* 'Grey Owl' is set off by the amber autumn foliage of *Cornus sanguinea* Winter Beauty. The dogwood's bright stems remain showy through winter.

Laburnum × *watereri* 'Vossii' ♛

Probably the most common cultivar of laburnum, or golden-chain, this deciduous tree produces a lavish display of long, handsome racemes of yellow flowers. Its growth habit is suitable for training over an arch, or it may be allowed to develop as a tree, either free-standing or within a very large shrub or mixed border to provide height. In more modest borders, a tree that is not top-grafted can be pruned back to encourage low branching, and will then make a bushy plant with flowers that can interact successfully with shrubs of intermediate size, such as early white or cream Shrub roses, snowball bush, and ceanothus cultivars. Its color harmonizes splendidly with yellow-green foliage, and with orange flowers such as those of some berberis species. Despite its long, graceful branches and dense foliage, it is a relatively dull tree when not in flower, but full-size plants can be used to host a late summer flowering climber, such as clematis or honeysuckle, to maintain color and interest as the leaves begin to lose their glossy freshness.

⬤ *Berberis darwinii*, *B.* × *stenophylla* 'Lemon Queen', *Ceanothus* 'Cascade', *Clematis montana* f. *grandiflora*, *Prunus padus* 'Watereri', *Rhododendron* 'Persil', *Rosa* × *fortuneana*, *R. primula*, *Rubus* 'Benenden', *Syringa vulgaris* 'Firmament', *S.v.* 'Primrose', *Wisteria floribunda* 'Alba', *W.f.* 'Multijuga'

H & S: 8m (26ft) ✿ **Late spring**
◊-◊◊ ▢-▢ **Z3 pH5–7.5**

This classic combination features a tunnel of *Laburnum* × *watereri* 'Vossii' woven with wisteria, with *Allium hollandicum*, contrasting in floral form and color, growing from below to frame porthole views to silvery *Brachyglottis* (Dunedin Group) 'Sunshine' in the garden beyond.

A

Lavandula angustifolia 'Hidcote' makes a telling contrast with gold-variegated sage (*Salvia officinalis* 'Icterina'), a popular combination both visually and for its fragrance. The partnership is useful equally in a herb garden, at the front of a border, or alongside a path, where passers-by will brush against the plants, releasing their aromatic scent.

Lavandula angustifolia 'Hidcote' ♀

L. angustifolia, an evergreen Mediterranean sub-shrub 15–90cm (6–36in) tall, has greyish leaves and flowers in pale to deep lavender, occasionally white or mauve-pink. 'Hidcote' is a richly colored dwarf cultivar, suitable for use at the front of a border, or for edging or a dwarf hedge. The true cultivar is difficult to obtain and is propagated by cuttings; seed-raised plants are more common, but tend to be variable and often lack the rich color of 'Hidcote'. It associates with mauve, pink, purple, or blue, and with purple or silver foliage, and contrasts well with yellow-green foliage and flowers. Like all lavenders, it can become leggy and die in patches unless pruned annually in early to mid-spring, although some gardeners prefer to prune as the blooms fade. Plants can be sheared over, removing most of the previous year's growth and maintaining a natural mounded form.

◐ *Anthemis* Susanna Mitchell, *A. tinctoria* 'E.C. Buxton', *Cistus* 'Grayswood Pink', *Convolvulus cneorum*, *Dianthus* 'Haytor White', *Sedum* 'Vera Jameson'

H: 60cm (24in) S: 75cm (30in)
❄ **Mid- to late summer**

Z6 pH5.5–7.5

Lavandula stoechas subsp. *pedunculata* combines agreeably with many alliums, whose round flower heads provide a contrast of form, while their colors are usually harmonious. In this informal patchwork of plants that are suited to Mediterranean conditions, the dying leaves of *Allium cristophii* are hidden by young shoots of gypsophila, with chives (*Allium schoenoprasum*) in the foreground.

The silvery foliage of *Lavandula lanata* is perhaps never more effective than when set against rich blue. *Ceanothus* 'Puget Blue', which grows with branches down to ground level, is a perfect companion in a sunny border backed by a wall.

Lavandula lanata ♀

The appeal of this lavender lies both in its purple flowers and in the broad, intensely silver foliage, which looks attractive at any time of year. A little more demanding than *L. angustifolia* cultivars (above), it requires good drainage, full sun, and freedom from winter damp. It is a superlative shrub for the front of a border, especially with grey-leaved plants or cool-colored flowers, and an asset in rock or gravel gardens, where it may be combined with other Mediterranean plants such as cistus, helianthemums, halimiums, and phlomis. It harmonizes well with yellow-green foliage and flowers, and contrasts with yellow flowers. Mid-spring is the best time to prune, to avoid fungal disease.

◐ *Anthemis punctata* subsp. *cupaniana*, *Artemisia schmidtiana*, *Halimium* 'Susan', *Phlomis chrysophylla*, *Salvia chamaedryoides*, *S. officinalis* 'Purpurascens'

H: 75cm (30in) S: 90cm (36in) ❄ **Late summer**

Z7 pH5.5–7.5

Lavandula stoechas subsp. *pedunculata* ♀

The flowers of this deep purple lavender, almost black and scarcely visible except at close range, sport a showy topknot of mauve bracts. The flower heads are born on long stems and are held well above the greyish evergreen foliage, unlike those of French lavender (*L. stoechas*), which have short stalks and less conspicuous bracts. The mauve coloring, useful for echoing similar tints in plants such as alliums, pinks, and cranesbills, combines well with cool shades such as lilac or lavender and with carmine, crimson, or rich purple. Attractive when partnered with silver or glaucous foliage, or with plants such as cistus and other lavenders, it is excellent for the front of a border or in gravel. 'James Compton' has particularly showy bracts.

◐ *Cistus* 'Grayswood Pink', *Crambe cordifolia*, *Dianthus* 'Becky Robinson', *D.* 'Musgrave's Pink', *Helianthemum* 'Wisley White', *Rosa* Flower Carpet

H & S: 60cm (24in)
❄ **Late spring to early summer**

Z8 pH5.5–7.5

Lavatera 'Barnsley' ♔

This floriferous, long-flowering, deciduous sub-shrub produces long annual stems from a woody base. It rapidly develops into a medium to large shrub, valuable for quickly filling gaps in a border, where it blends with cool colors and purple, silver, or glaucous foliage, and makes an excellent partner for old roses or a backdrop of clematis. Its slightly amorphous habit is best combined with architectural plants, or those with flower spikes or plates or other equally contrasting floral forms. 'Barnsley' may be pruned back to a basal framework of branches in mid-spring, but in cold climates, frost can cut growth to below ground level. As long as they are not severely frosted, plants will regenerate from the roots, although they do then tend to revert to the original clone, the deeper colored 'Rosea'. Protecting the base of the plant over the winter usually averts this danger, and spare plants can very easily be raised from cuttings.

⬤ *Aconitum* × *cammarum* 'Bicolor', *Buddleja davidii* 'Nanho Petite Purple', *Cistus* × *argenteus* 'Blushing Peggy Sammons', *Dahlia* 'Gerrie Hoek' p.372 **B**, *Hebe* 'Midsummer Beauty', *Romneya californica*, *Rosa* Iceberg, *Thalictrum delavayi* 'Hewitt's Double' ❑ p.178 **A**

H & S: 2m (6½ft) ❁ **Early to late summer**
◐◐ ▢-▨ **Z8 pH5.5–7.5**

Later clematis such as *C.* 'Perle d'Azur' make an ideal backdrop for *Lavatera* 'Barnsley'. Planted nearby, the odd trail of clematis, perhaps a Jackmanii, Viticella, or Texensis cultivar in carmine, crimson, or sumptuous burgundy, can be allowed to weave itself through the lavatera.

With identically shaped foliage in dramatically contrasting colors, *Ligustrum ovalifolium* 'Aureum' and *Prunus* × *cistena* make a striking combination. Pruning will keep both at comparable size, even to below 1m (3¼ft), allowing this partnership to be used in the smallest gardens.

Ligustrum ovalifolium 'Aureum' ♔
GOLDEN CALIFORNIA PRIVET

The foliage of this bright deciduous shrub can vary between uniform yellow-green and green with a yellow-green margin. If left unpruned, it makes a rather shapeless bush, whereas pruning in late winter or early spring to a framework of branches or a column stimulates long sprays of more definite form. In full sun its color approaches yellow, which is especially useful for mixing with hot yellows or oranges and red foliage or flowers, and with blue flowers such as delphiniums. The foliage is less markedly yellow in shade, but very attractive with sulfur-yellow or cream flowers. Plants can be used as specimens or as a repeated accent along a border, and make excellent hedges, both on their own and with other colored-foliage shrubs. They are valuable hosts for climbers whose flowers contrast or harmonize with the creamy white panicles of the privet – a blue clematis or cream honeysuckle, for example.

⬤ *Achillea* 'Lucky Break', *Clematis macropetala* p.113 **A**, *Delphinium* 'Butterball', *D.* 'Fenella', *Hemerocallis* 'Golden Chimes', *Kniphofia* 'Sunningdale Yellow', *Miscanthus sinensis* 'Strictus', *Phlomis russeliana*, *Rosa* Graham Thomas, *Tithonia rotundifolia*

H & S: 3m (10ft) ❁ **Mid-summer**
◐◐ ▢-▨ **Z6 pH5–7.5**

Lonicera nitida 'Baggesen's Gold' 🏆

When grown in full sun, the tiny, glistening leaves of this evergreen shrub are almost pure gold, with bronze tints developing in winter. In shady parts of the garden they are not so brightly colored, but their light green effect is still valuable for illuminating dark corners. Tiny cream flowers in spring are followed by translucent purple-blue berries, although neither are conspicuous. Plants quickly become shaggy unless trimmed frequently to maintain their crisp outline. Annual pruning back to a billowing mound or a geometric shape will encourage attractive feathery shoots to develop in the following season. Treated in this way, plants can be used to support elegant and wispy climbers such as tropaeolums and clematis, in contrasting or harmonious colors. If old plants become unruly, they may be restored by pruning back to about 15cm (6in) high, after which new growth will spring vigorously from the base.

The billowing pale foliage of *Lonicera nitida* 'Baggesen's Gold' makes a successful foil for boldly shaped flowers in contrasting colors. Provided the shrub is not kept too small by pruning, it can support a moderately vigorous climber – a perennial pea, for example, or a Viticella clematis, such as *Clematis* 'Venosa Violacea' shown here.

Achillea 'Hella Glashoff', *Aconitum hemsleyanum*, *A.* 'Ivorine', *Clematis* × *durandii* p.108 **B**, *Delphinium* 'Lord Butler', *Geranium* 'Johnson's Blue', *Hosta fortunei* var. *aureomarginata*, *Ipomoea tricolor*, *Lathyrus sativus*, *Miscanthus sinensis* 'Zebrinus', *Yucca flaccida* 'Golden Sword' p.293 **A** ❑ pp.43 **B**, 46 **B**, 93 **C**

H & S: 1.5m (5ft) **(Late spring)**
Z7 pH5.5–7.5

Lupinus arboreus 🏆

TREE LUPINE

A sunny, well-drained position best suits this short-lived, semi-evergreen lupine, which quickly grows into a large, sprawling shrub that looks extremely attractive when mixed with Mediterranean plants such as brooms and cistus. The spires of bloom born in early summer give it a distinctive structure, highly effective in contrasts with flowers of different shapes such as the plates of achilleas. The yellow form is most common, but named clones such as 'Mauve Queen' and 'Snow Queen' are also available. Other colors, especially blue and cream, are often grown from seed, but these may not come true to type; some blue shades can be slightly impure and therefore unsuited to brightly colored schemes or strong contrasts. The tree lupine is excellent with white or orange Oriental poppies, early-flowering annuals or biennials such as *Limnanthes douglasii* and California poppies, and yellow-green or glaucous foliage.

Anchusa azurea, *Aquilegia canadensis*, *Cistus* × *hybridus*, *Nigella damascena* 'Miss Jekyll', *Paeonia lactiflora* 'Jan van Leeuwen', *Papaver orientale* 'Black and White', *P.o.* 'May Queen', *Rosa* 'Frühlingsgold', *Thalictrum flavum* subsp. *glaucum* ❑ p.160 **A**

H & S 1.5m (5ft) **Early summer**
Z8 pH5.5–7

Purple smoke bush, dramatically back-lit by the sun, presents a striking contrast to the vertical spikes of this soft yellow tree lupine (*Lupinus arboreus*), which is planted in front with cushions of lady's mantle (*Alchemilla mollis*). A single white-flowered species rose of simple and ethereal beauty provides the background.

Magnolia × loebneri 'Leonard Messel' has blush-pink flowers that are often a deeper mauve-pink on the outside of the petals and in the buds. Here, it is combined with *M. × soulangeana* 'Etienne Soulange-Bodin', and topped by the evergreen foliage and white bark of the snowgum (*Eucalyptus pauciflora* subsp. *niphophila*).

Magnolia × loebneri 'Leonard Messel' ♀

This is a deciduous large shrub or small tree, with upright growth and delicate blush-pink flowers, deeper in color on the reverse of the petals and in the buds, which appear before the leaves in mid-spring. It makes a charming specimen plant, suitable even for relatively small gardens, and in a prominent position needs only to be surrounded by a carpet of spring flowers such as pulmonarias, cream or white narcissi, chionodoxas, erythroniums, or primroses. When grown in a border, it benefits from being placed in front of other plants of similar height, to avoid obscuring its structure and to encourage even flowering on all sides. Like all magnolias, early selection of main branches is essential to establish a well-shaped plant, since pruning larger branches causes internal rotting. Other attractive cultivars include white 'Merrill' and 'Snowdrift', and pink 'Raspberry Fun'.

🌼 *Amelanchier lamarckii*, *Camellia × williamsii* 'Donation', *Chionodoxa forbesii*, *Narcissus* 'Thalia', *Pulmonaria* 'Blue Ensign', *Rhododendron williamsianum*

H & S: 8m (26ft) ❄ **Mid-spring**
△△-△△△ ▢-■ ■ **Z5 pH5–7**

Magnolia × soulangeana

The blooms of this small deciduous tree are usually goblet-shaped and of superlative quality, varying in color between pure white and wine-red. The first flush appears in mid-spring; a few more flowers are born later on, with the unfurling leaves, but they are largely hidden. The tree's spreading growth habit is difficult to accommodate in a border, because the wide canopy usually branches near the ground, but it looks enchanting as a single tree with spring flowers planted beneath, including small shrubs. Useful cultivars include 'Alexandrina' ♀, which is rich pink and has relatively upright growth. 'Lennei' ♀ is one of the darkest, with wine-red blooms that are almost pure white inside, and 'Lennei Alba' ♀ is pure white.

🌼 *Camellia* 'Inspiration', *Malus × atrosanguinea*, *Narcissus* 'Empress of Ireland', *Primula* 'Iris Mainwaring', *Rhododendron schlippenbachii* ⌙ p.67 **A**

H: 5–8m (16–26ft) S: 8m (26ft)
❄ **Mid- to late spring**
△△-△△△ ▢-■ ■ **Z5 pH4.5–6.5**

The goblet-shaped flowers of *Magnolia × soulangeana* 'Rustica Rubra', elegantly shaded from their pink tips to burgundy bases, harmonize perfectly with *Clematis montana* var. *rubens*. Training the clematis over an adjacent tree, shrub, or structure works best; grown into the magnolia, it could mar the poise and rhythm of the evenly spaced, sumptuous blooms.

Mahonia aquifolium
OREGON GRAPE

This is an evergreen, suckering shrub, with glossy, rich green, holly-like leaves, and yellow flowers born in terminal panicles. It is happy in sun or shade, and is a good plant for a woodland garden or for positions towards the front of a shrub border. An attractive companion for spring flowers – especially blue, cream, white, palest yellow, and orange bulbs – it associates particularly well with bluebells, muscaris, smaller narcissi and tulips, and white flowering currants. Plants grown from seed are very unpredictable and hybridize freely with related species such as *M. pinnata* and *M. repens* to produce seedlings of varying height, foliage, and flower. In most cases, especially when more than one plant is required, it is preferable to use a named clone such as 'Apollo', which has large and prolific panicles of flowers.

🌼 *Cornus mas*, *Forsythia ovata* 'Tetragold', *Helleborus foetidus*, *Ilex aquifolium* 'Pyramidalis Aureomarginata' p.61 **C**, *Milium effusum* 'Aureum', *Vinca minor*

H: 1m (40in) S: 1.5m (5ft) ❄ **Early to mid-spring**
△△-△△△ ▢-■ ■ **Z5 pH5.5–7.5**

The mahonia cultivar 'Apollo', here contrasting spectacularly with *Muscari armeniacum* 'Blue Spike', has less glossy leaves and many more lateral flower clusters than typical *Mahonia aquifolium*, making it a good choice where uniformity or plentiful color is needed.

Above: The flowers of *Mahonia × media* emerge when many shrubs still bear colorful autumn fruits, including the European spindle (*Euonymus europaeus*), its deep pink fruits here split open to reveal vermilion seeds.

Below: Autumn foliage as well as fruits may remain as *Mahonia × media* 'Charity' comes into bloom, as here with *Malus* 'Professor Sprenger'. This crab apple's fruits will stay on the tree throughout the flowering of the mahonia.

Mahonia × media

There are at least a dozen clones of this autumn- to winter-flowering shrub, each varying slightly in flower color, growth habit, and hardiness. All form stiff, erect shrubs, with evergreen holly-like leaflets and intensely yellow flowers that smell like lily-of-the-valley. To appreciate this fragrance, they may be grown near the house, through a carpet of short evergreens such as *Euonymus fortunei* cultivars, mingling with variegated hollies, early-flowering winter heaths, evergreen ferns and sedges, and the earliest snowdrops. 'Lionel Fortescue' ♀ is one of the first to flower, with erect, bright yellow racemes; 'Underway' ♀ is more compact, with paler primrose-yellow flowers; and 'Winter Sun' ♀, also compact, is outstandingly fragrant.

 *Euonymus fortunei* 'Emerald 'n' Gold', *Galanthus* 'Atkinsii', *Hamamelis × intermedia* 'Pallida', *Hedera helix* 'Buttercup', *Helleborus niger*, *Sarcococca confusa*

H: 4–5m (13–16ft) **S: 3–4m** (10–13ft)
❀ **Late autumn to late winter**
◊◊ ▢-▤ **Z8 pH5–7**

Wall training hides the rather unappealing habit of *Malus × zumi* 'Golden Hornet', also allowing it to be lightly clad with an early-flowering clematis such as *C. alpina* 'Ruby'.

Malus × zumi 'Golden Hornet' ♀

Although grown principally for its attractive golden yellow fruits, this crab apple also has decorative white flowers, opening from pink buds. It can be grown as a free-standing tree – at the back of a border, perhaps, behind late-flowering helianthus and rudbeckias – or as an espalier trained on a wall or, if bottom-grafted, as a low, spreading shrub. For spring display it can be draped with an early-flowering clematis. The fruits remain on the bare branches for several months, looking particularly effective when sunlit against dark foliage. It combines well with other autumn-coloring trees including sorbus, maples, nyssas, hickories, cladrastis, parrotias, and oaks, along with many larger shrubs, such as Japanese maples, berberis, dogwoods, smoke bush, cotoneasters, deciduous euonymus, witch hazels, sumacs, roses, sorbarias, and larger deciduous azaleas and viburnums.

● *Aucuba japonica* 'Crotonifolia', *Clematis macropetala* 'Markham's Pink', *Cotoneaster salicifolius* 'Rothschildianus', *Hamamelis × intermedia* 'Advent', *Ilex aquifolium* 'Amber', *Mahonia × media*, *Pyracantha* 'Soleil d'Or', *Rosa helenae*, *Sorbus* 'Joseph Rock', *Taxus baccata* 'Semperaurea'

H: 10m (33ft) **S: 8m** (26ft) ❀ **Late spring**
◊◊ ▢-▤ **Z4 pH5.5–7.5**

Morus alba 'Pendula'

The branches of this small deciduous tree fall dramatically to form a dense curtain of glossy foliage, bright yellow in autumn, making an effective, mushroom-shaped backdrop for other plants with light foliage or pale flowers. Its own flowers are insignificant and the fruits are hidden by the foliage, but it is excellent for training over a tunnel or bower, combined with other autumn-coloring plants such as vines or parthenocissus, or with celastrus, whose orange fruits would also add to the display. It may be trained as a standard by tying one of the most vigorous stems to a post 4–6m (13–20ft) high, and then makes a strong visual impact in the very largest shrub or mixed borders; ultimately, however, it

forms a very spreading tree. Spring flowers like snowdrops, crocuses, wood anemones, and celandines grow happily beneath its canopy. Although very hardy, it needs warm sunlight to ripen the wood, and does not thrive in areas with cool summers.

⬤ *Ampelopsis glandulosa* var. *brevipedunculata*, *Aralia elata* 'Variegata', *Celastrus orbiculatus*, *Rosa* 'Pax', *Rubus cockburnianus* 'Goldenvale', *Vitis* 'Brant'

H: 3m (10ft) S: 5m (16ft) ❈ (Late spring)
◊◊ ▦-▦ Z5 pH5.5–7.5

The bold outline and dark foliage of *Morus alba* 'Pendula' act as a punctuation mark at the corner of this box-edged bed. Other plants that work well here are of striking growth habit and subdued coloring, including *Phormium cookianum* subsp. *hookeri* 'Tricolor', striped green, creamy yellow, and red, and the arching white plumes of *Ligustrum quihoui*.

In this combination of Japanese plants designed principally for foliage effect, the mahogany coloring of *Acer palmatum* Dissectum Atropurpureum Group is echoed by the fruits and some bronze-flushed leaves of heavenly bamboo (*Nandina domestica*). In winter, the nandina will adopt more bronze coloring, as will the cryptomeria (top right).

Nandina domestica ♔

HEAVENLY BAMBOO

This upright shrub, semi-deciduous to evergreen, has dainty compound leaves that often assume bright red or orange tints late in the year, and bears large panicles of white flowers, followed (in warm climates) by red fruits. Its elegant growth warrants a position among shorter plants that do not mask its appearance. The airy foliage harmonizes with Japanese maples and bamboos, and in autumn associates well with cercidiphyllums, smoke bush, sumacs, sorbus, clethras, deciduous dogwoods, cotoneasters, witch hazels, linderas, deciduous azaleas, and stephanandras. Chrysanthemums (Rubellum, Korean, or Charm) in sunset colors, Chinese lanterns, and hostas, particularly those turning butter-yellow in autumn, are all good herbaceous companions.

⬤ *Acer palmatum* 'Seiryû', *Cercidiphyllum japonicum*, *Cornus alba* 'Kesselringii', *Fatsia japonica*, *Miscanthus sinensis* 'Zebrinus', *Physalis alkekengi*, *Pleioblastus auricomus*, *Rhus typhina* 'Dissecta', *Sorbus vilmorinii*, *Xanthorhiza simplicissima*

H: 1.8m (6ft) S: 1.5m (5ft) ❈ Mid-summer
◊◊ ▦-▦ Z7 pH5–7.5

Neillia thibetica

With its quiet charm and gracefully arching habit, this deciduous shrub (closely allied to *Spiraea* and formerly known under this name) is very much at home in wilder and more natural parts of the garden. Its slender racemes of rose-pink flowers, emerging from rust-red calyces, are not obviously showy, but make a very attractive complement to species roses, philadelphus, deutzias, late azaleas in pastel colors, cranberry trees, cranesbills, cow parsley, and pink, white, or red columbines. If left untrimmed for three or four years, the shrub will tend to lose its distinctive arching habit, but this can be avoided by hard pruning occasionally, immediately after flowering. This will also stimulate plenty of young stems, whose bark is a conspicuous bright green in winter, and this could justify neillia's inclusion in a bed of shrubs with colored stems, such as dogwoods, willows, and stephanandras.

◑ *Chaerophyllum hirsutum* 'Roseum', *Philadelphus* 'Belle Etoile', *Rhododendron viscosum*, *Rosa glauca*, *Spiraea cantoniensis*, *Viburnum opulus* 'Roseum'

H & S: 2m (6½ft) ❀ **Early summer**

◊◊ ▢-▢ **Z6 pH5–7.5**

After flowering, the rose-pink inflorescences of *Neillia thibetica* take on reddish tints as its seeds ripen, and the same hues are echoed along its leaf veins and margins. The mauve-pink flowers of the vigorous cranesbill *Geranium × oxonianum* 'Claridge Druce' scrambling through its stems clash slightly but not disagreeably.

A

Philadelphus 'Beauclerk' ♛

This arching deciduous shrub has powerfully fragrant white flowers, each with a pinkish stain at its center. Although too vigorous for most mixed and shrub borders, it is perfectly suited to large-scale plantings in wilder, less formal parts of the garden. It blends successfully with almost any color, but especially with pink flowers that echo the stain at the base of the petals, and combines well with early species roses, cranesbills, pale columbines, early single peonies, and pink cow parsleys. It tends to look rather dull later

Scrambling among the lower branches and flowers of *Philadelphus* 'Beauclerk', the mauve-pink cranesbill *Geranium × oxonianum* 'Claridge Druce' proves itself an agreeable invader. When both plants are in bloom, the effect is pretty and informal, and well suited to the wilder parts of a garden.

in the year, and benefits from draping with a wispy climber such as a late-flowering clematis, or a climbing annual. As with all philadelphus, removing about a quarter of the least floriferous main stems each year, immediately after flowering, helps maintain a succession of vigorous new growth.

Anthriscus sylvestris 'Ravenswing', *Aruncus dioicus*, *Campanula latifolia* 'Gloaming', *Chaerophyllum hirsutum* 'Roseum', *Kolkwitzia amabilis*, *Rosa elegantula* 'Persetosa', *R.* 'Nevada', *Syringa × prestoniae* 'Elinor', *Thalictrum aquilegiifolium*

H & S: 2m (6½ft) ❀ **Early summer**
◊◊ ▢-■ **Z5 pH5.5–7.5**

Both contrast and harmony feature when you combine *Philadelphus coronarius* 'Aureus', *Narcissus* 'Hawera', and a pansy (*Viola*). Placing the narcissus irregularly through an extended carpet of the viola would keep it from being camouflaged by the philadelphus, whose bulk could be broken up by wisps of a blue-flowered Alpina clematis.

Philadelphus 'Belle Etoile' ♛

A little neater and more compact than 'Beauclerk' (above), this philadelphus suits smaller-scale plantings and more sophisticated displays. It has a slightly more pronounced pinkish stain at the base of the petals than 'Beauclerk', and excels in harmonies with pink flowers and silver or white-variegated foliage, although it will combine successfully with almost any color. 'Belle Etoile' mixes well with the same plants as 'Beauclerk', together with some of the more elegant Tall Bearded irises, camassias, semi-double and double peonies, and double roses. It should be pruned in the same way as 'Beauclerk', and can be draped in a similar fashion with climbers to enliven it later in the season. Since it is deciduous, it can be planted beneath with spring bulbs that flower early, before the philadelphus leafs up.

Ammi majus, Aquilegia vulgaris var. *stellata* 'Nora Barlow', *Campanula lactiflora, Clematis montana* var. *wilsonii, Geranium sylvaticum* 'Baker's Pink', *Hesperis matronalis, Paeonia lactiflora* 'White Wings', *Papaver orientale* 'Black and White', *Rosa* 'New Dawn' p.143 **A**

H & S: 2m (6½ft) ❀ **Early summer**
◊◊ ▢-■ **Z5 pH5.5–7.5**

Covered in headily fragrant, pink-stained white flowers in early summer, *Philadelphus* 'Belle Etoile' combines charmingly with *Spiraea canescens*, whose tiny, creamy white florets are massed along arching sprays.

Philadelphus coronarius 'Aureus' ♛

GOLDEN MOCK ORANGE

This philadelphus is grown principally for the brightness of its foliage, rather than for its white flowers. The leaves are vivid yellow-green in spring, and approach full yellow later on when grown in sun, although they can scorch in areas with hot summers. Shade reduces flowering and turns the leaf color more towards green, but the foliage is still bright enough to have an impact and lighten a dark corner. Pleasing combinations include harmonies with yellow, cream, and white flowers, and contrasts with blue, orange, or scarlet flowers and bronze foliage. The shrub forms an excellent background for late-flowering spring bulbs such as camassias; and, although it lacks an attractive structure, it can be draped with wispy climbers such as clematis, honeysuckles, and morning glories.

Allium hollandicum p.301 **A**, *Berberis thunbergii* f. *atropurpurea* p.32 **C**, *Clematis × durandii, Consolida ajacis, Cytisus × praecox* 'Warminster' p.44 **C**, *Eryngium × tripartitum, Ipomoea tricolor* 'Heavenly Blue', *Primula veris* p.279 **A** ⌐ p.41 **A**

H: 2.5m (8ft) **S: 1.5m** (5ft) ❀ **Early summer**
◊◊ ▢-■ **Z4 pH5.5–7.5**

Philadelphus intectus

One of the larger, more vigorous mock oranges, this deciduous shrub produces strong, arching stems. The flowers are short-lived but prolific and marvellously fragrant. A free-standing specimen creates a graceful cascade when in bloom but is rather undistinguished in leaf alone. The shrub is most effective scrambling into a crab apple, pear, or birch 9–15m (30–50ft) high, where it will be less conspicuous after its few weeks of flowering glory. A wild garden is the best site and avoids any need for hard pruning. Alternatively it can be included in a scented floral hedge or walkway, entwined with honeysuckle, eglantine roses, and pink early-flowering Rambler roses.

◗ *Lonicera periclymenum* 'Graham Thomas', *Rosa* 'Cerise Bouquet', *R. nutkana* 'Plena', *Styrax japonicus* 'Pink Chimes', *Syringa × josiflexa* 'Bellicent'

H: 6m (20ft) S: 5m (16ft) ❀ **Early summer**
⬤⬤ ▦ **Z5 pH5–7.5**

The creamy plumes of handsome *Aruncus dioicus* contrast in form with *Philadelphus intectus*, here unpruned and so remaining leafy to ground level with flowering stems.

Phillyrea latifolia

Sometimes called mock privets, phillyreas are handsome, slow-growing shrubs or small trees closely related to osmanthus. *P. latifolia* resembles a small olive tree, with intriguingly gnarled and twisted branches, bending under their weight of glistening evergreen leaves to produce a softly billowing outline. Although scented white flowers appear in late spring, the strongly sculptural shape of the shrub has always been its irresistible appeal, and it is traditionally planted as an architectural feature – to soften the corner of a building, for example, or create a focal point at the end of a border. It has particularly dramatic impact when planted to contrast with the formal shape of a boxwood or yew hedge. It is perhaps best planted with bulbs, short herbaceous plants, and low shrubs that do not obscure its unique branch structure. In warm gardens, small black fruits can sometimes develop in autumn.

◗ *Arctostaphylos uva-ursi*, *Epimedium × versicolor* 'Sulphureum', *Euonymus fortunei*, *Shibataea kumasasa*, *Stephanandra incisa*, *Viburnum davidii*

H & S: 9m (30ft) ❀ **Late spring**
 ⬤⬤ ▢-▦ **Z7 pH5–8**

Placed towards the corner of a house to divide views from two facades, *Phillyrea latifolia* has here achieved the size of a small tree. Its handsome clouds of evergreen foliage and attractive branch structure provide the perfect foil to the severe lines of the building and to the paler, smooth-surfaced hedge of boxwood (*Buxus sempervirens*).

The mounded growth habit of *Phlomis fruticosa* makes it useful toward the front of a border, with taller shrubs behind. Here, its bright flowers harmonize with cream-variegated *Ligustrum sinense* 'Variegatum' and are set off by purple smoke bush (*Cotinus coggygria* 'Royal Purple').

Phlomis fruticosa ♛

JERUSALEM SAGE

Even when out of flower, this popular Mediterranean shrub catches the eye in a gravel bed or at the front of a border, where its spreading mound of felted greyish leaves makes a strong evergreen statement. In summer, whorls of bright yellow flowers are held high above the foliage and appear in huge numbers. It combines naturally with other hot-climate plants such as sages, white cistus, and ornamental grasses; it blends well with other yellow or orange flowers; and it makes an effective contrast with blue and mid-purple and with silver or purple foliage. It can become leggy unless pruned almost back to the previous year's growth in early spring; alternatively, large portions can be cut out every one or two years. Dwarf *P. italica* is slightly less hardy, with soft mauve blooms.

◗ *Artemisia stelleriana* 'Boughton Silver', *Festuca glauca* 'Blaufuchs', *Geranium* 'Johnson's Blue' p.227 **A**, *Hakonechloa macra* 'Aureola', *Iris* 'Jane Phillips', *Nepeta* 'Six Hills Giant' p.267 **B**, *Salvia lavandulifolia*

H: 1m (40in) S: 1.5m (5ft) ❀ **Early summer**
⬤ ▢ **Z7 pH5.5–7.5**

Photinia × fraseri

This photinia and its cultivars are evergreen shrubs or small trees, primarily used as foliage plants. They are most striking in spring, when their young shoots appear flushed brilliant red, later turning bronze and then green. New red sideshoots continue to form throughout the season, but without the startling impact of the spring flourish. Small white flowers are produced freely in warm, dry areas, less prolifically elsewhere.

The plants' vigorous growth habit suits a wild or informal garden rather than a shrub border, and their open base makes them ideal for planting with smaller shrubs and bulbs such as red crown imperials. For maximum effect, they can be combined with other hot colors such as red, vermilion, or scarlet azaleas and rhododendrons. *P. × fraseri* 'Red Robin' ♀, 'Robusta' ♀, and 'Rubens' are all popular choices for their flaming red growth, while 'Birmingham' is a darker coppery red. All can suffer from the bacterial disease fireblight, and early-morning spring sunshine can cause frost damage.

🌑 *Fritillaria imperialis* 'Aurora', *Geum* 'Beech House Apricot', *G. chiloense*, *Rhododendron* 'Coccineum Speciosum', *Tulipa* 'Prinses Irene' ⌐ p.344 **A**

H & S: 5m (16ft) ❈ **Early summer**
 ◊◊ ■ **Z7 pH5–7**

The coppery red spring shoots of *Photinia × fraseri* 'Birmingham' have here lost their initial brilliance but still remain in perfect harmony with *Euphorbia griffithii* 'Dixter'.

Phygelius aequalis '**Yellow Trumpet**' ♀

This remarkable phygelius produces creamy yellow-green, trumpet-shaped blooms that nod gently on one side of tall, angular stems, rather like those of a penstemon. In frost-free gardens, especially in a sheltered site such as the foot of a warm wall, this graceful South African sub-shrub is reliably evergreen or semi-evergreen and forms suckering clumps of upright stems. Elsewhere it may be cut down by frost and so start flowering later, producing even larger flower heads; hard annual pruning will have the same effect.

The soft, magical coloring goes well with both hot and cool shades, but it looks particularly breathtaking when partnered by magenta, blue, gold, or scarlet. More rounded flowers contrast well with the prominent spikes of the phygelius, which is equally at home near the front of a mixed or herbaceous border, or in a shrubbery.

🌑 *Argyranthemum maderense*, *Euphorbia seguieriana* subsp. *niciciana*, *Felicia amelloides* 'Santa Anita', *Geranium* 'Ann Folkard', *Nicotiana* 'Lime Green', *Petunia* Surfinia Purple, *Salvia greggii*, *S. patens*

H: 1m (40in) S: 50cm (20in)
❈ **Mid-summer to early autumn**
 ◊◊ □-■ **Z8 pH5.5–7.5**

The soft yellow florets of *Phygelius aequalis* 'Yellow Trumpet', born along one side of the stem, contrast dramatically in color and form with *Geranium psilostemon*.

Phygelius × rectus

Greater vigor and larger size distinguish this evergreen or semi-evergreen hybrid shrub from its parents, *P. aequalis* and *P. capensis*. There are several cultivars in a range of sizes and colors, and some are noted for their large, flared trumpet flowers with attractive markings. Outstanding cultivars include light red 'African Queen' ♀, salmon 'Pink Elf', and 'Moonraker', which is a similar creamy yellow to *P. aequalis* 'Yellow Trumpet' (above) but has blooms all round the stems. Because of their size, plants are best sited towards the middle of a border, perhaps among bronze or silver shrubs or with herbaceous plants in fairly warm colors.

🌑 *Achillea* 'Lachsschönheit', *Argyranthemum* 'Peach Cheeks', *Dianthus* 'Doris', *Diascia barberae* 'Blackthorn Apricot', *Euphorbia seguieriana* subsp. *niciciana*, *Heuchera* 'Smokey Rose', *Kniphofia* 'David'

H: 75–150cm (30–60in) S: 60cm (24in)
❈ **Mid-summer to early autumn**
 ◊◊ □-■ **Z8 pH5–7.5**

A gentle contrast between two harmonies, silver and blue versus coral-salmon and red-purple, from four plants of markedly differing form: from front to back, *Senecio viravira*, *Phygelius × rectus*, *Eryngium alpinum* 'Amethyst', and *Berberis thunbergii* 'Rose Glow'.

Physocarpus opulifolius 'Dart's Gold' ♀

A neat plant with gracefully arching branches, this deciduous shrub is brightest in spring, with its radiant yellow young foliage, and in early summers when the stems are packed with dense clusters of tiny white flowers. The plant needs space to display its shapeliness, so should not be overcrowded by competitive neighbors, although surrounding low-growing ground-cover plants can emphasize the arching growth habit. A slender Alpina Group clematis growing through the branches is a good companion, and purple foliage plants nearby contrast dramatically. 'Dart's Gold' also harmonizes well with other yellow-leaved plants such as euphorbias and decorative grasses. 'Luteus' is a more subdued shade of yellow; 'Diabolo' has leaves flushed dusky purple, especially when young.

◉ *Agapanthus* 'Loch Hope', *Clematis alpina* 'Frances Rivis', *Cotinus coggygria* 'Royal Purple', *Ipomoea tricolor* 'Heavenly Blue', *Miscanthus sinensis* 'Strictus' ❑ p.50 **B**

H & S: 1.5m (5ft) ❀ **Early summer**
◌◌ ▨ **Z3 pH5–6.5**

The essentially horizontal branches and silvery grey-green foliage of *Picea pungens* 'Globosa' contrast dramatically with weeping, green-leaved *Juniperus recurva* var. *coxii*.

When in flower, *Physocarpus opulifolius* 'Dart's Gold' has dazzlingly bright yellow-green leaves, here making a striking contrast with purple filbert (*Corylus maxima* 'Purpurea'). The leaves become greener as the season advances.

Picea pungens Pendula Group
WEEPING BLUE SPRUCE

This elegant group, based on the variable cultivar previously known as *P.p.* 'Glauca Pendula', has irregular weeping growth, more vigorous than that of *P.p.* 'Globosa' (above) and other small spruces, and with a loose growth habit. The best forms retain their glaucous coloring well, although not as permanently as smaller forms. The group's graceful growth and conical shape give it great distinction, making it effective as a focal point or vertical accent in larger gardens. Space and light are critical for producing a well-shaped plant, and a position away from competition is essential. Prostrate conifers, heathers, and low herbaceous plants can be grown around but not beneath them. The central stem should be trained vertically on a tall cane to encourage good height early on.

Other choice glaucous spruces include 'Procumbens' ♀, a dwarf, spreading cultivar with pendulous branches; 'Hoopsii' ♀, brilliant blue and densely conical in shape; and 'Koster' ♀, also conical with silvery blue foliage. Two other conical cultivars are 'Moerheimii', with tight, intensely blue foliage, and 'Montgomery', bright greyish blue and a little more rounded in shape.

Picea pungens 'Globosa' ♀

A compact blue-green form of the blue spruce, 'Globosa' is often planted as an evergreen focal point in gardens. It makes a dense bush, globe-shaped but with a flat top, and can take as long as 15 years to reach 1.5m (5ft) in height and spread. It sits easily with other conifers, especially junipers, and looks particularly good as a specimen in a bed of heathers. It needs space to grow symmetrically: crowding it in a small border or using it to support climbing plants can spoil the satisfying geometrical shape. For this reason it should be sited where sunlight and fresh air reach all sides. It is effective surrounded by low-growing herbaceous plants, especially bugleweeds, omphalodes, and other blue-flowered plants, or those with soft yellow flowers such as primroses.

◉ *Carex oshimensis* 'Evergold', *Erica carnea* 'Cecilia M. Beale', *Hosta* (Tardiana Group) 'June', *Juniperus horizontalis* 'Mother Lode', *Omphalodes cappadocica*

H & S: 1.5m (5ft) ❀ **(Late spring)**
◌◌ ▨ **Z2 pH5–6.5**

Winter-flowering heaths such as *Erica* × *darleyensis* 'Arthur Johnson' make an effective foil for *Picea pungens* Pendula Group, leafy to the ground with glaucous foliage.

◉ *Ajuga genevensis*, *Calluna vulgaris* 'Beoley Gold', *Euonymus fortunei* 'Emerald 'n' Gold', *Hakonechloa macra* 'Aureola', *Rhododendron* 'Sarled'

H: 10m (33ft) S: 3m (10ft) ❀ **(Late spring)**
◌◌ ▨ **Z2 pH5–6.5**

Pieris formosa is of comparable size and growth to many rhododendrons, making possible some dazzling combinations with its brilliant young shoots – as with the lilac-flowered cultivar here. A rhododendron or perhaps a deciduous azalea with peach, orange, apricot, or salmon blooms would make an equally satisfying partner.

Pieris formosa

Pieris are some of the loveliest evergreen shrubs, with handsome foliage and long trusses of usually white, spring flowers, reminiscent of lily-of-the-valley. The blooms of *P. formosa* are exceptionally beautiful, and its young leaves take on vivid red tints in mid- and late spring, making it one of the most striking shrubs for an early display. It needs to be positioned carefully, where it can be appreciated fully, and is best combined with salmon, apricot, cream, and yellow flowers, or contrasted with the apple-green of hellebores. It flowers well in full sun, although light overhead shade provides useful protection from frost, which can be especially damaging in late spring. As with all pieris, it must be grown in acid soil or compost.

⬤ *Amelanchier lamarckii*, *Camellia* 'Black Lace', *Crinodendron hookerianum*, *Dryopteris erythrosora*, *Embothrium coccineum*, *Euphorbia griffithii*, *E. palustris*, *Helleborus argutifolius*, *Paeonia delavayi*, *Rhododendron* 'Gloria Mundi', *R.* 'Golden Torch' ⬏ p.84 **B**

H: 5m (16ft) S: 4m (13ft) ❋ **Mid- to late spring**
Z8 pH4–6

Pieris japonica

One of the easiest and hardiest of pieris, this is a compact evergreen shrub with glossy foliage and masses of very sweetly scented white flowers gathered in heavy, branching trusses. The buds form early in autumn and, in a mild season, can open from late winter onwards. It is effective in small gardens, in mixed borders or in large containers, and also in woodland or wild garden settings. It can be combined with spring bulbs of all kinds, and other ericaceous shrubs such as heathers or rhododendrons. Acid soil or compost is essential, as is plenty of light for prolific flowering, although plants are happy in dappled shade. There are several popular cultivars such as 'Firecrest' ♥ and 'Red Mill' that produce flamboyant red new leaves as the flowers open.

⬤ *Camellia japonica* 'Hagoromo', *C.* × *williamsii* 'J.C. Williams', *Cryptomeria japonica* Elegans Group, *Erica* × *darleyensis* 'Silberschmelze', *Helleborus hybridus*, *Magnolia kobus*, *Narcissus* 'Mrs R.O. Backhouse', *Rhododendron arboreum*, *Skimmia japonica* 'Rubella'

H: 4m (13ft) S: 3m (10ft)
❋ **Late winter to early spring**
Z5 pH4–6.5

Drooping panicles of creamy white flowers on a young *Pieris japonica* are partnered prettily by *Corydalis solida* 'Lahovice'. A mature pieris would need larger companions.

The yellow-green foliage of *Pinus mugo* 'Winter Gold' mixes agreeably with the blue flowers of *Lithodora diffusa* 'Grace Ward'. The lithodora prefers neutral to alkaline soil.

Pinus mugo 'Winter Gold'

P. mugo, the mugo pine, is a very variable conifer from Central Europe that has produced numerous dwarf cultivars ideal for garden use. 'Winter Gold' is particularly useful, with an open arrangement of many low branches. These are thickly leaved and resemble bottle-brushes, upturned at their tips, giving strong textural impact. The foliage is fresh greenish yellow from late spring until early autumn, but it is at its best in winter when the whole conifer turns a brilliant and sunny shade of golden yellow. The spreading plant needs space to achieve its full beauty, and should not be hemmed in by other shrubs; annual pruning is recommended if a compact plant is needed. It can be surrounded with low-growing blue, cream, or yellow herbaceous flowers, spring bulbs, or combined with foliage plants such as heathers, gaultherias, and bergenias.

⬤ *Campanula poscharskyana*, *Corydalis ochroleuca*, *Festuca glauca* 'Blaufuchs', *Geranium* Rozanne, *Omphalodes cappadocica*, *Tulipa* 'Spring Green'

H: 60cm (24in) S: 1m (40in)
❋ **(Late spring to early summer)**

Z2 pH4.5–7.5

The small, white-mottled leaves of *Pittosporum tenuifolium* 'Irene Paterson' contrast effectively in both form and color with a dark-leaved phormium – both are New Zealanders with similar hardiness and cultivation requirements.

Pittosporum tenuifolium 'Irene Paterson' ♛

The variegated foliage of this evergreen shrub emerges cream, matures to deep green mottled with white, and becomes flushed with pink in winter. Its pale markings, most noticeable in spring, provide a lighter tone that is useful for harmonies with other pale foliage and for contrasts with darker plants. *P. tenuifolium* and all its cultivars thrive in maritime climates, where they can be grown with other pittosporums, olearias, hoherias, smaller or pruned eucalyptus, larger hebes, griselinias, and atriplex; other good partners include brachyglottis, choisyas, cordylines, escallonias, ozothamnus, corokias, tamarisks, and smaller phormiums. Larger cultivars look good draped with small-flowered clematis; shorter, silver-variegated kinds blend well with blue *Hydrangea macrophylla* cultivars.

 Agapanthus inapertus, *Ceanothus* 'Delight', *Choisya* Goldfingers, *Dodonaea viscosa* 'Purpurea', *Maurandya barclayana*, *Pseudopanax lessonii* 'Purpureus'

H: 1.5m (5ft) S: 60cm (24in)
❀ Late spring to early summer
▨▨▨ ◌◌ ▢-▨ Z9 pH5–7

Pittosporum tenuifolium 'Tom Thumb' ♛

This compact evergreen shrub has a neat shape and glistening foliage flushed bronze-purple. It makes dramatic contrasts with pale-leaved plants, and suits sumptuous color schemes featuring other plants with dark foliage such as purple or bronze cannas, sages, or dahlias, as well as flowers in hot colors or purple shades. Other good companions include smaller, deep purple or pink *Hydrangea serrata* or *H. macrophylla* cultivars, corokias, crocosmias, and smaller escallonias and phormiums, especially those with bronze, purple, or pink-striped leaves. 'Purpureum' is larger, with very dark purple leaves.

 Celmisia semicordata, *Dahlia* 'Moonfire', *Diascia barberae* 'Ruby Field', *Hebe speciosa* 'La Séduisante', *Nicotiana* 'Lime Green', *Phormium* 'Maori Sunrise'

H: 90cm (36in) S: 60cm (24in)
❀ (Late spring to early summer)
▨▨▨ ◌◌ ▢-▨ Z9 pH5–7

Pittosporum tenuifolium 'Tom Thumb' and *Corokia × virgata* harmonize in leaf color. Their similar textures might benefit from an intervening plant of contrasting form, perhaps with strap-like or grassy leaves.

Pleioblastus auricomus ♛

Grown for its bright, gold-variegated leaves, this evergreen bamboo spreads slowly to form a large clump that looks effective toward the front of a shrub border or in a woodland garden, mixed with hot colors, blue flowers, and glaucous foliage. Its foliage is brightest in late spring and early summer, when it is striking with yellow or orange azaleas, hostas, euphorbias, bluebells, and blue poppies; in mid-summer it combines well with blue or white hydrangeas, and later with autumn-coloring shrubs. Acanthus and larger ferns, grasses, and bergenias make good contrasts.

At the front of a border filled primarily with herbaceous plants, the slightly invasive, brightly variegated bamboo *Pleioblastus auricomus* provides an attractive contrast with the soft orange flowers of *Geum* 'Dolly North'. The bamboo's foliage is at its brightest in early summer when the geum is in full bloom. In a woodland garden it is best grown in an open area to ensure it receives partial sun.

 Corydalis flexuosa, *Euphorbia griffithi* 'Dixter', *Helleborus foetidus*, *Hosta* (Tardiana Group) 'Halcyon', *Hydrangea arborescens* subsp. *discolor* 'Sterilis', *H. macrophylla* 'Blue Bonnet', *Meconopsis grandis*, *Ophiopogon planiscapus* 'Nigrescens', *Phormium* 'Dark Delight', *Rhododendron augustinii*, *R.* 'Coccineum Speciosum', *R.* 'Narcissiflorum'

H: 1.2m (4ft) S: 1.5m (5ft) ❀ (Summer)
▨▨▨ ◌◌-◌◌◌ ▢-▨ ▨ Z7 pH5–7

A

The pale yellow-green foliage of annually pruned *Populus alba* 'Richardii' contrasts sharply with a purple *Cleome hassleriana*, the magenta flowers of *Geranium* 'Ann Folkard', and mauve *Allium carinatum* subsp. *pulchellum*.

Populus alba 'Richardii' ♡

When pollarded or pruned, this deciduous, medium-sized tree or large shrub has particularly large, vivid yellow-green leaves, and makes a handsome foliage plant for a mixed or shrub border, especially when ruffled by a breeze to reveal the downy white underside of its foliage. Its bright leaves make striking contrasts with hot colors such as magenta, scarlet, or orange, and they also associate well with white, yellow, or pure blue flowers – delphiniums, for example – and silver, yellow-green, or yellow-variegated foliage. It is outstanding as a companion for lavender-blue buddlejas and yellow or orange *Buddleja* × *weyeriana* cultivars, and it also succeeds as a support for a wispy flowering climber such as a morning glory or a Viticella clematis. Other suitable partners include yellow-green catalpas, honey locust, and robinias; silver atriplex, elaeagnus, and hippophae; and tall yellow flowers such as rudbeckias and helianthus.

◐ *Buddleja* 'Lochinch', *Clematis* 'Rhapsody', *Delphinium* 'Blue Jay', *Euphorbia sikkimensis*, *Ipomoea tricolor* 'Heavenly Blue', *Rosa* 'Golden Wings', *R.* 'Sally Holmes', *Rudbeckia* 'Juligold', *Tithonia rotundifolia*

H: 15m (50ft) S: 12m (40ft) ❀ (Early spring)
◊◊-◊◊◊ ▢-■ Z2 pH5–7.5

Potentilla fruticosa

SHRUBBY CINQUEFOIL

This variable deciduous shrub may have an erect or prostrate habit, deep green or silvery leaves, and flowers that are white to golden yellow, sometimes orange-red or peach. Rarely profuse enough to make a solid block of color, the flowers and dainty filigree foliage excel at close range, especially with plants of more definite form such as hostas, grasses, day lilies, eryngiums, and crocosmias. The flowers suit combinations with warm colors and yellow-green, gold-variegated, or glaucous foliage, and they contrast well with blue flowers, such as caryopteris, perovskias, or ceratostigmas. Good partners include old shrub roses, lavenders, lavender-blue or white hebes, hydrangeas, olearias, catmints, buddleias, and hypericums. Among the most useful cultivars are 'Beesii' ♡ (60cm/24in), with silvery leaves and golden flowers; 'Abbotswood' ♡ (75cm/30in), with bluish green leaves and white flowers; the free-flowering 'Goldfinger' ♡ (75cm/30in), with

Right: The silvery leaves of *Potentilla fruticosa* 'Primrose Beauty' and its pale flowers blend with almost any other color. Here, it spreads over edging stones at the front of a border among flowers of varied colors and forms – *Rosa* 'Felicia', purple-leaved *Actaea simplex* Atropurpurea Group, blue *Polemonium foliosissimum*, coral kniphofias, white violas, and variegated *Phlox paniculata* 'Norah Leigh'.

Below: In a simple but striking combination, *Potentilla fruticosa* 'Tangerine' is draped gracefully with the cream-edged foliage of *Vinca major* 'Variegata'.

large golden flowers; 'Elizabeth' ♡ (1m/3¼ft), in rich yellow; 'Maanelys' ♡, Moonlight (1.2m/4ft), with soft yellow flowers until late autumn; and 'Katherine Dykes' ♡ (up to 2m/6½ft), in primrose-yellow.

◐ *Agapanthus* 'Donau', *Caryopteris* × *clandonensis*, *Eryngium* × *tripartitum*, *Hakonechloa macra* 'Aureola', *Helictotrichon sempervirens*, *Hemerocallis* 'Corky', *Hosta* 'Big Daddy', *Lavandula angustifolia* 'Hidcote', *Nepeta* × *faassenii*, *Perovskia* 'Blue Haze', *Rosa* 'Sally Holmes' p.161 **A**, *Sedum* 'Herbstfreude' p.285 **B**

H: 30cm–2m (1–6½ft) S: 1–2m (3¼–6½ft)
❀ Late spring to mid-autumn
◊◊ ▢-■ Z3 pH5–7.5

B

C

The ornamental cherry *Prunus pendula* 'Pendula Rosea', grown as a specimen tree, is planted with crocuses below in purple, lilac, and white. The effect is pleasing for its subtlety – adding golden yellow crocuses here would be too strident.

Prunus pendula 'Pendula Rosea' ♀

The rose-pink flowers of this deciduous ornamental cherry appear before the leaves, in early and mid-spring, coinciding with crocuses, narcissi, and early tulips, any of which can be used to create a tapestry of flowers beneath its spread. With its elegantly weeping habit, it makes a fine specimen tree, but it may also be grown in a large border above shade-tolerant plants and spring flowers, preferably where it is screened from early morning sun to avoid frost injuring the blooms. The flowers blend well with red-flushed evergreen foliage such as that of bergenias, and with other short spring flowers, including wood anemones, *Cyclamen coum* variants, and hellebores. This charming tree also associates well with camellias, such as *Camellia × williamsii* cultivars, and with *Viburnum tinus* cultivars and early rhododendrons. *Prunus × subhirtella* 'Autumnalis' ♀ is a slightly less graceful *P. pendula* hybrid, with white or palest blush flowers through the winter and into spring; the blooms of *P. × s.* 'Autumnalis Rosea' ♀ are a more definite pink, while those of *P. × s.* 'Fukubana' ♀ are dark rose-pink.

○ *Camellia japonica* 'Hagoromo', *C. × williamsii* 'J.C. Williams', *Helleborus × hybridus*, *Rhododendron dauricum*, *R. mucronulatum*, *Viburnum × bodnantense*

H & S: 10m (33ft) ※ **Early to mid-spring**
◊◊ ▨-▨ **Z5 pH5.5–7.5**

Prunus Sato-zakura Group
JAPANESE FLOWERING CHERRY

The Japanese cherries are popular, spring-flowering deciduous small trees, with single, semi-double, or double flowers in white to deep pink, and green, bronze-flushed, or purple foliage. Upright or columnar cultivars are useful in restricted spaces or formal arrangements, whether as focal points or repeated accents; where there is plenty of room, they look more effective as a group than planted singly. Spreading kinds can be trained up high enough to be planted with shrubs below or to allow a walkway beneath, or they can arch gracefully above their neighbors. Strongly colored cultivars can be used for dramatic partnerships with other small trees and large shrubs such as flowering crab apples, lilacs, hawthorns, magnolias,

○ *Amelanchier × grandiflora* 'Rubescens', *Camellia japonica* 'Alba Simplex', *Crataegus monogyna* 'Biflora', *Magnolia kobus*, *Malus floribunda*, *Rhododendron schlippenbachii*, *Syringa oblata*, *Viburnum × burkwoodii*

H: 6–10m (20–33ft) S: 3–10m (10–33ft)
※ **Early to late spring**
◊◊ ▨-▨ **Z5 pH5.5–7.5**

rhododendrons, and *Camellia japonica* or *C. × williamsii* cultivars. Specimen trees look particularly fine carpeted beneath with spring flowers such as narcissi, tulips, pulmonarias, brunneras, forget-me-nots, wood anemones, cardamines, corydalis, and bluebells.

Attractive white cultivars include 'Shirotae' ♀, with single and semi-double flowers; single 'Taihaku' ♀ (the great white cherry); 'Ukon' ♀, a spreading tree with double flowers that are white-flushed yellow-green; and 'Shirofugen' ♀, whose blush-white flowers open from pink buds. Among pale pink cultivars are semi-double 'Accolade' ♀; narrowly columnar 'Amanogawa' ♀, double; 'Ichiyo' ♀, double; and the late-flowering 'Taoyame', semi-double. The weeping double 'Kiku-shidare-zakura' ♀ (syn. 'Cheal's Weeping'), semi-double 'Chôshû-hizakura', and double 'Pink Perfection' ♀ are all bright pink. Double 'Kanzan' ♀ is outstanding for the sheer abundance of its deep pink flowers, while the otherwise similar 'Royal Burgundy' has purple foliage.

Prunus 'Shirotae' makes a widely spreading tree, with pure white, single and semi-double flowers emerging from palest pink buds. It is planted beneath here with uneven clumps and drifts of cream *Narcissus* 'February Silver'.

Even without a companion, the potential of *Pyracantha angustifolia* for combining with autumn foliage or fruits is apparent, with its glossy evergreen leaves showing pale undersides and copious berries on arching stems.

Pyracantha angustifolia

This is a variable evergreen shrub, erect or prostrate, with creamy white flowers followed by orange-yellow to orange-red berries. It can be grown as a freestanding shrub, trained against a wall, or used to make a hedge, perhaps with winter jasmine or ivy. The persistent berries look striking in winter, and are usually still plentiful and attractive when spring bulbs such as narcissi and tulips are in bloom. This pyracantha combines well with prostrate junipers, other berrying shrubs such as cotoneasters, white-flowered winter heaths, ground-covering ivies, evergreen euonymus, and dogwoods, willows, and other deciduous shrubs with colored stems. For autumn effect it may be combined with late-coloring deciduous shrubs such as Japanese maples, smoke bush, fothergillas, witch hazels, sumacs, and azaleas.

⬤ *Amelanchier laevis, Berberis wilsoniae, Cotinus coggygria, Cryptomeria japonica* Elegans Group, *Fothergilla major, Hedera canariensis* 'Gloire de Marengo', *H. colchica* 'Sulphur Heart', *Rhododendron luteum, Rosa* 'Alchymist', *R.* 'Golden Wings'

H & S: 3m (10ft) ❀ **Early summer**
◊◊ ▢-■ **Z6 pH5.5–7.5**

Pyracantha coccinea

This large deciduous shrub differs from *P. angustifolia* (above) in having broader leaves, deeper red berries, and slightly later, creamy white flowers. Although the species itself is rarely available, there are a few valuable cultivars, including 'Lalandei', a more vigorous, erect plant, with larger berries thickly covering its branches. 'Red Column', with heavy clusters of early scarlet berries, is dense and erect, while the low 'Red Cushion' is useful for a ground cover. Hybrids include vigorous 'Orange Glow' ♡, with plenty of orange-red berries that last well into winter; 'Golden Charmer', with arching branches and orange-yellow berries; 'Mohave', which is orange-red and has early ripening berries; and its white-edged variant 'Mohave Silver'.

⬤ *Acer palmatum* 'Ôsakazuki', *Buddleja × weyeriana, Cotoneaster frigidus* 'Cornubia', *Euonymus europaeus* 'Red Cascade', *Juniperus × pfitzeriana* Gold Sovereign, *Photinia beauverdiana, Rhododendron calendulaceum, Rhus typhina, Rosa* 'Blanche Double de Coubert'

H & S: 4m (13ft) ❀ **Early summer**
◊◊ ▢-■ **Z5 pH5.5–7.5**

The arching sprays of blossoms of *Pyracantha coccinea*, harmonizing here with *Elaeagnus* 'Quicksilver', are as appealing as its berries, although shorter-lived. The effect is most dramatic on fairly young or recently pruned bushes.

A classic element of the white garden, where it can be combined with foliage in silver, glaucous, or plain green and with white flowers, *Pyrus salicifolia* 'Pendula' here harmonizes with the foliage of sea kale (*Crambe maritima*) in front. *Leucojum aestivum* and the contrasting form of ostrich fern (*Matteuccia struthiopteris*) sit to one side.

Pyrus salicifolia 'Pendula'
WEEPING WILLOW-LEAF PEAR

This is an elegant, weeping deciduous tree, with narrow silver-green leaves and white flowers that appear as the leaves emerge. Although pretty at close range, its blooms are slightly camouflaged by the pale foliage, which is this plant's chief attraction. The most common form produces a low mushroom of foliage suitable for smaller gardens, but for larger plantings trees can be trained to a taller stake to allow planting beneath with shade-tolerant evergreens and spring flowers such as anemones and celandines. It associates well with cool colors, white flowers, and other silver foliage plants, and makes a dramatic contrast with dark green or dark purple foliage. In a large border, it can stand in front of other plants of similar size. Occasional removal of stems from the crown will provide a more graceful appearance. If a larger, non-weeping tree is needed, the plain species or the similar *P. elaeagnifolia* can be grown.

⬤ *Clematis alpina* 'Ruby' p.107 **B**, *Cosmos bipinnatus* 'Purity', *Crambe cordifolia, Delphinium* 'Lilian Bassett', *Digitalis purpurea* f. *albiflora, Miscanthus sinensis* 'Morning Light', *Onopordum nervosum, Rosa* Iceberg, *R.* 'Lavender Lassie' p.157 **C**

H: 5m (16ft) S: 4m (13ft) ❀ **Mid-spring**
◊◊ ▢-■ **Z4 pH5.5–7.5**

Rhododendrons
including Azaleas

RHODODENDRONS COMPRISE one of the most important genera of garden plants. There are approximately 4,000 types available, flowering from late winter to mid-summer, in every color except pure blue. They vary greatly in growth habit, from low, carpeting cultivars suitable for ground covers to large, tree-like species; many have an open, branching habit. Rhododendron foliage is almost always respectable and sometimes exceptionally handsome, as in larger species such as *R. macabeanum* ♀ and *R. rex*. A few, for instance *R.* Shilsonii Group, have attractive bark. Most rhododendrons in this book fall into three groups: evergreen hardy hybrids (or "iron clads") and their parent species; deciduous azaleas; and evergreen azaleas.

All rhododendrons prefer moist, acid soil with high humus content and dappled shade, suiting them ideally to a woodland garden. Many evergreen rhododendrons make useful screens or informal hedges, although large expanses of their foliage can look dull through summer and autumn unless brightened by more varied leaf textures. Summer-flowering types include selections of some of the North American azaleas and their hybrids, as well as the sweet-scented *R. auriculatum* and its hybrid 'Polar Bear'. Most deciduous azaleas have a rich and pervasive scent; many also have brilliant autumn color, provided they are not grown in dense shade.

In cool climates, rhododendrons described as sun-tolerant can be grown in almost full sun, although this may result in a very tight habit and unnaturally dense flower cover. More shade can help to loosen the habit of excessively spherical types: birches provide good quick cover in a rhododendron garden, as do oaks for the longer term (beech should be avoided, as the dense canopy and dry soil it creates are not suitable for rhododendrons). An

evergreen windbreak is vital for the more tender evergreen rhododendrons, the large-leaved kinds usually needing the most shelter. Most rhododendrons prefer an acid soil with a pH of 4.5–5.5 but will tolerate a pH of 4–6. However, some nurseries may offer a new kind of rhododendron, grafted onto lime-resistant rootstocks, and these will grow on even quite alkaline soil.

When planting rhododendrons, it is useful to bear in mind that irregular groups tend to look more natural, and that the scale of the group needs to relate to its setting (in a large area, single plants can create a "spotty" effect). The very brightly colored and most floriferous types, particularly if they have a densely spherical habit, can seem out of place in a natural setting such as a woodland garden, and tend to look better near the house. Rules decreeing that azaleas should not be combined with other rhododendrons should be ignored; however, it is worth

In an intimate garden, a jumble of deciduous azaleas in harmonious, sugared almond colors can look charming. The true *Allium aflatunense*, with its spherical, pinkish purple heads, almost matches the azaleas in height.

noting that combinations of flowers in the yellow to scarlet range with those in crimson through magenta to lavender can clash horribly or excitingly, depending on personal preference.

Rhododendrons are surface-rooting, with a spreading, fibrous root system: even mature specimens can be transplanted without impairing their growth, allowing plants to be eased out when they become congested and colors to be rearranged. Leggy plants, if growing vigorously, can be restored to shape by hard pruning in late winter, although smooth-barked types do not regenerate easily and should not be cut back so severely. New strains of rhododendron powdery mildew mean that regular use of fungicides is essential for some species. Deadheading significantly increases the following year's bloom.

Rhododendron 'Amethyst'

The brilliant violet-blue of this sun-tolerant hardy hybrid makes a dazzling contrast with greenish yellow, and a slightly less punchy one with sulfur-yellow flowers. It also combines pleasantly with carmine, campanula-blue, mauve-pink, or lilac blooms. Extremely pale colors, such as light blues, mauves, and pinks, as well as white, tend to be less successful, since they do not contrast or harmonize as effectively. However, the tiniest of flowers in these colors – cow parsley, for example – can work well.

The feathery, bright yellow-green new leaves of *Acer palmatum* 'Linearilobum' provide delicate texture and a striking color contrast with *Rhododendron* 'Amethyst'.

Generally, the fine texture and relatively amorphous habit of 'Amethyst' demand companions of definite form to avoid an excessively diffuse effect.

◐ *Allium hollandicum, Anthriscus sylvestris* 'Ravenswing', *Lunaria annua, Meconopsis integrifolia, Milium effusum* 'Aureum', *Smyrnium perfoliatum*

H & S: 1.5m (5ft) ✽ **Mid- to late spring**
 ◊◊-◊◊◊ ▨-▨ ▨ **Z6 pH4–6**

Hosta fortunei 'Crowned Imperial' adds bold structure here, its glaucous leaves with yellow-green margins contrasting with the lilac flower heads of *Rhododendron* 'Blue Peter'.

Rhododendron 'Blue Peter' ♔

The bold lilac flower heads of 'Blue Peter', with their repeated pattern of dark basal blotches, are almost too sumptuous and sophisticated for the wilder parts of the garden. This is one of the bluest hardy hybrids; it makes attractive contrasts with pale yellow, apricot, and yellow-green flowers, and harmonizes with pink, carmine, and campanula-blue. It is especially effective as a quieter foil for some of the intense violet-blue, smaller-flowered species rhododendrons such as *R. fastigiatum* ♔, *R. impeditum* ♔, and *R. russatum* ♔ and their hybrids, including *R.* 'Amethyst' (above left). Combinations with glaucous blue-green, yellow-green, purple, and smoky purple-grey foliage also work well. 'Blue Peter' is one of the most sun-tolerant hardy hybrids, and becomes leggy and shy-flowering if deprived of adequate light.

◐ *Camassia leichtlinii, Euphorbia amygdaloides* var. *robbiae, Heuchera* 'Can-can', *Hyacinthoides non-scripta, Mertensia virginica, Milium effusum* 'Aureum', *Prunus spinosa* 'Purpurea', *Smyrnium perfoliatum*

H & S: 3m (10ft) ✽ **Late spring**
◊◊-◊◊◊ ▨-▨ ▨ **Z5 pH4–6**

Rhododendron Blinklicht Group

Like many other hardy hybrids, Blinklicht Group has a fairly solid habit, bold leaves, and large flower heads, giving it more definite form than small-leaved rhododendrons with few flowered inflorescences. Its solidity can be offset by partners with a more elegant, open growth habit, and its strong color looks best in areas that do not lean toward wildness. It contrasts well with soft yellow and yellow-green flowers and leaves, and harmonizes with rich peach, apricot, soft orange, deep salmon-pink, and deep rose-pink blooms. Combinations with bronze foliage also need lighter colors to brighten them.

◐ *Aquilegia canadensis, Euphorbia amygdaloides* 'Purpurea', *Helleborus* × *sternii, Hosta* 'Sum and Substance', *Physocarpus opulifolius* 'Luteus', *Rhododendron* 'Elizabeth Lockhart', *R.* 'Fabia'

Rhododendron Blinklicht Group, planted under with *Tiarella cordifolia*, harmonizes with *Acer palmatum* f. *atropurpureum. Polygonatum* × *hybridum* gives a graceful contrast of form.

H: 2.5m (8ft)   S: 1.5m (5ft) ✽ **Mid- to late spring**
 ◊◊-◊◊◊ ▨-▨ ▨ **Z6 pH4–6**

Rhododendron campylocarpum

The soft yellow blooms and slightly lax, informal growth habit of this evergreen species suit it to wild gardens, where it can mingle prettily with the most humble flowers such as meadow buttercups, cow parsley, and bluebells. It also combines agreeably with gold, apricot, white, and chartreuse flowers and yellow, chartreuse, and glaucous foliage. Pure blue flowers, for instance blue poppies or *Corydalis flexuosa*, contrast well; purplish blue cranesbills and campanulas are also effective. Good frost drainage helps prevent damage to the flowers from late frosts.

○ *Brunnera macrophylla, Hosta sieboldiana* var. *elegans, Meconopsis betonicifolia, Milium effusum* 'Aureum', *Myosotis sylvatica, Smyrnium perfoliatum*

H: 5m (16ft) **S: 4m** (13ft) ❀ **Mid-spring**
○○-○○○ ■-■ ■ **Z6 pH4–6**

The ivory-white flowers of *Fothergilla gardenii*, emerging from greenish yellow buds, create a color harmony with *Rhododendron campylocarpum* and a contrast of floral form.

Rhododendron Cilpinense Group ♈

The pale, sugary pink of the floriferous, evergreen Cilpinense Group looks good with darker pink, white, or deep crimson flowers (bright crimson can overwhelm it), and with red-tinted foliage. Harmonies with mauve, lilac, peach, and pale apricot also work well. Its color is not strong enough for extreme contrasts, except possibly with pale apple-green. Flowering earlier than most hardy hybrids, it blooms before most deciduous or herbaceous foliage unfurls, although it can be

Pulmonaria 'Lewis Palmer' makes a superb ground cover beneath the pink bloom of *Rhododendron* Cilpinense Group.

used successfully with a wide range of spring bulbs – narcissus cultivars are particularly effective. The young foliage and flower buds of this rhododendron are susceptible to damage from late frosts.

○ *Anemone nemorosa* cultivars, *Helleborus argutifolius, H. × hybridus, Narcissus* 'February Silver', *Primula* 'Old Port', *Rhododendron* 'Elizabeth Lockhart' ❏ p.35 **B**

H & S: 1m (40in) ❀ **Early spring**
○○-○○○ ■-■ ■ **Z6 pH4–6**

Rhododendron 'Fandango'

Like many other evergreen azaleas, 'Fandango' (not to be confused with the hardy hybrid of the same name) makes a spreading, compact plant that is covered by dazzling flowers in spring. Its deep purplish pink can be used with great panache and brilliance, mixed with other bright flowers and foliage, to make an impact when seen in passing; however, such intense combinations can pall if the plant is sited where it will be viewed for longer periods of time. The solid sheets of purplish pink can be rendered more acceptable by using a scattered group rather than a single block, by combining it with soft bronze or glaucous foliage, or by adding slightly paler, dusky mauve-pink flowers. Clashes with vermilion or chartreuse might appeal to the daring. Although 'Fandango' is a neat shrub, it lacks distinction when not in flower; neighbors with a strong growth habit or textured foliage should be chosen to extend the period of interest.

○ *Dicentra* 'Stuart Boothman', *Helleborus × sternii, Primula* 'Guinevere', *Pulmonaria saccharata* Argentea Group, *P.s.* 'Dora Bielefeld'

H: 90cm (3ft) **S: 1.2m** (4ft) ❀ **Late spring**
○○-○○○ ■-■ ■ **Z6 pH4–6**

The colors and textures of *Acer palmatum* f. *atropurpureum* and *Rhododendron* 'Fandango' mix well. An additional, intermediate shrub would balance the difference in height.

Rhododendron 'Kirin' ♔

This brilliant rich cerise evergreen azalea has hose-in-hose flowers (with two flower tubes, one inside the other). Its color and uses are similar to those of the lower-growing 'Fandango' (facing page); however, whereas 'Fandango' can be used to make up the pattern of a richly colored carpet of perennials and shrubs, the taller 'Kirin' is more suited to working into borders and shrubberies. The strong colors of both azaleas are their greatest assets and their chief limitations: although their brilliance can be moderated by combining them with more muted, harmonious tones, they can seem brash if used with other strong colors and are more suited to momentary spectacle than to contemplative, wild or woodland gardens.

◉ *Bergenia* 'Bressingham Bountiful', *Dicentra spectabilis*, *Helleborus argutifolius*, *Heuchera* 'Can-can', *Prunus* × *cistena*, *Pulmonaria* 'Vera May'

H & S: 1.5m (5ft) ❄ **Mid-spring**
◊◊-◊◊◊ ▨-▪ ◼ Z6 pH4–6

Rhododendron 'Kirin' creates a dazzling combination with *Hosta undulata* var. *undulata*: its all panache and pizzazz, but is not for those who seek tranquillity in the garden.

Helleborus × *hybridus* is a good companion for *Rhododendron hippophaeoides*. Cultivars in clear pink, plum, soft yellow, or white work best with the rhododendron's bright violet.

Rhododendron hippophaeoides

This sun-tolerant evergreen rhododendron can vary in color between lavender-blue, as seen in the superlative clone 'Habashan' ♔, and mauve-pink. It tends to be upright when young, becoming more spreading with age. Lavender-blue variants form striking contrasts with greenish yellow and sulfur-yellow, and combine attractively with mauve-pink, lilac, carmine, and campanula-blue flowers; they work less well with paler blues, mauves, pinks, and whites, unless the flowers of the companion plants are very small. The pinkish variants combine well with white, purple, and darker blue shades, and contrast effectively with light apple-green, but not yellow. Its tolerance of sunnier situations suits it to more open, heath-like areas rather than to a woodland garden, and its neat growth habit makes it suitable for smaller gardens.

◉ *Allium aflatunense*, *Corydalis solida*, *Euphorbia amygdaloides* var. *robbiae*, *E. polychroma* 'Major', *Helleborus argutifolius*, *H.* × *hybridus* (primrose), *Narcissus* 'Liberty Bells', *N.* 'Pipit'

H: 1.5m (5ft) S: 75cm (2½ft) ❄ **Mid-spring**
◊◊-◊◊◊ ▨-▪ ◼ Z6 pH4–6

Rhododendron 'Linda'

The sumptuous cerise of this hardy hybrid and its tight, compact growth habit make it effective in more cultivated areas near the house, where it might be combined with Lily-flowered tulips and pink and white forget-me-nots. In a wild or woodland garden, its tendency to brashness can be moderated by companion plants of looser growth habit and more delicate or duskier coloring. Although it combines attractively with carmine to lavender-blue flowers, it is perhaps most

Rhododendron 'Linda' and bluebells (*Hyacinthoides non-scripta*) make a lovely pairing for a woodland garden.

effective in harmonies with pale pink, mauve, or deep crimson blooms and purple-flushed leaves. Pale apple-green flowers or glaucous foliage could also provide a pleasant contrast.

◉ *Anthriscus sylvestris* 'Ravenswing', *Chaerophyllum hirsutum* 'Roseum', *Geranium sylvaticum* var. *wanneri*, *Helleborus* × *sternii*, *Hyacinthoides* 'Rose Queen'

H & S: 1.2m (4ft) ❄ **Mid-spring**
◊◊-◊◊◊ ▨-▪ ◼ Z6 pH4–6

Rhododendron luteum ♔

Perhaps the most common deciduous azalea species in cultivation, this is often known by its former name, *Azalea pontica*. Showy, intensely fragrant, easy to grow, and not too stiff in growth habit, it is eminently suitable for a wild or woodland garden. Its flowers are usually golden yellow, although there is some variation in both flower and autumn leaf color when raised from seed. This is an advantage if it is to be used extensively in a large area, the occasional individuals with paler yellow flowers helping to lighten the ensemble. *R. luteum* combines well with palest yellow, cream, peach, and apricot flowers, including other deciduous azaleas, and with yellow-green foliage and flowers, blue flowers, and yellow-variegated or glaucous foliage. For a more dramatic effect, it can be combined

Rhododendron luteum and bluebells (*Hyacinthoides non-scripta*) are effective partners; including another plant of intermediate height for spring and one or more for autumn would provide additional interest.

with orange or vermilion flowers and bronze foliage; yellow-green also works well with this color range. It benefits from neighbors with good autumn color but contrasting leaf shape, such as Japanese maples or some of the larger grasses. A fairly sunny situation is needed for maximum flowering and autumn color, but it will tolerate some shade.

◐ *Camassia quamash* 'Orion', *Euphorbia griffithii* 'Dixter', *Hosta* 'Sum and Substance', *Luzula sylvatica* 'Hohe Tatra', *Miscanthus sinensis* var. *purpurascens*, *Rhododendron* 'Klondyke', *Symphytum caucasicum*

H & S: 4m (13ft) ❋ **Late spring**
⬛▬▬ ◊◊-◊◊◊ ◼-◼ ◼ **Z5 pH4–6**

Rhododendron 'May Day' ♔

Tolerant of full sun, this spreading evergreen hybrid has deep scarlet flowers backed by petal-like calyces of the same shade. Its rich color suits it to displays of unashamed, even unnatural, sumptuousness – either with hot colors such as flame, orange, and bronze foliage and sharply contrasting yellow-green leaves and flowers, or in slightly less punchy combinations with warm coral, peach, and apricot. Such vibrant hues can look brash and over-sophisticated in a wild or woodland garden but are suitable in more cultivated arrangements, perhaps near the house. 'May Day' is best planted in loose groups, combined with less dense foliage such as that of ferns, sedges, Japanese maples, and grasses, including those with a bronze flush. Although its foliage is always respectable, the spring flowers are its chief glory, and it contributes little in other seasons. Regular spraying with fungicide may be necessary to protect it from rhododendron powdery mildew.

◐ *Acer palmatum* 'Corallinum', *Calluna vulgaris* 'Red Carpet', *Dryopteris erythrosora*, *Leucothoe* Scarletta, *Photinia* × *fraseri* 'Red Robin', *Rhododendron* 'Fabia'

H: 1.2m (4ft) S: 1.5m (5ft) ❋ **Mid- to late spring**
⬛▬▬ ◊◊-◊◊◊ ◼-◼ ◼ **Z7 pH4–6**

Bright new shoots of *Pieris formosa* var. *forrestii* 'Wakehurst' harmonize with *Rhododendron* 'May Day', while the feathery heads of *Fothergilla major* Monticola Group provide contrast.

Rhododendron orbiculare

This sun-tolerant evergreen species has neat, oval leaves and attractively flared pink flowers that merit close-range inspection. It is slow-growing, ultimately becoming a large shrub, with a dense growth habit and formal, domed shape that make it especially suitable for use as a specimen. If grown in this way, it benefits from sun and air on all sides to ensure even growth and a uniform covering of flowers. It can look charming surrounded by a carpet of lower plants such as winter heaths, spring bulbs, bergenias, and hellebores. Its flowers

The sugar-pink flowers of *Rhododendron orbiculare* form a close harmony with the deeper pink blooms produced by a shorter-growing hybrid of *R. williamsianum*.

harmonize well with those in carmine, cerise, crimson, or white, and with purple foliage, and are just sufficiently strongly colored to contrast with light apple-green.

◕ *Bergenia* 'Sunningdale', *Erica erigena* 'Irish Dusk', *Fritillaria verticillata*, *Helleborus* × *hybridus*, *H.* × *sternii*, *Narcissus* 'Thalia', *Pulmonaria* Opal

H & S: 3m (10ft) ✿ **Mid-spring**
◌◌-◌◌◌ ▪-▪ ▪ Z6 pH4–6

The glowing orange flowers of *Rhododendron* 'Spek's Brilliant' clash dazzlingly with the magenta-purple of the evergreen azalea *R.* 'Chanticleer' – an exhilarating effect, but one that is perhaps too stimulating for those areas of the garden intended for repose.

Rhododendron 'Spek's Brilliant' ♛

This vibrant orange deciduous azalea can bring richness to warm color schemes with apricot, peach, and soft yellow flowers, and bronze foliage. Pacified by such gentle colors, it is good in a woodland garden, where some shade will moderate its flowering and help to prevent it from being overbearing. It can also be used for hot color schemes with vermilion, scarlet, and gold flowers and bronze foliage, with yellow-green leaves and flowers and gold-variegated leaves added for contrast. Its orange flowers can also make an explosive combination with magenta blooms – even more daring is the mixture of orange, magenta, and yellow-green. Such fiery associations require profuse flowering to look their best, and therefore demand more light than for subdued woodland displays – fortunately, this cultivar tolerates full sun.

◕ *Acer palmatum* 'Sango-kaku', *Fritillaria imperialis* 'The Premier', *Geum* 'Werner Arends', *Trollius* × *cultorum* 'Orange Princess', *Tulipa* 'Apricot Beauty'

H & S: 2.5m (8ft) ✿ **Late spring**
◌◌-◌◌◌ ▪-▪ ▪ Z7 pH4–6

Rhododendron pseudochrysanthum ♛

Trusses of pale rose-pink or white flowers, lined deep pink on the outside and spotted dark pink within, adorn this sun-tolerant evergreen species. Its chief glory, however, is its handsome foliage, covered with buff down when young, and later becoming deep green. It ultimately forms a medium-sized, dense, dome-shaped bush, which is good as a specimen if surrounded by lower plants. Pink-flowered selections harmonize with rose-pink, white, salmon, or red flowers, although it is easier to find companion plants to blend with the white-flowered clone. This allows harmonies with apricot, peach, and pale yellow flowers, and with bronze foliage.

◕ *Acer palmatum* f. *atropurpureum*, *Carex brunnea*, *Dryopteris wallichiana*, *Epimedium* × *warleyense*, *Geum* 'Beech House Apricot', *Narcissus* 'Geranium'

H & S: 3m (10ft) ✿ **Mid-spring**
◌◌-◌◌◌ ▪-▪ ▪ Z7 pH4–6

The glossy, bright green young leaves of a Japanese shield fern (*Dryopteris erythrosora*) provide an ideal contrast of form and color for *Rhododendron pseudochrysanthum*.

Rhus × *pulvinata* Autumn Lace Group

The sumacs are most striking in autumn, when their attractively feathered, deciduous leaves assume glorious seasonal tints of rich yellow, orange, and red. They are extremely handsome for the rest of the year, the large shrubs or small trees branching freely to produce a widely spaced canopy of decorative foliage that provides an exotic sense of luxuriance from spring until the tints appear with the first frosts. For a really fiery effect, they can be combined with plants that turn different but complementary colors; for example, 'Red Autumn Lace' ♀ with an orange or yellow maple. For maximum color, they should be grown at the back of a border, where they may be left to sucker freely. Plants sometimes appear under other guises; for example, 'Red Autumn Lace' may be sold as *Rhus glabra* 'Laciniata', which is a much rarer but equally choice cultivar.

These plants are related to poison ivy and their sap may cause skin irritation.

Acer palmatum 'Sango-kaku', *Cortaderia selloana* 'Sunningdale Silver', *Helianthus* 'Monarch', *Rudbeckia fulgida* var. *sullivantii* 'Goldsturm'

H: 3m (10ft) S: 5m (16ft) Mid-summer
Z3 pH5–7.5

The distinctive foliage of *Rhus* × *pulvinata* Autumn Lace Group provides a backdrop for *Geranium* 'Ann Folkard', *Salvia officinalis* 'Purpurascens', and *Artemisia abrotanum*.

Ribes sanguineum
FLOWERING CURRANT

A popular choice for spring color, this easy, fast-growing deciduous shrub has slightly drooping racemes of flowers, in shades from white to pink and red, which appear with the first tiny leaves. From late spring onward, it is relatively undistinguished; however, it will blend satisfactorily into a general planting arrangement for the rest of the season, and it may be used to support a honeysuckle or summer-flowering clematis. The species itself can be indifferent, and the best display will be given by a superior cultivar such as – 'Pulborough Scarlet' ♀ or 'King Edward VII', planted in full sun with other spring-flowering shrubs and bulbs.

Forsythia × *intermedia* 'Lynwood', *Helleborus foetidus*, *Muscari latifolium*, *Narcissus* 'Ice Follies', *Spiraea* 'Arguta', *Tulipa* 'Golden Oxford'

H & S: 2m (6½ft) Mid- to late spring
Z6 pH5–7.5

Ribes sanguineum 'Brocklebankii' ♀

One of the best flowering currants for a long season of color, this compact, relatively slow-growing, deciduous shrub bears attractive bright yellow-green foliage that is particularly striking in late spring and summer. The contrast with its pink flowers does not suit everyone's tastes, but growing the shrub in shade will partially suppress flowering and emphasize the yellow foliage, which can scorch in bright sun. Useful for brightening up dark areas, dull corners, and dappled shade, it works well with plants that have purple foliage or purple, blue, yellow, or white flowers such as anchusas, bugleweeds, or ceanothus. It is smaller than other flowering currants, but it develops a similar shape and requires occasional hard pruning, removing the oldest wood to maintain a high proportion of vigorous young stems.

Anchusa azurea 'Loddon Royalist', *Berberis thunbergii* 'Rose Glow', *Camassia leichtlinii* 'Semiplena', *Ceanothus* 'Cascade', *Cotinus coggygria* 'Royal Purple', *Narcissus* 'Irene Copeland', *Tulipa* 'Burgundy'

H & S: 1.2m (4ft) Mid- to late spring
Z6 pH5–7.5

A mature flowering currant (*Ribes sanguineum*) is large enough to support an Alpina clematis such as *C.* 'White Swan', creating a charming contrast of floral form. Mid- to deep pink cultivars of the currant, or white with a blue or ruby clematis, are perhaps more effective than paler pink ones, emphasizing the different flower shapes.

The gold leaves of the flowering currant *Ribes sanguineum* 'Brocklebankii' contrast with the lavender-blue flowers and purple calyces of *Ajuga* 'Tottenham'. Using a darker-leaved bugleweed such as *A. reptans* 'Atropurpurea' would give a more striking foliage contrast after flowering has finished.

Robinia pseudoacacia 'Frisia' ♔

There are several attractive forms of the black locust (*Robinia pseudoacacia*), a large, rugged tree that suckers freely. Probably the most valuable of these for general garden use is 'Frisia', a much smaller and more versatile deciduous tree with rich yellow-green foliage turning golden yellow in autumn. It has an informal, irregularly branching shape and makes a bold impact wherever it is grown, fully deserving its status as one of the most popular gold-leaved garden trees.

This dominating tree needs plenty of space to show itself to best effect, and is often planted as a bold punctuation mark in a large border, standing slightly in front of other plants of similar height. Contrasting shrubs with green or purple foliage may be planted beneath, or a summer-flowering rose can be grown through the branches. White, cream, or apple-green flowers, together with a late-flowering white clematis or a cream or white Rambler rose, would make perfect partners. Young plants should be staked and the brittle stems sheltered from strong winds, and suckers should be removed as they appear.

In restricted spaces, the feathery *Gleditsia triacanthos* or honey locust will provide a similar effect, especially the golden-leaved 'Sunburst' ♔, which withstands hard pruning.

⬤ *Allium hollandicum* p.301 **A**, *Anchusa azurea* 'Loddon Royalist', *Geranium* 'Johnson's Blue', *Rosa* 'Sander's White Rambler', *Sedum telephium* p.286 **A**

H: 15m (50ft)   S: 8m (26ft)
❀ **Early to mid-summer**
◌ ⬜ **Z3   pH5.5–7.5**

Robinia pseudoacacia 'Frisia' can be used to support a contrasting clematis, in this case *C.* 'Etoile Violette', one of the earlier-flowering Viticella Group cultivars.

A

Rosmarinus officinalis
ROSEMARY

This is an aromatic evergreen shrub that flowers from mid-spring to early summer, continuing in some varieties until late autumn. While most have blue flowers, several types are mauve-pink, but these are generally not as effective as the blues. Rosemary is slightly tender, and proves hardiest in sunny positions in relatively poor, well drained soil. Here, whether in a border or in a pot, it can be combined with other Mediterranean shrubs including lavenders, cistus, and phlomis, and makes a wonderful addition to a sunny sitting area, where its fragrance can be fully appreciated.

One of the best rich blue types is 'Miss Jessopp's Upright' ♀, a relatively hardy, columnar shrub that can grow exceptionally tall if sheltered on a warm wall. Its brittle main branches tend to twist and bend under the weight of foliage, so that it ages to a broad bush; occasional pruning immediately after flowering helps maintain a balanced shape. The rather more tender *R.o.* var. *angustissimus* 'Benenden Blue' is also rich blue, and similar in habit, with narrow leaves. The upright 'Sissinghurst Blue' ♀ is fairly hardy, whereas the long-flowering 'Severn Sea' ♀ can be rather tender. Prostratus Group ♀ is tender but useful for sprawling on a sunny bank or tumbling over a low wall. The gold-variegated rosemary, 'Aureus', is an ancient pale blue-flowered garden variety whose intricately yellow-banded foliage suits combinations with other gold-leaved plants, while Silver Spires ('Wolros') recreates the silver-variegated "striped rosemary" popular in the seventeenth century.

With its long tradition of cultivation, rosemary is an especially appropriate plant for old-fashioned gardens, and hardier kinds can be used for short hedges or knots if clipped once a year after flowering. All blue cultivars make good harmonies with blues, mauves, and pinks, and contrast with soft yellow or yellow-green. Sages, teucriums, catmints, and Bearded irises are excellent partners.

◑ **Prostrate:** *Cytisus* × *kewensis*, *Helianthemum lunulatum*, *Iris* 'Curlew', *Nepeta* × *faassenii*
Upright: *Genista hispanica*, × *Halimiocistus wintonensis* 'Merrist Wood Cream', *Lavandula stoechas* subsp. *pedunculata* 'James Compton', *Santolina chamaecyparissus* p.92 **A**, *Stipa tenuissima* p.289 **B**

H: 15cm–2m (6in–6½ft) **S: 1.2–1.8m** (4–6ft)
❀ **Mid-spring to early summer**
 ◊◊ ▢-▪ **Z8 pH5.5–7.5**

Top: Sprawling rosemaries – here *Rosmarinus officinalis* 'McConnell's Blue' with the perennial candytuft *Iberis sempervirens* 'Schneeflocke' – tend to be less hardy than more upright types but are immensely useful plants for clothing a bank or tumbling over a low wall. They can also be attractive grown in a large pot or container.

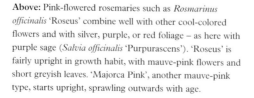

Above: Pink-flowered rosemaries such as *Rosmarinus officinalis* 'Roseus' combine well with other cool-colored flowers and with silver, purple, or red foliage – as here with purple sage (*Salvia officinalis* 'Purpurascens'). 'Roseus' is fairly upright in growth habit, with mauve-pink flowers and short greyish leaves. 'Majorca Pink', another mauve-pink type, starts upright, sprawling outwards with age.

Above: Blue-flowered rosemaries combine especially well with silver or glaucous leaves and with white or cream flowers, and can contrast with yellow-green, for instance euphorbias – as in this combination of *Rosmarinus officinalis* 'Sissinghurst Blue' with purple wood spurge (*Euphorbia amygdaloides* 'Purpurea'). Only the most floriferous or richest blue types contrast well with yellow.

Rubus cockburnianus 'Goldenvale' is combined here with lady's mantle (*Alchemilla mollis*) – the leaves of the two plants contrast markedly in shape, while the flowers of the alchemilla harmonize with the rubus foliage. Both are deciduous, allowing room for early bulbs to be planted beneath.

Rubus cockburnianus 'Goldenvale'

The yellow-green fern-like foliage of this deciduous shrub (syn. 'Wyego') is brightest in a sunny site, but even in shade it provides useful lighter tones. Its arching white stems make a dramatic winter tracery, particularly if set against a dark evergreen background. Its impact is greatest in borders if the bare stems are not hemmed in by other shrubs, but it can be planted with an evergreen ground cover or with spring bulbs such as snowdrops beneath. In winter it is particularly effective with winter heaths, prostrate dwarf conifers, and *Cyclamen coum*, and makes a stark contrast with red or orange dogwoods. From late spring it combines well with blue-flowered plants like aconitums, and with glaucous foliage such as that of hostas. Stems lose their white bloom during their second season and should then be pruned out.

◉ *Ajuga reptans* 'Catlin's Giant', *Bergenia cordifolia* 'Purpurea', *Elaeagnus* × *ebbingei* 'Gilt Edge' p.46 **A**, *Erica carnea* 'Vivellii', *Galanthus nivalis*, *Gentiana asclepiadea* p.223 **C**, *Hosta sieboldiana* var. *elegans*, *Muscari latifolium*, *Ranunculus ficaria* 'Brazen Hussy', *Viburnum tinus* 'Eve Price'

H: 1.8m (6ft) **S: 1.2m** (4ft) ❋ **Mid-summer**
◊-◊◊◊ ▢-▮ **Z6 pH5–7.5**

Rubus thibetanus ♛

An erect deciduous shrub with white winter stems and greyish pinnate leaves, this bramble is used and pruned for winter color in the same way as *R. cockburnianus* 'Goldenvale' (above), removing second-year stems to leave only the newest, brightest shoots. The effect of its foliage, through late spring and summer into the autumn, is less obviously showy, and plants are better suited to more subdued displays and styles of planting, especially in wilder and more natural parts of the garden. It succeeds in the same winter combinations as 'Goldenvale', but for summer use it is best associated with white, pale or rich blue flowers and dark green foliage. From a distance its foliage is somewhat amorphous, but closeup is quietly pretty, especially if draped with an annual or perennial white-flowered climber, such as a sweet pea.

◉ *Clematis heracleifolia*, *Cornus alba* 'Sibirica', *C. sanguinea* 'Midwinter Fire', *Crocus tommasinianus*, *Eranthis hyemalis*, *Helleborus atrorubens*, *Juniperus horizontalis* 'Bar Harbor', *Lathyrus latifolius* 'White Pearl', *Lobelia siphilitica*, *Narcissus* 'Actaea'

H & S: 2.5m (8ft) ❋ **Mid- to late summer**
◊-◊◊◊ ▢-▮ **Z6 pH5–7.5**

Striking white stems of *Rubus thibetanus* harmonize with the pale-spotted leaves and white flowers of *Pulmonaria* 'Sissinghurst White'. The combination depends on the stems of the rubus not being pruned away until they start to be hidden by its leaves (usually in mid- to late spring). Later-flowering bulbs can be planted through the pulmonaria to add height while the rubus is laid low.

The yellow-green flowers of *Ruta graveolens* 'Jackman's Blue' perfectly match the foliage of *Choisya ternata* Sundance, while the rue's foliage provides a gentle and pleasant contrast. To produce so much bloom, the rue should receive only the minimum of pruning. Larger cream flowers would be effective for lightening the display, while strong blue could be used for contrast.

Ruta graveolens 'Jackman's Blue' ♛

This is a superlative, compact evergreen sub-shrub that enjoys a sunny position on well-drained soil. It may be sited towards the front of a border or in a gravel garden, and mixes well with Mediterranean plants such as sages, halimiums, and white-flowered cistus. Its intensely blue-green foliage makes a good contrast with its yellow-green flowers, which help it to relate to other plants with yellow-green foliage or flowers, such as alchemillas and golden marjorams, and to those in white, yellow, or blue. Annual pruning in mid-spring can maintain shapeliness and qualify plants for use as a semi-formal edging, although the flowers may be sacrificed; alternatively, selective pruning after flowering can prevent plants from sprawling and developing gaps. 'Variegata', with foliage heavily splashed with white, has a more open growth habit, better suited to single planting than as hedging.

◉ *Ajuga reptans* 'Atropurpurea', *Cistus* × *cyprius*, *Euphorbia myrsinites*, *Halimium ocymoides*, *Iris* 'Joyce' p.321 **C**, *Nepeta* 'Six Hills Giant', *Rosmarinus officinalis* Prostratus Group, *Salvia officinalis* 'Icterina', *Symphytum* × *uplandicum* 'Variegatum'

H & S: 60cm (24in) ❋ **Mid-summer**
◊-◊◊◊ ▢-▮ **Z5 pH5–7.5**

Salix alba var. *vitellina* ♔
GOLDEN WILLOW

Boggy situations and moist soils suit this medium to large deciduous tree, noted for its feathery, fairly pale green foliage and orange-yellow stems that look striking when they catch the winter sun. It can be grown to full size in a wild garden, but is usually regularly pruned to encourage the production of bright new shoots. As a waterside or winter garden plant, it mixes well with dogwoods and other bright-stemmed deciduous shrubs to make a harmonious display of warm colors, and may be planted with ground-cover plants such as ivies. Good companions include evergreen *Euonymus fortunei* cultivars, bergenias, winter heaths, heucheras, forsythias, and early-flowering bulbs such as narcissi, scillas, snowdrops, and winter aconites. 'Britzensis' ♔ is a rich red clone, often sold as 'Chermesina' (a different plant with bright red winter stems).

⊙ *Bergenia cordifolia* 'Purpurea', *Cornus stolonifera* 'Flaviramea', *Erica carnea* 'Springwood White', *Hedera colchica* 'Dentata Variegata', *Narcissus* 'February Silver', *Viburnum tinus* 'Eve Price'

H & S: 25m (80ft) ❀ **(Mid-spring)**

Z2 pH5.5–7.5

Pruned plants of *Salix alba* var. *vitellina* 'Britzensis' glow in the low light of the winter sun, their rich red stems, golden yellow at the base, showing up effectively against the shady side of a cypress. Winter-flowering heaths make an ideal carpet: here *Erica* × *darleyensis* 'Darley Dale' is used; a white cultivar would be an attractive alternative.

A Spanish clone of the Rubens willow *Salix* × *rubens*, pruned to produce bright winter stems, is here planted with the lungwort *Pulmonaria angustifolia* subsp. *azurea* and crocuses beneath. Relatively late pruning makes the most of the combination with the lungwort.

Salix × *rubens*
HYBRID CRACK WILLOW

This cross between the white willow (*Salix alba*) and the crack willow (*S. fragilis*) occurs naturally wherever the two parents are found together. The best selections belong to *S.* × *r.* 'Basfordiana' ♔, which has more brightly colored winter twigs, most commonly a glowing yellowish orange; nurseries often offer a female clone with showy, bright red catkins in early spring. The rather slower-growing var. *rubens* has reddish winter twigs.

All variants of *S.* × *rubens* are suited to the same combinations as *S. alba* var. *vitellina* (above), including evergreen ground-cover plants and early-flowering spring bulbs. They are easily propagated from hardwood cuttings taken in autumn and inserted quite deep in a mixture of sand and peat, or soil mix.

⊙ *Chionodoxa forbesii*, *Erica* × *darleyensis* 'Silberschmelze', *Galanthus elwesii* var. *monostictus*, *Helleborus foetidus* Wester Flisk Group, *Rubus thibetanus*

H & S: 25m (80ft) ❀ **(Mid-spring)**

Z5 pH5.5–7.5

Salvia officinalis 'Purpurascens' ♔
PURPLE SAGE

The common sage (*Salvia officinalis*) is a more or less evergreen sub-shrub for well-drained sunny spots at the front of a border and in gravel or herb gardens, where it forms attractive greyish green mounds that associate well with other Mediterranean plants such as lavenders, cotton lavender, cistus, phlomis, and rosemaries. Purple sage is a spreading selection, its leaves lightly flushed with purple and combining happily with other purple-leaved plants, as well as with silver foliage and cool-colored flowers. Its lavender-blue florets, enhanced by reddish purple calyces, look particularly showy with harmonious cool colors, or with a contrasting color such as the pale sulfur-yellow of achilleas or the acid yellow-green of euphorbias. It is also handsome with glaucous fescues, silver artemisias, or sprawling cranesbills.

⊙ *Buddleja alternifolia* p.33 **B**, *Geranium riversleaianum* cultivars, *Hebe ochracea* p.56 **A**, *Limnanthes douglasii* p.384 **C**, *Rhus* × *pulvinata* Autumn Lace Group p.86 **A**, *Rosmarinus officinalis* 'Roseus' p.88 **B**

H: 80cm (31in) S: 1m (40in)
❀ **Early to mid-summer**

Z6 pH5.5–7

Purple sage (*Salvia officinalis* 'Purpurascens') makes an attractive contrast with variegated periwinkle (*Vinca major* 'Variegata'). Planted close to the sage, the periwinkle's slender stems push through its neighbor, the creamy margins on the leaves emphasizing their simple shape.

Sambucus nigra

EUROPEAN ELDERBERRY

This large deciduous shrub with pinnate leaves bears creamy white flowers in broad, flat heads, followed by nodding bunches of purple-black fruits. Although suitable for a wild garden, where its fruits benefit birds and other wildlife, it is a little coarse for general garden use, except as part of an informal hedge, perhaps mixed with other wildlife hedging species, such as beech, blackthorn, or wild roses, and embellished with climbing plants such as honeysuckles. A number of attractive and more refined cultivars have been developed, most notably 'Guincho Purple' 🏆, which has purple-flushed leaves, darker when grown in sun, and pink flowers. A newer cultivar, also purple-leaved but with deeper foliage and richer pink flowers, is Black Beauty ('Gerda'), a spreading bush that is useful where more somber foliage or brighter pink flowers are needed. Both can be planted in a mixed border or in a woodland garden (although the less dramatic color of 'Guincho Purple' might best suit wild settings), and as regularly pruned shrubs in larger herb gardens, where the simple species was traditionally grown for its many culinary and medicinal uses. Both dark-leaved cultivars combine well with Japanese maples, species roses, foxgloves, and other dark-leaved shrubs like purple berberis or sloe, and can be used to contrast with silver or yellow-green foliage, or to harmonize with flowers in white or pink; the slightly peachy tint in 'Guincho Purple' makes it less satisfactory when used with cool colors such as mauve, purple, or blue. For the most spectacular display of foliage, they are best pruned annually to a framework of branches, or pruned lower if required. This technique does, however, sacrifice the flowers; if both flowers and bold, well-colored foliage are required, stems can be removed on a two- or three-year cycle – the flowers are born on two-year-old stems.

Other pleasant cultivars include 'Aurea' 🏆, with yellowish green leaves (brightest in sun) that look attractive with blue flowers such as delphiniums, and also with hot colors or contrasted with purple foliage. *S.n.* f. *laciniata* 🏆 has narrow leaflets, darker than those of the typical species and very deeply divided if grown in shade, although plants flower more profusely in sun. While variants with purple-flushed or yellow-green leaves generally color better in sun, one of the most valuable features of European elderberry is its tolerance of dry shade, where some of the variegated cultivars excel: 'Marginata', with white-edged leaves, is outstanding, while white-speckled 'Pulverulenta' works well in shade where a lighter tone of green is needed.

Acer shirasawanum 'Aureum' *Ammi majus*, *Berberis × ottawensis* f. *purpurea* 'Superba', *Lonicera nitida* 'Baggesen's Gold', *Prunus spinosa* 'Purpurea'

H & S: 6m (20ft) **Early summer**

Z5 pH4.5–7.5

A

Right: The cut-leaved elderberry (*Sambucus nigra* f. *laciniata*) has leaflets larger than but otherwise similar to those of this Japanese maple (*Acer palmatum* Dissectum Viride Group), harmonizing but with the bonus of plentiful, flat, creamy white flower heads born on a taller bush.

B

Below: Horizontal flower heads of *Sambucus nigra* 'Guincho Purple' match the color of upright foxgloves *Digitalis purpurea* 'Sutton's Apricot', lightened by white *D.p.* f. *albiflora*. The elderberry's dark foliage adds rich depth.

Santolina chamaecyparissus 🏆
LAVENDER COTTON

An evergreen sub-shrub with intensely silvery foliage, this is a Mediterranean plant that revels in poor and well drained soils, whether at the front of a border or gravel garden, clipped in pots, or massed as a filler for parterres. As a foliage plant it blends well with cool colors such as mauves, blues, and pinks, and mixes with other silver-leaved or glaucous foliage plants and those with contrasting leaf form such as fescues or phlomis. It is a natural companion for other Mediterranean plants like lavenders, catmints, cistus, and helianthemums, and also looks agreeable in front of old-fashioned roses, perhaps partnered by pinks, particularly white-flowered cultivars, or euphorbias. If allowed to flower, its blooms can limit successful combinations, but it remains effective with blue flowers and glaucous leaves such as those of *Cerinthe* species. *S.c.* 'Lemon Queen' is a cultivar with paler flowers, while 'Lambrook Silver' has particularly silver foliage; var. *nana* 🏆 is a compact variety suitable for smaller gardens.

🌑 *Cerinthe major* 'Purpurascens', *Cistus* 'Silver Pink', *Dianthus* 'Haytor White', *Euphorbia myrsinites*, *Festuca glauca* 'Blaufuchs', *Helianthemum* 'Rhodanthe Carneum', *Nepeta* × *faassenii*, *Phlomis fruticosa*

H: 50cm (20in) S: 90cm (36in) ❀ **Mid-summer**
▦ 💧-💧💧 ▦-▦ **Z7 pH6–7.5**

In this Mediterranean planting, santolinas occupy the foreground, contrasting silver *S. chamaecyparissus* with deep green *S. rosmarinifolia*. A pale lavender and an upright rosemary fill the border against the wall. The attractive billowing masses of santolina will need occasional pruning to prevent them from becoming gappy.

The neat foliage and pretty flower heads of *Skimmia japonica* 'Rubella', effective at the front of a border, especially when viewed at close range, are here augmented by the marbled foliage of *Arum italicum* 'Marmoratum'.

Sorbus 'Joseph Rock' 🏆

An attractive small deciduous tree at any season, this sorbus stars in autumn when its bunches of small spherical fruits mature from green through white to soft amber-yellow, against a canopy of brilliant crimson, purple, and scarlet foliage. It succeeds in a large mixed border or a shrubbery, and as a specimen tree to interact with other plants with bright autumn fruits or foliage. Good companion trees include linderas, maples, amelanchiers, deciduous hollies, cladrastis, liquidambars, some crab apples, hawthorns, and other sorbus, particularly those with soft-colored fruits such as some of the Lombarts Hybrids. Among the most suitable shrubs are deciduous berberis and euonymus, witch hazels, sumacs, deciduous azaleas and vacciniums, roses, and stephanandras. Larger specimens can be lightly swagged with a vine or parthenocissus species.

🌑 *Amelanchier lamarckii*, *Cladrastis kentukea*, *Euonymus alatus* var. *apterus*, *Hamamelis* × *intermedia* 'Arnold Promise', *Lindera benzoin*, *Rhododendron luteum*

H: 10m (33ft) S: 7m (23ft) ❀ **Late spring**
▦ 💧💧 ▦-▦ **Z4 pH5–7.5**

Skimmia japonica 'Rubella' 🏆

This neat, non-fruit-bearing skimmia has rounded heads of rich red buds that color in early winter and remain attractive until spring, when they open to white-petaled flowers born above reddish stalks, giving an overall pinkish effect. A useful pollinator for fruit-bearing cultivars of skimmia, it is suitable for loose groups in mixed or shrub borders in partial or full shade. It is also fine for large containers, combined with other evergreens such as ivies and (in milder areas) winter cherries, cinerarias, smaller *Cyclamen persicum* cultivars, and variegated hebes. Good companions include other winter- or spring-flowering plants like viburnums, snowdrops, cyclamens, abeliophyllums, evergreens such as bergenias, heucheras, asarums, hollies, and *Euonymus fortunei* and *E. japonicus* cultivars, and contrasting foliage such as that of bamboos and evergreen grasses and sedges.

🌑 *Bergenia cordifolia* 'Purpurea', *Cyclamen coum*, *Erysimum* 'Bowles' Mauve' p.48 **A**, *Hebe* × *franciscana* 'Variegata', *Hedera canariensis* 'Gloire de Marengo'

H & S: 1.2m (4ft) ❀ **Mid- to late spring**
▦ 💧💧 ▦-▦ **Z7 pH5–7**

The rich autumn coloring of *Sorbus* 'Joseph Rock' lends itself to combinations with other large shrubs and small trees with contrasting leaf form, especially if these have foliage color matching the fruits of the sorbus.

The greyish leaves and pink fruits of *Sorbus vilmorinii* make it especially suitable for combinations with other large shrubs or small trees that have crimson autumn color and/or white or crimson fruits.

Sorbus vilmorinii ♚

This deciduous sorbus is a large shrub or small tree with leaves composed of pretty, tiny leaflets that assume autumn tints of orange, scarlet, crimson, and deep purple; its deep pink fruits mature to almost pure white, with occasional crimson flecks. It suits a mixed border, shrubbery, or woodland garden, and looks outstanding above lower-growing plants. It can be used with the same sort of combinations as *S.* 'Joseph Rock' (facing page), and may also be surrounded by shorter evergreens such as small hollies, junipers, and fruit-bearing skimmias and berberis, or planted in grass with white autumn crocuses and colchicums. In a mixed border it works well with larger, looser autumn daisies such as helianthus, larger Korean and Rubellum chrysanthemums, and *Leucanthemella serotina*, and with grasses such as miscanthus.

◉ *Berberis* × *carminea* 'Pirate King', *Colchicum speciosum* 'Album', *Helianthus* 'Monarch', *Ilex aquifolium* 'J.C. van Tol', *Juniperus squamata* 'Meyeri'

H & S: 5m (16ft) ✿ **Late spring to early summer**
◊◊ ☐-■ Z6 pH5–7.5

Spartium junceum ♚
SPANISH BROOM

Long flowering and tolerance of poor, dry soils distinguish this shrub, which has erect, cylindrical green stems and vestigial leaves. It bears its golden yellow flowers most profusely in early to mid-summer, when it combines successfully with other Mediterranean shrubs such as white cistus, coluteas, brooms, halimiocistus, halimiums, phlomis, genistas, and olearias. It works well with yellow-green foliage and flowers, and with blue flowers or glaucous foliage. Its slim stems harmonize with those of larger early-flowering grasses (stipas, for example), and also look good in seaside settings with New Zealand plants such as ozothamnus, or with large whipcord hebes. Other effective companions include laburnums, *Buddleja* × *weyeriana* cultivars, and yellow, peach, or apricot roses.

◉ *Cistus* × *cyprius*, *Colutea arborescens*, *Cytisus multiflorus*, *Genista hispanica*, × *Halimiocistus wintonensis* 'Merrist Wood Cream', *Hebe cupressoides*, *Olearia* × *haastii*, *Ozothamnus ledifolius*

H & S: 3m (10ft) ✿ **Early summer to early autumn**
◊-◊◊ ☐-■ Z6 pH5.5–7.5

In this relatively narrow border planned to provide color throughout summer and autumn, Spanish broom (*Spartium junceum*) is one of the longest-flowering and most reliable performers. It is topped by toetoe grass (*Cortaderia richardii*), and accompanied by yellow *Calceolaria angustifolia* and paler yellow *Achillea* 'Moonshine', together with the dark-leaved orange *Dahlia* 'David Howard'.

Spiraea japonica

With hard pruning in early spring, this deciduous spiraea blooms freely through the summer. Cultivars vary in flower color from white or pink to crimson, and a few have foliage emerging golden yellow flushed with orange and red. All are good near the front of a mixed or shrub border. Those with green leaves and pink flowers ('Bumalda' or dwarf 'Nana' ♚, for example) are effective with cool flowers and purple, glaucous, silver, or white-variegated foliage. Carmine or crimson cultivars such as 'Dart's Red', 'Anthony Waterer' ♚, and 'Walluf' contrast with sulfur-yellow or with yellow-green foliage and flowers. Golden-leaved 'Goldflame' ♚ and 'Gold Mound' ♚ are valuable for spring display in bright borders, together with bulbs such as tulips, narcissi, and crown imperials.

A bright-leaved cultivar of *Spiraea japonica*, its form contrasting with a neat globe of *Lonicera nitida* 'Baggesen's Gold', makes an attractive combination with the lilac pompons of *Allium cristophii*, lavender cranesbills (*Geranium* 'Johnson's Blue' and *G.* × *magnificum*) and a short blue *Anchusa azurea* cultivar. The white in the leaves of *Astrantia major* 'Sunningdale Variegated' lightens the planting.

◉ **Green-leaved:** *Berberis thunbergii* f. *atropurpurea*, *Caryopteris* × *clandonensis*, *Ceratostigma plumbaginoides*, *Coronilla valentina* subsp. *glauca* 'Variegata'
Golden-leaved: *Dicentra eximia* p.211 **B**, *Polemonium caeruleum* p.275 **B**, *Tulipa* 'Jewel of Spring' p.349 **A**

H: 30–150cm (12–60in) S: 50–150cm (20–60in)
✿ **Mid- to late summer**
◊◊ ☐-■ Z4 pH5.5–7.5

Spiraea nipponica 'Snowmound' ♈

Sometimes wrongly called *S. nipponica* var. *tosaensis*, this vigorous deciduous shrub makes a mound-like bush with arching branches, extremely pretty in early summer when smothered with white flowers. It mixes well with other early summer flowering shrubs, including Shrub roses, weigelas, hebes, and *Potentilla fruticosa* cultivars, and can be draped with annual or herbaceous climbers, such as sweet peas, to continue the display after the spiraea flowers have finished. Although perhaps a little stark to contrast with hot shades, its color will combine successfully with most others, especially blue flowers and silver or glaucous foliage. Good herbaceous companions include cranesbills, campanulas, later-flowering Tall Bearded irises, achilleas, paler day lilies, and most summer-flowering bulbs, particularly lilies. 'Halward's Silver' is more compact and erect, about 1m (3¼ft) high and wide.

⬤ *Berberis thunbergii* 'Aurea', *Geranium* × *riversleaianum* 'Mavis Simpson', *Iris* 'Cambridge', *Lathyrus latifolius* 'Rosa Perle', *Lilium pyrenaicum* var. *pyrenaicum*, *Potentilla fruticosa* 'Beesii'

H & S: 1.2m (4ft) ✽ **Early summer**
◦◦ ▢-▨ **Z5 pH5.5–7.5**

Grown in a narrow border and crowded with bloom from top to toe, the arching stems of *Spiraea nipponica* 'Snowmound' contrast with billowing masses of *Ceanothus* 'Puget Blue'. The yellow-green foliage beyond contrasts equally effectively with the ceanothus. Given a wider border, adding a shorter, yellow-flowered shrub or another with yellow-green leaves would unify the arrangement.

The informal growth habit of a *Syringa vulgaris* cultivar, massed with conical panicles of bloom, contrasts with neat columns of dark Irish yew (*Taxus baccata* 'Fastigiata'), which effectively counteract the lilac's amorphousness.

Syringa vulgaris
COMMON LILAC

Cultivars of this large deciduous shrub are essential plants for late spring display in a shrub or mixed border, their panicles of fragrant flowers in white, creamy yellow, pink, lavender-blue, or plum-purple combining well with ceanothus and the more sun-tolerant rhododendrons. Larger specimens can be lightly draped with white or pink *Clematis montana* cultivars. White or pale yellow lilacs contrast with colors closest to blue, and combine well with Lady Banks roses, laburnums, brooms, genistas, and berberis, yellow-green foliage and flowers, purple foliage, and white flowers such as exochordas and spiraeas. They also associate well with small flowering trees such as crab apples, Japanese cherries, and magnolias, osmanthus, amelanchiers, daphnes, dipeltas, early species roses, cercis, and hawthorns. Gently colored cultivars look charming in semi-natural settings, planted with cow parsley, bluebells, and pheasant's-eye narcissi beneath.

⬤ *Anthriscus sylvestris*, *Ceanothus* 'Cascade', *Clematis montana* var. *rubens* p.114 **C**, *Exochorda* × *macrantha* 'The Bride', *Hyacinthoides non-scripta*, *Laburnum* × *watereri* 'Vossii', *Rosa banksiae* 'Lutea'

H: 2–7m (6½–23ft) S: 1.5–5m (5–16ft)
✽ **Late spring to early summer**
◦◦ ▢-▨ **Z4 pH5–8**

Syringa vulgaris 'Charles Joly' ♀

With double, rich plum-purple flowers, this large deciduous shrub suits sumptuous late spring color schemes. It blends well with purple foliage, such as that of cherry plums or berberis, although dark colors may not show up well from a distance unless lifted by pink or mauve flowers, such as *Clematis montana* var. *rubens* cultivars. Good partners are euphorbias, shrubs with yellow-green leaves such as elderberry or philadelphus, and later-flowering, paler lilacs. It contrasts well with soft yellow – *Rosa xanthina* variants, for example – and with yellow-green foliage and flowers, and may be planted with late-flowering tulips in red, purple, or lilac, pink alliums, and early cranesbills beneath.

◗ *Euphorbia characias* subsp. *wulfenii* 'Lambrook Gold', *Physocarpus opulifolius* 'Dart's Gold', *Prunus cerasifera* 'Pissardii', *Rosa* × *fortuneana* p.141 **C**

H: 3m (10ft) **S: 2m** (6½ft)
❀ **Late spring to early summer**
◌◌ ▢-▨ ■ **Z4 pH5–8**

Rich, reddish purple *Syringa vulgaris* 'Charles Joly' is here woven through with Chinese wisteria (*W. sinensis*). It is hard to prune the wisteria in such situations, so it needs warm or hot summers if it is to flower reliably.

Tamarix tetrandra ♀

Like other tamarisks, this arching deciduous shrub is suited to well-drained soils, maritime sites, and gravel gardens. Although slightly ungainly, at flowering time the whole plant is wreathed in blooms. These open rose-pink and age to a reddish color, blending agreeably with plum-purple and partnering other rose-pink or red flowers such as pink alliums, astrantias, *Smyrnium perfoliatum*, late tulips, and pheasant's-eye narcissi. It is very effective with white flowers and purple or copper foliage, such as that of berberis.

A cloud of sugar-pink *Tamarix tetrandra* is here backed by the short-panicled *Laburnum alpinum*. Pink and yellow can be difficult to combine successfully, but the softness of the tamarisk's color makes this combination a happy one. A laburnum with longer panicles, such as *L. anagyroides* or *L.* × *watereri* 'Vossii', could be used for a more flamboyant effect. The spreading growth habit of both plants requires some planting beneath to complete and unify the scheme.

◗ *Anthriscus sylvestris* 'Ravenswing', *Chaerophyllum hirsutum* 'Roseum', *Cistus* × *hybridus*, *Cytisus* × *praecox* 'Allgold', *Hippophae rhamnoides*, *Narcissus poeticus* var. *recurvus*, *Tulipa* 'Queen of Night'

H & S: 3m (10ft) ❀ **Late spring**
◌-◌◌ ▢-▨ ■ **Z6 pH5.5–7.5**

Taxus baccata ♀
EUROPEAN YEW

This evergreen conifer is suited to clipping for hedges and topiary, and to planting beneath other trees and shrubs in a woodland garden, where it tolerates dry, dense shade. With its dark green feathery foliage it is excellent as a foil for other plants at the back of a border or as an architectural specimen, perhaps draped with a climber such as scarlet flame nasturtium. 'Fastigiata' ♀, the Irish yew, makes a fine specimen tree, as does the golden 'Fastigiata Aureomarginata' ♀. 'Dovastoniana' ♀ and the gold-variegated 'Dovastonii Aurea' ♀ are large, spreading shrubs with curtains of branchlets, while 'Repandens' ♀ and gold-edged 'Repens Aurea' ♀ are spreading, ground-cover shrubs. 'Semperaurea' ♀ is a slow-growing bush with ascending branches, its yellow color lasting through the year. All golden variants contrast well with blue flowers or glaucous foliage, and harmonize with hot color schemes.

◗ *Amelanchier lamarckii*, *Chamaecyparis lawsoniana* 'Pembury Blue', *Ilex* × *altaclerensis* 'Golden King', *Kniphofia* 'David' p.254 **C**, *Picea pungens* 'Koster', *Syringa vulgaris* p.94 **B**, *Tropaeolum speciosum* p.130 **B**

H: 1–12m (3¼–40ft) **S: 1–10m** (3¼–33ft)
❀ **(Early to mid-spring)**
◌◌ ▢-▨ ■ **Z5 pH5–8**

In late spring, the new shoots of the low, spreading yew *Taxus baccata* 'Summergold' emerge sulfur-yellow, making a striking contrast with the reddish purple young leaves of a purple smoke bush (*Cotinus coggygria* 'Royal Purple').

Ulmus minor 'Dicksonii'

DICKSON'S ELM

This is a slow-growing deciduous tree that seldom reaches sufficient size to be susceptible to Dutch elm disease. It is suitable for growing in a large border or shrubbery, but where space is restricted it can be reduced in size by pruning some of its outermost branches back into the center of the tree. Its bright yellow-green foliage is particularly effective in plantings designed around hot color schemes of yellow, orange, or scarlet, and can also be used as a striking contrast for blue flowers or purple foliage. Good companions include plants with silvery foliage, such as weeping willow-leaf pears or willows, and larger herbaceous plants like helianthus or delphiniums; it may also be draped with a clematis such as a Viticella cultivar in dusky red-purple or purplish blue.

○ *Clematis viticella* 'Mary Rose', *Delphinium* 'Alice Artindale', *Helianthus decapetalus* 'Soleil d'Or', *Pyrus salicifolia* 'Pendula', *Rosa* 'Frensham'

H: 10m (33ft) S: 6m (20ft)
✿ **(Early to mid-spring)**
◊-◊◊ ▢-▮ **Z4 pH5–8**

Adding dramatic height to a deep border, *Ulmus minor* 'Dicksonii' is contrasted with silver willow (*Salix alba* var. *sericea*), pollarded annually to prevent it becoming too large; lavender *Hebe* 'Jewel' furnishes the front. A lavender-blue Viticella clematis could also be included to drape the willow and elm, further unifying the design.

Viburnum × *bodnantense*

One of the most useful species for winter color, this large deciduous shrub has strongly fragrant blooms in white or pink. Three cultivars are often grown: 'Charles Lamont' ♀, with flowers in pure pink; 'Dawn' ♀, also pink; and 'Deben' ♀, with white flowers opening from pink buds. All are best sited close to an entrance or path, where their fragrance can be appreciated. They associate well with other winter-flowering plants such as *Prunus* × *subhirtella* cultivars, *Prunus pendula* cultivars, *Viburnum tinus*, *V. grandiflorum*, winter heaths, early-flowering camellias, and sarcoccoas, and with handsome evergreens like *Euonymus japonicus* cultivars, white-variegated hollies, fatsias, and garryas. Other good partners include *Daphne*

Viburnum × *bodnantense* 'Dawn' starts flowering in autumn, allowing it to be combined with fruit-bearing shrubs such as cotoneasters. Crab apples, euonymus, gaultherias, hollies, pyracanthas, roses, sorbus, and snowberries would also make good companions.

mezereum and *D. odora* cultivars, winter-flowering honeysuckles, and ground-covering ivies and bergenias. Thinning the branches helps prevent congestion, and the occasional removal of older branches encourages the growth of vigorous young flowering wood.

○ *Camellia* 'Cornish Snow', *Erica carnea* 'Springwood White', *Hamamelis* × *intermedia* 'Moonlight', *Ilex aquifolium* 'Silver Queen', *Lonicera fragrantissima*, *Rhododendron mucronulatum*, *Sarcococca confusa*

H: 3m (10ft) S: 2m (6½ft)
✿ **Late autumn to mid-spring**
◊◊ ▢-▮ **Z7 pH5–8**

Viburnum × *burkwoodii*

This is a useful evergreen or semi-evergreen shrub that produces intensely fragrant white blooms, opening from pink buds from mid- or late winter to late spring. It is a cross between deciduous *V. carlesii* and glossy evergreen *V. utile*, and some of the finest cultivars are the result of back-crossing this hybrid with one of the parents. 'Anne Russell' ♀, back-crossed with *V. carlesii*, is compact and semi-evergreen, with large, very fragrant flowers; fragrant 'Mohawk', another compact back-cross to *V. carlesii*, has bright red buds opening white, and orange-red autumn leaf tints; both are in bloom in mid- to late spring. 'Chenaultii' is typical of *V.* × *burkwoodii*, flowering at the same time, but more compact. Later-blooming 'Park Farm Hybrid' ♀ is vigorous and spreading, with dark pink flowers, fading to white. All but the last can be used like *V.* × *bodnantense* (left), combined with winter-flowering plants, evergreen shrubs, and ground covers. 'Park Farm Hybrid' associates well with spring bulbs such as hyacinths, tulips, and white or pink narcissi, pink forget-me-nots, rock cress, and white or pink erythroniums.

○ *Bergenia cordifolia* 'Purpurea', *Camellia* × *williamsii* 'Donation', *Erythronium californicum* 'White Beauty', *Myosotis sylvatica* 'Victoria Rose', *Narcissus* 'Ice Follies', *Rhododendron* × *mucronatum*

H: 1.5–2.5m (5–8ft) S: 2m (6½ft)
✿ **Mid-winter to late spring**
◊◊ ▢-▮ **Z5 pH5.5–8**

Facing page: The many-flowered heads of *Viburnum* × *burkwoodii*, here trained as a standard, provide a contrast of floral form with more solid blooms such as tulips.

A

Viburnum davidii ♆

Since this low, spreading evergreen shrub bears its flattened heads of white male and female flowers on separate bushes, a pollinator – ideally one male plant to about six females – is necessary if female plants are to produce their display of bright blue berries on reddish stalks. The handsome, boldly veined, glossy foliage makes a striking impression towards the front of a border and the fruits, which are produced in autumn, are carried for a long time, making this a useful plant for the winter garden. It may be grown with evergreens such as *Euonymus fortunei* cultivars, ivies, and winter heaths, and it is also valuable for providing a ground cover, especially when grown through a contrasting

The boldly structured foliage and domed flower heads of *Viburnum davidii* allow it to be used in combination with more diffuse and amorphous shrubs such as broom. Rich pink or white flowers are perhaps most flattering for the viburnum's subdued coloring.

cover of yellow-green or white-variegated foliage. However, a large, dense expanse can easily mask the individual character of each shrub, and extensive plantings are perhaps most effective with slightly wider spacings between bushes to ensure they do not completely coalesce.

◐ *Bergenia* 'Morgenröte', *Erica* × *darleyensis* 'Silberschmelze', *Euonymus fortunei* 'Emerald Gaiety', *Hedera helix* 'Glacier', *Ilex crenata* 'Golden Gem'

H & S: 1.2m (4ft) ✿ **Late spring**
◊◊ ☐-■ **Z7 pH5.5–8**

Viburnum opulus 'Roseum' ♆
SNOWBALL BUSH

This large, sterile form of the deciduous cranberry tree is a classic partner for other late spring flowering shrubs such as kolkwitzias, ornamental cherries and crab apples, larger deciduous azaleas, early species roses, hawthorns, and *Kerria japonica* cultivars. Its white flowers combine with any other color of flower or foliage, although they are especially attractive with yellow-green foliage and flowers, with blue flowers such as those of larger ceanothus, or with a draping of a light pink *Clematis montana* var. *rubens* cultivar. The bold shape of its flower heads (which are useful for cutting) provides an effective contrast in form with the flowers of other genera, such as lilacs and dipeltas, as well as ceanothus. Because the snowball tree is relatively large, it requires a position towards the back of a mixed border or shrubbery and, if used in combinations with herbaceous plants, benefits from an intervening group of smaller shrubs.

◐ *Crataegus laevigata* 'Rosea Flore Pleno', *Kolkwitzia amabilis* 'Pink Cloud', *Malus* 'Royalty', *Rosa* 'Complicata', *Syringa vulgaris* 'Firmament' ⌐ p.44 **A**

H: 5m (16ft) **S: 4m** (13ft)
✿ **Late spring to early summer**
◊◊ ☐-■ **Z3 pH5–8**

A billowing mass of evergreen ceanothus forms a dramatic dusky blue backdrop for the bold flower heads of *Viburnum opulus* 'Roseum'. Good as this grouping is, adding an early yellow rose would flatter both partners.

The large off-white flower heads and handsome leaves of *Viburnum rhytidophyllum* benefit from companions in subdued colors and of contrasting scale, as in this *Berberis thunbergii* f. *atropurpurea* in late spring bloom.

Viburnum rhytidophyllum

With its splendid glossy foliage, pale beige-colored flowers, and shiny fruits, this statuesque evergreen shrub is a magnificent plant for the back of large shrub or mixed borders, and for sunny glades in a woodland garden. The leaves are long and corrugated, deep green above with thickly felted grey undersides, providing a strong impact in winter like that of an impressive large-leaved rhododendron. The soft, subdued blooms are effective with subtle tones such as peach, buff-yellow, apricot, cream, and pale salmon, and with bronze-flushed foliage. Plants may be combined with gently colored roses such as some of the Hybrid Musks, dipeltas, kolkwitzias, later-flowering rhododendrons including deciduous azaleas, xanthoceras, *Buddleja globosa*, hybrid brooms, deutzias, large species hydrangeas, philadelphus, and hybrid lilacs. It also associates well with bronze-flushed hazels, maples, plums, and photinias, and with honeysuckles and early clematis on neighboring walls or shrubs.

◐ *Dipelta floribunda*, *Philadelphus coronarius*, *Photinia* × *fraseri* 'Birmingham', *Rhododendron* 'Irene Koster', *Rosa* 'Buff Beauty', *Syringa vulgaris* 'Primrose'

H: 5m (16ft) S: 4m (13ft)
❀ Late spring to early summer
Z6 pH5.5–7.5

Weigela florida 'Foliis Purpureis' ♔

This is a compact deciduous shrub with purplish grey-green leaves enhanced at flowering time by soft pink flowers. In partial shade the leaf color is less intense and flowering is diminished, and a site in full sun is preferable. It is excellent near the front of a shrub or mixed border, where it combines well with pink or crimson flowers and grey, glaucous, or deeper purple foliage. Attractive partners include pinks, old roses, cerise or carmine-pink achilleas, pink convolvulus, cistus, mauve-pink campanulas and mallows, cranesbills, heucheras, and plants with contrasting foliage, such as glaucous fescues or Tardiana Group hostas. Similar weigelas with purple-flushed foliage include 'Red Prince', with ruby-red flowers, and 'Victoria', compact but more upright, with deep bronze-purple foliage and purplish pink flowers.

◐ *Achillea millefolium* 'Cerise Queen', *Dianthus* 'Doris', *Geranium* 'Chocolate Candy', *Hosta* (Tardiana Group) 'Halcyon', *Rosa* 'Tuscany Superb'

H: 1m (3¼ft) S: 1.5m (5ft) ❀ Early summer
Z5 pH5.5–7.5

Weigela florida 'Foliis Purpureis' is combined with plants of similar dusky purple leaf color but contrasting form. Purple New Zealand flax (*Phormium tenax* Purpureum Group) provides a dramatic vertical accent, while the cow parsley *Anthriscus sylvestris* 'Ravenswing' contributes lacy white umbels of flowers over feathery foliage.

Weigela 'Florida Variegata' ♔

Leaves edged in creamy yellow and rose-pink flowers opening from deep pink buds make this small to medium-sized deciduous shrub a handsome candidate for growing in the front or second row of a shrub or mixed border. It associates well with salmon or cream flowers, and blends attractively with bronze-flushed foliage. In shade, flowering is suppressed, allowing it to be used in plantings intended mainly for foliage effect, combined with yellow-green foliage and flowers, or with cream, white, or soft yellow flowers. When used as a foliage plant, it can be pruned in mid-spring rather than at the usual time immediately after flowering.

Another excellent variegated weigela for similar use is 'Praecox Variegata' ♔, with creamy yellow leaf margins, turning white with age, and large fragrant blooms, rich pink with yellow throats, in mid-spring.

◐ *Choisya ternata* Sundance, *Euphorbia* × *martini*, *Geranium albanum* p.225 **A**, *Potentilla fruticosa* 'Tilford Cream', *Rosa* 'Carmenetta', *Tulipa* 'Elegant Lady'

H & S: 1.5m (5ft) ❀ Early summer
Z5 pH5.5–7.5

Weigela 'Florida Variegata' is planted in front underneath *Berberis thunbergii* 'Atropurpurea Nana', whose reddish purple foliage harmonizes with the weigela's rose-pink flowers, while contrasting strikingly with its leaves.

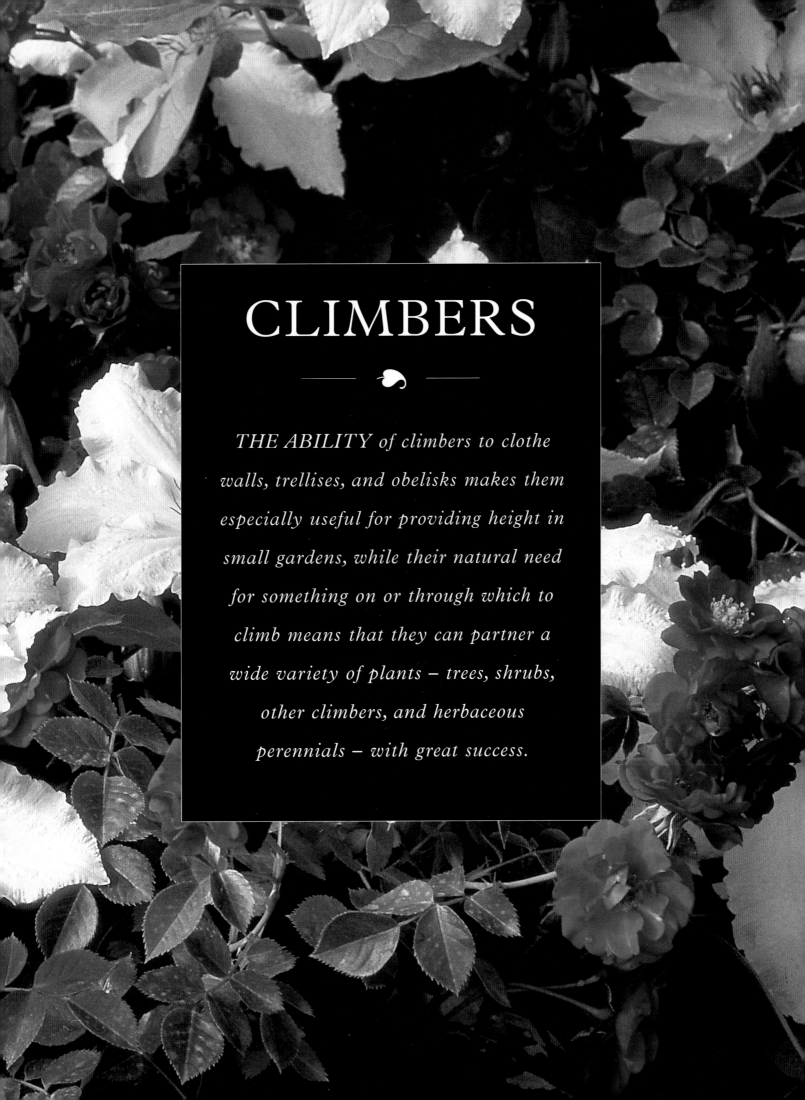

CLIMBERS

THE ABILITY of climbers to clothe walls, trellises, and obelisks makes them especially useful for providing height in small gardens, while their natural need for something on or through which to climb means that they can partner a wide variety of plants – trees, shrubs, other climbers, and herbaceous perennials – with great success.

IN THE WILD, climbers have adapted to scramble through other plants to reach the sun. It is vital to understand how these plants climb if they are to be used successfully in the garden: a wisteria planted at the base of a stout pergola pillar will writhe forever on the ground unless it is given a slimmer support, such as a wire, around which it can wind. It is also very important to match the vigor of the plant to its situation. Eccremocarpus will be satisfied with a bamboo cane 2–3m (6½–10ft) high, while crimson glory vine and wisterias will eventually climb to the top of the tallest tree. Finally, it makes sense to position those climbers that have scented flowers – honeysuckles, jasmines, sweet peas, wisterias – in sheltered situations where both their scent and those who appreciate it will be inclined to linger.

How climbers climb

Some climbers, such as clematis, sweet peas, or vines, climb by tendrils or leaf stalks which curl tightly around any convenient support. Others twine their whole stem spirally around thin supports – wisterias, honeysuckles, morning glories, and summer jasmine, for example. A third method of climbing is by aerial roots or suckers that adhere to and sometimes penetrate rough brick, stone, timber, or bark. Ivy climbs like this and can cling so tightly that it damages the wall when attempts are made to remove it; campsis, on the other hand, never seems to cling quite tightly enough – unless growth is lightened by regular pruning, whole branches will tear away from the wall in heavy rains or strong winds. If there is any concern about potential damage from this group of climbers, they can be grown on trellis: they will cling to the rough surface of the wood or can be tied in for additional support if needed, and the trellis can be lowered from the wall for painting or other maintenance from time to time. A few plants, roses and bougainvilleas among them, are scramblers rather than climbers, with long stems clothed with sharp thorns to hook on to their supports. Such plants are never secure until their stems can intertwine and form a self-supporting structure. Lastly, there are those plants – figs, forsythias, flowering quinces, and winter jasmine – that are naturally shrubs but which, in cultivation, are often fastened to a wall, either because they are decorative in such a position or because they benefit from the shelter and warmth offered by the wall. They can be held in place with twist ties or wires.

Because they take up very little space, climbers can be used in a variety of ways around even the smallest garden. They will disguise and decorate house walls, garages, sheds, fences, and eyesores. They can be trained on trellises, fences,

Facing page: Although often grown on its own, Japanese wisteria (*W. floribunda*) associates amicably with many of the other climbers and wall shrubs, such as this ceanothus, that flower in the same season.

Below: Few climbers are more versatile than the clematis, available in a host of colors, forms, and sizes for use as screens and backdrops or, in a more natural style, for encouraging to scramble through other plants.

arches, pergolas, and obelisks to provide a lighter and more colorful vertical emphasis than trees or walls. A pergola draped entirely in wisteria, a fragrant tangle of jasmine, billowing masses of ivy on an old stump, or a bower of cascading roses – each has a magic of its own. It is also possible to grow plants in combination: dark red clematis through purple-leaved vines; yellow or green vines with blue *Clematis macropetala*, or interwoven strands of early and late honeysuckles. Of course, with such mixtures, great care has to be taken to prevent the plants growing into an unruly mass. This is easier if each year one of the partners can be cut to the ground, as with many clematis, or back to a basic framework of older stems, as with vines.

Climbers in borders and pots

In a border, the teepees, obelisks, or single posts up which many climbers like to grow will add height while occupying minimal ground area, and the lighter-stemmed climbers can be used, without artificial support, to scramble through shrubs or over robust perennials to give a second period of interest. Gertrude Jekyll used to drape the dying stems of delphiniums with white sweet peas, then *Clematis* 'Jackmanii', and, finally, *Clematis flammula* to achieve a very long season. It is easy to think of other combinations: large-flowered clematis over peonies; white-flowered clematis through the grey leaves of *Brachyglottis* 'Sunshine', or the diminutive pink-flowered *Convolvulus althaeoides* through lavenders, for example.

Annual climbers, especially, are excellent in large pots. A tripod of canes will support sweet peas, eccremocarpus, canary creepers, or morning glories. These can also be allowed to trail down over the edge of the pot. Generous feeding of potted climbers will lead to prolific flowering, and the flowering season can often be prolonged by moving the pots into a greenhouse or sunroom at the end of the summer.

Finally, grown horizontally, many climbers will hide compost bins or other unattractive features with a blanket of foliage and flowers.

A purplish blue selection of *Aconitum hemsleyanum* contrasts with the pendant yellow flowers of climbing *Dicentra scandens*. Both have the same rate of growth, habit, and cultivation requirements, making them ideal partners for covering a wall (with support), trellis, or large shrub.

Aconitum hemsleyanum

Often wrongly identified as *A. volubile*, this scrambling herbaceous plant has broad, lobed, rich green leaves and racemes of large, hooded flowers that can vary considerably in color between shades of dull greenish grey, greyish lilac, lavender-blue, and a rich deep purple-blue. Recent introductions of the species from the wild have brought a number of more definite flower colors into cultivation, and for this reason it is best to check the catalogue description of the color before buying. The flowers are seldom bright enough to show well from a distance, but plants look charming when scrambling over a shrub with silver or yellow-green foliage, especially yellow-green maples, elders, physocarpus, philadelphus, and silver elaeagnus or willows. Although flowering will be diminished if planted in the densest shade, *A. hemsleyanum* is fairly shade-tolerant, and makes a good plant for a small town or courtyard garden, where its subdued charm can be appreciated at close quarters.

○ *Acer shirasawanum* 'Aureum', *Clematis* 'Prince Charles', *Elaeagnus* 'Quicksilver', *Ipomoea tricolor* 'Heavenly Blue', *Salix elaeagnos* subsp. *angustifolia*

H: 2–3m (6½–10ft) ✿ **Mid-summer to early autumn**
░░░ ◊◊ ▨ ■ **Z6 pH5.5–7.5**

Actinidia kolomikta ♀

Many of the leaves of this vigorous, deciduous twining climber have a white zone tipped with pink, producing an exotic effect found in few other plants. This leaf coloring is most pronounced on male specimens (the white male and female flowers grow on separate plants) and develops maximum intensity in full sun. Plants with pink, white, or crimson flowers and those with purple foliage make excellent associates. In areas with fairly cool summers, the actinidia benefits from being grown against a wall. With careful training it is possible to combine it with two or more other climbers quite uniformly, but for this to be effective at long range and to avoid visual confusion, the coloring of companion plants should not be too close to that of the actinidia – suitable partners include many roses, clematis, and pink or white jasmines. If trained on a wall, it is advisable to prune this actinidia every winter, leaving a framework of branches but shortening sideshoots to one or two buds.

○ *Clematis florida* var. *sieboldii* p.110 **B**, *C.* 'Madame Julia Correvon', *Jasminum* × *stephanense*, *Rosa* 'Madame Grégoire Staechelin', *Vitis vinifera* 'Purpurea'

H: 5m (16ft) ✿ **Early summer**
░░░ ◊◊ ▨-■ **Z5 pH5.5–7.5**

The boldly splashed leaves of *Actinidia kolomikta* (hardy kiwi), harmonize with the pink and red in the flowers of the honeysuckle *Lonicera* × *italica*, both supported by wires against a moderately sunny wall. The actinidia will remain colorful after the honeysuckle has finished flowering.

Ampelopsis glandulosa var. *brevipedunculata* 'Elegans'

A deciduous tendril climber with foliage irregularly splashed with white and pink, this cultivar has berries that turn a brilliant blue on ripening and look spectacular once the leaves are shed in autumn. Except in climates with hot summers, it usually needs to be grown against a warm wall to encourage fruit bearing. The filigree effect of its small, three-lobed leaves is best appreciated at close quarters, making it a useful plant for small gardens and patio areas, whether attached to wires or trellis on a wall or allowed to clamber over other wall plants, especially those with an early flowering season or with dark foliage. Suitable companions include dark-leaved ceanothus, smaller evergreen clematis such as some of the Forsteri Group, and climbers of similar vigor, like maurandyas, rhodochitons, pink- or red-flowered jasmines, and small-leaved ivies. Combinations with other variegated plants, although charming and intricate when seen close up, can look muddled from a distance.

⦿ *Billardiera longiflora fructu-albo*, *Ceanothus* 'Autumnal Blue', *Clematis* 'Duchess of Albany', *Ipomoea lobata*, *Jasminum beesianum*, *Maurandya barclayana*, *Tropaeolum tricolor*

H: 4m (13ft) ✿ **(Summer)**
◌◌ ▢-▇ Z9 pH6–7.5

This subtle tapestry of variegated foliage owes much of its charm to the different leaf shapes – palmate in *Ampelopsis glandulosa* var. *brevipedunculata* 'Elegans', pinnate in *Jasminum officinale* 'Aureum', and peltate in nasturtium. The mottled variegation lightens the color of the leaves without emphasizing their shape as white edges would, making this arrangement more effective seen at close range.

Campsis radicans
TRUMPET CREEPER

This vigorous deciduous climber uses aerial roots to attach itself to supports. It has pinnate leaves, and clusters of flowers, born on the current season's growth, that are usually scarlet shading to orange in the throat. Color variants include 'Atrosanguinea', which has deep blood-red blooms, and f. *flava* ♛, in rich yellow; *C.* × *tagliabuana* 'Madame Galen' ♛ is a similar hybrid with more spreading clusters of flowers in a rich salmon-red. All may be grown on walls, where they often flower more profusely, or allowed to climb into large shrubs or small trees. The flowers blend well with other hot colors and bronze foliage, and continue into autumn to partner with seasonally coloring shrubs and climbers such as crimson glory vine. Trumpet creeper is also effective with yellow-green foliage, including ivies, golden hops, and golden catalpas, and with deep red Viticella or Texensis clematis and purple vines.

⦿ *Clematis* 'Kermesina', *Cotinus obovatus*, *Hedera helix* 'Buttercup', *Parthenocissus himalayana* var. *rubrifolia*, *Rosa* Altissimo, *Vitis* 'Brant', *V. vinifera* 'Purpurea'

H: 10m (33ft) ✿ **Late summer to mid-autumn**
◌◌ ▢-▇ Z5 pH5.5–7.5

Trumpet creeper (*Campsis radicans*) gracefully clothes the top of a wall, its flowers harmonizing with the brick. From here it can scramble into the adjacent *Elaeagnus* 'Quicksilver', contrasting with its pale leaves. The foliage of the smoke bush (*Cotinus coggygria*) behind will assume autumnal tints that match the color of the vine's late flowers.

Clematis

THE GENUS *CLEMATIS* is immensely
diverse, with flowers, from large to tiny,
of almost every color except pure blue,
always presented with poise and elegance.
Most are moderately vigorous and easy
to keep in balance with other plants,
producing slender stems that can drape
themselves over or through their neighbors
without suppressing them. Along with
roses, they are the most useful climbers in
association with other plants. Yet clematis
are often grown in isolation, without any
attempt to allow them to interact with
their companions. It is true that the most
vigorous sorts – like *Clematis montana* var.
rubens ♀ – create such large areas of color
that any interaction is apparent only
around the fringes of the plant; and on
pillar or obelisk, a single clematis of
reasonable vigor allows little space for a
companion, except for wispy climbers such
as morning glories or perennial peas. A
clematis "balloon", however, gives scope
for two cultivars to be interwoven, perhaps
with another slender scrambler.

On a wall, different clematis can be
used to carry upwards the color scheme
of the border beneath, possibly mixed with
a bold-leaved vine or *Actinidia kolomikta* to
compensate for their lack of good foliage,
and enhanced by using clematis with
flowers of differing sizes. Small-flowered
C. × triternata 'Rubromarginata' ♀ or
C. × jouiniana 'Praecox' ♀, for example,
can be mixed with medium-sized Viticella
and larger Jackmanii cultivars.

Clematis may also be draped over
shrubs, to contrast with gold or silver
foliage or harmonize with purple, or to
add interest to shrubs that are dull after
flowering. A number of species and almost
all clematis in the Tangutica Group have
decorative seedheads, some persisting
through winter, and these are particularly
effective when in the open garden, rather
than on walls. Texensis cultivars have
upward-facing blooms, which are an asset

if grown across a carpet of ground cover.
Shorter clematis, such as *C. × bonstedtii*,
C. × durandii ♀, *C. heracleifolia*, and
C. recta, can be grown as border plants
with the help of brushwood stakes.

Clematis climb by means of their
twining leaf-stalks. They may be deciduous
or evergreen, although all those described
in this book are deciduous. Early-flowering
kinds with axillary flowers (for example

Above: Summer-flowering Jackmanii and Viticella clematis
(purple *C.* 'Jackmanii Superba', crimson 'Ville de Lyon',
and pink 'Comtesse de Bouchaud') mingle harmoniously
here against a dry stone wall.

Left: Combining clematis of different flower sizes and
distinct colors can add sparkle, as here with red Texensis
'Gravetye Beauty', soft lavender Jackmanii 'Perle d'Azur',
and white Viticella 'Huldine'.

Alpina Group cultivars and *C. montana*)
are pruned after flowering, while large- or
later small-flowered cultivars are pruned in
late winter or early spring. Regularly tying
in new shoots, ideally at least once every
two weeks, helps to spread out the stems
for maximum floral display and prevents
kinking at the base, which encourages
clematis wilt disease. If the rootball is set
8cm (3in) or so below the soil surface, the
plant will usually regrow after an attack by
wilt. Mildew can be a problem for groups
such as Jackmanii, Texensis, and some
Viticellas, particularly if grown on a wall.
Bare stems at the base of the clematis are
best hidden by other plants, casting the
roots into the shade they prefer.

Clematis 'Alba Luxurians' ♀

From mid-summer onwards, *C.* 'Alba Luxurians' produces flowers of the purest white, its sepals often having a leafy green tip and/or central section. These are not shed as the flowers age but wither and turn brown, although this does not usually disfigure the plant. As with its parent *C. viticella*, some of its flowers nod gracefully downwards: the reverse of the flower is not such a pure white, but the plant is still attractive if grown across the ground. A vigorous grower, the plant can smother smaller shrubs and ground covers; if used with these, some thinning of its shoots might be needed. It combines well with pink, mauve, blue, or soft yellow flowers and looks pleasing when grown through gold foliage. Gentle harmonies with silver-leaved shrubs are also possible, although the overall color tones of clematis and shrubs are often so similar that such combinations are best seen at close range. It flowers well in areas where summers are hot, but in cooler regions it may not be so floriferous unless given the sunniest position. Like all other members of the Viticella Group, this clematis should be pruned hard in early spring.

🌑 *Buddleja* 'Lochinch', *B.* 'Pink Delight', *Ceanothus* × *delileanus* 'Gloire de Versailles', *Clematis* 'Prince Charles', *Hippophae rhamnoides* p.58 **A**, *Prunus spinosa* 'Purpurea', *Salix elaeagnos* subsp. *angustifolia*

H: 4m (13ft) ❀ **Mid-summer to early autumn**
◌◌ ☐-☒ **Z5 pH5–8**

Clematis 'Alba Luxurians' scrambles among pretty blue periwinkle (*Vinca major*) and arching white *Lysimachia clethroides*, with spiky-leaved *Astelia chathamica* behind.

Clematis alpina ♀

C. alpina and the other species and hybrids of the Alpina Group, including *C. macropetala* (p.113), usually have nodding blue flowers, with white petal-like staminodes at the center, although many mauve-pink, light purplish red, purple, and white variants also occur. The single, bell-shaped blooms of *C. alpina* have a charming simplicity, while those of *C. macropetala* variants and hybrids are more showy, with numerous sepals making them appear double, and staminodes extending beyond these. All Alpina Group clematis produce their flowers in spring, and tend to carry a few more later in the year.

The best blue cultivars are bright enough to stand up to combinations with yellow flowers or foliage, particularly soft, light lemons such as in *Forsythia suspensa* f. *atrocaulis*. However, clematis alpina do not usually bloom profusely enough for really showy display. Nor are pinkish, purplish, or most white cultivars sufficiently pure for shining color combinations – although the best whites, *C.a.* 'White Columbine' ♀ and subsp. *sibirica* 'White Moth', are excellent with the blue of early ceanothus or the rich

The soft, light purplish red of *Clematis alpina* 'Ruby' creates a subdued harmony with the unfurling leaves of weeping silver willow-leaf (*Pyrus salicifolia* 'Pendula'). A combination with any strong color would have overwhelmed the delicate tints of the clematis.

pink of the better *Ribes sanguineum* cultivars. The repeat-flowering white subsp. *sibirica* 'Riga' is sweetly scented, as are other Alpina cultivars, such as 'Columella' and 'Propertius'.

Alpina Group clematis do not need regular pruning unless intertwined with another plant, when pruning will help keep the two in balance, and prevent the buildup of a "nest" of dead clematis stems, which may cause the death of sections of the supporting shrub. Stems that have bloomed should be cut out immediately after flowering.

🌑 **Blue:** *Amelanchier lamarckii*, *Chaenomeles* × *superba* 'Issai White', *Philadelphus coronarius* 'Aureus', *Prunus glandulosa* 'Alba Plena', *Ribes sanguineum* 'Tydeman's White', *Rosa primula*, *Viburnum opulus* 'Roseum'
Pink/Ruby: *Berberis thunbergii* 'Rose Glow', *Exochorda* × *macrantha* 'The Bride', *Malus* × *zumi* 'Golden Hornet' p.68 **C**
White: *Chaenomeles* × *superba* 'Pink Lady', *Ribes sanguineum* p.86 **B**, *R.s.* 'Poky's Pink', *Rosa xanthina*

H: 3m (10ft) ❀ **Mid- to late spring**
◌◌ ☐-☒ **Z5 pH5–8**

Clematis 'Comtesse de Bouchard' ♛

This is a vigorous and justly popular cultivar, whose color tends towards mauve. Good harmonies can be achieved with mauve-pink, crimson, or burgundy flowers, especially roses or other clematis; added interest comes by varying the flower size, combining it with a small-flowered Viticella cultivar for example. Deep purple, rich blue, or white make good contrasts, and it is effective grown over purple foliage. Those who dare mixing pink and yellow might try it with soft sulfur; it does not, however, sit happily with rose-pink, salmon, or scarlet. Like all other Jackmanii cultivars this needs pruning in early spring, cutting it close to the ground.

◑ *Clematis* × *triternata* 'Rubromarginata', *C. viticella* 'Mary Rose', *Ipomoea batatas* 'Blackie', *Lathyrus rotundifolius* 'Albus', *Maurandya barclayana*, *Prunus cerasifera* 'Nigra', *Rosa* 'Brenda Colvin' p.140 **A**

H: 4m (13ft) ❄ **Early summer to early autumn**
▬▭ ◌◌ ▢-▨ **Z5 pH5–8**

Grown with *Clematis* 'Jackmanii', *C.* 'Comtesse de Bouchaud' gives a good color contrast, while erect stems of white *Actaea cordifolia*, yellow *Thalictrum flavum* subsp. *glaucum*, and magenta lythrum provide variety of form.

Clematis × *durandii* ♛

With the exception of some of the Alpina cultivars, this is one of the bluest clematis, its relative lack of purple providing better contrasts with yellow flowers or foliage. It is also stunning against silver leaves. The deep ridges on its sepals cast dark shadows, emphasizing the shape of the flower. It can be grown in a border, with support, as a herbaceous perennial up to 1.5m (5ft); it may also be trained against a wall or allowed to sprawl over a ground cover. It will scramble happily over medium-sized shrubs without smothering them. Hard autumn pruning gives an early to mid-summer flush of flowers with only a few blooms later on. For mid- to late summer flowers and a more prolonged season, it should be pruned in spring.

◑ *Achillea* 'Lucky Break', *Atriplex halimus*, *Berberis temolaica*, *Calluna vulgaris* 'Gold Haze', *Lonicera periclymenum* 'Graham Thomas', *Philadelphus coronarius* 'Aureus', *Rosa* 'Leverkusen', *R. multiflora* p.142 **C**, *Verbascum* 'Gainsborough'

H: 2m (6½ft) ❄ **Early summer to mid-autumn**
▬▭ ◌◌ ▢-▨ **Z5 pH5–8**

Above: *Clematis* × *durandii* looks effective trained over gold-leaved shrubs such as *Lonicera nitida* 'Baggesen's Gold'.

Right: Grown as a herbaceous perennial on tall branched stakes, *Clematis* × *durandii* harmonizes with purplish red *Knautia macedonica*, violet *Nepeta sibirica*, and pinkish purple *Stachys macrantha*, with vivid *Rosa* News behind.

Clematis × *eriostemon* 'Blue Boy'

Although this clematis is as near to true blue as *C.* × *durandii* (facing page), it differs from it in its strongly recurved sepals and paler tone, which give it an altogether daintier appearance. This and its smaller flower size make it suitable for smaller-scale groupings to be seen at closer range. Its color is gentle enough to be overpowered by strong yellows, but it combines attractively with yellow-flushed or silver foliage and soft yellow, white, palest blue, or deep blue flowers.

'Blue Boy' clematis shares the herbaceous character of *C.* × *durandii*, and its pruning requirements are identical. The grace with which the flowers are carried can be a little hampered by training the plant to stakes or fixing it tightly to a wall: if it is allowed to scramble over a ground cover or shrubs, its flowers will display themselves more elegantly.

○ *Achillea* 'Lucky Break', *Brachyglottis* 'Sunshine', *Calluna vulgaris* 'Gold Haze', *Crocosmia* 'Honey Angels', *Philadelphus coronarius* 'Aureus', *Rosa* Iceberg

H: 2m (6½ft) ❀ **Mid-summer to early autumn**
◌◌ ▢-▇ **Z5 pH5–8**

Clematis × *eriostemon* 'Blue Boy' presents its flowers with poise when allowed to scramble freely over bright yellow-green *Choisya ternata* Sundance. The rich, dark leaves and flowers of *Bupleurum fruticosum* provide an excellent foil, while the whole is leavened by creamy white *Anthemis tinctoria* 'Sauce Hollandaise'.

Clematis 'Etoile Rose'

Most Texensis cultivars have upward-facing blooms, making them ideal for growing across ground-covering plants, but the flowers of 'Etoile Rose' nod downwards so that they are perhaps best seen from beneath. The deep rose-pink petals have paler margins, helping to emphasize the elegant shape of the flower. As with *C.* × *eriostemon* 'Blue Boy' (above), the grace with which the flowers hang can be lost if the plant is trained too tightly against a wall; it is also more prone to mildew here than in an open situation (protective spraying in early summer helps). A much more pleasing effect is obtained if the clematis can arrange itself loosely over a wall plant or a tall, free standing shrub. 'Etoile Rose' works well with silver or purple foliage, or with mauve, purple, crimson, or pale pink flowers, including larger-flowered Viticella clematis. Like all Texensis cultivars, it needs hard pruning to about 35cm (14in) in early spring.

○ *Ceanothus* × *pallidus* 'Marie Simon', *Clematis* 'Hagley Hybrid', *C.* 'Prince Charles', *Cotinus coggygria* 'Royal Purple', *Hibiscus syriacus* 'Hamabo', *H.s.* 'Red Heart', *Prunus spinosa* 'Purpurea', *Rosa* Super Dorothy, *Salix alba* var. *sericea* (pollarded)

H: 2.5m (8ft) ❀ **Mid-summer to mid-autumn**
◌◌ ▢-▇ **Z5 pH5–8**

The mix of *Clematis* 'Etoile Rose' and *Buddleja* 'Lochinch' benefits from the excellent contrast of flower form, size, and color as well as from the buddleja's silver foliage.

Clematis 'Etoile Violette' ♈

Creamy anthers enliven the rather somber violet flowers of this Viticella cultivar, which have six sepals, unlike *C. viticella* which has four. Very floriferous and capable of achieving an almost solid expanse of bloom with little leaf showing, its rich color is scarcely visible from a distance, making it more suitable for viewing at close range. It is useful for adding resonant depth to larger-flowered clematis of medium tone such as 'Perle d'Azur' or 'Victoria'. While it can be used for opulent and dusky harmonies, it is perhaps most often seen with lighter colors such as mauve, carmine, or blue. The lightest colors can present too stark a contrast: yellow and the palest blues or mauves work best if supplied by flowers much smaller than the clematis itself, such as honeysuckles or smaller species clematis. 'Polish Spirit' ♈ is similar to 'Etoile Violette' but has red anthers.

⊙ *Buddleja davidii* 'Dartmoor', *Ceanothus* × *delileanus* 'Gloire de Versailles', *Clematis* 'Perle d'Azur' p.116 **B**, *Hebe* 'Midsummer Beauty' p.55 **A**, *Hosta* 'August Moon' p.243 **A**, *Lathyrus latifolius*, *Lophospermum erubescens*, *Passiflora caerulea*, *Robinia pseudoacacia* 'Frisia' p.87 **A**

H: 4m (13ft) ❀ **Mid-summer to early autumn**
◊◊ ☐-☐ **Z5 pH5–8**

The sumptuous but recessive tone of *Clematis* 'Etoile Violette' provides a good foil for honeysuckles such as *Lonicera* × *americana*. Although their flower shape is very different, they have similar foliage texture; contrasting daylily leaves beneath help to prevent monotony.

Clematis florida var. *sieboldii* is flattered here by the bold pink-tipped foliage of *Actinidia kolomikta*. Such a vigorous companion could overwhelm it unless regularly pruned.

Clematis florida var. *sieboldii*

The most appealing of all clematis, *C. florida* var. *sieboldii* has greenish cream flowers with a central boss of inky purple petaloid stamens, which blend well with almost any color save scarlet or orange. A weak grower, resenting root competition and drought, it is not entirely hardy and in cooler gardens is best against a warm wall. In milder climates with hotter summers, it can be used to scramble into shrubs such as roses of moderate size. It can also be grown in a large pot, outside or in a greenhouse, and is effective trained into a tall cone or to cover an obelisk, combined with, for example, large fuchsias and good foliage plants such as *Melianthus major*. *C.f.* var. *flore pleno* is an exquisite double.

⊙ *Fuchsia magellanica* var. *gracilis*, *Lathyrus odoratus* 'Matucana', *Rosa* 'Climbing Pompon de Paris', *R.* 'Leverkusen', *R.* 'Reine Victoria'

H: 2.5m (8ft) ❀ **Early summer to early autumn**
◊◊ ☐-☐ **Z8 pH5.5–7.5**

Clematis 'Gravetye Beauty'

With their pinched sepals the cross-shaped flowers of this crimson Texensis cultivar are very effective seen from above but not from below, making it best suited to growing across a ground cover. Its slender growth keeps it from smothering companions, and it will sprawl elegantly over low shrubs, especially Ground Cover roses such as Immensee. Although the blooms clash with mauve-pink, they harmonize with gold, orange, or other rich red flowers, and with bronze foliage.

The combination of *Clematis* 'Gravetye Beauty' with summer-flowering heathers is a classic one – although white or deepest red-purple heathers might be more agreeable than the mauve-pink *Calluna vulgaris* cultivar used here. Heaths with colored foliage, groups of bergenias, or carpeting conifers, such as some of the junipers, could also be attractively draped with this clematis.

⊙ *Bergenia* 'Sunningdale', *Calluna vulgaris* 'Beoley Gold', *Clematis* 'Huldine', *C.* 'Perle d'Azur', *Erica carnea* 'Vivellii', *E. cinerea* 'Pentreath', *Juniperus horizontalis* 'Wiltonii', *J. sabina* var. *tamariscifolia*

H: 5m (16ft) ❀ **Mid-summer to early autumn**
◊◊ ☐-☐ **Z6 pH5.5–7.5**

Clematis integrifolia is similar in height to *Rosa gallica* var. *officinalis* and sets off the rich carmine color of its blooms as well as providing a contrast of flower shape.

Clematis integrifolia

This lax herbaceous plant can be encouraged to scramble into shrubs of similar height or trained on stakes for use as a conventional border plant. Four twisting sepals give the blooms an attractive, lively shape. The dusky blue flowers are not very visible from a distance and are best seen at close range. Their gentle shade combines happily with lighter or brighter blues, mauves, and pinks but is not best used with the deepest blues, purples, and crimsons. It is especially effective as a foil for soft, light yellows. If it is grown over a gold-leaved shrub, its subtle color may be overwhelmed, but it works well with silver foliage. Where a taller scrambler is needed, *C.* × *eriostemon* cultivars could be substituted. As a border plant, *C. integrifolia* (solitary clematis) is best supported with hazel twigs inserted through the clump when 50cm (20in) high, the twig tops bent over just above this height.

◉ *Achillea* 'Credo', *Artemisia ludoviciana* 'Silver Queen', *Iris* 'Jane Phillips', *Nepeta sibirica* 'Souvenir d'André Chaudron', *Stachys macrantha* 'Robusta'

H: 70cm (27in) ☼ **Mid- to late summer**
◌◌ ▢-▧ **Z3 pH5–8**

Clematis 'Jackmanii' ♈

Each flower of 'Jackmanii' usually has four rhomboid blue-purple sepals, making it seem almost square in outline. This and the gaps between the sepals give a distinct pattern to the mass of blooms. 'Jackmanii Superba' is similar, although slightly less blue in color and with a greater number of six-sepalled flowers, in which the more oval sepals overlap slightly. Because of this, although ostensibly larger and showier, the flowers do not provide the same patterned effect as 'Jackmanii'. They may even produce too solid a block of color, making integration and interaction with another climber or shrub less complete. Both plants are good combined with a bold and greyish-leaved vine, late-flowering Rambler roses in rich pink, or other clematis cultivars in lighter shades such as mauve, powder-blue, or mid- to deep rose-pink. Startling contrasts can be achieved by partnering 'Jackmanii' with gold *Senecio doria*, strong pink *Phlox paniculata* 'Bright Eyes' or 'Windsor', and white *Hydrangea arborescens* 'Annabelle'.

◉ *Buddleja* 'Lochinch', *Ceanothus* × *pallidus* 'Perle Rose', *Clematis* 'Comtesse de Bouchaud' p.108 **A**, *C.* 'Ville de Lyon' p.118 **B**, *C. viticella* 'Purpurea Plena Elegans' p.119 **A**, *Rosa* 'Lavender Lassie', *R.* Super Dorothy, *Salix alba* var. *sericea*, *Vitis vinifera* 'Incana'

H: 4m (13ft) ☼ **Early summer to early autumn**
◌◌ ▢-▧ **Z4 pH5–8**

Above: *Luma apiculata* 'Variegata' makes an effective backdrop for *Clematis* 'Jackmanii Superba', with orange *Lilium pardalinum* adding a touch of brightness.

Below: Arching gracefully above a wrought-iron gate, *Clematis* 'Jackmanii' contrasts dramatically with the gold-variegated ivy *Hedera colchica* 'Sulphur Heart'.

Clematis × jouiniana 'Praecox' ♔

The delicate blue of *C. × jouiniana* 'Praecox' might seem indistinct in isolation but can leaven sugary or heavily sumptuous colors without the harsh contrast of pure white. While admirable with mauves, and deep pinks and blues, it is not flattered by yellow, orange, or scarlet, and its subtle coloring would be overwhelmed by gold foliage and lost against white-variegated or silver leaves. Its small flowers provide a dainty setting for Viticella and Jackmanii clematis or morning glories, although several well-grown plants of the latter would be needed to match its volume. A strong-growing, woody-based, semi-

herbaceous plant, which needs pruning to about 30cm (12in) in late winter or early spring, it is too vigorous for draping shrubs, but it can be trained on a wall with other clematis and climbers, or used as a ground-covering carpet through which perennials, shrubs, or bedding plants may be grown.

Clematis × jouiniana 'Praecox' acts as foil for *C.* 'Victoria', toning down its possible excess of gorgeousness.

⬤ *Buddleja davidii* 'Dartmoor' p.33 **C**, *Caryopteris × clandonensis* 'Pershore', *Ipomoea tricolor* 'Heavenly Blue', *Monarda* 'Beauty of Cobham', *Pulmonaria saccharata* p.279 **C**

H: 6m (20ft) ✿ **Mid-summer to mid-autumn**
▰▰▱▱ ◊◊ ▢-▣ **Z4 pH5–8**

Clematis 'Kermesina'

The slightly nodding flowers of this purple-crimson Viticella cultivar, and of the very similar 'Viticella Rubra', retain much of the grace and poise of their parent *C. viticella*. Their slender habit of growth allows them to be draped over shrubs, although they will scarcely show against purple foliage and contrast too starkly against silver or gold leaves. They are especially effective with deep to mid-pink or mauve flowers, but salmon-pink does not flatter them. Partners in light orange are particularly striking; those in pale yellow are less attractive, but still agreeable. When *Clematis* 'Kermesina' is grown across a ground cover, it displays the silver-pink reverse of its flowers rather than their faces, which has a slightly unnerving effect. It perhaps looks best if the flowers are at eye level or above, whether grown over shrubs or trained with other climbers against a wall.

⬤ *Clematis* 'Victoria' p.118 **A**, *Eccremocarpus scaber*, *Humulus lupus* 'Aureus', *Lathyrus odoratus* 'Noel Sutton', *Rosa* 'Climbing Madame Caroline Testout', *R.* 'Mermaid', *R.* Super Dorothy

H: 4m (13ft) ✿ **Mid-summer to early autumn**
▰▰▱▱ ◊◊ ▢-▣ **Z5 pH5–8**

The gently nodding blooms of *Clematis* 'Kermesina' mingle well with the old, richly scented sweet pea *Lathyrus odoratus* 'Matucana'. The sweet pea was sown in spring to make its flowering coincide with that of the clematis.

Above: A rich blue variant of *Clematis macropetala* here balances the brightness of golden California privet (*Ligustrum ovalifolium* 'Aureum'). These will not remain in equilibrium without careful management. The easiest method is to clip both after the privet's first flush of growth, but this can reduce the flowering of the clematis. Otherwise, the clematis can be removed from the privet and the latter clipped after its first flush; or individual bits can be pruned out of the privet without disturbing the clematis.

Right: *Clematis macropetala* 'Markham's Pink' with *C.* 'Blue Bird' is a subtle charming mixture, seen best close up.

Clematis macropetala

This Alpina Group clematis has double flowers, frillier than the C. *alpina* (p.107) but not so bold in shape or distinctive at a distance. Ideas for grouping it with other plants are given under C. *alpina*. Among the best cultivars are 'Maidwell Hall' hort. ♀ in rich blue ('Lagoon' and 'Pauline' are similar), 'Markham's Pink' ♀, and 'Snowbird' in pure white. 'Ballet Skirt' opens rich pink and fades paler as the flowers age. Mauve-purple 'Jan Lindmark' is one of the first to bloom, while 'Purple Spider' is the richest of its color. *C.* 'Blue Bird', pale blue 'Floralia', 'Rosie O'Grady', and 'White Swan' are good hybrids with *C. alpina*.

◐ **Blue:** *Amelanchier lamarckii*, *Chaenomeles × superba* 'Issai White', *Philadelphus coronarius* 'Aureus', *Prunus glandulosa* 'Alba Plena', *Ribes sanguineum* 'Tydeman's White', *Rosa primula*, *Viburnum opulus* 'Roseum'
Pink/Ruby: *Berberis thunbergii* 'Rose Glow', *Exochorda × macrantha* 'The Bride', *Lathyrus odoratus* 'Noel Sutton' p.125 **A**
White: *Chaenomeles × superba* 'Pink Lady', *Ribes sanguineum* 'Poky's Pink', *Rosa xanthina*

H: 4m (13ft) Mid- to late spring
Z6 pH5–8

Clematis 'Margot Koster'

Unlike most other Viticella clematis, this cultivar has flowers that face outwards and slightly upwards rather than nodding, suiting it to use below eye level on shrubs and over a ground cover as well as at a greater height on a wall. Its bright cerise flowers are light enough to show against a background of purple foliage and make effective contrasts with pale peach roses (three rose plants would be needed if of moderate size such as *R.* 'Penelope'), light sky-blue clematis, or chartreuse flowers or leaves. 'Madame Julia Correvon' ♀ is a similar Viticella cultivar that blooms even longer and may be used in the same way. Both are valuable for their color rather than their rather irregular flower shape.

◐ *Ceanothus × delileanus* 'Gloire de Versailles', *C. × pallidus* 'Perle Rose', *Cercis canadensis* 'Forest Pansy', *Clematis* 'Prince Charles', *Euphorbia schillingii*

H: 3m (10ft) Mid-summer to early autumn
Z4 pH5–8

Both the contrasting form and soft peach coloring of *R.* 'Gloire de Dijon' make a telling combination with *Clematis* 'Margot Koster'.

Clematis montana

This sweet-scented species typically has white flowers, but most of its cultivars are pink, derived from var. *rubens*. Free-flowering and easy to grow, it is admirably suited to bold planting on the largest scale. It is almost uncontrollably vigorous, tending to form a large sheet of growth that is covered in bloom in late spring; the white var. *wilsonii* flowers two weeks later, allowing different combinations with the first of the summer flowers. Although *C. montana* can produce the most exquisite late spring partnerships, its vigor is its greatest limitation in achieving them. It is almost impossible to get it to mix intimately with another plant without smothering it; nor does a great expanse of white or pink blooms make for good associations, for the interplay between clematis and its neighbor is effective only around the edges. Stunning combinations are sometimes seen – with wisteria, for example, or when the clematis drapes itself into a small or moderately sized tree. However, the chances of achieving a successful balance without careful management of the clematis and often its partner too are very small; even if such a balance is found, it is not likely to last more than a few years. On a wall or a large pillar, it is possible to spur-prune the clematis as if it were a grape vine, allowing only five to ten main stems to develop and cutting back all lateral shoots close to these after flowering. In this way a wall can be lightly clad with swags of clematis mixed with another climber that flowers at the same time. If *C. montana* is grown over a large shrub or small tree, pruning can be less draconian, but considerable thinning is advisable after flowering each year. White variants mix well with pale lilacs, or early yellow or pink roses, as well as mauve wisteria. Light pink cultivars of var. *rubens* are attractive with white wisteria or early white roses, or scrambling across palest or mid-mauve to deep purple lilacs, while rich pink variants are effective trained into purple plums or crab apples.

⬤ **White:** *Ceanothus arboreus* 'Trewithen Blue', *Lonicera* × *americana* p.126 **A**, *Rosa banksiae* 'Lutea', *Syringa vulgaris* 'Madame Antoine Buchner', *Wisteria sinensis* p.131
B Pink: *Choisya ternata* p.38 **A**, *Malus* × *zumi* 'Golden Hornet', *Prunus cerasifera* 'Nigra', *P.* 'Shirotae', *P.* 'Shôgetsu', *Rosa* 'Cooperi', *Syringa vulgaris* 'Congo', *S.v.* 'Krasavitsa Moskvy', *Wisteria floribunda* 'Alba'

H 10m (33ft) ❀ **Late spring to early summer**
 ◊◊◊ ▢-■ **Z6 pH5–8**

Top: A harmonious pairing of *Clematis montana* var. *rubens* 'Tetrarose' and *Spiraea* 'Arguta' needs regular attention to maintain the balance and attractive mingling of both plants.

Above: *Clematis montana* var. *rubens* drapes itself over *Syringa vulgaris*. The relatively small flowers of the clematis contrast with the bold panicles of the lilac.

Left: *Clematis montana* var. *rubens* forms a backdrop to *Allium hollandicum*, white-variegated moneyplant (*Lunaria annua* var. *albiflora* 'Alba Variegata'), and wood forget-me-nots.

Facing page: A fence clothed with a pale form of *Clematis montana* var. *rubens* provides an effective backdrop for purple and white moneyplant (*Lunaria annua* var. *albiflora*).

A

Clematis 'Moonlight'

One of very few light yellow clematis, 'Moonlight' has twisted buds opening into large, showy blooms in palest lemon-yellow with yellow stamens. Although full sun encourages flowering, the delicate coloring of this charmingly informal cultivar is liable to fade, and flowering is poor if it is grown in shade. The elegance of its gently cupped blooms can be heightened by training it on an open shrub such as a branching rhododendron, while their pale color is particularly effective with blue or gold flowers. Brighter yellow flowers such as *Acacia pravissima* and softly colored hellebores make good companions.

◑ *Ceanothus* 'Cascade', *Genista tenera* 'Golden Showers', *Kerria japonica* 'Golden Guinea', *Lonicera* × *tellmanniana*, *Rosa* × *odorata* 'Pseudindica'

H: 2.5m (8ft) ❁ **Late spring to early summer**
◌◌ ◻-▦ **Z4 pH5–8**

Clematis 'Moonlight' grows gloriously with *Ceanothus impressus* and a burnt-orange hybrid *Paeonia delavayi*.

Above: *Clematis* 'Perle d'Azur' is used to extend a border's color scheme upwards, above the pink-purple spikes of *Stachys macrantha*, and the red heads of *Monarda* 'Prärienacht'.

Left: *Clematis* 'Etoile Violette' makes a good match for 'Perle d'Azur', although here both are so large that the supporting obelisk is hidden beneath them. With a bigger support, the clematis could produce a more spectacular display.

Clematis 'Perle d'Azur'

Among the most floriferous and spectacular of the Jackmanii clematis, 'Perle d'Azur' is capable of making almost too solid an expanse of bloom. Such indigestible and excessive gorgeousness can be relieved by intermingling it with another climber such as a vine, honeysuckle, perennial pea, rose, or small-flowered clematis. It is paired with the winegrape (*Vitis vinifera* 'Purpurea') in the celebrated Rose Garden at Sissinghurst Castle in Kent, England, using several plants to cover a large curved wall with a sheet of bloom – an effect that would be totally overpowering in smaller gardens. It looks marvellous with pink, purple, and pale or rich lavender-blue flowers, and with soft purple or silver foliage. Its blue is not sufficiently strong or pure to balance golden yellow, although it is effective with pale lemon. Ideal for walls, it can also be allowed to scramble over large shrubs.

◑ *Clematis tibetana* subsp. *vernayi* 'Orange Peel' p.117 **B**, *C.* 'Ville de Lyon' p.118 **B**, *C. viticella* 'Purpurea Plena Elegans' p.119 **B**, *Hemerocallis* 'Hyperion' p.239 **A**, *Lavatera* 'Barnsley' p.65 **A**, *Lonicera sempervirens* f. *sulphurea*, *Prunus spinosa* 'Purpurea', *Rosa* 'Sander's White Rambler', *Vitis vinifera* 'Purpurea' p.131 **A**

H: 4m (13ft) ❁ **Mid-summer to late autumn**
◌◌◌ ◻-▦ **Z5 pH5–8**

Clematis 'Prince Charles'

Compared to 'Perle d'Azur' (facing page), this Jackmanii cultivar has slightly paler, smaller, more delicate flowers with four or six sepals, making it perhaps more interesting in flower shape, and better suited to smaller-scale plantings seen at closer range. While 'Perle d'Azur' is just strong enough in color to be used in bright harmonies with magenta and cerise and contrasts with lemon, *Clematis* 'Prince Charles' is best in gentler color schemes with white, soft pinks, mauves, and blues, or with smoky purple or silver foliage.

Clematis 'Prince Charles' is shorter than most other Jackmanii or Viticella cultivars, allowing it to be draped over shrubs of moderate size, such as *Berberis thunbergii* 'Golden Ring'. The rich color of the berberis is not a true purple and contrasts with the gentle lavender of the clematis. The smoky hue of purple sloe would be thoroughly harmonious here and equally effective.

◗ *Buddleja* 'Lochinch', *Ceanothus delileanus* 'Gloire de Versailles', *Clematis* 'Alba Luxurians', *C. triternata* 'Rubromarginata', *Hydrangea aspera* Villosa Group, *Lavatera* 'Barnsley', *Prunus spinosa* 'Purpurea', *Rosa* 'Climbing Iceberg', *Salix elaeagnos* subsp. *angustifolia*

H: 2.5m (8ft) ❀ **Early summer to early autumn**
◊◊ ■-■ **Z5 pH5–8**

Clematis 'Venosa Violacea' provides a contrast of floral form with *Lonicera tragophylla*. After its spring pruning, the clematis should be trained to grow into the honeysuckle, with care being taken to maintain a balance between the two, neither plant being allowed to crowd out the other.

Clematis 'Venosa Violacea' ♛

One of the most vigorous Viticella cultivars, 'Venosa Violacea' also has as large a flower as any in its class. The white center to each purple sepal gives a pronounced accent, although the variable number of sepals (from four to six) fails to establish a pattern across the plant; the bicolored effect can also be fussy in larger gardens or at long range and too insistent close up. The flowers look good grown over a background of purple-flushed foliage, although if the purple is too solid, the darker zone of the flower will almost disappear at middle range. Contrasts with yellow or white are attractive in detail but may lose their appeal over the large area that this cultivar can fill. Harmonies with deep mauve or dusky carmine are more successful. 'Minuet' ♛ is similar, having flowers with four sepals and of a slightly lighter tone.

Clematis tibetana subsp. *vernayi* 'Orange Peel'

Often sold under the collectors' number LS&E 13342, this Tangutica clematis has finely divided, glaucous leaves, and bell-shaped flowers that open chartreuse, are pure yellow in full bloom, and age to orange-brown. Partners in cream, pale yellow, or orange will flatter all these color phases. Light pruning in spring results in flowers from early summer to mid-autumn. If grown through shrubs or wall plants, its height can be restricted to about 4m (13ft) by pruning more severely and it will flower a month or so later. Its silky white seed heads appear before flowering finishes and last through winter.

◗ *Campsis radicans*, *Eccremocarpus scaber*, *Hedera colchica* 'Sulphur Heart', *Helianthus debilis* subsp. *cucumerifolius* 'Italian White', *Ipomoea lobata*, *Tithonia rotundifolia* 'Torch', *Tropaeolum majus* 'Gleam Mixed'

H: 6m (20ft) ❀ **Early summer to mid-autumn**
◊◊ □-■ **Z6 pH5–8**

The yellow of *Clematis tibetana* subsp. *vernayi* flatters *C.* 'Perle d'Azur', but its greenish young flowers and orange-brown older ones mix less pleasantly.

◗ *Clematis* × *triternata* 'Rubromarginata', *C. viticella* 'Purpurea Plena Elegans', *Lonicera nitida* 'Baggesen's Gold' p.66 **A**, *Prunus spinosa* 'Purpurea', *Rosa glauca*, *R.* 'Karlsruhe' p.142 **A**, *R.* 'Sophie's Perpetual' p.145 **C**

H: 4m (13ft) ❀ **Mid-summer to mid-autumn**
◊◊ □-■ **Z5 pH5–8**

This harmonious mixture of *Clematis* 'Victoria' (right),
an unnamed Viticella cultivar (center), and *C.* 'Kermesina'
(left), also of the Viticella Group, offers blooms of varying
size. It is chosen so that all three plants flower together.

Clematis 'Victoria'

The Jackmanii cultivar 'Victoria' matches
'Perle d'Azur' (p.116) in the quality and
quantity of its blooms, although it has never
gained the same popularity – perhaps because
the mauve of 'Victoria' is not as rare as the
lavender-blue of 'Perle d'Azur' and does
not contrast pleasantly with light yellow.
Nevertheless, its color combines agreeably
with pinks, carmines, crimsons, lavender-
blues, and purples, as well as with purple
foliage, but its vigorous growth suits it to
draping only larger shrubs or small trees.
Like all cultivars with regularly shaped
flowers, the repeated pattern of its blooms
enhances the display. 'Victoria' is superb
planted in association with late-flowering
Rambler roses and smaller-flowered clematis.

◐ *Clematis* 'Huldine', *C.* × *jouiniana* 'Praecox' p.112 **A**,
C. × *triternata* 'Rubromarginata', *C.* 'Venosa Violacea',
Lathyrus grandiflorus, *L. latifolius*, *L. odoratus* 'Matucana'
(spring sown), *Maurandya barclayana*, *Prunus cerasifera*
'Nigra', *P. spinosa* 'Purpurea', *Rosa* Super Dorothy, *R.*
Super Excelsa, *Vitis vinifera* 'Purpurea'

H: 4m (13ft) ❊ **Mid-summer to early autumn**
▰▰▰▱ ◊◊ ▱-▰ **Z4 pH5–8**

Clematis 'Ville de Lyon'

'Ville de Lyon' is a Jackmanii cultivar with
six slightly overlapping sepals. The rather
solid outline of the flower is alleviated by
the color gradation within each sepal, dark
at the edge with a bright crimson center,
contrasting the central boss of creamy yellow
stamens. Its color is just light enough to
show up against deep purple foliage and it
is attractive combined with pink, mauve, or
lavender-blue flowers. Acid contrasts with
chartreuse flowers or foliage are good,
although few climbers have this coloring.
'Ville de Lyon' can, however, be trained
over shrubs of moderate size, or against a
wall with tall herbaceous plants in front. This
helps hide its worst defect, the bareness of

Clematis 'Ville de Lyon' with *C.* 'Comtesse de Bouchaud'
and *C.* 'Jackmanii Superba' provide an eye-catching
combination of sumptuous crimson, pink, and purple.
Greater variety of flower size might give even more impact.

the lower parts of the stems by late summer.
While usually hard-pruned in early spring,
this clematis can be treated less severely,
shortening stems to the uppermost pair of
plump buds, and it will then produce flowers
in early summer.

◐ *Aconitum* 'Newry Blue', *Cercis canadensis* 'Forest
Pansy', *Clematis* 'Hagley Hybrid', *C.* 'Minuet',
C. 'Prince Charles', *C.* 'Victoria', *Eupatorium
purpureum*, *Filipendula rubra*, *Foeniculum vulgare*,
Humulus lupulus 'Aureus', *Prunus cerasifera* 'Nigra'

H: 3m (10ft) ❊ **Mid-summer to mid-autumn**
▰▰▰▱ ◊◊ ▱-▰ **Z4 pH5–8**

Clematis viticella '**Purpurea Plena Elegans**' 🏆

Although lacking the elegantly nodding flowers of the plain species, *C. viticella* 'Purpurea Plena Elegans' and the similar, larger-flowered, deep lavender-blue *C.v.* 'Mary Rose' are both plants of considerable charm. Their blooms usually have four larger outer sepals, giving them a roughly square outline, the pale reverse of the unopened sepals providing a contrasting button centre. Soft plum-purple 'Purpurea Plena Elegans' is the more vigorous, although 'Mary Rose' has perhaps a more effective color for contrasts with soft yellow or yellow-green.

Both plants carry their flowers with a poise that can be lost if they are trained too tightly against a wall. Their slender growth habit makes them ideal for growing through shrubs and wall plants and into small trees; they rarely produce a solid canopy of foliage and so do not harm their companions. Their muted colors and complex flowers make them most effective when seen at close range, for instance on a pergola. They are excellent with late-blooming Rambler roses or clematis with larger, brighter flowers, but they can be overwhelmed by the most dazzling colors. Like all Viticella clematis, these plants need pruning in early spring.

⬤ *Actinidia kolomikta*, *Clematis* 'Hagley Hybrid', *C.* 'Little Nell', *C.* 'Prince Charles', *C.* 'Victoria', *Hydrangea aspera* Villosa Group, *Ipomoea purpurea*, *I. tricolor* 'Crimson Rambler', *Jasminum officinale*, *Lophospermum erubescens*, *Mutisia oligodon*, *Rosa* Super Dorothy, *Salix alba* var. *sericea*, *S. elaeagnos* subsp. *angustifolia*, *Vitis vinifera* 'Purpurea'

H: 4m (13ft) ❄ **Mid-summer to early autumn**
▬▬▬ ◌◌ ☐-◼ **Z5 pH5–8**

Right: A successful blend combines *Clematis viticella* 'Purpurea Plena Elegans' with the bolder, dark purple *C.* 'Jackmanii', grown together on an iron "balloon".

Below: The colors, sizes, and growth habits of *Clematis viticella* 'Purpurea Plena Elegans' and *C.* 'Perle d'Azur' are ideally suited to each other. After pruning, both cultivars need careful training and tying to their supports to ensure they are well blended and balanced.

A

B

Eccremocarpus scaber ♈

GLORY FLOWER

The flowers of this rather tender semi-evergreen climber are usually orange, but several variants exist, including gold f. *aureus*, carmine-red f. *carmineus*, f. *roseus* with deep carmine-pink flowers, and an unnamed apricot variant. All produce a cheerful and continuous display over a long season, from late spring through to the autumn frosts. In cold areas the plant may be grown as a half-hardy annual, and where summers are cool it benefits from a warm site against a sunny wall. It climbs by means of leaf tendrils and so needs wires on a wall or trellis; in the open it will climb up a tepee of poles or drape over a large shrub. It combines well with hot colors, and with yellow-green, purple, or bronze foliage, and contrasts with pure blue or blue-green, for example glaucous-leaved shrubs or blue-green painted trellis. If grown in containers, plants can be overwintered in frost-free conditions, and then will flower earlier the following year. Where winters are mild, plants often self-seed freely.

Ceanothus × *delileanus* 'Gloire de Versailles', *Clematis* 'Perle d'Azur', *Cotinus coggygria* 'Royal Purple', *Solanum crispum* 'Glasnevin'

H: 5m (16ft) Late spring to mid-autumn
Z9 pH5.5–7.5

Typical orange-flowered *Eccremocarpus scaber* is matched in growth by the Tangutica clematis 'Bill MacKenzie', the two mingling together without either being suppressed by the other. The flowers of the eccremocarpus harmonize in color and contrast in form with those of the clematis.

A

B

Hedera canariensis 'Gloire de Marengo' ♈

The severity of a house wall is here softened by a covering of pale *Hedera canariensis* 'Gloire de Marengo', contrasting with the bright berries of a pyracantha. Purple smoke bush (a cultivar of *Cotinus coggygria*) and *Juniperus chinensis* 'Plumosa Aurea' attractively fill the space in front.

Like all other ivies, this is an evergreen climber, with large handsome leaves, shallowly lobed and deep green with grey-green and creamy white variegation. It is one of the least hardy of commonly grown ivies, and its foliage is easily damaged during a cold winter, but plants recover rapidly in spring. Even so, in cold areas it benefits from wall training, perhaps with foliage of a different color such as purple or yellow-green, or as a contrast to bright flowers. In favored localities it is an excellent ground-cover plant, valuable as winter cover through which to grow evergreen shrubs, early-flowering perennials such as hellebores, and plants like dogwoods and willows with colorful winter stems. It may also be combined with another climber against a trellis or chain-link fence.

Although blending well with any color, it looks outstanding with cool colors like carmine-pink, and harmonizes with silver foliage and white flowers. Good companions include pyracanthas and plants with large flowers or inflorescences, especially clematis and climbing hydrangeas; it will also contrast effectively with autumn-coloring climbers such as parthenocissus or a vine.

Fuchsia magellanica var. *gracilis* p.53 **B**, *Hedera helix* 'Buttercup' p.122 **A**, *Parthenocissus quinquefolia*, *P. tricuspidata*, *Vitis vinifera* 'Purpurea'

H: 5m (16ft) (Autumn)
Z8 pH5.5–7.5

Hedera colchica ♔

PERSIAN IVY

This handsome evergreen climber with deep green, shiny, heart-shaped leaves is a vigorous, relatively hardy plant valuable both for training on wires against a wall and for use as a ground cover over a large area. It is immensely useful for a woodland garden or border planted for spring or winter, particularly where foliage effect is needed before deciduous plants have come into leaf. When used as a ground cover, and kept close to the ground by occasional cutting back in spring, it can be underplanted with bulbs such as lilies or narcissi. Its variegated forms bring welcome light to dark corners, especially if underplanted with colchicums

and autumn-flowering crocuses, their lilac blooms producing a striking effect against the creamy yellow mat of foliage. An effective foil for plants of any color, it is outstanding with pale flowers, and lighter green, yellow-green, silver, or variegated foliage.

Among numerous cultivars are 'Dentata' ♔, which has lobed leaves and less of a tendency to climb, a useful characteristic where trees might be invaded; and 'Dentata Variegata' ♔, with yellow-edged leaves dazzlingly variegated with pale green shot with yellow – this can be used in the same way as *H. canariensis* 'Gloire de Marengo' (facing page), especially with hot colors or for contrasts with purple or blue. In 'Sulphur Heart' ♔, the center of the leaf is greenish yellow, only slightly less brilliant than 'Dentata Variegata', but with a more definite

shape to the variegated zone. It makes a handsome backdrop for a richly colored climber, such as a red rose or purple clematis, remaining attractive in winter when its companion is leafless.

◐ *Bergenia cordifolia* 'Purpurea', *Clematis* 'Jackmanii' p.111 **C**, *Cornus stolonifera* 'Flaviramea', *Lonicera × tellmanniana* p.127 **C**, *Parthenocissus henryana* p.128 **A**, *P. quinquefolia* p.128 **B**, *Rosa* 'Mermaid' p.142 **B**, *Salix alba* subsp. *vitellina* 'Britzensis'

H: 10m (33ft) ❀ **(Autumn)**
◌◌ ▢-▧ ■ **Z6 pH5.5–7.5**

Grown across a carpet of winter heaths, the bright variegation of *Hedera colchica* 'Sulphur Heart' can add sparkle in winter, especially if the heaths have such richly colored flowers as this *Erica × darleyensis* 'Arthur Johnson'. Heathers with colored foliage could also be used.

A

Above: *Hedera helix* 'Buttercup', rather pale through being grown in sun, and white-variegated *H. canariensis* 'Gloire de Marengo' here show the shrubby or "arborescent" habit characteristic of mature ivies, producing attractively billowing branches. Such a partnership could serve as an effective backdrop for blue flowers or dark foliage.

Below: Ivies such as *Hedera helix* 'Manda's Crested' can provide a carpet of attractive ground-covering foliage, even spreading across paving as here. Used in this way, the ivy acts as a foil for a formal globe of dwarf boxwood (*Buxus sempervirens* 'Suffruticosa') and a loose lime green mound of lady's mantle (*Alchemilla mollis*).

Hedera helix
EUROPEAN IVY

There are hundreds of cultivars of this evergreen self-clinging climber, including some with variegated foliage in yellow-green, gold, or silver, and many with differently shaped leaves. It thrives in sun or shade, although yellow-green cultivars are brightest in full sun. Because it attaches itself permanently to walls, it does not combine easily with other climbers, but different ivies planted near each other can create a tapestry of varied leaf forms, and once these are established other climbers can be trained in – parthenocissus is a particularly striking partner, especially in full autumn color. Ivy also makes an effective ground-covering foil for herbaceous plants and bulbs, although hormones from its roots can suppress and even kill competing shrubs such as yew. However the plant is grown, annual clipping is necessary to keep it in trim; mid-summer is the best time for this, or early to mid-spring if another climber is used with the ivy.

Anemone blanda, Calluna vulgaris 'Robert Chapman', *Ceanothus* 'Cascade' p.36 **A**, *Galanthus elwesii* var. *monostictus, Lonicera caprifolium* p.126 **B**, *Parthenocissus quinquefolia* p.129 **A**, *P. tricuspidata* p.128 **C**, *Schizophragma hydrangeoides* 'Roseum', *Solenostemon scutellarioides* (mixed) p.401 **C**

H: 5m (16ft) ❀ **(Autumn)**
🌢🌢 ◼ - ◼ **Z5–7 pH5–8**

The bright yellow-green foliage of *Humulus lupulus* 'Aureus' contrasts with a carpet of long-flowering, perennial *Viola* 'Huntercombe Purple'. Another climber with flowers that harmonize with the viola, such as a clematis or morning glory could be, planted a little distance away from the roots of the hop and trained into it, to help break up the mass of hops leaves and unify the arrangement.

Humulus lupulus 'Aureus' ♛
GOLDEN HOP

This is a rampant herbaceous climber, with yellow-green leaves and greenish yellow flowers in summer. Although it tolerates some shade, it is most colorful in full sun. Its vigorous growth makes partnerships with other climbers difficult, and it can smother any shrub over which it is grown, so it is most useful as a background to contrasting flowers or foliage – to the tall spikes of aconites, for example, or to late-flowering blue shrubs such as *Ceanothus* × *delileanus* cultivars. It is not self-clinging, but may be trained on wires or trellis on a wall or pillar, perhaps as a foil for dark green evergreens, or behind columns or obelisks of climbers with richly contrasting flowers such as clematis. It tends to grow straight upwards on a wall, forming a fairly dense mass of growth, and it is helpful to train it out sideways at frequent intervals from the time it starts growing in spring.

Aconitum hemsleyanum, Campanula latifolia, Ceratostigma willmottianum, Clematis 'Kermesina', *Coronilla valentina* subsp. *glauca* 'Variegata' p.42 **A**, *Delphinium* 'Alice Artindale' p.208 **B**, *Lonicera* × *heckrottii* 'Gold Flame' p.126 **C**, *Phormium tenax* 'Veitchianum', *Rosa* 'Frensham', *Tolpis barbata* p.403 **A**

H: 6m (20ft) ❀ **(Summer)**
🌢🌢 ◼ - ◼ **Z5 pH5.5–7.5**

Morning glory (*Ipomoea lobata*) can be used to weave through much shorter herbaceous plants or shrubs, including bush roses. Here, its flowers create a brilliant contrast of color and form with a rich rose-pink cultivar of *Phlox paniculata*. For a more subtle effect, a cream phlox could be used, or a magenta one for even more pizzazz.

Ipomoea lobata

SPANISH FLAG

Although it is strictly a perennial climber, the morning glory (syns *I. versicolor, Mina lobata*) is usually treated as an annual. Its flowers are formed in a spike, with florets along one side and becoming smaller towards the tip; these range in color from red through orange and yellow, to soft cream on the mature flowers. Probably unique in the plant world, this arrangement has a charming effect and makes an excellent contrast for flowers of larger size and more solid outline. Grown as an annual, the morning glory makes a wispy climber, suitable for training into shrubs and over herbaceous plants, or for growing against a wall or another support. It is particularly effective combined with hot colors, set against bronze, purple, or dark red foliage, or contrasted with lime green, carmine-pink, or magenta flowers. The cultivar 'Citronella' is predominantly pale yellow, and useful for combinations with rich gold or contrasts with blue.

⦿ *Atriplex hortensis* var. *rubra, Berberis thunbergii* f. *atropurpurea, Dahlia* 'Bishop of Llandaff', *Lychnis coronaria, Nicotiana* 'Lime Green', *Parthenocissus tricuspidata, Rosa* 'Frensham', *Tropaeolum speciosum*

H: 3m (10ft) ❀ **Mid-summer to mid-autumn**
◊◊ Z10 pH6–7.5

Ipomoea tricolor 'Crimson Rambler'

Although sky-blue morning glories are perhaps the most familiar, purple, red, and even light brown cultivars are also available. Despite its name, 'Crimson Rambler' is almost primary red, and mixes well with both hot colors and cool shades such as true crimson, purple, and lavender. Like *I. lobata* (above), it is a tender perennial, usually grown from seed as an annual for planting out when temperatures are warm enough for it to grow vigorously (mid-summer in cooler regions). It stands out most conspicuously against flowers of significantly different size, form, or color, and contrasts well with silver foliage (but is too dark to show up against dark red or purple). Good partners are small-flowered clematis, flamboyant climbers including campsis, lophospermums, and *I. lobata*, and contrasting yellow-green climbers such as golden hop (facing page). Morning glories are at their best early in the day, closing their blooms in the afternoon.

Trained tall to be seen against the blue of the sky, red *Ipomoea tricolor* 'Crimson Rambler' and yellow canary creeper (*Tropaeolum peregrinum*), with their contrasting flower shapes and compatible growing habits, create a striking combination of primary colors.

⦿ *Abutilon vitifolium* 'Veronica Tennant', *Artemisia ludoviciana* 'Silver Queen', *Clematis* 'Etoile Violette', *Crocosmia* 'Lucifer', *Lophospermum erubescens, Pyrus salicifolia* 'Pendula'

H: 3m (10ft) ❀ **Mid-summer to mid-autumn**
◊◊ Z10 pH6–7.5

A cascade of *Ipomoea tricolor* 'Heavenly Blue' tumbles through a wall-trained *Plumbago auriculata* in matching azure. Broad-leaved *Fatsia japonica*, grey-green *Brachyglottis* (Dunedin Group) 'Sunshine', and pots of agapanthus provide a contrast of foliage and form to decorate the base.

Ipomoea tricolor 'Heavenly Blue' ♀

A tender perennial often grown as an annual, this is perhaps the best known morning glory, with exquisite sky-blue flowers with a white eye – a coloring so striking that it is highly valued in spite of its fleeting beauty. Like the other ipomoeas on this page, it needs warm summer weather to thrive, but can be a superb climber for draping over shrubs or to intertwine with other wall plants, and also looks outstanding scrambling up an obelisk or pillar, against a contrasting background. It combines well with glaucous, silver, or yellow-green foliage and cream or white flowers, and contrasting with yellow flowers. The best partners are those with flowers of differing sizes or forms – the tiny white blooms of the climber *Solanum laxum* or the yellow ones of canary creeper, for example, or a small-flowered white clematis such as *C. flammula* or a yellow clematis like those in the Tangutica Group.

⦿ *Argyranthemum* 'Jamaica Primrose', *Artemisia ludoviciana, Coronilla valentina* subsp. *glauca, Elaeagnus* 'Quicksilver', *Fremontodendron californicum, Hedera helix* 'Buttercup', *Hemerocallis* 'Golden Chimes', *Hippophae rhamnoides, Kniphofia* yellow cultivars, *Lonicera caprifolium, Philadelphus coronarius* 'Aureus'

H: 3m (10ft) ❀ **Mid-summer to mid-autumn**
◊◊ Z10 pH6–7.5

Jasminum nudiflorum ♔
WINTER JASMINE

The green winter stems of this sprawling deciduous shrub provide a satisfying contrast to the bright yellow flowers. Its habit of growth makes it an easy plant to train up against a wall, allow to tumble downwards from the top of a wall or bank, or even grow in the mortar of an old wall. It can be used as a flowering backdrop for hellebores, winter irises, and snowdrops, and combines well with evergreen wall plants such as ivies, or with berry plants that retain their fruits over winter, including pyracanthas and *Cotoneaster horizontalis*. Although this jasmine flowers best in sun, it tolerates some shade. While the plant itself is relatively hardy, the flowers can be harmed by severe frost – where this may be a problem, a west-facing aspect should be chosen to avoid morning sun damaging frosted buds and flowers.

◐ *Galanthus nivalis*, *Garrya elliptica* 'James Roof', *Hedera colchica*, *Helleborus* × *hybridus*, *Ilex aquifolium* 'J.C. van Tol', *Pyracantha coccinea* 'Lalandei'

H & S: 3m (10ft) ❀ **Late autumn to early spring**
◌◌ ▨ ▰ **Z6 pH5.5–8**

Trained low across a wall, winter jasmine (*Jasminum nudiflorum*) can interact with even the shortest early-flowering plants such as this winter iris, *I. unguicularis*. Used in this way, the jasmine could equally be combined with snowdrops, hellebores, or Reticulata irises.

The blooms of the white Chilean bellflower (*Lapageria rosea* var. *albiflora*) are strikingly pure in form and color, contrasting well with darker flowers such as *Rhodochiton atrosanguineus*. To succeed, they need a site with enough sun for the rhodochiton but not too much for the lapageria.

Lathyrus latifolius '**Albus**' ♔

The slender growth of this white variant of the broad-leaved everlasting or perennial pea allows it to be draped over other shrubs and climbers without smothering them. It can be used to scramble through plants on a wall, and will enliven early-blooming shrubs whose foliage is relatively dull, such as flowering currant, philadelphus, deutzias, or lilacs. The flower color permits combinations with almost any other, but is perhaps most effective with cool-colored flowers, in contrasts with the foliage of dark evergreens, and in subtle or subdued harmonies with silver-leaved plants. It combines successfully with flowers of contrasting shape and color, such as Viticella clematis cultivars or pure blue morning glories. 'White Pearl' ♔ is similar but with larger flowers, while 'Rosa Perle' ♔ has pale pink flowers.

◐ *Artemisia ludoviciana*, *Clematis* 'Venosa Violacea', *Deutzia scabra*, *Elaeagnus* 'Quicksilver', *Lavandula lanata*, *Paeonia lactiflora* 'Albert Crousse', *Ribes sanguineum*, *Rosa* 'Carmenetta', *R.* 'Cerise Bouquet', *R.* 'Constance Spry', *R.* 'Pink Perpétué', *Santolina chamaecyparissus*, *Syringa vulgaris*

H: 1.8m (6ft) ❀ **Early summer to early autumn**
◌◌ ▨ **Z5 pH5.5–7.5**

Lapageria rosea ♔
CHILEAN BELLFLOWER

This evergreen climber is a variable species in the wild, and although its large, bell-shaped flowers are normally rich crimson, color variations include 'Flesh Pink' ♔, 'Nash Court' ♔, in which the flowers are delicately marbled in pale pink, and the creamy white var. *albiflora*. It is quite demanding in its cultivation and needs moisture, a mild climate, and preferably some shade, requirements that often make it most suitable for growing in a greenhouse. There (and outdoors in favored localities) it may be combined with smilax species with marbled leaves, berberidopsis, billardieras, vine-like plants such as some species of cissus and parthenocissus, mandevillas, sollyas, maurandyas, rhodochitons, and silver- or white-variegated foliage.

◐ *Asparagus densiflorus* Sprengeri Group, *Cissus rhombifolia*, *Euonymus fortunei* 'Silver Queen', *Hedera helix* 'Glacier', *Smilax aspera*

H: 5m (16ft) ❀ **Early summer to late autumn**
◌◌ ▨ ▰ **Z9 pH5–6.5**

Herbaceous (or annual) climbers such as *Lathyrus latifolius* 'Albus' are in many respects easier to use for draping shrubs such as *Berberis* × *ottawensis* f. *purpurea* 'Superba' than are woody climbers like clematis or honeysuckle: each can be managed between leaf fall and spring, pruning the shrub or removing some of the pea to maintain balance without the need for difficult disentanglement. A dark-leaved shrub such as this berberis makes a superb foil for the pea.

Above: Sweet peas combine well with clematis flowers or seedheads, as here with *Lathyrus odoratus* 'Noel Sutton' and the silvery heads of *Clematis macropetala*, but the seedheads tend to lose their sheen before the pea stops blooming.

Below: *Lathyrus odoratus* 'Matucana', a sweet pea with small, unruffled but intensely fragrant flowers in maroon and light pinkish violet, here blends well with soft magenta *Geranium psilostemon* 'Bressingham Flair' and *Erysimum* 'Bowles' Mauve'. The round seedheads of *Allium hollandicum* repeated throughout add interest and unity.

Lathyrus odoratus

SWEET PEA

Modern sweet peas, all classed as Spencer cultivars, come in a wide range of colors, from white to deep indigo-blue and plum-purple, as well as cream, scarlet, and salmon-pink. These climbers, grown as biennials from an autumn sowing to flower in early to mid-summer, or as spring-sown annuals to flower from mid-summer to early autumn, may be grown on supports such as trellises, tepees or brushwood, or be allowed to scamble over shrubs. Some cultivars are strongly scented and ideally these should be positioned near a window or sitting area to appreciate the fragrance. Partnerships should be with plants that flower at about the same height and time – possibly other annual climbers such as lophospermums and morning glories or, for a contrast, eccremocarpus or perennial peas. Dwarf cultivars can tumble over a low wall or be grown in containers, either trained upward on short supports – for instance a tripod up to about 60cm (24in) high – or allowed to trail over the edge to intermingle with other plants. All benefit from regular deadheading to encourage prolonged flowering.

Clematis 'Kermesina' p.112 **B**, *Crambe maritima*, *Gypsophila paniculata*, *Lathyrus rotundifolius* p.125 **C**, *Lophospermum erubescens*, *Verbena bonariensis*

H: 60cm–2.5m (2–8ft)
Early summer to early autumn
Z6 pH5.5–7.5

The rather small flowers of *Lathyrus rotundifolius* provide subtle variety when scrambling together with those of a sweet pea (*L. odoratus*) cultivar. Beneath, the imposing flower heads of spider flowers (*Cleome hassleriana*), in a mixture of perfectly harmonious colors, offer a more striking contrast of form.

Lathyrus rotundifolius

This is a slender herbaceous perennial pea, useful for planting so that it twines over small or medium shrubs, or covers the base of a wall. The brick coloring of its flowers blends with other warm hues such as dusky red, burnt orange, salmon-pink, peach, or apricot, and mixes well with bronze foliage, such as some berberis or cotinus. It will also scramble over a Ground Cover or Patio roses, and it is slender enough to be allowed to twine into herbaceous plants with flowers in sympathetic colors, such as achilleas. 'Tillyperone', which is vibrant magenta-pink, combines successfully with purple foliage and cool colors such as mauve, paler pink, crimson, lavender, and lilac, and can be planted against shrubs such as cistus, lavenders, olearias, and any with silver or purple leaves.

Achillea 'Lachsschönheit', *Berberis thunbergii* f. *atropurpurea*, *Cotinus coggygria* 'Royal Purple', *Rosa* 'Buff Beauty', *R.* Sweet Dream

H: 1.8m (6ft) Early to late summer
Z5 pH5.5–7.5

The dainty blooms of *Lonicera × americana* mingle freely with those of *Clematis montana* var. *wilsonii*. Maintaining a balance between two such vigorous climbers is difficult unless the two are planted some distance apart and trained towards each other. Hard pruning will be needed every few years, being more severe on the dominant climber. Instead, each could be trained to horizontal wires on a wall, but an unnatural effect, with honeysuckle and clematis alternating evenly, is best avoided.

Lonicera × heckrottii 'Gold Flame' here contrasts with golden hop (*Humulus lupulus* 'Aureus'). The hop dies back in winter, allowing the honeysuckle, which should be planted some distance away, to be pruned or retrained. The hop's vigorous new shoots need to be trained out sideways from the time they emerge and thinned occasionally later.

Lonicera × americana

Like most deciduous climbing honeysuckles, *L. × americana* can be draped over a large shrub or small tree, or mingled with other climbers on a wall. Its long, elegant florets give a filigree effect, contrasting well with flowers of more solid outline, and they have a strong scent that carries well, especially in the evening. Harmonies with similar tones, such as mid-pink roses, are best seen at close range, while a more contrasting companion works better from a distance – carmine, strong red, white, palest buff, pink, or yellow flowers, and purple foliage, all mix effectively at longer range. After an abundant early summer flush, there is still enough bloom to combine with late summer flowering Viticella clematis. The similar *L. × italica* ♀ is often supplied under this name.

◉ *Clematis* 'Etoile Violette' p.110 **A**, *C.* 'Kermesina', *Cotinus coggygria* 'Royal Purple', *Prunus cerasifera* 'Nigra', *Rosa* 'Climbing Iceberg', *R.* 'Goldfinch'

H: 9m (30ft) ❀ **Early summer to autumn**
◊◊ ▢-▧ **Z6 pH5–8**

Lonicera caprifolium ♀

ITALIAN WOODBINE

Vigorous enough to scramble into a small tree, this deciduous woodbine has a creamy yellow tint that suits it to combinations with white, rich gold, and even soft orange, or with purple foliage. Close-range harmonies with pale yellow or peach are attractive. Most clones have a pink tint in their florets; 'Anna Fletcher' lacks this, and therefore may be used in contrasts with light to mid-blue flowers. As with all the more vigorous honeysuckles, this species needs to be trained outwards when young to prevent its growing straight up and forming a congested clump at the top. Occasional pruning is needed to prevent its overwhelming a supporting shrub, or to maintain balance with another climber.

◉ *Clematis montana*, *Corylus maxima* 'Purpurea', *Eccremocarpus scaber*, *Magnolia grandiflora*, *Rosa* 'Madame Alfred Carrière', *R.* 'Maigold', *R.* 'Paul Noël'

H: 6m (20ft) ❀ **Late spring to late summer**
◊◊ ▢-▧ **Z6 pH5–8**

Lonicera caprifolium has been trained out across *Cotinus coggygria* 'Royal Purple' to stop it smothering the bush. European ivy (*Hedera helix*) provides winter color.

Lonicera × heckrottii

The coral-red trumpets of the deciduous or semi-evergreen *L. × heckrottii* have golden orange mouths, giving a rich coral-orange effect, a good contrast for chartreuse foliage. Freely produced in summer, they are brilliant carmine in bud, and fragrant. The oval or elliptical leaves, reddish purple when they emerge in spring, mature to a lustrous blue-green, especially on their underside, making a striking combination with the flower color. The flower heads are a little congested and less elegant than in some honeysuckle species, making them less effective for leavening a display of large, round flowers. *L. × heckrottii* combines well with salmon-pink, peach, or apricot flowers, and is also pleasing with buff or gold, and with bronze or purple foliage. The more vigorous 'Gold Flame' is brighter and more yellow in the mouth.

◉ *Berberis × ottawensis* f. *purpurea* 'Superba', *Cotinus coggygria* 'Royal Purple', *Philadelphus coronarius* 'Aureus', *Rosa* 'Buff Beauty', *R.* 'François Juranville'

H: 4m (13ft) ❀ **Early to late summer**
◊◊ ▢-▧ **Z6 pH5–8**

Above: *Lonicera periclymenum* 'Belgica' in its second flush of flower, with Viticella clematis 'Polish Spirit'. The clematis does not show up well from afar, so this grouping is best seen close up. *L.p.* 'Graham Thomas' would also succeed here, flowering more profusely with the clematis.

Right: Soft yellow *Lonicera periclymenum* 'Graham Thomas' pairs well with cream *Lilium* 'Roma'; both do well in sun or partial shade. The less formal *L. martagon* var. *album* better match the woodbine's semi-wild habit.

Lonicera periclymenum
WOODBINE

The semi-wild appearance of this vigorous deciduous woodbine suits it to wilder parts of the garden – in lightly canopied woodland for instance. It has tubular, two-lipped flowers, which are white to crimson or soft yellow on the outside, and white aging to yellow within. The flowering season differs according to variety: 'Belgica' ♀ (early Dutch honeysuckle) flowers mainly in early summer, with some later blooms; the creamy yellow 'Graham Thomas' ♀ flowers from mid-summer to early autumn, as does the crimson and cream 'Serotina' ♀. Yellow sorts combine well with white, gold, or soft blue; pink and cream clones can be used with white or mid- to deep pinks; and crimson and cream ones are especially good with peach or rich pink.

◉ *Ceanothus* × *delileanus* 'Gloire de Versailles', *Clematis* 'Kermesina', *Rosa* 'Cerise Bouquet', *R.* 'Climbing Iceberg', *R.* 'François Juranville'

H: 7m (23ft) ❀ **Early summer to autumn**
◊◊ ☐-■ **Z5 pH4–8**

Lonicera × tellmaniana ♀

This superb but scentless deciduous hybrid has a single flush of flowers in golden orange, a color so rich that it can look out of place in wilder parts of the garden, and is perhaps best in more cultivated areas. It contrasts well with chartreuse foliage or purple flowers, and harmonizes with cream, yellow, orange, or red flowers, and with bronze or purple foliage. The plant is rather too big and vigorous to grow over shrubs, and its display can be too diffuse if grown through a small tree. It is, however, ideal for a shady wall, tolerating shade better than most other honeysuckles; it will also thrive in sun, provided the root run is cool and moist. Its slightly more vigorous parent *L. tragophylla* ♀, which can be used in the same ways, produces flowers that are closer to pure yellow.

◉ *Clematis* 'Moonlight', *C.* 'Niobe', *Fremontodendron* 'California Glory', *Hedera helix* 'Buttercup', *Philadelphus coronarius* 'Aureus', *Rosa* 'Leverkusen'

H: 5m (16ft) ❀ **Late spring to early summer**
◊◊ ☐-■ **Z6 pH5–8**

Lonicera × *tellmanniana* and *Hedera colchica* 'Sulphur Heart' make a pleasing partnership, but are best planted some distance apart to avoid root competition. The ivy will cling to the wall, allowing the honeysuckle to be trained over it.

Varied leaf shapes and sizes create a pretty pattern when *Parthenocissus henryana* is grown with the ivy *Hedera colchica* 'Sulphur Heart'. A sunny site intensifies the colors of both.

Parthenocissus henryana ♔

Like most others of its genus, this self-clinging deciduous climber can attach itself to walls or tree trunks without support. The silvery markings at the center of the leaflets are more pronounced when grown in shade, although the fiery scarlet autumn color tends to be brighter in sun. When the stems have climbed to the top of their support, they will flow gracefully downwards, making a veil of subdued but dainty foliage. It can also be grown over a ground cover, but if this is too flat the elegantly draped effect may be lost. Its growth is not as profuse and blanketing as that of its relatives, Boston ivy and Virginia creeper (right), making it much more amenable to combinations, and it is especially effective with gold autumn color or berrying plants such as the larger pyracanthas. Since the foliage of *Parthenocissus henryana* is small and delicate, it is best seen at close range. In colder gardens it succeeds best on a wall.

Celastrus orbiculatus, *Cotoneaster salicifolius* 'Rothschildianus', *Juniperus × pfitzeriana* 'Pfitzeriana Aurea', *Lindera obtusiloba*, *Vitis* 'Pulchra'

H: 10m (33ft) ❀ **(Summer)**

◊◊ ◻-◼ **Z7 pH5.5–8**

Parthenocissus quinquefolia ♔
VIRGINIA CREEPER

This deciduous self-clinging climber is extremely useful for covering brickwork and tall fences, although it looks more natural tumbling downwards, through large trees, for example, than growing tightly up against a wall. Its divided leaves make for a fairly delicate effect, and provide superb autumn color. It works best mixed with a companion plant that grows away from the wall a little, allowing Virginia creeper to cascade from its partner's outermost twigs, forming intriguing, uneven patterns. Its vigorous growth can be a problem, but regular pruning (preferably not to an unnaturally straight line) will maintain the balance with neighboring plants, and prevent it from blocking gutters.

Ilex × altaclerensis 'Camelliifolia', *Juniperus squamata* 'Blue Carpet' p.62 **A**, *Malus × zumi* 'Golden Hornet', *Pyracantha* 'Soleil d'Or', *Robinia pseudoacacia* 'Frisia'

H: 15m (50ft) ❀ **(Summer)**

◊◊ ◻-◼ **Z4 pH5.5–8**

Above: The autumn color of *Parthenocissus quinquefolia* breaks up an expanse of a cream-variegated ivy (*Hedera colchica* 'Dentata Variegata'), creating attractive patterns.

Facing page: A mature English ivy (*Hedera helix*) produces elegant sprays of rich green foliage, seen distinctly against Virginia creeper's bright autumn leaves.

Parthenocissus tricuspidata ♔
BOSTON IVY

The lobed leaves of Boston ivy turn a brilliant red to purple color in autumn. The uses and cultivation requirements of this vigorous, self-clinging deciduous climber are similar to those of Virginia creeper (above). However, the greater vigor and more solid outline of the leaves of Boston ivy make it harder to integrate with other plants. In particular it looks good planted on the back of a wall and allowed to fall over the top to form a curtain across the face, thinning as necessary for the

The lobed leaves of *Hedera helix* 'Oro di Bogliasco' sit easily with *Parthenocissus tricuspidata*, fiery red in autumn.

benefit of other plants trained there. 'Lowii' is less vigorous with smaller, deeply lobed leaves, best at closer range; 'Veitchii' turns deep purple in autumn, forming a striking contrast with scarlet-tinted foliage.

Celastrus orbiculatus, *Fraxinus excelsior* 'Jaspidea', *Liriodendron tulipifera*, *Pyracantha atalantioides* 'Aurea', *P. rogersiana* f. *flava*

H: 20m (65ft) ❀ **(Summer)**

◊◊ ◻-◼ **Z5 pH5.5–8**

The large, pink-tinted flower heads of *Schizophragma hydrangeoides* 'Roseum', grown at the foot of a sunny wall, contrast in form with the tiny stars of *Trachelospermum jasminoides*. The grassy leaves of *Iris unguicularis* add foliage contrast and promise a winter display.

Schizophragma hydrangeoides 'Roseum'

A deciduous climber that attaches itself by means of aerial roots, this is a hydrangea relative with "lacecap" flowers, creamy white in the species and soft rose-pink in this cultivar. It is a fairly tender plant that needs a mild climate with plenty of moisture and ideally some shade. In areas where frost is a possibility, it is best planted on a west-facing wall to avoid sun-scorch on frosted shoots and to minimize any rain-shadow effects caused by the wall. It can also be grown up the trunk of a tree, initially attached firmly to a support until climbing freely. It combines well with pink or red flowers, such as berberidopsis and mandevillas, with purple foliage, and with white-variegated ivies, and is effective with other climbers that have contrasting leaves, such as some ampelopsis or parthenocissus. The creamy white flowers of *Schizophragma hydrangeoides* ♥ itself can be combined effectively with gold-variegated or yellow-green foliage.

⬤ *Ampelopsis glandulosa* var. *brevipedunculata* 'Elegans', *Hedera canariensis* 'Gloire de Marengo', *H. helix* 'Buttercup', *Sambucus nigra* 'Guincho Purple'

H: **12m** (40ft) ❀ **Mid- to late summer**
⬤⬤ ☐-☐ ☐ **Z8 pH5.5–7.5**

Tropaeolum speciosum ♥
FLAME NASTURTIUM

This perennial relative of the annual nasturtium, with herbaceous stems growing from fleshy tuberous roots, flowers most prolifically if the roots are kept cool and moist, with the shoots in full sun. It can be used to stunning effect with the roots protected by the base of a broad hedge, while the stems grow over the face of the hedge, especially one with fine, dark foliage such as yew – however, clipping needs to be timed after the yew's flush of new growth but before the tropaeolum stems begin to climb. This combination of hedge and elegant creeper is immensely effective and hard to improve upon, although flame nasturtium can also be used to form an integral part of a hot-colored scheme. A partially shaded woodland garden is a suitable setting, with the climber draped across shrubs, especially those with bronze foliage or dark evergreens, or as a striking contrast with yellow-green foliage.

⬤ *Acer palmatum* (purple-leaved), *Amelanchier lamarckii*, *Hydrangea serrata* 'Rosalba' p.60 **C**, *Ilex aquifolium*, *Rhododendron luteum*, *Tropaeolum tuberosum* p.130 **C**

H: **4m** (13ft) ❀ **Mid-summer to mid-autumn**
☐☐ ◇◇ ☐-☐ ☐ **Z7 pH5–6.5**

Spectacular trails of *Tropaeolum speciosum* drape themselves across a somber hedge of common yew (*Taxus baccata*). The surface of the hedge is angled towards the sun, encouraging the flame nasturtium to bloom profusely.

Tropaeolum tuberosum 'Ken Aslet' flowers from mid-summer, coinciding with the entire season of the flame nasturtium (*T. speciosum*). Its trumpet-shaped blooms and peltate leaves harmonize with those of its companion but differ sufficiently to create a very effective combination.

Tropaeolum tuberosum
AÑU

This is a tuberous herbaceous perennial with twining stems, and relatively small yellow, orange, or red flowers. The most commonly grown sort, var. *lineamaculatum*, does not flower until autumn, but 'Ken Aslet' ♥ is in bloom from mid-summer. Although it blends with hot colors, it is more useful with warm hues like red, salmon, peach, apricot, and burnt orange, with bronze foliage, and yellow-green foliage or flowers. It can be planted on supports such as twiggy stakes, or allowed to trail over shrubs such as bronze-leaved berberis, warm-colored roses, and golden elderberries or philadelphus. It combines well with red-, yellow-, or orange-flowered morning glories, nasturtiums, canary creeper, and other tropaeolums, and golden hops.

⬤ *Berberis* × *ottawensis* f. *purpurea* 'Superba', *Humulus lupulus* 'Aureus', *Rosa* 'Geranium', *Sambucus nigra* 'Aurea', *Vitis vinifera* 'Purpurea'

H: **4m** (13ft) ❀ **Early to mid-autumn**
⬤⬤ ☐-☐ ☐ **Z8 pH5.5–7**

When *Clematis* 'Perle d'Azur' starts to bloom in mid-summer, the leaves of *Vitis vinifera* 'Purpurea' are downy grey, becoming gradually less so but more flushed with purple as the season advances. At all stages, the color of the vine and its handsome leaves flatter the clematis and punctuate its almost too solid sheet of bloom.

Vitis vinifera 'Purpurea' ♛

The leaves of this tendril climber emerge downy and grey, and only start to assume purplish tints from mid-summer, becoming deep maroon-purple before they are shed. This handsome foliage is a good foil for cool-colored flowers in early summer, including clematis and roses, and continues to blend with these colors in late summer as it turns purple; by late autumn the tone is distinctly reddish and blends equally well with autumn-coloring foliage and hot colors. During the summer its greyish coloring complements climbers such as *Solanum crispum* and its cultivars, maurandyas, and wall-trained buddlejas. Its autumn tints provide a deeper tone to complement the lighter, brighter colors of other true vines, parthenocissus and celastrus species, and free-fruiting species or Rambler roses. Good drainage is a strong influence on fine autumn color, so heavy soils should be lightened by incorporating coarse gravel at planting time.

Acanthus spinosus, Buddleja fallowiana, Celastrus orbiculatus Hermaphrodite Group, *Clerodendrum bungei* p.39 **B**, *Parthenocissus henryana, Rosa* 'Albertine' p.138 **A**, *R. rugosa* p.160 **B**, *Vitis coignetiae*

H: 7m (23ft) ❀ **(Early summer)**
Z6 pH5–7.5

Wisteria sinensis ♛
CHINESE WISTERIA

This is a vigorous, deciduous twining climber suitable for growing on trellises, pergolas, and walls; it can also be trained as a standard, used perhaps as a focal point or at intervals to punctuate a border, while in areas with hot summers it may be allowed to scramble into trees. The long racemes of usually lilac-blue flowers are born with extraordinary profusion and combine well with early-flowering clematis such as *C. montana* cultivars, early Rambler roses like the Lady Banks cultivars, ceanothus, and laburnums. (However, laburnums' strong yellow can slightly overwhelm the more delicate coloring of the wisteria and might be better partnering *W. sinensis* 'Alba' ♛.) Chinese wisteria is a superb plant for pergolas or arcades because the pendant racemes of flowers hang down within the framework, although *W. japonica* 'Multijuga' ♛, with racemes 45cm (18in) long, is sometimes even more spectacular. Where trained lower down a wall or other structure, or when used as a standard, wisteria's pendulous blooms can interact with shorter shrubs, such as genistas or berberis, or with herbaceous or bulbous plants, such as taller alliums or (especially with white wisteria) crown imperials. Wisteria enjoys plenty of moisture at its roots and is a classic climber for training along rustic bridges and fences near ponds, where its lavish display can be reinforced by reflections in the water.

Allium hollandicum, Ceanothus 'Concha', *Euphorbia griffithii* 'Dixter', *Fritillaria imperialis, F.i.* 'Maxima Lutea', *Syringa vulgaris* 'Charles Joly' p.95 **A** ⌐ p.63 **A**

H: 9m (30ft) ❀ **Late spring**
◊◊ Z5 pH6–8

In areas with warm summers, *Wisteria sinensis* will produce plentiful bloom without severe annual pruning, allowing a much more informal effect than would be seen on spur-pruned plants kept trained close against a sunny wall. This delightful informality is here beautifully enhanced by swags of white *Clematis montana*, which is of comparable vigorous growth and will remain, at least for a few years, in equilibrium with the wisteria.

ROSES

THE MOST VERSATILE of garden plants, roses are capable of climbing boldly to the top of a tall tree or decorating a small pot with elfin charm. Their popularity is ensured by their ability to blend subtly with other shrubs and climbers or to be the focal point of a display that includes less flamboyant companions.

FOR CENTURIES, the rose has intrigued gardeners and plant breeders alike. As a result of this fascination and the untiring work of the plant breeders, there are now roses for almost every garden situation: swooning shrubs laden with scented flowers for borders and shrubberies, elegant climbers to festoon pergolas and arches, rampant ramblers to adorn trees and walls, neat and tidy bushes to use as bedding, and minute patio plants to fill pots, window boxes, and raised beds.

Rose flowers come in an enormous variety of colors and forms, and many are beautifully fragrant. Some rose plants flower only once a year while others bloom sparsely but more-or-less continuously over a long period or produce several flushes of blooms. While the leaves are rarely the reason they are grown, plenty of roses do have attractive and healthy foliage. A few species and varieties also have brightly colored hips that extend the season of interest.

Because the rose genus is so large, horticulturists have divided it into different categories according to habit of growth and the form and presentation of the flowers. These categories include Climbing and Rambler roses,

Long after their flowers have faded, many Shrub and Climbing roses continue to delight the eye with their late summer and autumn display of colorful hips, while also offering sturdy support for later-flowering climbers such as clematis and perennial sweet peas, as here in a border in Vita Sackville-West's Sissinghurst garden.

old and modern Shrub roses, Hybrid Teas and Floribundas, and Ground Cover roses. Many of the categories are further subdivided. All this can make choosing a rose seem a difficult task. However, it simplifies matters to consider the two main ways that roses are used in gardens: the shrubby roses and many of the climbers are perfect for integrating into the garden as a whole, while the larger-flowered roses, such as the Hybrid Teas and Floribundas, are suitable for more formal presentations.

Roses in beds and borders

The type of rose that is ideal for growing in mixed borders or shrubberies tends to produce large trusses of fairly informal, softly colored flowers on plants with ample foliage. Apart from the modern "old" roses, most of these are shrubs that have one main flush of bloom with perhaps a second sprinkling later in the season. There is also a huge variety of species roses that are excellent used in this way.

All these roses will complement a wide variety of herbaceous plants, as well as each other, and they are very versatile because they may be left to grow into large masses or pruned regularly to produce small plants with more blooms. They are less useful as accent plants as their soft forms and usually indistinct foliage mean they are not very remarkable once flowering is over.

Although a little too brash for some tastes, the bright scarlet, white-eyed blooms of Floribunda rose Eye Paint can provide a racy element in imaginative combinations with softer colors such as the delicate pink of Silene dioica.

Rosa Pink Symphony, a small Floribunda or Patio rose of great quality, has the perfect combination of dense and shrubby but informal growth and outstanding flower color to be a success in a container, especially beside a border of complementary coloring.

Although often used for formal arrangements (see below), some of the larger-flowered roses with their clear colors and freedom of flowering can be invaluable in mixed borders. Memorable and long-lasting effects can be achieved by interspersing the strong-colored types with cannas, dahlias, and scarlet salvias, or using the paler-colored ones with grey foliage plants – artemisias, cranesbills, or pinks, for example.

Formal rose beds

Roses suitable for planting alone or in geometric beds usually produce large flowers of exquisite shape in a steady trickle over long periods. Unlike many of their forebears, most of the recent introductions have compact growth, numerous flowers, and good resistance to disease. However, their habit of growth is gaunt and their foliage is sparse and, therefore, formal rose gardens require careful complementary planting if they are to be attractive for more than a few weeks of the year. Edging the beds with box or lavenders or, less formally, with stachys, saxifrages, or other low-growing evergreens will provide a longer season of interest as well as emphasize the geometry of the beds in a way that the roses themselves cannot. In the summer, carpets of violas or cranesbills will decorate the garden more fully at ground level and will harmonize with most rose colors. As in mixed borders, standard roses can be used to introduce greater height, and climbers – roses or others – can be grown up obelisks, over arches, or on trellises to ensure year-round structure.

Planting notes

Roses are grown for their flowers, so they are always best where these can be fully appreciated, especially if they are fragrant. Even the taller shrubs should be planted near the front of borders, where they will also produce a useful variation in height. Where roses are grown over arches, careful tying in is necessary to keep the thorns away from eyes, skin, and clothes.

Climbing & Rambler Roses

CLIMBING ROSES may be divided into two main classes: Ramblers and Large-flowered Climbers (including Climbing Hybrid Teas and Climbing Floribundas). Among the old roses, all Noisettes and Boursaults are Climbers, while Bourbons, Chinas, Hybrid Perpetuals, and Teas include a few climbing varieties.

Ramblers include hybrids of the fragrant *R. multiflora* and glossy-leaved *R. wichurana*, as well as the stronger-growing species roses, including rampant kinds like *R. filipes* (known botanically as *Synstylae* roses). They produce vigorous new shoots near the base of the plant each year, which flower the following year. Flowered stems are normally cut out immediately after flowering, but this can be difficult if the rose is entwined with another climber; in this case, it is usually possible to prune both rose and companion in late winter. Shorter-growing Ramblers are ideal for obelisks and as ground covers or, if grafted onto tall stems, as weeping standards. Varieties of average vigor make stems long enough to reach over a pergola or arch, or along a trellis; they can also sprawl into large shrubs or small trees; some may be trained against walls, although disease can be a problem here. The most vigorous sorts are best in a wild garden, where they can be left to scramble unrestrained into trees.

Large-flowered Climbers usually have fewer main stems, each of which provides flowering sideshoots for several years. Pruning, in late winter, consists of cutting back both main stems and sideshoots, and removing some older stems to encourage strong new growth. With their few stems and often coarse foliage these roses can look somewhat gaunt on a pergola or obelisk, and less so on a wall, but growing them in close association with another climber can improve their appearance.

A

Rosa 'Albertine' ♕

A rose that has found a special place in gardeners' affections, this Wichurana Rambler flowers just once, at the height of summer, but so lavishly that the dark green foliage can disappear beneath the exuberant display. The fully double salmon-pink blooms, born singly or in small sprays, emerge from copper-red buds and are deliciously scented.

The rose is vigorous enough to be grown on a pergola or an arch, and also succeeds trained against a wall. It is outstandingly effective when associated with purple, bronze, red, or copper-flushed foliage, and combines particularly well with blood-red, peach, apricot, cream, or white flowers. Yellow-green flowers make good partners, but yellow-green foliage may tend to overwhelm it.

Trained to mingle agreeably against a wall, the double flowers of *Rosa* 'Albertine' and the lobed leaves of the ornamental vine *Vitis vinifera* 'Purpurea' complement each other beautifully in both color and shape. It is unusual for this vine to be so strongly purple-flushed when *R.* 'Albertine' is in full bloom, except when grown in a nutrient-poor soil in a dry, sunny situation or hot climate.

This rose is fairly prone to mildew, particularly when grown against a wall, where air flow is restricted, but is relatively healthy if allowed to scramble freely into small trees or to develop as a sprawling, rather lax bush in the open garden.

○ *Jasminum officinale* 'Aureum', *Lonicera* × *italica* Harlequin, *Photinia* × *fraseri* 'Red Robin', *Physocarpus opulifolius* Diabolo, *Rosa* 'American Pillar' p.139 **A**

H: 5m (16ft) S: 4m (13ft) ❀ **Mid-summer**
◐◐ ▣-▣ **Z5 pH5.5–7.5**

Rosa 'American Pillar'

This robust Wichurana Rambler has clusters of single, white-eyed, rich carmine flowers born in one exuberant summer display, and glossy, deep green foliage. It is excellent for growing on pergolas or in trees, and may be trained on walls, although here it tends to suffer from mildew. It is valuable for creating brilliant, large-scale effects, but at close range its flowers are marred by the anthers turning brown before the petals are shed. Partnerships with lighter carmine or crimson flowers and purple or red-flushed foliage work well, and the blooms make pleasant contrasts with yellow-green flowers or dazzling clashes with orange. Its brashness can be tempered by combining it with silver foliage.

◉ *Acacia baileyana* 'Purpurea', *Cotinus coggygria* 'Royal Purple', *Eucalyptus kybeanensis*, *Euphorbia sikkimensis*, *Knautia macedonica*, *Senecio viravira*

H: 5m (16ft) S: 4m (13ft) ❄ **Mid- to late summer**
◌◌ ▤-▤ **Z5 pH5–7.5**

The strongly colored single blooms of *Rosa* 'American Pillar' are here combined with the more delicate pink rose *R.* 'Albertine' and *Helichrysum petiolare*. The helichrysum, with its elegant sprays of grey-green foliage tipped with clusters of creamy flowers, is an ideal companion for the roses in warmer climates, where it can be grown outdoors year-round, trained against a wall for shelter.

Rosa banksiae 'Lutea' ♕
YELLOW LADY BANKS ROSE

The graceful, arching stems of this lovely Banksian rose look best if they are trained only loosely against a wall, allowing the swags and sprays of soft butter-yellow flowers to display themselves with a natural informality.

Each tiny bloom is fully double and lightly scented. This rose makes good contrasts with blue flowers, and harmonizes with white, cream, peach, and apricot. Plants with yellow-variegated foliage, variegated ivies, and many kinds of clematis are excellent partners.

This is the hardiest of the Banksian roses, suitable for growing against a sheltered, sunny wall. In areas with cool summers, plants may thrive but tend not to flower so profusely. Unlike most other Ramblers, this does not need annual pruning; once every five to ten years is usually enough.

The charming single yellow Banksian rose, *R.b.* 'Lutescens', is more fragrant than 'Lutea', as are the white Banksian roses, namely *R.b.* var. *banksiae* (formerly known as *R.b. alba* or *R.b. alba-plena*), which is double, and the original wild, single-flowered *R.b.* var. *normalis*. None of these is as hardy as the double yellow form.

◉ *Acacia dealbata*, *Aquilegia chrysantha*, *Ceanothus arboreus* 'Trewithen Blue', *Euphorbia characias* subsp. *wulfenii* 'Purple and Gold', *E. griffithii* 'Dixter', *Hedera colchica* 'Dentata Variegata', *Kerria japonica* 'Pleniflora', *Ribes × gordonianum*, *Wisteria sinensis*

H & S: 6m (20ft) ❄ **Late spring**
◌◌ ▤-▤ **Z7 pH5.5–7**

Many evergreen ceanothus coincide with *Rosa banksiae* 'Lutea'. Here, the rich blue flowers of *Ceanothus* 'Concha' contrast perfectly with the rose's butter-yellow blooms. Looser training of the rose would also be effective, resulting in trails of blooms cascading over the clouds of blue.

Rosa 'Brenda Colvin'

This *Synstylae* Rambler, with single pale pink flowers that fade as they age, inherits the vigor of its parent, *R. filipes* 'Kiftsgate' (facing page). This is both an asset and a limitation. Too vigorous to respond to annual pruning, it is not recommended for use on a wall; however, it can cover the largest pergola, will scramble through a medium-sized tree in a wild garden or orchard, and may be used on a large, informal hedge. Here, strongly colored flowers and foliage can seem unnaturally bright, so it is best combined with white flowers and with grey or delicately red-flushed foliage. Bolder pairings with, for example, rich pink flowers or strongly red-flushed foliage would be more successful on a large pergola; a robust vine would be a good companion, as would another Rambler of equal vigor, perhaps with pure white or smaller, double flowers.

Chamaecyparis lawsoniana 'Pembury Blue', *Lonicera japonica* var. *repens*, *Prunus cerasifera* 'Pissardii', *Pyrus salicifolia* 'Pendula', *Rosa* 'Seagull'

H: 9m (30ft) S: 6m (20ft) ❀ **Mid-summer**
◊◊ ■-■ **Z5 pH5–7.5**

The large-flowered *Clematis* 'Comtesse de Bouchaud' is an excellent partner for *Rosa* 'Brenda Colvin', echoing the rose's pink buds and the palest blush of its young blooms. However, the rose is so vigorous that the clematis will occupy only a part of its spread.

Rosa 'Climbing Paul Lédé' harmonizes beautifully with the cinnamon-pink of *Verbascum* 'Helen Johnson', bronze fennel (*Foeniculum vulgare* 'Purpureum') in the foreground, and distant red-leaved Japanese maples, brightened by the greyish shoots of *Cotoneaster simonsii* and white-variegated holly (*Ilex aquifolium* 'Silver Queen'). The blue-green of the obelisk and seat complement the arrangement perfectly.

Rosa 'Constance Spry' ♛

The large, fully double pink blooms of this versatile, once-flowering modern Shrub rose have the sweet fragrance of myrrh, like those of 'Félicité Perpétue' and 'Splendens'. The first of David Austin's English roses (see p.152), this is an unruly cultivar with long pliable branches that demand a lot of space and management when grown as a shrub, and it is often treated to great effect as a climbing rose instead. When trained against a wall, it tends to bloom a little before the main flowering season of old roses, and so is best positioned behind the earliest of these, together with other precocious plants such as philadelphus or early-flowering clematis, and those with silver or purple-flushed foliage. With its vigorous habit and large flowers, it is suited to large-scale plantings, although its short flowering season may be a limitation. This can be redeemed by training a Viticella or similar late-flowering clematis over and through the rose stems.

Clematis 'Princess Diana', *C.* 'Venosa Violacea', *Deutzia* × *elegantissima* 'Rosealind', *Philadephus* 'Manteau d'Hermine', *Vitis vinifera* 'Purpurea'

H & S: 3m (10ft) ❀ **Early summer**
◊◊ ■-■ **Z5 pH5–7.5**

Rosa 'Climbing Paul Lédé'

The first flush of double, yellowish buff blooms on this Climbing Tea rose is highly prolific, and may be followed by occasional later flowers right through until autumn. It is particularly attractive combined with warm tints such as copper, peach, and apricot, and is also good with glaucous foliage. Since its flowers are quite large, it may be used for contrast with a smaller-flowered climber, and looks outstanding when positioned behind tall herbaceous plants with differently shaped flowers, such as those with slender spikes or flat heads. It is deliciously scented and is useful for training on a tall trellis, obelisk, or pergola, and may also be grown against a wall, although here it is prone to fungal diseases.

Achillea 'Inca Gold', *Agastache* 'Firebird', *Elaeagnus* 'Quicksilver', *Hemerocallis* 'Penelope Vestey', *Hosta sieboldiana* var. *elegans*, *Stipa arundinacea*

H: 3.5m (11ft) S: 2.5m (8ft)
❀ **Mid-summer to mid-autumn**
◊◊ ■-■ **Z7 pH5.5–7**

Although *Rosa* 'Constance Spry' flowers earlier than many of the large-flowered Climbing roses, if moderately pruned (with all sideshoots cut back substantially), it will coincide in season with *R.* 'Rambling Rector', whose small, informal white florets contrast effectively in size and color with the lush and glorious blooms of its partner.

The delicate butter-yellow of *Rosa* 'Easlea's Golden Rambler' is a rare choice to combine with rich pink and red. This partnership with red valerian (*Centranthus ruber*) succeeds only through the sheer size, sumptuousness, and profusion of the rose: smaller flowers of this hue would be visually overwhelmed by their more colorful partners.

Swags of *Rosa* × *fortuneana*, studded with charmingly informal, evenly spaced, creamy white blooms, drape themselves through the sumptuous purple flowers of the lilac *Syringa vulgaris* 'Charles Joly'. The rose could also be allowed to tumble through a large, blue-flowered, evergreen ceanothus or a purple-leaved shrub, or used on a wall or pergola together with a purple wisteria.

Rosa 'Easlea's Golden Rambler'

The fragrant, soft butter-yellow flowers of this Wichurana Rambler grow singly or in a cluster, in a single flush in early summer; they are large and fully double, with long, strong stems, and are excellent for cutting. This is a vigorous plant, suitable for training on a pergola or large trellis, and also against a wall, although here it may suffer from fungal diseases. It combines well with gold, white, and warm colors such as peach or apricot, and with bronze-flushed, yellow-green, glaucous, or gold-variegated foliage. Blue flowers make a fine contrast. Because this rose has a limited flowering season, it is perhaps best planted as an ingredient of the early summer garden. If grown where continual display is important, it can be used to support a later-flowering clematis.

◐ *Clematis* 'Alba Luxurians', *Cornus alba* 'Spaethii', *Cotinus* 'Grace', *Digitalis purpurea* 'Sutton's Apricot', *Euphorbia griffithii* 'Dixter', *Lonicera periclymenum* 'Belgica', *Paeonia delavayi*, *Philadelphus* 'Innocence', *Potentilla fruticosa* 'Primrose Beauty'

H: 6m (20ft) **S: 5m** (16ft) ❀ **Early summer**
◌◌ ■-■ **Z5 pH5–7.5**

Rosa filipes 'Kiftsgate' ♛

This is the most vigorous of all the *Synstylae* Ramblers, and in time it can spread to astonishing proportions, smothering even a moderately large tree. Because it is too territorial to be manageable when grown against a wall, and annual pruning and training make little impact on its vigor, it is perhaps best planted in a wild garden, where it can be allowed to scramble harmlessly into medium-sized or large trees (preferably robust, locally native species rather than cultivated ornamentals). Its spectacular flush of single, sweetly scented, creamy white blooms is followed in autumn by a glittering display of sprays of orange-red hips. These combine well with Virginia creeper, Boston ivy, and other plants with fine autumn tints that can be trained through the same trees as the rose.

◐ *Acer platanoides* 'Crimson King', *Ampelopsis megalophylla*, *Fagus sylvatica*, *Fraxinus angustifolia* Raywood, *Parthenocissus quinquefolia*, *Vitis coignetiae*

H: 10m (33ft) **S: 20m** (65ft) ❀ **Mid-summer**
◌◌ ■-■ **Z5 pH5–7.5**

The dark, richly colored foliage of a cherry plum (*Prunus cerasifera* 'Pissardii') makes a dramatic foil for the profuse, creamy white flowers of *Rosa filipes* 'Kiftsgate'. The rose will ultimately suppress even the largest plum unless pruned, although a comparable combination of the rose with a fairly mature, purple-leaved maple or beech, or even a large, dark green conifer, would work well.

Rosa × *fortuneana*

The great virtue of this lovely Chinese hybrid is that it flowers early, in late spring, when its informal, ruffled, double creamy white, scented blooms can be draped like swags over larger shrubs in flower at the same time. It can also be trained against a wall, although here it is most successful if its attractive growth is allowed to cascade freely over other climbers and wall shrubs, rather than being tied tightly to a framework.

The origin of this pretty rose is obscure, although it is generally believed to be a cross between the double white Banksian rose (*R. banksiae* var. *banksiae*) and the Cherokee rose (*R. laevigata*). As such it requires a warm climate with mild winters, so is not suited to north-eastern or Midwestern states, except in particularly warm, sheltered positions.

◐ *Abutilon* × *suntense* 'Jermyns', *Allium hollandicum* 'Purple Sensation', *Ceanothus* 'Dark Star', *Clematis* 'Niobe', *Iris* 'Victoria Falls', *Paeonia rockii*, *Vitis vinifera* 'Purpurea', *Wisteria floribunda* 'Domino'

H: 4.5m (15ft) **S: 2.5m** (8ft) ❀ **Late spring**
◌◌ ■-■ **Z7 pH5.5–7**

The rich, recessive purple of the late-flowering *Clematis* 'Venosa Violacea', its blooms enlivened by their star of pale petal centers, makes an attractive foil for *Rosa* 'Karlsruhe', providing a contrast of floral form. They make excellent companions, both remaining in flower for several months.

Rosa 'Karlsruhe'

This is a moderately vigorous modern Climber, suitable for training on a trellis or against a wall, although its stems are not quite long enough to be trained satisfactorily on a pergola. It has masses of handsome, glossy dark green foliage, and its scented, fully double pink flowers, born in clusters of up to ten, appear in a prolific early flush, with some later blooms occurring throughout the season. It combines well with coral-red, peach, apricot, cream, or white flowers and with red-flushed or bronze foliage, and makes an excellent companion for deep red flowers, such as some clematis cultivars.

One of the parents of this rose is *R. × kordesii*, a hybrid between *R. wichurana* and *R. rugosa*, both noted for their hardy nature.

⊙ *Clematis* 'Rouge Cardinal', *Lilium* Pink Perfection Group, *Phlox paniculata* 'Windsor', *Phygelius × rectus* 'Salmon Leap', *Weigela florida* 'Foliis Purpureis'

H: 2.5m (8ft) S: 1.8m (6ft)
✿ **Mid-summer to mid-autumn**
◖◗ ◊◊ ▪-▪ **Z5 pH5.5–7**

Left to its own devices to form a mound of stems, *Rosa multiflora* is charming in more informal parts of the garden, with the added bonus of powerful fragrance. Here, white foxgloves (*Digitalis purpurea* f. *albiflora*) echo its color and add bold vertical accents, while *Clematis × durandii* provides a gentle contrast in flower shape and color.

Rosa multiflora

This intensely fragrant Japanese species can be grown as a Rambler or as a free-standing shrub, when it will form a broadly spreading mound. It is most at home in a wild garden, where it can be left to scramble informally over hedges and into small trees. Its large clusters of single creamy white blooms are followed in autumn by tiny orange-red hips – very decorative in themselves, especially where they are well lit by the sun – and these can be worked into a planting scheme with other fruit-bearing or autumn-coloring plants. In a wild garden it perhaps looks most effective with plants of contrasting floral form or growth habit such as honeysuckles, foxgloves, cow parsley, and bold grasses. 'Grevillei' (syn. 'Platyphylla'), or the seven sisters rose, is an old Chinese cultivar of similar habit, with sweetly scented blooms in shades of soft pink, deep lilac, and white.

⊙ *Cotoneaster lacteus*, *Eremurus robustus*, *Lunaria rediviva*, *Paeonia lactiflora* 'Bowl of Beauty', *Philadelphus coronarius* 'Variegatus', *Selinum wallichianum*, *Verbascum* 'Gainsborough', *Viburnum rhytidophyllum*

H: 5m (16ft) S: 3m (10ft) ✿ **Mid-summer**
◖◗ ◊◊ ▪-▪ **Z5 pH5–7.5**

Rosa 'Mermaid' ♔

The Macartney rose (*R. bracteata*) and an unknown double yellow Tea rose are the parents of this vigorous but slightly tender hybrid, which bears large, scented, single, pale canary-yellow flowers with a central disk of golden anthers. It is perpetual-flowering and in mild climates holds its glossy, dark green foliage all winter. Where summers are hot, it may thrive in the open garden or over a pergola, but in cooler climates flowering may be sparse unless it is given the protection of a warm wall. Although rather slow to establish a framework of large branches,

The bold boss of stamens at the center of each bloom of *Rosa* 'Mermaid' and the hint of yellow in its petals harmonize with the variegation of the ivy *Hedera colchica* 'Sulphur Heart'. Keeping the latter pruned close to the wall with the rose stems held just clear of the ivy allows occasional pruning or retraining of the rose and facilitates maintenance.

it should be given plenty of space while young because ultimately growth is very vigorous and can cover a large wall area. Its flowers blend well with golden yellow, peach, or apricot flowers and yellow-green foliage, and contrast dramatically with soft blue and the most sumptuous purples and blues.

⊙ *Ceanothus* Zanzibar, *Clematis* 'Helios', *Corokia × virgata* 'Red Wonder', *Cytisus battandieri*, *Fremontodendron* 'Pacific Sunset', *Jasminum officinale* Fiona Sunrise, *Lilium lancifolium* 'Flore Pleno', *Phygelius × rectus* 'African Queen', *Piptanthus nepalensis*

H & S: 6m (20ft) ✿ **Early summer to mid-autumn**
◖◗ ◊◊ ▪-▪ **Z6 pH5.5–7**

Rosa 'New Dawn' 🏆

Although sometimes classed as a Rambler, this is a Climbing rose with relatively large, semi-double, pale pink flowers, often born singly but also in clusters, particularly earlier in the summer. After a prolific early flush of freshly fragrant blooms, it continues to flower, rather less profusely, until autumn. With its vigor and delicate coloring, 'New Dawn' is a good choice for a wild garden, scrambling into trees or over hedges. It may be grown as a lax bush, and is also effective trained on a pergola, but it is too vigorous for even tall pillars or obelisks. Some shade is acceptable, so a wall facing away from the sun is another possible site. It combines especially well with white, lime green, deep pink, or red flowers, and with purple-flushed foliage; honeysuckles make exceptionally attractive partners. 'New Dawn' is a sport of 'Doctor W. Van Fleet', an even more vigorous, once-blooming rose that might be used as an alternative if flowers are needed only in early summer.

🔵 *Centranthus ruber, Cestrum parqui, Deutzia × hybrida* 'Mont Rose', *Lonicera periclymenum* 'Belgica', *Persicaria bistorta* 'Superba', *Viburnum sargentii* 'Onondaga'

H: 3m (10ft) **S: 2.5m** (8ft)
❀ **Early summer to mid-autumn**
⬛⬛⬜⬛ ◇◇ ⬛-⬛ **Z5 pH5.5–7**

In this pleasantly delicate association, the marks at the base of the florets of *Philadelphus* 'Belle Etoile' echo the color of the buds and flowers of *Rosa* 'New Dawn'. This combination would be easier to manage if only a few odd stems of roses were trained from a nearby wall rather than allowing the two plants to tangle.

A

Roses grown on a wall are not limited to combinations with other wall plants. Free-standing shrubs often make good companions as do biennials such as this Scotch thistle (*Onopordum nervosum*), which punctuates the rich blooms of *Rosa* 'Pink Perpétué' with a bold structure of pale leaves.

Rosa 'Pink Perpétué' ♔

A hybrid derived from crossing 'Danse du Feu' with 'New Dawn', this Climbing rose has fully double, deep pink flowers with a pleasant fragrance said to be of green apples, born in clusters from summer into autumn. The stems, which are moderately vigorous and bear small, glossy leaves with purple tints, are too short to reach across the top of a pergola, but provide good coverage for obelisks or for the lower part of a sunny wall. The latter is a particularly good site, encouraging free production of the charming flowers, which have a slight touch of iridescence, making 'Pink Perpétué' equally useful for brightening darker corners and walls. It looks good with late-flowering clematis and Ramblers with smaller flowers, and mixes well with dark red or light to mid-pink flowers, and with red or silver foliage.

🔵 *Berberis thunbergii* 'Rose Glow', *Clematis* 'Duchess of Albany', *Cotinus coggygria* 'Royal Purple', *Phygelius aequalis* Sensation, *Rosa* 'Narrow Water'

H: 3m (10ft) S: 2.5m (8ft)
❋ **Mid-summer to mid-autumn**

 ◊◊ ■-■ **Z5 pH5.5–7**

Rosa 'Rambling Rector' ♔

This is a once-flowering Rambler, with the vigor and powerful, delicious fragrance of its parent, *R. multiflora* (p.142). Its large clusters of small, semi-double flowers open cream and age to white. The central disk of golden anthers is initially attractive, when the flowers first open, but they turn brown with age and are then not so appealing at close range. This is scarcely significant for large-scale effects in sites such as a wild garden, and an established plant in full bloom is a breathtaking sight. The display continues into autumn as polished, rounded red hips follow the flowers. The rose's extraordinary vigor makes pruning and training difficult, and it is perhaps best planted where it can be allowed to grow without restraint – scrambling into a small or medium-sized tree, for example, or tumbling over an unsightly wall as an effective screen. It combines well with honeysuckles and small-flowered clematis.

🔵 *Clematis* 'Perle d'Azur', *Lonicera periclymenum* 'Graham Thomas', *Parthenocissus henryana*, *Rosa* 'Constance Spry' p.140 **C**, *Vitis vinifera* 'Purpurea'

H & S: 6m (20ft) ❋ **Mid-summer**
◊◊ ■-■ **Z5 pH5–7.5**

An intimate combination of three different flowers usually succeeds if each is distinct in at least two of the three major characteristics – size, shape, and color – while achieving pleasant harmonies or contrasts. This combination of *Rosa* 'Rambling Rector', the potato vine cultivar *Solanum crispum* 'Glasnevin', and *Clematis* 'Hagley Hybrid' meets this criterion, creating an attractive, harmonious effect.

Grafted onto a standard-sized stock (1.2m/4ft), *Rosa* 'Sander's White Rambler' makes a dome of cascading white blooms, here surrounded by a contrasting carpet of lavender (*Lavandula angustifolia*). A taller stock would give longer, more dramatic trails of blooms, the curtain of stems broken in places towards the ground, allowing planting to continue beneath the rose.

Rosa 'Sander's White Rambler'

This superlative Wichurana Rambler is fairly late-flowering, producing sprays of formal, double, scented white blooms once in mid- to late summer. The flowers work well with almost any color, but are especially attractive with mid-blues and pastels, and with glaucous or silver foliage. The moderate growth is suitable for obelisks and for training on pergolas. It is also superb for growing as a weeping standard, making good punctuation marks in beds and borders, where plants should stand well in front of others of similar height, leaving the cascades of bloom uncluttered by neighbors. It is an excellent choice for a ground cover, both on the level, with its long, relaxed stems fanned out evenly and pegged down, and over banks, where it can be allowed to trail informally.

Acanthus mollis, Campanula lactiflora, Catananche caerulea, Clematis 'Silver Moon', *Cynara cardunculus, Delphinium* 'Blue Nile', *Lupinus arboreus* (blue), *Miscanthus sinensis* var. *condensatus* 'Cosmopolitan', *Rhamnus alaternus* 'Argenteovariegata', *Salvia aethiopis*

H & S: 4m (13ft) **Mid- to late summer**

 **Z5 pH5–7.5**

Rosa 'Seagull'

The vigor of this Multiflora Rambler, which bears large sprays of mainly single but also semi-double creamy white blooms with prominent golden stamens, makes it suitable for planting in a wild garden, where it can grow freely through a medium-sized tree or scramble over a large hedgerow. It is equally useful for covering a large pergola or expanse of wall, although its strong growth is difficult to prune and train, particularly if it has been combined with another climber. In wilder areas of the garden it is an excellent companion for honeysuckles or the yellow-green foliage of golden hops. It combines well with white, peach, or apricot flowers, and with silver foliage. Its greyish green foliage and rich scent add to its virtues.

Campanula latifolia 'Gloaming' p.200 **B**, *Elaeagnus* 'Quicksilver', *Eryngium × oliverianum, Humulus lupulus* 'Aureus', *Jasminum officinale* Fiona Sunrise, *Ligustrum lucidum* 'Excelsum Superbum', *Lonicera periclymenum* 'Belgica', *Philadelphus* 'Innocence'

H: 6m (20ft) **S: 4m** (13ft) **Mid-summer**
Z5 pH5-7.5

Rosa 'Seagull', growing along a suspended swag from the left of the picture, makes a charming combination where it meets the luscious pink blooms of the Climbing Bourbon rose *R.* 'Blairii Number Two', growing from the right. The vigor of 'Seagull' is more than enough for it to grow up its supporting pole and more than halfway along the rope slung between this and the next pole – an essential requirement for roses used in this way.

Rosa 'Sophie's Perpetual'

This perpetual-flowering Climbing China rose, sometimes classed as a Hybrid Perpetual, is a very old rose of unknown origin. It bears small, deliciously fragrant, loosely double flowers, cerise-carmine on their outer petals and shading to a rich pink center with silvery highlights. It is moderately vigorous and ideal for growing on obelisks, pergolas, and walls, where it combines well with other climbers such as clematis or honeysuckles of similar growth habit. Its color blends with deep crimson or pale pink flowers, and with silver or deep purple foliage, and makes effective contrasts with yellow-green foliage or flowers.

Buddleja fallowiana var. *alba, Cotinus coggygria* 'Royal Purple', *Geranium × oxonianum* 'Winscombe', *Liatris spicata, Ruta graveolens, Weigela* 'Victoria'

H: 2.5m (8ft) **S: 1.2m** (4ft)
Early summer to mid-autumn
Z6 pH5.5–7

The vibrant cerise blooms of *Rosa* 'Sophie's Perpetual' glow against the dusky purple of the Viticella clematis *C.* 'Venosa Violacea'. The pruning of the clematis, cutting it almost to the ground in late winter, is easier than that of a woody climber intertwined with the rose.

Old shrub roses

NO GROUP OF GARDEN PLANTS has a greater power for evoking the romance of the past than the old shrub roses. Their intricately shaped blooms, heady fragrance, and petals with sumptuous textures of satin or velvet are exquisite at close range, yet born in enough profusion for grand effect. Although some do have a short flowering season – just a few glorious weeks at the height of summer – the beauty and quality of these plants offer more than adequate compensation.

The style of the flowers usually reflects the taste of the age when they were bred. Early nineteenth century varieties, such as 'Charles de Mills', generally have formal, flat, intricately quartered blooms; later Victorian types, such as Bourbons, are usually globular and opulent; while those of the *fin de siècle* often have narrower, more elegant buds from which unfurl gracefully scrolled petals. A few (*R. gallica* 'Versicolor', for example) are even more ancient, associated with the Wars of the Roses, the Crusades, or even the world of classical antiquity. Mixed with other old-fashioned plants, they are essential for bringing old-world charm into any garden.

Hard annual pruning is seldom necessary; removal of weak, old, or spindly stems and shortening the longest ones will usually suffice, although occasionally removing large old branches helps to ensure a succession of vigorous flowering stems. However, where smaller bushes are needed, many respond to harder pruning, giving a later, longer flush of larger blooms. Those with long, slender stems benefit from training, either to a frame or by building up a structure from the branches. If the flowers nod, higher training ensures that they face the viewer.

Their foliage is generally uninteresting and tedious when they are planted *en masse*; their appearance is much improved by combining them with plants of boldly contrasting leaf form or color.

Rosa 'Charles de Mills' ♔

The flat, formally quartered, fully double blooms of this fragrant rose are perhaps the most perfect and fascinating of all the Gallica roses. Like its relatives, it flowers just once, in a color that varies according to climate and situation, from deep carmine to crimson, sometimes taking on attractive purplish tints as the blooms age. Relatively short in height, it is suitable for the second or third row of a border, and may be pruned quite severely each year to less than 1m (40in) high, when it is ideal for flower beds or rose displays and for interplanting with alliums such as *A. cristophii*. It blends well with mauve, purple, and pink flowers and, for the duskiest and most sumptuous displays, with purple foliage. It can be contrasted with lime green, yellow-green and, in areas and climates where it takes on the darkest tints, with soft pale yellow. Sometimes said to be the same as 'Charles Lemayeux', 'Charles Lemoine', or 'Charles Wills', in fact the parentage and origin of this rose are not known for certain.

⦿ *Allium × hollandicum* 'Purple Sensation', *Aquilegia* 'Apple Blossom', *Knautia macedonica*, *Salvia nemorosa* 'Rose Queen', *S. officinalis* 'Purpurascens', *Sambucus nigra* Black Beauty

H & S: 1.2m (4ft) ❅ **Early to mid-summer**
◊◊ ▢-▨ **Z4 pH5.5–7**

The superlative rich crimson blooms of *Rosa* 'Charles de Mills' contrast in size and color with the pale-leaved white rose campion (*Lychnis coronaria* 'Alba'), which is echoed in the distance by a white Rambler rose. Harmonious crimson Texensis Group clematis *C.* 'Gravetye Beauty' winds around the nearby post.

A

Purplish crimson *Rosa* 'De Rescht' clashes gently with Shirley poppies, most of which are a bright scarlet color. A hedge of dwarf boxwood (*Buxus sempervirens* 'Suffruticosa') grows at the front of the border, adding a touch of crisp formality lacking in the other plants.

Rosa 'De Rescht' ♔

This is a recurrent-flowering Portland Damask rose of short to moderate height. Its fully double flowers are exquisitely scented and formally quartered, and vary in color from deep carmine to rich crimson, taking on purplish tints as they age. It suits the same combinations as 'Charles de Mills' (facing page), but its ability to flower repeatedly is an added virtue. Other excellent repeat-flowering Portland Damasks include 'Arthur de Sansal', which is compact with upright growth and slightly deeper in color, and 'Indigo' (syn. 'Pergolèse'), 1.2m (4ft) high, with smaller and more distinctly quartered flat flowers. There are two excellent pink Portland Damasks: rose-pink 'Madame Knorr' ♔ (syn. 'Comte de Chambord'), and soft pink 'Marchesa Boccella' ♔ (syn. 'Jacques Cartier').

🌑 *Cleome hassleriana* 'Cherry Queen', *Geranium phaeum*, *Monarda* 'Prärienacht', *Stachys macrantha*, *Teucrium hircanicum*, *Veronica spicata* 'Rotfuchs'

H: 90cm (36in) S: 60cm (24in)
❀ **Mid-summer to mid-autumn**

◊◊ ▢-▦ Z5 pH5.5–7

Rosa 'Fantin-Latour' ♔

Although sometimes classed as a Centifolia, the handsome foliage of this superlative once-flowering, pale rose-pink variety shows the influence of a China-derived rose such as a Bourbon. It is quite vigorous, allowing it to be used in the middle or toward the back of a mixed border, and its fully double flowers, which are very sweetly perfumed and flat when fully open, harmonize well with white, deep pink, light crimson, mauve, lavender, or lime green, and have just enough strength of color to contrast effectively with yellow-green foliage and flowers. It is also very good with silver, red, or purple-flushed foliage. Its strong upright growth will support a Viticella clematis such as 'Minuet' to add later color.

🌑 *Alchemilla mollis*, *Digitalis purpurea*, *Eremurus robustus*, *Euphorbia palustris*, *Geranium* × *oxonianum* 'Julie Brennan', *Lychnis coronaria* Oculata Group, *Rosa* × *francofurtana* 'Empress Josephine' p.147 **C**

H: 1.5m (5ft) S: 1.2m (4ft)
❀ **Early to mid-summer**

 ◊◊ ▢-▦ Z5 pH5–7.5

The charming, soft pink blooms of *Rosa* 'Fantin-Latour' contrast in size and form with the slender spires of the perennial toadflax *Linaria purpurea* 'Canon Went' while matching its color exactly. Mixed foxgloves (*Digitalis purpurea*) echo the shape of the toadflax, which has a slender enough growth habit to weave itself through the rose, integrating the whole arrangement perfectly.

Rosa × *francofurtana* 'Empress Josephine' ♔

The Frankfurt rose, *R.* × *francofurtana*, is thought to be the result of a cross between *R. gallica* and possibly *R. pendulina* (syn. *R. alpina*). Formerly known as a Turbinata rose and now classed as a Gallica, this exists in two clones, by far the superior being 'Empress Josephine', a sprawling, healthy shrub with plentiful, almost thornless stems and fairly dense, large foliage. Its semi-double (sometimes fully double) rose-pink flowers, shaded and veined with lilac, are large,

fragrant, and loosely formed, with slightly wavy petal margins. Although not recurrent, they are so beautiful that this plant deserves to be placed near the front of a border, where it can be appreciated at close range. It combines well with white, crimson, mauve, lilac, and lavender flowers, and with purple, red-flushed, or yellow-green foliage.

🌑 *Centaurea hypoleuca* 'John Coutts', *Hosta* 'Buckshaw Blue', *Hyssopus officinalis* 'Roseus', *Lonicera nitida* 'Red Tips', *Salvia sclarea*, *Viburnum sargentii* 'Onondaga'

H & S: 1.2m (4ft) ❀ **Early to mid-summer**
◊◊ ▢-▦ Z4 pH5.5–7

Sumptuous blooms of *Rosa francofurtana* 'Empress Josephine' are here set above a sea of silvery rose campion (*Lychnis coronaria* 'Alba' and pink-eyed *L.c.* Oculata Group), with a bush of the paler pink *R.* 'Fantin-Latour' behind (top left). A yellow-green leaved shrub in the background provides piquancy, saving the display from potential blandness.

Rosa gallica 'Versicolor' ♔

ROSA MUNDI

This ancient Gallica rose, believed to be medieval, is easy to grow, very floriferous and, like all roses of its class, flowers only once. Its virtually unscented loosely semi-double blooms are reddish pink, striped pale pink, with conspicuous golden anthers. In some seasons, many or most of the blooms can be an unmarked red. It is compact and grows densely enough to make a hedge. Since it responds well to fairly hard pruning it can also be used for a parterre, where it looks effective with the apothecary's rose (*R. gallica* var. *officinalis* ♔), the earliest known Gallica, of which it is a sport. Also sometimes called the red rose of Lancaster, it has light red, fragrant blooms and more vigorous growth, up to 1.5m (5ft) tall. Pruning needs to take into account the differences in growth habit where they are grown together. Both combine well with crimson, pale pink, white, and yellow-green flowers, and with red-flushed or yellow-green foliage. Good companions include alliums and nicotianas.

◉ *Campanula latiloba* 'Hidcote Amethyst', *Dianthus* 'Pink Mrs Sinkins', *Galega* 'His Majesty', *Geranium sylvaticum*, *Lilium candidum*, *Viola cornuta*

H: 80cm (31in) **S: 1m** (40in)
✿ **Early to mid-summer**
◌◌ ▦-■ **Z4 pH5.5–7**

Right: The large, informal blooms of *Rosa gallica* 'Versicolor', extravagantly splashed and striped with palest pink, contrast in size with the slightly taller cranesbill *Geranium psilostemon*, its magenta flowers veined and eyed with glistening black.

Below: The recessive tints of blue love-in-a-mist (*Nigella damascena*) and dusky crimson-purple *Rosa* 'Tuscany Superb' set off the bright flowers of *Rosa gallica* 'Versicolor', while the white rose campion (*Lychnis coronaria* 'Alba') lightens the ensemble. Fairly hard annual pruning has kept 'Tuscany Superb' at about the same height as *Rosa gallica* 'Versicolor'.

Rosa 'Madame Pierre Oger'

A rose of flawless beauty, 'Madame Pierre Oger' benefits from being seen at close range rather than from a distance. Like most other Bourbons, it is repeat-flowering, with fragrant, nodding, globular, double blooms, in white shaded with the most delicate pink. It makes quite long, slender growth that is well suited to training, preferably on a fence or trellis rather than the wall of a house, where it can suffer from blackspot. The subtle pink and white flowers can easily be upstaged by strong colors, so they are best combined with flowers in cool pastel colors and silver or smoky purple-grey foliage. 'Madame Pierre Oger' is a sport of 'Reine Victoria', which has flowers of similar shape but in rose-pink, born on a more vigorous bush.

⊙ *Achillea* 'Forncett Candy', *Aconitum napellus* subsp. *vulgare* 'Carneum', *Berberis temolaica*, *Campanula lactiflora* 'Loddon Anna', *Lavatera maritima*

H: 2m (6½ft) **S: 1.2m** (4ft)
✾ **Early summer to mid-autumn**
◐◐ ▨-▨ Z5 pH5–7

Rosa 'Madame Pierre Oger', its slender stems here bowed by the weight of its full, globular blooms, has flowers of great delicacy, their faint hint of pink toning with the red in the striking, contrasting dark leaves of purple berberis (*B. thunbergii* f. *atropurpurea*).

The chameleon colors of *Rosa* *odorata* 'Mutabilis' embrace the soft yellow, pink, and red found in the blooms of *Alstroemeria* 'Charm', creating a perfect harmony. Both contrast gently with the lilac blooms of the herbaceous *Clematis* 'Arabella' and spires of the perennial toadflax *Linaria purpurea*.

Rosa × *odorata* 'Mutabilis' ♛

Also known as 'Tipo Ideale', this floriferous China rose blooms from early summer until fall frosts, producing scarcely fragrant single flowers that open apricot and age through rich pink to red. With its shrubby habit, it can be grown in borders, including lightly shaded ones, as hedging, and in containers. Its coloring combines well with warm colors such as cream, apricot, peach, coral-pink, and soft red, and it is strong enough to survive partnerships with hot colors such as orange, vermilion, and scarlet. It makes fine contrasts with yellow-green, and associates well with purple or deep red foliage. Like many China roses, it is a little slow to build up into a full-sized bush, and needs very little pruning in its formative years. Even mature bushes flower on very spindly shoots and require minimal seasonal attention.

⊙ *Asclepias curassavica*, *Canna* 'Durban', *Eccremocarpus scaber*, *Fuchsia magellanica* 'Versicolor', *Penstemon barbatus*, *Phygelius* × *rectus* 'African Queen'

H: 1–1.2m (3¼–4ft) **S: 60–90cm** (24–36in)
✾ **Early summer to mid-autumn**
◐◐ ▨-▨ Z7 pH5–7

Rosa 'Prince Charles'

This is a vigorous Bourbon rose, with veined and crinkled double flowers that open light crimson and assume maroon then lilac-magenta tints as they age. Unlike most other Bourbons, it rarely blooms after mid-summer, but it is excellent in an early summer border, combining well with purple foliage and mauve, lilac, or pink flowers, and making an attractive contrast with yellow-green or lime green. Its arching growth is strong enough to support a clematis that will supply color after the roses have finished. Viticellas are outstanding for this purpose, especially a white cultivar such as *C.* 'Little Nell', or purple *C.v.* 'Purpurea Plena Elegans', both of which will complement any late rose flowers.

⊙ *Centaurea montana*, *Geranium sanguineum* 'Cedric Morris', *Linaria purpurea*, *Malva moschata*, *Phuopsis stylosa*, *Verbascum* 'Megan's Mauve'

H: 1.5m (5ft) **S: 1.2m** (4ft)
✾ **Early to mid-summer**
◐◐ ▨-▨ Z5 pH5–7

The purplish crimson blooms of *Rosa* 'Prince Charles' blend perfectly with the pink Damask rose *R.* 'La Ville de Bruxelles' and the large amethyst flower heads of *Allium cristophii*, backed by a cloud of white *Crambe cordifolia*. Adding another relatively tall allium, for example *A.* 'Globemaster', between the roses would help break up their undistinguished foliage and unify the display.

Rosa 'Reine des Centifeuilles'

Centifolia roses are once-flowering shrub varieties derived from the cabbage rose (*R.* × *centifolia*). One of the best Centifolias is 'Reine des Centifeuilles', of superlative floral quality (although unscented) with double blooms that are flatter, larger, and more formal than is usual for this class. The petals are also more open and less tightly packed. A good rose for a mixed border, its clear pink color blends well with white, crimson, deep pink, lilac, lavender, and mauve flowers, and with purple-flushed foliage.

Centifolias do not usually perform well in wet, cool summers of the Pacific Northwest, but 'Reine des Centifeuilles' is more tolerant of cool weather than most.

◉ *Cirsium rivulare* 'Atropurpureum', *Corylus maxima* 'Purpurea', *Erigeron* 'Quakeress', *Eryngium giganteum*, *Salvia verticillata* 'Purple Rain', *Silybum marianum*

H & S: 1.5m (5ft) ❀ **Early to mid-summer**
⬛⬛⬜⬛ ◌◌ ⬜-⬛ **Z5 pH5–7.5**

The intricately pleated blooms of *Rosa* 'Reine des Centifeuilles' harmonize perfectly with the pink toadflax *Linaria purpurea* 'Canon Went'. The toadflax contrasts in shape, as does the lavender goat's rue (*Galega orientalis*), which adds a second harmonious color.

A

B

Rosa 'Tuscany Superb' ♛

The strongly fragrant, semi-double deep crimson blooms of this once-flowering Gallica rose assume purplish tints as they age. They are flat and slightly larger than those of 'Tuscany' (the old velvet rose, from which this was originally a sport), and display fewer prominent anthers at their center. The velvety blooms merit inspection at close range, and combine particularly well with pink, purple, lilac, and mauve flowers, and with purple foliage; they also make effective contrasts with yellow-green foliage or flowers, and with white-flowered, silver-leaved plants.

Although this rose is commonly grown as a freestanding shrub – most often in a border, hedge, or tub – it produces numerous new upright canes from the base each year, and so lends itself to formal training – against a fence, for example. In this case, it may be pruned like a Rambler, by removing all the older canes after flowering.

The bright blooms of white rose campion (*Lychnis coronaria* 'Alba'), and its silvery stems and leaves, help lift the sumptuous but recessive colors of *Rosa* 'Tuscany Superb'. Sky-blue love-in-a-mist (*Nigella damascena*) is even more recessive in color than the rose, letting its partners dominate, although its blooms and feathery leaves add charm to the arrangement.

◉ *Aquilegia vulgaris* var. *stellata* 'Royal Purple', *Astrantia major* 'Ruby Wedding', *Galactites tomentosa* 'Alba', *Geranium* 'Sirak', *Rosa gallica* 'Versicolor' p.148

H & S: 1.2m (4ft) ❀ **Early to mid-summer**
⬛⬛⬜⬛ ◌◌ ⬜-⬛ **Z4 pH5–7.5**

Rosa 'Zéphirine Drouhin' ♛

This is a repeat-flowering Bourbon rose with attractive foliage, tinged bronze-purple when young, and completely unarmed stems, hence its popular name of the thornless rose. Its sweetly fragrant semi-double blooms, which appear continually until fall frosts, have an unsophisticated charm that suits cottage gardens, and they vary in color between carmine-pink and carmine-magenta. They combine effectively with crimson, purple, lavender, and lilac flowers, and with purple foliage; they also make good contrasts with yellow-green foliage and flowers. Excellent companion plants include alliums, nicotianas, and cranesbills.

'Zéphirine Drouhin' may be pruned in the form of a shrub for growing in larger borders or as a tall hedge; alternatively, it can be grown as a fairly short climber, up to about 3m (10ft) in height. If trained against a wall, it can suffer from mildew and blackspot, but on a obelisk or pergola or trained on an open wire fence, where the flow of air is less restricted, it is relatively healthy. Its paler-flowered sport, 'Kathleen Harrop', is equally attractive but slightly less vigorous.

◉ *Cotinus coggygria* 'Royal Purple', *Lupinus* 'Blueberry Pie', *L.* 'Plummy Blue', *Nicotiana sylvestris*, *Persicaria bistorta*, *Phlox paniculata* 'Mother of Pearl'

H 3m (10ft) **S: 2m** (6½ft)
❀ **Mid-summer to mid-autumn**
⬛⬛⬜⬛ ◌◌ ⬜-⬛ **Z5 pH5–7**

Facing page: *Rosa* 'Zéphirine Drouhin', variable in color and here almost at the palest end of its potential color range, blends perfectly with the rich crimson blooms of the Viticella clematis *C.* 'Madame Julia Correvon', which also provides a contrast of flower shape.

Larger species & larger modern Shrub roses

APART FROM THEIR SIZE, the roses in this section have no shared characteristics but fall into a number of categories, each with its own distinct traits and uses.

The species and their primary hybrids tend to be more elegant than the highly bred cultivars. Many are single-flowered and often attractive also for their hips and autumn color. Some, such as *R. moyesii* and *R. glauca* ♀ and their hybrids, have a vase-shaped growth habit, with tall, arching stems that are bare at the base. The ruggedness of such stems can seem out of place in sophisticated borders, but in naturalistic planting is a virtue.

The Rugosa roses, many of them raised around 1900, and so on the cusp of old and modern, have glistening parsley-green foliage that, for some, is almost too vibrant for soft, old-fashioned displays. They are, however, immensely useful for their hardiness, fragrance, continual blooming, and autumn color. They can make an impenetrable thorny hedge.

Hybrid Musk roses, their rich fragrance derived not from the musk rose but mainly from *R. multiflora* (p.142), usually have loosely double blooms in clusters born continually from summer to autumn. Their colors include peach, apricot, and soft yellow, rare in old roses but gentle enough to blend with them, as well as vibrant carmines and scarlets suited to more flamboyant plantings.

David Austin's English roses were bred to combine the floral form of the old roses with the colors and continual flowering of modern varieties. Selected for the English climate, many perform even better in hotter areas such as California, South Africa, or the Mediterranean. Meilland's Romantica Series produces similar roses for the Mediterranean climate.

A

Rosa Bonica ('Meidomonac') ♀

This is a superlative modern Shrub rose, growing to a moderate height and bearing clusters of slightly fragrant, fully double, rose-pink flowers from mid-summer to mid-autumn. The color is close enough to primary pink to be used with both salmons and peaches, and also with cool colors such as mauve, lilac, and lavender. It looks attractive, too, with crimson or white flowers, and silver, glaucous, or red foliage, and makes effective contrasts with yellow-green foliage and flowers. It is excellent for use as a hedge, or in the second row of a mixed border, either as a single plant or in loose groups, preferably with contrasting foliage such as that of day

The large, loosely but charmingly informal pink flowers of *Rosa* Bonica contrast effectively with the dark, dusky pincushion blooms of *Knautia macedonica*, which cover the rose's stems. Light pruning has allowed the rose to grow bigger than usual, making it suitable for combinations with other companion plants on a correspondingly larger scale.

lilies or miscanthus. To hide the base of the shrub, it can be allied with lavenders, catmints, hostas, shorter grasses, or a similar mound-forming plant in front.

◑ *Cosmos bipinnatus* 'Daydream', *Nepeta* 'Six Hills Giant', *Penstemon* 'Alice Hindley', *Phlox paniculata* 'Eventide', *Verbena bonariensis*, *Vernonia noveboracensis*

H: 90cm (3ft) S: 1.2m (4ft)
❀ **Mid-summer to mid-autumn**
 ◌◌ ■-■ Z5 pH5–7.5

The buff-apricot blooms of *Rosa* 'Buff Beauty' are here complemented by the boldly contrasting flower and leaf shape of the bright yellow columbine *Aquilegia chrysantha*. Several other columbines, particularly the North American species and their long-spurred hybrids, have warm-colored flowers, suiting them perfectly to combinations with soft yellow, peach, or apricot roses.

Rosa 'Buff Beauty' ♡

From early summer through to autumn, this handsome Hybrid Musk rose bears large clusters of sweetly scented double blooms that vary in color from pale or medium buff-yellow to buff-apricot, making it especially suitable for blending with white or warm tints such as apricot, soft yellow, or burnt orange, as well as with bronze foliage and yellow-green foliage or flowers. Associations with Spuria irises, daylilies, and bronze sedges are excellent. It makes a large, branching shrub with strong, arching growth that bends gracefully under the weight of its heavy flower trusses, and attractive dark green, sometimes purple-tinted foliage. This can be prone to mildew close to walls and in other positions where airflow is restricted, but in an open border it provides a handsome background to the superb autumn flower display.

⬤ *Alchemilla mollis, Amaranthus hybridus* 'Hot Biscuits', *Bupleurum fruticosum, Carex testacea, Eupatorium rugosum* 'Chocolate', *Foeniculum vulgare* 'Purpureum', *Hemerocallis* 'Cynthia Mary', *Iris* 'Elixir'

H & S: 1.5m (5ft) ❈ **Early summer to mid-autumn**
◊◊ ■-■ **Z5 pH5–7.5**

Rosa 'Carmenetta'

This hybrid between *R. glauca* and *R. rugosa* inherits the typical Rugosa hardiness and vigor, combined with the foliage and loose, open clusters of single, unscented carmine-pink flowers characteristic of *R. glauca* (p.155). In 'Carmenetta', the flowers are followed by an attractive autumn display of hips. Slightly coarser than *R. glauca* in appearance, its thorny stems tend to become bare at the base. This can be perfectly in keeping in a wild garden, where it can make a statuesque, vase-shaped shrub, arching above cranesbills, campanulas, Spuria irises, or glaucous hostas. It is stronger-growing than *R. glauca*, especially on light sandy soils where the good drainage can protect it against rust, and makes an excellent tall windbreak.

⬤ *Clematis × durandii, Geranium phaeum* 'Rose Air', *G. pyrenaicum* 'Bill Wallis', *Hesperis matronalis, Hosta sieboldiana* 'Blue Angel', *M. sinensis* 'China'

H: 2.5m (8ft) S: 2m (6½ft)
❈ **Early to mid-summer**
◊◊ ■-■ **Z4 pH5–7.5**

Although the bare stems of *Rosa* 'Carmenetta' may seem a little rugged for the most sophisticated sites, in more informal settings they can be dramatic and attractive, lifting a cloud of smoky foliage and pink flowers above the carpet of plants beneath. Here, the display includes large pinkish purple alliums (*Allium cristophii*), a variegated weigela, and the upright *Campanula latiloba* and *C.l.* 'Hidcote Amethyst'.

Crambe cordifolia is one of relatively few herbaceous plants that can match the gigantic scale of *Rosa* 'Cerise Bouquet', particularly if several plants are grouped together. Here, the vibrant blooms of the rose are contrasted with the crambe's clouds of tiny white flowers against an azure sky.

Rosa 'Cerise Bouquet' ♡

This is a large, sturdy modern Shrub rose, with greyish leaves and clusters of loosely double, but fairly refined, unscented carmine-red flowers. These appear in a main flush in summer, with a few more in autumn. One of its parents is *R. multibracteata*, from which it inherits its curiously bracted flower stalks. It is very vigorous, able to hold its own in a wild garden, although here the brightly colored flowers might be hard to place. It makes an arching, sprawling shrub for the back of a border or for a large-scale planting with big, bold shrubs and larger herbaceous plants.

It may also be trained on a wall, but the stiff stems can be intractable. 'Cerise Bouquet' combines well with crimson, cerise-pink, or purple flowers and purple foliage, and makes a fine contrast with yellow-green foliage and flowers. Sweet peas can be allowed to climb through its stems, and a pink Rambler rose scrambling into it looks marvelous, although pruning may prove difficult.

⬤ *Achillea* 'Summerwine', *Atriplex hortensis* var. *rubra, Lychnis coronaria, Malva sylvestris* 'Zebrina', *Persicaria amplexicaulis, Weigela florida* 'Foliis Purpureis'

H & S: 4m (13ft) ❈ **Early summer to mid-autumn**
◊◊ ■-■ **Z5 pH5–7.5**

With the simplicity of a briar rose but with larger, more strongly colored blooms, *Rosa* 'Complicata' is ideally suited to a more natural style of gardening using semi-wild flowers, for example this cultivated variant of foxglove (*Digitalis purpurea*).

Rosa 'Complicata' ♈

Although classed as a Gallica rose on the grounds of having *R. gallica* in its parentage, this vigorous shrub is quite unlike other Gallica hybrids in that it has large single flowers and a lax, arching growth habit capable of scrambling into large shrubs and even small trees. The solitary, pale-centered pink blooms, which are delicately scented, are followed by conspicuous round orange hips.

The charm and simplicity of this rose make it especially suitable for inclusion in a wild garden, where it can be grown as a sprawling shrub, associated with flowers such as foxgloves and oxeye daisies. It can also be incorporated successfully into a flowering hedgerow, perhaps combined with other roses such as Ramblers and woven through with honeysuckles, and looks good in a mixed border, where it combines well with contrasting spikes of flowers.

Filipendula rubra 'Venusta', *Leucanthemum* × *superbum* 'Horace Read', *Leuzea centauroides*, *Lonicera periclymenum*, *L. tatarica* 'Hack's Red', *Lythrum salicaria*

H: 2m (6½ft) S: 2.5m (8ft) ✿ Early to mid-summer
◊◊ ■-■ Z4 pH5–7.5

Rosa 'Excellenz von Schubert'

Variously identified as a Polyantha rose or as a Lambertiana, derived from a cross between 'Madame Norbert Levavasseur' and 'Frau Karl Druschki', this Shrub rose may be regarded as a forerunner of the Hybrid Musks. Its sturdy arching stems bear large clusters of very lightly scented, fully double flowers, varying between dark carmine-rose and deep lavender-pink, shaded with lilac, and born recurrently into autumn. If not deadheaded, it will also produce a heavy crop of scarlet hips. Although it starts flowering later than most, this is a rose to be cherished for its continual display. It combines pleasantly with red or purple foliage, and with deep crimson, purple, or pink flowers. It can also be grown by itself as a loose hedge.

Dianthus 'Laced Monarch', *Galtonia candicans*, *Heuchera* 'Magic Wand', *Lamium maculatum* 'Beacon Silver', *Lavandula angustifolia* 'Hidcote Pink'

H & S: 1.5m (5ft) ✿ Mid-summer to late autumn
◊◊ ■-■ Z5 pH5.5–7

The stems of *Rosa* 'Excellenz von Schubert' arch down to meet snow-in-summer (*Cerastium tomentosum*), its silver foliage and white flowers contrasting with the rich coloring of the rose. The ground-covering snow-in-summer could be combined with bulbs.

Extended groups of roses are often more attractive and effective than single ones dotted around the garden. Here, a simple display depends on the repetition of delicate pink *Rosa* 'Felicia' and the contrasting green seedheads of *Allium hollandicum*. These draw the eye along the group towards the bright Hybrid Musk rose 'Vanity'.

Rosa 'Felicia' ♈

This is a superlative Hybrid Musk rose, with clusters of strongly scented, double, soft rose-pink blooms, with salmon and silver overtones, that blend charmingly with white, deep pink, crimson, or soft red flowers, with warm colors such as peach or coral, and also with apple-green. One of the more vigorous Hybrid Musks, it is a bushy, wide-spreading shrub with strong branching stems and plenty of dark green leaves. It is useful in the second row of a border, combined with silver or bronze foliage, or planted behind contrasting foliage such as that of Tall Bearded irises, catmints, or lavenders. Noted for its long flowering season which ends with a flourish, bushes often blooming lavishly in mid-autumn – it is handsome as a specimen shrub – and is good for cutting. It also makes a sturdy, weather-proof hedge, even on light, dry soils where other classes of rose might become thin and unhealthy.

Eupatorium capillifolium 'Elegant Feather', *Iris* 'Jane Phillips', *Nepeta grandiflora* 'Dawn to Dusk', *Potentilla nepalensis* 'Miss Willmott' ❑ p.77 **B**

H: 1.5m (5ft) S: 2m (6½ft)
✿ Mid-summer to late autumn
◊◊ ■-■ Z5 pH5–7.5

Rosa 'Geranium' ♛

The single, soft cherry-red flowers of this
R. moyesii seedling bloom from early to mid-
summer. Although charming, the unscented
flowers are relatively short-lived and are rarely
produced in sufficient profusion to make a
powerful impact. They are followed, however,
by a display of pendant, urn-shaped scarlet
hips, which are among the showiest of the
genus. Coloring in late summer and lasting
well into the winter, they make a distinctive
contribution to hot color schemes and to
autumn plantings, harmonizing with orange
or scarlet flowers and bronze foliage, and
contrasting with yellow-green, blue, or
purple. The plant grows into a tall, arching
bush, often bare at the base, with delicate,
ferny foliage. It makes an impressive autumn
feature when planted with larger miscanthus,
Rubellum or Korean chrysanthemums, and
asters. Occasionally, one of the older, woodier
branches should be pruned out to encourage
a constant supply of vigorous, young, flower-
bearing wood.

◉ *Achillea* 'Fanal', *Canna* 'Wyoming', *Crocosmia*
'Lucifer', *Helenium* 'Bruno', *Helianthus* 'Monarch'
p.235 **A**, *Kniphofia* 'Timothy', *Lobelia* 'Cherry Ripe'
p.259 **B**, *Phygelius capensis* ⊔ p.374 **C**

H: 2.5m (8ft) S: 1.5m (5ft)
❀ **Early to mid-summer**
△△ ■-■ **Z4 pH5.5–7**

The scarlet hips of *Rosa* 'Geranium' are born in sufficient
profusion to make a bold effect, their uniformly nodding
pose giving a distinct pattern to the bush. Here, they
harmonize with other reds – *Penstemon* 'Andenken an
Friedrich Hahn' and the unusual Anemone-flowered
Group dahlia *D.* 'Comet' – together with maiden grass
(*Miscanthus sinensis* 'Gracillimus') for foliage contrast.

In autumn, the vermilion hips of *Rosa glauca* are fully
formed – plump and glistening – and the foliage is glaucous
overlaid with a purple flush, turning to shades of orange,
red, and amber towards the end of the season. The
orange flowers of montbretias (*Crocosmia* × *crocosmiiflora*)
harmonize perfectly with the rose's fruits, while the leaves
provide good contrast in color and form.

Rosa glauca ♛

This is one of a few roses that are grown
mainly for their foliage, which in this species
is glaucous blue-green, flushed with purplish
red if sited in full sun. Like *R. moyesii* and its
hybrids, it tends to make a vase-shaped,
arching shrub that is often bare at the base,
although this can be hidden by surrounding
plants. Small, single, slightly fragrant flowers,
carmine-pink with white centers, appear in
early summer, followed by a lavish display
of orange-red hips; the leaves, too, assume
autumnal tints. In summer it combines well
with cool colors, purples, blues, mauves,
carmine-pinks, and white, and with purple
foliage; if grown in light shade to avoid the
red foliar flush, it is also effective with yellow
flowers. In autumn it makes a brilliant display
with hot-colored crocosmias, Korean and
Rubellum chrysanthemums, and dahlias, as
well as other autumn-coloring shrubs such as
smoke bush, berberis, or euonymus, and with
larger grasses such as miscanthus.

◉ *Crocosmia* 'Dusky Maiden', *Euonymus alatus*,
Kniphofia 'Sunningdale Yellow' p.255 **B**, *Lilium
speciosum* p.329 **B**, *Miscanthus sinensis* 'Malepartus',
Onopordum nervosum p.391 **A**, *Salvia guaranitica*

H: 2m (6½ft) S: 1.5m (5ft) ❀ **Early to mid-summer**
△△ ■-■ **Z4 pH5.5–7**

Rosa Graham Thomas ('Ausmas') ♔

This is one of David Austin's English roses, producing flattish flowers like those of many old Shrub roses. The fully double blooms have a good Tea rose fragrance and are born singly and in clusters, from early summer through to autumn, in a color that varies according to climate and situation from light to mid butter-yellow, occasionally taking on amber tints. The plant is excellent for creating harmonies with warm colors – soft orange, peach, apricot, and cream – and makes a fine contrast with blue. It combines well with yellow-green flowers and foliage, and with silver or glaucous foliage. Vigorous and freely branching as a specimen shrub, it may also be trained against a fence or trellis, up to about 2m (6½ft), especially in warmer climates where it can produce very long stems.

🌐 *Aquilegia vulgaris* 'Mellow Yellow', *Eschscholzia californica* 'Apricot Flambeau', *Hemerocallis* 'Golden Chimes', *Nigella damascena* 'Oxford Blue', *Salvia patens*

H: 1.2m (4ft) S: 1.5m (5ft)
❀ **Early summer to mid-autumn**
◐◐ ▨-▨ Z5 pH5–7.5

Right: Rich blue, columnar flower heads, such as the vertical spikes of *Delphinium* 'Cristella', make a highly effective contrast with the large, round blooms of the yellow rose *R.* Graham Thomas, while the horizontal plates of *Achillea* 'Coronation Gold' provide another contrast of form in a harmonious color. The cone-shaped panicles of lavender *Buddleja* 'Lochinch' behind the delphinium will continue the contrast after the delphinium has finished.

Below: In a combination similar in some ways to the one shown on the right, but this time in harmonious colors, *Rosa* Graham Thomas contrasts in form with the horizontal plates of creamy *Tanacetum macrophyllum* and the sulfur-yellow spikes of *Lupinus* 'Chandelier'.

A

B

In this hot-colored scheme, *Rosa* 'Helen Knight' is paired with the wallflower *Erysimum cheiri* 'Fire King' and the creamy yellow goblets of the peony *Paeonia mlokosewitschii*. The rose has been encouraged to produce blooms on the lower part of the bush by pruning some of the main stems back by about two-thirds of their length.

Rosa 'Helen Knight' ♛

This early-flowering species hybrid, usually classed as a Shrub rose, is the result of a cross between the upright yellow-flowered species *R. ecae* and the sprawling Scotch rose (*R. pimpinellifolia*). 'Helen Knight' has single, unscented, saucer-shaped yellow flowers in one flush, on arching stems that bear the typical ferny leaves of *R. ecae*. The stems themselves are reddish brown or maroon and contribute to the elegance of this unusual rose, which is equally successful trained as a climber on walls and obelisks. It may be combined with warm- or hot-colored, late spring flowers such as wallflowers, tulips, late narcissi, early peonies, and crown imperials. Early cranesbills, brunneras, omphalodes, deeper colored forget-me-nots, and similar blue flowers make attractive companions, as do yellow-green plants such as euphorbias.

◉ *Erysimum × allionii, Euphorbia polychroma, Filipendula ulmaria* 'Aurea', *Fritillaria imperialis, Iris* 'Saltwood', *Polemonium caeruleum, Potentilla recta, Tanacetum vulgare* 'Isla Gold', *Tulipa* 'Golden Artist'

H & S: 2m (6½ft) ❀ Late spring
◌◌ ▣-▪ Z4 pH5.5–7

Rosa 'Highdownensis' ♛

A seedling from *R. moyesii*, this is a handsome, large Shrub rose with copper-flushed foliage, especially on the new growth, and in summer deep cerise-pink, unscented single flowers born on arching stems. These are followed by large, urn-shaped plum-red hips. As with *R. glauca* (p.155), this shrub's summer display makes it suitable for combinations with cool colors, whereas in autumn it blends particularly well with hot shades. Its stems, like those of its parent, are covered with colorful bristles and prickles. Occasional pruning out of one of the large, old branches towards the base of the bush can help to maintain a continuous supply of vigorous, flowering and fruit-bearing stems with the brightest coloring.

◉ *Chrysanthemum* 'Mary Stoker', *Crocosmia × crocosmiiflora* 'Queen of Spain', *Kniphofia* 'Royal Standard', *Rudbeckia fulgida* var. *sullivantii* 'Goldsturm', × *Solidaster luteus, Stokesia laevis, Strobilanthes attenuata*

H: 3m (10ft) S: 2m (6½ft) ❀ Early to mid-summer
◌◌ ▣-▪ Z4 pH5–7.5

Towards the back of a mixed border, *Rosa* 'Highdownensis' displays its elegant, rich pink blooms on a gracefully arching bush. The tender, shrubby *Artemisia arborescens* grows at the foot of the rose with attractive silvery foliage. In front, the ancient double red campion *Silene dioica* 'Flore Pleno' has blooms that match exactly those of the rose, unifying the arrangement.

The mauve-pink blooms of *Rosa* 'Lavender Lassie' combine well with the foliage of the weeping willow-leaf pear (*Pyrus salicifolia* 'Pendula'), contrasted here with a dark green yew. With lighter pruning, the rose could scramble to the top of the pear, studding its entire surface with flowers.

Rosa 'Lavender Lassie' ♛

A hybrid Shrub rose of similar parentage to the Hybrid Musks, 'Lavender Lassie' produces a compact bush of moderate size, with large trusses of fragrant, mauve-pink pompon flowers opening continually from mid-summer through to autumn. Their pretty, fully double shape and delicate coloring makes this a suitable candidate for mixing with old roses or for combining with cool colors, particularly pastel shades, and also with cerise. 'Lavender Lassie' is an outstanding partner for plants with silver, purple, or glaucous foliage. Light pruning can emphasize its upright growth and encourages long stems, allowing it to be trained like a climbing or trailing rose or to scramble freely into a shrub, such as a silver elaeagnus or a purple sloe.

◉ *Campanula punctata* 'Pantaloons', *Hebe* 'Mrs Winder', *Hemerocallis* 'Grape Velvet', *Monarda* 'Aquarius', *Saponaria officinalis* 'Rosea Plena', *Sidalcea* 'Elsie Heugh', *Thalictrum delavayi* 'Hewitt's Double'

H: 2m (6½ft) S: 1.2m (4ft)
❀ Mid-summer to late autumn
◌◌ ▪-▪ Z5 pH5–7.5

Rosa 'Nevada' ♛

This is a vigorous modern Shrub rose whose arching branches are studded with flowers, and can be trained against a wall to produce a short climber about 2.5m (8ft) high. It has an obscure parentage, although it is reputedly derived from a cross between a Hybrid Tea and *R. moyesii*, from which it gets its arching growth habit. Its lightly scented, semi-double blooms open palest yellow, fading in cool climates to white, while in hot situations they take on pinkish tints. In warm climates, they appear repeatedly from summer through to autumn, but in cooler areas there are few flowers after the first flush. Whatever the temperature, rain will often mark the blooms with red spots, and this can limit the possible color combinations. 'Nevada' is perhaps most successful with warm-colored flowers, from yellow through apricot to peach. It also works well with silver or bronze foliage.

⬤ *Eucalyptus gunnii*, *Hemerocallis* 'Prairie Sunset', *Lupinus* 'African Sunset', *Potentilla fruticosa* 'Abbotswood', *Rhamnus alaternus* 'Argenteovariegata'

H & S: 2m (6½ft)
✽ **Early summer to early autumn**
◐◐ ■-■ **Z4 pH5–7**

Newly opened blooms of *Rosa* 'Nevada', each with a central disk of golden anthers, retain a hint of yellow in their petals, harmonizing here with yellow and orange Welsh poppies (*Meconopsis cambrica*). Other white flowers, namely white sweet rocket (*Hesperis matronalis* var. *albiflora*) and, across the path, *Spiraea* 'Arguta', unify the arrangement.

Rosa 'Maigold' ♛

The strong, upright growth of this Climbing Pimpinellifolia Hybrid rose is useful for fanning out and training against a fence or wall, or for arranging around an obelisk. Without support, it is also an attractive shrub, its prickly stems arching gracefully to form a large sprawling bush, well furnished with healthy foliage. Its large amber-yellow blooms are semi-double or loosely double and very fragrant, most of them born in clusters in a single flush in late spring or early summer, before most other roses are in flower. Their gentle color and a relaxed growth habit make 'Maigold' suitable for less formal areas of the garden, even for a wild garden, where it can scramble through other

The soft amber-yellow, loosely informal blooms of *Rosa* 'Maigold', born on an arching bush, here contrast effectively with the blue flowers of *Iris sibirica*. The subdued blooms of the allium relative *Nectaroscordum siculum*, naturalized throughout the area, neither add to nor detract from the color scheme but provide a quiet charm.

shrubs or over a hedge. It blends well with warm colors, glaucous foliage, and yellow-green foliage or flowers, and makes a stunning contrast with blue flowers. Attractive partners include Bearded and Siberian irises, larger euphorbias, and early peonies.

⬤ *Euphorbia sikkimensis*, *Geranium himalayense*, *Iris* 'Blenheim Royal', *I.* 'Butter and Sugar', *Lupinus arboreus*, *Scrophularia buergeriana* 'Lemon and Lime'

H & S: 2.5m (8ft) ✽ **Late spring to early summer**
◐◐ ■-■ **Z5 pH5–7.5**

In this pleasantly subtle combination, the delicate pink of *Rosa* Peach Blossom is echoed in the pink-flushed leaves of *Fuchsia magellanica* 'Versicolor'. A carpet of silver-green woolly lamb's ears (*Stachys byzantina*) decorates the front of the bed, while a cloud of *Crambe cordifolia* fills the background.

Cranesbills are effective plants for carpeting in front of and beneath roses. Here, *Geranium clarkei* 'Kashmir Purple' – a useful cultivar flowering from early to late summer – weaves itself through the arching stems of the cherry-red Hybrid Musk rose *R.* 'Robin Hood'.

Rosa Peach Blossom ('Ausblossom')

This David Austin English rose is fairly upright in growth, and produces blush-pink flowers with a light almond fragrance. Deadheading the earliest blooms will encourage the plant to produce more later on, or the spent flowers can be left to form an autumn crop of attractive hips. The loosely semi-double blooms have an informal charm that suits them to planting in cottage garden style. Their delicate coloring combines well with other cool pastels such as pink, mauve, lilac, and pale lavender, and with white flowers and silver or purple-flushed foliage, such as silvery white stachys, or purple ajugas and smoke bush, and dark-leaved *Viola riviniana* Purpurea Group. With its upright, bushy growth habit and size, this is a rose for the second row of a border.

Achillea 'Apfelblüte', *Astrantia maxima, Lavatera* 'Pavlova', *Malva moschata* f. *alba, Phlox maculata* 'Rosalinde', *Saponaria officinalis* 'Rosea Plena'

H: 90cm (3ft)   S: 1.2m (4ft)
Mid-summer to mid-autumn
Z5   pH5–7.5

Rosa 'Penelope'

One of the most reliable Hybrid Musks, 'Penelope' flowers prolifically and continually from mid-summer until late autumn, especially if deadheaded after the first main flush. It makes a fairly dense, spreading bush and bears large trusses of exceptionally fragrant, semi-double blooms that can vary in color according to climate and situation from pale peach to cream, with deeper shading towards the center. Its color is delicate enough to go with almost any other, but it is especially effective with warm colors such as peach, apricot, and pale pink, and with bronze-flushed foliage. It associates well with daylilies that have bronzy copper flower tones, red-flushed berberis, or bronze sedges. Blue flowers also make good companions, particularly delphiniums, and salvias such as *S. nemorosa* and *S.* × *superba* cultivars.

Berberis thunbergii 'Pink Queen', *Carex comans* (bronze), *Hemerocallis* 'Ruffled Apricot', *Iris* 'Champagne Elegance', *Persicaria virginiana* Compton's form, *Stokesia laevis* 'Peach Melba', *Uncinia egmontiana*

H & S: 1.5m (5ft)   Mid-summer to late autumn
Z5   pH5–7.5

Trained to cover a wire fence, this fairly yellow *Rosa* 'Penelope' is seen here in a classic partnership with a columnar flower, the relatively short foxglove *Digitalis purpurea* Foxy Group. This shorter variant interacts with the rose more effectively than a taller sort, such as *D.p.* 'Sutton's Apricot', would have.

Rosa 'Robin Hood'

A neat and sturdy Hybrid Musk rose, 'Robin Hood' has small flowers, freely born in clusters over a long season. Unlike most of the other Hybrid Musks, the flowers are only faintly scented. They are a slightly dusky shade of cherry-red, which forms an effective background for other, brighter shades – although it is not quite brilliant enough for dazzling color schemes. The flowers deepen with age and are followed by clusters of tiny brown hips. Being close to primary red, this rose is equally suited to growing with vermilion or bright carmine-pink flowers, and also combines well with purple or red foliage. Yellow-green foliage or flowers make an excellent contrast. It is wonderful as a flowering hedge and also looks attractive planted in tubs and other large containers.

Cotinus coggygria Golden Spirit, *Geranium* 'Lydia', *Hypericum androsaemum* 'Albury Purple', *Leycesteria formosa* Golden Lanterns, *Sidalcea* 'Mrs Borrodaile'

H: 1.2m (4ft)   S: 90cm (3ft)
Mid-summer to late autumn
 Z5   pH5–7.5

Rosa 'Roseraie de l'Haÿ' ♡

Constantly in flower from early summer until autumn, this is a very rewarding Rugosa rose, with semi-double, rich magenta-crimson blooms, unfurling from narrow buds and strongly scented. Unlike most Rugosas, it produces very few hips, so it is grown mainly for its flowers rather than for autumn color, although the foliage does assume good autumn tints. It makes a handsome, very thorny bush that can be used as a hedge. If not grafted onto a rootstock, its own roots will produce suckers that eventually form an impenetrable barrier that tolerates some shade. Its rich color can be used in harmonies with cool shades such as blue and purple, or in contrasts with bright yellow, vermilion, or yellow-green. It works well with purple or glaucous foliage, and looks very attractive with a sweet pea or small-flowered clematis scrambling through it.

Atriplex hortensis var. *rubra*, *Clematis* 'Princess Diana', *C. recta* 'Velvet Night', *Hypericum androsaemum* 'Albury Purple', *Lathyrus grandiflorus*, *Nepeta govaniana*

H & S: 2m (6½ft) **Early summer to late autumn**
Z4 pH5.5–7

If *Rosa* 'Roseraie de l'Haÿ' is pruned only lightly or not at all, it will bloom in late spring, making possible dazzling combinations such as this with tree lupine (*Lupinus arboreus*), the young leaves of *Lysimachia ciliata* 'Firecracker', and a richly colored broom. Each brings its own contrasting texture and structure to the ensemble.

A

B

In autumn, the flowers of *Rosa rugosa* become few and far between and its fat, glistening hips take over the display. Here, the hips harmonize with the mahogany leaves of the vine *Vitis vinifera* 'Purpurea' and the rusty seedheads of *Sedum* 'Herbstfreude', whose glaucous foliage and that of *Hebe albicans* provide gentle contrast.

Rosa rugosa

In cultivation *R. rugosa* has single, mid-carmine flowers with broad petals, crinkled and thin-textured, and a prominent central disk of golden yellow anthers. The blooms, born singly or in small clusters, are followed in autumn by large, round orange-red hips, and the leaves turn butter-yellow. Its flower color suits it to summer combinations with cool shades such as pale carmine-pink, magenta, crimson, mauve, lilac, lavender, blue, or purple, together with purple or silver foliage, and to contrasts with yellow-green. In autumn it combines well with warm colors such as peach, apricot, and soft orange, and bronze or red-flushed foliage. Like 'Roseraie de l'Haÿ' (left), it makes a suckering shrub if grown on its own roots, and may be used as a tough, impenetrable barrier. Variants include 'Rubra', with slightly deeper, light magenta flowers, and 'Alba', which has large, very delicate single flowers with pure white petals.

Crocosmia 'Mars', *Kniphofia rooperi*, *Miscanthus sinensis* 'Sioux', *Phormium* 'Pink Panther', *Phygelius* × *rectus* 'Salmon Leap', *Rudbeckia* 'Herbstsonne'

H & S: 1–2.5m (3¼–8ft)
Early summer to mid-autumn
Z3 pH5.5–7

Rosa 'Sally Holmes' ♚

This is an outstanding Shrub rose for the second row of a border. Its flowers, creamy white and single with a central disk of golden anthers, are born in large clusters in summer and autumn, and make a strong visual impact, particularly when the plants are organized in loose groups. Its parentage is similar to that of the Hybrid Musk roses, hence its rich fragrance. If pruned fairly hard, it may be treated as a Floribunda, whereas lighter pruning allows it to achieve more substantial size. It is a versatile rose that mixes successfully with almost any color, and looks especially effective with silver or glaucous foliage. Dramatic combinations can be made with yellow flowers that reflect the golden centers of the rose blooms, or with blue flowers to create a contrast to the anthers. Annual climbers such as morning glories can be planted as companions and allowed them to weave informally across and through medium- to large-sized groups.

⊙ *Campanula lactiflora* 'Prichard's Variety', *Clematis* × *durandii*, *Consolida ajacis*, *Convolvulus tricolor* 'Royal Ensign', *Coreopsis verticillata* 'Grandiflora', *Geranium* 'Brookside', *Geum* 'Lady Stratheden'

H: 2m (6½ft) **S: 1m** (3¼ft)
❀ **Mid-summer to late autumn**
◖▬▬▭ ◊◊ ■-■ **Z5 pH5–7.5**

Rosa 'Sally Holmes' is here pruned hard, as for a Floribunda, keeping it compact and spectacularly floriferous. *Potentilla fruticosa* 'Goldfinger' decorates the rose's base and harmonizes with its golden yellow anthers. Deadheading the rose encourages plentiful later bloom.

A

Hybrid Teas & Floribundas

HYBRID TEAS (Large-flowered roses), popular for the size and often superb shape of their blooms, and the very floriferous Floribundas (Cluster-flowered roses) are the largest and most commonly grown classes of bush rose, both of them available in a wide range of colors. Generally, bush roses are best combined with plants of other genera rather than planted in the traditional way – massed in beds or as a series of sentry singletons in clashing colors, with their usually coarse foliage and stiff growth habit on display. Mound-forming plants, or even boxwood edging, in front of the roses can mask their unsightly bases, while foliage of attractive texture or architectural form on either side and behind will ensure that the onlooker scarcely notices the leaves of the roses but instead concentrates on the undoubted beauty of the flowers.

The scale of the flowers and the bushes themselves also needs consideration. Large blooms, particularly if brightly colored, can look far too big in a tiny garden, unless there is a deliberate attempt to use oversized plants throughout. A single bush, or a whole bed of them, might not match the scale of planting of the rest of the garden: three, five, or more bushes, perhaps loosely grouped, and with other plants woven through them, might provide a more suitable scale.

Hybrid Teas are traditionally pruned in late winter, removing weak or spindly shoots, shortening the main stems and sideshoots to outward-facing buds, and removing occasional older main stems to ensure a constant supply of vigorous flowering wood. For Floribundas, the main stems are pruned more severely to encourage larger new shoots, each of which will provide a cluster of blooms in early summer, followed later in the season by smaller sprays on the sideshoots.

A

Pruning in this way allows light and air between the plants, making it possible to plant beneath with spring flowers, such as bulbs, wood anemones, or primroses. The young rose leaves, if red, can harmonize attractively or clash dramatically with the plants beneath. If rose bushes are planted under, pruning may need to take place earlier than usual, even in autumn in mild climates; it is usually difficult to mulch in spring, but a loose organic mulch that will not impede their emerging shoots of spring flowers could be applied in autumn instead.

If the scale of the planting requires a bigger or taller rose than the traditional

The tall Floribunda *Rosa* Anne Harkness blooms a little later than others of its group, continuing into the autumn. Its growth habit makes it eminently suitable for use in a mixed border, where it can be combined with mid-summer or later flowers in warm or hot colors, ideally using several bushes of the rose to relate the scale of the group to that of other planting and to avoid a spotty effect. Here, Anne Harkness is partnered by vermilion sprays of *Crocosmia paniculata* and the acid yellow-green buds of goldenrod; it would also combine well with dahlias.

Floribunda, then lighter pruning can be a solution. The cultivars 'Chinatown' ♀, 'Frensham', Iceberg ('Korbin') ♀, and 'Yesterday' ♀ work particularly well on a larger scale. More sizable bushes look very effective lightly draped with annual or herbaceous climbers, for instance morning glories or sweet peas.

Rosa Avalanche ('Jacay')

Very popular in New Zealand, this Floribunda rose has cream flowers fading to white. The flowers are not fully double and often reveal the yellow anthers at the center of the bloom. The shade of cream is inclined more towards apricot or peach than yellow, so this rose tends to combine best with warm tints such as peach or apricot, although it will blend with virtually any flower color and works well with glaucous or silver foliage, as well as with bronze-flushed or white- or gold-variegated leaves. It looks particularly attractive planted with other white flowers, especially umbellifers, gypsophilas, sea kale, and other plants with flower heads of similarly contrasting form or size.

◑ *Achillea* 'Hella Glashoff', *A.* 'Hoffnung', *Artemisia* 'Powis Castle', *Eschscholzia californica* 'Alba', *Hakonechloa macra* 'Alboaurea', *Verbascum* (Cotswold Group) 'Gainsborough'

Rosa Avalanche is here combined with the charming annual umbellifer *Orlaya grandiflora*, its lacy flowers and fern-like foliage contrasting with the altogether more solidly substantial rose. Other annual umbellifers such as *Ammi majus* could be used in the same way with roses.

H: 1.2m (4ft) **S: 90cm** (3ft)
❀ **Mid-summer to late autumn**
◊◊ ▥-▥ **Z5 pH5–7.5**

The flat, formal, rich red flowers of *Rosa* 'Europeana' and its red-flushed young leaves combine perfectly with the salmon and scarlet, dark-centered blooms of sprawling *Potentilla nepalensis* 'Roxana'.

Rosa 'Europeana' ♡

Opulent and richly colored, this fine Floribunda rose has fully double, relatively flat blooms, and profuse foliage that emerges dark red and matures to green. The flower color suits sumptuous displays, especially plantings with coral, rich salmon-pink, or vermilion flowers, and contrasts with lime green or yellow-green foliage and flowers. The young red leaves make an eye-catching combination with late spring bulbs such as narcissi, tulips, or crown imperials, perhaps planted under with Cowichan polyanthus or primroses. For impact from a distance, its colors are a little dusky and do not show up as well as lighter reds, but its attractive flower formation is very striking at close range. Relatively upright and tall for a Floribunda, it is good for the second or third row of a border, where it mixes well with bronze- or purple-leaved plants including medium-sized shrubs and phormiums, and dark-leaved dahlias and crocosmias.

◑ *Alchemilla mollis*, *Dahlia* 'Tally Ho', *Lychnis* × *arkwrightii* 'Vesuvius', *Narcissus* 'Ambergate', *Nicotiana* 'Lime Green', *Primula* Cowichan Venetian Group, *Tulipa* 'Couleur Cardinal'

H & S: 60cm (24in)
❀ **Mid-summer to late autumn**
◊◊ ▥-▥ **Z5 pH5–7.5**

Rosa 'Chinatown' ♡

Although classed as a Floribunda, this is a vigorous, disease-resistant rose that may be lightly pruned for use as a shrub rose, or a medium-sized hedge, or even espaliered like a short climbing rose on a wall or fence. Owing to its large size, it may be grown in the second or third row of a border. Its very large, fully double yellow flowers have notched and slightly crimped petals, giving each bloom a rather frilly outline, and they appear continuously throughout the summer. The yellow of the flowers is pure enough to contrast well with blue, and it also looks good with pale yellow, cream, and warm colors

Pruned hard, as usual for a Floribunda, *Rosa* 'Chinatown' is compact with a prolific first flush of flowers, produced at an ideal height to contrast with those of the catmint *Nepeta* 'Six Hills Giant'. Deadheading the rose will encourage blooming into the autumn. The catmint will also produce later flowers if cut back after its first flush.

such as peach and apricot, as well as yellow-green foliage and flowers or gold-variegated leaves. Good companions include gold-variegated grasses, Spuria irises, *Iris sibirica* cultivars, and hosta cultivars that tolerate strong sun. If allowed to grow to a large size, this rose looks effective draped with an annual or herbaceous climber.

◑ *Achillea* 'Lucky Break', *Delphinium* Summer Skies Group, *D.* 'Sungleam', *Hosta* 'Sum and Substance', *Iris* 'Cambridge', *I. orientalis*, *Miscanthus sinensis* 'Strictus', *Nigella damascena* 'Miss Jekyll', *Verbascum* (Cotswold Group) 'Cotswold King'

H: 1.2m (4ft) **S: 90cm** (3ft)
❀ **Early summer to late autumn**
◊◊ ▥-▥ **Z5 pH5–7.5**

Rosa Evelyn Fison ('Macev')

The rich scarlet, double blooms of this handsome, slightly fragrant Floribunda rose lend it to sumptuous combinations with salmon-pink, coral, or vermilion, and striking contrasts with yellow-green or lime green. With its even, compact growth habit, it is suitable for positions at the front of a border, perhaps behind a row of mounded, sprawling plants. It may also be used as a bedding rose, especially if widely spaced at about 60cm (24in) or slightly more, when it can be interspersed with another plant of similar height and contrasting foliar or floral form. This might be an annual such as an alonsoa or zinnia, one of the taller French marigolds, or a tall nicotiana in lime green or rich salmon-pink. Other suitable companions

In this hot-colored scheme, the orange flowers of *Crocosmia* 'Vulcan' and its bold, pleated leaves contrast in form with scarlet *Rosa* Evelyn Fison, with golden *Ligularia dentata* and yellow *Verbascum chaixii* adding further warmth. The deep purplish blue flowers of *Aconitum* 'Spark's Variety' and dark-leaved *Berberis thunbergii* f. *atropurpurea* provide a foil for the brighter blooms.

might include a hardy herbaceous plant such as a crocosmia, a tender perennial such as a dahlia (perhaps with dark foliage), a grass such as a pennisetum or, for contrast, a yellow-green foliage plant.

🌑 *Cosmos sulphureus* 'Polidor', *Eupatorium capillifolium* 'Elegant Feather', *Lupinus* 'African Sunset', *Potentilla* 'Monsieur Rouillard', *Tagetes patula* 'La Bamba'

H: 70cm (27in) **S: 60cm** (24in)
❀ **Mid-summer to late autumn**

 🌢🌢 ■-■ Z5 pH5–7.5

Rosa 'Frensham'

This outstanding rose, with its pure scarlet, semi-double flowers, was the first truly popular red-flowered Floribunda and is wholly evocative of its era (it was introduced in 1946). If only lightly pruned, this vigorous cultivar can achieve the size of a Shrub rose, allowing its use toward the back of a border and in larger-scale plantings. With its exceptionally strong, robust growth habit and very prickly stems it makes a good hedge, although it can be prone to mildew if grown this way. Its bright coloring works well with hot tints such as orange, vermilion, and golden yellow, or warm colors such as peach and coral. It also combines happily with bronze, purple, or red-flushed foliage, and makes effective contrasts with yellow-green flowers and leaves and lime-green flowers.

🌑 *Dahlia* 'Bednall Beauty' p.371 **B**, *Hemerocallis* 'Root Beer', *Kniphofia* 'Green Jade', *Nicotiana langsdorffii* 'Cream Splash', *Persicaria microcephala* 'Red Dragon'

H: 1.2m (4ft) **S: 75cm** (30in)
❀ **Mid-summer to late autumn**

■■■■ 🌢🌢 ■-■ Z5 pH5–7.5

In this border of red, yellow, and creamy white flowers combined with dusky foliage, the rich scarlet *Rosa* 'Frensham' and the dark-leaved loosestrife *Lysimachia ciliata* 'Firecracker' are lightened by the sulfur-yellow candelabra of *Verbascum* 'Vernale' and the fluffy yellow panicles of the meadow rue *Thalictrum flavum* subsp. *glaucum*. White roses in the background complete the arrangement.

Rosa 'Gruss an Aachen' can vary a little in color according to climate and situation and is here pale pink, rather than its usual pale apricot-blush, allowing it to combine even more harmoniously with the foxglove *Digitalis purpurea* Foxy Group. Because the foxglove is relatively short, its spires of bloom can be seen in close conjunction with the rose, providing a contrast of form.

Rosa 'Gruss an Aachen'

This attractive and fragrant perpetual variety, perhaps best classed as a Hybrid Tea, makes a fairly short, upright bush, with flattened, fully double blooms opening from apricot-pink buds to creamy white with a pale apricot-pink center. Its old-fashioned floral form associates well with old roses and with David Austin's English cultivars. The delicate flower color mixes with almost any other shade, but it is especially attractive with other warm tints, such as apricot, pink, salmon-pink, coral, peach, or yellow, and with bronze-tinted or silver foliage. Its neat growth habit suits it to bedding and, if fairly widely spaced, this rose can be intermingled with other harmonious flowers or foliage, or it may be planted with pinks, for example, beneath.

⬤ *Campanula punctata* 'Bowl of Cherries', *Dianthus* 'Doris', *Geranium* × *riversleaianum* 'Mavis Simpson', *Lavandula angustifolia* 'Miss Katherine'

H & S: 45cm (18in)
✿ Mid-summer to late autumn
 🌢🌢 ▨-▨ Z6 pH5.5–7

Rosa Lilli Marlene is here combined with other red flowers, including bold-leaved *Crocosmia* 'Lucifer' (behind), its red tending slightly towards orange, and in front a carpet of sprawling *Potentilla* 'Gibson's Scarlet', with the foliage of cherry plum (*Prunus cerasifera* 'Pissardii') providing a strong, dusky background.

Rosa Iceberg ('Korbin') 🏆

One of the most beautiful and elegant of the Floribundas, the slightly fragrant, relatively thin-petaled, loosely double flowers of this rose are born singly or in graceful sprays over a long period from mid-summer, with a particularly strong flush in autumn. Their color is usually almost pure white, occasionally with a faint pinkish ivory flush towards the center, and blends with almost any other shade, although it is particularly suitable for lightening plantings of pink and darker-colored roses. It is also very attractive with silver or glaucous foliage and lime green or yellow-green flowers.

This rose may be lightly pruned to produce a shrub up to about 1.8m (6ft) high, perfectly at home when planted among old-fashioned roses; it also makes a good hedge, which benefits from having short, cushion-forming plants such as lavenders in front to disguise its unsightly vase-shaped bases.

⬤ *Echinops sphaerocephalus* 'Arctic Glow', *Hemerocallis* 'Gentle Shepherd', *Lobelia* × *gerardii* 'La Fresco', *Lupinus* 'Storm', *Salvia nemorosa* 'Ostfriesland', *Sidalcea candida*

H: 1.2–1.8m (4–6ft) S: 90cm (3ft)
✿ Mid-summer to late autumn
 🌢🌢 ▨-▨ Z5 pH5–7.5

In a pretty planting display that depends solely on flowers rather than foliage, the large white blooms of *Rosa* Iceberg and deep pink *R.* Mary Rose and the dense flower heads of red valerian (*Centranthus ruber*) contrast in form with the more diffuse pink blooms of *Kolkwitzia amabilis* and *Gypsophila elegans* 'Giant White'. The cranesbill *Geranium* 'Johnson's Blue' carpets the foreground.

Rosa Lilli Marleen ('Korlima')

This is a compact Floribunda with large, semi-double, velvety bright crimson blooms, born in clusters. With its neat and strongly branching growth habit, it is useful both as a bedding rose and as a sturdy hedge. The sumptuous coloring of its flowers, set against the dark, slightly bronzy foliage, is enhanced in combinations with purple, mauve, and strong pink. It can be a dusky foil for brighter red or vermilion, and for yellow-green and yellow flowers. Although a rich enough shade to act as a stabilizing component of red borders, this tends to make the flowers less visible from a distance, and specimen plants are best positioned where they can be seen at close range. This rose is prone to mildew and blackspot, and should be treated routinely for these disorders.

⬤ *Anthemis tinctoria* 'Sauce Hollandaise', *Coreopsis verticillata* 'Moonbeam', *Hemerocallis* 'Golden Chimes' p.238 **B**, *Hypericum frondosum*, *Lathyrus chloranthus*

H: 75cm (30in) S: 60cm (24in)
✿ Mid-summer to late autumn
 🌢🌢 ▨-▨ Z5 pH5–7.5

Rosa 'The Fairy' ♛

Best classed as a Polyantha rose, this hybrid derives from a cross between a Polyantha (a small-flowered ancestor of Floribundas) and a Wichurana Rambler. From the latter it inherits a rather lax but graceful growth habit that suits it for use as a bush rose towards the front of a border, for a ground cover, or cascading over the edge of a dwarf wall; it may also be grafted as a semi-weeping standard. The foliage is neat and attractive, with tiny, glossy leaflets. Its large clusters of lightly fragrant blooms, each lasting for several weeks, comprise numerous pompon-like, double, rose-pink florets. These are most attractive combined with warm colors such as coral, apricot, peach, and cream; they also look good with white or rich deep scarlet flowers and silver or red-flushed foliage, and form striking contrasts with yellow-green and lime green. Combinations with cooler shades, such as lavender, blue, mauve, and lilac, tend to be less effective. Pleasant companions include miscanthus, hostas, alstroemerias, and old roses.

● *Carex muskingumensis* 'Ice Fountains', *Diascia barberae* 'Blackthorn Apricot', *Hosta* 'Krossa Regal', *Scabiosa* 'Chile Pepper', *Senecio cineraria*, *Stachys coccinea*

H: 60cm (24in) S: 1.2m (4ft)
❀ **Mid-summer to late autumn**
⬛⬜⬛ ◊◊ ⬜-⬛ **Z5 pH5–7.5**

Facing page: A cascading mound of *Rosa* 'The Fairy' here harmonizes perfectly with the blooms of *Alstroemeria* 'Charm'. The combination would be further enhanced by the addition of some handsome foliage, perhaps in darkest red or silvery green.

Rosa Westerland ('Korwest') ♛

This is a vigorous, branching rose that may be pruned firmly as a Floribunda for beds and the front rows of a border, or more lightly as a Shrub rose for positions further back in borders and for flowering hedges. Its stiff, upright stems are also suitable for training on walls and fences, where it can exceed its usual height by 60cm (24in) or more. Its loose sprays of pleasantly scented, ruffled double apricot blooms blend happily with other warm colors, such as cream, peach, coral, buff-yellow, soft orange, or soft red, and contrast prettily and gently with yellow-green or lime green. Since its color is in the same range as many of David Austin's English roses, it associates well with many of

The soft apricot blooms of *Rosa* Westerland are born on a bush tall enough to top the other, scarlet-flowered border plants in this display, which includes an opium poppy (*Papaver somniferum*), Jerusalem cross (*Lychnis chalcedonica*), and a climbing nasturtium (*Tropaeolum majus*). All of the flowers harmonize attractively with the orange-red bricks of the wall behind.

these. It may also be combined in plantings with day lilies, lilies, and taller grasses, or with bronze-flushed shrubs such as smoke bush and *Berberis thunbergii* cultivars.

● *Hemerocallis* 'Lemon Bells', *Hypericum androsaemum* 'Albury Purple', *Lilium henryi*, *Miscanthus sinensis* 'Zebrinus', *Rosa* Molineux, *R.* Pat Austin ⌐ p.392 **C**

H: 1.8m (6ft) S: 1.2m (4ft)
❀ **Mid-summer to late autumn**
⬛⬜⬛ ◊◊ ⬜-⬛ **Z5 pH5–7.5**

Rosa 'Yesterday' ♛

Taller than most Floribundas, this is an upright bushy Polyantha or modern Shrub rose which, depending on the severity of pruning, may be grown in the middle of a border or close to the front, or as a mounded ground-cover rose. Its numerous small, lightly scented flowers, which open flat, at first magenta and fading to a soft lilac-pink, are born in sprays, generally toward the top of the bush, so this rose benefits from other plants growing in front to disguise its bare stems. Apart from a tendency to become chlorotic in alkaline or poor soils, causing the foliage to clash with the flowers, it is an excellent trouble-free variety that combines well with cool colors such as mauve, lilac,

lavender, or blue, and with white or crimson flowers and purple or silver foliage. Lime green or pale lemon-yellow flowers contrast effectively with the magenta blooms.

● *Indigofera amblyantha*, *Lavandula stoechas* subsp. *pedunculata* 'Pukehou', *Lupinus* 'Storm', *Lysimachia ephemerum*, *Physostegia virginiana* 'Summer Snow'

H: 1.5m (5ft) S: 1.2m (4ft)
❀ **Mid-summer to late autumn**
⬛⬜⬛ ◊◊ ⬜-⬛ **Z5 pH5–6.5**

In this planting, which succeeds solely on flowers in soft magenta, ruby, and contrasting white, *Rosa* 'Yesterday' rises above the exotic-looking Chinese foxglove (*Rehmannia elata*) behind a carpet of *Diascia barberae* 'Ruby Field' and *Viola cornuta* Alba Group. The rehmannia and diascia are perennial plants, but would need to be treated as annuals in cooler climates.

Smaller species & smaller modern Shrub roses

IN TINY GARDENS and small-scale areas within larger ones, conventional bush and shrub roses can sometimes seem coarsely oversized, and roses that are smaller in height and spread, and often in flower and leaf, may look more appropriate.

Among these are the Scotch or Burnet roses, slender shrubs derived from *R. pimpinellifolia*, with tiny flowers born in great profusion in early summer, sometimes followed by rounded hips. Thriving in light soil and tolerant of some shade, they are ideal plants for a natural garden, suckering steadily but controllably into wide colonies.

R. 'Cécile Brunner' is entirely different in form, a diminutive China rose with perfect, high-pointed buds unfurling to pale pink flowers on frail-looking stems. Many of the Miniature and Patio roses follow in its train. These are hybrids between the very tiny sports of China roses and the more robust and free-flowering modern Floribunda roses.

The smallest of the Miniatures, only 23–45cm (9–18in) tall, are pretty little roses best used in pots so that they may most easily be appreciated at close range – and in colder climates be moved to shelter in winter since the roots are intolerant of freezing. The simpler roses among these may also find a home in a rock garden.

The somewhat larger Patio roses look more like plants than scale models or toys and can be used effectively in raised beds or containers, or perhaps along the outer edge of a terrace so that they can be viewed in detail from below. Many small rock plants, ground-cover plants, and annuals are delicate enough in appearance to associate with Patio roses in these situations without overwhelming their small flowers and fine-textured foliage.

A

Rosa elegantula 'Persetosa'
THREEPENNY BIT ROSE

Sometimes listed as *R. farreri* var. *persetosa*, this is a dainty early-flowering species Shrub rose, with tiny fern-like leaflets that are purple-flushed in full sun and turn purple and crimson in the autumn, and arching stems densely covered with bristles. In time it can form a fairly large shrub, studded in late spring with tiny, lightly scented pink flowers – seldom in sufficient profusion to make a dazzling display – and later with small orange hips. A graceful rose for the front of a shrub or mixed border, and for wilder, more natural parts of the garden, it combines well with purple foliage and with other flowers that bridge the gap between spring and summer, for example columbines, violas, early cranesbills, and bugleweeds planted as a carpet under its rather sparse growth. It

Although it can become a moderately sized shrub in time, the tiny flowers and leaves of *Rosa elegantula* 'Persetosa' suit it to a smaller scale of planting and to close-range viewing, for instance at the front of a bed or border. Here, its relatively sparse branches let enough light through for a complete carpet of mixed violas.

is attractive with plants of different floral form, such as umbellifers, including cow parsley, and with contrasting foliage such as the grassy leaves of earlier-flowering herbaceous irises. Compatible partners include sweet rocket, purple-leaved berberis, glaucous-leaved hostas, dipeltas, exochordas, kolkwitzias and other early roses in white, pink, or crimson shades.

◐ *Anthriscus sylvestris* 'Ravenswing', *Aquilegia vulgaris* 'Royal Purple', *Hosta* var stellata (Tardiana Group) 'Halcyon', *Iris* 'Banbury Beauty', *Salvia lyrata* 'Burgundy Bliss'

H & S: 1.5m (5ft) ❊ **Late spring to early summer**
◌◌ ▣-■ **Z4 pH5.5–7**

The sprawling growth habit of *Rosa* 'Raubritter' allows other flowers to be woven through its outer fringes. Here, dainty blue love-in-a-mist (*Nigella damascena*) mingles with the globular blooms of the rose.

Rosa 'Raubritter'

This *R.* 'Macrantha' hybrid is an arching Shrub rose, useful for early and mid-summer plantings for slopes, ground covers, and the front of beds and borders. Its extremely pretty spherical flowers, reminiscent of 'Reine Victoria', are shapely and sophisticated, a rich enough pink in color to suit dazzling combinations with cool-colored flowers, glaucous, silver, red, or purple-flushed foliage, and other roses with a contrasting color or flower size, such as small-flowered white or deep red Ground Cover cultivars. It also contrasts effectively with yellow-green flowers, such as alchemillas or nicotianas. Good partners include pinks, irises (including late-flowering Tall Bearded kinds), hebes, cranesbills such as *Geranium* × *riversleaianum* cultivars, shrubby lavateras, eryngiums, campanulas, and dictamnus. If planted close to a large shrub or small tree, its branches can be encouraged to scramble upward, and they are sufficiently flexible to be trained as a semi-weeping standard or to sprawl over the edge of a low wall.

◐ *Achillea* 'Apfelblüte', *Hebe* 'Pink Pixie', *Iris* 'Pacific Mist', *I.* 'Dreaming Spires', *Lavatera* 'Kew Rose', *Nicotiana langsdorffii*, *Physostegia virginiana* 'Bouquet Rose', *Ruta graveolens*

H: 1m (3¼ft) **S: 1.8m** (6ft) ❀ **Early to mid-summer**
◊◊ ▪-▪ **Z4 pH5.5–7.5**

Rosa Sweet Dream ('Fryminicot') ♚

Winner of numerous awards, this Patio rose is among the most popular rose varieties of all time. Like all Patio roses, its flowers and foliage are proportionately smaller than those of Hybrid Teas or Floribundas, making it especially useful for smaller gardens, intimate plantings, and for containers. Its neat and bushy, almost cushion-like growth habit and dense, glossy foliage make it a good choice for edging beds and paths, planted either in small groups or as a continuous low hedge. The soft apricot coloring of its fragrant, perfectly formed flowers is particularly suitable for combinations with other warm tints such as peach, salmon, soft yellow, and cream, as well as with bronze foliage and with yellow-green foliage and flowers. It contrasts memorably with the pure blue of plants like Belladonna Group delphiniums or *Salvia patens* cultivars. Despite its small size, it benefits from having low or cushion-forming plants in front, including smaller glaucous-leaved hostas, bronze sedges, a heuchera with purple or bronze foliage, and also diascias, especially a rich salmon or coral (so-called apricot-colored) cultivar.

This rose has been propagated by tissue culture, resulting in the distribution of several slightly different clones, some of which are exceedingly prone to blackspot and others that differ in flower color, tending more towards yellow. It would therefore be a good idea to buy container-grown flowering plants that can be checked for color and health.

◐ *Diascia barberae* 'Blackthorn Apricot', *Heuchera* 'Chocolate Ruffles', × *Heucherella* 'Chocolate Veil', *Hosta* 'Buckshaw Blue', *Lavandula* 'Sawyers', *Persicaria microcephala* 'Red Dragon', *Stokesia laevis* 'Peach Melba'

H: 40cm (16in) **S: 35cm** (14in)
❀ **Mid-summer to late autumn**
◊◊ ▪-▪ **Z5 pH5–7.5**

Rosa Sweet Dream blends harmoniously with a carpet of *Diascia* 'Salmon Supreme' and the loose, greenish cream panicles of dark-leaved *Heuchera micrantha* var. *diversifolia* 'Palace Purple', with the bold *Phormium* 'Sundowner' just visible behind. Deadheading the rose and shearing over the diascia after it has completed its first flush of flowers will ensure the display continues into the autumn.

Ground Cover roses

THERE ARE TWO main kinds of Ground Cover roses. Some are vigorous, decidedly prostrate plants, most flowering only once, in the summer. Others are neater and more compact, and rather like low, spreading modern Shrub roses; many of the more recent cultivars bloom repeatedly, producing showy flowers over a long season from summer into autumn.

The more prostrate types have trailing stems that often root where they touch the ground and usually form dense mats or mounds of cover. Some may be too strongly horizontal to associate well with border plants, but are excellent for covering banks or slopes, especially in more naturalistic parts of the garden.

The shrubby types have arching stems, giving a fairly mounded or dome-shaped habit. These roses are particularly attractive when allowed to tumble over a slope or low wall, or over the edge of a large container. Although their blooms are generally too sophisticated for the edge of a woodland garden, for example, they are useful in making the transition from formal to more relaxed and lower-maintenance areas. Great swathes of one variety are best avoided, unless planting on the largest scale, but groups of roses in harmonious colors weaving among arching shrubs can look very attractive.

Perhaps the main point to bear in mind when using Ground Cover roses is that most are too open to be really effective in smothering weeds. It is therefore vital to ensure there are no perennial weeds in the soil before planting and to control annual weeds meticulously in the first year.

These roses do not need regular pruning but they can be cut back severely every few years, using loppers or a brush cutter; this will rejuvenate the planting, and allow the removal of any intrusive upright branches to maintain a low profile.

Rosa 'Nozomi' ♔

This is a versatile Ground Cover or Miniature Climbing rose that can be trained against a low wall or fence, or as a weeping standard for use as a focal point or repeated accent in a border. It is effective draped over a bank, and in containers, where its branches will arch gracefully over the edge. The single, unscented flowers, which open palest blush-pink, take on greyish tints as they age, and the anthers turn black, giving the blooms a slightly subdued tone that blends well with white and muted colors such as old rose or dusky mauve, and also complements silver, purple, or red-flushed foliage. Although not as dense and wide-spreading as some Ground Cover roses, its trailing stems can be pegged down to improve coverage and these will often root, extending the spread. It is one of the best Ground Cover roses for use as a

Rosa 'Nozomi' here spreads itself gracefully across a carpet of yellow-green leaved heather (*Calluna vulgaris*), creating a pleasantly uneven mix of the two plants and a contrast of foliage and form. The rose will have almost completed its flowering before the heather starts to bloom.

background for clematis, both Viticellas such as purple 'Royal Velours' to provide exciting color combinations and later-flowering kinds like *C. integrifolia* 'Rosea', which bloom after 'Nozomi' has finished. In a wild garden this rose can be combined with white umbellifers such as wild carrots or cow parsley, and simple wild flowers, for example campions, cranesbills, and yarrows.

⊚ *Achillea* 'Apfelblüte', *Astrantia maxima, Geranium × antipodeum, Salvia nemorosa* 'Amethyst', *S. officinalis* 'Purpurascens', *Stachys byzantina, Veronica* 'Ellen Mae'

H: 90cm (3ft) **S: 1.8m** (6ft) ❀ **Mid-summer**
◊◊◊ ☐-■ **Z5 pH5–7.5**

The sprawling growth of Ground Cover roses allows them to mingle more effectively than bush roses, such as Floribundas, with neighboring plants. Here, *Rosa* Pink Bells blends harmoniously with a white musk mallow (*Malva moschata* f. *alba*) and a lilac-blue peach-leaved bellflower (*Campanula persicifolia*).

Rosa Pink Bells ('Poulbells')

The arching growth of this superlative Ground Cover rose is suitable for covering banks and low fences, and for training as a weeping standard. It is equally effective for large plantings and small groups. The dainty, fully double, rich pink flowers, with a mild fragrance, combine well with flowers in cool colors – rich pink, white, mauve – and with red, purple, or silver foliage. Effective partners include sages, catmints, lavenders, pinks in white or crimson, smoke bush, and lime green nicotianas. It will host a white or deep carmine sweet pea or a Texensis or Viticella clematis, while its repeat-flowering into autumn combines with later flowers such as penstemons, white Japanese anemones, and white or crimson cosmos.

⬤ *Lavandula angustifolia* 'Imperial Gem', *Monarda* 'Aquarius', *Nepeta* 'Six Hills Giant', *Penstemon* 'Evelyn', *Salvia verticillata* 'Purple Rain', *Sidalcea candida*

H: 75cm (30in) S: 1.5m (5ft)
✽ **Mid-summer to early autumn**
◊◊ ▢-▨ **Z5 pH5–7.5**

Rosa Suffolk ('Kormixal')

This relatively prostrate Ground Cover rose bears small, lightly scented, rich scarlet single flowers in large clusters almost continuously until autumn. Their slightly cut petals enclose a disk of golden anthers, and their florets tend to close as the anthers blacken with age. This dramatic coloring suits hot color schemes with yellow, orange, or yellow-green flowers, and looks effective with lime green flowers and with yellow-green or red-flushed foliage. It is an excellent rose for interplanting with larger phormiums, dark-leaved heucheras, berberis, and smoke bush, and with climbers such as tropaeolums, Texensis clematis, or glory flower. Since this cultivar is rather prone to blackspot it needs a good, moist soil; extended plantings or very enclosed areas are best avoided.

⬤ *Hakonechloa macra* 'Aureola', *Hemerocallis* 'Lemon Bells', *Heuchera* 'Chocolate Veil', *Hypericum frondosum*, *Lamium maculatum* Golden Anniversary

H: 45cm (18in) S: 90cm (36in)
✽ **Mid-summer to late autumn**
◊◊ ▢-▨ **Z5 pH5–7.5**

The petals of *Rosa* Suffolk contrast dazzlingly with *Euonymus fortunei* 'Emerald 'n' Gold', while the golden anthers form a satisfying harmony with the variegation in the euonymus leaves. Both of these plants are low-growing and suited to the front of beds and borders.

The silvery foliage of *Artemisia* 'Powis Castle' provides an effective foil for the cascading blooms of *Rosa* Surrey, a better partnership for a more steeply sloped border than many of the other, lower-growing Ground Cover roses.

Rosa Surrey ('Korlanum') ♛

The frilly, double, richly colored blooms of this very fragrant Ground Cover rose are close enough to primary pink to mix well with colors such as mauve, carmine, or white, warm tints like peach, apricot, and cream, and more opulent shades. Associations with red, purple, silver, or glaucous foliage work well, as do contrasts with yellow-green flowers or foliage. It is suitable for larger plantings, punctuated with a climber such as a sweet pea or clematis. Flowering continues late into the season, and the rose can then partner penstemons, Japanese anemones, and other roses grown for late blooms – some China and Hybrid Musk cultivars, for example – or for early hips, such as *Rosa moyesii* hybrids and cultivars.

⬤ *Anemone hupehensis* 'Bowles' Pink', *Eryngium giganteum*, *Leymus arenarius*, *Penstemon* 'Osprey', *Sedum telephium* subsp. *maximum* 'Atropurpureum'

H: 80cm (31in) S: 1.2m (4ft)
✽ **Mid-summer to late autumn**
◊◊ ▢-▨ **Z5 pH5–7.5**

PERENNIALS

WITH THEIR DIVERSITY of foliage and often showy flowers, herbaceous perennials play an essential role in the garden, providing interest and beauty as they change dramatically through the seasons. A valuable component of borders, many can also be used for a ground cover, for naturalizing in a wild garden, or for containers.

STRICTLY, PERENNIALS are any plants that live for two years or more and flower each year. Gardeners use the word mainly for herbaceous, non-woody plants that die back to an overwintering rootstock.

The oldest herbaceous borders had single plants perfectly spaced on a rectangular grid, with no attempt to organize flower colors and little use of ornamental foliage. These were abandoned in Victorian times in favor of borders in which each species was massed in a group for maximum impact.

Gertrude Jekyll was perhaps the first to advocate borders based on a limited color range, with flowers of a single color, two pleasantly contrasting ones such as blue and yellow, or a spectrum of colors shifting gradually along the border's length. She recommended using hot colors near the house, passing from purple through orange to yellow, which would be contrasted with blue at the far end of the border to emphasize distance. Miss Jekyll was also an early advocate of the use of foliage color and form, both to enhance color schemes and to add structure to planting, a principle we regard as axiomatic today. She also favored the "drift", a long, narrow group of plants running at a shallow oblique angle to the border's front. This is especially useful in borders 3–4m (10–13ft) deep, planted traditionally with groups that gradually and uniformly rise in height from front to back.

Mixing form and color

Whatever the color scheme, a variety of flower shapes generally gives the most pleasant effect. Flowers born in spikes, such as those of lupines, delphiniums, verbascums, and hardy salvias, provide useful vertical accents and can be contrasted with the flat plates of achilleas and clouds of crambe, gypsophila, or thalictrum. Varied foliage helps too, for instance fine-textured grasses, straps of daylilies, spiky sword-shaped leaves of crocosmias, or handsomely architectural acanthus. Foliage color can also be used to complement a color scheme: silver,

glaucous, or purple leaves blend well with cool shades, while red, bronze, or yellow-green leaves are effective with hot ones. Pure blue flowers can be set off by yellow-green, glaucous, or silver leaves. Variegation can provide accents, emphasize a bold leaf shape, or give a lighter tone, but it can look frantic if used to excess.

Contrasts of form are easy to achieve and often successful. Harmonies are harder. A border planted solely with daylilies or hostas may become tedious, yet the gentle textures found in a grass garden can be very attractive, the result of the most subtle variations of leaf color and form, particularly when they soften a formal pattern of beds. Yet monocot borders, with only grassy, strap-shaped, and spiky leaves, seem to fall between two camps, having neither enough harmony nor sufficient contrast. Even Gertrude Jekyll could not make a success of a border consisting solely of New England

This planting in the style of Gertrude Jekyll uses most of the plants she favored for the blue border. Blue echinops, perovskias, eryngiums, and salvias are leavened by white cosmos, phlox, and anemones, with drifts of tall cream antirrhinums. Foliage plays an important role, with silver stachys and artemisias, glaucous lyme grass, and the bold thistle leaves of echinops providing structure and a variety of textures.

asters and had to resort to grasses such as miscanthus and an edging of neat foliage plants to provide the variations of form and texture that the asters lacked.

Even if we love a particular genus of perennials to the exclusion of all others, growing them in mixed company usually gives more satisfying results than a monoculture. The once-popular phlox border needs suitable companion plants both to hide the base of the phlox stems and to compensate for their rather dull leaves and amorphous flower heads. A bed of hostas alone risks camouflaging the bold shape of individual plants, whereas combined with the contrasting leaves of ferns and grasses, each hosta can be appreciated distinctly. Even plants of more definite form, such as daylilies, lupines, or delphiniums, benefit from two or three different companions to provide a foil. Many more than this, however, would risk diluting the essential character of the preferred genus, and result in something like any other border.

All-year appeal

The main challenge in designing a traditional herbaceous border is to ensure it performs for as much of the year as possible. Two factors help: one, as discussed, is to make the most of foliage, not just for architecture and structure, but for color, too; the second is to incorporate tender perennials such as dahlias, cannas, penstemons, or argyranthemums. These come from climates where frost does not curtail their yearly cycle: they do not have to rush to produce seed before the weather cuts them down, and so they may flower incessantly. Some annuals can also be used in this way (see pp.358–407).

For winter, there are a few precious evergreen perennials, including hellebores, epimediums, periwinkles, and bergenias and some of the newer heucheras. However, many gardeners relish the winter remains of herbaceous plants such as achilleas, sedums, cardoons, and larger grasses such as miscanthus. Although some prefer to cut back everything in autumn, those with a more relaxed attitude will

leave these skeletons, clearing them only to make room for bulbs and other early flowers. In this way the herbaceous border can retain some form and structure through the winter months.

For creating a large and imposing display with a long season of interest, a mixed border is especially valuable. Combining herbaceous perennials mainly with shrubs, it is potentially the most attractive synthesis of garden plants.

Numbers and spacing

There is a general convention among gardeners that perennials are best grouped in odd numbers and it is indeed difficult to avoid, say, a block of four or six plants looking self-consciously regular. Some, however, consider this a rule

Whereas a planting of variegated hostas alone would be tedious and would mask the individual beauty of the hosta, here the foliage of *H. crispula* is flattered by its companion plants, including ferns, *Hydrangea quercifolia*, Solomon's seal, and the whorled leaves of martagon lilies.

made to be broken. An irregularly shaped group with odd plants of the same sort a little distance from it gives a more natural effect, and groups of the same sort of perennial can be repeated at intervals along the length of a border to provide a unifying theme.

Many books on perennials and garden catalogues give a recommended spacing for plants within a group. Adjacent groups need spacing further apart than this if they are not to appear cramped. A rule of thumb is that the spacing between two groups should be three quarters the sum of their spacings: in other words, if one group has plants spaced at 40cm (16in) and its neighbor has plants spaced at 60cm (24in), the gap between the outermost plants of the two groups should be 75cm (30in).

An old convention for herbaceous borders was that they should be twice as wide as the height of their tallest plants, with a path at the back to allow maintenance of hedges or wall plants. This gives a spacious feel to the planting but is a counsel of perfection that those of us with smaller gardens and narrower borders will neither want nor feel obliged to follow. It is perfectly possible to devise perennial border planting that is as tall as, or even taller than, the width of the border, giving a dramatically steep, even towering, effect. However, plants for such borders should have long, leafy, preferably flowering stems and should not bear their flowers only at the top. Using such paragons of the plant world, it is possible to achieve a border only three groups deep but 1.5m (5ft) high with not a bare stem in sight.

Frontline candidates

The choice of perennials for the front of beds and borders is perhaps the most crucial. Generally they should be of neat growth habit and/or should have attractive foliage. Spacious and gently rising borders can have a low carpet of alpine pinks or woolly lamb's ears in front, with mound-forming plants in the second row to hide the stems of taller plants behind. If the border is steeply sloped, the ground cover must be dispensed with and the mounds must come to the front. Some bold foliage, such as that of bergenias or hostas, towards the front can help define the border, anchoring it and giving it presence. Fluffs like catmint and gypsophila can set a tone of amorphous anonymity if used to excess, although they have ethereal charm when used in moderation with bolder plants.

Rebels may wish to flout the convention of designing the border as an evenly graded bank of flowers, gradually rising in height, and allow some tall plants to grow well forward of others of their own size. By contouring the heights of perennials more irregularly and dramatically, it is possible to create bays within the planting whose innermost recesses are hidden when the border is viewed obliquely from a distance – their contents will be revealed as a delightful surprise as the viewer moves along the border.

Facing page: This planting of *Filipendula rubra* and *Potentilla nepalensis*, with flowers in perfectly matching shades of pink, is saved from dullness by drifts of purple orach woven through and behind the plants.

Below: Harmonies of yellow, with *Santolina pinnata* subsp. *neapolitana* 'Edward Bowles', *Anthemis tinctoria* 'E.C. Buxton', and spiky-leaved *Sisyrinchium striatum*, contrast with the rich purple-blue flowers of *Lavandula angustifolia* 'Hidcote'.

Acanthus spinosus ♀

This stately plant has large, divided leaves, glossy, deep green with paler veins, and spikes of pinkish white, foxglove-like florets, with magenta, purple-flushed calyces. It flowers profusely in sun, less so in shade, and while happy in poor, dry soil, it may lose its foliage there by mid-summer or develop mildew. It makes a bold focal point near the front of a border, especially when set off by paler leaves or flowers, and works well with pink, mauve, or mid- to light blue flowers or with soft yellow. Leaves of the Spinosissimus Group are deeply cut, with pale veins and almost white spines. *A. mollis* has less divided, glossier leaves; the more tender Latifolius Group is handsome but lacks the vertical accent and strong coloration of *A. spinosus*.

◐ *Allium cristophii*, *Geranium* 'Johnson's Blue', *G.* × *riversleaianum* 'Mavis Simpson', *Philadelphus coronarius* 'Aureus', *Rosa glauca*

H: 1.5m (5ft) S: 90cm (36in)

✿ **Early to late summer**

◊-◊◊ ☐-☐ Z7 pH5–7.5

The handsome, architectural leaves and bold flower spikes of *Acanthus spinosus* act as a focal point in a sunny border, backed by the shrubby pale mauve-pink *Lavatera* 'Barnsley' and furnished in front by contrasting golden feverfew (*Tanacetum parthenium* 'Aureum') and the yellow-green flower heads of lady's mantle (*Alchemilla mollis*).

In a garden of broad beds and hot-colored flowers in early summer, the horizontal plates of *Achillea* 'Coronation Gold' contrast with the vertical spires of a verbascum hybrid. The rich red flowers of Jerusalem cross (*Lychnis chalcedonica*), feathery heads of bronze fennel (*Foeniculum vulgare* 'Purpureum'), and orange-yellow *Ligularia dentata* fill the gap between the two.

Achillea 'Fanal'

Garden achilleas normally have a limited range of yellow or white flowers. *A.* 'Fanal', one of the Galaxy hybrids, was the first to have bright scarlet flowers, making it useful for hot color schemes. However, like many other colored hybrids, it fades with age through salmon-pink to buff, tints that make finding suitable neighbors a challenge. It is especially good with salmon-pink flowers and bronze foliage. If its older flowers do not harmonize with a particular arrangement, they may be cut off; this will encourage new blooms, so extending the flowering period until autumn. Some other richly colored variants age more pleasantly – 'Feuerland' and 'Walther Funcke', for example.

◐ *Dahlia* 'Bishop of Llandaff', *Diascia* 'Salmon Supreme', *Elymus magellanicus*, *Foeniculum vulgare* 'Purpureum', *Monarda* 'Cambridge Scarlet'

H: 75cm (30in) S: 45cm (18in)

✿ **Early summer to mid-autumn**

◊-◊◊ ☐-☐ Z3 pH5–7.5

Achillea 'Coronation Gold' ♀

Some of the most valuable garden achilleas are derived from yellow-flowered species such as *A. clypeolata*. However, these grey-leaved sun-lovers do not thrive in heavy or damp soil, or in cool summers, whereas hybrids from them can be more amenable. *A.* 'Coronation Gold' is one of the best of medium height, and therefore more suitable for a small garden. It is easier to grow, longer-flowering, and cleaner in color than its other parent *A. filipendulina*, and has better silver foliage. As with most achilleas, the flowers are held in horizontal plates, making it useful for balancing flower heads of other forms, especially spikes. It can produce good contrasts with mid-blue flowers, harmonizes well with hot colors, and is particularly attractive with silver-foliaged plants. Other compatible neighbors include kniphofias, salvias, and many grasses of moderate size such as *Miscanthus sinensis* 'Gracillimus'.

◐ *Artemisia ludoviciana*, *Campanula persicifolia*, *Coreopsis* 'Baby Gold', *Delphinium* 'Sabrina', *Hemerocallis* 'Sammy Russell' p.239 **C**, *Kniphofia* 'David' p.254 **C**, *Onopordum nervosum*, *Salvia nemorosa* 'Lubecca', *Stipa capillata*, *Viola cornuta*

H: 90cm (36in) S: 45cm (18in)

✿ **Early to late summer**

◊◊ ☐ ☐ Z4 pH5–7.5

The flower heads of *Achillea* 'Fanal' open rich scarlet and turn to terracotta before aging through salmon to chamois. Here, the terracotta tones with the distant wall, while the scarlet chimes with the flowers of bold-leaved *Crocosmia* 'Lucifer'. The curious spherical seedheads of *Allium cristophii* are just tall enough to appear behind the achillea, playing their part in the ensemble.

Grown at eye level, the flat heads of *Achillea filipendulina* 'Gold Plate' appear as narrow yellow lines, a distinctive pattern that is even more pronounced in bright sun when underlined by the rich olive-green of their undersides. The bold leaves of *Canna indica* 'Purpurea', *Dahlia* 'Blaisdon Red', orange heleniums, and the tall sunflower *Helianthus annuus* 'Velvet Queen' add exotic richness.

Achillea filipendulina 'Gold Plate' ♟

This is one of the taller achilleas, with broad heads of yellow flowers. Its great height makes a striking impact but also reduces the area presented to the eye to a narrow, arched line. This effect is offset by the underside of the flower heads, which in bright sunlight appear intense olive-green, emphasizing the graceful, arching growth habit. It is a good, drought-tolerant plant for the back of a border, especially pleasing when combined with blues and hot colors, spiked flower heads, and moderate to tall grasses such as *Miscanthus sinensis* 'Strictus' or 'Variegatus'. Shorter variants such as *A.f.* 'Neugold' and 'Altgold' bear their flowers below eye level and therefore appear considerably showier.

🌐 *Crocosmia* 'Lucifer', *Delphinium* 'Alice Artindale', *Eryngium* × *tripartitum*, *Hemerocallis* 'Stafford' p.239 **B**, *Salvia pratensis* 'Indigo' p.283 **A**

H: 1.5m (5ft) S: 60cm (24in)
❀ **Early to late summer**
◐-◊◊ ▢-▧ **Z4 pH5–7.5**

Achillea 'Lachsschönheit'

This delightful achillea, also known as Salmon Beauty, is one of the Galaxy hybrids, bred from *A. millefolium* and *A.* 'Taygetea' in order to bring intermediate shades into achilleas' limited yellow or white-to-crimson color range. Its flowers open as an attractive salmon-pink, eventually aging to beige. They are particularly effective with other salmon-pink or cream flowers, and also with bronze foliage. As with similar hybrids that change color as the flowers age, they should be deadheaded if they pass to a shade that does not sit happily with those of their neighbors. Like all Galaxy hybrids, this is a dependable choice for dry, sunny places and soils of poorer quality. 'Apfelblüte' (Appleblossom) is similar, with flowers aging from pink to greyish white.

🌐 *Berberis thunbergii* f. *atropurpurea*, *Delphinium* 'Sungleam', *Diascia barberae* 'Blackthorn Apricot', *Foeniculum vulgare* 'Purpureum', *Iris pallida* 'Variegata'

H: 75cm (30in) S: 45cm (18in)
❀ **Early to late summer**
◐-◊◊ ▢-▧ **Z3 pH5–8**

After opening rose-pink, the flowers of *Achillea* 'Lachsschönheit' age to pale beige tints, harmonizing with the bronze leaves of *Heuchera micrantha* var. *diversifolia* 'Palace Purple', which grows in front. Removing the heuchera's flowers ensures fresh and healthy foliage.

In this cool-colored arrangement, the profuse blooms of *Achillea millefolium* 'Cerise Queen' provide the mainstay of the display, aided by crimson *Knautia macedonica*, bold heads of agapanthus, and a carpet of pansies. An additional bold-leaved plant at the front, perhaps one with glaucous or silver foliage, would give structure and anchor the design.

Achillea millefolium 'Cerise Queen'

Pink variants of *A. millefolium* are common in the wild, but examples that retain their color without developing greyish tints are rare, as are those that stand upright with little need for staking. 'Cerise Queen' succeeds on both counts and keeps its rich cerise coloring quite well, the small but plentiful flower heads fading only slightly as they age. Many inferior variants can be found under its name, however, and it is advisable to see plants in flower before buying. It is a good companion for crimson, blue, or purple flowers, and for purple foliage; it also mixes well with white flowers and silver foliage. It tolerates hot, dry, or sunny sites and poor soils, and benefits from frequent dividing. Another superlative hybrid, 'Summerwine', has very deep crimson flowers that do not become paler with age.

🌐 *Artemisia schmidtiana* 'Nana', *Berberis thunbergii* 'Atropurpurea Nana', *Ruta graveolens* 'Jackman's Blue', *Salvia* × *superba* 'Superba'

H: 60cm (24in) S: 45cm (18in)
❀ **Mid-summer to early autumn**
◐-◊◊ ▢-▧ **Z3 pH5–8**

The sumptuous, deep purplish blue flowers of monk's hood (*Aconitum napellus*), born on a tall and slender plant, provide a contrast with the dainty pink flowers of *Astrantia major* var. *rosea* in a steeply planted narrow border.

Aconitum napellus
MONKSHOOD

The spiked flowers of many *Aconitum* species produce bold effects, especially in mid-border. *A. napellus* has light indigo-blue spires, which make a classic contrast with achilleas, particularly in soft yellow, and also work well with grasses, Japanese anemones, and paler shades of blue, mauve, soft yellow, and cream. Variants include subsp. *vulgare* 'Carneum', which is flesh pink, and greyish white subsp. *v.* 'Albidum', both producing the purest colors and largest flowers where summers are cool and moist. Annually dividing plants in early autumn ensures long spikes and prolonged flowering, provided only the biggest tubers are replanted. Other choice species and cultivars include mid-blue and white *A.* × *cammarum* 'Bicolor' ♀ and white *A.* × *c.* 'Grandiflorum Album'. *A.* 'Spark's Variety' ♀ is deep purplish blue.

◖ *Anemone* × *hybrida* 'Honorine Jobert', *A.* × *h.* 'Elegans', *Aster* × *frikartii* 'Mönch', *Choisya ternata* Sundance, *Digitalis purpurea* f. *albiflora*, *Hosta* 'August Moon', *Miscanthus sinensis* 'Sarabande', *Stipa capillata*

H: 1.5m (5ft)   **S: 30cm** (12in)

☼ **Mid- to late summer**
 ◊◊ ▨ **Z5 pH5–7.5**

Acorus gramineus 'Variegatus'

A variant of the Japanese rush (not a true rush, but a member of the arum family), *A. gramineus* 'Variegatus' (syn. *A.g.* 'Argenteostriatus') resembles a grass in impact, with its attractive cream-edged leaves and insignificant flowers. A dainty plant, ideal for small-scale plantings or viewing at close range, it enjoys moist, humus-rich soils, boggy sites, and waterside beds. It has a cleaner appearance than some grasses, which can be disfigured by dying leaves, and looks effective with Candelabra primulas, calthas, In rich, moist soil by a pond, *Acorus gramineus* 'Variegatus' can reach as high as 45cm (18in), allowing it to rise over the vibrant vermilion Candelabra primula *P.* 'Inverewe'.

smaller astilbes, and small hostas. There are also several gold-variegated cultivars such as 'Oborozuki' and 'Ôgon'. *A. calamus* is similar but larger, and its cultivar 'Argenteostriatus' is a good choice for larger-scale plantings.

◖ *Astilbe* × *crispa* 'Perkeo', *Caltha palustris* 'Flore Pleno', *Hosta* 'Buckshaw Blue', *Primula japonica* 'Miller's Crimson', *P.j.* 'Postford White'

H: 35cm (14in)   **S: 20cm** (8in)   ❀ **(Late spring)**
◊◊◊ ▨-▨ **Z5 pH5–7**

The elegant coppery fronds of *Adiantum aleuticum* 'Japonicum' emerge in mid-spring, contrasting attractively with the blue flowers of Siberian squill (*Scilla siberica*).

Adiantum aleuticum 'Japonicum'

The leaves of this dainty maidenhair fern are bronze when they unfurl in spring. It is then most attractive among pure or greenish blue flowers. It associates happily with the blue of plants such as *Scilla siberica*, and some corydalis species, and with other ferns such as hart's tongue; smaller hostas and small epimediums, too, offer contrasting foliage. This fern also combines well with soft orange, cream, and salmon-pink, but the bronze coloring is easily overpowered by brighter or stronger colors.

◖ *Corydalis flexuosa*, *Epimedium* × *versicolor* 'Cupreum', *E.* × *v.* 'Sulphureum', *Hosta* (Tardiana Group) 'Halcyon', *Pulmonaria saccharata*

H: 60cm (24in)   **S: 45cm** (18in)
 ◊◊-◊◊◊ ▨ ▨ **Z8 pH5.5–7.5**

Agapanthus 'Loch Hope' ♡

Agapanthus are relatives of onions and, like them, have slim, handsomely arching foliage, which is usually deciduous. Umbels of generally blue flowers are held well above the leaves. They are stately, imposing plants, ideally suited to growing in the front or second rank of a border and in containers.

Hybrids and cultivars are usually hardier than the parent species. 'Loch Hope' blooms later than most, in late summer and early autumn. It has tall, upright stems and deep blue flowers that do not develop the reddish tints that mar some hybrids as they age. It works well with grasses such as miscanthus, with silver foliage, and with blue, mauve, purple, or pink flowers, and contrasts well with soft yellow flowers and gold foliage, such as that of golden hostas (in situations where some midday shade can protect the hosta leaves from scorching). Agapanthus need space on all sides for their magnificent foliage and flower stems to have maximum impact, so they should stand towards the front of the border and not be surrounded by other plants of their own height.

⬤ *Elaeagnus* 'Quicksilver', *Euphorbia schillingii*, *Hosta* 'Sum and Substance', *Iris pallida* 'Variegata', *Miscanthus sinensis* 'Variegatus', *Sambucus nigra* 'Aurea', *Sisyrinchium striatum* 'Aunt May'

H: 1.5m (5ft) S: 60cm (24in)
※ **Late summer to early autumn**
◊◊ ▢-▉ **Z7 pH5–7.5**

Blue flowers and creamy yellow variegation can provide a pleasant contrast, as here with *Agapanthus* 'Loch Hope', the variegated pampas grass *Cortaderia selloana* 'Aureolineata', and *Helichrysum petiolare* 'Roundabout', each supplying a distinctive foliage effect.

The gentle coloring of *Agastache* 'Firebird' matches perfectly the variegation of *Berberis thunbergii* 'Rose Glow', whose darker tints and red stems add richness.

Agastache 'Firebird'

This erect, bushy perennial has greyish foliage and slightly diffuse heads of flowers of almost indefinable color, somewhere between deep salmon-pink, coral, and soft orange. It looks most effective with hot flower colors such as oranges and scarlets – calceolarias in burnt orange, for example, and scarlet penstemons – but is also attractive with peaches, apricots, and creams. It mixes well with bronze foliage and silver-leaved plants such as *Plectranthus argentatus*. Sunny, dry positions are best, where it may be combined with other sun-lovers such as hemerocallis, achilleas, and crocosmias. It may also be grown in containers, an advantage in colder gardens since plants can then be moved under cover for winter protection.

⬤ *Argyranthemum* 'Jamaica Primrose', *Artemisia* 'Powis Castle', *Crocosmia × crocosmiiflora* 'Lady Hamilton', *Dahlia* 'Bishop of Llandaff', *Diascia barberae* 'Ruby Field', *Foeniculum vulgare* 'Purpureum'

H: 60cm (24in) S: 30cm (12in)
※ **Mid-summer to late autumn**
◊-◊◊ ▢-▉ **Z7 pH5–7.5**

Above: The mildly invasive bugleweed (*Ajuga reptans*) is an excellent plant for providing a decorative filler between other late spring and early summer flowers, its recessive tints helping to highlight brighter blooms of bolder shape. Here, it harmonizes with pink, lilac, and white *Symphytum ibericum* and flatters the handsome flowers of the Lenten rose (*Helleborus × hybridus*).

Below: Bugleweeds can be used with other prostrate foliage plants to create a carpet of subtly varied textures and colors. Here, the dark foliage of *Ajuga reptans* 'Atropurpurea' is contrasted against the tiny, pale, glaucous leaves of *Hebe pinguifolia* 'Pagei'.

Ajuga reptans
COMMON BUGLEWEED

This European wild flower has dozens of cultivars that spread into carpets of evergreen foliage, often colored or variegated, with upright spikes of purple-blue, pink, or white flowers. Choice varieties include 'Variegata', with leaves edged irregularly with cream; 'Multicolor', mottled pink and cream; and compact 'Pink Elf', with soft pink flowers. Vigorous 'Catlin's Giant' ♀ and 'Jungle Beauty' have larger leaves and blooms.

Given good, rich soil, bugleweeds make an excellent ground cover in sun or shade, under shrubs or at the front of borders, combined with pink, pale blue, and mauve flowers. They make classic partnerships with late narcissi, soft yellow primroses, and cowslips, and later with autumn crocuses and colchicums. Dark-leaved cultivars such as 'Purple Torch' and 'Atropurpurea' ♀ can be used as a dramatic background for pale flowers.

○ *Chionodoxa forbesii* 'Pink Giant' p.308 **B**, *Colchicum agrippinum* p.309 **A**, *Dianthus* Allwoodii Alpinus Group, *Erysimum hieraciifolium*, *Iris pallida* 'Argentea Variegata', *Origanum vulgare* 'Aureum' p.268 **C**, *Primula veris*, *Tulipa clusiana* var. *chrysantha*

H: 15cm (6in) **S: 60–90cm** (24–36in)
✿ **Late spring to early summer**
 ◌◌-◌◌◌ ☐-■ **Z3 pH5–7.5**

In this grouping relying principally on foliage for its effect, billowing mounds of lady's mantle (*Alchemilla mollis*) flowers anchor the design at the front of the border. *Cornus alba* 'Aurea' provides matching yellow-green in the background, while the bold, bright green leaves of a crocosmia form a focal point. The pale foliage of *Rhamnus alaternus* 'Argenteovariegata' offers a gentler, lighter tone.

Alchemilla mollis ♀
LADY'S MANTLE

This ground-cover plant is much tougher than its demure beauty suggests. The downy, scalloped leaves hold glittering droplets of rain or dew on their grey-green surface and, in summer, airy sprays of greenish yellow flowers appear like masses of tiny stars.

A. mollis supplies piquant color for all planting arrangements in full sun or light shade, adding astringency to pink, mauve, and blue flowers such as anchusas, and enhancing the impact of yellow, orange, and scarlet. It can be planted in gravel, or used to soften the edges of paths, or small groups can be repeated along the front of a border, combined with lamb's ears, pinks, grasses, and other spiky-leaved plants.

Trimming plants after flowering prevents lavish seeding and stimulates fresh young foliage to appear about two weeks later.

○ *Calendula officinalis*, *Cotoneaster horizontalis* p.43 **C**, *Dianthus* Allwoodii Alpinus Group, *Elymus magellanicus*, *Euonymus fortunei* 'Emerald 'n' Gold', *Festuca glauca* 'Elijah Blue', *Geranium* 'Ann Folkard', *Lupinus arboreus* p.66 **B**, *Penstemon* 'Chester Scarlet' p.394 **C**, *Rosa* Graham Thomas, *Rubus cockburnianus* 'Goldenvale' p.89 **A**, *Viola cornuta* Lilacina Group

H: 40cm (16in) **S: 60cm** (24in) ✿ **Early summer**
◌◌-◌◌◌ ☐-■ **Z3 pH4–8**

Allium schoenoprasum
CHIVES

A traditional edging for beds of other herbs, chives deserve wider use elsewhere in the garden. Plants form neat clumps of deep green, grass-like foliage, topped by tight, rounded heads of honey-scented mauve flowers. There are also good decorative cultivars such as clover-pink 'Forescate' and 'Pink Perfection' ♀, and several white forms, although some of these can be weak-growing.

Clumps of chives increase freely in volume, especially in moist, fertile soil, and are readily divided to provide plenty of plants for the front of sunny beds and borders, either in formal rows or as repeated groups. Their spiky, tufted shape and rich coloring make an exciting contrast to leafy herbs such as marjorams and purple- or gold-leaved sages, and in flower borders blend well with stachys,

primroses, and *Alchemilla mollis*. Chives can also be used to echo the shape of other alliums of different sizes but with similar flower color and form.

Deadheading by pulling out the flower stalks prevents self-seeding.

In this extended grouping of plants of similar height, clumps of a vigorous, white-flowered form of chives (*Allium schoenoprasum*) and of a white columbine (*Aquilegia vulgaris* 'Nivea') are intermingled and repeated to give a ghostly harmony. Deadheading will keep the foliage of both plants healthy and encourage a little reblooming.

⦿ *Allium moly*, *Buddleja alternifolia* p.33 **B**, *Lavandula stoechas* subsp. *pedunculata* p.64 **C**, *Origanum vulgare* 'Aureum', *Salvia officinalis* 'Icterina', *S.o.* 'Purpurascens'

H: 30cm (12in) S: 23cm (9in)
❀ **Late spring to mid-summer**
◖◗ ◊-◊◊ ▨-▩ Z4 pH5.5–7.5

Alstroemeria 'Apollo' ♀

Alstroemerias or Peruvian lilies have beautiful, often extravagantly marked flowers, small and lily-like in shape, with a distinctly aristocratic air. The blooms of most common species, born on clumps of leafy, wiry stems, appear in early and mid-summer, although some modern hybrids bloom later when other herbaceous flowers may be sparse. 'Apollo', soft white with a yellow throat, is an excellent choice for any border and may also be used for cutting. Like most alstroemerias, it contrasts well with plants of radically different growth habits, especially delphiniums and others with tall, slim flower spikes, and may be planted in large groups in rose beds.

Other modern cultivars often have opulent coloring and contrasting markings – examples include the Princess and Little Princess Series, and broad-petalled Dutch hybrids such as 'Friendship' and 'Yellow Friendship'. Most benefit from brushwood stakes when stems are about two-thirds their eventual height.

⦿ *Aconitum napellus*, *Campanula persicifolia*, *Delphinium* 'Sabrina', *Hydrangea paniculata* 'Grandiflora', *Rosa* 'Albertine', *R.* 'Felicia', *R.* 'Frensham'

H: 90cm (36in) S: 75cm (30in) ❀ **Mid-summer**
◖◗ ◊◊ ▨-▩ Z7 pH5.5–7.5

Hydrangea arborescens provides bulk and solidity next to a group of *Alstroemeria* 'Apollo'. The hydrangea flower heads will mature to pure white while the alstroemeria remains in flower, harmonizing with its beautifully marked blooms.

This grouping of hot colors, with *Alstroemeria aurea* and harmonious *Crocosmia* 'Vulcan', is given greater depth by the recessive purplish blue tints of *Aconitum* 'Spark's Variety' in the background.

Alstroemeria aurea

One of the easiest alstroemeria species (syn. *A. aurantiaca*), this typically has orange flowers (although the cultivar 'Lutea' is bright yellow). 'Dover Orange' and 'Orange King' are particularly rich selections. It looks best with hot colors and bronze foliage, but also contrasts effectively with bright pure blue or magenta; it is especially good with kniphofias, and soft orange or pale yellow achilleas. The plants are very vigorous and benefit from brushwood stakes inserted when about two-thirds their final height. Clumps can become congested, flowering less freely and for a shorter time. The best method of dividing them is to cut out portions after flowering and transplant them with their soil – the roots will not tolerate being teased out, or being moved in autumn. In dry climates, plants are prone to infestation by red spider mite.

Achillea 'Moonshine', *Cotinus coggygria* 'Royal Purple', *Geranium* 'Johnson's Blue', *Kniphofia* 'David', *Lychnis* × *arkwrightii* 'Vesuvius', *Rosa* 'Prince Charles'

H: 90cm (36in) **S: 60cm** (24in) **Mid-summer**
Z7 pH5.5–7.5

Alstroemeria ligtu hybrids

These are hybrids between *A. ligtu*, which has flowers varying in color from white to pale lilac or pinkish red, and *A. haemantha*, a variable, spreading species, with orange or dull red flowers streaked and splashed with yellow, maroon, and purple. The hybrids vary considerably, but their most common color is salmon-pink with yellow inner petals marked with maroon. With their relatively short stature, they are well suited to the front ranks of a border, where they make an ideal combination with bronze-leaved heucheras. They are also very effective with white, soft orange, and blue flowers, such as day lilies and *Polemonium caeruleum* or its white form *P.c.* subsp. *caeruleum* f. *album*, perhaps with a refreshing background of acid green *Philadelphus coronarius* 'Aureus'.

Cistus × *cyprius* p.38 **B**, *Geranium renardii*, *Heuchera micrantha* var. *diversifolia* 'Palace Purple', *Macleaya microcarpa* p.263 **A**

H: 75cm (30in) **S: 60cm** (24in) **Early summer**
Z7 pH5.5–7.5

The color of *Penstemon* 'Andenken an Friedrich Hahn' in the foreground is close enough to primary red to blend agreeably with the salmon flowers of the *Alstroemeria ligtu* hybrids beyond. They themselves harmonize with the color of the brick wall behind.

The florets of *Alstroemeria psittacina* have their own internal contrast provided by the green tips on their red blooms. Mixing the alstroemeria with *Nicotiana* 'Lime Green', its flowers harmonizing with the tips but contrasting with the predominant scarlet, creates a striking combination. A background of *Berberis thunbergii* 'Rose Glow', its rich leaf color enlivened by splashes of pink, completes the picture.

Alstroemeria psittacina

This is not a showy plant, but it looks very appealing at close range. Its rich rust-red flowers with green-tipped segments are effective with lime green flowers, such as *Nicotiana langsdorffii* or the large-flowered *N.* 'Really Green'. Scarlet companions are suitable, provided they are not overpowering, and plants with many smaller scarlet blooms are best – alonsoas or *Salvia microphylla* cultivars, for example. It is also good with salmon-pink. It makes a sultry contribution to hot groupings, especially with tawny orange and yellow flowers such as day lilies, achilleas, or *Rudbeckia hirta*. The slender stems can give a slightly tousled effect, often making the best impression next to plants of more solid growth habits and bolder foliage.

Alonsoa warscewiczii, *Cotinus coggygria* 'Royal Purple', *Euphorbia schillingii*, *Heuchera* 'Plum Pudding', *Phygelius* × *rectus* 'Salmon Leap'

H: 90cm (36in) **S: 45cm** (18in)
Mid-summer to early autumn
Z7 pH5.5–7.5

Above: The elegant white flowers of *Anemone* × *hybrida* 'Honorine Jobert' rise above the spherical seedheads of *Allium cristophii*, nestling among the anemone's basal leaves. The allium just rises over the silvery edging provided by the foliage of *Senecio viravira* at the front of the border.

Below: The cross-banded *Miscanthus sinensis* 'Zebrinus' is the right height to provide excellent contrast of form with the late Japanese anemone *A.* × *hybrida* 'Elegans'.

Anemone × hybrida

JAPANESE ANEMONE

Japanese anemones derive mainly from two species: *A. hupehensis*, with its variant var. *japonica* which has many narrow petals, and *A. vitifolia*. Their hybrid *A.* × *hybrida* and its cultivars are perhaps the most beautiful and useful to gardeners. A number have white or pink flowers. The commonest include white 'Honorine Jobert' ♥ (sometimes called 'Alba', but not to be confused with the same named synonym of 'Lady Ardilaun'), and several good pinks. 'Paxton's Original' is typical, but there is also 'Elegans', mid-pink becoming paler with age; 'Lady Gilmour', with heavily frilled, light green leaves; and 'Margarete' (also incorrectly called 'Lady Gilmour'), with almost double, pale pink flowers.

Japanese anemones are good with late roses such as Chinas and Hybrid Musks, with penstemons, pink chrysanthemums, asters such as *A.* × *frikartii* cultivars, and New York asters, with smaller miscanthus cultivars such as *M. sinensis* 'Gracillimus', and with silver or purple foliage.

◐ *Arundo donax* var. *versicolor* p.364 **C**, *Aster novi-belgii* 'Marie Ballard', *Chrysanthemum* 'Clara Curtis', *Clematis* 'Alba Luxurians', *Rosa* 'Penelope' ❏ p.356 **B**

H: 1.2–1.5m (4–5ft) S: 60cm (24in)

 ✿ **Late summer to mid-autumn**

◊◊ ▦ ■ **Z6 pH5–8**

The cypress spurge (*Euphorbia cyparissias*) is slightly invasive, enabling it to grow through a carpet of *Anthemis punctata* subsp. *cupaniana*, punctuating it with its acid yellow-green flower heads.

Anthemis punctata subsp. *cupaniana* ♥

This is an attractive carpeting plant, grown as much for its neat silver foliage as for the white flowers with their yellow centers. These appear mainly in early summer, although some blooms may be produced later, even into the autumn, encouraged by shearing plants after the main flowering period. Shearing also helps to keep them tidy and improves their color late in the season; untrimmed plants often turn greyish green.

It is a satisfying plant when grown at the front of a border, where it can tumble over adjacent paving or edging stones, and it also succeeds well in a gravel garden. It looks good with other silver foliage, with lavenders, sages, and other Mediterranean plants, including Dwarf Bearded irises, and with lime green flowers such as euphorbias or compact grasses like the smaller *Stipa* species. In hot, dry beds it is effective when planted beneath agaves, such as *A. americana*, and even columnar cacti.

◐ *Festuca glauca* 'Elijah Blue', *Helleborus foetidus*, *Iris* 'Curlew', *Kniphofia* 'Goldelse' p.255 **A**, *Lavandula angustifolia* 'Hidcote', *Myosotis alpestris*, *Salvia* × *sylvestris* 'Mainacht', *Stipa tenuissima*, *Tulipa* 'Ballerina' p.344 **B**, *T.* 'Fantasy' p.347 **B**

H: 30cm (12in) S: 90cm (36in) ✿ **Early summer**
◊ ▢ **Z7 pH5.5–7.5**

In this richly colored combination at the front of a border, orange *Anthemis sancti-johannis* and its companions – light magenta *Stachys macrantha*, purplish blue *Campanula latiloba* 'Highcliffe Variety', and dusky pinkish crimson *Astrantia major* 'Rubra' – are allowed to flop forward over the adjoining path.

Anthemis sancti-johannis

The true species of this herbaceous perennial is distinctive for the richness and intensity of its orange flowers, with short petals surrounding a central disc, although plants sold under this name are sometimes inferior hybrid seedlings – and these often occur in gardens if the true plant is grown close to *A. tinctoria*. *A. sancti-johannis* is an outstanding source of hot color for the front of a border, harmonizing with other oranges, as well as scarlets, yellows, creams, peaches, and apricots. It makes a striking contrast with violet-blue flowers – some of the more richly colored, short campanulas, for example – and combines well with many geums as well as with bronze-leaved heucheras. It can be short-lived, especially where drainage is less than perfect, and can suddenly disappear unless cut back immediately after flowering.

Alonsoa warscewiczii, Calendula officinalis 'Gitana Orange', *Campanula glomerata* 'Joan Elliott', *Geum* 'Lady Stratheden', *G.* 'Mrs J. Bradshaw', *Hemerocallis* 'Golden Chimes', *Heuchera micrantha* var. *diversifolia* 'Palace Purple', *Lychnis* × *arkwrightii* 'Vesuvius'

H & S: 60cm (24in) ⚘ **Early to mid-summer**
 ○ ▢ **Z5 pH5.5–7.5**

Anthemis tinctoria
GOLDEN CHAMOMILE

The front or second row of a well-drained border or gravel garden suits this showy plant, also known as dyar's chamomile, oxeye chamomile, or yellow chamomile. The bright yellow flowers make excellent contrasts with blues and harmonize with hot orange and red. It flowers so prolifically that it may exhaust itself unless sheared back after its first flush. Plants may be even more short-lived on poorly drained clay, although they are easily propagated from cuttings.

Choice variants of the species include 'E.C. Buxton' and 'Wargrave Variety', both in pale creamy yellow, and the even paler 'Sauce Hollandaise' – all are very good with silver plants. The hybrid *A.* 'Grallagh Gold' is golden yellow, and *A.* Susanna Mitchell ('Blomit') has white flowers.

Achillea 'Moonshine', *Aconitum* 'Spark's Variety', *Bidens ferulifolia* p.365 **B**, *Centaurea macrocephala*, *Clematis* × *eriostemon* 'Blue Boy' p.109 **A**, *Lavandula angustifolia* 'Hidcote', *Mimulus cardinalis*, *Rosa* 'Buff Beauty', *R.* Graham Thomas, *Tanacetum parthenium*

H: 60–90cm (24–36in) S: 60cm (24in)
⚘ **Early to mid-summer**
 ○-○○○ ▢-� **Z4 pH5.5–7.5**

The soft yellow flowers of *Anthemis tinctoria* 'E.C. Buxton' here provide a contrast with the slender spires of purple toadflax (*Linaria purpurea*) and the magenta, black-eyed blooms of the cranesbill *Geranium* 'Ann Folkard'. The cranesbill's yellowish green foliage harmonizes with the lemon daisy-like flower heads while also contrasting with its own flowers and those of the toadflax.

Beneath a canopy of deciduous trees in late spring, *Aquilegia canadensis* and *Phlox divaricata* form a carpet of gently contrasting flowers.

Aquilegia canadensis 🏆
WILD COLUMBINE

This dainty perennial has finely divided leaves, fern-like and dark green, and elegant, nodding flowers with scarlet sepals and lemon-yellow petals tapering to red spurs. *A. formosa* is similar but has bluish green foliage. Both species flower in late spring and early summer, and produce a more refined effect than *Aquilegia vulgaris*, which is altogether bigger and beefier.

Plants associate well with Dwarf and Intermediate Bearded irises, wallflowers, and the bronze foliage of some heucheras, especially those with reddish flowers. They harmonize with hot or warm colors such as peach and scarlet, although too much strong color overpowers their natural daintiness. They are good with cream or lime green, but contrasts with other flower colors are difficult to achieve.

Erysimum × *allionii, Euphorbia amygdaloides* var. *robbiae, Heuchera micrantha* var. *diversifolia* 'Palace Purple', *Iris* 'Curlew', *I.* 'Rocket' p.252 **C**

H: 38cm (15in) S: 20cm (8in)
⚘ **Late spring to early summer**
○○ ▢-▢ **Z3 pH4.5–7.5**

Aquilegia vulgaris
COLUMBINE

This is a very variable species, with single or double flowers, with or without spurs, and in colors ranging from white, pink, and pale blue to deep blue, crimson, and purple-black. 'Nivea' ♀ (also known as 'Munstead White') has nodding, single white flowers and grey-green leaves. *A.v.* var. *stellata* has spurless double flowers, lacking some of the charm of the typical columbine but with a grace of their own. Its famous variant is 'Nora Barlow', with petals that are reddish pink at the base, passing through white to green at the tips.

Bold, single flowers and less double variants of var. *stellata* have most impact at a distance, whereas complex, fully double types work best at close range. They are all very effective with irises, early roses, early cranesbills, hostas, and martagon lilies, as well as with purple foliage and umbel-shaped flower heads such as pink cow parsley.

All these aquilegias tolerate shade but are not very long-lived. Periodically raising replacements from seed is advisable, but only a few will produce true seedlings, and only then if plants have been growing in isolation.

◉ *Allium schoenoprasum* (white) p.183 **A**, *Anthriscus sylvestris* 'Broadleas Blush', *Centaurea montana* 'Alba' p.201 **C**, *Hosta* (Tardiana Group) 'Halcyon', *Iris* 'Cambridge', *Paeonia lactiflora* 'Albert Crousse'

H: 60–90cm (24–36in) **S: 45cm** (18in)
✽ **Late spring to early summer**
◖◗ **Z3 pH4.5–7.5**

Right: A mauve-flowered strain of *Aquilegia vulgaris* var. *stellata* harmonizes perfectly with the spherical flower heads of *Allium hollandicum* 'Purple Sensation' around silvery *Seriphidium nutans*.

Below: An informal mix of *Aquilegia vulgaris* in pinks and whites, plus lavender-blue *A.* 'Hensol Harebell', combines pleasantly with cranesbills, including the mourning widow (*Geranium phaeum*) in the foreground, the wood cranesbill (*G. sylvaticum*) just behind it, and white *G. phaeum* 'Album'. All would flower equally well in semi-shade.

Arrhenatherum elatius subsp. *bulbosum* 'Variegatum'

VARIEGATED TALL OAT GRASS

The striped form of the tall oat grass is a brilliantly white-variegated plant for the front of a border. Ideally it will be grown in moist soil, and in full sun in areas where summers are cool; in hotter climates a little shade is advisable. Plants look attractive with dark or silver foliage, such as purple-grey *Sedum telephium* 'Matrona' or *Stachys byzantina* 'Big Ears', and contrast well with richly colored flowers including *Hemerocallis* 'Red Rum' and similarly sumptuous short daylilies, and harmonize with pastel blues and mauves.

This grass is best kept away from mat-forming plants because its rhizomatous roots spread fairly freely underground and may become entangled with those of its neighbors. The foliage is prone to rust, and it should be clipped back near or just after flowering time, otherwise by late summer the plant looks untidy. This is particularly so where the soil is dry or impoverished.

A

○ *Allium cristophii*, *Artemisia stelleriana* 'Boughton Silver', *Crocosmia* 'Lucifer', *Hemerocallis* 'Stafford', *Ophiopogon planiscapus* 'Nigrescens'

H & S: 30cm (12in)
✿ (Mid-summer to early autumn)
◇-◇◇ ▢-▨ **Z4 pH5–7.5**

Linear foliage, including the white-striped *Arrhenatherum elatius* subsp. *bulbosum* 'Variegatum', sword-shaped crocosmia, and arching, gold-banded pampas grass (*Cortaderia selloana* 'Aureolineata'), is contrasted with clouds of the goldenrod *Solidago* 'Goldenmosa' in a combination suitable for a broad, informally planted bed.

B

Artemisia alba 'Canescens' ♛

Few other silver foliage plants can rival the daintiness of this cultivar, whose remarkably lacy leaves are divided into thread-like sections that coil into twists and curlicues. The flowering stems form delicate spires, although the flowers themselves are insignificant, even slightly unattractive. This is a plant for well-drained soils, towards the front of a border. It is charming with cranesbills, pinks, smaller campanulas and, above all, old roses, and it makes pleasant harmonies with soft colors such as pinks, blues, and mauves. It also works well with less dainty artemisias such as *A. stelleriana* in white schemes. The foliage contrasts effectively with bolder shapes, and with dark or glaucous foliage, like that of Dwarf or Intermediate Bearded irises; companions of differing leaf forms but closely allied coloring, such as silver-green *Convolvulus cneorum*, can also prove satisfying.

○ *Campanula* 'Burghaltii', *Dianthus* 'Doris', *Geranium sanguineum* var. *striatum* p.230 **A**, *Iris* 'Grapesicle', *Nemophila menziesii*, *Nigella damascena*, *Rosa* 'Charles de Mills', *R.* 'Fantin-Latour'

H: 45cm (18in) **S: 30cm** (12in)
✿ Mid-summer to early autumn
◇ ▢ **Z5 pH5.5–7.5**

Deadheading *Artemisia alba* 'Canescens' after its first flush of flowers has here produced an uncharacteristically late second crop of filigree spires of buds in early autumn, contrasting with the solid, flat flower heads of *Sedum* 'Herbstfreude', nestling in front of the variegated dogwood *Cornus alba* 'Elegantissima'.

Artemisia ludoviciana

For much of the season, the slender stems of this attractive perennial bear willowy leaves, some with cut or forked ends in clear silvery white, although later they turn dull green as the white flowers assume brownish tints with age. The remedy is to cut growth back by half when about 75cm (30in) high, which stimulates plants to bush out and remain fresh and silver. 'Silver Queen' ♥ has lax, stems about 90cm (36in) high; the more refined var. *latiloba*, about 60cm (24in) tall, is broader, with more silvery leaves largely uncut. All are good in silver foliage displays or with plants such as lavenders and cistus, and work well with flowers in pastel pinks, mauves, and pale blues. They contrast well with richer colors like crimson, and with dark foliage, although care is necessary to avoid overwhelming their delicacy.

◐ *Cistus* × *purpureus*, *Geranium tuberosum* p.231 **A**, *Hebe* 'Watson's Pink' p.56 **C**, *Iris* 'Nightfall' p.250 **B**, *Penstemon* 'Chester Scarlet' p.394 **C**, *Rosa* 'Carmenetta', *Tulipa* 'Palestrina' p.352 **B**

H: 1.2m (4ft) S: 60cm (24in)
❀ **Mid-summer to early autumn**
 ◊-◊◊ ▣-▨ **Z4 pH5.5–7.5**

Above: A subtle interplay of leaf shapes in silvery grey-green is achieved by combining *Artemisia ludoviciana* var. *latiloba* and filigree *Senecio cineraria*, interlaced with bronze-tinged umbels of dill (*Anethum graveolens*), providing a delicate interplay best appreciated at close range.

Below: The typical species *Artemisia ludoviciana* has leaves more lobed and divided than its variety above, making a less bold but daintier effect. Here, wood forget-me-nots (*Myosotis sylvatica*), self-seeded the previous summer, spangle the young artemisia foliage with sky-blue flowers.

In a broad and shallowly banked grouping, a carpet of compact silvery *Artemisia schmidtiana* 'Nana' spreads before clumps of bronze sedge (*Carex flagellifera*), in front of the handsome spurge *Euphorbia characias*.

Artemisia schmidtiana ♥

The silky, glistening foliage of this silver plant makes a strong impact at the front of a border. Its best known variant is perhaps 'Nana' ♥, which is only 8cm (3½in) or so high and produces a very low, spreading mat of foliage. The small yellow flowers of this and the species itself are not especially attractive and are usually best cut off.

These are some of the easier, more tolerant silver plants to grow and, like many artemisias, may be used with a wide range of other silver-leaved plants and Mediterranean natives such as lavenders, sages, pinks, and cistus. They are very satisfying with flowers in pastel pinks, mauves, and pale blues, or contrasted with dark foliage and richly colored flowers.

◐ *Berberis thunbergii* 'Atropurpurea Nana', *Cistus* × *purpureus*, *Dianthus* Allwoodii Alpinus Group, *Lavandula lanata*, *Rosmarinus officinalis* Prostratus Group, *Rosa* Pink Bells, *Salvia officinalis* 'Purpurascens'

H: 30cm (12in) S: 45cm (18in)
❀ **(Mid- to late summer)**
 ◊-◊◊ ▣-▨ **Z4 pH5.5–7.5**

Artemisia stelleriana 'Boughton Silver' 🏆

Sometimes known as beach wormwood, this semi-evergreen (syns *A.s.* 'Mori' and 'Silver Brocade') is a sprawling, prostrate plant, much shorter than the typical species, with deeply indented silvery leaves, and flowers of similar color arrayed in sprays. It is an ideal choice for the front of a border, for a gravel or rock garden, or for softening the edge of an adjoining path. A good partner for cool-colored flowers and silver or glaucous foliage, it is attractive when fronting mound-forming plants such as smaller grey-leaved hebes, lavenders, sages, rosemaries, smaller cistus, helichrysums, perovskias, rue, lavender cottons, and other artemisias, together with dianthus, marjorams, and smaller irises. It also intermingles successfully with other sprawling plants that grow at a similar rate, including smaller cranesbills, grey-leaved veronicas, stachys, and sedums, and bulbs such as alliums planted beneath.

Dianthus Allwoodii Alpinus Group, *Hebe pinguifolia* 'Pagei', *Lavandula angustifolia* 'Hidcote', *Origanum vulgare* 'Aureum', *Perovskia* 'Blue Spire', *Salvia officinalis* 'Kew Gold', *Sedum spectabile* 'Brilliant'

H: 15cm (6in) **S: 40cm** (16in)

Mid-summer to early autumn

Z4 pH5.5–7.5

Although *Artemisia stelleriana* 'Boughton Silver' is far less vigorous than *Geranium* 'Ann Folkard', planting the artemisia near to the limit of the cranesbill's spread prevents it being overwhelmed by its neighbor and allows an attractive intermingling of the two.

Aruncus dioicus

GOATSBEARD

This statuesque herbaceous perennial has elegantly divided leaves and imposing plumes of tiny creamy white flowers, male and female on separate plants (as the females produce copious quantities of invasive seed, only the male form has the ♕). It is a choice plant for mixed or herbaceous borders, for waterside planting, or for use as a focal point, especially against a dark background. Its harmonizes with astilbes and contrasts prettily with delphiniums, achilleas, campanulas, and Shrub roses, while its color, which mixes with most others, is very effective with yellow, pure white, warm peach or apricot, and yellow-green foliage or flowers. Good partners include euphorbias, ligularias, telekias, golden philadelphus or elderberries, and medium-sized bamboos. Among its variants are 'Kneiffii', a smaller, dainty plant with leaflets that narrow to threadlike strips; upright 'Glasnevin', with narrower plumes; and 'Southern White', which has branching spikes and tolerates hot summers.

Achillea 'Lachsschönheit', *Astilbe* 'Red Sentinel', *Heuchera* 'Pewter Moon', *Ligularia dentata* 'Desdemona', *Philadelphus intectus* p.72 **A**, *Rosa* 'Highdownensis'

H: **1.8m** (6ft) **S:** **1.2m** (4ft)

Early to mid-summer

Z3 pH4.5–7.5

A

The splendid architectural form of goat's beard (*Aruncus dioicus*) makes it a good choice where a specimen plant is needed, as here where it contrasts with a crisply formal opening through a hedge of beech (*Fagus sylvatica*). A pair of clipped boxwoods (*Buxus sempervirens*) in containers, one on either side, echoes the formality of the beech.

Asclepias tuberosa

BUTTERFLY WEED

Hot summers and good drainage are essential for this tuberous herbaceous perennial if it is to continue flowering late in the season. Its flowers are usually vermilion with a golden yellow center, giving an overall impression of orange, but there are numerous selections with different colors, such as golden 'Hello Yellow', 60–75cm (24–30in) high, and Gay Butterflies Group, also 60–75cm (24–30in), in a range of colors including scarlet, gold, pink, and orange. It looks very effective with other hot-colored perennials, such as hedychiums with dahlias, late-flowering euphorbias and alstroemerias, kniphofias, leonotis, cannas, rudbeckias, heleniums, arctotis hybrids, salvias, and roses. It is also a good partner for bronze foliage, yellow-green foliage and flowers, and annuals such as salvias, tagetes, ursinias, and dimorphothecas.

Arctotis × hybrida 'Flame', *Canna indica* 'Purpurea', *Hedychium coccineum* 'Tara', *Kniphofia* 'Sunningdale Yellow', *Tagetes patula* 'Striped Marvel'

H: **45–90cm** (18–36in) **S:** **30cm** (12in)

Mid-summer to early autumn

Z4 pH5.5–7.5

B

This vibrant combination of orange butterfly weed (*Asclepias tuberosa*) and the mauve, dark-centered flowers of narrow-leaved *Echinacea tennesseensis* provides a contrast of floral form on plants of similar height. Both are wild flowers of the North American prairies.

C

Growing in a crevice in a limestone rockery, the bold unfurling fronds of hart's tongue fern (*Asplenium scolopendrium*) are furnished from spring into summer with the azure-blue blooms of *Lithodora diffusa* 'Heavenly Blue'.

Asplenium scolopendrium ♕

HART'S TONGUE FERN

This is a handsome, hardy evergreen fern, with strap-shaped leaves 5–60cm (2–24in) long, that are often crested, wavy, or forked. The simplest kinds are perhaps the most useful and can look almost tropical when grown well. It is a shade-loving species for moist conditions, and mixes well with hardier begonias, ivies, asarums, shade-tolerant sedges, and other ferns such as athyriums and polystichums. Its evergreen foliage complements spring bulbs such as snowdrops and cyclamens, and provides interest under deciduous shrubs when these are out of leaf. Good selections include the ruffled Crispum Group, including 'Crispum Bolton's Nobile' ♕; Fimbriatum Group, with narrow, deeply serrated fronds; and Ramocristatum Group, with divided, crested fronds. The leaves of 'Kay's Lacerated' ♕ are more or less triangular and deeply cut at the edges.

Asarum shuttleworthii, *Convallaria majalis* p.204 **A**, *Cyclamen coum*, *Galanthus nivalis*, *Hedera helix* 'Manda's Crested', *Lobelia richardsonii* p.385 **B**

H & S: **30–60cm** (12–24in)

Z4 pH4–8

Aster divaricatus

The wiry, nearly black stems of this aster (syn. *A. corymbosus*) bear heart-shaped leaves that are among the most handsome of the genus. From mid-summer onwards, they also carry starry white flowers that associate well with almost any other color. This shade-tolerant species has a graceful growth habit, and looks best when draping forward naturally over other plants, particularly if these will accept some shade later in the year. The sprawling aster growth might interfere with the flowers of its neighbors, unless these are produced earlier in the season – as with heucheras, bergenias, and bugleweeds, for example. *A. divaricatus* is perhaps at its best in a woodland garden, whose shade few late flowers tolerate so well. Although the rhizomatous roots eventually spread to form loose groups, for full impact it should be planted closely in generous drifts to produce a delicate haze of white stars. *A. macrophyllus* is a more robust plant of similar temperament, but its pale violet flowers, fading to white, are less magical in wooded situations.

Achillea millefolium 'Cerise Queen', *Anemone* × *hybrida* 'Elegans', *Deschampsia cespitosa*, *Miscanthus sinensis* 'Gracillimus', *Rhus* × *pulvinata* Autumn Lace Group, *Salvia* × *superba* 'Rubin'

In a classic combination, suitable for the front of a bed or border, the dainty flower stems of Aster divaricatus *drape themselves over the bold leaves of mixed bergenias. The star-like aster flowers will continue into autumn.*

H & S: 60cm (24in)

Mid-summer to mid-autumn

Z4 pH5–7.5

Aster × frikartii 'Mönch' ♔

Many consider this to be the finest aster for long display. Its soft lavender-blue flowers with a yellow disc go well with almost any color except lavender or lilac, which are too similar and may be diminished by close comparison. The flowers harmonize with blues and purples, and contrast dramatically with orange – some late-flowering crocosmias, for example, or the early autumn tints of the ornamental vine *Vitis coignetiae*. They also look very pleasing with silver foliage, chrysanthemums, or dahlias, particularly the soft pale yellow, rose-pink, and purple kinds.

This aster benefits from staking with brushwood, which should be worked into the plant when about two-thirds of its flowering height, and is best replanted in fresh ground every three years or so. There is a lot of unhealthy stock in circulation, and it is always advisable to buy plants from stock that is known to be vigorous and free-flowering.

Chrysanthemum 'Clara Curtis', *Dahlia* 'Pink Michigan', *Echinacea purpurea* 'Magnus', *Heliopsis helianthoides* 'Patula' p.236 **A**, *Rudbeckia fulgida* var. *sullivantii* 'Goldsturm', *Stipa tenuissima*, *Verbena bonariensis*

H: 80cm (31in) S: 40cm (16in)

Mid-summer to mid-autumn

Z5 pH5.5–7.5

Although the camera sees its color as lying between lilac and mauve, Aster × frikartii *'Mönch' has petals of soft lavender, contrasting with the flowers' yellow centers. In this lively, long-flowering summer grouping,* Aster novae-angliae *'Harrington's Pink' supplies abundant smaller harmonious blooms. Both asters are resistant to tarsonemid mite.*

Above: The lavender-blue *Aster novi-belgii* 'Marie Ballard' is sufficiently definite in color to be contrasted with the rich yellow, dark-centered daisy-like flowers of *Rudbeckia fulgida* var. *deamii*, also providing a contrast of floral form.

Left: *Aster novi-belgii* cultivars are often associated with impressionistic swirls of lavender and mauve, although bolder colors are available, such as the carmine 'Carnival' here. Adding plants of contrasting growth habits could give more structure to this border planting.

◐ *Anemone × hybrida* 'Honorine Jobert', *Chrysanthemum* 'Wedding Day', *Cortaderia selloana* 'Aureolineata', *Cotinus* 'Flame', *Dahlia* 'Pink Michigan' p.374 **C**, *Kniphofia rooperi*, *Miscanthus sinensis* 'Morning Light', *Vitis coignetiae*

H: 30–120cm (12–48in) S: 30–40cm (12–16in)

❋ **Late summer to mid-autumn**

▇▇▇▇▇▢ ◌◌-◌◌◌ ▨-▨ **Z3 pH4.5–8**

Aster novi-belgii

NEW YORK ASTER

New York asters provide immensely useful color from late summer to mid-autumn, although most cultivars bloom only for about a month. Colors range from crimson, purple, and nearly blue, through all the paler shades to white, with individual flowers varying from single to fully double, and from about 1cm to 7cm (½–2½in) across. They are good with other late summer and autumn flowers such as Japanese anemones, chrysanthemums, and dahlias, in pink, white, crimson, or soft yellow. They also work well with strongly textured or structured plants such as miscanthus, pampas grass, and some later-flowering kniphofias.

Plants may be attacked by aphids or aster wilt, and all but the shortest need staking. It is best to divide them annually in spring, replanting a vigorous section of rhizome, but they can be left undisturbed for up to three years before they start to decline.

Astilbe × arendsii hybrids

These astilbes need waterside or bog planting, or a damp border. They produce dazzling displays in colors from crimson and scarlet to mauve-pink, rose-pink, and salmon, and in white. Flamboyant cultivars may look unnaturally bright in waterside and boggy sites, and here the least vibrant colors are most useful, particularly if they also have a graceful, arching growth habit. They can be planted with water-loving iris species, *Ranunculus aconitifolius*, white zantedeschias, and glaucous-leaved hostas, with aruncus or sorbarias to echo their form.

For brighter, more highly colored schemes, crimson and rich pink cultivars can be grown with purple foliage and with flowers in similar tones. Scarlet cultivars may be mixed with

Soft pink *Astilbe × arendsii* 'Ceres' is a late-flowering, gently colored cultivar suited to subtle associations. Here, it harmonizes with the purplish, pink-splashed leaves of *Berberis thunbergii* 'Rose Glow'.

variegated and gold-leaved plants, such as hostas or dogwoods, with bronze foliage, or with ligularias. All contrast well with strap- or grassy-leaved irises.

Astilbes are best divided in early autumn and are very prone to vine weevil attacks.

◐ *Aruncus dioicus*, *Cornus alba* 'Elegantissima', *Hosta sieboldiana* var. *elegans*, *Iris pseudacorus* 'Variegata', *I. sibirica* 'Cambridge', *Ligularia dentata* 'Othello', *Lobelia* 'Queen Victoria', *Sorbaria sorbifolia*

H: 50–120cm (20–48in) S: 45cm (18in)

❋ **Late spring to mid-summer**

▇▇▇▇▢ ◌◌◌ ▨-▨ ▇ **Z5 pH5.5–7**

The erect, carmine-pink spires of *Astilbe chinensis* var. *taquetii* 'Superba', contrasted with orange *Crocosmia* 'Vulcan' and yellow kniphofias and day lilies, help to emphasize the straight geometric lines of this formal garden area.

Astilbe chinensis var. *taquetii* 'Superba' ♈

This astilbe, which flowers unusually late, has a stiffly upright growth habit useful for semi-formal accents in a formal border or at the water's edge. It tolerates full sun in moist soil, but its color is best in shade, next to mauve, lavender, lilac, purple, and other cool hues, and contrasting with soft yellow, yellow-green, and white flowers or variegated foliage; it also blends with silver or purple foliage. Effective companions are perennial lobelias, lythrums, lysimachias, filipendulas, monardas, and late-flowering euphorbias, and plants such as hostas or larger sedges and grasses, including bamboos. 'Purpurlanze' is tall and branching, with magenta spikes. Other good variants are mauve-pink *A.c.* var. *pumila* ♈; *A.c.* 'Visions', with spreading magenta-pink panicles; and 'Finale', with broad pink spikes.

◉ *Carex grayi*, *Euphorbia schillingii*, *Filipendula camtschatica*, *Hosta* 'Shade Fanfare', *Lysimachia clethroides*, *Mimulus aurantiacus*, *Phyllostachys nigra*

H: 1.2m (4ft) **S: 60cm** (24in)

❀ **Late summer to mid-autumn**

◊◊-◊◊◊ ☐-■ ■ Z4 pH5.5–7

Astilbe 'Red Sentinel'

An early-flowering astilbe, 'Red Sentinel' is suitable for bog gardens and waterside plantings, and also for borders where the soil does not become dry in summer. Its rich red flowers and dark foliage are very close to primary red, mixing happily with mauve-pink or rose-pink companions, including other astilbes and later-flowering primulas such as Candelabra hybrids, and with hot colors; it can also be contrasted with yellow-green foliage and flowers. It makes an effective partner for euphorbias, earlier-flowering ligularias, and mimulus, and combines well with the contrasting foliage of grasses, sedges, smaller bamboos, and hostas. Other good companions include plants with red-flushed foliage, including Japanese maples, and moisture-tolerant lilies such as *L. superbum* and *L.* Bellingham Group.

◉ *Acer palmatum* f. *atropurpureum*, *Euphorbia amygdaloides* var. *robbiae*, *Iris ensata*, *Primula* Inshriach hybrids, *Sasa veitchii*

H: 90cm (36in) **S: 50cm** (20in) ❀ **Early summer**

◊◊-◊◊◊ ☐-■ ■ Z4 pH5.5–7

In this brightly colored waterside planting, *Astilbe* 'Red Sentinel' stands out against the yellow-green foliage of the dogwood *Cornus alba* 'Aurea'. In between, the lofty flowers of *Hosta* 'Tall Boy' are starting to unfurl. All three plants benefit from the pond's moisture.

The intricate flowers of *Astrantia major* 'Hadspen Blood', their dusky pink umbels enclosed in a ruff of crimson bracts, harmonize perfectly with the dark foliage of *Berberis thunbergii* 'Atropurpurea Nana'.

Astrantia major 'Hadspen Blood'

Although blooming mainly in summer, this handsome astrantia will produce some autumn flowers, all in a dusky ruby-red that is an excellent foil for brighter colors, such as richer crimson and brighter carmine, magenta, and rich pink. It also combines effectively with white flowers and with dark-leaved heucheras and smaller purple-leaved berberis or ornamental cherries. It can be partnered by roses, especially old roses in crimson or dusky pink, shrubby lavateras, *Geranium psilostemon* cultivars and hybrids, *Achillea millefolium* cultivars, *Phlox maculata* cultivars, and reddish leaved phormiums, and looks very attractive with magenta species gladioli and light green *Gladiolus tristis* var. *concolor*. Other dark-flowered cultivars include 'Ruby Cloud', 'Ruby Wedding', and the rather variable 'Claret'.

◉ *Cotinus* 'Flame', *Foeniculum vulgare* 'Purpureum', *Heuchera micrantha* var. *diversifolia* 'Palace Purple', *Phormium* 'Bronze Baby', *Rosa* 'Charles de Mills'

H: 60cm (24in) **S: 45cm** (18in)

❀ **Early to late summer**

◊◊ ☐-■ ■ Z4 pH5–7.5

In this complex tapestry of varied leaf forms, the boldly margined foliage of *Astrantia major* 'Sunningdale Variegated' is the focal point. It is joined by pale-spotted lungwort and glaucous-leaved roseroot (*Rhodiola rosea*), nestling against wild marjoram (*Origanum vulgare* 'Aureum').

Astrantia major 'Sunningdale Variegated' ♀

This brightly variegated cultivar has spring foliage splashed with cream, darkening to green by mid-summer. It is a choice plant for spring edging and for sparkling combinations with white or yellow tulips and late narcissi, or with blue flowers such as brunneras or omphalodes. The dusky pink flowers that appear in early summer are quietly attractive, but by this stage the brightness of the leaves has diminished, so 'Sunningdale Variegated' is primarily a plant for early foliage effects, pale enough to go with almost any other, but especially satisfying with yellow, white, or blue flowers, and with yellow-green foliage and flowers. Among its many suitable partners are early-leafing hostas, bluebells, forget-me-nots, rock cress, aurinias, primroses, polyanthus, and euphorbias.

◑ *Acer palmatum* var. *dissectum, Aconitum napellus, Diascia barberae* 'Blackthorn Apricot' p.210 **C**, *Hebe ochracea* p.56 **A**, *Spiraea japonica* p.93 **C**

H: 60cm (24in) **S: 45cm** (18in)
❀ **Early to late summer**
 ◊◊ ◻-◼ ◼ **Z4 pH5–7.5**

Athyrium filix-femina ♀
LADY FERN

With its love of moisture, this elegant deciduous fern is a delightful plant for bog or waterside plantings, woodland gardens, and shady town gardens that are not too dry. It is perhaps most effective in subdued groupings based simply on shades of green, especially in late spring and early summer, when the lacy foliage is at its freshest. It contrasts well with smaller bamboos, hart's tongue ferns, grasses, and sedges, and may be grown through a carpet of low ground cover, when the repeated pattern of its shuttlecock-shaped clumps of fronds can make an arresting statement. There are several dozen strikingly different kinds, including the feathery 'Vernoniae' ♀; 'Frizelliae' ♀, the tatting fern, with fan-shaped lobes along the frond midribs; and 'Victoriae', which has narrow pinnae that branch to form crosses.

◑ *Asplenium scolopendrium, Carex grayi, Fargesia murielae* 'Simba', *Hedera canariensis* 'Ravensholst', *Milium effusum* 'Aureum', *Pachysandra terminalis*

H: 15cm–1.5m (6in–5ft) **S: 20cm–1m** (8in–3¼ft)
◊◊-◊◊◊ ◻-◼ ◼ **Z4 pH4–7.5**

On a shady bank in late autumn, the arching fronds of a lady fern (*Athyrium filix-femina* Cruciatum Group) form a delicate tracery of criss-crossed feathers above the autumn fern (*Dryopteris erythrosora*), an evergreen named for the bronze color of its young fronds.

Aubrieta 'Argenteovariegata'

This evergreen perennial with purple blooms and leaves edged in creamy white is an attractive plant for rock gardens, sunny banks, walls, troughs, and border edgings. If cut back after flowering, it produces a new crop of variegated leaves and shoots, which add interest when the plant is out of flower. Its color harmonizes with white, soft yellow, purple, or lilac flowers, and contrasts with yellow-green flowers and foliage. Good companions include early-flowering euphorbias, soft yellow wallflowers, aurinias, white rock cress, smaller narcissi, ipheions,

Purple *Aubrieta* 'Argenteovariegata' and white-flowered *Arenaria montana*, two plants of similar stature, flower shape, and size but of contrasting flower color, make a pleasant pattern on a sunny slope in spring.

chionodoxas, and small spring-flowering shrubs such as daphnes or spiraeas. Plants are short-lived and are best propagated from summer cuttings every three or four years.

◑ *Erysimum* 'Moonlight', *Euphorbia polychroma* 'Major', *Ipheion uniflorum, Narcissus bulbocodium, Spiraea japonica* 'Goldflame' (foliage)

H: 5cm (2in) **S: 60cm** (24in) ❀ **Mid- to late spring**
◊◊ ◻-◼ ◼ **Z5 pH5.5–8**

A

Rich lilac aubrieta makes an attractive foil for the bold white flower heads of perennial candytuft (*Iberis sempervirens*) in late spring.

Aubrieta cultivars

These easy, mat-forming, evergreen perennials are suitable for rock gardens, sunny banks, walls, hanging baskets, and spring bedding. Over a hundred cultivars are available, in showy colors from ruby-red to lavender-blue, and shades between these and white. They are effective with spring bulbs such as muscaris, smaller narcissi and tulips, and ipheions, and with rock cress, perennial candytufts, primroses, polyanthus, and smaller bedding violas. Plants in walls can become sparse in summer, but revive during winter to flower profusely in spring. Good seed-raised cultivars include the Royal Series, such as 'Royal Red' and 'Royal Purple'. 'Novalis Blue' ♀ is very close to sky-blue; the Bengal hybrids include semi-double flowers in red and purple; and the Cascade Series makes a floriferous ground cover.

◐ *Arabis alpina* subsp. *caucasica* 'Variegata', *Euphorbia amygdaloides* var. *robbiae* p.218 **B**, *Ipheion uniflorum*, *Muscari armeniacum*, *Narcissus* 'Hawera', *Primula* 'Guinevere', *Tulipa clusiana* p.346 **A**, *Viola tricolor*

H: 5–15cm (2–6in) S: 30cm (12in)
✿ **Mid- to late spring**
 ◊◊ ▢-◼ **Z4–5 pH5.5–8**

Aurinia saxatilis ♀

A sub-shrubby and mound-forming plant, this easy evergreen perennial (syn. *Alyssum saxatile*) suits the same situations as *Aubrieta* cultivars (left), with which it can be combined. It is an excellent edging plant for the front of a border, and associates well with small white or cream narcissi, smaller tulips, muscaris, ipheions, perennial candytufts, rock cress, primroses, polyanthus, and wallflowers. A large expanse of aurinias can appear dull in texture, so they are best arranged in diffuse groups, intermingled with other plants of contrasting form, such as bulbs or, in a larger rock garden, dwarf conifers. Cultivars include 'Citrina' ♀, an extremely attractive lemon-yellow; 'Compacta', which is shorter and neater, and more suitable for smaller planting groupings; apricot-colored 'Dudley Nevill', also relatively compact; and 'Variegata', with leaves edged in creamy white.

◐ *Cerastium tomentosum*, *Erysimum linifolium* 'Variegatum', *Ipheion uniflorum*, *Juniperus horizontalis* 'Bar Harbor', *Muscari armeniacum*, *Narcissus* 'Actaea'

H: 25cm (10in) S: 45cm (18in)
✿ **Late spring to early summer**
◼▨▢ ◊◊ ▢-◼ **Z4 pH5.5–8**

C

Two plants with attractive silvered foliage suited equally to containers or the front of beds and borders, *Ballota pseudodictamnus* and the feathery-leaved wormwood *Artemisia* 'Powis Castle' create a pleasing picture of contrasting foliage forms.

B

Grown through gravel scree at the front of a sunny bed, the compact lemon-yellow *Aurinia saxatilis* 'Citrina' and gold *A.s.* 'Compacta' form spreading mats smothered with bloom in late spring, with white-flowered perennial candytuft (*Iberis sempervirens*) and the slightly taller spurge *Euphorbia polychroma* 'Major' beyond. Deadheading the aurinias will encourage some later blooming.

Ballota pseudodictamnus ♀

Woolly grey-green leaves and white stems characterize this mound-forming, sub-shrubby perennial, which is an exceptionally useful plant for a white garden. It may also be grown in front of roses, in a gravel garden, and at the front of a border, where it associates well with cistus, lavenders, shrubby phlomis, helianthemums, and similar Mediterranean plants, as well as with silver foliage plants of contrasting form such as artemisias. Its white or pinkish white flowers are somewhat insignificant, but plants blend pleasantly with other blooms of almost any color, although less successfully with hot or strong shades. The plant keeps it leaves all through the year; annual clipping in spring helps to maintain a neat and tidy plant.

◐ *Cistus* × *purpureus*, *Helianthemum* 'Rhodanthe Carneum', *Lavandula angustifolia* 'Hidcote', *Phlomis fruticosa*, *Rosa* 'Felicia', *Rosmarinus officinalis* 'Roseus', *Salvia officinalis* 'Purpurascens'

H: 45cm (18in) S: 60cm (24in)
✿ **(Late spring to early summer)**
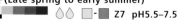 ◊◊ ▢-◼ **Z7 pH5.5–7.5**

The airy indigo spires of *Baptisia australis*, recessive in color and less visually insistent than the lupines they resemble, form an attractive background for the sumptuous cupped pink blooms of *Rosa* 'Aloha'.

Baptisia australis ♧

The indigo-blue flowers of this elegant herbaceous perennial are born in airy spikes, reminiscent of a lupine, but much more understated and less emphatically vertical. A plant for the second or third row of a border, it has a quiet charm that makes it suitable for supporting roles with foliage and flowers of more definite form and stronger color, such as delphiniums, roses, cranesbills, and Tall Bearded irises. It blends well with silver and glaucous foliage, and with other cool colors, especially cream – the flowers of some *Anthemis tinctoria* cultivars, for example. Its blooms are a little too diffuse and too subtly colored, however, to succeed in strong contrasts with colors such as yellow. Its spikes of large, dark grey seedpods are attractive in autumn, after the first frosts, and may be cut for indoor decoration.

⦿ *Artemisia ludoviciana*, *Dahlia* 'Requiem' p.375 **A**, *Delphinium* 'Sabrina', *Geranium × oxonianum* 'Wargrave Pink', *Rosa glauca*, *Spiraea nipponica* 'Snowmound'

H: 1.2m (4ft) S: 60cm (24in) ❈ **Early summer**
◌-◌◌ ▨-▨ **Z3 pH5.5–7.5**

Bergenia cordifolia 'Purpurea' ♧

This bergenia is one of the most outstanding foliage plants, pre-eminent in a genus noted for handsome leaves. Although attractive, its pink flowers are perhaps best regarded as a bonus, complementing the leathery, shiny, rounded leaves, which are deep green and assume a purple flush in winter. Tolerating soils ranging from dry to very moist, it is an indispensable plant for a woodland or gravel garden, and for the front of a border, especially in full sun, which encourages the richest purple coloring. Winter-flowering plants such as *Cyclamen coum* variants, early crocuses, winter heaths, snowdrops, and winter aconitums make the most satisfying companions, but this bergenia also combines well with evergreen heucheras, smaller evergreen shrubs such as euonymus, and dogwoods with colored winter stems, and with foliage of contrasting form – evergreen grasses, sedges, and ferns, for example. It will also tolerate, even thrive in, light shade, and so may be grown in front of a relatively lax plant, such as codonopsis or one of the floppier species of aster, that will sprawl over the bergenia for part of the year. It is propagated in early autumn by dividing clumps and replanting vigorous young sections of rhizome at the soil surface; this practice can prevent a build-up of vine weevil infestation if done once every five years or so.

⦿ *Carex comans* (bronze), *Codonopsis ovata*, *Cornus alba* 'Sibirica', *Crocus tommasinianus*, *Eranthis hyemalis*, *Erica carnea* 'Springwood White', *Euonymus fortunei* 'Silver Queen', *Hedera colchica* 'Sulphur Heart'

H: 60cm (24in) S: 75cm (30in)
❈ **Late winter to late spring**
◌◌ ▨-▨ **Z3 pH4.5–7.5**

Glossy purple above and red below, the foliage of *Bergenia cordifolia* 'Purpurea' (heartleaf bergenia) is most richly tinted in late winter and early spring, coinciding in season with delicate white snowdrops (*Galanthus nivalis*).

Bergenia 'Morgenröte' ♛

The rich carmine flowers of this evergreen perennial, born clear of the leaves on strong stems, appear in mid- to late spring and again in early summer or mid-autumn, especially if plants are deadheaded. 'Morgenröte' is an excellent partner for early irises and for crimson, purple, or pink primulas, including primroses, polyanthus, and Candelabra varieties. Its late flowers associate well with plants that have distinctly different form and foliage such as astilbes. It also makes striking contrasts with the bright yellow-green of euphorbias and *Alchemilla mollis*, orange Candelabra primulas, and crown imperials. This bergenia generally combines well with purple-leaved plants, especially *Berberis thunbergii* and *B.t.* 'Atropurpurea Nana' – although the effect may be leaden without the addition of some paler-colored foliage.

◐ *Erythronium revolutum*, *Euphorbia polychroma* 'Major', *Fritillaria imperialis* 'The Premier', *Primula* Cowichan Garnet Group, *Tulipa* 'Prinses Irene'

H & S: 45cm (18in) ✿ **Mid- to late spring**
◌◌ ▢-▢ ▆ **Z4 pH4.5–7.5**

Although in sunny situations and warm climates, the second flowering of *Bergenia* 'Morgenröte' can begin very shortly after the first flush ends (provided the plant has been deadheaded), it can sometimes reach a spectacular climax in mid-autumn, coinciding in season with *Sedum* 'Herbstfreude', as here. Both are handsome-leaved plants that work especially well at the front of a border.

Buphthalmum salicifolium

A remarkably long flowering season, from early summer to early autumn, and profuse flowering are notable qualities of this plant. It is a good choice for a sunny spot, ideally in poor soil. Its tendency to flop looks effective at the front of a border, spilling onto a path perhaps, or over edging. The rich gold flowers complement other hot colors, and also combine well with purple-leaved plants, such as heucheras, particularly those with scarlet flowers, or dwarf purple berberis. Fairly amorphous in appearance, this buphthalmum looks best with contrasting foliage, such as that of short, yellow-green or gold-variegated grasses or some irises – Tall Bearded irises flower at the same time, but look rather tall unless planted behind, whereas Intermediate and Dwarf Bearded irises flower earlier.

◐ *Achillea* 'Martina', *Crambe maritima*, *Delphinium* (Belladonna Group) 'Völkerfrieden', *Iris orientalis*, *Verbascum* (Cotswold Group) 'Gainsborough'

H & S: 60cm (24in)
✿ **Early summer to early autumn**
▆▆ ◌-◌◌ ▢-▢ **Z4 pH5–8**

The tiny sky-blue florets of *Brunnera macrophylla* harmonize with the larger, changeable pink to blue flowers of pulmonarias. This excellent combination is particularly suitable for positions near the front of a bed or border, in humus-rich soil and partial shade.

Brunnera macrophylla ♛

This herbaceous perennial has dainty blue forget-me-not flowers and bold, heart-shaped leaves, silver spotted in some variants. Its slightly coarse appearance makes it suitable for wilder settings, or for planting under roses in a rose garden, especially with early yellow roses. It blends well with other early yellow flowers, such as primroses and cowslips, with gold-edged hostas, and with golden millet grass. White or soft yellow tulips and late narcissi are also excellent partners.

Two brightly variegated cultivars, a little too extravagant for a wild garden, are good choices for more cultivated areas: 'Hadspen Cream' ♛ has yellowish, cream-edged leaves that tolerate full sunlight, unlike the bold, creamy white variegation of 'Dawson's White', which can burn in hot sun. This cultivar makes a very bright highlight, but needs moisture and grows relatively slowly.

◐ *Erythronium californicum* 'White Beauty' p.313 **A**, *Hosta* 'Zounds', *Juniperus squamata* 'Filborna' p.62 **B**, *Narcissus* 'Hawera', *Primula veris*, *Rosa pimpinellifolia* 'Grandiflora', *Tulipa* 'Golden Oxford' p.348 **A**

H: 45cm (18in) **S: 60cm** (24in)
✿ **Mid- to late spring**
◌◌ ▢-▢ ▆ **Z4 pH4–7.5**

In this long border entirely of yellow-flowered plants, *Buphthalmum salicifolium* (oxeye) is backed by evening primrose (*Oenothera biennis*), with the marigold *Tagetes tenuifolia* 'Lemon Gem' blooming in front. Bold or grassy foliage could be included to add varied form and texture.

Caltha palustris ♈
MARSH MARIGOLD

This member of the buttercup family is a showy, moisture-loving plant, equally successful in damp ground, bog gardens, and waterside sites, and even as a pond plant in shallow water up to 20cm (8in) deep. Its bold, golden yellow flowers and glossy, fleshy, round leaves, which form dramatic clumps, are particularly suited to naturalizing in small colonies in swampy or marginal positions. This plant makes satisfying partnerships with primroses and polyanthus, especially those in pale yellow or orange, with evergreen sedges and grasses with yellow-green or bronze foliage, and with early-leafing ferns.

'Flore Pleno' ♈ makes a smaller plant, with complex, fully double flowers that merit viewing from close range, while the variant often sold as *C. polypetala* is larger and more vigorous, with particularly large, single flowers. The creamy white *C. palustris* var. *alba* produces its flowers in early spring, often before the leaves appear. It is a compact plant, suitable for sheltered, moist or boggy situations, and looks especially attractive combined with *Primula denticulata* and *P. rosea*, its regular companions in the wild.

◉ *Brunnera macrophylla, Carex oshimensis* 'Evergold', *Hosta fortunei* var. *albopicta, Lysichiton americanus* p.262 **A**, *Ranunculus ficaria* 'Brazen Hussy'

H: 15–40cm (6–16in) **S: 45cm** (18in)
❀ **Early to late spring**
〇〇〇 ▪ Z4 pH5–7.5

Alongside a stream, the heart-shaped leaves and glossy yellow flowers of marsh marigold (*Caltha palustris*) emerge at the same time as the strikingly striped foliage of *Iris pseudacorus* 'Variegata'. The combination will remain colorful for some two months, although the iris's variegation will begin to fade by summer.

The dusky lilac-grey bells emerging from maroon buds of *Campanula* 'Burghaltii' are the only colored flowers in this arrangement of white blooms and silvery foliage, including feathery *Artemisia pontica*, spiky *Eryngium giganteum*, white *Papaver orientale*, and *Lychnis coronaria* 'Alba', but their muted color does not disturb its tranquillity.

Campanula 'Burghaltii' ♈

The upright stems of this unusual and striking hybrid bear long, tubular, pendent flowers in a subtle shade of lilac-grey. It is good at the front of a border, perhaps set off by a carpeting plant in the foreground. It can be grown in full sun in areas where summers are cool, but elsewhere it retains its color best when shaded from bright sun. Its delicate coloring is easily overwhelmed by strident neighbors, such as those with bright yellow flowers, and is most attractive partnered with rich shades of mauve, purple, and campanula-blue, or with pure white or cream. It makes a charming combination with silver-leaved plants such as artemisias, and with pale-colored pinks, and also works well with smoky purple foliage. 'Van-Houttei' is a similar hybrid but with darker flowers.

◉ *Artemisia ludoviciana, Dicentra* 'Stuart Boothman', *Geranium clarkei* 'Kashmir Purple', *G.* 'Sue Crûg', *Heuchera* 'Pewter Veil', *Nepeta* × *faassenii*

H: 60cm (24in) **S: 30cm** (12in)
❀ **Early to mid-summer**
〇〇 ▪-▪ Z4 pH5–7.5

A

This cool combination features *Campanula* 'Kent Belle' and the double-flowered feverfew *Tanacetum parthenium* 'Rowallane'. *Perovskia* 'Blue Spire' grows through the feverfew and will take over its display in late summer.

Campanula 'Kent Belle'

This superlative hybrid campanula tolerates shade sufficiently to merit a place in partially shaded borders or lighter parts of a woodland garden. Its rich purplish blue coloring mixes well with cool shades such as mauve, lilac, pink, and blue, as well as white, cream, or soft yellow, and looks very attractive with silver or glaucous foliage. It can partner hostas, cranesbills, silver-leaved lamiums, thalictrums, echinops, and aconitums, including cream and pale yellow cultivars, and can be planted among old roses, hydrangeas, and *Potentilla fruticosa* cultivars. It contrasts effectively with yellow-green flowers and foliage, including alchemillas and variegated grasses. If cut back in mid-summer, right after flowering, it will continue producing new flowering shoots into autumn.

◑ *Aconitum lycoctonum* subsp. *vulparia*, *Hosta fortunei* var. *albopicta* f. *aurea*, *Lamium maculatum* 'White Nancy', *Potentilla fruticosa* 'Primrose Beauty'

H: 90cm (36in) S: 60cm (24in)
✿ **Early to late summer**
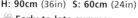 ○○ ☐-■ **Z5 pH5–7.5**

C

The sturdy and statuesque spikes of the pinkish buff perennial foxglove *Digitalis* × *mertonensis* give structure to this grouping, while the more diffuse stems of *Campanula persicifolia alba* planted through it leaven the effect.

Campanula latifolia
GIANT BELLFLOWER

Robust and shade-tolerant, this herbaceous campanula is suitable for perennial or mixed borders and wild or woodland gardens, and can be naturalized in coarse grass. Its flowers vary in color from white to deep purplish blue. White variants, sometimes known as 'Alba', are among the most useful – they are particularly good with other white or pale flowers, with contrasting dark foliage, and with orange lilies. The deep lavender-blue var. *macrantha* and rich lavender-blue 'Brantwood' are suitable for the same combinations as *C.* 'Kent Belle' (above). 'Gloaming', pale greyish lavender, is good with pure white and cream flowers; 'Pallida' is even paler and can be used in the same way where a ghostly effect is required. 'Roger Wood' has bicolored lavender and white flowers on 1m (3¼ft) stems.

◑ **White:** *Anthriscus sylvestris* 'Ravenswing', *Delphinium* 'Alice Artindale', *Lilium* 'Enchantment' **Blue:** *Aruncus dioicus*, *Geranium* × *oxonianum* 'Wargrave Pink', *Echinops bannaticus* 'Taplow Blue'

H: 90–120cm (36–48in) S: 60cm (24in)
✿ **Early to mid-summer**
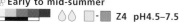 ○○ ☐-■ **Z4 pH4.5–7.5**

B

In a semi-wild setting, trailing stems of the white-flowered Rambler rose *R.* 'Seagull' drape down to the ground, from a bank of shrubs behind, to interact with the ghostly bells of *Campanula latifolia* 'Gloaming' planted at the front of the shrubbery in partial shade.

Campanula persicifolia
PEACH-LEAVED BELLFLOWER

Garden selections of this variable species have flowers that may be bell-shaped or almost flat, single or double, and pure white to campanula-blue. 'Hampstead White' is an extremely graceful double; 'Fleur de Neige' ♛ has well-formed white double flowers; and plants grown as *alba* are more or less pure white, blending with almost any color and excellent in white arrangements or with silver foliage. Blue-flowered variants combine with cool colors and with glaucous or silver foliage, and are effective with white, cream, or soft yellow Shrub and Ground Cover roses. All benefit from being placed in front of neighbors of their own height, and behind plants such as pinks, catmints, lavenders, or hostas. They complement plants of contrasting floral form, such as thalictrums and artemisias, the flat plates of achilleas, and the spiky flowers of veronicas or salvias.

◑ **Blue:** *Nepeta* 'Six Hills Giant', *Rosa* 'Nozomi', *Thalictrum delavayi* ☐ p.171 **A**
White: *Hosta fortunei*, *Scabiosa* Butterfly Blue p.284 **B**

H: 60–120cm (24–48in) S: 30cm (12in)
✿ **Early to mid-summer**
 ○○ ☐-■ **Z4 pH5–7.5**

Campanula takesimana

This herbaceous bellflower with a strong creeping rootstock grows best in light to partial shade, although it tolerates more sun in areas with cool summers. A pale greyish pink with maroon spots inside, its flowers cannot compete with bright, brash colors, but it combines effectively with plants with purple, red-flushed, or white-variegated leaves, including heucheras, bugleweeds, and rodgersias, and it is outstanding with white or deeper pink and with soft yellow-green or lime green flowers, such as nicotianas. It is an attractive partner for astilbes, lilies, and cranesbills, and good with contrasting foliage such as the strap-shaped leaves of larger grasses and the more shade-tolerant irises, or the bold leaves of hostas. In moist, humus-rich soils, it can become almost invasive.

🔘 *Ajuga reptans* 'Multicolor', *Astilbe × arendsii* 'Venus', *Helictotrichon sempervirens*, *Heuchera* 'Plum Pudding', *Lilium candidum*, *Rodgersia pinnata* 'Superba'

H: 60cm (24in) S: 45cm (18in)
✽ **Early to mid-summer**
◊◊ ▣-■ **Z5 pH5–7.5**

At the front of a semi-shady border, the substantial, dusky grey-lilac bells of *Campanula takesimana* harmonize perfectly with clouds of tiny heuchera flowers, providing a contrast of floral form.

A

B

The maroon calyces of *Cautleya spicata* 'Robusta' match the flowers of chocolate cosmos (*C. atrosanguineus*) in front, and harmonize with the foliage of *Dahlia* 'David Howard' behind. The color of its small, hooded, yellow flowers is reflected in those of *Heliopsis helianthoides* (left), *Hypericum kouytchense* (top right), and *Calceolaria angustifolia* (bottom right).

Cautleya spicata 'Robusta'

This is a handsome relative of ginger, growing from a tuberous rootstock and happy in partial shade, although in areas with cool summers it can be grown successfully in full sun. It is a plant for the second or third row of a border, where its broad handsome leaves, rather like those of a canna, and spikes of yellow florets emerging from rich maroon bracts have an almost tropical appearance that suits hot-colored schemes. Its two-toned flowers combine dramatically with yellows and maroons or scarlets, including plants such as late-blooming achilleas, dahlias, cannas, later-flowering crocosmias, chocolate cosmos, kirengeshomas, scarlet lobelias, and hedychiums. It is an attractive companion for tender perennials such as coleus, and for plants with deep red or bronze foliage – dark-leaved heucheras, for example – and makes effective contrasts with yellow-green, such as late-flowering euphorbias.

🔘 *Canna* 'Erebus', *Crocosmia × crocosmiiflora* 'Carmin Brillant', *Euphorbia schillingii*, *Hedychium coccineum* 'Tara', *Lobelia* 'Queen Victoria'

H: 90cm (36in) S: 45cm (18in)
✽ **Late summer to mid-autumn**
◊◊ ▣-■ ■ **Z7 pH5–7.5**

Centaurea montana

MOUNTAIN BLUET, PERENNIAL CORNFLOWER

The glory of this traditional cottage garden plant is the intricacy of its deep blue flowers, which deserve to be seen at close quarters. It is an attractive choice for the front of a border, together with pinks, lavenders, and columbines, or cushion-forming plants such as catmints, and is especially valuable for providing color between the main flush of spring flowers and most of the summer flowering plants. It can be combined with Bearded irises, achilleas, dicentras, early cranesbills, day lilies, and silver foliage plants such as artemisias, and used for contrasts with soft yellow including trollius. Useful variants include 'Alba', with pure white flowers; pink 'Carnea'; 'Gold Bullion', which is blue with yellow-green leaves; creamy white 'Ochroleuca'; and amethyst 'Parham'.

🔘 *Achillea* 'Moonshine', *Artemisia schmidtiana*, *Centranthus ruber* p.202 **A**, *Digitalis lutea* p.212 **B**, *Kniphofia* 'Atlanta', *Tulipa* 'Elegant Lady' p.347 **A**

H: 45cm (18in) S: 60cm (24in) ✽ **Early summer**
◊◊ ▣-■ **Z3 pH4.5–7.5**

C

In a sunny border in late spring, the boldly shaped flowers of white mountain bluet (*Centaurea montana* 'Alba'), extravagantly flared outwards from their black-netted knobs, bring light into this cottage garden mixture of columbines (*Aquilegia vulgaris*) in various colors.

A charming late spring display, with a variety of flower forms, mixes the typical rich pink valerian (*Centranthus ruber*), deep blue mountain bluet (*Centaurea montana*), and the long-flowering cranesbill *Geranium* 'Johnson's Blue'.

Centranthus ruber

RED VALERIAN

Easy to grow, and highly attractive to bees and butterflies, red valerian bears rose-pink flowers from late spring to late summer. It enjoys a position in a sunny border but is seen at its best when naturalized in walls or stony banks.

Two common color variants are the good white form 'Albus', with the most glaucous leaves, and the deep red 'Atrococcineus'. Each breeds true in isolation, but if grown near another variant seedlings can be mixed, with colors ranging from white to deepest black-red. Of these, the delicate pale pink form is one of the most desirable for planting with silver foliage and in soft color schemes. The rose-red form complements yellow-green and rose-pink flowers and bronze foliage, but does not mix well with strong, bright shades such as blue, purple, or crimson. Its slightly diffuse growth benefits from association with more structural plants such as Bearded irises.

⬤ *Deutzia longifolia* 'Vilmoriniae' p.45 **C**, *Euphorbia polychroma* 'Major' p.220 **B**, *Rosa* 'Easlea's Golden Rambler' p.141 **A**, *R.* Iceberg p.165 **B**

H & S: 90cm (36in)

✿ **Late spring to late summer**

░░░░░░ ◊-◊◊◊ ▢-▣ **Z5 pH5–8**

Chaerophyllum hirsutum 'Roseum'

The ferny foliage and lacy pink flowers of this cultivar are especially attractive in late spring, its main season; if plants are deadheaded, they will flower again on and off throughout the summer. It is a suitable candidate for fairly informal plantings and for a wild garden, although it is also valuable in more sophisticated arrangements – combined with white-edged hostas and late tulips, for example, perhaps in a bed nearer the house. It can look effective with contrasting foliage, such as that of Siberian irises, and with white flowers or purple foliage, and harmonizes prettily with columbines of all colors. Other good companions include late primulas (such as *Primula japonica* cultivars), *Paeonia officinalis* cultivars, and grasses, which provide a fine contrast in texture. It tolerates most sites, but prefers moist soil in a reasonably sunny position.

⬤ *Cotinus coggygria* 'Royal Purple', *Hosta fortunei* 'Francee', *Iris* 'Cambridge', *Miscanthus sinensis* 'Morning Light', *Tulipa* 'White Triumphator'

H & S: 60cm (24in)

✿ **Late spring to early summer**

░░░░░░ ◊◊ ▢-▣ **Z5 pH4–7.5**

This pleasant planting arrangement for spring, good in either sun or partial shade, combines lacy pink *Chaerophyllum hirsutum* 'Roseum' with the maroon flowers of the mourning widow (*Geranium phaeum*), to give a subtle and subdued combination suitable for wilder parts of a garden or even for naturalizing.

Chrysanthemum

Chrysanthemums are immensely useful for providing late color, with plants flowering from mid-summer until the onset of frost and even later in the case of the hardiest kinds. Thousands of cultivars are available, the majority of them raised specifically to produce cut flowers or pot plants and of only limited hardiness outdoors (usually Zone 9).

Varieties that belong to the Early-flowering Outdoor Groups may be used outdoors when grown from spring cuttings taken from roots overwintered indoors, but their hardiness is generally limited to Zone 9. A few varieties prove hardy enough for Zone 8, including the excellent scarlet 'Pennine Signal' ♥, 75cm (30in) tall and flowering in late summer and early autumn. Early-flowering kinds such as this should be deadheaded to extend their flowering period into autumn (this does not benefit later-flowering ones, however, since their season is limited by frost). Most early kinds flower for a month or two – pot-grown plants of these can be valuable for replacing summer bedding that is exhausted early.

The hardiest chrysanthemums are divided into three main groups: Pompon, Korean, and Rubellum chrysanthemums; all are generally hardy to Zone 5. Those in the Pompon Group have globular, tightly packed, fully double flower heads. Among those recommended are 'Anastasia' (pink, 60cm/24in, mid- to late autumn); 'Bronze Elegance' (60cm/24in, late autumn); 'Bronze Fairy' (45cm/18in, autumn); 'Jante Wells' (vivid golden yellow, 30cm/12in, mid-summer to autumn); 'Mei-kyo' (deep carmine, 60cm/24in, late autumn); 'Nantyderry Sunshine' ♥ (mid-yellow, 60cm/24in, mid- to late autumn); and 'Salmon Fairie' (45cm/18in, autumn). Korean chrysanthemums are early, outdoor spray chrysanthemums, mostly with single or semi-double flowers, and include 'Ruby Mound' (60cm/24in, autumn) and 'Wedding Day' (white with a green eye, 75cm/30in, autumn). Rubellum chrysanthemums, hybrids derived from *C. zawadskii* (syn. *C. rubellum*), have single, semi-double, or double blooms. They include 'Apricot' (single, 75cm/30in, autumn); 'Clara Curtis' (single, clear pink, 75cm/30in, late summer to mid-autumn); 'Emperor of China' (double pink with quilled petals, foliage red-tinted in autumn, 1.2m/4ft, late summer and autumn); 'Mary Stoker' (single pink, tinted apricot-yellow, 75cm/30in, late summer and early autumn); 'Mrs Jessie Cooper' (semi-double, red, 75cm/30in, late

summer and early autumn); and 'Nancy Perry' (semi-double, deep pink, 75cm/30in, late summer and early autumn).

A fourth kind that is increasingly used for outdoor display is the Charm Group ("cushion mums"), raised originally for pot-plant cultivation. They are generally compact and form neat mounds of single flowers. Although most are not hardy in areas colder than Zone 9, the Yoder Series contains many varieties claimed to survive in Zone 8 – Bravo ('Yobra'), which is deep red, 30cm/12in tall, and flowers in late summer to mid-autumn, is a typical example. They generally make dwarf plants that are good for carpeting and for bedding in the front of borders, but when massed in large groups the shortest varieties can appear unnaturally even. A more unaffected look can be achieved by planting irregular groups with a few single plants scattered away from the main colony. The shortest of the plants in this group, especially pale pink, crimson, or wine-purple kinds, would be very effective planted as a carpet beneath *Nerine bowdenii*.

The golden amber flowers of *Chrysanthemum* 'Honey', one of the Early-flowering Outdoor Intermediate Group, combine with the flat, deep rose flower heads of *Sedum spectabile* 'Septemberglut' to provide warm tints towards the front of a border in early autumn.

Chrysanthemums may be combined with asters – blue asters, for example, are good partners for wine-purple, carmine, crimson, white, or soft yellow chrysanthemums. They also work well with dahlias and Japanese anemones, and with schizostylis lilies or grasses for foliage contrast. Hot-colored chrysanthemums are particularly satisfying companions for grasses that are yellow-variegated or that turn red, bronze, or orange in autumn, and for shrubs that color well in autumn, such as smoke bush.

◉ *Anemone × hybrida* 'Honorine Jobert', *Aster novi-belgii* 'Ada Ballard', *Cortaderia selloana* 'Aureolineata', *Cotinus* 'Flame', *Dahlia* 'Requiem', *Rhus × pulvinata* Autumn Lace Group, *Schizostylis coccinea* 'Major'

H: 20–150cm (8–60in) S: 30–60cm (12–24in)

❅ **Mid-summer to mid-winter**

◌◌ ☐-■ Z5–9 pH5.5–7

Convallaria majalis ♔

LILY-OF-THE-VALLEY

Lily-of-the-valley has attractive foliage and pretty, richly scented white flowers, which are best appreciated at close range (they are also superb for cutting). It prefers partial shade, but tolerates almost full shade and also full sun where summers are cooler. Excellent in woodland gardens, it can also be planted in mixed or shrub borders under deciduous shrubs, such as azaleas and roses, or with violets, European wood anemones, spring bulbs, and primroses. It combines well with plants with contrasting foliage – for example, early or evergreen ferns, blue mertensias, and corydalis. It is quite invasive, and best grown away from choice, slow-growing plants.

'Fortin's Giant', 30cm (12in), is the largest and boldest variety, and the best at longer range; the bright, striped 'Vic Pawlowski's Gold' is only 15cm (6in), slow-growing, and good at close range; 'Hardwick Hall', 25cm (10in), has leaves with cream margins.

● *Anemone nemorosa, Arum italicum* 'Marmoratum', *Chelidonium majus, Corydalis flexuosa, Erythronium* 'Pagoda', *Mertensia virginica, Primula vulgaris*

H: 15–30cm (6–12in) **S: 30cm** (12in)
❁ **Late spring**

◊◊-◊◊◊ ☐-■ **Z4 pH4.5–7.5**

The bold leaves and bell-shaped florets of lily-of-the-valley (*Convallaria majalis*) combine with the unfurling fronds of hart's tongue fern (*Asplenium scolopendrium*) and the contrasting foliage of *Polystichum setiferum* Divisilobum Group, a hedge fern in which the tiny pinnules are separate and do not overlap, giving a lacy effect.

A

Although *Achillea* 'Coronation Gold' is rather taller than *Coreopsis lanceolata* 'Sterntaler', it nods down to mingle with its companion, their golden yellow flower heads producing a close color harmony.

Coreopsis lanceolata 'Sterntaler'

C. lanceolata is a long-flowering perennial that may be grown as an annual, with various cultivars available offering a range of heights from 25 to 60cm (10–24in). 'Sterntaler' forms clumps of numerous wiry stems, each sporting a bright golden yellow flower with a brown disc – these make fine, long-lasting cut flowers. In areas with hot summers, especially in dry soils, the display may be short-lived; but a cool season will prolong flowering, and deadheading will extend the display into autumn. It is an excellent choice for the front or second row of a border, and has maximum impact when combined with hot colors or in deliberate clashes with, for example, magenta or gentian-blue. Its rich color and the profusion of its flowers can overwhelm paler blues, however. Owing to its slightly amorphous shape, it benefits from a position next to plants with bold leaf forms or interesting textures, such as grasses.

◉ *Aconitum napellus*, *Delphinium* 'Blue Nile', *Geranium* 'Johnson's Blue', *G. psilostemon*, *Hakonechloa macra* 'Alboaurea', *Helictotrichon sempervirens*

H & S: 40cm (16in)

❀ **Late spring to late summer**

 ◊·◊◊ ☐-■ Z4 pH5.5–7.5

Cortaderia selloana
PAMPAS GRASS

Although its reputation has suffered slightly from crude and over-enthusiastic Victorian use, this is an excellent plant for dramatic focal points, catching the eye with its fountain of foliage and creamy plumes of flowers that remain attractive all winter.

Pampas grasses are extremely variable: they range in height from 1.2 to 3m (4–10ft), and in hardiness from Zone 5 to Zone 9; flowering times vary from late summer to mid-autumn. To be sure of selecting the most suitable variety, it is best to buy a named, predictable clone or acquire an offset of a suitable clone growing locally. This can be divided in late spring.

'Sunningdale Silver' ♀ is perhaps the tallest clone at 3m (10ft), with magnificent feathery, silvery white plumes in late autumn; however, it is hardy only to Zone 8, unreliable and shy-flowering in cool conditions. For paler tones, 'Albolineata' and 'Aureolineata' ♀ are effective variegated cultivars that flower in early autumn, are 2m (6½ft) high, and hardy only to Zone 8.

'Pumila' ♀, 1.5m (5ft) high and hardy to Zone 6, is very reliable, flowering profusely in early autumn. Its numerous stiff, silvery cream flower heads are upright and lack elegance, but the foliage, markedly shorter than in the larger cultivars, arches beautifully to produce a handsome specimen plant for smaller gardens, especially as a feature near water. *C. richardii*, 2.5m (8ft) high and hardy to Zone 8, flowers in mid-summer, producing slim, parchment-colored plumes that move freely in the breeze. It is earlier flowering, starting in mid-summer, and the plumes arch expansively so that flowering plants can occupy a significantly larger area of ground than their basal leaf clumps, and this should be allowed for when placing companions.

The arching growth habit of most pampas grasses needs space to display itself to full effect, so plants are best positioned slightly in front of their rank in the border, surrounded by shorter neighbors, including other grasses and stately herbaceous perennials such as inulas, thalictrums, *Knautia macedonica*, *Scabiosa japonica* var. *alpina*, and richly colored daylilies.

All pampas grasses look best in more natural plantings, in scattered or informal groups. They grow naturally in vast colonies spreading across South American plains, hence their slightly artificial appearance when grown as lonely specimens in a lawn or as a front garden centerpiece. This can be remedied by combining them within a community of larger grasses, where they create effective textural harmonies with plants such as miscanthus and molinias, perhaps against a background of bamboos, or by integrating them as focal points in lavish autumn planting schemes with New York asters, Japanese anemones, and taller chrysanthemum cultivars.

◉ *Acer griseum*, *Agapanthus* 'Loch Hope' p.181 **A**, *Anemone hybrida* 'Lady Gilmour', *Arrhenatherum elatius* subsp. *bulbosum* 'Variegatum' p.188 **A**, *Aster novi-belgii* 'Fellowship', *Chrysanthemum* Rubellum Group, *Cotinus* 'Flame', *Deschampsia cespitosa*, *Euonymus hamiltonianus* subsp. *sieboldianus* p.49 **C**, *Picea pungens* 'Koster', *Rhus pulvinata* Autumn Lace Group, *Sedum* 'Herbstfreude' p.285 **B**, *Stipa calamagrostis*

H: 1.2–3m (4–10ft) S: 1.8m (6ft)

❀ **Late summer to mid-autumn**

■ ◊◊·◊◊◊ ☐-■ Z5–9 pH4.5–8

In this combination of plants liking a sunny site, pampas grass (*Cortaderia selloana*) and the shorter, variegated Spanish dagger (*Yucca gloriosa* 'Variegata'), joined also by a relatively hardy opuntia cactus, have great similarity of coloring, proportions, and outline, making a harmonious grouping with a pronounced vertical emphasis.

Corydalis flexuosa and *Dicentra* 'Pearl Drops' harmonize well together, coming from related genera with the shared characteristics of compound pinnate leaves and relatively small florets. The dicentra's white flowers help leaven the intense blue of the corydalis.

Corydalis flexuosa

This exquisite plant, with its greenish blue flowers falling above daintily ferny foliage, brings a rare and spectacular color to late spring and early summer plantings. Each individual floret is enlivened by a white throat. The most common cultivars include 'Blue Panda', 'China Blue', 'Père David', and 'Purple Leaf', all of them effective when combined with soft yellow primroses and soft pink polyanthus, or harmonized with meconopsis. They make telling partners for yellow-green flowers or foliage, for example *Hosta fortunei* var. *albopicta* f. *aurea*, and look outstanding contrasted with the foliage of grasses or more boldly shaped plants. Corydalis flower longest in moist, cool conditions, and in hot, dry summers tend to die back, although they will sometimes revive in autumn and flower then as well.

○ *Leucojum aestivum* 'Gravetye Giant' p.323 **B**, *Meconopsis betonicifolia*, *Primula* 'Guinevere' p.277 **B**, *Roscoea cautleyoides* p.281 **A**, *Smilacina racemosa* p.287 **B**

H: 30–38cm (12–15in) **S: 20–30cm** (8–12in)

❀ **Late spring to early summer**

○○ ■ **Z5 pH4.5–7**

Crambe maritima

SEA KALE

The chief glory of sea kale is its dramatically curled, frilled glaucous foliage. It also bears small white flowers that are pleasant, but unexceptional; these are followed, however, by pea-sized glaucous pods, which when profuse are highly decorative. Sea kale is an effective subject for sunny gravel gardens and maritime sites, and enjoys the same conditions as many late spring and early summer flowering bulbs, which make excellent partners. A group will produce superlative foliage effects at the front of a border, especially if full and luxuriant growth is sustained by supplying the roots with plenty of well-rotted manure. It can be grown with restrained carpeting plants such as small-leaved sedums or low-growing nigellas, and harmonizes well with other brassicas such as curly or black kale.

○ *Brassica oleracea* (Acephala Group) 'Nero di Toscana', *Eryngium giganteum*, *Nigella damascena*, *Pyrus salicifolia* 'Pendula' p.79 **C**, *Sedum* 'Bertram Anderson'

H & S: 60cm (24in) ❀ **Early summer**

○-○○ ■-■ **Z5 pH5.5–8**

The burgeoning leaves and flower stems of sea kale (*Crambe maritima*) help to hide the dying foliage of *Allium hollandicum* while harmonizing with its mauve flowers and the foliage of an achillea behind.

Above: Among the many cultivars of *Crocosmia × crocosmiiflora*, 'Lady Hamilton' is one of the finest and is an ideal candidate for including in planting arrangements where hot, strong colors prevail. Here, its soft orange flowers combine effectively with bright yellow *Rudbeckia fulgida* var. *deamii* in a bold, long-lasting, mid-summer to early autumn display. The two contrast not only in the color of their flowers, but also in flower and foliage shape.

Left: *Crocosmia × crocosmiiflora* 'Solfatare' has a softer flower color than many other cultivars. Here, the pale orange-yellow flowers and bronze-flushed leaves combine well with *Sedum telephium* 'Arthur Branch'. *S.t.* subsp. *maximum* 'Atropurpureum', whose glaucous leaves and stems are flushed deep purple, also makes an effective companion. Ornamental grasses, preferably with plain green leaves, can be planted among groups of montbretias.

Crocosmia × crocosmiiflora cultivars

MONTBRETIA

C. × crocosmiiflora, the montbretia, is one of the most valuable plants for late summer and autumn display. The flowers are striking, especially as an ingredient of hot color arrangements, and the grassy foliage is useful for offering effective contrasts with other leaf textures. 'Carmin Brillant' is one of the easiest and most floriferous cultivars. Its color – almost pure red rather than carmine – harmonizes with yellows and oranges, and provides good contrasts with yellow-green flowers and golden or bronze foliage. It benefits from fairly frequent division and replanting, both to keep it flowering well and to ensure longer, more branched, and longer-lasting flower spikes. 'Lady Hamilton' is another fine cultivar with similar qualities of foliage and texture. Its soft orange color is effective not only with hot, strong colors – bright yellows, golds, and rich scarlets – but also the softer tones of peach and apricot; it is also very attractive with bronze foliage.

All montbretias prefer a moderately rich soil that remains reasonably moist at all times. They are prone to red spider mite in dry conditions, so are not suitable for hot sites such as at the foot of a sunny wall.

Aralia elata 'Aureovariegata' p.31 **B**, *Hypericum forrestii* p.61 **A**, *Persicaria amplexicaulis* p.272 **A**, *Rosa glauca* p.155 **B**, *Stipa calamagrostis*

H: 50–90cm (20–36in) **S:** 23cm (9in)

Mid-summer to early autumn

Z5–8 pH5–7.5

Crocosmia 'Lucifer'

This bold, vigorous crocosmia is one of the most striking and valuable of the genus. It has upward-facing vermilion flowers, and broad, pleated, sword-like foliage, which grows in bold, eye-catching clumps that look magnificent all summer and are an important ingredient of "tropical" foliage plantings. The strongly vertical accents of the leaves make an outstanding contrast with horizontal shapes, such as the plate-like flower heads of achilleas. The richly colored flowers produce superb hot harmonies with strong yellow, gold, or scarlet flowers, and with bronze or purple foliage; clashing contrasts with magenta or yellow-green flowers and yellowish foliage are also stimulating. Its flowering season is relatively short, but the otherwise similar 'Late Lucifer' can be grown as a substitute to produce the same kind of impact a month or so later, in late summer.

Dahlia 'Arabian Night' p.371 **A**, *Helenium* 'Wyndley' p.234 **B**, *Hemerocallis fulva* 'Flore Pleno' p.238 **A**, *Monarda* 'Adam' p.266 **C** pp.29 **A**, 165 **C**, 178 **C**, 324 **A**

H: 1.2m (4ft) **S:** 23cm (9in) Mid-summer

Z5 pH5–7.5

The widely planted *Crocosmia* 'Lucifer' is a deserved favorite for including in exotic foliage displays. To be really effective it needs to be planted in bold groups or drifts. Here, it combines well with the pinkish purple flowers of a perennial mallow (*Malva sylvestris* subsp. *mauritanica*) and the sword-like leaves of New Zealand flax (*Phormium tenax*), which echo those of the crocosmia. Various other phormiums would also make good companions, especially bronze- or purple-leaved cultivars.

Cynara cardunculus 🏆

CARDOON

This is an extremely variable herbaceous plant, with stems 1–2.5m (3¼–8ft) high bearing numerous thistle-like flowers, which emerge from a scaly head that is sometimes tinged purple. Its splendid, silvery grey leaves are deeply divided, usually spiny, and up to 1.2m (4ft) long at the base of the plant.

As a foliage plant the cardoon is handsomely architectural, at its best in late spring and early summer when the leaves are young. It is very impressive standing apart from other plants of similar height, such as one-year-old plants in white or blue spring bedding or in beds and borders to punctuate less dramatic foliage, or as part of a group of silver foliage and white flowers. Its season of maximum glory coincides with plants such as lupines, delphiniums, Oriental poppies, earlier cranesbills, peonies, columbines, foxgloves, early roses, and philadelphus. Cardoons can also be used with plants that look similar, such as centaureas and echinops, to give plantings a unifying theme. To prolong the season of good foliage effect, the flower stems can be removed in summer. Globe artichokes (Scolymus Group cultivars) have less silvery, sometimes green leaves that are not spiny, and, although less magnificent as foliage plants, may be used in similar situations.

Delphinium 'Sungleam', *Digitalis lutea*, *Geranium pratense* 'Mrs Kendall Clark', *Hemerocallis* red-flowered cultivars p.239 **C**, *Papaver orientale*

H: 1–2.5m (3¼–8ft) **S:** 1.2m (4ft)

Early summer to early autumn

Z7 pH5–7.5

In a complex grouping consisting principally of plants with silvery foliage, the large, boldly divided leaves of cardoon (*Cynara cardunculus*) form the focal point, decorated with the felted leaves of woolly lamb's ears (*Stachys byzantina*), and highlighted by the bright cream variegation of ribbon grass (*Phalaris arundinacea* var. *picta*) backlit by the sun.

A

B

The intricate blue pompon florets of *Delphinium* 'Alice Artindale', born on a narrow, erect spike, are given an effective backdrop by golden hops (*Humulus lupulus* 'Aureus'), trained against a wall.

Delphinium 'Alice Artindale'

The double flowers of this delphinium combine shades of grey, green, blue, and mauve, and have an old-fashioned formality that deserves to be seen at close quarters, especially with other old-fashioned plants such as double *Hesperis matronalis* or old roses. It benefits from combinations with cool mauve, rich blue (including other delphiniums, ideally of contrasting form, such as those of the Belladonna Group), purple, and white flowers, and is sufficiently strongly colored to be contrasted with soft pale yellow – with achilleas, for example. The bold shape of its tall slim flower spikes can provide vertical accents and focal points, especially if contrasted with clouds of crambe and horizontal flower heads, and can be echoed by the spikes of companions such as lupines or veronicas. It is an excellent partner for peonies, onopordums, and galegas, and for plants with glaucous or silver foliage.

Achillea 'Moonshine', *Galega orientalis*, *Hesperis matronalis* 'Lilacina Flore Pleno', *Lupinus* 'Polar Princess', *Onopordum nervosum*, *Rosa* 'Fantin-Latour'

H: 1.5m (5ft) **S:** 60cm (24in)

Early to mid-summer

Z3 pH5–7.5

Delphinium 'Sabrina'

This compact cultivar suits small-scale plantings and narrow borders and, if thinned at an early stage to avoid the flower stems becoming spindly, will usually stay upright without staking. It has broad, dense spikes of mid-blue white-eyed flowers that work well with other cool colors, especially other pure blue flowers and silver or glaucous foliage, and make an effective contrast with yellow-green or yellow, particularly yellow Shrub roses. It can be used with larkspurs, cornflowers, achilleas, campanulas, baptisias, smaller philadelphus, Tall Bearded irises, and taller cranesbills and euphorbias. Other relatively short cultivars are Blue Jade Group, 1.2m (4ft), pale blue with a brown eye; 'Blue Tit', 1m (3¼ft), indigo-blue with a black eye; 'Cupid', 90cm (3ft), pale sky-blue with a white eye; 'Lord Butler' ♀, also pale blue with a white eye, 1.4m (4½ft); and 'Mighty Atom' ♀, also 1.4m (4½ft), in deep lavender-blue.

◉ *Achillea* 'Coronation Gold', *Baptisia australis*, *Campanula persicifolia* 'Telham Beauty', *Iris* 'Jane Phillips', *Philadelphus* 'Beauclerk', *Rosa* 'Maigold'

H: 1.2m (4ft) **S: 60cm** (24in)
❀ **Early to mid-summer**
 ◊◊ ▢-▆ **Z3 pH5–7.5**

Although many delphiniums would be too tall to interact with the Peruvian lily *Alstroemeria* 'Vesuvius', the relatively short *Delphinium* 'Sabrina' scarcely rises over it and contrasts strikingly with its rich vermilion flowers.

Delphinium 'Sungleam' ♀

Perhaps the best of the yellow-flowered delphiniums, 'Sungleam' bears numerous stems of blooms in a soft pale butter-yellow that combines well with rich golden yellows, creams, whites, and yellow-green foliage or flowers. It produces stunning contrasts with blue flowers, especially those in pale to mid-blue (stronger blues can overwhelm it), and looks effective with glaucous foliage, yellow-green leaved shrubs such as golden elderberry or philadelphus, larger gold achilleas, and Shrub roses in warm tints of yellow, peach,

The vertical spikes of *Delphinium* 'Sungleam' are echoed by the upright racemes of golden-flowered, dark-stemmed *Ligularia stenocephala*. The round flower heads of the giant scabious (*Cephalaria gigantea*) exactly match the delphinium in color, while on the wall behind, pineapple broom (*Cytisus battandieri*) also has upright, albeit shorter, yellow racemes, unifying the design.

and apricot – some of David Austin's English roses, for example. Other good partners are crambes, spartiums, larger hypericums, earlier flowering kniphofias and, for contrast, baptisias and campanulas. 'Butterball' is similar but with flowers in a paler yellow.

◉ *Baptisia australis*, *Crambe maritima*, *Kniphofia* 'Goldelse', *Philadelphus coronarius* 'Aureus', *Potentilla fruticosa* 'Primrose Beauty', *Rosa* Graham Thomas, *Sambucus nigra* 'Aurea'

H: 1.5m (5ft) **S: 60cm** (24in)
❀ **Early to mid-summer**
◊◊ ▢-▆ **Z3 pH5–7.5**

Deschampsia cespitosa
TUFTED HAIR GRASS

This tussock-forming grass produces airy panicles of flowers that are typically purplish in color, although some sorts are greenish yellow. A good plant for moist borders, bog gardens, and waterside positions, it has a graceful symmetry that deserves prominence, among shorter plants such as heaths and heathers, other grasses, rushes, small gunneras, hostas, and ferns. It can also be used in beds with mound- or hummock-forming plants such as hardy salvias and rudbeckias. Selections include the early-flowering 'Goldschleier' (Golden Veil) (1.2m/4ft) and 'Bronzeschleier' (Bronze Veil) (90cm/3ft); 'Tardiflora' (90cm/3ft), starts flowering only in mid-summer. Blends of two or three cultivars are attractive, particularly if backlit by sun.

◉ *Arrhenatherum elatius* subsp. *bulbosum* 'Variegatum', *Calluna vulgaris* 'Blazeaway', *Juncus effusus* f. *spiralis*, *Rudbeckia hirta* 'Rustic Dwarfs', *Salvia nemorosa*

H: 60–150cm (24–60in) **S: 60–100cm** (24–40in)
❀ **Late spring to late summer**
 ◊◊-◊◊◊ ▢-▆ **Z4 pH4.5–7**

In autumn, the seedheads of tufted hair grass (*Deschampsia cespitosa*) take on parchment tints and glow against the sun, aided by the aging leaves and red stems of the dogwood *Cornus sanguinea* 'Winter Beauty', with the magenta flowers of *Geranium* 'Ann Folkard' for contrast.

A bed of China roses including *Rosa* 'Hermosa' is planted with mixed pinks (*Dianthus* Allwoodii Alpinus Group) beneath. The pinks have attractive glaucous foliage and include exactly the same range of colors as the roses, providing a neat filler between and in front of them.

Dianthus Allwoodii Alpinus Group

Complex hybridization a century ago between the pink 'Old Fringed White' and Perpetual-flowering Carnations produced the Allwoodii Pinks, once known as *D.* × *allwoodii*, and further crossing with the alpine pink (*D. alpinus*) resulted in this group of superb hybrids. Distinguished by compact growth, freedom from disease, and a long flowering season, these neat garden pinks have flowers in often brilliant colors, from white through pink to red, some with a contrasting eye.

They are versatile plants, at home in a gravel garden or at the front of a border, and may be used as edging or for carpeting beneath loosely branched China or Polyantha roses. They are good partners for other pink, red, and white flowers, and contrast well with acid yellow-green flowers such as *Alchemilla mollis*.

⊙ *Ajuga reptans* 'Atropurpurea', *Artemisia schmidtiana*, *Euphorbia seguieriana* subsp. *niciciana*, *Lavandula angustifolia* 'Hidcote', *Rosa* 'Cécile Brünner'

H: 15cm (6in) **S: 30–45cm** (12–18in)

❊ **Early to mid-summer**

◻◼◻ ◒-◒◒ ◻-◼ **Z4 pH5.5–8**

Diascia barberae 'Blackthorn Apricot' flowers freely at the feet of a clump of *Astrantia major* 'Sunningdale Variegated', whose bright leaf edges darken to green once spring passes into summer. The apricot-pink diascia harmonizes with the astrantia's pink-flushed flowers.

Dianthus 'Haytor White' ♔

This easy and floriferous cultivar, with pure white, sweetly scented flowers on tall stems, is one of the Devon Series, bred for the cut-flower market. It is equally successful as a garden plant – although it may need some staking – and can be grown in gravel or in a border, both at the front and in the second rank behind a low carpeting plant. It can be used to leaven rich colors or to form harmonies with paler tones, and is a good candidate for white and silver schemes. As with other Devon Series cultivars – 'Devon Cream', yellow with a light magenta flush, 'Devon Wizard', purple with a ruby eye, and rich crimson 'Devon General', for example – occasional high-potash feeding results in stouter, more numerous flower stems.

⊙ *Diascia barberae* 'Ruby Field', *Festuca glauca*, *Geum* 'Mrs J. Bradshaw', *Iris* 'White Swirl', *I.* 'Symphony', *Lavandula lanata*, *Papaver orientale* 'Cedric Morris', *Rosa* 'Frensham', *R.* Iceberg

H: 45cm (18in) **S: 40cm** (16in)

❊ **Early summer to early autumn**

◼◻◻ ◒-◒◒ ◻-◼ **Z4 pH5.5–8**

In this carpet of white flowers with silvery and white-variegated foliage, *Dianthus* 'Haytor White' supplies abundant bloom in front of the filigree leaves of *Senecio cineraria* and the neatly white-edged evergreen, *Euonymus fortunei* 'Emerald Gaiety'.

Diascia barberae 'Blackthorn Apricot' ♔

In common with many other diascia hybrids, this is a sprawling, mat-forming plant that suits positions near the front of a border where it can weave through its neighbors, especially restrained shrubs of similar height such as some of the smaller hebes. It flowers over a long season, covering itself with loose masses of apricot-pink blooms with downward pointing spurs well into autumn. Plants benefit from being cut back after the first main flush of bloom, but this should not be done during prolonged dry weather. It is good with grasses, small sedums, and dianthus, and makes attractive combinations with peach, cream, white, or brick-red flowers, and with bronze or glaucous foliage. Its strong, clear coloring is enhanced by partners with soft blue flowers or gold-variegated or yellow-green foliage, especially the contrasting forms of smaller ferns.

⊙ *Alchemilla mollis*, *Cerinthe major* 'Purpurascens', *Eryngium giganteum*, *Helichrysum petiolare*, *Lavandula angustifolia* 'Hidcote', *Plectranthus argentatus*

H: 25cm (10in) **S: 50cm** (20in)

❊ **Early summer to early autumn**

◒◒ ◻-◼ **Z8 pH5.5–7.5**

Diascia barberae 'Ruby Field' ♀

This popular cultivar of *D. barberae* bears masses of rich coral-colored flowers from early summer onwards. Like most other diascias, its slightly sprawling growth benefits from shearing after the first flush of bloom; provided there is adequate moisture at their roots, plants will quickly grow back to produce a strong second flush of flowers lasting into autumn. It is effective at the front of a border or for planting beneath loosely branched roses, making attractive harmonies with peach, cherry-red, salmon, or white flowers, and contrasts with pale sulfur-yellow or acid yellow-green. Since its growth is rather amorphous, it benefits from close association with plants of more definite form.

◐ *Euphorbia schillingii*, *Penstemon* 'Pennington Gem', *Phygelius aequalis* 'Yellow Trumpet', *P.* × *rectus* 'Salmon Leap', *Rosa* 'Yesterday' p.167 **B**

H: 25cm (10in) **S: 50cm** (20in)
❋ **Early summer to early autumn**
◌◌ ▨-▧ **Z8 pH5.5–7.5**

In a steeply sloped planting, coral-pink *Diascia barberae* 'Ruby Field' decorates the base of *Penstemon* 'Schoenholzeri', whose colorful racemes of flowers fill the gap at the foot of a wall-trained *Carpenteria californica*.

Dicentra 'Pearl Drops'

Like *D. eximia* (below left), this is a good choice for a woodland garden or semi-shady border, but it spreads rather more freely, its rhizomes tending to weave among neighboring plants. Its flowers are white with a hint of pink and brown, a subdued coloration that qualifies this cultivar for plant groupings where form and texture are paramount; it is effective with smaller grasses, for example, harmonizes with ferns and glaucous-leaved plants, and creates an exciting contrast of leaf form with hostas and other plants of dramatically different shape. Its glaucous leaf color blends well with pure blue flowers like brunneras, forget-me-nots, and omphalodes. Pink flowers are also attractive partners, but strong or hot colors can overwhelm its quiet charm.

◐ *Brunnera macrophylla*, *Corydalis flexuosa* p.206 **A**, *Hosta* (Tardiana Group) 'Halcyon', *Hyacinthoides hispanica*, *Myosotis sylvatica*, *Omphalodes cappadocica*

H: 30cm (12in) **S: 45cm** (18in)
❋ **Mid-spring to early summer**
◌◌ ▨ ■ **Z4 pH5.5–7.5**

Glaucous *Dicentra* 'Pearl Drops' weaves between mid-green male ferns (*Dryopteris filix-mas*) and epimediums to create a tapestry of shapes. This combination succeeds solely on the variety of foliage forms and colors, although it is not impaired by the dicentra's pinkish white flowers.

The fern-like leaves of *Dicentra eximia*, the broad, lobed foliage of the cranesbill *Geranium* × *oxonianum*, and the simple, lance-shaped leaves of *Spiraea japonica* 'Goldflame' combine in a pleasing interplay of different foliage forms at the front of a border. The dicentra's flowers clash gently with the spiraea's yellow-green young leaves.

Dicentra eximia

This rhizomatous dicentra has glaucous ferny foliage, and nodding racemes of pink flowers that are longer and more elegant than those of the otherwise similar *D. formosa*, with which it is often confused. It is a valuable plant for woodland gardens or semi-shady borders, and grows best in climates with cool summers and adequate moisture. In hotter, drier weather it will survive but tends to become unkempt by mid-summer, dying back and only reviving when cooler, moister conditions return. It is attractive with crimson, white, or palest pink flowers, and also with purple-flushed foliage such as that of some newer heuchera cultivars. It harmonizes well with ferns and looks effective with contrasting foliage – that of smaller grasses and hostas, for example. The richer pink forms may be contrasted with yellow-green flowers or foliage.

◐ *Arum italicum* 'Marmoratum', *Asplenium scolopendrium*, *Epimedium* × *versicolor* 'Neosulphureum' p.215 **A**, *Heuchera* 'Plum Pudding'

H: 60cm (24in) **S: 45cm** (18in) ❋ **Late spring**
◌◌ ▨ ■ **Z4 pH5.5–7.5**

Dicentra spectabilis ♀
BLEEDING HEART

This charming herbaceous perennial (syn. *Lampranthus spectabilis*) has elegant, divided leaves and heart-shaped, pendent flowers, strung out on slender, drooping stems like a row of rose-pink lockets; the shape of the individual florets is emphasized by the white inner petals. The plants form fairly upright clumps, the neat foliage and long flower stalks arching out from the center.

Bleeding hearts are desirable plants for a woodland garden, accompanied by heucheras, tellimas, tiarellas, and herbaceous saxifrages. They can be grown at or near the front of a lightly shaded border with plants of similar stature, or alone, surrounded by a carpet of white bugleweeds, creeping small-leaved gunneras, or *Mitella breweri*. They associate well with pale pink or crimson flowers or,

in brighter situations, with pale pink, white, or soft, pale yellow tulips.

In moist, cool growing conditions, bleeding hearts remain attractive for longer than in areas with hot summers, where they will die back by mid-summer. The pure white-flowered 'Alba' ♀ is more vigorous, with paler green leaves, while 'Goldheart' is an eye-catching gold-leaved variety, although the combination of foliage color with rich pink flowers does not suit everyone's taste.

◉ *Ajuga reptans* 'Variegata', *Gunnera magellanica*, *Heuchera* 'Pewter Moon', *Saxifraga granulata*, *Tellima grandiflora*, *Tiarella trifoliata*, *Tulipa* 'Spring Green'

H: 1.2m (4ft) S: 60cm (24in)
✾ **Late spring to early summer**
 ◊◊◊ ■ ■ **Z3 pH5.5–7.5**

The nodding pink and white racemes of *Dicentra spectabilis* create a contrast of form and color with the yellow-green flower heads of the spurge *Euphorbia polychroma*.

In an appealing combination for a lightly shaded position, the pale yellow flowers of small yellow foxglove (*Digitalis lutea*) are offset by the spidery, deep blue heads of mountain bluet (*Centaurea montana*).

Digitalis lutea
SMALL YELLOW FOXGLOVE

The small yellow foxglove is smaller and less showy than its more common cousin, the yellow foxglove (*D. grandiflora*), but it is more dependably perennial and has a compelling elegance. Plants form clumps of smooth, toothed leaves and discreetly pretty spikes of small, creamy yellow, tubular flowers. It makes very attractive vertical accents in a woodland garden, with blue cranesbills or meconopsis, or in a sunny or lightly shaded border, especially if given a position of prominence slightly in front of its peers. It may be contrasted with flowers or foliage of different form, such as grasses and ferns, and its soft yellow coloring works well with blue shades or with gold and white. It is also sufficiently muted to succeed close to pink.

Untidy, faded blooms should be removed, cutting back the main spikes after flowering. Feeding encourages secondary flower spikes.

◉ *Astrantia major* 'Sunningdale Variegated', *Corydalis flexuosa*, *Dryopteris affinis*, *Geranium* 'Johnson's Blue', *Meconopsis betonicifolia*, *Milium effusum* 'Aureum'

H: 60cm (24in) S: 30cm (12in)
✾ **Early to mid-summer**
 ◊◊ ■ ■ **Z4 pH5.5–7.5**

Dryopteris affinis ♔
WOOD FERN

Like all dryopteris ferns, this is a long-lived foliage plant. It is a handsome, robust species, cleaner and more refined than the common male fern (*D. filix-mas*). It is loveliest in spring, when its pale green fronds emerge, unfurling with contrasting golden brown scales on the leaf stalks and mid-ribs, and radiating outwards around a central hollow, producing a charming shuttlecock effect.

This fern contrasts well with broad-leaved plants such as hostas and bergenias, and with grasses. Attractive companions include gold, sulfur-yellow, apricot, and soft orange flowers, such as geums or trollius, and primulas – for instance *Primula bulleyana* or *P. cockburniana*. It is particularly effective with earlier-flowering lilies that tolerate shade, such as martagon lilies. The ferns are best grouped in irregularly scattered colonies, allowing each plant space to develop its distinctive shape. In late winter, surviving fronds should be cut off to make way for new spring growth.

🌑 *Geum rivale* 'Leonard's Variety', *Hosta* 'Gold Standard', *Lilium martagon* var. *album*, *Rodgersia pinnata* p.280 **B**, *Trollius* × *cultorum* 'Alabaster'

H: 15–120cm (6–48in) **S: 15–90cm** (6–36in)

◌◌-◌◌◌ ▨ ■ **Z4 pH5–7.5**

The emerging yellow-green, orange-flushed fronds of *Dryopteris affinis* create a striking contrast of form with the handsome bronze-tinged foliage of *Rodgersia podophylla*.

Echinacea purpurea
PURPLE CONE FLOWER

A slightly coarse but handsome perennial for sunny borders or prairie meadows, purple cone flower has slightly muted, deep magenta flowers, each with a central golden brown cone. Its petals may descend strongly to give the impression of a shuttlecock or, in some varieties, stand out almost horizontally, and the bold floral shape can be used to make a pronounced accent – such as when repeated along a border. Plants combine well with purple or crimson flowers, or with purple foliage and grasses such as silky brown-flowered *Calamagrostis* × *acutiflora*, and contrast effectively with soft pale yellow or rich deep orange flowers. Creamy white cultivars, such as 'White Lustre' and 'White Swan', are more successful than pure white flowers as contrasts in hot color groupings, and blend well with soft yellow, peach, and apricot, or with bronze foliage.

🌑 *Achillea* 'Summerwine', *A.* 'Taygetea', *Aster novi-belgii* 'Chequers', *Cotinus coggygria* 'Royal Purple', *Helenium* 'Kupferzwerg', *H.* 'Septemberfuchs', *Miscanthus sinensis* 'Sarabande', *Monarda* 'Prärienacht', *Rhus* × *pulvinata* Autumn Lace Group

H: 60–120cm (24–48in) **S: 45cm** (18in)

❄ **Mid-summer to mid-autumn**

◌◌ ▨ **Z3 pH5.5–7.5**

Above: In a border of mainly mauve-pink flowers, *Echinacea purpurea* provides bold floral shape behind a froth of tiny blooms of *Heuchera micrantha* var. *diversifolia* 'Palace Purple', with *Lychnis coronaria* Oculata Group, large heads of *Phlox maculata*, and the narrow, dark spikes of *Persicaria amplexicaulis* 'Atrosanguinea'.

Below: Floriferous *Echinacea purpurea* 'Magnus' is here joined by the smaller, harmoniously colored flowers of *Verbena bonariensis* and *Aster* × *frikartii*.

Echinops bannaticus 'Taplow Blue' ♔

With its rich steely blue flower heads and handsomely lobed leaves, this is a superlative selection of the commonest species of globe thistle, a splendid plant for borders and wild gardens and for naturalizing. It blends with cool mauve, lilac, lavender or purple, soft yellow or acid yellow-green, white, and pure blue, and with glaucous or silver foliage. The shapely leaves can be used to echo other thistle-like plants such as onopordums, eryngiums, cardoons, and centaureas, and contrast with miscanthus cultivars and other taller grasses, and shrubs such as silver-leaved elaeagnus or pollarded silver willow. Suitable partners are repeat-flowering Shrub roses, obelisk-trained clematis, taller campanulas such as *C. lactiflora* cultivars, and *Hydrangea paniculata* cultivars. *Echinops ritro* ♔ is similar but a little shorter, as are its rich blue variants subsp. *ruthenicus* ♔ and 'Veitch's Blue'.

◑ *Centaurea macrocephala*, *Cynara cardunculus*, *Eryngium bourgatii* 'Picos Blue', *Miscanthus sinensis* 'Morning Light', *Onopordum nervosum*, *Rosa* 'Felicia'

H: 1.2m (4ft)   S: 60cm (24in)
❀ **Mid- to late summer**
◖▬▬◗ ◊◊ ▨-▦ **Z3   pH5.5–7.5**

A cherry plum (*Prunus cerasifera* 'Pissardii') provides a sumptuous setting for the silvered leaves and steely blue globes of *Echinops bannaticus* 'Taplow Blue'. A shrub such as purple-leaved smoke bush (a *Cotinus coggygria* cultivar) could be used as an alternative to the plum.

A

B

Elymus magellanicus

This short-lived perennial grass differs from other elymus and leymus species in that it is relatively small, lax in growth habit, and prefers cool summers. Its foliage is a bright silvery blue, which is valuable at the front of a border or in a gravel garden for growing through low ground-cover plants such as acaenas, mondo grass, bugleweeds, or sedums. It combines effectively with glaucous- or silver-leaved plants such as woolly lamb's ears, smaller artemisias, smaller glaucous hostas, and glaucous oxalis species, with white or blue annuals like heliophilas and nigellas, and yellow-flowered annuals such as smaller California poppies and hunnemannias. Good contrasts can be made with yellow-green plants such as euphorbias, and with the soft yellow of some smaller

In a simple but effective combination using cool colors and contrasting form, the narrow blue-green leaves of *Elymus magellanicus* arch gracefully in front of mauve-flowered musk mallow (*Malva moschata*).

achilleas. Its flower spikes, which are narrow and the same color as the foliage, add little to the effect, although allowing the plant to seed can be the best means of ensuring its survival.

Similar species include *E. hispidus*, or blue wheatgrass, which is a more erect plant, and the blue fescues, which have narrower, stiffly upright leaves.

◑ *Achillea* 'Moonshine', *Eschscholzia caespitosa* 'Sundew', *Geranium × riversleaianum* 'Mavis Simpson' p.229 **C**, *Ophiopogon planiscapus* 'Nigrescens'

H: 15cm (6in)   S: 45cm (18in)
❀ **Early to late summer**
◖▬▬◗ ◊◊ ▨-▦ **Z4   pH5.5–7.5**

Epimedium × *versicolor*

This shade-tolerant hybrid is rather variable. Its typical cultivar, 'Versicolor', is deciduous, with young red leaves maturing to green and flowers of dusky deep pink and yellow, while the commonest cultivar, 'Sulphureum' ♀, is evergreen with elegant sprays of sulfur-yellow flowers. 'Neosulphureum' is similar but with fewer leaflets, and 'Cupreum' resembles 'Versicolor' but with coppery flowers. All are elegant ground-cover plants, the copper or pink cultivars succeeding in combinations with warm-tinted spring flowers, while the yellow ones blend with rich yellow narcissi, primroses, and rhizomatous anemones, yellow-green woodrushes, and blue flowers such as brunneras, omphalodes, and forget-me-nots. They are also attractive with euphorbias and white, cream, green, or soft yellow hellebores, or, for contrast, with early-leafing ferns, sedges, and grasses.

⊙ *Anemone ranunculoides*, *Brunnera macrophylla*, *Helleborus* × *hybridus* (primrose), *Luzula sylvatica* 'Aurea', *Milium effusum* 'Aureum', *Myosotis sylvatica*

H & S: 30cm (12in) ❊ **Mid- to late spring**

◊◊ ■-■ ■ Z5 pH5–7.5

This pleasant mixture combines two mildly invasive plants that have contrasting leaf shapes: *Epimedium* × *versicolor* 'Neosulphureum' with its red-flushed, heart-shaped leaflets and the feathery, glaucous-leaved *Dicentra eximia*.

In mid-spring, a carpet of *Epimedium* × *youngianum* 'Niveum' topped with tiny white florets forms a foil for a handsome rosette of *Meconopsis napaulensis*, which has yet to extend its summer flower spike. The dark green leaves and yellowish green flower heads of the hybrid spurge *Euphorbia* × *martini* make an effective backdrop.

Epimedium × *youngianum* 'Niveum' ♀

Generally small and gently spreading, the rather variable *E.* × *youngianum* is sometimes almost evergreen and bears flowers that may or may not have spurs. 'Niveum' is one of the prettiest cultivars, with small white flowers, few of which have spurs, and bronze-flushed young foliage. The flower color blends with any other, but the leaves are most effective with warm-tinted flowers, including tulips, primroses, and smaller narcissi, and with other plants with bronzed or reddish foliage, such as bugleweeds and some euphorbias and sedges. White flowers – wood anemones, cardamines, pachyphragmas, and narcissi – are also good partners. 'Merlin' has purple-flushed young leaves and large, short-spurred mauve flowers, while 'Roseum', also purple-flushed, has smaller mauve-pink flowers.

⊙ *Ajuga reptans* 'Atropurpurea', *Anemone nemorosa* 'Vestal', *Cardamine trifolia*, *Euphorbia amygdaloides* 'Purpurea', *Hosta fortunei* 'Albomarginata' p.244 **A**

H: 20cm (8in) **S: 30cm** (12in)
❊ **Mid- to late spring**
◊◊ ■-■ ■ Z5 pH5–7.5

Erigeron cultivars
FLEABANE

Most garden fleabanes are herbaceous plants for the front of borders, rock gardens, or gravel gardens. Their single or double daisy-like flowers have a central disc of yellow florets within petals that are usually in shades from white through rich carmine to lavender-blue. All blend with cool colors – purple, lavender, or lilac fleabanes being especially effective with other blooms in the same range and in yellow-green or soft yellow. Their slightly soft texture works well with plants of more definite form, such as eryngiums, fescues, artemisias, and sedums. Cultivars include deep lavender-blue 'Dunkelste Aller' ♀ (Darkest of All), 'White Quakeress', mauve-pink 'Foersters Liebling' ♀, and deep violet 'Schwarzes Meer' (Black Sea).

⊙ *Artemisia alba* 'Canescens', *Ballota pseudodictamnus*, *Eryngium* × *tripartitum*, *Euphorbia seguieriana* subsp. *niciciana*, *Festuca glauca* 'Elijah Blue'

H: 25–75cm (10–30in) **S: 30cm** (12in)
❊ **Early to mid-summer**
◊◊ ■-■ ■ Z5 pH5.5–7.5

The bright pink flowers of *Erigeron* 'Gaiety' and the magenta blooms of rose campion (*Lychnis coronaria*) are born at the same height and mingle together attractively if plants of each are grown close to each other.

Erodium trifolium

Plants in the genus *Erodium* are known as storksbills or heron's bills, and are close relatives of the very similar cranesbills. *E. trifolium* (syn. *E. hymenodes*) is a fairly sprawling species, its relaxed, spreading shape suiting it to the front of a border and to rock, scree, and gravel gardens. The soft coloring of its dull green toothed leaves and simple flowers in two shades of pink, delicately spotted with brown, blends amicably with most other shades, especially mauves, blues, carmines, and crimsons, and even soft yellows; purple-leaved plants are good companions, too. Plants tolerate most well-drained soils, but can be short-lived, lasting four to five years in light soils, and only two on clay. Fortunately, they self-seed readily, so replacements are always available.

🌕 *Dianthus* Allwoodii Alpinus Group, *Festuca glauca* 'Elijah Blue', *Geranium* 'Chocolate Candy', *Lysimachia nummularia* 'Aurea', *Molinia caerulea* 'Variegata'

H: 30cm (12in) S: 45cm (18in)
❋ **Early to late summer**
◊ ☐ **Z8 pH6–8**

Erodium trifolium will scramble into shrubby, yellow-flowered *Halimium lasianthum* to add its flowers to those of its support. Both like a sunny, well-drained site.

Eryngium alpinum ♧

There are two main groups of eryngiums. Those included in this book are European or Old World eryngiums, with rounded, lobed or pinnate leaves and flowers often flushed with blue as they age. American or New World species usually have strap-like leaves and smaller, green or cream flowers.

E. alpinum has striking, bold conical heads of florets in summer, each cone surrounded by a ruff of feathery bracts, and relatively plain, blue-tinted foliage. The maturing flowers assume clear blue shades, especially in superior cultivars such as 'Amethyst', 'Slieve Donard', and 'Superbum'. The cultivars are suitable for the second rank of a herbaceous border, combined with magenta, pink, mauve, purple, and soft (but not strong) yellow flowers, and purple-leaved plants. They are effective with other flowers of contrasting shapes, such as the flattened, soft yellow heads of some achilleas, and glaucous or yellow-banded grasses.

🌕 *Achillea* 'Taygetea', *Cotinus coggygria* 'Royal Purple', *Geranium pratense* 'Plenum Violaceum', *Lythrum virgatum* 'The Rocket', *Miscanthus sinensis* 'Strictus', *Phormium* 'Bronze Baby', *Phygelius × rectus* p.73 **C**

H: 50–75cm (20–30in) S: 45cm (18in)
❋ **Mid-summer to early autumn**
◊ ☐ **Z5 pH5.5–7.5**

The exquisitely shaped flower heads of *Eryngium alpinum* are perhaps most effectively displayed against a quite simple, contrasting background, as provided here by *Berberis thunbergii* 'Rose Glow'.

Eryngium bourgatii 'Picos Blue'

Even before its flowers appear, *E. bourgatii* is a handsome plant, its deeply divided, dark green leaves having a lighter central zone or veining that emphasizes the crisp outline. 'Picos Blue' retains this feature, together with its shapely, more strongly colored flowers, which age to a beautiful lavender-blue. With smaller blooms than *E. alpinum* (above), it needs to be seen at close quarters – the front of a border is ideal, particularly with grassy or sword-leaved companions such as Dwarf Bearded irises. 'Oxford Blue' is also excellent, a touch darker and a purer silvery blue.

🌕 *Berberis thunbergii* 'Aurea', *Iris* 'Harpswell Happiness', *Phalaris arundinacea* var. *picta* 'Feesey', *Philadelphus coronarius* 'Aureus', *Phormium* 'Yellow Wave', *Potentilla fruticosa* 'Primrose Beauty', *Sisyrinchium striatum* 'Aunt May'

H: 45cm (18in) S: 30cm (12in)
❋ **Mid- to late summer**
◊ ☐ **Z5 pH5.5–7.5**

The color of *Eryngium bourgatii* 'Picos Blue' is strong enough to contrast with yellow-green dogwood (*Cornus alba* 'Aurea') and box (*Buxus sempervirens* 'Latifolia Maculata').

Eryngium maritimum
SEA HOLLY

This outstandingly handsome species has superb, greyish blue-green foliage and bracted grey-green flowers with a slightly blue cast, contributing a silvery, leafy element to planting arrangements. These striking plants belong at the front of a border, where they blend well with pink, magenta, mauve, purple, and soft yellow flowers, and purple foliage. They look most effective with achilleas and glaucous and yellow-banded grasses. Their rather open, irregular growth habit can be disguised by growing them through gravel or a carpet of prostrate plants, such as alpine pinks. They tolerate the salt-laden winds of coastal gardens but are not always easy to establish; like most eryngiums, they need very porous soil and may rot in moist conditions.

Achillea filipendulina 'Gold Plate', *Dianthus* 'Doris', *Helictotrichon sempervirens*, *Miscanthus sinensis* 'Zebrinus', *Tamarix ramosissima* 'Pink Cascade'

H & S: 30cm (12in) ✷ **Mid- to late summer**
◊ ☐ **Z5 pH5.5–7.5**

The silvery blooms of *Eryngium maritimum*, here supported by encircling *Lavandula angustifolia*, are strikingly decorative; they become tinged with blue as they age.

Left: Even before its stems and flower heads flush blue, the pale, glaucous *Eryngium* × *tripartitum* makes an effective display against a dark background of *Salvia* × *superba*.

Right: The wiry habit of *Eryngium* × *tripartitum* allows it to support scrambling plants such as *Rehmannia elata* and the cranesbill *Geranium* × *riversleaianum* 'Russell Prichard'.

Eryngium × *tripartitum* ♔

This is one of the easiest eryngiums to grow. Its prettily divided leaves are arranged in a basal rosette, which develops numerous widely spaced, pale grey-green flowering shoots that assume blue tints as buds develop. The dainty flowers are violet-blue, with darker bracts, and are born in great profusion. As they fade, they develop parchment-colored tints lasting into autumn, and they deserve to be left through winter until the spring. The tallish clumps look well combined with magenta, pink, mauve, purple, and soft yellow flowers, and with some of the larger grasses. They will also support restrained climbers and scramblers, for example the smaller convolvulus species.

Achillea 'Moonshine', *Allium sphaerocephalon* p.303 **B**, *Eupatorium purpureum* subsp. *maculatum* 'Atropurpureum', *Geranium* 'Ann Folkard', *Hemerocallis* 'Golden Chimes', *Miscanthus sinensis* 'Morning Light'

H: 75cm (30in) **S: 45cm** (18in)
✷ **Mid-summer to early autumn**
◊ ☐ **Z5 pH5.5–7.5**

Eupatorium purpureum subsp. maculatum 'Atropurpureum' ♛

E. purpureum, or boneset, is a large, imposing perennial with tall, stout stems that sport pointed leaves arranged in neat whorls. In the choice form 'Atropurpureum', the leaves are purple-tinted, while the rounded heads of the tiny florets are a dusky purplish pink and born in two main flushes, first in mid-summer and again in early autumn when there is a shortage of herbaceous flowers.

This cultivar thrives in rich soil with plenty of moisture, and so makes a good choice in a moist wild garden or beside water, planted in bold groups; it also stands out at the back of a moist border. It is best combined with muted colors, such as dusky pink or cream, since more brightly colored neighbors can make it look dirty. Good companions include Japanese anemones, pampas grass and similar tall grasses, and plumed or spiky flowers such as artemisias and later aconitums.

◑ *Aconitum napellus* subsp. *vulgare* 'Carneum', *Anemone* × *hybrida* 'Lady Gilmour', *Cortaderia selloana* 'Pumila', *Sedum* 'Herbstfreude' p.285 **B**

H & S: 30cm (12in)
✾ **Mid-summer to early autumn**

◊◊-◊◊◊ ▨-▩ Z5 pH5.5–7.5

The creamy plumes of *Artemisia lactiflora* provide a contrast of form next to the rounded, dusky pink heads of *Eupatorium purpureum* subsp. *maculatum* 'Atropurpureum'.

Euphorbia amygdaloides var. robbiae ♛
MRS ROBB'S BONNET

Mrs Robb's bonnet is a robust, low-growing euphorbia with short, upright stems that bear extremely handsome rosettes of glossy, dark green foliage, capped in mid-spring by rounded heads of acid green flowers. It is a meandering plant that dies out and then moves elsewhere, best in an informal tapestry of low-growing plants in a woodland setting – perhaps infiltrating carpets of other flowers, such as aubrietas or violas – rather than as a ground cover in a border, where it lacks persistence. It combines well with wood anemones, golden millet grass and other early-leafing grasses, and with some evergreen sedges. The combination of deep green foliage and yellow-green flowers harmonizes well with hot colors, and makes an attractive contrast with blues, purples, cream, and pale yellow.

Grown beneath aubrietas on a dwarf wall, the yellow-green flowers of *Euphorbia amygdaloides* var. *robbiae* provide a sharp color contrast through mid- and late spring.

◑ *Allium hollandicum* 'Purple Sensation', *Anemone sylvestris*, *Arum creticum* p.306 **C**, *Berberis thunbergii* f. *atropurpurea*, *Carex elata* 'Aurea', *Geranium phaeum* p.228 **A**, *Rosmarinus officinalis* 'Sissinghurst Blue', *Viola* 'Huntercombe Purple'

H & S: 50cm (20in)
✾ **Mid-spring to early summer**

◊◊ ▨ ▦ Z7 pH5–8

Euphorbia cyparissias
CYPRESS SPURGE

This wandering species is quite variable in form. It is characterized by its decorative foliage, which is slender, feathery, and dense, with less glaucous coloring than many other euphorbias. In late spring it bears yellow-green flowers, sometimes tinged with orange. This plant can intermingle freely with bugleweeds and other mat-forming plants of comparable vigor and size to create a tapestry effect near the front of a border or in gravel. It contrasts with blues and purples, and combines well with cream, pale yellow, and hot colors. Plants tolerate some shade, but are more colorful in full sun, when they may develop fine autumn tints. Less invasive kinds include upright 'Bushman Boy'; 'Fens Ruby' (syns 'Clarice Howard', 'Purpurea'), with purple-flushed leaves; and 'Orange Man', with brilliant orange autumn tints.

The slightly sprawling growth habit of cypress spurge (*Euphorbia cyparissias*) allows it to meander through the variegated *Hosta* (Tardiana Group) 'June' and the contrasting cranesbill *Geranium himalayense* 'Plenum'.

◑ *Anthemis punctata* subsp. *cupaniana* p.185 **C**, *Geranium pratense* 'Mrs Kendall Clark' p.228 **B**, *Helianthemum* 'Fire Dragon' p.57 **B**

H: 15–50cm (6–20in)   **S: 30–60cm** (12–24in)
✾ **Late spring to mid-summer**

 ◊ ▦ Z5 pH5.5–8

Euphorbia dulcis 'Chameleon'

The small-growing euphorbia *E. dulcis* is noted for its autumn coloring, which is richest in the cultivar 'Chameleon'. Its loose, airy clouds of small leaves are bronze-green flushed purple, turning to shades of orange, scarlet, and crimson in autumn, especially if grown in full sun. By comparison, the heads of yellowish green flowers, aging to bronze-purple in early summer, are insignificant. 'Chameleon' can be planted in a woodland garden or near the front of a border, to mingle with more structured neighboring plants, and also in gravel, where it can seed itself. It is attractive in hot-colored groupings, and mixes well with orange, scarlet, and yellow flowers, or with silver foliage.

◐ *Allium nigrum* p.303 **A**, *Brachyglottis* (Dunedin Group) 'Sunshine', *Erysimum cheiri* (mixed) p.378 **C**, *Euphorbia griffithii* 'Dixter', *Geranium sylvaticum* f. *albiflorum*, *Tulipa* 'Orange Favourite'

H: 40cm (16in) S: 30cm (12in)
✻ **Mid-spring to early summer**
◊-◊◊ **Z4 pH5–8**

In a sunny position, *Euphorbia dulcis* 'Chameleon' assumes dark bronze tints, contrasting dramatically with the silvery wormwood *Artemisia* 'Powis Castle'.

Left: In spring, the orange and bronze tints of *Euphorbia griffithii* 'Dixter' harmonize with golden feverfew (*Tanacetum parthenium* 'Aureum'), tulips, and the wallflower *Erysimum cheiri* 'Fire King'.

Above: In mid- to late autumn, *Euphorbia griffithii* 'Dixter' turns fiery scarlet, harmonizing with the golden blooms of *Bracteantha bracteata* 'Dargan Hill Monarch'.

Euphorbia griffithii 'Dixter' ♔

E. griffithii is a very variable species that has given rise to numerous superior clones, of which 'Dixter' is probably the best. It has dark foliage with a distinct red flush, turning dazzling orange and scarlet in autumn. From late spring or early summer, it is crowned by heads of orange-red bracts that look good as part of a hot color arrangement. It makes an outstanding partner for contrasting leaf shapes such as those of grasses.

Other commendable cultivars include 'Fern Cottage', with burnt orange bracts and yellow and gold autumn shades; 'King's Caple', with brick-red flowers and good autumn color, and taller and bushier than the otherwise similar but invasive 'Fireglow'; and 'Robert Poland', a strong plant with bright red bracts.

◐ *Berberis thunbergii* f. *atropurpurea*, *Cytisus* × *praecox* 'Warminster', *Helictotrichon sempervirens*, *Photinia* × *fraseri* 'Birmingham' p.73 **A**, *Primula* Inshriach hybrids p.277 **A**, *Pyrus salicifolia* 'Pendula'

H: 60cm (24in) S: 45cm (18in)
✻ **Late spring to mid-summer**
◊◊ **Z5 pH5–7.5**

Euphorbia myrsinites ♈
MYRTLE SPURGE

This Mediterranean species is a sun-lover for hot, dryish sites. Its serpentine stems are covered with glaucous leaves, evergreen or semi-evergreen, and from late spring they produce rounded, greenish yellow flower heads, which in some forms turn pink or purple as they age. Growth trails all round, like Medusa's head, creating an attractive, open mat of stems. If grown on its own in bare soil, the gaps between the stems would be too noticeable, so it is best planted in gravel, or where it can sprawl over the edge of borders; or it can be combined with aubrietas and other smaller carpeters. It mixes well with hot colors, purple or bronze foliage, and blue or purple flowers. Good partners include smaller fescues and other glaucous grasses, and small, sun-loving bronze sedges.

◐ *Aubrieta* 'Argenteovariegata', *Carex comans* (bronze), *Festuca glauca* 'Elijah Blue', *Muscari latifolium* p.330 **B**, *Sedum* 'Bertram Anderson' p.285 **A**

H: 15cm (6in) S: 30cm (12in)
❀ Late spring to mid-summer
◻◼ ◊ ◻ Z6 pH5.5–8

A Spreading clumps of donkeytail spurge (*Euphorbia myrsinites*), grown through gravel in a border, contrast with *Berberis thunbergii* 'Atropurpurea Nana' in late spring.

B

Euphorbia polychroma 'Major' ♈

E. polychroma (syn. *E. epithymoides*) is a dome-shaped euphorbia, treasured for its bright greenish yellow bracts. 'Major' is shorter and more compact than the species, and has striking autumn color. Its solid clumps are best grown as individual mounds rather than massed in blocks, and they make superb repeated accents to enliven muted color schemes. Plants mix well with many mid- or late spring bulbs. Pale yellow, cream, apricot, peach, orange, and scarlet are all satisfying harmonies, while blue makes a fine contrast. Other recommended clones include 'Midas', which is a little taller; 'Orange Flush', with darker foliage, orange flower tints, and bright autumn color; and 'Sonnengold', which is shorter and broader, tinted purple in spring, and rich orange or brown in autumn.

◐ *Aurinia saxatilis* 'Citrina' p.196 **B**, *Deutzia longifolia* 'Vilmoriniae' p.45 **C**, *Dicentra spectabilis* p.212 **A**, *Euphorbia characias* subsp. *wulfenii* 'Lambrook Gold' p.50 **A** and **B**, *Fritillaria pyrenaica* p.315 **C**, *Tulipa* 'Spring Green' p.353 **C**

H: 40cm (16in) S: 50cm (20in)
❀ Mid-spring to early summer
◻◼ ◊-◊◊ ◻ Z5 pH5.5–8

Euphorbia polychroma 'Major' sets off *Centranthus ruber* in late spring, while spires of foxgloves add vertical accents.

Euphorbia rigida

Also sold under the name *E. biglandulosa*, this is a remarkable euphorbia of superior form, most impressive when out of flower. It has very glaucous, upright stems that bear plenty of pointed, very fleshy glaucous leaves, and yellowish green flower heads from early spring. It is similar in many ways to *E. myrsinites* (left), but its large, bold leaves make a stronger statement, and it has fewer, more succulent stems, so clumps reveal even larger gaps and are less likely to develop into a solid circle of radiating branches. For this reason, plants are rarely able to make a balanced composition on their own. They are best grown through carpets of very small prostrate plants at the front of a border; they will also sprawl satisfactorily through gravel. This species combines well with blue, purple, and yellow flowers, and with bronze foliage such as that of smaller sedges; while in flower, it makes a dramatic partnership with orange.

C

The fleshy glaucous rosettes of *Euphorbia rigida* make a bold, small-scale accent between the diminutive cranesbill *Geranium cinereum* var. *subcaulescens* 'Splendens' and violas.

◐ *Acaena microphylla* 'Kupferteppich', *Aubrieta* cultivars (blue or purple), *Carex comans* (bronze), *Erodium trifolium*, *Sedum* 'Bertram Anderson'

H & S: 45cm (18in)
❀ Early spring to early summer
◻◼ ◊ ◻ Z7 pH5.5–8

Euphorbia schillingii contrasts strikingly with scarlet Jerusalem cross (*Lychnis chalcedonica*) in mid-summer.

Euphorbia schillingii ♔

E. schillingii makes an impressive and colorful statement in mixed and herbaceous borders. It increases freely into clumps of tall, upright stems, with deep green, elliptical leaves highlighted by conspicuous white veins. The bright greenish yellow, branching heads of flowers are large and eye-catching, and last over a long season from mid-summer into autumn. The foliage produces good autumn tints, scarlet in hot climates or buttery yellow where summers are cooler.

This euphorbia can be planted in the middle ranks of a border, ideally in loose, scattered groupings since it looks better as a repeated accent than as a solid block. It is an extremely useful ingredient of hot color schemes, and makes a startling contrast with blues and purples. Hostas, other glaucous foliage plants, and grasses are good companions. In exposed borders it benefits from a little brushwood staking when stems are two-thirds their eventual height.

◐ *Asclepias tuberosa*, *Cerinthe major* 'Purpurascens', *Helictotrichon sempervirens*, *Hosta sieboldiana* var. *elegans*, *Lobelia siphilitica*, *Ruta graveolens* 'Jackman's Blue', *Salvia nemorosa* 'Ostfriesland'

H: 90cm (36in) S: 60cm (24in)
❀ **Mid-summer to mid-autumn**
⬛⬛⬜ ◐◐ ⬛ Z8 pH5–7.5

Euphorbia seguieriana subsp. *niciciana*

This is an easy to grow euphorbia from southeast Europe, with lively coloring and supremely elegant form. It produces clumps of slender, woody-based stems, well clad with narrow blue-green foliage and topped by large heads of vibrant yellow-green bracts of exceptional intensity. Plants need space to develop into impressive clumps, which look best when surrounded by shorter neighbors, well away from the competition of other tall plants. It combines well with purples and blues, as well as mid- to pale yellows, cream, and orange. Fescues and other grasses are perfect companions, sharing its love of sunshine and good drainage.

◐ *Allium cristophii*, *Crocosmia* 'Lucifer', *Festuca glauca* 'Elijah Blue', *Heuchera* 'Plum Pudding', *Nepeta* 'Six Hills Giant', *Leymus arenarius*, *Miscanthus sinensis* 'Zebrinus', *Monarda* 'Prärienacht'

H: 50cm (20in) S: 45cm (18in)
❀ **Early summer to early autumn**
⬛⬛⬜ ◐ ⬛ Z8 pH5.5–8

In a gravel garden, *Euphorbia seguieriana* subsp. *niciciana* provides contrasting color and variety of form with the purple racemes of *Salvia nemorosa* 'Ostfriesland' and the white-flowered rock rose *Helianthemum* 'The Bride'.

Ferula communis
GIANT FENNEL

This majestic perennial is highly prized as a foliage plant, its broad clump of feathery green leaves building up over several seasons to make an impressive mound of lacy, finely cut plumes. From its center, a robust stem eventually soars to 2–3m (6½–10ft), even to 5m (16ft) in some cases, bearing masses of umbels of yellow-green flowers. After this, plants usually die, although they can be allowed to self-seed or a few extra specimens may be grown to perpetuate the foliage effect. Giant fennel can be planted in the middle or near the front of a border, behind more solid neighbors with broad or spiky leaves such as hostas or irises; the flowers are so airy and softly colored that they combine well with most colors except pink. As a foliage plant it will tolerate a fair amount of shade, but to flower it should be grown in full sun.

In mid-spring, the common giant fennel (*Ferula communis*) makes a dramatic fountain of feathery fronds among the strap-shaped leaves of bulbs such as snowdrops and eye-catching foliage plants including the boldly variegated *Arum italicum* 'Marmoratum'.

◐ *Dicentra* 'Pearl Drops', *Hosta* (Tardiana Group) 'Halcyon', *Iris* 'Jane Phillips', *I. pallida* 'Variegata', *Miscanthus sinensis* 'Variegatus', *Onopordum nervosum*, *Phormium tenax* 'Veitchianum', *Yucca gloriosa*

H: 3.5m (11ft) S: 1.2m (4ft)
❀ **Early to mid-summer**
 ◐·◐◐ ⬛ Z6 pH5.5–8

Festuca glauca

BLUE FESCUE

This small grass has softly arching blue-green foliage (becoming greener in winter) that is evergreen in climates with relatively mild winters. Especially suited to small-scale plantings, it is attractive in gravel gardens, at the front of borders, and as an edging to beds. It combines well with blue, soft yellow, cream, or white flowers, other glaucous or silver-leaved plants, and foliage of contrasting form, such as that of smaller glaucous hostas, artemisias, smaller yellow-flowered achilleas, anthemis, and eryngiums. Good, intensely blue-green cultivars are 'Azurit', slightly more upright than most, 'Blaufuchs' ♀ (Blue Fox),

and 'Blauglut' (Blue Glow). Perhaps most vivid of all is 'Elijah Blue', bright silvery blue-green and long-lived; 'Harz' is a deeper, duller color with purple-tipped leaves, good for contrast and variation in tone in beds of mixed blue-green fescues.

◐ *Achillea* × *lewisii* 'King Edward', *Anthemis punctata* subsp. *cupaniana*, *Artemisia schmidtiana*, *Eryngium maritimum*, *Hosta* (Tardiana Group) 'Halcyon'

H: 10–30cm (4–12in) **S: 20–50cm** (8–20in)
✵ **Late spring to mid-summer**

◇-◇◇ ☐-■ **Z4 pH5.5–7.5**

The leaves of *Festuca glauca* 'Blauglut' are sufficiently blue to be set off companions with yellow-green foliage and flowers, as here with *Juniperus* × *pfitzeriana* Gold Sovereign among a carpet of heathers.

In a waterside planting in mid-summer, the feathery, rich rose-pink flower heads of *Filipendula* 'Kahome' provide a contrast of form with the delicately colored day lily *Hemerocallis* 'Dresden Dream'.

Filipendula 'Kahome'

This hybrid meadowsweet, with rose-pink flowers and slightly bronze-flushed foliage, suits bog gardens, waterside sites, and beds or borders that do not dry out. Its rich flower color is useful in blends with cool colors such as mauve, purple, lilac, lavender, and white, and contrasts with yellow-green foliage and flowers. The deeply cut leaves and fluffy flower heads allow harmonies with the similar form of astilbes and can be contrasted with the more solid outline of hostas or the elegant foliage of moisture-loving irises, sedges, and grasses such as phalaris, and ferns like *Athyrium filix-femina* cultivars or osmundas. Good companions include lythrums, monardas, moisture-loving persicarias and perennial lobelias, white filipendulas, and purple, glaucous, or grey foliage.

◐ *Carex grayi*, *Hosta fortunei* 'Francee', *Iris pseudacorus* 'Variegata', *Lythrum salicaria* 'Morden Pink', *Phalaris arundinacea* var. *picta* 'Feesey'

H: 40cm (16in) **S: 45cm** (18in)
✵ **Mid- to late summer**

◇◇ ☐-■ ■ **Z4 pH5–7.5**

Filipendula ulmaria 'Aurea'
GOLDEN QUEEN-OF-THE-MEADOW

The yellow-green leaves of this herbaceous plant, which approach pure gold in fairly well-lit positions, are at their brightest in late spring and early summer, when the creamy white flowers appear. It is then very effective for harmonies with hot colors or contrasts with blue in bog gardens, waterside plantings, and moist borders, especially with early-leafing ferns, ranunculus, moisture-loving irises, Candelabra and Sikkimensis primulas, and late spring bulbs like crown imperials, bluebells, muscaris, and late narcissi or tulips. It is an attractive partner for euphorbias, brunneras, omphalodes, forget-me-nots, wallflowers, moneyplant, sweet rocket, blue, yellow, or red columbines, and shrubs such as spiraeas, especially cultivars of *Spiraea japonica* with yellow-green leaves.

Aquilegia vulgaris (blue), *Brunnera macrophylla*, *Hyacinthoides hispanica*, *Iris sibirica* 'Cambridge', *Matteuccia struthiopteris*, *Myosotis sylvatica*, *Omphalodes cappadocica*, *Primula* Inshriach hybrids

H: 75cm (30in) S: 45cm (18in)
Late spring to early summer

Z3 pH4–7.5

In early summer, the bright foliage of golden meadowsweet (*Filipendula ulmaria* 'Aurea') contrasts with the flowers of the cranesbill *Geranium* 'Johnson's Blue'. The combination will remain colorful for several months.

Gentiana asclepiadea
WILLOW GENTIAN

One of the easiest gentians to grow, this is a graceful herbaceous perennial with intense, deep pure blue flowers. It can be grown in borders in partial or full shade, but seems to perform best in a woodland setting, in the shade of beech or oak. Its elegant arching growth habit looks best surrounded by shorter plants such as ferns, late-flowering saxifrages, shade-loving grasses and sedges, late-flowering cranesbills, and Japanese anemones, particularly white cultivars. It combines effectively with white or pale blue flowers and contrasts with yellow flowers like patrinias, or yellow-green foliage and flowers. Good companions include white or yellow tricyrtis, yellow-green hostas and ground-covering ivies, kirengeshomas, hydrangeas, late-flowering lilies, white-variegated grasses, and plants with white or yellow berries.

Anemone × *hybrida* 'Honorine Jobert', *Geranium* 'Johnson's Blue', *Hedera helix* 'Buttercup', *Hosta* 'Sum and Substance', *Lilium lancifolium* var. *splendens*

H: 90cm (36in) S: 60cm (24in)
Mid-summer to early autumn

Z6 pH5–7.5

In this mixture of herbs, a pleasant effect is achieved solely through the use of different kinds of foliage. The feathery leaves of fennel and bronze fennel (*Foeniculum vulgare* and 'Purpureum') are joined by the larger, bolder leaflets of angelica (*Angelica archangelica*) and by the narrow-leaved Spanish sage (*Salvia lavandulifolia*).

Foeniculum vulgare
COMMON FENNEL

This aromatic herbaceous perennial can be grown in wild or gravel gardens, and in borders. Its feathery foliage is most attractive in late spring and early summer, when spangled with the flowers of companions such as moricandias, *Omphalodes linifolia*, *Gladiolus tristis*, calochortus, alliums, nigellas, forget-me-nots, and heliophilas. Its own flowers, born later in the season, are yellowish green and have a quiet charm. Fennel can also be used purely as a foliage plant, providing a complete contrast with grasses and sedges, ferns, angelicas, or hostas. Bronze fennel, *F.v.* 'Purpureum', combines well with mauve, purple, and hot-colored flowers to give a dusky bronze background.

Achillea 'Coronation Gold' p.178 **B**, *Dahlia* 'Glorie van Heemstede' p.373 **A**, *Geranium* × *oxonianum* f. *thurstonianum* p.227 **B**, *Hedychium coccineum* 'Tara' p.234 **A**, *Rosa* 'Climbing Paul Lédé' p.140 **B**

H: 1.8m (6ft) S: 50cm (20in)
Mid- to late summer

Z4 pH5.5–8

The rich blue flowers of *Gentiana asclepiadea* stand out dramatically against the yellow-green foliage of *Rubus cockburnianus* 'Goldenvale'. Grown in light shade, the rubus leaves remain bright and avoid being scorched by the sun.

Geraniums

GERANIUMS or cranesbills are among the most popular herbaceous plants, reflecting their versatility and prettiness, and the fact that they are generally easy to cultivate. Many grow naturally in dappled shade in woods or hedgerows. Others are meadow plants, upright in growth and suitable for a herbaceous border. Some are scramblers, able to weave through shrubs and across banks or providing a good ground cover. There are clump-forming alpine species, superb for a gravel garden, rock garden, or (the easier ones) the front of a border. A few, such as the monocarpic, tender *G. maderense* ♥ and the rather hardier, longer-lived *G. palmatum* ♥, are not herbaceous but form bold rosettes of leaves born on a woody stem. There are also some annuals, although these tend to be rather straggly with tiny flowers.

The flowers of cranesbills are cool-colored, from soft lavender-blue to magenta and paler tints to white; they are often attractively veined – dramatic black on magenta, for example. The blooms are born scattered across the clump, seldom in such profusion that they overwhelm their neighbors, making them ideal in a supporting role to stars of the border such as delphiniums, peonies, or old roses. One exception is *G. × magnificum* ♥, which for a brief couple of weeks can produce a solid sheet of blue capable of disrupting the balance with and between its companions, unless used in a scattered drift or grown in partial shade to control its flower production. There is a handful of *G. pratense* cultivars that have double flowers; although these perhaps lack the pleasant simplicity of the single blooms, they have their own charm and are longer-lasting.

The foliage of cranesbills is usually tidy and respectable, without showing any strong form or texture, which must be supplied by companion plants such as irises, daylilies, or grasses. There are some silvery leaved sorts, and chocolate-

Above: An informal mix using cranesbills in a sunny glade, including pale greyish blue *Geranium pratense* 'Mrs Kendall Clark' (foreground and center), magenta *G. psilostemon*, and rich blue *G. × magnificum*, with cardoons (*Cynara cardunculus*), delphiniums, lupines, poppies, and roses.

Left: Deep pink *Geranium × oxonianum* f. *thurstonianum* and lavender-blue *G. ibericum* mingle harmoniously in this border planting, with contrasting iris leaves and the erect, deep blue spikes of *Veronica austriaca* subsp. *teucrium*.

or purple-leaved cultivars are on the increase. Most are sufficiently late-leafing to be planted with spring bulbs, wood anemones and celandines beneath.

Many cranesbills are excellent when used as a ground cover, although the vigor and ultimate size of the chosen sort need to be carefully tailored to the neighboring plants. While smaller kinds such as *G. × cantabrigiense* are not problematic, the larger *G. macrorrhizum* and *G. × oxonianum* cultivars are so large and vigorous that they can suppress nearby roses, for example. *G. procurrens* is beautiful but irrepressible, rooting wherever it touches the ground, and only practical where there is plenty of space.

Deadheading is usually desirable to keep the clumps looking neat, prevent excess seedlings, and maintain good basal foliage; it can sometimes encourage repeat-flowering. Snapping off the spent flower stems within the dome of basal foliage leaves no trace of interference. However, cutting the whole group to the ground with shears may be simpler. New foliage is usually produced within a couple of weeks.

Geranium albanum weaves through the outer branches of *Weigela* 'Florida Variegata', beneath which grows a carpet of self-seeded wood forget-me-nots (*Myosotis sylvatica*). The sprawling growth habit of this cranesbill allows it to meander through its neighbors, its scattering of dainty flowers uniting them all into an intimately mixed ensemble.

Geranium albanum

A rather sprawling cranesbill, with bright pink flowers, this species is suitable for the front of a border or for a ground cover, especially when intermingled with neighbors such as small shrubs with a fairly open growth habit, or small species or Ground Cover roses. It also looks effective with periwinkles, *Omphalodes linifolia*, cistus, lavenders, and low-growing annuals such as forget-me-nots. The cranesbill's blooms are rather small, and the foliage can predominate in nitrogen-rich soil, so for a good flowering display plants are perhaps best grown in poor soil or even in gravel. Because growth tends to die back during the summer, it is a good idea to combine this species with a late-blooming plant such as *Aster divaricatus*, which can fill the cranesbill's space in late summer and autumn.

◐ *Cistus × cyprius*, *Convolvulus cneorum*, *Erysimum* 'Bowles' Mauve', *Lavandula lanata*, *Rosa* 'Nozomi', *R.* 'The Fairy', *Vinca minor* 'La Grave'

H & S: 45cm (18in) ❀ **Late spring to mid-summer**
◊◊ ▢-▩ **Z7 pH5.5–7.5**

Geranium × cantabrigiense

This is a fairly dwarf, mat-forming cranesbill, capable of making dense carpets of ground cover and useful for planting under shrubs that tend to have clear stems such as some roses. It has neat, glossy foliage that assumes tints of scarlet, flame, and yellow before it dies in autumn, and flowers that vary from palest pink to a rich carmine-pink. It thrives in sun or partial shade, and is suited to the front of a border. The commonest cultivars are 'Biokovo', in palest blush-pink; 'Cambridge', in a richer shade of pink; and 'Karmina', which is a deeper carmine-pink. All combine well with heucheras, bergenias, and plants with contrasting foliage such as ferns, sedges, and smaller or glaucous grasses. They also make a superb foil for summer-flowering bulbs such as lilies.

◐ *Bergenia* 'Abendglut', *Carex comans* 'Frosted Curls', *Dryopteris affinis*, *Festuca glauca* 'Elijah Blue', *Heuchera cylindrica* 'Greenfinch', *× Heucherella alba* 'Rosalie', *Lilium* 'Joy', *Molinia caerulea* 'Variegata', *Rosa glauca*

H: 30cm (12in) S: 60cm (24in)
❀ **Early to mid-summer**
◊◊ ▢-▩ **Z5 pH5–7.5**

Geranium × cantabrigiense 'Cambridge', grown through gravel to edge a bed, is infiltrated by the mildly invasive variegated apple mint, *Mentha suaveolens* 'Variegata'. The cream edges to the mint's leaves highlight their shape, producing an attractive pattern.

Geranium 'Ann Folkard' is, like *G. albanum* above, a plant that will sprawl through its neighbors, unifying the whole. Its flowers contrast with its foliage: combining it with the mauve blooms of *Allium cristophii* and yellow-green leaves of wild marjoram (*Origanum vulgare* 'Aureum') gives an arrangement in which all the flowers contrast with all the leaves.

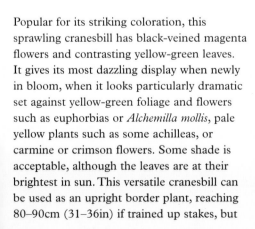

Geranium 'Ann Folkard' ♛

Popular for its striking coloration, this sprawling cranesbill has black-veined magenta flowers and contrasting yellow-green leaves. It gives its most dazzling display when newly in bloom, when it looks particularly dramatic set against yellow-green foliage and flowers such as euphorbias or *Alchemilla mollis*, pale yellow plants such as some achilleas, or carmine or crimson flowers. Some shade is acceptable, although the leaves are at their brightest in sun. This versatile cranesbill can be used as an upright border plant, reaching 80–90cm (31–36in) if trained up stakes, but it is most suitable for a ground cover or as a carpet through which other plants can be grown – these may be herbaceous perennials, small shrubs such as *Potentilla fruticosa* cultivars, or summer bulbs such as lilies.

◐ *Anthemis tinctoria* p.186 **B**, *Artemisia stelleriana* 'Boughton Silver' p.190 **A**, *Cytisus nigricans* p.44 **B**, *Deschampsia cespitosa* p.209 **C**, *Geranium sylvaticum* 'Mayflower' p.230 **C**, *Heuchera micrantha* var. *diversifolia* 'Palace Purple' p.240 **A**, *Lilium* 'Joy' p.327 **A**, *Populus alba* 'Richardii' p.77 **A**, *Rhus × pulvinata* Autumn Lace Group p.86 **A**, *Rosa* 'De Rescht'

H: 60cm (24in) S: 90cm (36in)
❀ **Mid-summer to mid-autumn**
◊◊ ▢-▩ **Z5 pH5–7.5**

Geranium 'Chocolate Candy'

This low-growing herbaceous plant is suitable for rock gardens and sunny borders with good drainage, where it associates most easily with plants from a similar climate and needing similar conditions – plants from New Zealand or the Chilean Andes, for example. Its deeply colored foliage, among the darkest of any cranesbill, looks best in a position near the front, in combinations with mondo grass, heucheras, and other dark-leaved cranesbills such as *G. pratense* Midnight Reiter strain. Its flowers are a strong enough pink to contrast with yellow-green flowers (but large areas of yellow-green foliage might overwhelm it) or, even more dramatically, with silver foliage, and they also work well with crimson and other cool colors such as mauve, lilac, or purple. Good partners include small euphorbias, oxalis, campanulas, marjorams, smaller penstemons, alchemillas, celmisias, erodiums, smaller hebes, and other small or prostrate cranesbills.

◑ *Artemisia alba* 'Canescens', *Celmisia spectabilis*, *Hebe ochracea*, *Heuchera* 'Plum Pudding', *Ophiopogon planiscapus* 'Nigrescens', *Spiraea japonica* 'Goldflame'

H: 25cm (10in) **S: 50cm** (20in)
✿ **Early summer to early autumn**
◊◊ ▢-▮ **Z8 pH5.5–7.5**

Facing page: The variety of flower and foliage sizes and colors adds interest to this pretty mixture of three cranesbills, in which soft pink *Geranium* 'Dusky Crûg', bright pink *G.* 'Chocolate Candy', and soft magenta *G. psilostemon* 'Bressingham Flair' all harmonize agreeably.

Geranium 'Johnson's Blue' ♔

With flowers as near to true blue as any cranesbill, this is a superlative hybrid that performs well in partial shade and also tolerates full sun. Combinations with yellow flowers are perhaps the most striking, especially early-flowering roses, daylilies, columbines, and Bearded irises; it is also attractive with yellow-green foliage or flowers and with white and other cool-colored flowers. It mixes well with baptisias, centaureas, anthericums, philadelphus, alchemillas, catmints, pinks, and campanulas, as well as with contrasting foliage plants, including yellow-green, glaucous, or variegated hostas and glaucous grasses such as elymus and helictotrichons. It makes dramatic partnerships with flowers of contrasting shape and size – camassias or veronicas, for example – and with those of similar shape but distinctively different color, such as violas in soft yellow, purple, and deep or very pale blue. If cut to the ground immediately after flowering, plants will usually bloom again later on.

◑ *Allium hollandicum* p.301 **A**, *Centranthus ruber* p.202 **A**, *Filipendula ulmaria* 'Aurea' p.223 **A**, *Iris chrysographes* p.249 **A**, *Lamium maculatum* p.256 **A**, *Lilium pyrenaicum* var. *pyrenaicum* p.328 **C**, *Rosa* Iceberg p.165 **B**, *Spiraea japonica* p.93 **C**

H: 40cm (16in) **S: 60cm** (24in)
✿ **Early summer to mid-autumn**
◊◊◊ ▢-▮ **Z4 pH5–7.5**

Geranium 'Johnson's Blue' is a superlative and floriferous mound-forming plant for the front of beds and borders, flowering profusely over several months, especially if grown in a fairly sunny situation. Here, it is used beneath Jerusalem sage (*Phlomis fruticosa*), providing a charming contrast of color and floral form.

Geranium × *oxonianum*

This clump-forming plant is useful for a woodland garden and for naturalizing, and can be used in a mixed border, beneath roses, or to create a tapestry of ground cover, perhaps with other cranesbills of contrasting form and color. Its flowers are various shades of pink: cultivars tending towards rose-pink mix well with warm colors such as peach and apricot, but are often close enough to primary pink not to clash with mauves and blues; mauve-pink cultivars are best with cool- or white-flowered plants; pale rose-pink cultivars combine with soft yellow. All blend with silver, glaucous, or purple-flushed foliage – artemisias or glaucous hostas, for example, and especially with heucheras and bergenias – and with contrasting foliage such as that of irises. 'A.T. Johnson' ♔ is silvery pink; 'Claridge Druce' is mauve-pink and vigorous; 'Phoebe Noble' is deep magenta, and 'Prestbury Blush' is almost white; 'Rose Clair' and 'Wargrave Pink' ♔ are both rose-pink.

In this subtly subdued but satisfying combination, the dusky magenta-pink flowers of the cranesbill *Geranium* × *oxonianum* f. *thurstonianum* harmonize with the purple-flushed leaves of bronze fennel (*Foeniculum vulgare* 'Purpureum'). The squirting cucumber (*Ecballium elaterium*) provides foliage interest in front, while the white flowers of the love-in-a-mist *Nigella damascena* 'Miss Jekyll Alba' leaven the whole.

◑ *Cotinus coggygria* 'Royal Purple' p.42 **B**, *Dicentra eximia* p.211 **B**, *Hebe stenophylla* p.56 **B**, *Hosta* 'Sum and Substance' p.247 **A**, *Kniphofia* 'Atlanta' p.254 **B**, *Philadelphus* 'Beauclerk' p.71 **A** ❏ p.70 **A**

H: 30–60cm (12–24in) **S: 40–75cm** (16–30in)
✿ **Late spring to mid-autumn**

◊◊ ▢-▮ ▮ **Z5 pH4.5–8**

The somber maroon flowers of the mourning widow (*Geranium phaeum*) are not easily visible from a distance, and tend to be upstaged by dazzling colors such as magenta, but combining them, as here, with Mrs Robb's bonnet (*Euphorbia amygdaloides* var. *robbiae*) draws attention to them without their being overwhelmed.

Geranium phaeum
MOURNING WIDOW

This rather variable herbaceous perennial holds itself with great poise and beauty. It tolerates dry shade well, but also performs well in full sun and is vigorous enough to be naturalized in grass and in a woodland garden. Its flowers, usually purplish black with a white center, are best appreciated at close range and are useful for providing a base note for plantings with brighter flowers, such as pink, mauve, or purple, and with purple-flushed foliage. 'Album' is a charming white cultivar for lighting up a shady corner; 'Blue Shadow' appears dusky amethyst or lavender depending on light levels; 'Joan Baker' is pale lavender-blue; and 'Lily Lovell' is dusky purple with yellowish green leaves.

Aquilegia vulgaris p.187 **B**, *Chaerophyllum hirsutum* 'Roseum' p.202 **B**, *Digitalis purpurea* f. *albiflora*, *Heuchera* 'Plum Pudding', *Tellima grandiflora*

H: 70–90cm (27–36in) S: 45cm (18in)
❀ Late spring to early summer
◊◊ ☐-■ Z4 pH4.5–7.5

In a steeply sloped, sunny planting of mainly cool but rich colors, *Geranium psilostemon* grows beneath blush-pink *Rosa* Heritage, with *Sedum* 'Herbstfreude' in front. *Viola* 'Mercury' and *Dianthus* 'Laced Monarch' decorate the front of the border. In a less steep position, a plant of intermediate height could be used between the cranesbill and the viola.

Geranium pratense
MEADOW CRANESBILL

This cranesbill is choice enough for a border in sun or partial shade, yet sufficiently robust to be naturalized in long grass and woodland gardens. It mixes with white flowers, silver foliage, and Shrub roses in cool colors and warm peach or apricot, and contrasts with soft yellow flowers and yellow-green foliage or flowers. It works well with glaucous hostas and larger grasses, especially white- or gold-variegated miscanthus. In grass, it looks effective with variants of *Achillea millefolium*. Attractive selections are *G.p.* f. *albiflorum*, which embraces white-flowered variants such as 'Galactic'; 'Mrs Kendall Clark' ♀, pale greyish blue; Victor Reiter strain, lavender-blue with bronze or purple-flushed foliage; subsp. *stewartianum* 'Elizabeth Yeo', almost pure pink; and the robust, double-flowered lavender 'Plenum Violaceum' ♀.

Achillea millefolium 'Lilac Beauty', *Artemisia alba* 'Canescens', *Hosta* (Tardiana Group) 'Halcyon', *Miscanthus sinensis* 'Variegatus', *Rosa* 'Buff Beauty'

H: 60–90cm (24–36in) S: 60cm (24in)
❀ Early to mid-summer
 ◊◊ ☐-■ Z4 pH4.5–8

The streaked, soft blue flowers of *Geranium pratense* 'Mrs Kendall Clark' are contrasted with the yellow-green inflorescences of cypress spurge (*Euphorbia cyparissias*). A deeper blue cranesbill would also be effective.

Geranium psilostemon ♀

One of the most spectacular herbaceous cranesbills and also one of the tallest, this is a candidate for the middle rows of a border. Its flowers are intense magenta, accentuated by shining black veins and a black center, making it suitable for combinations with cool colors and for almost shocking contrasts with soft yellow, yellow-green, or orange. It combines well with glaucous, silver, or purple foliage, and creates good contrast with yellow-green foliage. Striking effects can be achieved with partners of contrasting form and foliage – larger miscanthus cultivars or larger hostas, for example. 'Bressingham Flair' is a lighter magenta and slightly shorter – although this is less effective for striking contrasts, it is a more peaceful color where harmonies of cool shades are being used.

Cotinus coggygria 'Royal Purple', *Foeniculum vulgare*, *Geranium* 'Chocolate Candy' p.226 **A**, *Gladiolus communis* subsp. *byzantinus* p.318 **A**, *Hosta sieboldiana* var. *elegans*, *Iris* 'Braithwaite', *Lathyrus odoratus* 'Matucana' p.125 **B**, *Miscanthus sinensis* 'Zebrinus', *Papaver orientale*, *Phygelius aequalis* 'Yellow Trumpet' p.73 **B**, *Rosa gallica* 'Versicolor' p.148 **A**

H: 1m (40in) S: 60cm (24in)
❀ Early to late summer
 ◊◊ ☐-■ Z4 pH5–7.5

Geranium renardii ♔

A charming plant for the front of a border or for rock gardens, this short, clump-forming herbaceous perennial flowers best in a sunny site. Its downy leaves are sage-green, almost silvery in relatively nutrient-poor soil, and incised with a network of deep veins, while the white flowers are veined with lavender, details that demand to be appreciated at close range. It is an excellent partner for silver foliage and cool-colored flowers, especially those in the blue to violet range. Its lavender-blue variant, 'Whiteknights', is more richly colored and will stand combinations with cream and contrasts with delicate yellow. Lilac-colored 'Tcschelda', and 'Zetterlund', also lilac but with violet veins, are attractive with smaller catmints, pinks, artemisias, and glaucous hebes, blue fescues, sages, and the silver (or lime-encrusted) *Ligulatae* saxifrages.

◖ *Anthemis tinctoria* 'E.C. Buxton', *Festuca glauca* 'Blaufuchs', *Hebe pinguifolia* 'Pagei', *Nepeta* × *faassenii*, *Salvia officinalis* 'Purpurascens'

H & S: 30cm (12in) ❀ **Early summer**

◊◊ ▢-■ **Z6 pH5.5–7.5**

Geranium renardii, with its fascinatingly felted and netted leaves and pale blooms, is an excellent plant for the front of a border, here harmonizing with the coppery flowers of *Geum rivale* 'Leonard's Variety'.

Geranium × riversleaianum

This hybrid between *G. endressii* and *G. traversii* has produced several cultivars, two of which are particularly valuable for ground covers and for the front of a border, or rock or gravel garden. 'Mavis Simpson' is a sprawling plant that will also scramble effectively over its neighbors and into small open shrubs like cistus, olearias, tree poppies, and escallonias. Its satiny rose-pink flowers and greyish green foliage are excellent with cool purple foliage plants such as heucheras and purple sage, glaucous dwarf fescues, and flowers such as pinks, catmints, campanulas, bugleweeds, smaller penstemons, and violas. The more robust 'Russell Prichard' ♔ has bright magenta flowers that look dramatic with cool colors, purple, silver, or glaucous foliage, and yellow-green, soft yellow, or orange flowers. Good companions include soft yellow achilleas, agapanthus, alchemillas, crocosmias, day lilies, and euphorbias.

◖ *Achillea* 'Moonshine', *Dianthus* 'Doris', *Eryngium* × *tripartitum* p.217 **C**, *Festuca glauca* 'Elijah Blue', *Heuchera micrantha* var. *diversifolia* 'Palace Purple' p.240 **A**, *Lilium speciosum* p.329 **B**

H: 23cm (9in) S: 1m (40in)
❀ **Early summer to early autumn**

 ◊◊ ▢-■ **Z6 pH5.5–7.5**

Above: In an attractive partnership for the front of a border, *Geranium × riversleaianum* 'Russell Prichard' weaves among the stems of tricolor sage (*Salvia officinalis* 'Tricolor'), its magenta flowers matching the flushed tips of the sage's young shoots.

Below: The soft pink flowers and slightly grey foliage of *Geranium × riversleaianum* 'Mavis Simpson' are suited to more delicately colored arrangements and combinations with silvery or glaucous foliage, as here with the contrasting form of the grass *Elymus magellanicus*.

The delicate blooms of *Geranium sanguineum* var. *striatum* show among a tracery of silvery *Artemisia alba* 'Canescens', the artemisia's filigree foliage letting through the light the cranesbill needs to flower.

Geranium sanguineum var. striatum ♗

With its sprawling mound of deeply cut, dark green leaves, this charming herbaceous perennial is a valuable addition to the front of a border or a rock garden. It tolerates a little shade, but in full sun gives the best display of its delicate pink, crimson-veined flowers. These combine pleasantly with cool colors or purple leaves, and their color is usually strong enough to contrast with yellow-green flowers – euphorbias, for example – or with very pale yellow flowers such as those of some violas. It combines well with heucheras, polemoniums, dictamnus, violas in dusky deep pink, mauve, purple, and blue, and shorter alliums that flower in early summer. Other good companions include early roses and campanulas, dicentras, and columbines.

🌑 *Allium cristophii*, *Berberis thunbergii* 'Atropurpurea Nana', *Dictamnus albus* var. *purpureus*, *Euphorbia schillingii*, *Salvia nemorosa* 'Lubecca' p.282 **B**

H: 15cm (6in) **S: 20cm** (8in)
❀ **Early summer to late autumn**

 ◊◊ ☐-■ **Z4 pH5.5–7.5**

Geranium sylvaticum
WOOD CRANESBILL

The wood cranesbill is a versatile plant that tolerates some shade and may be naturalized in sunnier parts of woodland or wild gardens. It blooms after most spring flowers but before the bulk of summer ones, so its natural allies include violas, polemoniums, columbines, and brunneras, as well as shrubs like brooms, rhododendrons, daphnes, and lilacs. Blue-flowered sorts, including the superlative 'Mayflower' ♗, are very effective with cool colors, glaucous, silver, or variegated foliage, and yellow-green foliage and flowers. White umbellifers, soft yellow deciduous azaleas, ceanothus, and early yellow roses are excellent partners. White-flowered variants (f. *albiflorum*) mix especially well with silver, glaucous, or white-variegated foliage and blue flowers, and with contrasting floral forms, such as the lacy heads of umbellifers or the spikes of lupines and camassias.

🌑 *Anthriscus sylvestris* 'Ravenswing', *Aquilegia vulgaris* (mixed) p.187 **B**, *Milium effusum* 'Aureum', *Polemonium caeruleum*, *Rhododendron* 'Narcissiflorum'

H: 75cm (30in) **S: 60cm** (24in)
❀ **Late spring to early summer**

 ◊◊ ☐-■ **Z4 pH5–7.5**

Above: The relatively upright *Geranium sylvaticum* f. *albiflorum* is tall enough to mingle with the lower branches of this purple smoke bush (*Cotinus coggygria* 'Royal Purple'), its flowers contrasting with the dark foliage.

Below: In a semi-shady border in late spring, the harmonious, similarly sized blooms of *Geranium sylvaticum* 'Mayflower' and *Viola cornuta* 'Rosea', enlivened by their white eyes, are separated by the contrasting yellow-green leaves of *Geranium* 'Ann Folkard'.

Geranium tuberosum

This tuberous-rooted perennial has deeply divided leaves and rosy-purple flowers that appear in late spring and early summer, and can therefore partner the same plants as *G. sylvaticum* and its derivatives (facing page), together with biennials such as sweet William. It dies back quickly after blooming, and then needs to be followed by another plant to continue the display – this successor might be a late-sown annual like nicotiana, a perennial bedding plant, or a pot-grown tender perennial. *G. tuberosum* also thrives when naturalized in sunnier parts of a wild or woodland garden, where it mixes well with later-flowering rhododendrons and azaleas. Too muted to be satisfactory in strong contrasts, it succeeds with cool colors and white flowers, including early white roses and philadelphus, and purple foliage such as that of purple cow parsley and some heucheras.

Dianthus barbatus, *Heuchera micrantha* var. *diversifolia* 'Palace Purple', *Nicotiana* Domino Series, *Philadelphus* 'Belle Etoile', *Rosa* × *fortuneana*

H & S: 30cm (12in) **Late spring to early summer**
Z7 pH5.5–7.5

The mauve flowers of *Geranium tuberosum* match those of trailing *G. pyrenaicum* 'Bill Wallis', although the two differ substantially in scale. In late spring, the silvery foliage of *Artemisia ludoviciana* is just emerging; as *G. tuberosum* dies back, the artemisia will become much taller, largely filling the gap left by the cranesbill.

A

At the peak of their flowering in early summer, yellow *Geum* 'Lady Stratheden' and scarlet *G.* 'Mrs J. Bradshaw' combine to give a dazzling display. Deep red or yellow-green foliage or blood-red flowers could enhance the effect.

Geum 'Lady Stratheden' ♛

This hybrid thrives at the front of a sunny or partially shaded border, where it will flower all summer long. Its ruffled, semi-double blooms are a rich, soft yellow that works well with hot colors and bronze foliage, and with warm shades such as apricot, peach, and buff. Roses in these colors make good companions, as do early lilies, daylilies, and achilleas. It blends with cream flowers such as cream aconitums and *Paeonia × lemoinei* cultivars, and looks effective with mid-blue or lavender-blue flowers such as cranesbills, columbines, *Trachymene coerulea*, *Nigella damascena*, and *Salvia pratensis* Haematodes Group. Its slightly coarse foliage benefits from finer or contrasting neighbors, including yellow-green grasses. 'Mrs J. Bradshaw' ♛ is similar, but with scarlet flowers. Both hybrids come true from seed.

◉ *Achillea* 'Fanal', *Aconitum* 'Ivorine', *Aquilegia* 'Hensol Harebell', *Geranium* 'Johnson's Blue', *Hakonechloa macra* 'Alboaurea', *Lilium* 'Enchantment', *Phormium* 'Bronze Baby', *Rosa* 'Buff Beauty'

H: 50cm (20in) S: 60cm (24in)
✿ Early summer to early autumn

 ◊◊ ▮ Z5 pH5.5–7.5

Gunnera manicata ♛

Often called giant rhubarb, this magnificent monster of a plant can make gardens of more modest size look jungle-like and mysterious. Its conical flower spikes, 1m (40in) high and covered with frilled reddish bracts, sometimes nestle invisibly beneath the leaves. It revels in moist situations, especially waterside positions where reflections double its impact. It is best combined with similarly dramatic plants – bamboos and other large grasses, such as arundos or the biggest miscanthus – and with plants of semi-tropical appearance, such as bananas, cannas, colocasias, palms, tetrapanax, the biggest ligularias and eupatoriums, and stooled paulownias or catalpas. Companions should be grouped on a similar scale to avoid being overwhelmed. The young foliage is sensitive to frost damage. *G. tinctoria* (syn. *G. chilensis*) is similar, but shorter at 1.5m (5ft) high.

◉ *Canna* 'Erebus', *Catalpa bignonioides* (stooled), *Eupatorium purpureum*, *Hosta sieboldiana* var. *elegans* p.246 **C**, *Ligularia stenocephala*, *Miscanthus sacchariflorus*, *Tetrapanax papyrifer* (stooled)

H: 2.5m (8ft) S: 4m (13ft) ✿ (Early summer)
◊◊◊ ▮ Z7 pH5.5–7.5

Backed by the elegant, arching canes of the bamboo *Fargesia murielae*, *Gunnera manicata* creates an exotic, almost tropical effect. Its leaves are echoed by the much smaller umbrella-like foliage of *Darmera peltata* that grows at the front of the planting.

In this pleasant late spring arrangement for partial shade, the oak fern (*Gymnocarpium dryopteris*) unfurls lacy new fronds between the lavender-speckled blooms of *Viola sororia* 'Freckles' and the sky-blue flowers of the wood forget-me-not (*Myosotis sylvatica*).

Gymnocarpium dryopteris ♛

OAK FERN

This hardy deciduous fern has divided, wavy-edged fronds, resembling tiny, unfurling oak leaves, that become a bright, rich green with age. It is an attractive plant for moist, shady situations, especially as a ground cover, either alone or partnered with contrasting foliage such as grasses and sedges, or the loose shuttlecocks of the hart's tongue fern. Shade-loving companions with white or very pale flowers that appear in late spring look most effective. The classic partner for the oak fern is *Ornithogalum nutans*, whose nodding, silvery white flowers stand above the fern's emerald-green new foliage, masking the bulb's somewhat unkempt leaves. In cool soils the fern's slender, creeping rhizomes will eventually produce a carpet of dainty foliage that looks fresh and deceptively fragile throughout the season, but in drier soils and warmer summers or where there is too much lime in the ground, growth is usually sparser.

🌣 *Asplenium scolopendrium*, *Carex siderosticha* 'Variegata', *Hesperis matronalis* var. *albiflora*, *Lunaria annua* var. *albiflora*, *Milium effusum* 'Aureum'

H: 20cm (8in)   **S: 45cm** (18in)
 Z3 pH5–7.5

Gypsophila paniculata 'Compacta Plena'

The airy clouds of blushed white, formal, double blooms produced by this slow-growing, spreading form of baby's breath are indispensable for softening hard edges, such as those at the side of paths or against edging stones. It is very much a front-of-border plant, ideal for growing next to spring bulbs or biennials such as sweet William or early perennials such as Oriental poppies, since it will happily fill the gap that is left once these have been removed or died back.

'Compacta Plena' makes a good foil for plants with deeper pink, carmine, or crimson flowers, and with glaucous or silver foliage, particularly if they have a bold, substantial form. 'Bristol Fairy' ♛ is taller at 60cm (24in), with larger, double white flowers up to 1.5cm (3/4in) across, but it is inclined to be short-lived, except on sharply drained, alkaline soils. G. 'Rosenschleier' (syn. 'Rosy Veil') ♛ is a hybrid with double pink flowers and will grow 40–50cm (16–20in) high by about 1m (31/4ft) wide.

The airy, delicate blush flowers of *Gypsophila paniculata* 'Compacta Plena' help to soften the almost too solid color of the annual Chinese pink *Dianthus chinensis* (Princess Series) 'Princess Salmon', in this pretty combination for summer display at the front of a border.

🌣 *Convolvulus cneorum*, *Dahlia* 'Bednall Beauty', *Diascia rigescens*, *Geranium* × *riversleaianum* 'Mavis Simpson', *Helianthemum* 'Ben Hope'

H: 25cm (10in)   **S: 60cm** (24in)
✽ **Mid- to late summer**
 Z4 pH6–8

The gracefully arching leaves of *Hakonechloa macra* 'Alboaurea', with their striking variegation of yellow and white, decorate the front of a border beneath the bold, dark green foliage of *Hosta tardiflora*.

Hakonechloa macra 'Alboaurea'

This is a gracefully arching, deciduous grass that has green and gold leaves occasionally streaked with white. It is attractive at the front of a border or cascading down a moist bank, and looks effective in containers, where it is best grown on its own, with suitable companions in adjacent pots. It mixes easily with glaucous foliage and the contrasting leaf shapes of ferns, hostas, or bergenias, and contrasts well with bronze or purple foliage. Blue flowers such as lower-growing veronicas and corydalis are good partners, but pairings with early spring flowers should be avoided since these tend to bloom before the leaves of the grass have expanded. The plant may become flat in the center unless stakes are worked in throughout the foliage. 'Aureola' ♛ is very similar but has slightly shorter, wider leaves without the white streaks.

🌣 *Bergenia cordifolia* 'Purpurea', *Corydalis flexuosa*, *Cotinus coggygria* Rubrifolius Group, *Erodium glandulosum*, *Festuca glauca*, *Lychnis* × *arkwrightii* 'Vesuvius', *Veronica austriaca* subsp. *teucrium*

H: 23cm (9in)   **S: 45cm** (18in)
✽ **Early to mid-autumn**
 Z5 pH5–7.5

Hedychium coccineum 'Tara' ♔

This is a superlative and relatively hardy orange-flowered cultivar of the red ginger lily, *Hedychium coccineum*. It is a rhizomatous herbaceous perennial that can be grown in beds and borders, in a greenhouse, or in large containers, and its handsome foliage and flowers add an exotic ingredient to plantings.

It may be used with other hot-colored plants, including tender species such as shrubby and sub-shrubby salvias, dahlias, phygelius, leonotis, and cannas, as well as with hardier plants such as ligularias, crocosmias, or kniphofias, and with bright annuals and bedding plants such as alonsoas, impatiens, and larger tagetes. The flowers contrast very effectively with the glaucous foliage of plants like *Nicotiana glauca* and hostas. They are also good with yellow-green foliage and flowers, including late-flowering euphorbias, cautleyas, and later-flowering lilies. Deep orange *H. densiflorum* 'Assam Orange' is another large, clump-forming ginger lily of similar hardiness.

◗ *Alonsoa warscewiczii*, *Canna* 'Striata', *Kniphofia caulescens*, *Leonotis leonurus*, *Phygelius* × *rectus* 'Moonraker', *Salvia coccinea* 'Lady in Red'

H: 2m (6½ft) S: 90cm (3ft)
✿ **Late summer to mid-autumn**
◊◊ ☐-■ **Z8 pH5.5–7.5**

The tropical-looking spikes of *Hedychium coccineum* 'Tara' are here set in a haze of seedheads of fennel (*Foeniculum vulgare*), beneath the golden honey locust (*Gleditsia triacanthos* 'Sunburst').

Helenium 'Wyndley'

Sneezeweeds are invaluable late-flowering hardy herbaceous perennials, providing solid color in a range from yellow through orange to rusty red and mahogany. 'Wyndley' has yellow petals flushed and streaked with orange, and makes a strong impact in hot color schemes in mixed or herbaceous borders with plants of more definite form, such as crocosmias, dahlias, kniphofias, cannas, tender shrubby salvias, hedychiums, and late-flowering lilies. Other good partners include yellow-green foliage and flowers such as hostas and late-flowering euphorbias, bronze foliage, yellow-variegated grasses like miscanthus cultivars, and annuals such as larger tagetes, alonsoas, rudbeckias, coreopsis, and sunflowers. Other excellent cultivars are 'Blütentisch', golden yellow flecked with brown; and mahogany-red 'Moerheim Beauty', flowering in early to mid-summer.

◗ *Euphorbia sikkimensis*, *Hosta* 'August Moon', *Kniphofia* 'Wrexham Buttercup', *Miscanthus sinensis* 'Zebrinus', *Tagetes patula* 'Striped Marvel'

H: 60cm (24in) S: 45cm (18in)
✿ **Early to late summer**
◊◊ ☐-■ **Z4 pH5.5–7.5**

In this glowing combination for mid-summer, the flowers of the sneezeweed *Helenium* 'Wyndley', with golden petals shaded warm orange around a mahogany disc, are just topped by the vermilion *Crocosmia* 'Lucifer'.

The rich golden yellow, outward-facing flowers of *Helianthus decapetalus* 'Soleil d'Or', seen here with *Helenium* 'Mahogany', bloom on the upper half of an erect plant, allowing it to punctuate borders with bright highlight.

Helianthus decapetalus 'Soleil d'Or'

A tall, upright plant with fully double golden yellow flowers, this perennial sunflower is useful in a herbaceous or mixed border, especially where the intricacy of its flowers can be appreciated at fairly close range. It associates well with hot-colored flowers, including dahlias, cannas, kniphofias, crocosmias, and later-flowering daylilies, and with yellow-green foliage, including that of shrubs such as golden elders. Effective contrasts can be made with glaucous foliage and with blue flowers such as *Ceanothus* × *delileanus* cultivars and with taller late-flowering salvias such as *Salvia uliginosa* or *S. guaranitica*. Good companions include repeat-flowering Shrub roses in white, cream, or soft yellow, larger grasses such as miscanthus cultivars, and other late-flowering daisies such as rudbeckias and heleniums. 'Loddon Gold' is similar, with more reflexed petals of a slightly paler yellow.

◗ *Canna* 'Striata', *Coronilla valentina* subsp. *glauca*, *Hemerocallis fulva* 'Flore Pleno', *Kniphofia rooperi*, *Rosa* Graham Thomas, *Sambucus nigra* 'Aurea'

H: 1.5m (5ft) S: 90cm (3ft)
✿ **Late summer to mid-autumn**
◊◊ ☐-■ **Z5 pH5–7.5**

Helianthus 'Monarch' ♧

The impressive semi-double golden yellow flowers of this tall herbaceous perennial sunflower make a strong statement in hot-colored schemes, such as those suggested for *Helianthus decapetalus* 'Soleil d'Or' (facing page) – with dahlias, crocosmias, cannas, and kniphofias for example. In addition, the yellowish brown disc at the center of each flower helps it harmonize with tawny colored flowers, such as heleniums and some annual sunflowers, and with bronze-colored foliage, including purple smoke bush and bronze or purple cultivars of hazel and larger berberis. The quality of its blooms is so high that 'Monarch' was traditionally grown for

exhibition, disbudding each stem to leave a single bloom, which grew to an impressive 15cm (6in) or more across. As with other sunflowers, its height can be reduced and its flowering delayed slightly by pinching back in late spring and early summer.

◐ *Berberis* × *ottawensis* f. *purpurea* 'Superba', *Corylus maxima* 'Purpurea', *Cotinus coggygria* 'Notcutt's Variety', *Helianthus* 'Pastiche'

H: 2m (6½ft) S: 90cm (3ft) ❀ Early to mid-autumn
◌◌ ▣–▣ **Z5 pH5–7.5**

The golden yellow flowers of *Helianthus* 'Monarch' lose some impact from being upward facing, although their size and profusion compensate. Here, they make a fine show with the yellow-edged leaves of the dogwood *Cornus alba* 'Spaethii' and the vermilion hips of *Rosa* 'Geranium'.

The blue-green leaves of blue oat grass (*Helictotrichon sempervirens*) harmonize with the fleshy foliage of *Sedum spectabile* 'Rosenteller', while contrasting gently with its rich rose flower heads in late summer and early autumn.

Helictotrichon sempervirens ♧
BLUE OAT GRASS

This tufted evergreen grass bears silvery blue-green leaves and spikes of flowers that mature to straw-yellow tinged with purple. Like other blue-green grasses such as elymus species and *Festuca glauca* cultivars, it is a good plant for use towards the front of a border or in a gravel garden, especially if surrounded by shorter plants. It looks very handsome with cool colors, particularly in harmonies with blue, white, or pink flowers and silver or glaucous foliage, and contrasts well with yellow-green foliage or flowers. When the seedheads assume their straw tints, blue oat grass can also produce attractive combinations with apricot-colored flowers such as repeat-flowering roses, *Mimulus aurantiacus* (syn. *M. glutinosus*), verbenas, and achilleas, or with the giant feather grass (*Stipa gigantea*) and other grasses that have seedheads of a similar color. Plants benefit from being shorn almost to ground level in late winter, to allow room for new growth.

◐ *Achillea* 'Walther Funcke', *Centranthus ruber* 'Albus', *Euphorbia polychroma* 'Major', *E. rigida*, *Geranium* 'Johnson's Blue', *G.* × *oxonianum* 'Wargrave Pink'

H & S: 1m (40in) ❀ Late spring to mid-summer
◌–◌◌ ▣–▣ **Z4 pH6–8**

Heliopsis helianthoides 'Patula'

This reliable long-flowering daisy, with rich golden yellow blooms, semi-double and gently frilled, is a valuable plant for hot borders, perhaps combined with other yellow or orange flowers such as ligularias or inulas, especially if their flamboyance is slightly soothed by plum or brown foliage – as in *Dahlia* 'Bishop of Llandaff', for example – and grasses like carex or miscanthus. It is also good in late herbaceous or mixed borders, especially on clay. This heliopsis can be mixed with perennials such as cannas, larger hypericums, later-flowering daylilies and kniphofias, late lilies in yellow or orange, heleniums, and other daisies in warm colors.

It works well with gold-variegated foliage and yellow-green foliage or flowers, and with blue or purplish blue, including echinops, *Buddleja davidii* cultivars, and late-flowering ceanothus. *H.h.* var. *scabra* 'Benzinggold' is another fine cultivar, producing large golden single blooms into mid-autumn.

◐ *Ceanothus × delileanus* 'Gloire de Versailles', *Echinops bannaticus* 'Taplow Blue', *Hypericum forrestii*, *Rosa* 'Grace', *Rudbeckia* 'Herbstsonne'

H: 90–120cm (3–4ft) S: 60cm (24in)
❀ **Early summer to early autumn**
◊◊ ▦- ■ **Z4 pH5–7.5**

In a partnership that will last from summer into autumn, the softly frilled, golden yellow, daisy-like flowers of *Heliopsis helianthoides* 'Patula' mingle easily with the lavender-blue blooms of *Aster × frikartii* 'Mönch'.

In a semi-shady border, the profuse, apple-green, dark-rimmed flowers of hellebore (*Helleborus foetidus*) contrast gently with the pale pink flowering currant *Ribes sanguineum* 'Carneum'.

Helleborus foetidus ♔
STINKING HELLEBORE

With its handsome foliage and early, apple-green flowers, stinking hellebore is an essential element of the winter garden. It is an evergreen perennial that is strictly herbaceous because it produces leafy stems in one season that flowers the next before dying. It combines well with bergenias, evergreen heucheras, ground-covering ivies, *Euonymus fortunei* cultivars, fatshederas, sarcococcas, and galax, and with early-flowering bulbs such as snowdrops, *Crocus tommasinianus* variants, and winter aconitums. Other early hellebores, such as *H. niger* variants, *H. × nigercors*, and *H. × ericsmithii*, also make good companions. The most common of its variants is the Wester Fisk Group, in which the leaf stalks and especially the flower stems are flushed with rich deep red. However, this is a very variable group, so it is best to select the most richly colored plants from those offered in flower. 'Green Giant' is larger in all its parts.

◐ *Cornus alba* 'Sibirica' p.40 **B**, × *Fatshedera lizei*, *Galanthus nivalis*, *Galax urceolata*, *Heuchera* 'Plum Pudding', *Iris unguicularis* p.253 **B**, *Mahonia aquifolium* 'Apollo', *Sarcococca hookeriana* var. *humilis*, *Tulipa* 'White Triumphator' p.355 **B**

H & S: 45cm (18in) ❀ **Mid-winter to mid-spring**

◊◊ ▦- ■ **Z6 pH5.5–8**

Helleborus hybridus

LENTEN ROSE

This name covers all the hybrid stemless hellebores, available in a huge range of floral forms, markings, and colors ranging from nearly black through deep wine-purple to crimson, pink, and white, together with cream, soft yellow, and yellow-green, often with dark blotches or spots. They are excellent plants for the front of a border or a woodland garden, and excel in small town gardens, especially if sited where their blooms can be enjoyed from indoors during the colder part of the year. They can be combined with much the same late winter and spring flowers as for *H. foetidus* (facing page) – galax, snowdrops, *Crocus tommasinianus* variants, and winter

aconitums – but their flowers often continue appearing later and so are also effective with small to medium-sized bulbs such as narcissi, scillas, smaller tulips, muscaris, and erythroniums, as well as with primroses and polyanthus, brunneras, omphalodes, and winter heaths. They also associate well with hepaticas, pachyphragmas, cardamines, corydalis, and epimediums, and with the contrasting foliage of sedges and evergreen grasses and ferns. Other good partners include witch hazels, magnolias, mahonias, early cyclamens, anemones including wood anemones, pulmonarias, evergreen heucheras, and smaller early-flowering rhododendrons. Named cultivars are becoming available, including rich deep purple 'Thanksgiving', which is in bloom on Thanksgiving Day.

Left: The pale green flowers of *Helleborus × hybridus* are enlivened by the bright yellow-green of golden millet grass (*Milium effusum* 'Aureum').

Right: This near-black selection from *Helleborus × hybridus* Ballard's Group would scarcely be visible from a distance but is fascinating at close range, especially when partnered by the distinctively marked snowdrop *Galanthus* 'Armine'.

Below: Recent hellebore breeding has resulted in strains with stronger yellow flowers that are more outward-facing, allowing the speckling at the center of the bloom to be seen. Here, a primrose *Helleborus × hybridus* is joined by *Narcissus* 'Tête-à-tête' and *Cyclamen hederifolium*.

🔵 *Ajuga reptans* p.182 **A**, *Buxus sempervirens* 'Marginata' p.34 **A**, *Eranthis hyemalis*, *Erythronium* 'Pagoda', *Magnolia × soulangeana* 'Alba', *Narcissus* 'February Silver', *Primula vulgaris* subsp. *sibthorpii*, *Rhododendron hippophaeoides* p.83 **A** ❏ p.256 **B**

H: 45cm (18in) S: 60cm (24in)
❀ Mid-winter to mid-spring

◊◊ ▨-▨ ■ Z4 pH5–7.5

Hemerocallis fulva 'Flore Pleno'

Daylilies are accommodating, almost indestructible plants. They are valuable assets in any garden, producing superlative single or double flowers – some deliciously scented – in a wide range of colors, from late spring to late summer depending on the cultivar. Although individual blooms are short-lived, a constant succession of buds ensures a long display of color. (The flowers are worth cutting while still in bud.) The leaves provide a useful shape and texture, punctuating expanses of dull, broad-leaved foliage and harmonizing with grasses and spiky irises. Plants are hardy and vigorous, quickly multiplying into fat clumps, and although not always floriferous in colder regions, they flower profusely in warm sites.

'Flore Pleno' is a double cultivar with a long flowering season. The advantage of double flowers is that the individual florets last for two days, twice as long as those of most single cultivars. Whereas many modern varieties have ceded the classic daylily flower shape to a more rounded outline, congested in the center in the case of double flowers, 'Flore Pleno' retains the clear lily-like symmetry of six outer petals. Its color – soft orange with deeper red markings at the base, sometimes hidden by other petals – blends well with bronze foliage and flowers in hot colors, such as shades of red, yellow, or orange. Dahlias are particularly good companions – the dark-leaved 'Bishop of Llandaff', for instance. The base of the plants is not especially attractive, but in the second row of a border will be discreetly hidden.

 Cotinus coggygria 'Notcutt's Variety', *Iris pallida*, *Kniphofia* 'Bees' Sunset', *Lilium* African Queen Group p.324 **A**, *L.* 'Connecticut King' p.326 **B**, *Lobelia* 'Cherry Ripe' p.259 **B**

H: 75cm (30in) S: 1.2m (4ft)
Mid- to late summer
 Z3 pH5–7.5

In this hot-colored scheme, *Hemerocallis fulva* 'Flore Pleno' harmonizes with vermilion *Crocosmia* 'Lucifer', while the superlative lemon-yellow *Lilium* Citronella Group echoes the flower shape of the daylily. Adding a bronze foliage plant with more rounded leaves could be effective.

The rufous-red reverses to the outer petals of *Hemerocallis* 'Golden Chimes' unite this combination with the richly colored *Rosa* Lilli Marleen and the deep bronze foliage of *Heuchera micrantha* var. *diversifolia* 'Palace Purple'.

Hemerocallis 'Golden Chimes'

The species *H. dumortieri* produces rich, deep yellow blooms, dark brownish or mahogany on the reverse, with buds of the same dark color. It has passed these qualities on to 'Golden Chimes', a dainty, long-flowering cultivar, with slender, grassy foliage, especially suitable for small gardens. The elegant, trumpet-shaped blooms, each lasting into a second day, are comparatively small, but they are produced in copious numbers in generously branching sprays. 'Corky' is similar, but with paler, lemon-yellow flowers.

Plants belong in the second row of a border, together with hot colors and bronze foliage, and also cream flowers. Purple or blue flowers are best avoided, as they make the brownish reverse of the petals look grubby. Bronze-leaved heucheras with coral-red or scarlet flowers are superb companions.

 Canna 'Wyoming', *Dahlia* 'Moonfire', *Fuchsia* 'Thalia', *Phygelius aequalis* 'Yellow Trumpet', *Rosa* Westerland, *Sisyrinchium striatum* 'Aunt May'

H: 90cm (36in) S: 60cm (24in)
Early to late summer
 Z4 pH5–7.5

The elegant, starry flowers of *Hemerocallis* 'Hyperion' seem to leap forwards when set against a contrasting background of recessive, soft lavender *Clematis* 'Perle d'Azur'.

Hemerocallis 'Hyperion'

This well-loved daylily is an historic hybrid, and one of the oldest still in existence. It retains its popularity because of its valuable fresh coloring – a clear, sharp yellow without a trace of orange – but it is its bold and elegant flower shape that makes it so useful.

The flowers are held well above the slim, grassy foliage, making this a good plant for the middle rows of a border where it can mix with tall neighbors more successfully than other daylily cultivars. The refreshing color goes well with all kinds of blue, even shades with a hint of lavender. The flowers are especially effective grown among those of a contrasting shape – roses, for example, particularly a very pale yellow such as Windrush ('Ausrush'), or with orange, peach, apricot, and red. Another classic daylily of similar coloring is 'Marion Vaughn' ♥, very fragrant and flowering well into late summer.

⬤ *Agapanthus* 'Lilliput', *Aralia elata* 'Aureovariegata', *Clematis* 'Prince Charles', *Helictotrichon sempervirens*, *Kniphofia* 'David', *Miscanthus sinensis* 'Zebrinus', *Phormium* 'Duet', *Rosa* Benjamin Britten, *R*. 'Grace', *Yucca flaccida* 'Golden Sword'

H: 90cm (36in) S: 75cm (30in) ❀ **Mid-summer**
◌◌ ▢-▮ **Z5 pH5–7.5**

Hemerocallis red-flowered cultivars

There are numerous attractive red daylilies, ranging in color from light rust and flame-red through to deepest mahogany. They are generally very hardy, but the blooms of many are easily blemished in cold or wet weather. Evergreen red cultivars are particularly sensitive to the cold, although a few such as rich scarlet 'Amadeus' are markedly more weatherproof. Some of the oldest are among the best, including 'Cherry Cheeks', cherry-red with a prominent white midrib down each petal; 'Stafford' in a rich opulent shade with contrasting midribs; and 'Sammy Russell', with smaller star-like tile-red blooms. Red cultivars are a favorite choice for the second or third rank of red borders, and they mix well with dark blue, yellow, and cream (but not white, which can be too harsh), together with bronze foliage.

⬤ *Artemisia ludoviciana*, *Corylus maxima* 'Purpurea', *Deschampsia cespitosa*, *Heuchera micrantha* var. *diversifolia* 'Palace Purple', *Kniphofia* 'Wrexham Buttercup', *Ligularia dentata* 'Desdemona' p.258 **A**

H: 15–120cm (6–48in) S: 30–90cm (12–36in)
❀ **Mid-summer**
 ◌◌ ▢-▮ **Z5 pH5–7.5**

Above: In a relatively steeply sloped border, tall stems of *Achillea filipendulina* 'Gold Plate' provide a contrast of floral and foliage form with the rich red *Hemerocallis* 'Stafford'. They are backed by purple smoke bush (*Cotinus coggygria* 'Royal Purple'), whose foliage harmonizes perfectly with the daylily.

Below: *Hemerocallis* 'Sammy Russell' is here combined with *Achillea* 'Coronation Gold', showing the effective use of the achillea's greyish, feathery leaves and flat flower heads as a contrast for the gently flared blooms of the daylily. Cardoons (*Cynara cardunculus*) provide bold, architectural foliage behind.

A

Heuchera micrantha var. *diversifolia* 'Palace Purple' ♛

In its best selections, chosen for outstanding leaf color, this popular heuchera is a handsome plant with metallic, deep coppery bronze foliage. There are numerous inferior seedlings, less richly colored than 'Palace Purple', but *H.m.* var. *d.* Bressingham Bronze ('Absi') is particularly fine, with shiny, almost black leaves that provide reliable foliage cover. It is an excellent choice where dramatic dark foliage is needed, perhaps for contrast with lighter leaves or flowers. Both plants enjoy a position in sun or partial shade (although full sun produces the most opulent coloring), and both can be grown at the front of a border, in a lightly shaded woodland garden, or as a ground cover.

These plants associate well with late spring bedding, providing a foil for lighter or brighter bulbs and biennials, including late-flowering narcissi, tulips, hyacinths, wallflowers, epimediums, and erythroniums, combining with both cool-colored flowers and those in warmer shades such as burnt orange, apricot, and peach. White or cream flowers and white-variegated leaves create dramatic contrasts. Other attractive companions include low-growing plants such as cranesbills, bergenias, shorter ferns and sedges, and hostas. Exciting contrasts can be made with silver-leaved plants or yellow-green foliage and flowers.

The tiny heuchera flowers are born in airy sprays, but their brownish buff color is neither showy nor effective. If they are thought to detract from the impact of the foliage, the stems can be removed as they start to develop. Plants can be left for three to four years before division is necessary. This should be done in early autumn, when pieces of vigorous stem quickly form new roots and become established before the onset of winter.

● *Achillea* 'Lachsschönheit' p.179 **B**, *Aralia elata* 'Aureovariegata', *Echinacea purpurea* p.213 **B**, *Hemerocallis* 'Golden Chimes' p.238 **B**, *Pelargonium* 'Paul Crampel' p.394 **A**, *Rosa* Sweet Dream p.169 **B**

H: 50cm (20in) S: 45cm (18in)
❀ **Late spring to early summer**
◌◌ ▢-◼ ◼ Z4 pH5.5–7.5

At its best, the foliage of *Heuchera micrantha* var. *diversifolia* 'Palace Purple' is glistening and sumptuously dark, and, as here, makes a fine contrast with the yellow-green leaves of *Geranium* 'Ann Folkard'. Sprawling *G. × riversleaianum* 'Russell Prichard' displays its flowers in front, a touch paler than those of 'Ann Folkard' but in perfect harmony.

The extraordinarily rich foliage color of *Heuchera* 'Plum Pudding' makes it suitable for opulent arrangements with other dark foliage and flowers intended to be seen at close range. Here, its companions are *Tulipa* 'Queen of Night' and the wallflower *Erysimum cheiri* 'Purple Queen'.

Heuchera 'Plum Pudding'

The leaves of this neat heuchera are distinctly lobed, and have a strong purple overlay to their metallic silver flush, making them a superb choice for rich color schemes with purple, magenta, carmine, crimson, pink, or mauve flowers. The foliage is at its most colorful from late spring to early summer as the new leaves expand, and it is then very attractive with late spring flowering plants such as tulips, wallflowers, polyanthus, and primroses, both in spring bedding schemes and as an edging plant. Its flowers are not especially appealing and the flower spikes are best removed as they develop, to encourage the production of good foliage. Plants benefit from division every three years.

◉ *Crocus goulimyi* p.310 **B**, *Erysimum* 'Bowles' Mauve', *Gaura lindheimeri* 'Siskiyou Pink', *Primula* 'Tawny Port', *P.* 'Wanda', *Tulipa* 'Red Shine'

H: 40cm (16in) **S: 30cm** (12in)
❀ **Late spring to late summer**

 ◊◊ ▢-▨ ■ **Z4 pH5.5–7.5**

Heuchera 'Rachel'

This outstanding compact heuchera is a fairly recent introduction and widely regarded as an improvement on *H. micrantha* var. *diversifolia* 'Palace Purple' (facing page). Its rounded, maple-like leaves are rich copper-bronze, with a gleaming metallic finish between the veins and fine rosy-purple undersides. The small coral-pink flowers are born in tall airy sprays, with some repeat flowering after the first flush. It is a neat plant, useful for the front of a border and for edging, and is particularly effective with flowers in coral, peach, or apricot, and with red-flushed or dark purple foliage. It is excellent used beneath roses, especially those with small, soft-colored flowers and dark foliage.

◉ *Allium cristophii*, *Festuca glauca* 'Elijah Blue', *Geranium* × *riversleaianum* 'Russell Prichard', *Rosa* Pink Bells, *Stachys byzantina*, *Tulipa* 'Burgundy'

H: 30cm (12in) **S: 45–60cm** (18–24in)
❀ **Early to late summer**

 ◊◊ ▢-▨ ■ **Z4 pH5.5–7.5**

The warm yet not too strongly colored leaves of *Heuchera* 'Rachel' work well with cool flowers such as this white musk mallow (*Malva moschata* f. *alba*). Warm "fruity" colors of high summer also make effective partners for this heuchera.

× Heucherella alba 'Rosalie'

This hybrid between a heuchera and a tiarella is grown mainly for its flowers, which appear as a froth of pale pink spikes, with a modest charm well suited to subdued schemes or as a foil for larger, showier flowers. Although it needs reasonably good light to flower profusely, it will thrive satisfactorily in lightly shaded woodland, perhaps growing beneath pink or white azaleas. It is a good plant for the front of a border or for a ground cover, and combines prettily with columbines, dicentras, pink geums, smaller violas, and *Primula sieboldii* cultivars. Its cultivation requirements are the same as those of *Heuchera micrantha* var. *diversifolia* 'Palace Purple' (facing page), except that it needs dividing every two to three years in autumn.

In a lightly shaded bed in late spring, the dainty, star-like pink flowers of × *Heucherella alba* 'Rosalie' harmonize with the much larger blooms of the strikingly variegated red campion *Silene dioica* 'Clifford Moor'. Bigger groups of each, planted further apart so that they remain more distinct, would allow the attractive foliage and blooms of both to be more clearly seen and make the harmony between them even more apparent.

◉ *Aquilegia vulgaris* (mixed), *Dicentra spectabilis*, *Geum rivale* 'Leonard's Variety', *Rhododendron* 'Palestrina', *Rosa glauca*, *Stachys byzantina* 'Silver Carpet'

H: 40cm (16in) **S: 30–45cm** (12–18in)
❀ **Late spring to mid-summer**

◊◊ ▢-▨ ■ **Z4 pH5.5–7.5**

Hostas

HOSTAS, OR PLANTAIN LILIES, are very popular plants for shade, and several thousand new varieties have been developed in the last few decades. They are useful for their tiny or exotically large foliage, which can be green, glaucous, or yellow-green, often variegated with white or yellow. Most also flower prolifically, and the beauty of the blooms can rival that of the leaves. Some hostas, such as *H. plantaginea* and its hybrids, benefit from fragrant flowers.

All hostas grow well in partial shade and some even in full shade; some can take full sun, although variegated or yellow-green kinds can become scorched, except in areas with the coolest summers. Hostas are superlative plants for a woodland garden, and are also excellent for beds and borders but can look unnaturally exotic in a wild garden. Particularly associated with Japanese gardens, they look at home with other Japanese plants with contrasting foliage, including bamboos, smaller maples, moisture-loving irises, primulas, sedges, ferns, and hydrangeas. Hostas work well when planted with late winter or spring bulbs, wood anemones, or celandines beneath – as the bulbs enter their summer dormancy, the hosta's leaves unfurl to hide their dying foliage. They are also excellent in containers, where they are perhaps most effective planted alone, with harmonies or contrasts provided by different subjects in adjacent pots.

In small gardens, the biggest sorts such as *H. sieboldiana* and its hybrids tend to be too large for general use or a ground cover, although they are useful as strong accents, repeated if necessary at intervals along a border. Similarly, variegated or yelow-green cultivars can be strident if used to excess, although they too make effective accents; green- or glaucous-leaved hostas are perhaps the best for extensive plantings such as a ground cover. The tiniest species and cultivars are well suited

A

to small-scale schemes and to groupings that are to be viewed at close range.

Some, especially the largest-leaved sorts, can take up to five years to adopt their full size and characteristic growth habit. Conversely, if left many years without division, the leaves can become congested and reduced in size, obscuring the shape of individual leaves. Tiny species such as *H. venusta* ♀, often dismissed for use as a ground cover because so many plants are needed for a reasonably sized group, can be propagated by division up to three times a year, even in full growth, provided the offsets are kept moist. In fact the neat, dark green leaves and entrancing flowers of this species make it exceptionally beautiful for large drifts of ground cover. This method also works for

This planting mainly of hostas, including (clockwise from right) the cream-edged *H. fortunei* 'Spinners', bright blue-grey *H.* (Tardiana Group) 'Halcyon', yellow-green variegated *H. sieboldiana* 'Frances Williams', and the large, deeply puckered *H.s.* var. *elegans*, is saved from monotony by the addition of the contrastingly smaller leaves and flowers of cranesbills, including *Geranium × oxonianum*.

suckering cultivars such as 'Ginko Craig'. With slow-growing cultivars the quickest means of propagation is to cut the central bud from a healthy crown and divide the remaining base plate with its octopus of roots vertically into three.

Slugs and snails can ruin the effect of hostas, particularly those with delicate, thin leaves. They should be controlled, especially when their populations start to increase in late winter and spring. Alternately, grow hostas in containers or in raised beds.

Hosta 'August Moon'

Grown for its large yellow-green leaves and pale lavender, nearly white flowers, this is one of the most sun-tolerant yellow-green hostas, its fine color appearing less striking when plants are grown in shade. Although not the biggest of the yellow-green cultivars, 'August Moon' is bold enough for a large garden or for use as a strong accent in a medium-sized or small site. It makes good harmonies with gold or white flowers, and contrasts strikingly with blue or purple, or with foliage that differs markedly in color (purple, glaucous, and bronze) or form (grasses, sedges, and ferns). Japanese maples, berberis, and other smaller shrubs are an excellent background for this hosta. Other yellow-green cultivars of similar size include 'Birchwood Parky's Gold', with lavender flowers and slightly smaller, heart-shaped, wavy-edged leaves, and 'Gold Edger', similar in size and appearance but with thicker, more slug-resistant leaves. 'Aspen Gold' spreads about 90cm (36in) wide, with rounded, cupped, puckered leaves; *H. tokudama* 'Golden Medallion', similarly cupped and crimped, makes a slightly taller, less broad mound of foliage; while 'Golden Prayers' is smaller, with thick leaves. *H. nakaiana* 'Golden Scepter' has thin leaves that emerge chartreuse, turning bright yellow.

◖ *Acer palmatum* f. *atropurpureum*, *Berberis thunbergii* f. *atropurpurea*, *Carex oshimensis* 'Evergold', *Gentiana asclepiadea*, *Hakonechloa macra* 'Alboaurea', *Hosta sieboldiana* var. *elegans*, *Matteuccia struthiopteris*, *Primula japonica* 'Postford White'

H: 70cm (27in) **S: 75cm (30in)** ❀ **Mid-summer**
◌◌-◌◌◌ ■-■ **Z3** **pH5–7.5**

Although even a wispy clematis planted among hostas could obscure the pattern of their handsome rosettes of leaves, the occasional trailing stem wandering from an adjacent wall or supporting shrub can create a charming incident. Here, *Clematis* 'Etoile Violette' contrasts with the bright foliage of *Hosta* 'August Moon'.

In this dramatic grouping, handsome foliage, some of it glaucous or yellow-green, is contrasted with the salmon-pink flowers of the Hybrid Musk rose *R.* 'Cornelia' and *Rodgersia pinnata* 'Maurice Mason'. The striking blue-green *Hosta* 'Buckshaw Blue' contrasts with Bowles' golden sedge (*Carex elata* 'Aurea'), while the spurge *Euphorbia palustris* fills the space beneath the rose.

Hosta 'Buckshaw Blue'

This is a striking plant for sun or shade, with attractive, pale lilac-colored flowers and strongly blue-green leaves that are ribbed and puckered, producing a bold shape that makes a memorable statement towards the front of a border. It combines well with other glaucous or silver foliage and with pink, lilac, or white flowers, and stands out against yellow-green foliage or flowers and leaves of contrasting shape, such as those of grasses, ferns, rodgersias, or astilbes. It is an excellent choice for a woodland garden, especially with blue flowers, although it leafs too late to be combined effectively with late spring flowers such as omphalodes or forget-me-nots. It associates well with old roses, and the bronze or purple leaves of Japanese maples, berberis, and similar smaller shrubs.

◖ *Acer palmatum* 'Bloodgood', *Astilbe chinensis* var. *taquetii* 'Superba', *Euphorbia schillingii*, *Festuca glauca* 'Elijah Blue', *Meconopsis betonicifolia*, *Milium effusum* 'Aureum', *Rodgersia pinnata* 'Superba', *Rosa* 'Reine des Centifeuilles'

H: 35cm (14in) **S: 60cm (24in)** ❀ **Mid-summer**
◌◌-◌◌◌ ■-■ **Z3** **pH5–7.5**

Hosta fortunei

One of the great benefits of this pale lilac-flowered hosta is that its leaves appear early enough to be combined with late spring flowers, unfolding while wood anemones and celandines are still in bloom, and associating pleasantly with azaleas, bluebells, omphalodes, forget-me-nots, brunneras, epimediums, and meconopsis.

The species itself is rarely seen compared to its many variants. One of the most common of these is var. *albopicta* ♀, with very striking and dramatic young leaves that emerge with green edges and a pale yellow center, darkening to green in summer. Its foliage can be a little strident in some settings – for instance, in a woodland garden – but it is useful where an emphatic plant of moderate size is needed. Another good choice is var. *albopicta* f. *aurea* ♀, which emerges brilliant light yellow-green, making dramatic combinations with blue spring flowers and striking contrasts with dark ground covers such as purple bugleweeds. One of the most floriferous variants is var. *hyacinthina* ♀, with lilac blooms and glaucous leaves with a narrow silvery edge. Its sports include 'Gold Standard', with yellow, green-edged leaves, the centers aging to cream and so remaining brightly variegated during the summer. 'Crowned Imperial' has white-edged leaves, while 'Aoki' has very puckered, less glaucous leaves and mauve flowers. The leaves of 'Albomarginata', white-edged and often quite narrow, are not so extroverted, thus suitable where a less emphatic note is needed, while 'Antioch' has even longer, more pointed leaves, with a broader cream margin fading to white. 'Francee' is another white-variegated sport with bold, white-edged leaves emerging later than most *H. fortunei* variants; it is among the best of the white hostas and makes a good specimen plant for pots or containers. With leaves narrowly edged in yellow, var. *aureomarginata* ♀ (syn. 'Obscura Marginata') is useful where more subtle variegation is needed, such as in a woodland garden.

◖ *Acer palmatum* Dissectum Atropurpureum Group, *Anemone nemorosa* 'Leeds' Variety', *Brunnera macrophylla*, *Chelidonium majus*, *Dryopteris erythrosora*, *Epimedium* × *versicolor*, *Geranium* × *oxonianum*, *Hyacinthoides non-scripta*, *Myosotis sylvatica*, *Omphalodes cappadocica*, *Primula* 'Rowallane Rose' p.278 **B**, *Ranunculus ficaria* 'Brazen Hussy', *Rehmannia elata*, *Rhododendron* 'Blue Peter' p.81 **C**, *R. luteum*, *Viburnum plicatum* 'Mariesii'

H & S: 60–90cm (24–36in)　❀ **Mid-summer**
▰▰▱▱ 　◊◊-◊◊◊ 　▪-▪ 　**Z3** 　**pH5–7.5**

Top: The white margins of *Hosta fortunei* 'Albomarginata' strikingly accentuate each rosette of leaves among a carpet of woodland plants – *Viola sororia* 'Freckles' and the dainty white *Epimedium* × *youngianum* 'Niveum'.

Above: Brightly white-variegated *Hosta fortunei* 'Francee' nestles against leaves that contrast in color and form. The pale deadnettle *Lamium maculatum* 'Beacon Silver' grows in front, while the attractively lobed leaves of *Kirengeshoma palmata* provide pleasantly different foliage to the left.

Left: Newly emerging *Hosta fortunei* var. *albopicta* f. *aurea*, placed where it is lit by the sun, is given yet more prominence by being set within a contrasting carpet of bluebells (*Hyacinthoides non-scripta*), whose recessive tints make the hosta seem even brighter.

Facing page: Hostas are useful for planting beneath the spreading branches of their compatriots, the Japanese maples. Here, *Hosta fortunei* var. *hyacinthina* and *H.f.* var. *aureomarginata*, edged in creamy yellow, cover the ground beneath *Acer palmatum* Dissectum Atropurpureum Group, which is echoed in hue by *Plantago major* 'Rubrifolia'.

A

The yellow-green, brightly gold-tipped leaves of *Hosta* 'Hydon Sunset' contrast with the soft lavender, red-eyed flowers of another inhabitant of deciduous woodland, *Phlox divaricata* subsp. *laphamii* 'Chattahoochee'. Both need relative freedom from slugs and snails if they are to succeed.

Hosta 'Hydon Sunset'

The foliage of this small hosta – probably a derivation from *H. nakaiana* – emerges brilliant yellow-green, but darkens to green during the summer. Its diminutive leaves, perfectly to scale with smaller gardens and intimate planting arrangements, display the brightest coloring early in the year and therefore combine well with plants intended for late spring and early summer impact. The foliage scorches in sun and needs shade for best results, as in a woodland garden, for example, where the plant combines well with corydalis, small ferns such as maidenhairs, smaller tiarellas, heucheras, and bugleweeds. It is also a good container plant.

A similar but rather smaller hosta, confusingly called just 'Sunset', has leaves of paler gold, a color that is maintained throughout summer and into autumn.

🌑 *Adiantum aleuticum* 'Japonicum', *Ajuga reptans* 'Atropurpurea', *Asplenium scolopendrium* 'Kaye's Lacerated', *Corydalis flexuosa* 'China Blue', *Heuchera micrantha* var. *diversifolia* 'Palace Purple', *Pulmonaria saccharata*, *Tiarella wherryi* 'Bronze Beauty'

H: 35cm (14in) S: 20cm (8in) ❀ **Mid-summer**
� ⬤⬤-⬤⬤⬤ ▪-▪ **Z3 pH5–7.5**

Hosta 'Shade Fanfare' ♔

This large-leaved hosta has bright yellow-green foliage, edged with creamy white, and turning white with age; lavender-colored flowers are born in summer. Because it scorches badly in full sun it needs to be grown in shade, but it is such a lively and brilliantly colored cultivar that, unlike 'Hydon Sunset' (above), it may look out of place in a woodland garden. Instead, it can be used as a bold focal point in a shady border, or as the focus of a group of containerized plants. It associates best with blue, white, or yellow flowers, including companions such as cranesbills and forget-me-nots, as well as with ferns. Against a background of dark foliage, plants make a particularly striking impact that is almost too dramatic for some tastes.

🌑 *Dryopteris affinis*, *Fatsia japonica*, *Geranium* 'Johnson's Blue', *Hedera canariensis* 'Ravensholst', *Hydrangea macrophylla* 'Mariesii Perfecta', *Lobelia siphilitica*, *Myosotis sylvatica*, *Primula florindae*, *Schizophragma hydrangeoides*

H: 50cm (20in) S: 45cm (18in) ❀ **Mid-summer**
⬤⬤-⬤⬤⬤ ▪-▪ **Z3 pH5–7.5**

Three harmonious hostas – (from front to back) the white and creamy yellow variegated 'Shade Fanfare', gold-edged 'Yellow Splash', and yellow-green 'Sun Power' – provide a contrast with the rich mauve flowers of the cranesbill *Geranium nodosum*. Placing 'Shade Fanfare', the largest and boldest of the three, at the back might help to draw the eye into the grouping.

Hosta sieboldiana var. *elegans* is a large and splendid hosta, capable almost of matching in magnificence the *Gunnera manicata* towering above it in this waterside planting. In front, the variegated yellow iris (*Iris pseudacorus* 'Variegata') provides a vertical accent, while *Primula vialii* adds a bold focus of color, with rich mauve flowers emerging from startlingly contrasting scarlet calyces.

Hosta sieboldiana var. *elegans* ♔

This large hosta, with conspicuously veined and puckered glaucous foliage and attractive lilac-colored blooms, enjoys shaded sites of all kinds, but will tolerate full sun in areas with cool summers. Its size suits the second row of a border, in large-scale plantings and combinations with bold, even tropically lush plants. It is very successful with blue, purple, white, yellow, or yellow-green, and combines with *Iris sibirica* cultivars, larger ferns, Japanese maples, smaller bamboos, and larger grasses. There are many similar large cultivars: 'Big Daddy', with cupped, rounded, very veined, crinkled leaves; 'Big Mama', with smoother, less glaucous leaves; 'Blue Angel' ♔, with nearly white flowers; sun-tolerant 'Blue Umbrellas'; and narrower-leaved 'Blue Seer'.

🌑 *Acer shirasawanum* 'Aureum', *Euphorbia schillingii*, *Iris* 'Harpswell Happiness', *Lilium leichtlinii* var. *maximowiczii* p.328 **B**, *Miscanthus sinensis* 'Zebrinus', *Philadelphus coronarius* 'Aureus', *Pleioblastus auricomus*, *Rosa glauca*

H: 1m (3¼ft) S: 1.2m (4ft) ❀ **Mid- to late summer**
⬤⬤-⬤⬤⬤ ▪-▪ **Z3 pH5–7.5**

Big and bold *Hosta* 'Sum and Substance' is covered from the top to the ground with leaves and so can be used at the very front of steeply sloped borders. Here, the vigorous, tall cranesbill *Geranium × oxonianum* 'Claridge Druce' leavens the hosta's solidity with contrastingly small foliage and flowers.

Hosta 'Sum and Substance' ♛

This very large hosta is perhaps the most sun-tolerant of the yellow-green kinds, with thick leaves that are relatively unpalatable to slugs and snails. Except in areas with particularly hot summers, a position in full sun is beneficial, producing a brighter, richer yellow coloring that combines effectively with purple, blue, yellow, or white flowers, and with glaucous foliage. It is an impressive plant, both in large pots or containers and in partnership with the largest, most exotic kinds of foliage plant, such as gunneras, bamboos, large grasses and ferns, herbaceous aralias, cannas, sumacs, aruncus, pruned catalpas and paulownias, and tree of heaven. As with other very large-leaved cultivars, such as glaucous grey-green 'Snowden', deep watering is essential in dry weather.

⊙ *Ailanthus altissima* (stooled), *Aruncus dioicus*, *Gunnera manicata*, *Hosta sieboldiana* var. *elegans*, *Lysimachia punctata*, *Miscanthus sacchariflorus*, *Paulownia tomentosa* (stooled), *Phyllostachys nigra*

H: 75cm (30in) S: 1.2m (4ft)
❀ **Early to mid-summer**
 ◊◊ □-■ **Z3 pH5–7.5**

Hosta (Tardiana Group) 'Halcyon' ♛

Most Tardiana Group hostas combine the glaucous foliage of one parent, *H. sieboldiana* var. *elegans*, with the prolific flowers and neat, relatively small leaves of the other, the late-flowering *H. tardiflora*. The majority are glaucous-leaved, although a few have yellow-green or variegated foliage. The leaves of 'Halcyon' – intensely blue-green when grown in shade, more grey-green in full sun – are lance-shaped when young, becoming broader with age. It is a neat plant, ideal for a woodland garden or the front of a border, and is very effective with blue, purple, yellow, or white flowers; it makes good contrasts with yellow-green foliage and flowers, and with feathery, grassy, or pinnate foliage. As an edging with roses, it is the right height to mask the base of bushes, from shorter Patio roses to Floribundas of moderate height.

⊙ *Aralia racemosa*, *Astilbe* 'Red Sentinel', *Campanula* 'Kent Belle', *Choisya ternata* Sundance, *Gentiana asclepiadea*, *Lysimachia clethroides*, *Rosa* 'Frensham'

H: 60cm (24in) S: 1m (40in)
❀ **Early to late autumn**
■■■□ ◊◊ □-■ **Z5 pH5–7.5**

The broad, glaucous foliage of *Hosta* (Tardiana Group) 'Halcyon' makes a fine contrast with the feathery mid-green fronds of fennel (*Foeniculum vulgare*). It would be possible to use this combination on a larger scale, planting mature clumps of the hosta, irregularly spaced, with larger plants of the fennel in the gaps, although the site must not be too shady for the sun-loving fennel. In this way, the characteristic rosettes of the hostas would give a pattern to the planting, while the fennel would form billowing mounds of soft green plumes between. The fennel would flower before its companion but would retain lacy seedheads that rise over the hosta as it came into bloom.

Rhizomatous anemones such as the wood anemone (*A. nemorosa* and its cultivars) flower at the same time as early-leafing hostas such as *Hosta undulata* var. *albomarginata* emerge, making them excellent and attractive companions, especially in a woodland garden.

Hosta undulata var. *albomarginata*

The bright, white-edged leaves of this variety emerge light yellowish green in mid-spring, early enough to combine with spring flowers such as wood anemones and celandines. Its coloring is highly effective with blue or yellow flowers such as brunneras, omphalodes, meconopsis, yellow epimediums, and doronicums; it is also outstanding planted under yellow-flowered deciduous azaleas. Its spikes of flowers have attractive purple, trumpet-shaped florets, while its leaves darken to rich green in summer. Other variants of *H. undulata* include var. *univittata* ♛, with a central white stripe; all-green var. *erromena* ♛; and var. *undulata* ♛, with yellow-green streaks and a central area of white.

⊙ *Epimedium × versicolor* 'Sulphureum', *Hydrangea macrophylla* 'Générale Vicomtesse de Vibraye' p.59 **A**, *Rhododendron* 'Kirin' p.83 **B**

H: 90cm (36in) S: 45cm (18in)
❀ **Early to mid-summer**
 ◊◊ □-■ **Z3 pH5–7.5**

Irises

THE VERY DIVERSE genus *Iris* embraces several thousand immensely useful garden plants. Herbaceous and rhizomatous sorts are considered here; those that grow from corms are discussed under Bulbs (see pp.321–323). *I. ensata* ♀, *I. japonica* ♀, and their hybrids and cultivars enjoy moist conditions and are superlative plants for waterside planting. Cultivars of *I. ensata* have large, exotically marked flowers, showy from a distance but needing close-range inspection for their intricacy to be appreciated. *I. chrysographes* cultivars and the related *I. delavayi* ♀ tend to be taller with grassier leaves and flowers in sumptuously dark colors; they too benefit from moist or waterside conditions and close-range viewing, their dusky blooms being scarcely visible from a distance. The hundreds of cultivars and hybrids of *I. sibirica* ♀ are also excellent marginal plants, but can be grown in a border provided the soil does not dry out. They make a classic combination with late-flowering deciduous azaleas in situations that are neither too arid nor too shady.

Species such as the evergreen *I. unguicularis* ♀, a precious winter-flowering iris, are suited to dry, sun-baked spots. *I. foetidissima* ♀ is invaluable in dry shade, and has attractively glossy, dark evergreen foliage and brilliant vermilion seeds, displayed for several months after its pods split open in autumn. It will grow happily at the foot of a hedge where few other plants would survive.

The Californian Hybrids, derived from species such as *I. douglasiana* ♀, *I. innominata*, and *I. chrysophylla*, make evergreen, fairly low-growing clumps of foliage with flowers in a range of colors, often attractively veined, usually in mid- to late spring but occasionally into summer.

Spuria irises, which are derived from species such as *I. crocea* ♀, *I. monnieri*, *I. orientalis* ♀, and *I. sanguinea* ♀, are the tallest and latest-flowering irises, making

narrow clumps with deciduous grassy foliage. Tolerating light shade, their growth habit suits them to planting in borders.

Perhaps the most valuable irises are the sun-loving Bearded cultivars, which vary in size from the Miniature Dwarf Bearded sorts at about 20cm (8in) high to Tall Bearded kinds at 70cm (27in) or more. As a rough rule, the shortest sorts flower earliest, in mid-spring, while the tallest

Above: The Tall Bearded iris *I.* 'Kent Pride' is classed as a Plicata cultivar (having a pale ground edged with a darker color). Brown varieties such as this can be combined with bronze or purple foliage (here, *Heuchera* 'Rachel') and purple or warm-colored flowers.

Left: Tall Bearded irises such as *I.* 'Nightfall' can supply an accent among lower planting, as here with poached egg flower (*Limnanthes douglasii*) and dark-leaved heucheras.

continue into early summer, their foliage providing useful contrast for old roses.

Irises are propagated by division after flowering, with young, short sections of vigorous rhizome replanted at the surface (not buried). Care should be taken not to arrange them all facing the same way, so that they move dependably in one direction, leaving bare rhizome behind. The base of the plants, particularly if they are used towards the front of a border, can look unattractive but can be masked by interplanting with a low carpeting plant such as an acaena, or with a later-flowering bulb such as *Allium flavum*. Some varieties are remontant, flowering reliably a second time in late summer.

At the front of a border in early summer, the deep purple-black flowers of *Iris chrysographes*, although recessive in color and hard to see from a distance, show distinctly against the much paler flowers of *Geranium* 'Johnson's Blue', and their upright stems provide a strong vertical accent.

Iris chrysographes ♛

A waterside position is ideal for this moisture-loving species, which usually has deep ruby-red or dark purple flowers (approaching black in some cases), although it also occurs in paler tones such as yellow and violet. While fascinating on close inspection, the flowers barely show up at a distance. Plants with purplish blooms look most effective with other mauve or lighter purple flowers, such as cranesbills and tradescantias (provided the ground is not too waterlogged), while the red variants work well with astilbes, monardas, lythrum cultivars, and late-flowering primulas. Related species that enjoy similar conditions include the purple *I. delavayi* ♛, 1.5m (5ft) tall, and yellow *I. forrestii* ♛, 40cm (16in), both flowering in mid-summer.

◐ *Astilbe* 'Red Sentinel', *Lythrum virgatum* 'Dropmore Purple', *Monarda* 'Cambridge Scarlet', *Primula capitata*, *Tradescantia* (Andersoniana Group) 'Purple Dome'

H: 40–50cm (16–20in) S: 30cm (12in)
✿ **Early to mid-summer**

◊◊·◊◊◊ ■-■ **Z4 pH5.5–7**

The rich purple blooms of *Iris* 'Grapesicle' dominate the smaller but harmoniously colored flowers of moneyplant (*Lunaria annua*) and wood forget-me-nots (*Myosotis sylvatica*) in this late spring border, with the glaucous foliage of opium poppy (*Papaver somniferum*) behind.

Iris 'Curlew'

This outstanding Intermediate Bearded iris blooms, like most of its class, after the bulk of spring flowers but before the main flush of summer bloom, making it a particularly valuable source of color for combining with late wallflowers, columbines, species roses, euphorbias, and early peonies. It is a superlative plant for the front of a border, where its soft yellow blooms blend well with cream, orange, and yellow-green flowers, together with warm colors such as peach and apricot, and with yellow-green or bronze foliage, including bronze-flushed cultivars of *Euphorbia griffithii* and sedges. Blue is an effective contrast, with the exception of the strongest blues, which can dominate the soft coloring of the iris.

◐ *Aquilegia vulgaris* (blue or yellow), *Carex oshimensis* 'Evergold', *Euphorbia griffithii* 'Dixter', *E. polychroma* 'Major', *Heuchera micrantha* var. *diversifolia* 'Palace Purple', *Paeonia mlokosewitschii*, *Rosa* 'Helen Knight', *Valeriana phu* 'Aurea'

H: 45cm (18in) S: 40cm (16in)
✿ **Late spring to early summer**

 ◊·◊◊ □-■ **Z4 pH5.5–8**

In a bed of relatively low plants in late spring, *Iris* 'Curlew' stands above the golden orange wallflower (*Erysimum* × *allionii*), with golden feverfew (*Tanacetum parthenium* 'Aureum') adding piquancy.

Iris 'Grapesicle'

This Standard Dwarf Bearded iris blooms in mid- and late spring, coinciding with flowers such as late spring bulbs and forget-me-nots. With is relatively small, rich plum-purple flowers, it is more graceful than some other modern cultivars which have disproportionately large flowers. It is an elegant plant for gravel gardens or the front of borders, where it may be planted with smaller columbines, ipheion cultivars, biennial moricandias, shorter perennial wallflowers, and mauve flowers such as early cranesbills. It combines well with purple foliage, and may be contrasted with soft yellow – *Limnanthes douglasii*, for example – or with acid yellow-green foliage and flowers, such as euphorbias. *I. pumila atroviolacea* is a darker purple alternative.

◐ *Aquilegia canadensis*, *Erysimum* 'Wenlock Beauty', *Geranium tuberosum*, *Heuchera micrantha* var. *diversifolia* 'Palace Purple', *Ipheion uniflorum* 'Wisley Blue', *Limnanthes douglasii*, *Moricandia moricandioides*

H & S: 30cm (12in) ✿ **Mid- to late spring**

◊·◊◊ □-■ **Z4 pH5.5–8**

Iris 'Lavinia'

The gentle coloring and pretty markings of this Californian Hybrid are very attractive with mauve or lilac, and with purple-flushed foliage; stronger colors may prove a bit overwhelming, although effective contrasts can be made with rich deep purple. It works well at the front of a border, with erodiums, ipheions, dicentras, columbines, moricandias, early cranesbills, prostrate rosemary, and chives. All Californian Hybrids need well drained soil, dry at the surface but with adequate moisture beneath, and with that proviso they can be grown in a gravel garden. Derived originally from West Coast and Californian species, they are not very hardy and some need warm summers to flower well; in cooler regions, cultivars derived mainly from selections from Oregon or Washington State, such as *I. tenax*, tend to flower better.

◑ *Allium schoenoprasum, Dicentra peregrina, Erodium trifolium, Geranium tuberosum, Heuchera* 'Plum Pudding', *Rosmarinus officinalis* Prostratus Group

H & S: 40cm (16in)
❀ **Late spring to early summer**
◌◌ ■-■ **Z7 pH5–7**

In early summer, the maroon markings of *Iris* 'Lavinia' match those of *Erodium pelargoniiflorum*, while their flowers and foliage provide a contrast of size and form.

Iris 'Nightfall'

A Tall Bearded iris, 'Nightfall' has light purple standard petals and deep purple, almost black falls. Its flowers retain some of the distinctive grace and classic fleur-de-lis outline of older Tall Bearded cultivars, and associate happily with old roses and alliums such as *A. aflatunense* or *A. hollandicum* and its cultivars. It harmonizes with mauve, pink, and crimson, and looks opulent planted beside pale yellow flowers such as achilleas, and with yellow-green foliage and flowers. Purple or silver foliage plants are effective partners, as are lupines, cranesbills, shorter delphiniums, and peonies, Mediterranean plants such as cistus, phlomis, and santolinas, and plants of more diffuse habit, such as variants of *Thalictrum aquilegiifolium*.

◑ *Cistus* × *argenteus* 'Silver Pink', *Delphinium* 'Mighty Atom', *Lupinus* 'Chandelier', *Paeonia lactiflora* 'Albert Crousse', *Rosa* 'Tuscany Superb'

H: 75cm (30in) **S: 60cm** (24in)
❀ **Late spring to early summer**
◌◌ □-■ ■ **Z4 pH5.5–8**

The sumptuous two-toned purple blooms of *Iris* 'Nightfall' contrast dramatically with the pale silvery leaves of *Artemisia ludoviciana*.

Iris orientalis ♔

This splendid Spuria iris is tall and elegant, with grassy foliage that makes a good foil for old roses, and with white and yellow flowers that work well with rich crimson, purple, or blue. They harmonize with white and cream, soft colors such as peach and apricot, rich golden yellow, and yellow-green, and with glaucous foliage such as that of larger hostas. Suitable companions include peonies, lupines, and delphiniums, and medium-sized shrubs such as berberis, philadelphus, and rhododendrons. Like most Spuria irises, it prefers a fairly moist site, but will tolerate all but very dry soil. 'Shelford Giant' ♔ is about twice as high as *I. orientalis*, with creamier flowers. Other choice Spuria irises are *I. spuria* itself, in various colors such as blue, white, violet, or yellow; *I.* Monspur Group, which comprises blue and violet hybrids including the superlative 'Cambridge Blue'; *I.* 'Sunny Day' ♔, with rich yellow flowers; and 'Clarke Cosgrove' ♔, which is lilac with yellow on its falls. 'Lydia Jane' ♔ is yellow shading to cream, a coloring shared by the more substantial 'Sierra Nevada'.

◑ *Berberis thunbergii* 'Aurea', *Delphinium* 'Sabrina', *D.* 'Sungleam', *Hosta sieboldiana* var. *elegans, Lupinus* 'Polar Princess', *L.* 'Thundercloud', *Paeonia lactiflora* 'Instituteur Doriat', *Rhododendron* Blinklicht Group, *Rosa* 'Charles de Mills'

H: 1m (40in) **S: 60cm** (24in)
❀ **Late spring to early summer**
◌◌-◌◌◌ □-■ **Z4 pH5–7.5**

Facing page: This combination is unified by the golden markings on the falls of *Iris orientalis* and traces of yellow, in the anthers of *Clematis* 'Sylvia Denny' and in the cream variegation of *Philadelphus coronarius* 'Variegatus'.

A

Iris pallida

This is a Bearded iris which in the typical subspecies *I.p.* subsp. *pallida* ♀ has grey-green leaves and elegant, soft lavender-blue blooms. It is one of the best for general use, effective with cool colors or white flowers and with silver, grey, or purple foliage, and a pleasant partner for early roses, lupines, delphiniums, and Mediterranean plants such as phlomis, cistus, or rosemary. The foliage of *I.p.* subsp. *cengialtii* ♀ is less grey, and its flowers violet-blue with slightly paler standard petals. There are two variegated cultivars: *I.p.* 'Variegata' ♀, with yellow-striped leaves that make a strong accent and contrast gently with its flowers; and 'Argentea Variegata', with poorly shaped flowers but attractive white-striped leaves. Both supply bold accents towards the front of a border, and can be repeated at intervals to give a unifying theme.

◉ *Anemone apennina* p.304 **A**, *Cistus* × *skanbergii*, *Lupinus* 'Gallery White', *Phlomis fruticosa*, *Rosa* 'Maigold', *Rosmarinus officinalis* 'Aureus'

H: 90cm (36in) S: 60cm (24in)
❀ **Late spring to early summer**

▦ ◊-◊◊ ▢-◼ **Z4 pH5.5–8**

The boldly striped sword-like leaves of the Bearded iris *I. pallida* 'Variegata' supply strong form to this grouping with *Penstemon* 'Pink Endurance', whose diffuse flower spikes open after those of the iris have faded.

Iris pseudacorus 'Variegata' ♀
VARIEGATED YELLOW FLAG

Like *I. pseudacorus* itself, this is a moisture-loving plant which also thrives in ordinary border soil that is not too dry. Its leaves emerge boldly variegated with yellow, but become greener during summer; the flowers are yellow with brown markings. It makes a strong accent in waterside plantings, especially when grown through darker-leaved plants such as purple bugleweeds or heucheras, and mixes well with warm or hot colors, yellow-green foliage and flowers, and white flowers. Suitable partners include

When its shoots are still bright in late spring, *Iris pseudacorus* 'Variegata' contrasts dramatically with purple bugleweed (*Ajuga reptans* 'Atropurpurea').

hostas, Candelabra primulas, euphorbias, ligularias, calthas, and trollius cultivars. It contrasts beautifully with meconopsis, and with the markedly different foliage of ferns.

◉ *Caltha palustris* p.199 **A**, *Hosta sieboldiana* var. *elegans* p.246 **C**, *Hydrangea arborescens* p.58 **B**, *Lysichiton americanus* p.262 **A**, *Primula florindae*

H: 1.2m (4ft) S: 75cm (30in)
❀ **Early to mid-summer**

▦ ◊◊-◊◊◊ ◼-◼ **Z5 pH4–7.5**

Iris 'Rocket'

The lovely and profuse apricot-colored flowers of this Tall Bearded iris blend particularly well with warm colors such as peach, apricot, soft yellow, or soft scarlet, and with bronze foliage and yellow-green foliage or flowers. Plants can be combined with early yellow roses, euphorbias, columbines in warm colors, geums, and dark-leaved heucheras, as well as with shrubs such as brooms, helianthemums, halimiums and halimiocistus, phlomis, and santolinas. Other good Tall Bearded irises with similar warm coloring include 'Supreme Sultan', butterscotch-yellow with crimson-brown falls, and creamy apricot-yellow 'Beyond'.

◉ *Aquilegia chrysantha* 'Yellow Queen', *Berberis thunbergii* f. *atropurpurea*, *Cytisus* × *praecox* 'Warminster', *Helianthemum* 'Ben Hope'

H: 75cm (30in) S: 60cm (24in)
❀ **Late spring to early summer**

▦ ◊-◊◊ ▢-◼ **Z4 pH5.5–8**

In late spring, the warm amber tints of *Iris* 'Rocket' blend perfectly with a bicolored columbine (a hybrid of *Aquilegia canadensis*), while providing a contrast of floral form.

Iris sibirica ♔
SIBERIAN IRIS

The Siberian iris has graceful, rich purplish blue flowers, smaller and less showy than most cultivars, but still valuable for waterside planting in wild gardens. Flowering profusely in sunny, moist sites, it tolerates light shade and ordinary border soil that is not too dry. Its hybrids have flowers that are prettily marked and veined at the top of their broad, nearly horizontal falls. Among the best are 'Cambridge' ♔, which is almost pure light blue; 'Oban' ♔, rich blue edged with white; 'Dreaming Spires' ♔, with deep purple falls and mid lavender-blue standards; the reddish purple 'Ruffled Velvet' ♔; 'Shirley Pope' ♔, which is very dark purple with a white flash; 'Crème Chantilly' ♔, pale cream fading to white; the cream and yellow 'Harpswell Happiness' ♔; 'White Swirl' ♔, with dramatic flaring falls; and 'Wisley White' ♔, white with yellow markings. All look effective with deciduous azaleas, meconopsis, euphorbias, trollius, astilbes, Candelabra primulas, and larger ferns, as well as small to medium-sized shrubs such as philadelphus, variegated dogwoods, deutzias, and silver-leaved willows. Other partners could include peonies, sweet rocket, columbines, and cranesbills.

◐ *Astilbe* 'Fanal', *Cornus alba* 'Sibirica Variegata', *Rhododendron* 'Narcissiflorum', *Rosa* 'Maigold' p.158 **A**, *Salix exigua*, *Trollius* × *cultorum* 'Canary Bird'

H: 50–120cm (20–48in) S: 45cm (18in)
❀ **Early to mid-summer**

○○-○○○ ■-■ **Z4 pH5–7.5**

In early summer, the flowers of *Iris sibirica*, born above its leaves, combine attractively with those of white sweet rocket (*Hesperis matronalis* var. *albiflora*).

Iris unguicularis ♔
ALGERIAN IRIS

An evergreen, winter-flowering iris from the Mediterranean, *I. unguicularis* has sweetly scented flowers in colors ranging from white through pale lilac to violet-blue. It is slightly tender and in cooler climates needs to be grown at the foot of a warm, sunny wall; it also prefers a soil fairly low in nutrients, because too much nitrogen can result in masses of leaves and very few flowers. It is an attractive plant for combining with other winter-flowering subjects such as snowdrops, *Cyclamen coum* variants, early crocuses, and hellebores; the more richly colored forms also pair well with corylopsis. 'Alba' has white thin-petalled flowers that are rather poorly shaped; 'Mary Barnard' is rich violet; and 'Walter Butt' has large pale lilac flowers. All are best propagated by lifting and dividing clumps of rhizomes in late summer.

◐ *Corylopsis pauciflora*, *Crocus chrysanthus* hybrids, *Galanthus nivalis*, *Helleborus* × *hybridus* (yellow), *Jasminum nudiflorum* p.124 **A**, *Lonicera* × *purpusii* ☐p.130 **A**

H: 40cm (16in) S: 60cm (24in)
❀ **Late autumn to early spring**

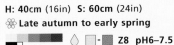 ○ ☐-■ **Z8 pH6–7.5**

A lilac-flowered variant of *Iris unguicularis* contrasts gently with the pale apple-green, maroon-lipped flowers of stinking hellebore (*Helleborus foetidus*) in late winter.

In early spring, the white of the snowdrop *Galanthus elwesii* var. *monostictus* leavens the rich lavender flowers of *Iris unguicularis* 'Mary Barnard', behind silvery cyclamen leaves.

A purple smoke bush (*Cotinus coggygria* 'Royal Purple') forms a harmonious backdrop for the crimson pincushion-like flower heads of *Knautia macedonica*.

Knautia macedonica

This clump-forming herbaceous perennial, a close relative of scabious, has pincushion flower heads usually of the deepest crimson, but in the wild it varies from crimson to pale pink or mauve, and these variants are sometimes available as Melton Pastels. It needs to be seen at close range and is a good plant for the front of a border, where it will blend with other cool colors and can be used as a foil for flowers of a brighter red. It contrasts well with peach-colored flowers, including roses, and yellow-green or lime green flowers (but it can be overwhelmed by solid areas of yellow-green foliage), and also with glaucous or silver foliage, such as that of grasses and artemisias. Exceptionally pretty partnerships can be made with nicotianas, penstemons, eryngiums, day lilies, phlox, thalictrums, and pinks, and with flowers of contrasting form, including pink gypsophilas, linarias, and veronicas.

Achillea millefolium 'Cerise Queen' p.179 **C**, *Allium sphaerocephalon* p.303 **C**, *Clematis* × *durandii* p.108 **C**, *Malva sylvestris* p.386 **B**, *Rosa* Bonica p.152 **A**

H: 60cm (24in) S: 45cm (18in)
❁ **Mid- to late summer**
◊◊ ▢-■ **Z5 pH5–7.5**

Kniphofia 'Atlanta'

A vigorous and hardy evergreen perennial, this red hot poker bears yellow flowers that open from orange-red buds, favoring combinations with bronze foliage or yellow, orange, or scarlet flowers, and making a telling contrast with blue flowers or yellow-green foliage and flowers. Its spiky grey-green leaves look imposing at the front of a border, especially with glaucous foliage plants. It is effective with late spring and early summer bulbs such as camassias and earlier daylilies, Bearded irises, and early Shrub roses in yellow or other warm tints, and produces thrilling clashes with magenta species gladioli. Other good partners are euphorbias, sea kale, anthericums, baptisias, alchemillas, and *Paeonia* × *lemoinei* cultivars, as well as delicate woodland plants like columbines.

Camassia cusickii 'Zwanenburg', *Gladiolus communis* subsp. *byzantinus*, *Hemerocallis* 'Golden Chimes', *Iris pallida* 'Variegata', *Rosa* 'Maigold'

H: 1.2m (4ft) S: 60cm (24in)
❁ **Late spring to early summer**
◊◊ ▢-■ **Z7 pH5.5–7.5**

Groups of yellow and red *Kniphofia* 'Atlanta', repeated at intervals and contrasted with silvery evergreen *Brachyglottis* (Dunedin Group) 'Sunshine', provide rhythm and accent along this border in late spring, together with lavender catmints and the pink cranesbill *Geranium* × *oxonianum*.

Kniphofia 'David' ♛

This superlative red hot poker is a mid-season herbaceous perennial with flowers that open soft yellow from coral-red buds, and slender green foliage that can be a little unkempt and is therefore best hidden by other plants in front. The color of its flowers suggests much the same combinations as for 'Atlanta' (below left), but its later timing also allows associations with achilleas, lilies, phygelius, later roses including larger bush roses, and even crocosmias. With its festive coloring, it is a good partner for annuals and bedding plants such as *Mimulus aurantiacus* and its variants, arctotis hybrids, poppies, verbascums, penstemons, alonsoas, calceolarias, and larger French marigolds. Its spiky outline is valuable punctuation in a border and can add rhythm to a landscape of mainly round or branching flowers, such as rudbeckias or heliopsis.

Alonsoa warscewiczii, *Arctotis* × *hybrida* 'Flame', *Papaver rhoeas* Shirley Group (double mixed), *Rosa* 'Chinatown', *Tagetes patula* 'Striped Marvel'

H: 75cm (30in) S: 45cm (18in)
❁ **Early to mid-summer**
◊◊ ▢-■ **Z6 pH5.5–7.5**

In this early summer planting of warm-colored flowers at the foot of a sentinel Irish yew (*Taxus baccata* 'Fastigiata'), the flat flower heads of *Achillea* 'Coronation Gold' contrast with the vertical pokers of *Kniphofia* 'David' and the yew, joined by the coral blooms of *Phygelius aequalis*.

Kniphofia yellow cultivars

Red hot pokers in pure yellow are remarkably versatile plants that can be used for fiery hot-colored displays and equally effectively as brilliant highlights among softer blue or cream flowers. Many excellent cultivars are available, flowering at different times, so their contribution to color schemes can be extended over a long season.

K. 'Goldelse' flowers fairly early, and has grassy foliage and narrow spikes of golden yellow blooms that combine well with earlier flowers such as catmints, baptisias, cranesbills, campanulas, Tall Bearded irises, and smaller delphiniums such as Belladonna Group cultivars, and they will coincide with many shrub and bush roses in warm colors. 'Goldelse' is also a good partner for shrubs such as hebes, halimiocistus, hypericums, lavenders, and *Potentilla fruticosa* cultivars.

K. 'Wrexham Buttercup' is an excellent plant, beefier and more substantial than 'Goldelse', with broader foliage and solid spikes of flowers that open yellow from yellow-green buds, and age to gold. It starts flowering with the roses and delphiniums, but continues into the season of later summer bedding plants and tender perennials.

K. 'Sunningdale Yellow' ♀ is a superlative pure yellow poker that remains in bloom longer than most other cultivars, coinciding with blue flowers such as cultivars of *Salvia farinacea* and *S. patens*, argyranthemums in white, cream or yellow, later-flowering euphorbias or cannas, and bedding plants such as smaller-flowered zinnias.

All these kniphofias provide strong vertical accents in borders and they can make memorable statements among agapanthus, daylilies, smaller grasses such as hakonechloas and smaller *Miscanthus sinensis* cultivars, and blue-green grasses, including elymus species, helictotrichons, and larger fescues. Other good companions include glaucous-leaved hostas (together with yellow-green and gold-variegated hostas in areas with cool summers), later-flowering catmints including yellow-flowered species, achilleas, and nicotianas in white or green.

 Early cultivars: *Baptisia australis*, *Campanula latifolia* 'Gloaming', × *Halimiocistus wintonensis* 'Merrist Wood Cream', *Nepeta* 'Six Hills Giant'
Later cultivars: *Agapanthus* 'Loch Hope', *Canna* 'Striata', *Salvia* × *superba*

H: 75–120cm (30–48in) S: 45–75cm (18–30in)
 Early summer to early autumn

 Z6 pH5.5–7.5

Above: In early summer, an imposing clump of *Kniphofia* 'Goldelse' rises from a carpet of white-flowered *Anthemis punctata* subsp. *cupaniana*, the kniphofias harmonizing with the golden centers of the daisies.

Above: Vertical accents of *Kniphofia* 'Sunningdale Yellow', backed by dusky *Rosa glauca*, echo the primrose blooms of *Anthemis tinctoria* 'Wargrave Variety', joined by golden feverfew (*Tanacetum parthenium* 'Aureum').

Below: The vertical pokers of *Kniphofia* 'Wrexham Buttercup' contrast with the horizontal layers of the variegated dogwood (*Cornus controversa* 'Variegata') and the flat plates of a creamy achillea.

Above: The dusky magenta blooms of the spotted dead nettle (*Lamium maculatum*) mingle and harmonize with the long-flowering cranesbill *Geranium* 'Johnson's Blue'.

Below: Mixing different sorts of spotted dead nettle (*Lamium maculatum*) introduces variety to a carpet of ground cover: here, the plain species is joined by *L.m.* 'Album' beneath a Lenten rose. A silver-leaved dead nettle could also be used.

Lamium maculatum

SPOTTED DEAD NETTLE

This is a low-growing rhizomatous perennial, with flowers in dusky magenta, pink, or white, and silver-marked leaves. Cultivars with almost entirely silver leaves, such as 'White Nancy' ♀ and pink-flowered 'Beacon Silver', tolerate shade and are useful for ground cover, effective with cool-colored flowers and white-variegated or darkest green foliage. They can be grown with other ground-covering plants such as heucheras, saxifrages, ivies, asarums, tiarellas, sedges, hostas, and bugleweeds. Gold-variegated kinds such as 'Anne Greenaway' and Golden Anniversary ('Dellam') and yellow-green 'Aureum' mix well with hot-colored flowers, yellow-green or gold-variegated foliage, and contrasting foliage, such as smaller glaucous hostas, dicentras, or early-leafing ferns.

⬤ *Asarum europaeum, Colchicum autumnale* p.309 **B**, *Dicentra eximia, Hosta fortunei* 'Francee' p.244 **C**, *Saxifraga fortunei, Tiarella cordifolia*

H: 15–30cm (6–12in) **S:** 90cm (36in)
❀ **Late spring to late summer**

 ◌◌ ◻-◼ ◼ Z4 pH4.5–8

By adding a shorter aster such as lilac *Aster turbinellus* in front of tall and narrow *Leucanthemella serotina*, a steep slope of autumn flowers can be created with blooms of matching form but contrasting size.

Leucanthemella serotina ♀

An impressively tall rhizomatous herbaceous perennial, this is a very erect plant that is immensely useful for its late white daisy-like flower heads, each with a central yellowish green disc. Formerly *Chrysanthemum uliginosum*, it is as choice as any white chrysanthemum, its 8cm (3½in) blooms lasting until the first frosts. It can be used in a wild garden or in a bog garden, or at the back of a moist border, where it combines well with taller, late-flowering perennials such as boltonias, helianthus, and the tallest asters. Late flowering and hip bearing roses such as some of the Hybrid Musks and cultivars or hybrids of *R. moyesii* make good companions, as does a wide range of autumn-coloring shrubs, including amelanchiers, sumacs, aronias, berberis, callicarpas, clethras, and cotinus, together with enkianthus, deciduous euonymus, linderas, deciduous azaleas, and cranberry trees. It is also attractive with taller eupatoriums, actaeas, and late aconitums.

⬤ *Actaea simplex* (Atropurpurea Group) 'Brunette', *Amelanchier lamarckii, Aster novi-belgii* 'Sarah Ballard', *Euonymus alatus, Helianthus* 'Monarch'

H: 1.8m (6ft) **S:** 90cm (3ft)
❀ **Early to late autumn**

 ◌◌-◌◌◌ ◻-◼ Z4 pH4.5–7.5

Leucanthemum vulgare

OXEYE DAISY

Although normally a little too coarse for use as a border plant, this herbaceous perennial is admirably suited to a wild garden and for naturalizing in grass, competing successfully even with vigorously growing grass. In these wild situations it can be used with other fairly strong-growing perennials, such as some umbellifers (it can bloom after cow parsley, for example), meadow buttercups and other robust species of ranunculus, and other naturalized or wild flowers such as red or white campions and yarrows; it also combines well with heracleums, columbines, chaerophyllums, trollius, and vigorous cranesbills. More refined forms suitable for including as part of a border scheme are 'Maistern' (May Star), which is 50cm (20in) high and produces large early flowers, and 'Maikönigin' (May Queen), also very early and taller, at 70cm (27in).

◖ *Anthriscus sylvestris, Aquilegia vulgaris, Chaerophyllum hirsutum* 'Roseum', *Geranium phaeum, Heracleum mantegazzianum, Ranunculus repens* var. *pleniflorus, Silene dioica, Trollius europaeus*

H: 30–90cm (12–36in) **S: 45–60cm** (18–24in)
❁ **Late spring to early summer**
◐◐ ▢-▇ **Z3 pH4.5–7.5**

In grassland that is neither nutrient rich nor very impoverished *Leucanthemum vulgare* can be naturalized attractively with wild flowers of similar regimes, such as meadow buttercup (*Ranunculus acris*).

Leymus arenarius

BLUE LYME GRASS

This is a vigorous herbaceous rhizomatous grass (syn. *Elymus arenarius*) with vividly blue-grey leaves and stiff wheat-like flower spikes. It can be grown in a border or a gravel garden, but it is invasive and needs confining or siting away from less robust plants, ideally in fairly nutrient-poor, well drained soil. It mixes happily with other blue plants and contrasts well with yellow, and, where it can be left to spread freely, combines attractively with plants such as sea kale, thrifts, horned poppies, pinks, eryngiums, and other grasses. If restricted in a border, it can partner similar plants, together with other blue-flowered or

Spreading clumps of *Leymus arenarius* are usually loose enough to allow slender plants of contrasting form and color, such as purple toadflax (*Linaria purpurea*), to be grown between, creating a pleasant mixture.

glaucous-leaved plants and, for contrast, silver foliage or yellow flowers. Examples include artemisias, catmints, smaller euphorbias, glaucous hebes, irises, ballotas, anthemis, erigerons, gypsophilas, and yellow achilleas.

◖ *Achillea filipendulina* 'Gold Plate', *Anthemis tinctoria, Armeria pseudarmeria, Ballota pseudodictamnus, Glaucium corniculatum, Nepeta* 'Six Hills Giant' p.267 **C**

H: 1.2m (4ft) **S: 90cm** (3ft)
❁ **(Mid-summer to early autumn)**

◐-◐◐ ▢-▇ **Z4 pH5.5–7.5**

Ligularia dentata
BIGLEAF GOLDENRAY

The leaves of this handsome if slightly coarse plant (syns *L. clivorum*, *Senecio clivorum*) are kidney-shaped or rounded, and heart-shaped at the base. Their color is green in the typical species, purplish green in 'Othello', and bronze-green with purple undersides in 'Desdemona' ♔. Bigleaf goldenray is very successful in waterside plantings and as a ground cover but also proves useful as a border plant where there is adequate moisture. Ideally it should receive morning sun but needs some shade in the afternoon to prevent leaves wilting. It blends well with other hot colors, or soft yellow, apricot, or peach, as well as with purple foliage and other plants with a similarly bold, almost tropical effect. Satisfying contrasts can be achieved with the foliage of daylilies, irises, ferns, and grasses, and with flowers in blue, purple, yellow-green, or even shocking pink.

🌑 *Achillea* 'Coronation Gold' p.178 **B**, *Camassia leichtlinii* 'Semiplena' p.307 **C**, *Iris pseudacorus* 'Variegata', *Rosa* Evelyn Fison p.164 **A**

H: 90–150cm (3–5ft) S: 90cm (3ft)
❀ **Mid-summer to early autumn**

◊◊◊ ■-■ **Z4 pH4.5–7.5**

Top: In this combination of dark leaves and hot colors, bronze-green leaved *Ligularia dentata* 'Desdemona' is joined by the yellow spires of *L. stenocephala*, the flat heads of *Achillea filipendulina* 'Gold Plate', and a rich red daylily (*Hemerocallis* 'Stafford'), against a background of purple smoke bush (*Cotinus coggygria* 'Royal Purple').

Above: Mauve-pink and orange can be difficult colors to combine well but can be less contentious if slightly muted tones are used, as in this selection of *Ligularia dentata* and *Clematis* 'Hagley Hybrid'. They sit easily alongside *Hydrangea aspera* subsp. *sargentiana*, with its felted leaves and lilac flower heads edged with white.

Ligularia stenocephala

This is an impressive plant for large-scale effects by water, where reflections can double the impact of its bold spikes of yellow flowers, which are born on dark stems above triangular leaves with jagged edges. It combines well with hot colors but also with pale yellow, cream, and yellow-green, and may be contrasted with blue or purple flowers, with bronze foliage plants, and with the different leaf forms of plants such as grasses, ferns, irises, daylilies, and astilbes. Like *L. dentata* (left), it needs moisture and sun, with afternoon shade to prevent wilting.

L. przewalskii is a similar species, but with much more jagged leaves and a less solid flower spike, while their hybrid *L.* 'The Rocket' ♔ is intermediate between the two.

🌑 *Astilbe* 'Red Sentinel', *Carex pendula*, *Delphinium* 'Sungleam' p.209 **B**, *Deschampsia cespitosa*, *Lobelia* 'Cherry Ripe', *Rodgersia pinnata* 'Superba'

H: 1.5m (5ft) S: 90cm (3ft)
❀ **Early to late summer**

◊◊◊ ■-■ **Z5 pH4.5–7.5**

In this classic combination of moisture lovers, *Ligularia stenocephala* towers over *Lysimachia ciliata*, a contrast in form but a blend of colors. The loosestrife, whose star-shaped flowers have red-brown centers, grows up to 1.2m (4ft) tall. Other large-scale plants to combine with these two include *Gunnera manicata* and *Rodgersia podophylla*.

In this combination for a well-drained sunny site, blue *Linum narbonense* contrasts with the yellow-flowered, prostrate broom *Genista sagittalis*. An attractive, subshrubby spurge, *Euphorbia characias*, gives bold architectural form to the planting.

Linum narbonense

This sun-loving flax has delicate, saucer-shaped flowers in silky blue, with a white eye. It is at its best in the morning, since the color tends to fade by the afternoon. It needs good drainage and prefers an open site, although it can be grown at the front of a border among low, carpeting plants. It is good with other sun-lovers such as lavenders, phlomis, cistus, helianthemums, and similar plants from the Mediterranean, South Africa, and California. It harmonizes with glaucous or silver foliage, and pink, white, or mauve flowers, and makes a fine contrast with sulfur-yellow flowers. The dome-shaped plants look effective with others of contrasting form – grasses, for example, or shorter achilleas with plate-like flower heads. 'Heavenly Blue' ♕ is a superlative selection.

◉ *Achillea* 'Moonshine', *Cistus* × *cyprius*, *Hakonechloa macra* 'Alboaurea', *Phlomis fruticosa*, *Rosmarinus officinalis* 'Roseus', *Ruta graveolens* 'Jackman's Blue'

H: 30–60cm (12–24in) **S: 45cm** (18in)
✿ **Early to mid-summer**
◊-◊◊◊ ▨-▨ **Z5 pH5.5–8**

Lobelia 'Cherry Ripe'

The exotic flower spikes of this bronze-leaved herbaceous perennial are cherry-red, and suited not only to hot color schemes but also to more subtle plantings with peach, apricot, or soft orange flowers and purple or bronze foliage. It is a shade of red that mixes equally well with scarlet or crimson. Like most of the herbaceous lobelias, the plant enjoys plenty of moisture (although in order to thrive it does need fairly good drainage and it cannot tolerate either stagnant or boggy conditions). This makes it suitable both for waterside schemes and for herbaceous borders provided the soil is adequately moist.

As with all the older lobelia clones, viral disease can be a problem, and any plants with symptoms such as distorted leaf blades or streaks in the flowers should be destroyed.

◉ *Carex pendula*, *Corylus maxima* 'Purpurea', *Hosta sieboldiana* var. *elegans*, *Iris pseudacorus* 'Variegata', *Ligularia dentata* 'Desdemona', *Lysimachia ciliata* 'Firecracker', *Mimulus aurantiacus*, *Osmunda regalis*

H: 90cm (36in) **S: 30cm** (12in)
✿ **Mid-summer to early autumn**
◊◊-◊◊◊ ▨ **Z6 pH5–7.5**

The narrow, upright growth habit of *Lobelia* 'Cherry Ripe' and its long racemes of blooms make it especially useful for steeply sloped borders such as this. In a predominantly red scheme, the lobelia is joined by *Dahlia* 'Grenadier', the scarlet hips of *Rosa* 'Geranium', and the double-flowered daylily *Hemerocallis fulva* 'Flore Pleno'.

In this extensive planting of hot-colored flowers, *Lobelia* 'Queen Victoria' has to be grouped several plants deep for its slender spikes to give the impression of solid color. Its partners here include *Dahlia* 'Bishop of Llandaff', heleniums, and crocosmias.

Lobelia 'Queen Victoria' ♕

Brilliant scarlet flowers and purple foliage make this a fine candidate for hot color schemes and red borders, and for dramatic contrasts with yellow-green foliage or flowers. It is also effective with plants of contrasting form, such as grasses and golden hostas or ligularias. Plants tend to look unsatisfactory on their own and are better arranged in fairly generous groups. Deadheading encourages further flowering, and plants benefit from frequent division. Most are now grown from seed, sown in early spring to flower by mid- to late summer. Other useful seed-raised lobelias include the Fan and Kompliment Series, both best treated as annuals or biennials. They are available in blue, purple, and pink, as well as scarlet and deep red.

◉ *Canna* 'Erebus' p.367 **B**, *Dahlia* 'Alva's Doris' p.370 **A**, *Hosta* 'Sum and Substance', *Ligularia dentata* 'Desdemona', *Molinia caerulea* 'Variegata'

H: 90cm (36in) **S: 30cm** (12in)
✿ **Mid-summer to mid-autumn**
◊◊-◊◊◊ ▨ **Z6 pH5–7.5**

A

Lupinus hybrids

Among the most popular of border perennials, lupines are often showy plants, on average 90–120cm (3–4ft) high, with densely packed spikes of bloom arising from clumps of soft green palmate leaves. The large pea flowers come in a vast range of colors – varying tones of pink and red, lilac and blue, orange and yellow – as well as white, and including bicolors (often white with another color). The main flowering period is early summer, but if the first flush is removed as the flowers fade, further spikes will usually be produced in late summer and autumn.

White cultivars generally are good partners for silver foliage and other white flowers, and combine agreeably with almost any other color, although they perhaps make most

B

impact with pastel shades. They can be used with richer colors, but the contrast can be a little severe, particularly with hot colors, and a cream or a broken white lupine might be a more satisfactory choice. Good white cultivars include 'Pope John Paul' ♀, 'Noble Maiden' in the Band of Nobles Series, and 'Gallery White' in the shorter (50cm/20in) Gallery Series. 'Polar Princess (1.2m/4ft) is one of the finest, with magnificent spikes of pure white flowers, but these are followed by relatively little secondary branching, so the flowering season is comparatively short.

Far left: Vigorously grown young lupines, such as the superb *Lupinus* 'Polar Princess', here making strong vertical accents against the silvery foliage of *Elaeagnus commutata*, will produce solid, columnar racemes of almost unnatural regularity in their first year of flowering, although they will bear numerous spires of varied size in subsequent years.

Left: In this purple, lavender, and yellow-green scheme, *Euphorbia characias* subsp. *wulfenii* echoes the bold verticals of *Lupinus* 'Thundercloud', along with catmint (*Nepeta* 'Six Hills Giant') and *Erysimum* 'Bowles' Mauve'.

'Thundercloud' is one of the best purple lupines, its color being effective not only when combined with harmonious tones such as those of blue cranesbills, or mauve or crimson flowers, but also when contrasted with yellow-green flowers or foliage, and with soft yellow flowers such as some achilleas.

All of the taller lupines are very useful for adding vertical accents and subdued focal points to a border, although they may need staking. They are best positioned in the second or third rank, slightly forward from other plants of similar height to give their spikes more prominence. They associate well with euphorbias and catmints, and make an arresting contrast with the globe-shaped flowerheads of early alliums.

Lupine aphid can disfigure plants and introduce viral disease, causing mottling of the leaves; slugs may also be a problem, and may require controlling.

◉ *Allium cristophii, A. sphaerocephalon, Artemisia ludoviciana, Iris orientalis, Paeonia lactiflora* 'Duchesse de Nemours', *Papaver orientale* 'Black and White', *Rosa* Graham Thomas p.156 **A**

H: 90–120m (36–48in) S: 60cm (24in)
❋ **Early summer**
◊◊ ▣-▨ ■ **Z3 pH5.5–7.5**

Lychnis × *arkwrightii* 'Vesuvius'

With its rich bronze-purple foliage and red-vermilion flowers, this eye-catching perennial (syn. *Silene* × *arkwrightii* 'Vesuvius') is an ideal ingredient of a hot color scheme, and also makes a startling contrast with acid yellow-green flowers or foliage. There are cultivars of *L.* × *haageana* that are very similar in coloring and growth habit, and these include seed-raised 'Molten Lava' which can be used in the same way as *L.* × *arkwrightii* 'Vesuvius'. Neither plant has great refinement of form and their impact is improved by being placed next to a plant of more definite structure or with interestingly textured foliage, such as a

grass or smaller phormium. These *Lychnis* cultivars require fairly rich soil and a sunny location, and often suffer from slug damage.

◉ *Berberis thunbergii* f. *atropurpurea, Choisya ternata* Sundance, *Euphorbia schillingii, Hemerocallis* 'Golden Chimes', *Phormium* 'Bronze Baby', *Stipa gigantea*

H: 45cm (18in) S: 30cm (12in)
❋ **Early to mid-summer**
◊◊ ▣-▨ ■ **Z6 pH5.5–7.5**

In this dramatic grouping reminiscent of a Japanese ikebana arrangement, the vivid flowers of *Lychnis* × *arkwrightii* 'Vesuvius' contrast with the brightly variegated grass *Hakonechloa macra* 'Aureola', around the spiky foliage of a dark form of *Eucomis comosa*. The arrangement could be repeated in a larger planting, replacing the grass with a less fiercely contrasting one if desired.

C

Lychnis coronaria

ROSE CAMPION

This lovely, easily grown, silver-leaved plant is long-flowering and profuse, with flowers in a range of colors. The species itself is usually magenta-pink, and combines well with pink, crimson, mauve, or purple flowers, and with silver or glaucous foliage of contrasting form, such as that of artemisias and grasses; soft yellow makes a pleasing contrast. It is best placed in the front or second rank of a border, and also succeeds in gravel gardens since it prefers good drainage – in heavier soils it tends to have a shorter life. It is in any case fairly short-lived, but self-seeds freely, and since the foliage of older plants is less satisfactory, it pays to allow seedlings to replace these regularly. To keep colored forms separate, however, plants of different shades should be grown apart. The many variants include the Atrosanguinea Group, which is purplish red, and contrasts well with salmon or soft yellow; it is excellent with old roses, catmints, and lavenders. Pure white 'Alba' ♀ can partner yellows, apricots, and peaches, as well as all the other cooler colors from pink and red through to blue.

⬤ *Campanula* 'Burghaltii' p.199 **B**, *Echinacea purpurea* p.213 **B**, *Erigeron* 'Gaiety' p.215 **C**, *Gladiolus communis* subsp. *byzantinus* p.318 **A**, *Malva sylvestris* p.386 **B**, *Rosa* 'Charles de Mills' p.146 **A**, *R.* × *francofurtana* 'Empress Josephine' p.147 **C**, *R. gallica* 'Versicolor' p.148 **B**, *R.* 'Tuscany Superb' p.150 **B**

H: 80cm (31in) S: 45cm (18in)
❊ **Mid- to late summer**
⬛⬛▨▧ ◊-◊◊◊ ▢-▨ ⬛ **Z4 pH5–8**

Right: A gently contrasting salmon pelargonium scrambles into rose campions (magenta *Lychnis coronaria* and white *L.c.* 'Alba') to give a vibrant color combination.

Below: In a sunny display in mid-summer, *Lychnis coronaria* 'Alba' combines with a lemon daylily (*Hemerocallis* 'Baroni'), the bold and elegant shape of the daylily blooms contrasting with those of the campion.

In boggy ground alongside a stream in early spring, the handsome golden spathes of the skunk cabbage (*Lysichiton americanus*) harmonize with the cream and yellow stripes of the variegated yellow iris (*Iris pseudacorus* 'Variegata'), planted with marsh marigolds (*Caltha palustris*) beneath.

Lysichiton americanus ♔
YELLOW SKUNK CABBAGE

This waterside plant has an alien appearance in spring when its hooded yellow spathes emerge, surrounding upright greenish flowers with a slightly unpleasant scent. The large, glossy leaves, which are rather coarse but nonetheless handsome, appear much later. It is an excellent companion for water irises, whose foliage provides contrast both at flowering time and later when the yellow skunk cabbage is in leaf. The foliage is particularly useful for creating a luxuriant primeval effect with other large-leaved partners such as gunneras. Plants harmonize with early yellow flowers such as calthas and the moisture-loving *Narcissus bulbocodium* and *N. jonquilla*, and also look appealing growing beneath dogwoods with colored bark. They provide good contrast with blue flowers such as brunneras and forget-me-nots, and with larger evergreen ferns. *L. camtschatcensis* ♔ is similar but smaller, with white spathes.

◉ *Brunnera macrophylla*, *Caltha leptosepala*, *C. palustris* var. *alba*, *Cornus alba* 'Sibirica', *Dryopteris affinis*, *Gunnera manicata*, *Iris chrysographes*, *I. ensata* cultivars, *Myosotis sylvatica*, *Osmunda regalis*, *Primula rosea*, *Rodgersia pinnata* 'Superba'

H: 1m (3¼ft) S: 1.5m (5ft) ❀ Early to mid-spring
◊◊◊ ▣-▢ Z7 pH5–7

Lysimachia ciliata 'Firecracker' ♔

Although producing pretty, nodding yellow flowers in summer, 'Firecracker' is primarily grown for its attractive foliage, reddish purple in closely space whorls. It is a useful plant from spring, when it can make a harmonious or contrasting backdrop to tulips and late narcissi, until autumn, when the leaves take on attractive tints. It looks good with pink, salmon-pink, or mauve flowers before its own flowers appear, and makes a fine subject for hot color schemes. It needs a moist site and will not tolerate summer drought, so boggy or waterside situations are ideal. Because it is invasive and needs to be kept under control, it should not be grown where the questing roots are likely to tangle with those of neighbors that resent disturbance.

◉ *Hemerocallis* 'Stafford', *Ligularia stenocephala*, *Narcissus* 'Actaea', *Rosa* 'Frensham' p.164 **B**, *R.* 'Roseraie de l'Haÿ' p.160 **A**, *Tulipa* 'Palestrina'

H: 1.2m (4ft) S: 60cm (24in)
❀ Mid- to late summer
◊◊-◊◊◊ ▣ Z3 pH5–7.5

The emerging chocolate shoots of *Lysimachia ciliata* 'Firecracker' in late spring provide a strong color contrast in this mixed planting of yellow tulips, which includes the Lily-flowered cultivar *T.* 'West Point' (top), emphasizing the bold shape of the flowers.

The bright yellow-green foliage and pale stems of golden creeping Jenny (*Lysimachia nummularia* 'Aurea') mingle with the glaucous, pinnate foliage of *Acaena saccaticupula* 'Blue Haze' to create a carpet that could be planted under with blue, white, or yellow bulbs. Although both plants have similar vigor, maintaining a balance between the two might require occasional division and replanting.

Lysimachia nummularia 'Aurea' ♔
GOLDEN CREEPING JENNY

The bright yellow-green foliage of this superb carpeting plant spreads rapidly, making an effective foil for plants such as white colchicums – even magenta ones, to be daring – or around splendidly symmetrical clumps of ferns. It will intermingle with other carpeters of comparable vigor, for example contrasting purple bugleweeds, bronze acaenas, or the white-splashed wild strawberry, *Fragaria × ananassa* 'Variegata', and may be used in hanging baskets, although it must have moist soil and can scorch in full sun. The flowers are yellow and camouflaged by the color of the leaves, adding little to the impact of the foliage. They are more charming seen against the fresh green foliage of the simple species, *L. nummularia*, which is a more rampant carpeter for cool, damp places.

◉ *Acaena microphylla* 'Kupferteppich', *Ajuga reptans* 'Atropurpurea', *Colchicum speciosum*, *C. s.* 'Album', *Hebe pinguifolia* 'Pagei', *Lobelia richardsonii*, *Matteuccia struthiopteris*, *Muscari armeniacum*, *Myosotis sylvatica*, *Scilla siberica* 'Spring Beauty', *Viola* 'Huntercombe Purple' p.292 **B**

H: 5cm (2in) S: indefinite ❀ Mid-summer
◊◊-◊◊◊ ▢-■ Z4 pH4.5–7.5

The tall plumes of *Macleaya microcarpa* in early summer harmonize both with the brick wall behind and with the group of mixed *Alstroemeria* ligtu hybrids in front. A hedge fern (*Polystichum setiferum*) decorates the base of the alstroemerias, while *Convolvulus sabatius* provides a splash of contrasting blue in the foreground.

Macleaya microcarpa

The color of the tall, airy flower spikes of this plume poppy lies somewhere between brick-red, coral, and salmon. It harmonizes with other flowers in all these colors, and contrasts with soft blue ones. It can, however, be slightly overwhelmed by brilliant scarlet or orange blooms. With its handsome, scalloped foliage, the plant is very effective among or in front of shrubs, and with perpetual-flowering roses such as some old Chinas, Teas, and Hybrid Musks, and many of the David Austin English rose cultivars. It combines well with alstroemerias, and with grasses, hostas, and other contrasting glaucous or silver-leaved plants, and its form is enhanced by a background of bronze or purple foliage. The cultivar 'Kelway's Coral Plume' ♀ is particularly fine. The rootstock is restlessly invasive so plants tend to wander from their original positions.

🔘 *Alstroemeria aurea*, *Campanula latifolia* 'Gloaming', *Cotinus coggygria* 'Notcutt's Variety', *Dahlia* 'Glorie van Heemstede' p.373 **A**, *Rosa* Peach Blossom

H: 2.2m (7ft) S: 90cm (3ft)
✺ **Early to mid-summer**
◊◊-◊◊◊ ■ Z4 pH5.5–7.5

Malva moschata f. alba ♀

The white form of the musk mallow varies in growth habit and in the size and number of its blooms. The best forms produce neat plants that are almost covered with broad, glistening white flowers in summer. The purity of the color, set against the deep green of the crisp, prettily cut leaves, can produce rather harsh contrasts with strong colors, but the plants are immensely effective with other white flowers, pastel shades, and silver foliage, and with yellow-green or glaucous leaves. They are excellent at the front of a border, growing with companions such as pinks, alchemillas, and catmints.

Cultivated forms of musk mallow, selected for their neat, compact growth habit, are only about half the height of the wild species, which can reach 90cm (36in).

🔘 *Artemisia schmidtiana*, *Astrantia maxima*, *Heuchera* 'Rachel' p.241 **B**, *Hydrangea arborescens*, *Rosa* Pink Bells p.171 **A**, *Veronicastrum virginicum album*

H: 90cm (36in) S: 60cm (24in)
✺ **Early summer to early autumn**
◊◊ ▢-■ Z4 pH5.5–7.5

An upright *Miscanthus sinensis* cultivar produces a fountain of foliage behind *Malva moschata* f. *alba* in a simple display of subdued colors. The deeply cut leaves of the musk mallow give a strong contrast of form with the ribbon-like foliage of the grass.

In early spring at the front of a border alongside a path, the young shuttlecocks of the ostrich fern (*Matteuccia struthiopteris*) make a bold statement and help draw attention to an imposing terracotta pot. Pure blue-flowered *Omphalodes cappadocica* 'Cherry Ingram' sits at the base of the ferns and hides the edge of the path.

Matteuccia struthiopteris ♀
OSTRICH FERN

Spring is the most beautiful season for this deciduous fern, when the young extending foliage forms a plume of light yellowish green shuttlecocks. It is also attractive in autumn as the fronds assume russet tints, and the dark brown fertile fronds will often persist through much of the winter. It perhaps looks its best combined with yellow or blue spring flowers, such as forget-me-nots, omphalodes, brunneras, epimediums, and erythroniums, and is very effective with a carpet of lower-growing plants beneath and between the plumes. This moisture-loving fern is an excellent choice for bog gardens or waterside plantings, and for moist, dappled shade, especially with deciduous azaleas. The underground shoots spread freely in all but the heaviest soils, where growth and height tend to be more restricted.

🔘 *Arum italicum* 'Marmoratum' p.307 **A**, *Erythronium revolutum* p.313 **C**, *Pyrus salicifolia* 'Pendula' p.79 **C**, *Tulipa* 'Sweet Harmony' p.354 **A**

H: 1.2m (4ft) S: 90cm (3ft)
◊◊-◊◊◊ ■ Z2 pH5.5–7

Meconopsis betonicifolia ♔
TIBETAN BLUE POPPY

The exquisite flowers of this species (syn. *M. baileyi*) are a rare pure blue, slightly greenish in areas with moist soils and cool summers, a little more purple after a hot or dry spring. It tends to be short-lived so is best divided or resown every two years or so in early to mid-spring. It is superlative with light yellow, white, or cream flowers, and with yellow-green foliage or flowers and bronze foliage. It is especially attractive with ferns with light green spring foliage, and with other greenish blue flowers on plants of contrasting form, such as corydalis.

M. grandis ♔ is perhaps even more handsome, with larger, more symmetrical flowers, but it is not so perennial. The hybrid between the two species, *M.* × *sheldonii* ♔, combines superior flower shape and size with longer life, although it is sterile and must be raised vegetatively. *M.b.* var. *alba* has delicate, purest white flowers, born over good foliage that is more glaucous than the typical species.

◖ *Astilbe* × *arendsii* 'Irrlicht', *Corydalis flexuosa*, *Hosta fortunei* var. *albopicta* f. *aurea*, *Matteuccia struthiopteris*, *Primula florindae*, *Rhododendron* 'Polar Bear', *Rodgersia pinnata* 'Superba'

H: 1.2m (4ft) S: 45cm (18in) ✿ **Early summer**
◊◊◊ ▨ ■ **Z7 pH5–6.5**

In a partially shaded glade blessed with moist, humus-rich soil, blue poppies (*Meconopsis betonicifolia*) and white foxgloves (*Digitalis purpurea* f. *albiflora*) create a classic combination of blue and white, the spikes of the foxgloves providing bold accents and contrast of form.

Milium effusum 'Aureum'
GOLDEN MILLET GRASS

Woodland gardens and shady borders are the best sites for this pretty yellow-green grass, which can become unkempt and scorched when planted in full sun. It is easy to grow and showiest in mid- to late spring, but its fine color will persist into summer if grown in moist cool conditions. With its readiness to self-seed, it may become a weed, although cutting the flower stems before seeds are shed can prevent this. It is best treated as a short-lived perennial, as older plants tend to look rather dishevelled. Blue, pale yellow, cream, or white flowers, glaucous foliage, and yellow-green foliage of contrasting form – hostas, for example – are all outstanding partners. Mass planting in blocks hides its natural grace, and

Golden millet grass (*Milium effusum* 'Aureum') has sown itself through silverweed (*Potentilla anserina*), an invasive plant with silvery glaucous foliage, to create a charming spring mixture.

it looks better scattered as individual clumps, perhaps through a carpet of low-growing plants such as bugleweeds. It is very effective, too, growing through forget-me-nots, blue corydalis, geums, bluebells, brunneras, and omphalodes, and with white, cream, or yellow erythroniums.

◖ *Ajuga reptans* 'Atropurpurea', *Geranium* 'Johnson's Blue', *Geum* 'Lady Stratheden', *Helleborus* × *hybridus* p.237 **A**, *Hosta* (Tardiana Group) 'Halcyon'

H: 60cm (24in) S: 30cm (12in)
✿ **Late spring to mid-summer**

◊◊-◊◊◊ ▨ ■ **Z5 pH5–7.5**

By late autumn, the dry seedheads of *Miscanthus sinensis* take on parchment tints but remain attractive, especially if rimed with frost or lit by the sun. The faded heads of other border plants can, if left, combine with them to create interesting patterns of contrasting forms in subdued fawns and russets, as here with the flat plates of *Achillea filipendulina*.

Miscanthus sinensis

This grass varies wildly in height, growth habit, hardiness, and flowering, so it is advisable to choose a named cultivar with particular qualities, rather than buy a plant simply as *Miscanthus sinensis*. There are narrow forms that can be incorporated into borders, whereas more arching cultivars need space to show their natural grace. Most hold their seedheads well and so are very useful for a winter garden, particularly if sited where they are backlit by the sun or sunlit against a dark evergreen backdrop. The most floriferous are so prolific that the individual grace of the flower heads or seedheads is lost: maroon-flushed 'Gewitterwolke', for example, although impressive at 1.8m (6ft) and with excellent foliage, bears flowers in such profusion that it can look very congested.

All cultivars may be grown with autumn-flowering plants such as helianthus, asters, and chrysanthemums, but with their loosely informal growth and subtle colorings, they are more effective where not overwhelmed by strong color. The following cultivars are all hardy to Zone 5. Some of the most useful non-variegated kinds include 'Gracillimus' (maiden grass), which is narrow-leaved with a pale central vein, 1.8m (6ft) tall, and good for planting in borders, but shy to flower where summers are cool. 'Sarabande', 1.2m (4ft), has similar narrow grey-green foliage but is floriferous, with flowers that emerge pink-flushed, aging to silver. 'Graziella', 1.5m (5ft), is also narrow-leaved with prolific pink-flushed flowers that turn silver, as do the spreading pink panicles of neat 'Flamingo', 1.2m (4ft). For imposing height there is 'Silbeturm' at 2.5m (8ft), with silvery plumes. The plumes of 'Grosse Fontäne', 2m (6½ft), cascade in a fountain of long fingers; 'Kleine Fontäne' is smaller at 1m (3¼ft). Free-flowering and also 1m (3¼ft) high is 'Kleine Silberspinne', with narrow leaves held horizontally and maroon-flushed plumes aging to silver. *M.s.* var. *condensatus* with broad leaves and thick, silvery stems, reaches 3m (10ft) and flowers in mid-autumn with an almost tropical effect. Diminutive kinds, such as 'Little Kitten', 30cm (12in) tall, narrow-leaved, and flowering in early autumn, are valuable for smaller gardens and for containers.

🔵 *Aster* × *frikartii* 'Mönch', *Eupatorium purpureum* subsp. *maculatum*, *Helianthus decapetalus* 'Soleil d'Or', *Malva moschata* f. *alba* p.263 **B**, *Rosa* 'Geranium' p.155 **A**, *Verbascum* 'Helen Johnson' p.291 **B**

H: 30cm–3m (1–10ft) S: 60cm–1.8m (2–6ft)
❀ **Mid-summer to late autumn**

◻◻◻◻◻◻ 🜄🜄 ◻-◼ ◼ **Z5–7 pH5–7.5**

In mid-autumn, *Miscanthus sinensis* 'Undine' stands gracefully behind lilac-tinted *Aster lateriflorus* 'Horizontalis' in front of creamy plumes of *Artemisia lactiflora*, with silvery *M.s.* 'Silberfeder' silhouetted against a dark yew hedge.

The cream-striped *Miscanthus sinensis* 'Variegatus' here seems almost identical in tone to silvery *Elaeagnus* 'Quicksilver', differing in form and texture, but blending to give a gentle and elegant combination.

Miscanthus sinensis 'Variegatus'

This is an arching foliage plant that needs space, but looks good surrounded by lower plants. Narrower variegated kinds for growing in borders include 'Silberpfeil', 2.2m (7ft), fairly free-flowering but fairly bare at the base. 'Morning Light', 1.5m (5ft), has narrow, elegant, white-edged leaves. More spreading cultivars with marginal variegation include 'Dixieland', 1.5m (5ft), a brighter and stronger plant than 'Variegatus'. *M.s.* var. *condensatus* 'Cabaret', 2.5m (8ft), has broad, white-centered leaves, while equally tall var. *c.* 'Cosmopolitan' is green with white edges. Several cultivars have transverse gold or beige variegation: best known of these is 'Zebrinus', 2.2m (7ft), with arching leaves and a spreading growth habit. 'Strictus' (porcupine grass), is similar, about the same height, with stiffly angled leaves that give a prickly effect.

🔵 *Anemone* × *hybrida* 'Elegans' p.185 **B**, *Chrysanthemum* Rubellum Group, *Crocosmia* 'Lucifer', *Echinacea purpurea*, *Rhus* × *pulvinata* Autumn Lace Group, *Rodgersia podophylla* p.280 **C**

H: 1.5m (5ft) S: 1m (3¼ft)
❀ **Early to mid-autumn**

◻◻◻◻◻◻ 🜄🜄 ◻-◼ ◼ **Z6–7 pH5–7.5**

A

This mid-autumn scheme has a strong vertical theme. *Molinia caerulea* 'Variegata' in the foreground growing at the base of *Actaea simplex* Atropurpurea Group, its white bottle-brushes born above dark leaves. In the distance are the upright buff seedheads of the feather reed grass, *Calamagrostis × acutiflora* 'Karl Foerster'.

Molinia caerulea 'Variegata' ♔
VARIEGATED MOOR GRASS

This is a neat and showy herbaceous grass, with clumps of brightly cream-striped leaves and spikes of purplish flowers that turn parchment color in winter. Tolerant of a wide range of soils, it can be used at the front of a border and as an edging to beds. Its top growth is usually shed by late winter, allowing it to be under- or interplanted with early-flowering bulbs such as snowdrops, and since it is rather late leafing in spring, it suits summer and autumn schemes. It harmonizes with warm-colored flowers, particularly yellow or cream, and contrasts with blue flowers or glaucous foliage. Other effective partners include lavenders, nigellas, smaller yellow tagetes, heliophilas, nemophilas, California poppies, fescues, and lyme grasses.

⬤ *Delphinium grandiflorum* 'Blue Butterfly', *Heliophila coronopifolia*, *Hosta* (Tardiana Group) 'Halcyon', *Nemophila menziesii*, *Nigella damascena* 'Miss Jekyll'

H: 90cm (36in) S: 60cm (24in)
�֎ **Mid-summer to mid-autumn**

◌◌-◌◌◌ ▨-▨ ■ Z5 pH5.5–7.5

C

Pale pink *Monarda* 'Beauty of Cobham', used towards the front of a border of predominantly purple flowers and dark foliage, helps to leaven an otherwise leaden combination featuring purple smoke bush (*Cotinus coggygria* 'Foliis Purpureis') and purple loosestrife (*Lythrum salicaria* 'Feuerkerze').

Monarda 'Adam'

One of the most outstanding red bergamot cultivars, this is a fairly compact, clump-forming rhizomatous perennial, with sturdy upright square stems bearing fragrant, dark green mint-like leaves. The comparatively large, hooded flowers appear in dense terminal whorls that have a pleasantly shaggy appearance. Although not sufficiently intense for hot-colored schemes, their sumptuous shade of cherry-red is a color that deserves prominence, and plants make exciting accents and highlights within borders, especially if partnered by acid yellow-green foliage and flowers or soft yellow flowers, such as some achilleas and day lilies, or euphorbias. Other good companions include liatris, catmints, hardy salvias, and eryngiums. Like many red monardas, it tends to be susceptible to powdery mildew, especially on dry soils or if massed within a tightly packed border.

⬤ *Achillea filipendulina* 'Gold Plate', *Aster divaricatus*, *Deschampsia cespitosa*, *Rudbeckia fulgida* var. *deamii*, *Salvia coccinea* 'Coral Nymph'

H: 80cm (31in) S: 45cm (18in)
✖ **Mid- to late summer**

◌◌ ▨-▨ ■ Z4 pH5–7.5

B

In this border of brightly colored flowers for mid-summer to autumn, the relatively compact, cherry-red *Monarda* 'Adam' takes center stage. In front are golden heleniums and crimson *Phlox paniculata*, while behind, *Crocosmia* 'Lucifer', achilleas, and dark-leaved *Ricinus communis* provide both structure and bold color.

Monarda 'Beauty of Cobham' ♔

Although tolerating any soil that does not dry out in summer, this rhizomatous herbaceous perennial prefers damp conditions, in which it will gradually spread to form a moderately sized clump. It is an attractive subject for moist herbaceous or mixed borders, and also for waterside plantings. The pale pink flowers suit combinations with other cool colors, such as purple, mauve, crimson, white, and lavender, while the purple calyces harmonize particularly well with purple foliage. Wherever summers are cool enough for hostas to grow successfully in full sun, 'Beauty of Cobham' can be partnered very pleasantly with the glaucous foliage of *Hosta sieboldiana* or *H.* Tardiana Group. It is an outstanding partner for astilbes, filipendulas, perennial lobelias, lythrums, later-flowering thalictrums, persicarias, plume poppies, and grasses such as *Miscanthus sinensis* cultivars. Like most monardas, it benefits from frequent division.

⬤ *Aster × frikartii* 'Mönch', *Astilbe × arendsii* 'Ceres', *Lobelia* 'Fan Scharlach', *Lythrum virgatum* 'Dropmore Purple', *Thalictrum delavayi* 'Hewitt's Double'

H: 90cm (36in) S: 45cm (18in)
✖ **Mid- to late summer**

◌◌ ▨-▨ ■ Z4 pH5–7.5

Nepeta govaniana

This is a beautiful Himalayan herbaceous perennial that expands in moist cool conditions to form a clump of erect pointed foliage and airy racemes of subdued creamy yellow flowers, born over a long period in summer. Although never showy, it is a charming companion plant for brighter, bolder flowers, particularly those in yellow or yellow-green, white, or warm colors such as apricot, and glaucous, gold-variegated, or yellow-green foliage, including hostas with yellow-green leaves and grasses such as miscanthus or molinia cultivars. It combines well with later-flowering daylilies, repeat-flowering shrub roses, agapanthus, willow gentians, hedychiums, and ligularias. Other good partners include asters, such as *A. amellus* and *A.* × *frikartii* cultivars, blue or white hydrangeas, kniphofias, and later-flowering lilies. It is very attractive with hypericums, *Ceanothus* × *delileanus* cultivars, caryopteris, perovskias, and similar shrubs.

The airy primrose flowers of *Nepeta govaniana*, rising above a cushion of feathery *Artemisia* 'Powis Castle' and a cream achillea, contrast with the nearby lavender-blue catmint *Nepeta* 'Six Hills Giant' in mid-summer.

🌑 *Agapanthus* 'Loch Hope', *Caryopteris* × *clandonensis* 'Heavenly Blue', *Hydrangea macrophylla* 'Mariesii Perfecta', *Lilium* African Queen Group, *Perovskia* 'Blue Spire', *Rosa* Crown Princess Margareta

H: 90cm (36in) S: 60cm (24in)
✿ Mid-summer to early autumn

◊◊ ▨-▦ ■ Z5 pH5.5–7.5

Nepeta 'Six Hills Giant'

Much larger than other popular catmints, this vigorous herbaceous perennial succeeds in large-scale plantings, with shrubs such as roses or philadelphus, or in front of moderately tall herbaceous plants like *Phlox paniculata* cultivars and some campanulas. It is particularly good with cool colors and soft yellow, especially flowers such as day lilies or achilleas that contrast with its own slightly amorphous form. Where summers are cool, it associates well with glaucous-leaved hostas. Many Mediterranean plants, including cistus and lavenders, make pleasant partners; grasses such as blue fescues, helictotrichons, or lyme grasses are also effective, as are Bearded irises, cranesbills, and peonies. The lavish top growth of 'Six Hills Giant' benefits from being cut hard back after the first flush of bloom. It will at once start to revive, quickly producing a new crop of foliage and blooming again in late summer, when it can combine attractively with later flowers such as Japanese anemones and penstemons.

🌑 *Geranium* × *oxonianum* 'A.T. Johnson', *Lupinus* 'Thundercloud' p.260 **B**, *Paeonia lactiflora* 'Albert Crousse', *Rosa* 'Chinatown' p.163 **B**

H: 75cm (30in) S: 90cm (36in)
✿ Early to late summer

◊-◊◊ ▨-▦ ■ Z5 pH5.5–7.5

The lavender-blue flowers of the catmint *Nepeta* 'Six Hills Giant' sprawl across a gravel path next to the contrasting yellow blooms of Jerusalem sage (*Phlomis fruticosa*), harmonizing with the glaucous lyme grass (*Leymus arenarius*), confined in a weathered copper tub.

Oenothera speciosa 'Siskiyou'

Good drainage and a sunny site are essential for this rhizomatous, clump-forming herbaceous perennial, so it is well suited to a rock or gravel garden, where it can be combined with Mediterranean plants such as helianthemums, cistus, lavenders, marjorams, and teucriums. Its delicate pink flowers, attractively veined and embellished with a yellow base, are perhaps most successful with cool-colored flowers, since the yellow eye scarcely provides enough color to participate in associations with warmer tints such as peach or salmon. Plants can be grown at the front of a border, preferably far enough away from neighbors to allow the cushions of growth to develop symmetrically. They look best in evenly spaced groups, perhaps interplanted with carpeting or cushion-forming plants, rather than in extensive drifts.

🌑 *Cistus* × *argentus* 'Silver Pink', *Helianthemum* 'Wisley White', *Lavandula* 'Regal Splendour', *Origanum* 'Kent Beauty', *Stipa gigantea*, *Teucrium fruticans*

H & S: 30cm (12in) ✿ Early to late summer
◊-◊◊ ▨-▦ ■ Z5 pH5.5–7.5

Allium senescens has here grown through the edges of *Oenothera speciosa* 'Siskiyou', its mauve flower heads harmonizing with the satin-pink blooms of the oenothera but providing a contrast of floral form.

Siberian springbeauty (*Claytonia sibirica*) has here sown itself around *Omphalodes cappadocica* and mingles its mauve flowers with those of the omphalodes to give a charming and harmonious combination.

Omphalodes cappadocica

With its preference for moisture and partial shade, this clump-forming rhizomatous evergreen succeeds in woodland gardens, beneath deciduous trees where it gets winter sun and some summer shade; it also makes a neat edging plant in shady borders. Its early flowering season allows combinations with spring bulbs such as narcissi, early yellow or white tulips, and pale yellow epimediums. The rich blue of its pretty flowers contrasts charmingly with yellow or white flowers, such as celandines and primroses. Other good partners are pale or very dark blue muscaris, scillas, and evergreen sedges and ferns. Notable selections are intense blue 'Cherry Ingram' ♥, white-centered 'Starry Eyes', rich blue 'Parisian Skies', and 'Lilac Mist'.

● *Carex oshimensis* 'Evergold', *Epimedium × versicolor* 'Sulphureum', *Hosta fortunei* var. *albopicta*, *Matteuccia struthiopteris* p.263 **C**, *Muscari latifolium*

H: 23cm (9in) S: 40cm (16in)
❀ **Late spring to early summer**
 ◊◊-◊◊◊ ▢-◼ ◼ **Z6 pH5.5–7.5**

Ophiopogon planiscapus 'Nigrescens' ♥
MONDO GRASS

This is an evergreen perennial lilyturf (also available as 'Arabicus', 'Black Dragon', and 'Kokuryû') that spreads slowly but steadily by means of rhizomes. Its glistening strap-like foliage is closer to black than almost any other plant, while its insignificant flowers – small, white, and sometimes tinged with lilac – are followed by fascinating dark green berries that are shaded black with turquoise undertones. It is a superlative ground-cover plant and a good foil for contrasting foliage and flowers, especially bulbs such as colchicums, and for specimen shrubs like

The glistening dark foliage of black mondo grass (*Ophiopogon planiscapus* 'Nigrescens') contrasts with the glaucous leaves of acaenas, forming a carpet beneath. The cranesbill *Geranium sessiliflorum* subsp. *novae-zelandiae* 'Nigricans' has smoky foliage intermediate in color between that of its two companions.

Japanese maples. It can also be used to make a patchwork of ground-cover foliage with leaves of contrasting form, either in harmonizing dusky colors such as those of dark-leaved heucheras, or together with contrasting pale-leaved plants like smaller yellow-green hostas or silver lamiums. Planted lavishly as an infill for parterres, it is an excellent choice for creating abstract carpet bedding designs on a large scale.

● *Acer palmatum* Dissectum Atropurpureum Group p.29 **B**, *Cyclamen hederifolium* f. *albiflorum* p.312 **A**, *Heuchera micrantha* var. *diversifolia* 'Palace Purple', *Iris* 'George' p.321 **B**

H: 20cm (8in) S: 30cm (12in) ❀ **Mid-summer**
◊◊ ▢-◼ ◼ **Z6 pH5–7**

Origanum vulgare 'Aureum' ♥
GOLDEN CREEPING OREGANO

The bright yellow-green young foliage of this rhizomatous, clump-forming, aromatic perennial approaches pure gold in sunny sites, deepening to green by mid-summer. Cutting plants to the ground when the foliage becomes lackluster produces a second crop of young leaves and removes the mauve-pink flowers, which tend to clash with the foliage. It associates well with anthemis, sisyrinchiums, annual or clump-forming convolvulus, blue-green fescues, and smaller achilleas, and is attractive with nasturtiums, rosemary, borage, hyssop, and white-flowered herbs such as chamomile and feverfew. It tolerates clipping as a component of a knot garden, and can be used to fill a parterre or create bright patches at the front of borders, mixed with glaucous foliage or blue flowers, hot colors such as orange and gold, or gold-variegated foliage.

● *Anthemis punctata* subsp. *cupaniana*, *Astrantia major* 'Sunningdale Variegated' p.195 **A**, *Geranium* 'Ann Folkard' p.225 **B**, *Salvia officinalis* 'Purpurascens'

H & S: 45cm (18in) ❀ **Early to late summer**
◊◊ ▢-◼ ◼ **Z4 pH5.5–8**

The new foliage of wild marjoram (*Origanum vulgare* 'Aureum') is brightest in late spring to early summer when, as here, it contrasts dramatically with the flowers and foliage of purple bugleweed (*Ajuga reptans* 'Atropurpurea').

In a glade in a woodland garden, the double-flowered evergreen azalea *Rhododendron* 'Amoenum' provides dramatic color behind a carpet of *Paeonia emodi*. A paler azalea, perhaps in soft yellow, would also be attractive.

Paeonia emodi

Despite its relatively short flowering season, this elegant herbaceous perennial has prettily divided foliage that remains attractive all summer. Its deliciously scented, pure white flowers have golden anthers, a combination that perhaps works best with blue, yellow, or yellow-green flowers, or with warm colors; it also looks attractive with glaucous or yellow-green foliage. Compatible partners are trollius, smilacinas, dicentras, columbines, corydalis, epimediums, and early cranesbills, together with shrubs like deciduous azaleas, early yellow roses, *Potentilla fruticosa* cultivars, and kerrias. It can be combined with plants of contrasting foliage, including early-leafing hostas, golden millet grass, and yellow-green sedges. Some shade is preferred, but full sun is tolerated where summers are cool.

Carex elata 'Aurea', *Corydalis flexuosa* 'China Blue', *Epimedium* × *versicolor* 'Sulphureum', *Hosta fortunei* var. *albopicta* f. *aurea*, *Rosa* 'Helen Knight'

H & S: 75cm (30in) Late spring

Z5 pH5.5–7.5

Paeonia lactiflora

Possibly the most popular herbaceous species, the Chinese peony is a graceful perennial, with beautiful single white blooms, 8–10cm (3½–4in) across, with a central mass of pale yellow stamens. It is the parent of several thousand cultivars in a wide range of floral forms – single, semi-double, double (sometimes ruffled), and 'Imperial' cultivars, in which the stamens are transformed into a nest of smaller petals – and in colors from white to deep red and soft yellow. Most retain the species' mahogany-tinted foliage, which often colors brightly in autumn, together with a wonderful lingering fragrance. Among the best cultivars are 'Bowl of Beauty', soft pink with a creamy white center; 'Festiva Maxima', double white with red flecks; and 'Sarah Bernhardt', double pink fading at the edges. The rich spring leaf tints combine prettily with forget-me-nots and make a fine setting for gold foliage and bright spring bulbs, especially crown imperials and tulips.

Alstroemeria 'Apollo', *Aquilegia vulgaris* (mixed), *Chionodoxa forbesii* p.308 **A**, *Iris* 'Jane Phillips', *Papaver orientale* 'Black and White', *Rosa* 'Charles de Mills'

H: 75–90cm (30–36in) S: 60cm (24in)
Early to mid-summer

Z6 pH5.5–7.5

In early summer, the rose-pink blooms of *Paeonia lactiflora* 'Albert Crousse' harmonize closely, both in color and floral form, with those of *Rosa* Gertrude Jekyll. Upright alliums in purplish mauve (*Allium aflatunense* and the taller *A. giganteum*) add contrast of form, their ramrod stems providing repeated vertical accents, while distant dark foliage gives depth to the perspective.

Carmine *Paeonia lactiflora* 'Auguste Dessert' is here daringly juxtaposed with yellow loosestrife (*Lysimachia punctata*). Although the contrast of form certainly succeeds, some gardeners might prefer to achieve it with spires of a more harmonious color, using perhaps a lupine or delphinium that would also blend agreeably with pale pink *P.l.* 'Noemi Demay' behind.

Paeonia lactiflora 'Auguste Dessert'

One of the most pleasing cultivars of this glorious and highly variable species, 'Auguste Dessert' has deep green foliage that assumes crimson tints in autumn, and vivid carmine flowers, shaded rose-pink and edged with silvery white. Its floral form resembles that of many old roses, with which it can produce attractive harmonies, but it is even more outstanding when contrasted with rose cultivars of distinctly different flower size, color, or form. The hint of blue in its coloring makes white too stark a contrast, but the shade suits combinations with cool colors – especially purple, crimson, and magenta – or contrasts with yellow-green or soft yellow, such as euphorbias or achilleas. Other fine partners include larger pinks such as *Dianthus* Devon Series, dictamnus, mauve-pink campanulas, cranesbills, centaureas, thalictrums, Tall Bearded irises, and alchemillas. Like all double peonies, the full blooms are heavy, especially after rain, and plants benefit from a wire hoop support.

◐ *Centaurea montana*, *Delphinium* 'Bruce', *Dictamnus albus* var. *purpureus*, *Lupinus* 'Thundercloud', *Potentilla fruticosa* 'Primrose Beauty', *Rosa* 'Complicata'

H & S: 75cm (30in) ✿ **Early to mid-summer**
◊◊ ☐-■ ■ Z5 pH5.5–7.5

Paeonia mlokosewitschii ♛
MOLLY THE WITCH

This is an outstanding herbaceous peony, with downy greyish green foliage that remains handsome throughout the summer. It has a relatively short flowering season, but its soft yellow blooms with their golden anthers are superlative, combining particularly well with warm-colored flowers, such as early yellow and cream roses, wallflowers, geums, columbines, brooms, chaenomeles, kerrias, and *Potentilla fruticosa* cultivars. It makes satisfying harmonies with yellow-green foliage and flowers, including euphorbias, perfoliate alexanders, golden millet grass, yellow-green sedges, and early-leafing hostas, as well as glaucous plants like dicentras. For contrast it can be partnered with blue flowers, such as brunneras, omphalodes, and forget-me-nots.

◐ *Brunnera macrophylla*, *Carex elata* 'Aurea', *Cytisus* × *praecox* 'Warminster', *Dicentra eximia*, *Kerria japonica* 'Picta', *Rosa* 'Helen Knight' p.157 **A**

H & S: 75cm (30in) ✿ **Late spring**
◊◊ ☐-■ ■ Z5 pH5.5–7.5

In this delightful, late spring planting arrangement, soft yellow *Paeonia mlokosewitschii* sits companionably with the moisture-loving *Euphorbia palustris* behind, while the dark blue Tall Bearded iris in front makes a subtle contrast.

Double-flowered *Papaver* 'Fireball' is here combined with the yellow-green leaves of golden feverfew (*Tanacetum parthenium* 'Aureum'), lemon Welsh poppies (*Meconopsis cambrica*), and yellow and red columbines. In a slightly less sunny site, the fading of 'Fireball' from vermilion to salmon might be lessened and the effect improved.

Papaver 'Fireball'

A hybrid of the Oriental poppy, 'Fireball' has informal double flowers that open vermilion and age (in sunny sites and warm climates) to salmon-pink. These colors allow it to mix well with flowers in warm tints such as peach, salmon, or apricot; however, in areas where it does fade, association with hot colors can make it seem jaded by comparison. Effective partners include geums, columbines, *Potentilla fruticosa* cultivars, Dwarf and Intermediate Bearded irises, and bronze foliage plants such as heucheras, bronze sedges, and *Berberis thunbergii* cultivars. This herbaceous plant produces stems from a running rootstock that can be invasive in its preferred sharply drained conditions. It needs a situation where its roots can spread without overwhelming its neighbors, and this, together with its slightly ragged and informal charm, suits it to a cottage garden style of planting.

◐ *Aquilegia canadensis*, *Berberis thunbergii* 'Rose Glow', *Carex comans* (bronze), *Geum* 'Coppertone', *Iris* 'Golden Muffin', *Potentilla fruticosa* 'Sunset'

H & S: 30cm (12in)
✿ **Late spring to early summer**
◊-◊◊ ☐-■ ■ Z4 pH5.5–7.5

Papaver orientale cultivars

Garden hybrids of the Oriental poppy vary in height from 60 to 150cm (2–5ft), and may be any shade between white, vermilion, blood-red, and crimson. A few have double flowers, and these bloom for slightly longer, but they lack the charming simplicity of the single flowers. All can be grown in herbaceous or mixed borders and gravel gardens, ideally set in front of companions of their own height so that the leaves at the base of the plants get plenty of sunlight. Their spectacular glistening blooms, often marked with an attractive dark basal blotch, appear before most other summer flowers, but plants have a tendency to die back after flowering, leaving an awkward gap in borders. One solution is to plant poppies in drifts, flanked by annuals or summer bedding plants that later grow into the vacant space: dahlias, nicotianas, argyranthemums, osteospermums, and cosmos are all suitable for this purpose.

The more intense poppy colors are suited to hot schemes with, for example, columbines, lupines, wallflowers, Bearded irises, and early alstroemerias, and for contrasts with yellow-green foliage and flowers. Those tending towards orange contrast effectively with blue flowers such as delphiniums and baptisias, while white-flowered cultivars combine well with silver, bronze, or purple foliage plants. Cultivars with salmon flowers can be combined with warm tints such as peach and apricot, while those in the color range mauve-pink to carmine blend pleasantly with cool colors. All are good with roses, brooms, and tree peonies.

Above: Along the length of a narrow border beside a gravel path, the extravagantly ruffled salmon flowers of *Papaver orientale* 'Prinz Eugen' are joined by the lilac blooms of sweet rocket (*Hesperis nationalis*).

Above left: In an eye-catching early summer combination, the scarlet black-blotched flowers of *Papaver orientale* 'Avebury Crimson' are contrasted with the gentian-blue flowers of a compact *Anchusa azurea* cultivar.

◉ *Alstroemeria ligtu* hybrids, *Campanula* 'Burghaltii' p.199 **B**, *Delphinium* 'Alice Artindale', *Iris* 'Symphony' p.322 **A**, *Lupinus* 'The Governor'

H: 60–150cm (2–5ft) S: 45–90cm (18–36in)
✽ **Late spring to mid-summer**
◐ ◌-◌◌ ◻-◼ Z4 pH5.5–7.5

In this striking partnership that will last into the autumn, the acidic, slightly greenish yellow blooms of *Patrinia scabiosifolia* are set off by the purple-flowered *Verbena bonariensis*, both plants of similar branching growth habit.

Patrinia scabiosifolia

This elegant herbaceous perennial, valuable for providing late flower color, has deeply divided leaves and loose, airy heads of small yellow flowers, tinted slightly with green. It makes a fairly narrow plant that is useful for weaving in drifts through herbaceous or mixed borders, where it can harmonize with hot colors such as orange, yellow, and scarlet, and with yellow or yellow-green plants, especially late-flowering euphorbias, larger hostas with yellow-green or gold-variegated leaves, and yellow-variegated grasses such as miscanthus or cortaderia cultivars. Effective contrasts can be made with blue or rich purple, using late aconitums for example, and with the quite different form of late-flowering daisies in hot colors, including heleniums, rudbeckias, and helianthus. It is particularly successful combined with salvias, dahlias, and many other late-flowering tender perennials used as bedding plants.

◉ *Aconitum napellus*, *Cortaderia selloana* 'Aureolineata', *Crocosmia* × *crocosmiiflora* 'Lady Hamilton', *Euphorbia schillingii*, *Helenium* 'Septemberfuchs'

H: 90cm (36in) S: 45cm (18in)
✽ **Late summer to mid-autumn**
 ◌◌ ◻-◼ ◼ Z6 pH5.5–7.5

The brick-red flower spikes of *Persicaria amplexicaulis* harmonize with sprays of burnt orange montbretia (*Crocosmia* × *crocosmiiflora*) in late summer.

Persicaria amplexicaulis

The flowers of this moisture-loving knotweed (syn. *Polygonum amplexicaule*) are a slightly muddy brick-red, and appear prolifically in sunny sites. Although unsatisfactory with clear pink or with strong, hot colors, they work well with salmon, peach, or burnt orange and with bronze foliage, and may be contrasted with yellow-green foliage or flowers. With its rather divergent flower stems and slightly coarse leaves, the plant is most at home in informal, waterside or bog gardens. It is best combined with plants of bold form – rodgersias, ligularias, or white-flowered hostas, for example – or with contrasting foliage such as that of grasses, ferns, and crocosmias. 'Firetail' ♡ has brighter red flowers, and 'Inverleith' is a rich deep red. The flowers attract wasps, so planting near sitting areas should be avoided.

◉ *Euphorbia schillingii*, *Hosta* 'Honeybells', *Ligularia dentata* 'Desdemona', *Phalaris arundinacea* var. *picta* 'Feesey', *Rodgersia pinnata* 'Elegans'

H: 30–120cm (12–48in) S: 45–120cm (18–48in)
❊ Mid-summer to early autumn

◖▮▮▯▯ ◊◊·◊◊◊ ▢-▮ ▮ Z5 pH5–7.5

Phalaris arundinacea var. *picta* 'Picta' ♡

RIBBON GRASS

This is a bright, variegated grass of medium size. The stripes in the leaves carry a hint of cream, which enhances their appearance when grown among plants with yellow, apricot, or peach-colored flowers.

There are a number of other similar variegated clones. 'Aureovariegata' and 'Luteovariegata' are both more yellow; the leaves of 'Tricolor' have a distinct pink flush for combining with purple foliage and pink, red, or mauve flowers; 'Feesey' is shorter, brighter with a faint pink flush, and less invasive. Plants are best in moist, rich situations: in poor or dry soil in the sun, the foliage can become unkempt in summer.

◉ *Achillea* 'Lachsschönheit', *Crocosmia* × *crocosmiiflora* 'Solfatare', *Cynara cardunculus* p.208 **A**, *Hemerocallis fulva*, *Tulipa* 'Ballerina' p.344 **B**

H: 75–100cm (30–40in) S: 1m (40in)
❊ Late spring to early summer

◖▮▮▯▯ ◊◊ ▢-▮ ▮ Z4 pH5–7.5

The bright variegation of *Phalaris arundinacea* var. *picta* 'Picta' contrasts boldly with the dark foliage of *Berberis thunbergii* 'Rose Glow'. Behind, carmine *Clematis* 'Madame Julia Correvon' harmonizes with the berberis.

This selection of *Phlomis russeliana* has flowers of clear yellow, rather than brownish buff, which make a fine contrast with lavender-blue flowers such as those of the catmint *Nepeta sibirica*. The phlomis is sufficiently strongly colored to be seen against a background of the harmonious cream variegation of the privet *Ligustrum ovalifolium* 'Argenteum'.

Phlomis russeliana ♡

This variable species has handsome leaves – mid-green and long, with a heart-shaped base – and hooded flowers that can range from almost pure light yellow to fawn. They are born in dense whorls on upright stems, producing a distinct rhythm and pattern when plants are grown in large groups. This is the best way to make an impact because single specimens tend to have too few flowers to be effective. The color is not usually bright enough to withstand association with fiery reds, oranges, and golds, but it is very good with warm hues such as soft yellow, apricot, peach, and cream, as well as with yellow-green flowers or foliage.

Since the species varies in the number of flowers it bears, it is best to obtain plants from a clone of known quality. Plants can tolerate some shade, although they produce more flowers when in full sun.

◉ *Cornus alba* 'Spaethii', *Cytisus* × *kewensis*, *Digitalis purpurea* f. *albiflora*, *Euphorbia characias* subsp. *wulfenii*, *Geranium sanguineum* var. *striatum*, × *Halimiocistus wintonensis* 'Merrist Wood Cream'

H: 90cm (36in) S: 75cm (30in)
❊ Late spring to early autumn

◖▮▮▯▯ ◊ ▢-▮ ▮ Z4 pH5.5–7.5

Phlox divaricata subsp. *laphamii* 'Chattahoochee' ♔

With its purple-tinted stems and long, prolific display of lavender flowers with purplish red eyes, this prostrate plant is a good subject for growing with purple foliage – purple-leaved heucheras, for example – or with crimson, purple, mauve, or mauve-pink flowers. It is also valuable for planting under sparsely branched roses in these colors. It looks effective in a woodland garden, at the front of a border, and in containers, and makes a pretty carpeting plant, but it lacks definite form and would benefit from more structured partners such as green hostas with a narrow white leaf edge. The color is generally too delicate for bold contrasts, although it goes well with yellow-green foliage or flowers. Partial shade is the best aspect, but it will tolerate full sun where summers are cool. Plants are relatively short-lived, and very susceptible to slug damage.

◖ *Alchemilla mollis, Aquilegia canadensis, Cornus florida, Heuchera* 'Plum Pudding', *Hosta* 'Hydon Sunset' p.246 **A**, *Primula japonica, Rosa* 'Charles de Mills', *Symphytum* 'Goldsmith' p.289 **C**

H: 15cm (6in) **S: 30cm** (12in)
❀ **Late spring to early autumn**
◊◊-◊◊◊ ◻-◼ ◼ **Z4 pH5.5–7.5**

As the first blooms of *Phlox divaricata* subsp. *laphamii* 'Chattahoochee' open, they are set off by the salmon flowers and cream variegation of *Pulmonaria rubra* 'David Ward'.

Phlox maculata

WILD SWEET WILLIAM

This is an upright perennial with narrow, conical flowerheads, loosely branched in some cultivars, in colors from mauve to lilac. These shades are good with purple, white, crimson, or blue flowers and with purple foliage, and contrast well with sulfur- or lemon-yellow. There are several excellent cultivars: 'Alba' is white, 'Alpha' ♔ mauve, and 'Omega' ♔ white with a magenta eye. 'Natascha', slightly shorter than the species, has cylindrical spikes of white and pink striped flowers, a slightly busy scheme best at close range. 'Princess Sturdza' is one of the finest selections with a color between mauve and lilac. All are suitable for borders in sun or partial shade, and for waterside planting, although the flowers may look too bright and solid in informal sites unless the plants are scattered or sparsely grouped.

Although strong yellow and mauve can make an uneasy alliance, the slightly paler yellow daylily *Hemerocallis* 'Marion Vaughn' and *Phlox maculata*, here with teasel (*Dipsacus fullonum*), make a more pleasant contrast.

◖ *Achillea* 'Moonshine', *Atriplex hortensis* var. *rubra*, *Campanula latifolia* 'Brantwood', *Cotinus coggygria* 'Royal Purple', *Echinacea purpurea* p.213 **B**, *Lupinus* 'Polar Princess', *Macleaya cordata*

H: 90cm (36in) **S: 45cm** (18in)
❀ **Early to mid-summer**
◊◊-◊◊◊ ◻-◼ ◼ **Z4 pH5.5–7.5**

In mid-summer, the cream-variegated foliage of *Phlox paniculata* 'Norah Leigh' harmonizes with a white agapanthus, while its mauve-pink flowers blend happily with the Oriental hybrid lily *Lilium* 'Black Beauty' and the Regal pelargonium *P.* 'Pompeii', a cultivar that will bloom out of doors even in climates with barely warm summers.

Phlox paniculata 'Norah Leigh'

This perennial phlox is grown for its brilliant creamy white foliage rather than for its flowers, which are mauve-pink with magenta eyes. It is good in borders, placed a little forward so the leaves are clearly visible. This also benefits growth because, with so little green in the leaves, the plant's constitution is slightly weakened and it is less able to compete with its neighbors. The flower color restricts partners to crimson, purple, pink, mauve, or blue flowers and contrasting purple foliage; it tends to clash with yellows, oranges, scarlets, and yellow-green flowers or leaves. Other variegated cultivars include 'Pink Posie', in deeper pink, and 'Harlequin', in magenta-purple, both less brightly variegated and therefore a little more vigorous. It is essential to get stock free from stem nematode, which kills the lower leaves.

◐ *Campanula* 'Kent Belle', *Corylus maxima* 'Purpurea', *Geranium* × *oxonianum* 'Claridge Druce', *Heuchera* 'Plum Pudding', *Rosa* 'De Rescht'

H: 1m (40in) **S: 60cm** (24in)
✿ **Mid-summer to mid-autumn**

 ◊◊ ▨-■ **Z4 pH5.5–7.5**

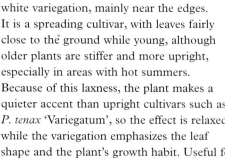

A pale blend of green and cream, *Phormium* 'Duet' and the scented pelargonium *P.* 'Lady Plymouth' make a good focal point for a container where subtle color is needed.

Phormium 'Bronze Baby'

The New Zealand flax (*Phormium tenax* ♀) is a dramatic plant, with upright, sword-like leaves. As one of its smallest cultivars, 'Bronze Baby' is useful as a focal point in smaller gardens or for containers. It is not as emphatic as larger phormiums, because of its size and also because it grows unevenly, with some leaves arching and others born at an angle. It is best used as a secondary accent, such as in a bedding scheme to echo a focal point provided by a larger purple phormium or a cordyline, and also as a contrast with paler foliage and flowers, especially in sky-blue or yellow-green. It is good with soft orange or peach, with hot colors such as scarlet, and with coral or apricot diascias. A loose group may be planted with carpeting plants such as red or purple verbenas or Million Bells Series petunias.

◐ *Diascia* 'Dark Eyes', *Phygelius* × *rectus* 'Pink Elf', *Potentilla fruticosa* 'Tangerine', *Skimmia japonica* 'Rubella', *Verbena* 'Lawrence Johnston'

H & S: 60cm (24in) ✿ **Mid-summer**

To produce a sumptuous effect at the height of the summer, in either a bed or a good-sized container, the richly colored *Phormium* 'Bronze Baby' can be planted through a carpet of flaming scarlet verbenas.

■■□ ◊◊-◊◊◊ ▨-■ **Z8 pH5–7.5**

Phormium 'Duet' ♀

The leaves of this phormium bear creamy white variegation, mainly near the edges. It is a spreading cultivar, with leaves fairly close to the ground while young, although older plants are stiffer and more upright, especially in areas with hot summers. Because of this laxness, the plant makes a quieter accent than upright cultivars such as *P. tenax* 'Variegatum', so the effect is relaxed, while the variegation emphasizes the leaf shape and the plant's growth habit. Useful for the front of a border or for growing in gravel, especially through a contrasting carpet of Tapien Series verbenas or purple bugleweeds, it combines well with paler blue flowers such as pimpernels, and with rich yellow or warm colors such as apricot and peach. It is more drought tolerant than *P. tenax* cultivars, but still needs adequate moisture to develop into impressive clumps.

◐ *Ajuga reptans* 'Atropurpurea', *Anagallis monellii*, *Hemerocallis* 'Golden Chimes', *Lysimachia nummularia* 'Aurea', *Verbena* Tapien Pink

H: 1m (3¼ft) **S: 1.2m** (4ft) ✿ **Mid-summer**

■■□ ◊◊-◊◊◊ ▨-■ **Z8 pH5–7.5**

Phormium tenax 'Veitchianum'

This variegated cultivar of the New Zealand flax (*Phormium tenax*) is extremely spiky, and therefore suitable for the most emphatic accents or focal points. With the broad, creamy yellow stripes on its dark green leaves, it is especially effective when used to contrast with plants with purple foliage, and when grown with strong blue flowers or in harmonies with gold or yellow-green. As with most other plants, the price of brighter variegation is reduced hardiness. *P.t.* 'Variegatum' ♀ has narrower creamy yellow stripes and is less striking (or less strident, depending on taste) than more brightly variegated clones, but it is hardier. Purple-flushed forms are also less hardy. Purpureum Group ♀ is recommended and has some variation in intensity of color; it harmonizes with flowers in hot colors and makes a fine contrast with yellow-green foliage.

⬤ *Bergenia cordifolia* 'Purpurea', *Penstemon* 'Andenken an Friedrich Hahn' p.394 **B**, *Pittosporum tenuifolium* 'Purpureum', *Verbena* Tapien Violet

H: 2.5m (8ft) S: 1.8m (6ft) ✿ **Mid-summer**
◊◊-◊◊◊ ⬜-■ **Z7 pH5–7.5**

In this striking combination relying on foliage effect alone, the creamy yellow striped leaves of *Phormium tenax* 'Veitchianum' make a bold statement between dark-leaved cannas and *Berberis* × *ottawensis* f. *purpurea* 'Superba'.

Jacob's ladder (*Polemonium caeruleum*) contrasts with *Spiraea japonica* 'Gold Mound', accompanied by black pansies, achilleas, and wood forget-me-nots (*Myosotis sylvatica*) in a charming incident that could be equally effective used on a larger scale.

Polemonium caeruleum

JACOB'S LADDER

The flowers of this easy herbaceous perennial have cool campanula-blue petals and orange anthers. They form effective contrasts with soft yellow flowers and yellow-green flowers or foliage, and harmonize with mauve or purple flowers or silver foliage. Garden forms are usually about 40cm (16in) tall, suiting them to the front rows of a border. They can seem rather leafy and a little coarse, and are best used in more informal parts of the garden. Other polemoniums of merit include subsp. *caeruleum* f. *album*, with pure white flowers prolonged by deadheading (which also prevents self-seeding), and *P. foliosissimum* subsp. *foliosissimum*, which is soft lavender, flowers longer, and is self-sterile so seeding is not a problem.

⬤ *Achillea* 'Moonshine', *Allium cristophii*, *Artemisia schmidtiana*, *Euphorbia characias* subsp. *wulfenii*, *Stachys byzantina* 'Silver Carpet'

H: 60cm (24in) S: 40cm (16in) ✿ **Early summer**
◊◊-◊◊◊ ⬜-■ **Z4 pH5–7.5**

In a lightly shaded site, the hedge fern (*Polystichum setiferum*) contrasts strongly in form with the sub-shrubby spurge *Euphorbia characias*. This is a simple but striking combination that needs no color other than green.

Polystichum setiferum ♔

SOFT SHIELD FERN

An elegant evergreen that tolerates a wide range of conditions, including dry shade, this is a valuable fern for use in woodland and rock gardens, at the front of borders, and in small city gardens, where its intricate foliage repays close inspection. The soft fronds are bright green and arranged like a shuttlecock, with dense brown scales on the stems and leaf buds. There are several cultivars, all of which grow successfully through low ground covers such as acaenas, bugleweeds, or small spreading ivies, or with ferns of contrasting form – hart's tongues, for example. Among the most attractive variants are Acutilobum Group, with erect fronds and wedge-shaped pinnules; Congestum Group, with attractive overlapping pinnae; lacy Divisilobum Group and crested 'Divisilobum Iveryanum' ♔; and the very feathery Plumosodivisilobum Group. 'Pulcherrimum Bevis' ♔ is tall and bold, with handsome, evenly spaced fronds.

◐ *Acaena saccaticupula* 'Blue Haze', *Ajuga reptans* 'Catlin's Giant', *Arisaema erubescens* p.306 **A**, *Convallaria majalis* p.204 **A**, *Macleaya microcarpa* p.263 **A**

H: 60–120cm (24–48in) S: 45–90cm (18–36in)
 Z5 pH4.5–7.5

Potentilla 'Etna'

This remarkable clump-forming plant has mid- to dark green leaves overlaid with silver hairs, and sprawling stems bearing semi-double, blood-red flowers, a color so deep that it is scarcely visible from a distance. It is most effective against a lighter background, such as silver or yellow-green foliage or paler flowers, in hot yellow or orange, or warm peach, apricot, and rich salmon. At the front of a border, it can trail over carpeting plants such as variegated ivies, acaenas, or golden creeping Jenny, or scramble into a small glaucous hebe, hypericum, or phygelius. It mixes well with violas, pinks, and zinnias, alchemillas, tagetes, smaller pelargoniums, coleus, and California poppies, and with plants of similar habit, such as nasturtiums, bidens, and *Helichrysum petiolare* cultivars.

◐ *Artemisia ludoviciana* 'Silver Queen', *Berberis thunbergii* 'Aurea', *Hebe* 'Red Edge', *Hedera helix* 'Glacier', *Phygelius × rectus* 'Pink Elf'

H: 45cm (18in) S: 60cm (24in)
✿ Early to late summer

 Z5 pH5–7.5

Against a background of dark foliage, blood-red *Potentilla* 'Etna' scrambles forwards across the floriferous seed-raised *Viola* 'Prince John', whose bright yellow blooms highlight those of the potentilla.

In two colors that lie to either side of primary deep pink, coral *Potentilla nepalensis* 'Miss Willmott' and soft magenta *Stachys macrantha* 'Superba' contrast gently, the potentilla scrambling around, into, and over its companion.

Potentilla nepalensis 'Miss Willmott' ♔

This clump-forming perennial makes a looser plant than *P.* 'Etna' (above), and its flowers vary from salmon-pink to deeper cherry-pink. It is just as effective trailing over other plants at the front of a border, although its color is more telling from a distance. Its flowers combine well with warm tints such as peach and apricot, and with purple foliage plants like dark-leaved heucheras. It can be contrasted with yellow-green flowers, but not large areas of yellow-green, which would tend to overwhelm it. Good partners are diascias, soft orange or ruby-red violas, smaller purple- or bronze-leaved shrubs such as *Berberis thunbergii* cultivars, and silver foliage plants, including *Senecio viravira* and *Helichrysum petiolare* cultivars. For dramatic effect, it can be trained into low-growing roses of significantly different color, such as very pale pink or rich red.

◐ *Berberis thunbergii* 'Atropurpurea Nana', *Diascia barberae* 'Blackthorn Apricot', *Heuchera micrantha* var. *diversifolia* 'Palace Purple', *Rosa* 'Europeana'

H: 45cm (18in) S: 60cm (24in)
✿ Early to late summer

Z5 pH5–7.5

Primula elatior ♀

OXLIP

Like its cousin *P. vulgaris*, the common primrose, this charming herbaceous perennial tolerates heavy soils and wet conditions. It is suitable for naturalizing in grass or in sunny glades in a woodland garden, as well as more subdued plantings at the front of a border. It combines well with white, blue, or yellow flowers, and also blends attractively with warm-colored tints such as peach and apricot. It can be naturalized with lady's smock, pasque flowers, and smaller narcissi, including jonquils if the site is very moist. In less natural settings it looks attractive with

In this pleasant mixture naturalized in long grass, soft yellow oxlips (*Primula elatior*) are joined by the distinctive purple checkered blooms of checker lily (*Fritillaria meleagris*) and white *F.m.* var. *unicolor* subvar. *alba*, along with a semi-wild, self-seeded pink polyanthus.

such spring plants as brunneras, omphalodes, wood anemones, muscaris, and forget-me-nots, and with foliage of contrasting form, particularly yellow-green grasses and sedges.

◐ *Anemone nemorosa* 'Allenii', *Cardamine pratensis*, *Milium effusum* 'Aureum', *Narcissus* 'Sun Disc', *Omphalodes cappadocica*, *Pulsatilla vulgaris*

H: 30cm (12in) **S:** 25cm (10in)
❋ **Mid-spring to early summer**

◊◊ ☐-■ ■ Z5 pH5.5–8

Primula 'Guinevere' ♀

One of the older cultivars of polyanthus, this is a herbaceous perennial with dark foliage and freely born pink flowers, which looks most attractive at the front of a border. As it tolerates some shade, especially in summer when it is relatively dormant, it may also be used for a ground cover between deciduous shrubs such as shrub or bedding roses. It blends well with cool colors such as blue, mauve, deeper pink, crimson, and white, and purple or red-flushed foliage. Its flower color is strong enough to contrast effectively with yellow-green flowers such as early euphorbias, and can hold its own in a ground-cover carpet of other primroses and polyanthus in distinctly different colors, such as rich magenta-purple. Good companions include pulmonarias, epimediums, cardamines, corydalis, and hellebores, and bulbs such as muscaris, scillas, ipheions, checker lilies, and smaller white narcissi.

The smoky bronze foliage and soft pink flowers of *Primula* 'Guinevere' harmonize with the dainty blue blooms and feathery leaves of *Corydalis flexuosa*.

◐ *Euphorbia polychroma* 'Major', *Heuchera micrantha* var. *diversifolia* 'Palace Purple', *Primula* 'Wanda', *Pulmonaria saccharata*, *Scilla siberica*

H: 15cm (6in) **S:** 20cm (8in) ❋ **Early to late spring**

◊◊ ☐-■ ■ Z5 pH5.5–7.5

Growing in moist ground, the warm colors of *Primula* Inshriach hybrids blend agreeably with the bronze leaves and vermilion bracts of *Euphorbia griffithii* behind.

Primula Inshriach hybrids

These are herbaceous perennial Candelabra primulas, available mainly in colors that range from yellow through orange to scarlet, together with paler tones such as apricot and coral-pink. All blend well with warm colors, bronze foliage, and white or yellow-green flowers. They thrive in waterside positions, in bog or woodland gardens, and in very moist borders, where they can associate with bronze rodgersias, yellow or white moisture-loving irises, yellow-green hostas, *Euphorbia griffithii* cultivars, and the contrasting foliage of stenanthiums, veratrums, and yellow-green or bronze moisture-loving ferns and sedges. Other good partners include early-flowering astilbes, ligularias, gold-variegated or yellow-green leaved dogwoods, and Sikkimensis primulas that have a contrasting floral form.

◐ *Carex elata* 'Aurea', *Cornus alba* 'Spaethii', *Iris orientalis*, *Matteuccia struthiopteris*, *Primula sikkimensis*, *Rodgersia pinnata* 'Superba', *Veratrum nigrum*

H: 75cm (30in) **S:** 45cm (18in)
❋ **Late spring to early summer**

◊◊ ☐-■ ■ Z6 pH5–7.5

Primula japonica ♀

With its tiers of flowers in purplish red to white, this Candelabra primula is superb for naturalizing in a bog garden, beside water, or in dappled shade. It combines best with pink, crimson, and purple flowers, purple-leaved plants, and the contrasting foliage of Siberian or *Laevigatae* irises, sedges, grasses, and ferns. Yellowish green spring foliage, such as the fronds of ostrich ferns, makes a good contrast. While the plant mixes well with other primulas such as polyanthus and primroses, hybrids may result from association with fellow Candelabras, possibly marring color schemes. 'Miller's Crimson' is richly hued with deep crimson eyes; 'Postford White' has florets with carmine eyes and is excellent for delicately colored plantings.

● *Astilbe × arendsii* 'Venus', *Dryopteris affinis*, *Iris ensata* cultivars, *I.* 'Cambridge', *Ligularia dentata* 'Othello', *Molinia caerulea* 'Variegata'

H & S: 45cm (18in)
✿ **Late spring to early summer**
▬▬▬ ◊◊◊ ☐-■ ■ Z6 pH5–7.5

In this streamside planting through a woodland glade, soft crimson *Primula japonica* stands above a carpet of *Phlox divaricata* in cool lavender, growing in moist ground by the water's edge.

Primula 'Rowallane Rose'

This Candelabra primula, producing rich salmon flowers with a yellow eye, thrives in waterside or bog gardens and other similarly moist situations. It looks most attractive with soft orange, salmon, or peach companions, with soft yellow flowers such as those of geums and deciduous azaleas, and with bronze foliage. For contrast it may be planted with grasses, including those with yellow-green leaves, and yellow-green or yellow-variegated hostas.

'Rowallane Rose' is a sterile hybrid that needs propagating by division. 'Inverewe' ♀ (syns 'Keillour Copper' and 'Ravenglass

In a warm-colored waterside arrangement, the rich salmon candelabra of *Primula* 'Rowallane Rose' rises over the soft yellow-edged leaves of *Hosta fortunei* var. *aureomarginata*, both plants supplying strong architectural form.

Vermilion') is also sterile, with dark flower stems 60cm (24in) tall, and intense vermilion flowers that make it suitable for hot color schemes or combinations with bronze foliage.

● *Carex comans* (bronze), *Geum* 'Lady Stratheden', *Hakonechloa macra* 'Alboaurea', *Ligularia dentata* 'Desdemona', *Rhododendron* 'Narcissiflorum'

H & S: 45cm (18in)
✿ **Late spring to early summer**

▬▬▬ ◊◊◊ ☐-■ ■ Z6 pH5–7.5

Primula veris ♔
COWSLIP

The rich yellow petals of cowslip flowers emerge from pale apple-green calyces, suggesting harmonies with other apple-green flowers such as *Helleborus × sternii* and some selections from *H. × hybridus*. Plants may be naturalized in grass (which should not be cut until the cowslip has shed its seeds), in borders in a wild garden, or in light, dappled shade in woodland. Here it is effective with blue flowers such as forget-me-nots, omphalodes, or brunneras, and with other primulas such as primroses. It harmonizes with glaucous-leaved plants, and with yellow-green foliage, although this might camouflage the cowslip so the two are best separated with a contrasting plant. It combines well with hot colors, but bold or sophisticated displays can overwhelm its modest charm.

⬤ *Brunnera macrophylla*, *Dicentra eximia*, *Hyacinthoides hispanica*, *Omphalodes cappadocica*, *Primula vulgaris* subsp. *sibthorpii*, *Pulmonaria angustifolia*

H & S: 25cm (10in) ❀ **Mid-spring to early summer**
◊◊ ☐-■ ■ Z5 pH6–8

At the edge of a border, cowslips (*Primula veris*) are contrasted with wood forget-me-nots (*Myosotis sylvatica*), while the yellow-green leaved *Philadelphus coronarius* 'Aureus' behind harmonizes with the cowslips.

Pulmonaria 'Lewis Palmer' ♔

One of the showiest lungworts, 'Lewis Palmer' (syn. 'Highdown') has flowers that open dusky carmine touched with purple, aging to rich blue, and leaves lightly spotted with silver-green. Growing best in full spring sunshine, with light shade in summer, it is effective in woodland gardens and semi-shady borders, and as a ground cover under late-leafing deciduous shrubs, such as *Hibiscus syriacus*, that do not hide the flowers. It contrasts well with soft yellow or yellow-green flowers, and with golden grassy foliage such as golden millet grass and Bowles' golden sedge, and it harmonizes with ferns, early-leafing hostas, and white or sulfur narcissi.

⬤ *Carex elata* 'Aurea', *Hosta fortunei* var. *albopicta* f. *aurea*, *Milium effusum* 'Aureum', *Narcissus* 'Tête-à-tête' p.337 **A**, *Rhododendron* Cilpinense Group p.82 **B**

H: 35cm (14in) S: 25cm (10in)
❀ **Early to mid-spring**
◊◊-◊◊◊ ☐-■ ■ Z5 pH5–7.5

In a sumptuous but cool-colored combination for moist, humus-rich soil, *Pulmonaria* 'Lewis Palmer' is set against the glowing crimson winter heath, *Erica carnea* 'Myretoun Ruby'.

Pulmonaria saccharata
BETHLEHEM SAGE

The flowers of this lungwort open pink and mature to blue, over leaves that are spotted with silvery green. The mix of pink and blue in the flowers prevents satisfying contrasts with yellow or yellow-green, but it works well with blue, pink, crimson, purple, or white flowers, and with purple or glaucous foliage. It is a good partner for polyanthus and primroses in these colors, and for foliage of contrasting form, such as grasses and ferns. Like all lungworts, it prefers spring sun, with dappled shade in summer, and is suitable for a woodland garden or for planting under late-leafing deciduous shrubs. The silvery leaf spots coalesce in Argentea Group ♔, the best clones of which have leaves that are entirely silvery green. 'Alba' has pure white flowers.

⬤ *Anemone nemorosa* 'Leeds' Variety', *Bergenia cordifolia* 'Purpurea', *Corydalis flexuosa* 'Purple Leaf', *Dicentra eximia*, *Erythronium californicum* 'White Beauty', *Primula* 'Guinevere', *P.* 'Tawny Port'

H: 30cm (12in) S: 60cm (24in)
❀ **Early to late spring**
◊◊-◊◊◊ ☐-■ ■ Z4 pH5–7.5

If cut back after flowering in spring, Bethlehem sage (*Pulmonaria saccharata*) will bear handsome, healthy foliage into the autumn. Here, it forms a carpet for the scrambling, herbaceous *Clematis × jouiniana* 'Praecox', whose milk-white blooms in late summer create a pleasing pattern with the spots on the pulmonaria's leaves.

Standing prominently at the edge of a bed, in front of a carpet of pure blue *Ceratostigma willmottianum* and a sentinel clump of New Zealand flax (*Phormium tenax*), the exotic trumpets of *Rehmannia elata* mingle with racemes of the smaller, paler pink blooms of *Diascia rigescens*.

Rehmannia elata

The large, showy flowers of this rehmannia, appearing in early summer, resemble those of incarvilleas, and are rich carmine-pink tending towards magenta, with yellow markings in the throat. Most attractive with cool colors and purple foliage, they also contrast well with soft yellow or yellow-green. They are superb in semi-tropical plantings, and good partners for flowers of contrasting form, such as pink gypsophilas, thalictrums, and purple salvias that produce flowers in a spike. Although the woody stems are relatively tender, plants grow again readily from shoots produced from the rootstock, provided the cold does not penetrate too deeply into the soil. If plants are seriously injured by frost, flowering may be delayed until late summer. Where the rootstock is likely to become frozen in winter, plants are best treated as annuals for summer display.

Eryngium × *tripartitum* p.217 **C**, *Gypsophila* 'Rosenschleier', *Nigella damascena* p.390 **B**, *Rosa* 'Yesterday' p.167 **B**, *Salvia nemorosa* 'Ostfriesland'

H: 60cm (24in) **S: 45cm** (18in)
Early to late summer
Z9 pH5.5–7.5

Rodgersia pinnata

This rhizomatous herbaceous perennial is a superb plant for watersides and bog gardens, although it will tolerate any border soil that does not dry out. It has handsome pinnate foliage and pyramidal panicles of flowers in yellowish white, pink, or red, later developing mahogany-red seedheads that remain decorative into autumn. It is an attractive plant that can complement pink and crimson flowers, and pink- or red-flowered sorts may be contrasted with yellow-green flowers such as late euphorbias. Good partners include filipendulas, persicarias, lilies, and perennial lobelias, cannas, later-blooming monardas, and contrasting foliage such as grasses and ferns. 'Alba' is yellowish white; 'Buckland Beauty' is rosy-red; 'Elegans' has sweet-scented, creamy white flowers; and 'Superba' ♈ is relatively tall, with red-flushed leaves and bright pink flowers.

Hosta 'Buckshaw Blue' p.243 **B**, *Lilium speciosum*, *Lobelia* 'Queen Victoria', *Mimulus cardinalis*, *Monarda* 'Beauty of Cobham', *Persicaria amplexicaulis*

H: 90–120cm (36–48in) **S: 60–75cm** (24–30in)
Mid- to late summer
Z5 pH5–7.5

Ferns are classic partners for rodgersias, liking similar conditions and providing an effective contrast of form. In this moist, semi-shady bed, the bold leaves of *Rodgersia pinnata* surround the base of wood fern (*Dryopteris affinis*), its orange-tinged fronds just unfurling.

Grasses, like ferns, provide a telling contrast of form with rodgersias. Here, the bronze-flushed palmate foliage of *Rodgersia podophylla* is joined by the elegant cream-striped *Miscanthus sinensis* 'Variegatus'.

Rodgersia podophylla ♈

This rodgersia is a rhizomatous herbaceous perennial that thrives in the same conditions as *R. pinnata* (above), preferring damp or moist sites but tolerating any position as long as the soil does not dry out completely. It produces panicles of greenish cream flowers that suit combinations with warm tints and yellow-green foliage and flowers. Its handsome palmate leaves, usually with five leaflets, are bronze when young, maturing to green, and later providing bright reddish bronze autumn tints that harmonize successfully with a whole range of late-coloring trees and shrubs, including maples, linderas, aronias, clethras, and stephanandras, as well as deciduous berberis, euonymus, and azaleas, smoke bush, kirengeshomas, sumacs, and autumn-coloring grasses.

Acer palmatum 'Ôsakazuki', *Deschampsia cespitosa*, *Dryopteris affinis* p.213 **A**, *Euphorbia schillingii*, *Kirengeshoma palmata*, *Rhododendron luteum*

H: 90–150cm (3–5ft) **S: 60–75cm** (24–30in)
Early to late summer
Z5 pH5–7.5

Roscoea cautleyoides ♔

This exotic-looking relative of ginger is a tuberous herbaceous perennial, with white, yellow, or magenta-purple flowers. Although it will tolerate full sun in areas where summers are cool, it generally prefers humus-rich soil, good drainage, and some shade, and so makes an excellent plant for woodland gardens, partially shaded rockeries, and shady borders. The commonest variant is 'Kew Beauty', with large, pale creamy yellow flowers that suit combinations with flowers in warm tints, stronger yellows, yellow-green, or white, and yellow-green or gold-variegated foliage. It is particularly attractive grown with ferns, smaller sedges, grasses, and hostas (especially purple-flowered cultivars), later-flowering woodland plants including patrinias, and later-flowering lilies, as long as these are not too strongly colored. Good magenta-purple selections are available, including 'Early Purple' and 'Purple Giant'.

◐ *Acer palmatum* var. *dissectum, Carex siderosticha* 'Variegata', *Dryopteris affinis, Hosta* 'Ginko Craig', *Lilium regale, Meconopsis betonicifolia, Molinia caerulea* 'Variegata', *Patrinia triloba* var. *palmata*

H: 45cm (18in) S: 30cm (12in)
❁ **Early to mid-summer**

◊◊ ▦-▪ **Z6 pH5–7.5**

In a semi-shaded bed of moist, humus-rich soil in early summer, the soft, creamy yellow, orchid-like blooms of *Roscoea cautleyoides* contrast in size, shape, and color with the striking blue flowers of *Corydalis flexuosa*. A shady rock garden also makes a good home for roscoea.

The combination of black-eyed Susan (*Rudbeckia fulgida* var. *deamii*) with a richly colored *Aster amellus* or *A. × frikartii* cultivar provides months of dramatically contrasting display, as here with *A.a.* 'King George'.

Rudbeckia fulgida var. *deamii* ♔

A strong rival to many of the showiest bedding plants, this clump-forming herbaceous perennial has neat growth and a long succession of prolific, bright golden yellow single daisy flowers, each with a mahogany-colored center. It is very useful for hot-colored schemes and contrasts with blue or purple, and also succeeds in the wild style of gardening with perennials and grasses planted in a naturalistic way in relatively nutrient-poor soil. It combines well with heleniums, daylilies, later-flowering crocosmias, dahlias, and other yellow daisies such as coreopsis, and looks outstanding with the contrasting foliage of larger grasses like *Miscanthus sinensis* cultivars. Effective with bronze shrubs and sedges, and yellow-green foliage and flowers such as nicotianas or feverfews, it can also be used with annuals – including larger tagetes, zinnias, and annual coreopsis – and with tender perennials like coleus, *Helichrysum petiolare* cultivars, argyranthemums, and osteospermums.

◐ *Aster novi-belgii* 'Marie Ballard' p.193 **B**, *Bidens ferulifolia, Crocosmia × crocosmiiflora* 'Lady Hamilton' p.207 **A**, *Hemerocallis fulva* 'Flore Pleno', *Nicotiana langsdorffii, Plectranthus argentatus* p.397 **A**, *Rudbeckia* 'Herbstsonne', *Zinnia* 'Chippendale'

H & S: 90cm (36in)
❁ **Late summer to mid-autumn**

◊◊ ▦-▪ **Z4 pH5.5–7.5**

Rudbeckia 'Herbstsonne'

Long-flowering and unusually tall, this herbaceous perennial is a good candidate for the widest herbaceous borders, mixed borders, and even shrubberies. Its rich yellow flowers with yellowish green centers blend well with hot-colored flowers and yellow-green, red, or bronze foliage, and create memorable contrasts with blue flowers such as echinops or aconitums. Suitable partners include taller heleniums, *Ceanothus* × *delileanus* cultivars, and larger *Miscanthus* cultivars, and shrubs with colored foliage such as smoke bush, deciduous dogwoods, philadelphus, hazels, physocarpus, or elderberries. It may be used imaginatively with pollarded trees with colored leaves – for example, poplars or catalpas kept to a comparable height by yearly pruning. Like many of the taller rudbeckias, the spreading rhizomes tolerate most moist soils as well as competition from other plants, making them an excellent choice for wildflower arrangements in tall, rough grass. There, they associate well with New York asters,

goldenrods, elecampanes, and eupatoriums to produce an exuberant late-season display. In a border, the imposing plants need staking, but can be made bushier by pinching out the flowering stems at the end of spring – this encourages profuse but slightly delayed flowering, and reduces the final height by 30–50cm (12–20in). *R. maxima* with drooping golden central cone is even taller at 2.7m (9ft) and may be shortened in the same way.

🌐 *Echinops bannaticus* 'Taplow Blue', *Nicotiana* 'Domino Red' p.389 **A**, *Populus alba* 'Richardii' (pollarded), *Sambucus nigra* 'Guincho Purple'

H: 2.2m (7ft) S: 90cm (3ft)
❀ **Mid-summer to early autumn**
▬▬▬ ◊◊ ▨-■ **Z5 pH5.5–7.5**

In this grouping from a border filled with hot-colored flowers, *Rudbeckia* 'Herbstsonne', with broad, reflexed, golden yellow petals surrounding a prominent green cone, is the tallest element of the display. The variegated dogwood (*Cornus alba* 'Spaethii'), here partly mutated to an all-gold sport, provides bulk to its left, while *Heliopsis helianthoides* var. *scabra* 'Spitzentänzerin' echoes the color of the rudbeckia at a shorter height, with a coppery helenium to its left.

At the height of summer, the violet flowers of *Salvia nemorosa* 'Lubecca', born on a 60cm (24in) plant, are surrounded at the base by a cushion of the delicate pink cranesbill, *Geranium sanguineum* var. *striatum*.

Salvia nemorosa

This variable herbaceous perennial has a narrow, upright growth habit that suits herbaceous and mixed borders, where its shape can be echoed by veronicas, delphiniums, and lupines, for example, and steeply sloped borders, perhaps set against the horizontal plates of achilleas and the diffuse flowers of crambes or thalictrums. It is also good for informal planting arrangements in the natural style, combined with grasses and daisy-like flowers such as rudbeckias on free-draining, fairly nutrient-poor soil. Its long, narrow racemes of flowers, usually mauve-pink to lavender-blue and emerging from dark calyces, harmonize with cool colors and purple foliage and contrast with soft yellow, particularly old shrub roses. Other suitable companions are silver-leaved artemisias, *Salvia officinalis* cultivars, campanulas, cranesbills, alchemillas, and Tall Bearded irises, biennials such as blue phlox, and early-flowering annuals like nigellas. Useful cultivars include 'Amethyst' ♀, violet 'Lubecca' ♀, and purple 'Ostfriesland' ♀.

🌐 *Achillea* 'Coronation Gold', *Delphinium* 'Sungleam', *Deschampsia cespitosa*, *Euphorbia seguieriana* subsp. *niciciana* p.221 **B**, *Rudbeckia fulgida* var. *deamii*

H: 45–90cm (18–36in) S: 45–60cm (18–24in)
❀ **Early summer to early autumn**
 ◊-◊◊ ▨-■ **Z5 pH5.5–7.5**

Salvia pratensis
MEADOW CLARY

The rather diffuse spikes of this lavender-blue herbaceous salvia make a good foil for larger flowers like roses or those with more solid blooms such as delphiniums. It naturalizes well with achilleas or can be used in open plantings with other hardy salvias, grasses, and daisy-like flowers. Haematodes Group ♥ has showy, pale lavender-blue flowers, mixing well with cool colors and silver or purple foliage, contrasting with soft yellow, and excellent with cranesbills, alchemillas, lavateras, eryngiums, and Tall Bearded irises. 'Indigo' ♥ has rich lavender blooms.

◑ *Alchemilla mollis*, *Anthriscus sylvestris* 'Ravenswing', *Artemisia* 'Powis Castle', *Delphinium* 'Butterball', *Eryngium alpinum*, *Iris* 'Nightfall', *Rosa* 'Buff Beauty', *Stipa tenuissima*, *Thalictrum flavum*

H: 75–100cm (30–40in) S: 45cm (18in)
❋ **Early to mid-summer**

 ◊◊ ▢-▨ **Z3–4 pH5.5–7.5**

The long-flowering, airy, lavender blooms of *Salvia pratensis* 'Indigo' provide a pleasant contrast, of both color and form, beneath the horizontal flower heads of *Achillea filipendulina* 'Gold Plate'.

In mid-summer, the richly colored flowers of *Salvia* × *superba* look striking beside the copper-red blooms of *Helenium* 'Moerheim Beauty'. Deadheading the salvia will encourage it to produce further flowers, prolonging the display.

Salvia × *superba* ♥

This hybrid species of herbaceous salvia has narrow spikes of lavender-blue flowers emerging from deep reddish purple calyces. Its upright growth habit is similar to that of *S. nemorosa* (facing page) and it may be used in the same situations, especially in borders where it can provide a useful leitmotif with other vertical plants along the border, or a contrast to horizontal flower heads or diffuse clouds of tiny blooms. The typical lavender-blue clone of the species, sometimes distinguished as *S.* × *s.* 'Superba', is sterile,

although many inferior plants are available as *S.* × *superba* raised from seed. Another superlative cultivar is *S.* × *s.* 'Rubin' ♥ which, at 75cm (30in) tall, is compact and bushy, and produces spikes of mauve-pink flowers emerging from purple calyces.

◑ *Achillea millefolium* 'Cerise Queen', *Echinacea purpurea*, *Eryngium* × *tripartitum* p.217 **B**, *Rudbeckia fulgida* var. *deamii*, *Thalictrum delavayi* 'Album', *Verbascum* (Cotswold Group) 'Gainsborough'

H: 60–90cm (24–36in) S: 45–60cm (18–24in)
❋ **Mid-summer to early autumn**

 ◊-◊◊ ▢-▨ **Z5 pH5.5–7.5**

Salvia × *sylvestris* 'Mainacht' ♥

An outstanding and floriferous herbaceous perennial, this salvia blooms about two weeks before *S.* × *superba* and *S. pratensis* and their variants (left), and therefore suits slightly different combinations with earlier-flowering shrubs and perennials in herbaceous and mixed borders. Its blooms are rich deep lavender-blue emerging from purplish black calyces, and it can be used with cool colors or contrasts with yellow or yellow-green. It combines well with moneyplant, sweet rocket, columbines, earlier cranesbills and peonies, early yellow Shrub roses, and day lilies, camassias, and Intermediate Bearded irises. Other good selections include the slightly lighter 'Blauhügel' ♥, and 'Tänzerin' ♥, with lavender flowers emerging from purple calyces – both in bloom a little later.

◑ *Aquilegia vulgaris* (mixed), *Camassia leichtlinii* 'Semiplena', *Geranium* × *oxonianum* 'A.T. Johnson', *Hemerocallis* 'Golden Chimes', *Hesperis matronalis* var. *albiflora*, *Lunaria annua* 'Variegata', *Paeonia lactiflora* 'Emperor of India', *Rosa* 'Maigold'

H: 60cm (24in) S: 30cm (12in) ❋ **Early summer**
◊◊ ▢-▨ **Z5 pH5.5–7.5**

The sumptuous dark blooms of *Salvia* × *sylvestris* 'Mainacht' harmonize perfectly with *Geranium* 'Kashmir Blue'. The near-black calyces remain attractive after flowering and should be left, rather than deadheaded.

In this display using bold form and primary colors, the nodding white flower heads of *Sanguisorba tenuifolia* 'Alba' are backed by the stiffly upright grass *Calamagrostis × acutiflora* 'Karl Foerster', with red *Papaver commutatum* 'Ladybird' and *Crocosmia masoniorum* 'Dixter Flame', blue *Campanula lactiflora*, and yellow *Oenothera biennis*.

Sanguisorba tenuifolia 'Alba'

This elegant herbaceous perennial bears white, drooping, almost catkin-like inflorescences, enhanced by their prominent anthers. It is a valuable component of white-flowered schemes, especially when combined with silver or glaucous foliage, but its color allows partnerships with almost any other. It looks most effective when grown in a naturalistic way, with artlessly arranged plants emerging from a carpet of smaller flowers – these could be annuals like nigellas and poppies, or perennials such as shorter catmints, salvias, and cranesbills, or the Little Princess Series of alstroemerias. Other good companions include artemisias, *Coreopsis verticillata* cultivars, later-flowering heucheras, and annuals such as taller ageratums, coreopsis, spring-sown nigellas, and clarkias.

Ⓖ *Artemisia ludoviciana*, *Clarkia amoena* Satin Series, *Geranium × oxonianum* 'Prestbury Blush', *Nepeta × faassenii* 'Alba', *Nigella damascena*, *Salvia × superba*

H: 1.2m (4ft) S: 60cm (24in)
✽ **Mid- to late summer**

 ◊◊ ▢-■ **Z4 pH5.5–7.5**

Scabiosa Butterfly Blue

The blooms of this long-flowering herbaceous perennial scabious are generally soft lavender, but may tend towards lilac in some climates and situations. They combine well with contrasting floral forms – the spikes of smaller penstemons, veronicas, or salvias, for example – and with cool-colored flowers and silver foliage; but, while successfully partnered with cream, they are perhaps too soft a color to contrast effectively with yellow. Attractive companions include shorter-growing roses, such as Ground Cover and Patio cultivars, artemisias, pinks, shorter eryngiums, and gypsophilas, and annuals such as brachyscomes, clarkias, annual gypsophilas, and *Salvia farinacea* cultivars. It also looks effective with tender perennials such as white or pink argyranthemums and purple or pink osteospermums.

Ⓖ *Artemisia schmidtiana*, *Brachyscome iberidifolia*, *Eryngium bourgatii* 'Picos Blue', *Gypsophila paniculata* 'Compacta Plena', *Rosa* Pink Bells

H & S: 45cm (18in)
✽ **Mid-summer to early autumn**

◊◊ ▢-■ **Z5 pH5.5–8**

In this complex combination of cool-colored flowers graded in height at the front of a border, *Scabiosa* Butterfly Blue is bordered in front by the glaucous foliage of *Mertensia simplicissima* and the brilliant crimson heads of *Dianthus deltoides* 'Leuchtfunk', and behind by the white *Campanula persicifolia alba*. Two alliums, blue *Allium caeruleum* and large-headed mauve *A. cristophii*, push their way through the other plants.

Schizostylis coccinea 'Major' ♛

This red-flowered rhizomatous herbaceous perennial, is immensely useful for its late flowers. It prefers moist soil, a sheltered site in cold gardens, and full sun, although in areas with hot summers it will tolerate dappled shade. It can be grown in mixed borders and at the foot of a sunny wall, although there it must be kept moist, both to sustain growth and keep flowering unchecked and to prevent attacks by red spider mite, its most serious pest. It is effective with other late flowers such as nerines, liriopes, asters (especially white-flowered cultivars),

In a simple but effective partnership, the soft scarlet blooms of the lily *Schizostylis coccinea* 'Major' harmonize with the tiny red berries of the herringbone cotoneaster (*C. horizontalis*), trained against a wall behind.

chrysanthemums, and fuchsias, and combines well with autumn-coloring plants including grasses. Other good partners include late-flowering sedums and smaller late roses, white autumn crocuses and colchicums, and plants with bronze or purple foliage. It appears to grow best with a companion, rather than on its own.

Ⓖ *Colchicum speciosum* 'Album', *Crocus speciosus* 'Conqueror', *Fuchsia magellanica* var. *gracilis*, *Nerine bowdenii*, *Sedum* 'Herbstfreude', *Stipa tenuissima*

H: 60cm (24in) S: 30cm (12in)
✽ **Late summer to late autumn**

 ◊◊ ▢-■ **Z6 pH5.5–7.5**

The warm, rosy-red flowers and purple foliage of *Sedum* 'Bertram Anderson', meandering through a clump of harmonious mauve *Allium senescens*, contrast with the glaucous foliage of the spurge *Euphorbia myrsinites*.

Sedum 'Bertram Anderson' ♛

The fleshy leaves of this superlative herbaceous perennial are perhaps its most outstanding feature. They are best described as glaucous and flushed strongly with deep purple, a coloring that suits associations with both glaucous-leaved plants and other purple foliage plants, and with cool-colored flowers. It is attractive throughout the time it is in leaf and has the bonus of conspicuous pink flowers. It is good for rock and gravel gardens, and for the front of a border, where its slightly sprawling growth habit does not look untidy. Even out of flower, it is a handsome plant for combining with pinks, catmints, glaucous fescues, and sea kale, silver foliage such as that of anthemis, sprawling cranesbills, and smaller hebes, dwarf hardy fuchsias, and smaller hostas, provided these do not shade the sedum. It contrasts well with yellow-green foliage and flowers, including many smaller euphorbias.

⬤ *Anthemis punctata* subsp. *cupaniana*, *Festuca glauca* 'Elijah Blue', *Fuchsia* 'Tom Thumb', *Geranium sanguineum* var. *striatum*, *Nepeta* × *faassenii*

H: 25cm (10in) S: 40cm (16in)
❀ **Late summer to mid-autumn**
⬤·⬤⬤ ▢-▣ **Z4 pH5.5–8**

Sedum 'Herbstfreude' ♛

Alternatively called Autumn Joy, this fleshy herbaceous perennial has glaucous foliage that is handsome throughout the season, and decorative glaucous green buds opening into flat flower heads that start pink, slightly to the mauve side of primary pink, and age to brick-red. This color change makes combinations with all but primary pink or red flowers difficult, but plants look very effective with white flowers – including chrysanthemums, asters, Japanese anemones, colchicums, and autumn crocus – and with lavender-blue flowers such as caryopteris and ceratostigmas. The flower heads remain attractive throughout winter, when they become rusty-red and make colorful partners for the dried leaves and stems of small to medium-size grasses. 'Herbstfreude' excels in gravel gardens and at the front of borders, especially if surrounded by low carpeting companions.

⬤ *Allium karataviense* p.302 **A**, *Artemisia alba* 'Canescens' p.188 **B**, *Bergenia* 'Morgenröte' p.198 **A**, *Rosa rugosa* p.160 **B** ⊿ 228 **C**

H: 45cm (18in) S: 60cm (24in)
❀ **Early to mid-autumn**
⬤⬤ ▢-▣ **Z3 pH5.5–8**

By mid-autumn, the brick red flowers of *Sedum* 'Herbstfreude', here at the front of a border, match those of *Eupatorium purpureum* subsp. *maculatum* 'Atropurpureum' behind, leavened by a white shrubby cinquefoil (*Potentilla fruticosa*), with dwarf pampas grass (*Cortaderia selloana* 'Pumila') supplying a bold focal point.

The glaucous, fleshy foliage and developing flower heads of *Sedum spectabile* 'Iceberg' look attractive for many months, but the plant has a brief moment of true glory when the flowers open to a rich cream. Soon, however, they turn a less appealing brown. Here, they provide a contrast for the bold, light magenta racemes of *Physostegia virginiana* 'Vivid'.

Sedum spectabile ♛

This is one of the parents of *S.* 'Herbstfreude' (above), sharing the qualities of its glaucous foliage, but flowering a little earlier, with bright mauve-pink blooms that combine well with cool colors and silver-grey, purple, or glaucous leaves. It mixes well with Japanese anemones, earlier-flowering chrysanthemums, asters, perovskias, and blue fescues. Later-flowering cranesbills, eryngiums, penstemons, and tender perennials like argyranthemums are other good partners. The flowers attract butterflies, and the seedheads remain decorative well into winter. Useful cultivars are 'Album', which opens pure white; bright pink 'Brilliant' ♛; rich carmine 'Carmen' and 'Meteor', and 'Septemberglut' (September Glow), with flowers in light purplish crimson.

⬤ *Anemone* × *hybrida* 'Honorine Jobert', *Aster* × *frikartii* 'Mönch', *Chrysanthemum* 'Clara Curtis', *Festuca glauca* 'Blaufuchs', *Perovskia* 'Blue Spire' ⊿ pp.203 **A**

H: 30–50cm (12–20in) S: 45cm (18in)
❀ **Late summer to early autumn**
⬤⬤ ▢-▣ **Z4 pH5.5–8**

Sedum telephium

ORPINE, LIVE-FOREVER

This extremely variable species has fleshy, glaucous leaves and light to rich carmine-pink flowers, which mix well with cool colors, purple foliage, and mauve, blue, or carmine flowers. Forms with salmon or brick-red flowers are perhaps best with warm tints such as blood-red, salmon, peach, or apricot, and with bronze foliage. Most are erect but some tend to sprawl – subsp. *ruprechtii*, for example, which has attractive glaucous foliage and pale yellowish green flowers. Dark-leaved variants include subsp. *maximum* 'Atropurpureum' ♀, which is slightly lax with very dark purplish red leaves, and *S.t.* 'Arthur Branch', with similar leaves, glowing red stems, and a more upright growth habit. These are good clump-forming plants for the front of a dry, sunny border or for growing in gravel. In winter the seedheads turn a beautiful rusty red.

Crocosmia × *crocosmiiflora* 'Solfatare' p.207 **B**, *Dahlia* 'Bishop of Llandaff' p.371 **C**, *Nemesia* 'Innocence' p.388 **B**, *Verbena* 'Lawrence Johnston' p.405 **A**

H: 45–60cm (18–24in) S: 30–45cm (12–18in)
❈ Late summer to early autumn

 ◊-◊◊ ☐-☐ **Z4 pH5.5–8**

In this pair of matching mixed borders, the flowers of orpine (*Sedum telephium*) harmonize with the distant brick wall and with purple-leaved *Berberis* × *ottawensis* f. *purpurea* 'Superba', while contrasting with the yellow-green leaves of false acacia (*Robinia pseudoacacia* 'Frisia').

A

At the front of a border adjoining a stone path, the erect stems of creamy yellow *Sisyrinchium striatum* provide a strong accent. The plant's base is covered by a carpet of rich blue-flowered *Veronica austriaca* subsp. *teucrium*, which spills over onto the path.

Sisyrinchium striatum

The pale creamy yellow flowers of this clump-forming perennial (a relative of the iris) will blend with almost any color and especially with blue. It is a good plant for the front of a border, where its grassy, upright growth habit can offer useful contrasts of texture and form with, for example, santolinas, violas, or agastaches, and satisfying harmonies with glaucous or silver foliage, rich yellow flowers, and yellow-green flowers or foliage. It thrives in gravel, perhaps with a carpeting plant at its base, and will tolerate fairly heavy soils, although in these conditions may be shorter-lived. It seeds itself readily, sometimes too readily. Timely deadheading can prevent this and help to produce flowers into late summer or autumn. The variegated 'Aunt May' is less hardy and requires good drainage.

Achillea 'Moonshine', *Artemisia* 'Powis Castle', *Campanula persicifolia*, *Kniphofia* 'David', *Lavandula angustifolia* 'Hidcote', *Papaver orientale* cultivars

H: 60cm (24in) S: 30cm (12in)
Early to mid-summer

  Z7 pH5.5–8

Smilacina racemosa
FALSE SPIKENARD

This handsome, clump-forming perennial (syn. *Maianthemum racemosum*) is valuable for a partially shaded woodland garden or border, especially if surrounded by shorter plants to display its graceful, slightly arching growth habit. Its creamy white flowers will blend with almost any other color, perhaps most effectively with blue, yellow, or yellow-green, and with contrasting strong-colored flowers such as a carpet of purple bugleweeds or blue corydalis. It is good with contrasting foliage such as ferns, grasses, and sedges. Sometimes it produces red berries, and those that fruit well are particularly pleasant for associations in late summer and early autumn; the fruits do not, however, always last long enough for reliable combinations with autumn-coloring deciduous shrubs.

Ajuga reptans 'Atropurpurea', *Brunnera macrophylla*, *Erythronium* 'Pagoda', *Euphorbia characias* subsp. *wulfenii* 'Lambrook Gold' p.50 **B**, *Polystichum setiferum*

H: 75cm (30in) S: 60cm (24in)
Mid- to late spring

 Z4 pH5–7

Towards the front of a bed in partial shade, a boldly arching clump of false spikenard (*Smilacina racemosa*), topped with creamy plumes of flower, is carpeted beneath with blue *Corydalis flexuosa*. A hedge fern adds foliage of contrasting form in front and, like the smilacina, will remain handsome when the corydalis has finished flowering.

The plumed flower heads of the goldenrod *Solidago* 'Crown of Rays' contrast in color and form with the tender, sub-shrubby, fragrant, deep purple *Heliotropium* 'Marine', both of them exactly matched in height.

Solidago 'Crown of Rays'

The dense flowering display of this relatively short goldenrod (also known as Strahlenkrone) is seen at its best in loosely spaced or scattered groups, with other plants threaded through; if grown in larger groups, the shape of the individual flower heads is easily masked. Alternatively, it may be grown in partial shade, which limits the profusion of its flower spikes. It is valuable for the second row of a herbaceous border, the golden yellow of its flowers looking especially good with hot colors such as orange and scarlet, or with bronze foliage. Effective contrasts with blue or purple flowers can be achieved with shorter dahlias and *Aster × frikartii* cultivars, or some taller *Aster amellus* cultivars. It is also good with shorter heleniums and early-flowering New York asters, and with contrasting textures such as those provided by grasses of similar height.

Aster amellus 'King George', *Crocosmia* 'Lucifer', *Dahlia* 'Grenadier', *Helenium* 'Wyndley', *Sambucus nigra* 'Guincho Purple' (stooled), *Stipa capillata*

H: 60cm (24in) S: 45cm (18in)
Mid- to late summer

Z4 pH5.5–7.5

In late spring, the emerging flower stems of woolly lamb's ears (*Stachys byzantina*) harmonize with the grey-leaved willow *Salix hastata* 'Wehrhahnii' behind. They are joined by self-seeded wood forget-me-nots (*Myosotis sylvatica*) and giant eryngo (*Eryngium giganteum*).

Stachys byzantina

WOOLLY LAMB'S EARS

An excellent carpeting plant, *S. byzantina* (syns *S. lanata*, *S. olympica*) is suitable for the front of a border and for gravel gardens, its rosettes of silvery grey leaves merging to form soft woolly mats, above which greyish white hairy stems bear whorls of small magenta flowers. It mixes well with other silver-leaved plants such as artemisias, and with lavenders, pinks, and catmints. 'Big Ears' (syn. 'Countess Helen von Stein') has larger leaves that are slightly less white but very effective for longer-range viewing. 'Cotton Boll' (syn. 'Sheila McQueen') has longer leaves and abortive flower stalks studded with cottony balls. 'Silver Carpet' is also non-flowering and produces a very flat mat of growth. 'Primrose Heron' has yellow-green leaves, so combines well with gold or yellow-green flowers and adds piquancy to pink, mauve, and soft blue displays. Over-feeding and too much water encourages mildew, which can mar the leaves.

⬤ *Allium moly* p.302 **B**, *Crocus vernus* 'Jeanne d'Arc' p.311 **B**, *Cynara cardunculus* p.208 **A**, *Rosa* Peach Blossom p.159 **A**, *Tulipa* 'Palestrina' p.352 **B**

H & S: 45cm (18in)
✾ **Early summer to early autumn**
▬▬▬▭▬ ◊-◊◊ ◻-◼ **Z4 pH5.5–7.5**

Stipa calamagrostis

The habit of this grass varies from almost upright, with its bottle-brush spikes scarcely branching, to gracefully arching, with stems of fully branched blooms. The spikes start light green and age to beige, and at mid-season both colors appear on a mix of young and old spikes. The glaucous foliage turns warm brown by autumn. This is a drought-tolerant species that thrives in gravel gardens; it also looks attractive near the front of a border, especially surrounded by plants such as the shortest sedums or Charm chrysanthemums, or colchicums growing through acaenas or bugleweeds. The warm beige color blends with other warm tints, especially peach, copper, and apricot flowers, and bronze foliage, and contrasts well with blue flowers such as ceratostigmas. A stout wire hoop can provide support for the stems.

⬤ *Acaena microphylla* 'Kupferteppich', *Ajuga reptans* 'Atropurpurea', *Ceratostigma willmottianum*, *Chrysanthemum* 'Bronze Fairy', *Colchicum autumnale*

H: 90cm (3ft) **S: 1.2m** (4ft)
✾ **Early summer to early autumn**
▬▬▬▭▬ ◊◊ ◻-◼ **Z6 pH5.5–7.5**

In this subtle arrangement relying on contrasting form and subdued coloring, the parchment plumes of *Stipa calamagrostis* arch over the pink-flushed flowers of *Sedum* 'Strawberries and Cream'.

Left: The glistening seedheads of *Stipa capillata* shimmer against the sun, providing a contrast of form with *Eryngium planum* 'Blaukappe', its flower heads flushed steely blue.

Stipa capillata

Like most stipas, *S. capillata* prefers full sun and good drainage and tolerates drought, so it is a superb plant for a gravel garden. It is a tough grass, developing into tall clumps with hair-like, almost white seedheads that are so fine and insubstantial that, from a distance, they resemble a shimmering cloud. Plants look best in scattered groups, loosely woven through slightly taller companions, forming a radiant foil for plants with a more definite structure. Single plants are ineffective, and solid groups are too nebulous to make a strong impact. Eryngiums are perhaps the supreme partners for them. Others include phormiums (but only cultivars of moderate height, and those in muted colors), kniphofias, and the more handsome salvias, such as *Salvia candelabrum*, *S. leucantha*, *S. splendens* 'Van-Houttei', and the densest white selections of shrubby *S. canariensis*.

Above: *Stipa tenuissima* differs from *S. capillata* in its smaller size, narrower habit of growth, and denser panicles, suiting it to a smaller scale, including containers. Here, it is joined by the starry heads of *Eryngium variifolium* and spiky stems of rosemary (*Rosmarinus officinalis*).

◑ *Achillea* 'Fanal', *Aster* × *frikartii* 'Mönch', *Echinops ritro*, *Kniphofia* 'Sunningdale Yellow', *Phormium* 'Duet', *Rudbeckia fulgida* var. *sullivantii* 'Goldsturm'

H: 90cm (36in) S: 60cm (24in)
✳ **Early to late summer**

 ◌-◌◌ ▪-▪ Z7 pH5.5–7.5

Symphytum 'Goldsmith'

This spreading rhizomatous perennial has brightly variegated foliage, edged at first with gold but aging to cream, and bears pale blue, white-tipped flowers. Its bright young foliage works well with blue spring flowers, such as brunneras, forget-me-nots, omphalodes, meconopsis, and corydalis, and it harmonizes with cream, white, or yellow flowers – doronicums, trollius, or geums, for example. It is also effective with plants of contrasting form such as ferns and grasses. 'Goldsmith' is a good ground-cover plant, but it is very vigorous and large and can threaten the scale of other plant groups or the garden itself. In full sun and dry conditions the leaf margins can turn brown, so it is best grown in partial shade with adequate moisture. The foliage stays brightest, with less mildew, if the flowers are removed as they appear.

◑ *Corydalis flexuosa* 'China Blue', *Forsythia* × *intermedia* p.52 **A**, *Myosotis sylvatica*, *Omphalodes cappadocica*, *Viola* 'Molly Sanderson'

H: 35cm (14in) S: 45cm (18in)
✳ **Mid- to late spring**

◌◌-◌◌◌ ▪-▪ ▪ Z5 pH5–7.5

The gold-edged leaves of *Symphytum* 'Goldsmith' contrast with the red-eyed, soft lavender flowers of *Phlox divaricata* subsp. *laphamii* 'Chattahoochee'. Both are plants that relish partial shade and a moist, humus-rich soil.

In a semi-shaded site, the airy, pale green racemes of fringe cups (*Tellima grandiflora*) and the purple globes of *Allium hollandicum* contrast in color and form.

Tellima grandiflora
FRINGE CUPS

This modest perennial, bearing kidney-shaped leaves, with scalloped edges, and dainty spikes of pale green flowers, tolerates dry shade and so makes a valuable ground cover for a woodland garden. With its quiet, unpretentious charm, it is an excellent foil for plants of bolder shape or brighter color, especially red, orange, and purple, as in alliums that flower in late spring. It associates well with most late spring bulbs, although it is best to avoid the largest, showiest kinds, such as Darwinhybrid Group tulips, which are likely to overwhelm the tellima. Forms with red-flushed stems and leaves, such as 'Pinky' and 'Purpurteppich', have attractive pinkish flowers, but the variable Rubra Group will probably contain individuals that, neither a distinct green nor pink, are a slightly grubby brown. Plants have no serious pests or diseases and can be grown as a solid mat of ground cover.

Bergenia 'Morgenröte', *Euphorbia griffithii* 'Dixter', *Hedera canariensis* 'Gloire de Marengo', *Hyacinthoides hispanica*, *Narcissus* 'Actaea'

H: 60cm (24in) S: 45cm (18in)
❀ **Late spring to early summer**

 ◊◊-◊◊◊ ◼-◼ ◼ Z4 pH5–7.5

Trillium chloropetalum
GIANT WAKE-ROBIN

The stems of this shade-loving perennial each bear three leaves, marbled with silver-green and/or maroon, and arranged in a triangle around an upright flower, which can be greenish white, yellow, or maroon-red. This trillium is at its best in humus-rich soil in a woodland garden, surrounded by lower-growing plants such as *Anemone nemorosa* cultivars, and looks very effective with smaller, pale yellow, cream, or white narcissi, such as some of the Triandrus Group. Like all trilliums, the plants have the greatest impact when grown in groups of 15 or more crowns. They are slow to increase, but may be divided after flowering. To multiply plants quickly, the crowns can be lifted in early spring, the growing point excised, and the remaining stock cut vertically into three sections, which can then be replanted.

Alchemilla mollis, *Anemone nemorosa* 'Leeds' Variety', *Arum italicum* 'Marmoratum', *Myosotis sylvatica*, *Narcissus* 'Hawera', *Omphalodes cappadocica*

H: 50cm (20in) S: 30cm (12in)
❀ **Late spring to early summer**

◊◊-◊◊◊ ◼-◼ ◼ Z4 pH5.5–7.5

Grown in shade among a carpet of ground cover, the bold foliage and upright red flowers of giant wake-robin (*Trillium chloropetalum*) make a strong statement. Its companions are the yellow archangel *Lamium galeobdolon* 'Silberteppich' – one of very few shade-tolerant plants with silvery leaves – and foamflower (*Tiarella cordifolia*).

In the temporary light beneath deciduous trees in late spring, an imposing group of white trilliums (*Trillium grandiflorum*) covers the ground in front of an elegant trumpet daffodil.

Trillium grandiflorum 🏆
WHITE WAKE-ROBIN

Perhaps the easiest trillium to grow, this also has the largest flowers, usually pure white but sometimes ageing with a pink flush. Unlike on *T. chloropetalum* (above), the leaves are only loosely arranged around each stem. Excellent in a woodland garden, combined with other spring flowers or growing through a carpet of bugleweeds or wood anemones, it is also robust enough to associate with plants of similar height such as smaller pulmonarias or epimediums. It mixes well with almost any color, but it is perhaps best with pink, mauve, or blue if its flowers have a pink flush. Good variants include the formal double 'Snow Bunting' (sometimes sold as 'Flore Pleno') and the rose-pink 'Roseum'. Plants can be propagated as for *T. chloropetalum*, and should be protected from slugs.

Ajuga reptans 'Catlin's Giant', *Anemone nemorosa* 'Robinsoniana', *Dicentra eximia*, *Epimedium* × *versicolor* 'Versicolor', *Pulmonaria saccharata*

H: 40cm (16in) S: 30cm (12in)
❀ **Late spring to early summer**

 ◊◊ ◼ ◼ Z4 pH5.5–7.5

In this use of contrasting bold foliage but harmonious flowers, *Veratrum nigrum* grows in front of the elegant hybrid plume poppy, *Macleaya × kewensis*. The poppy's beige-colored flowers are born in panicles similar in shape to those of the veratrum.

Veratrum nigrum ♕

This stunningly architectural plant has broad, deeply pleated basal leaves, topped by tall, branched panicles of deep maroon flowers in summer. With its handsome appearance, it merits space away from other plants that might vie for attention. Combinations with bright colors and bronze- or purple-leaved shrubs tend to camouflage its grandeur, and it is best associated with more subdued tones, such as soft brick-red or orange, peach, apricot, or light to mid-blue; it also benefits from a background of pale foliage to show off its flowers. Asiatic or martagon lilies in warm shades make excellent companions. Partial shade is ideal for this plant, but it can tolerate full sun if the soil is sufficiently moist. It is very prone to slug and snail damage, especially when young.

◑ *Cercidiphyllum magnificum*, *Cornus alba* 'Sibirica Variegata', *Lilium* 'Enchantment', *L. martagon*, *Meconopsis betonicifolia*, *Saxifraga fortunei*

H: 1.8m (6ft) S: 60cm (24in)
❀ **Mid- to late summer**

◊◊-◊◊◊ ▨ ■ Z4 pH5.5–7.5

Verbascum 'Helen Johnson'

The unusually subtle coloring of this lovely perennial – warm, peachy buff flowers born over silver grey-green, woolly leaves – is difficult to combine effectively, since it is easily overwhelmed by brighter, brasher tones. Plants look most effective when associated with warm colors such as peach, apricot, or soft orange, and with bronze or silver foliage, and they make a telling contrast with pale to mid-sky-blue flowers. Warm-colored achilleas, artemisias, or glaucous grasses make pleasant companions; in fact, glaucous foliage generally offers the most attractive and gentle contrast to the color of the flowers. Some stocks have mutated during micropropagation to lose much of their silvery hairy covering, turning the foliage a darker, duller grey-green – these are best avoided. The plants need sun and good drainage if they are to thrive, and may suffer from spider mites in hot areas.

◑ *Anthriscus sylvestris* 'Ravenswing', *Artemisia ludoviciana*, *Clematis integrifolia* 'Pastel Blue', *Rosa* 'Climbing Paul Lédé' p.140 **B**, *Stipa calamagrostis*

H: 90cm (36in) S: 30cm (12in)
❀ **Early to late summer**

 ◊-◊◊ ▢-■ Z4 pH6–7.5

In this charming mix of flowers, *Verbascum* 'Helen Johnson' stands behind young leaves of the grass *Miscanthus sinensis* and the yellow plate-like heads of *Achillea clypeolata*, with white sweet rocket (*Hesperis nationalis* var. *albiflora*) in the background. The grouping would be most effective on a larger scale, with more space given to each plant.

A

Rich blue, low-growing *Veronica austriaca* subsp. *teucrium* 'Crater Lake Blue' provides a foil for the flowers of *Osteospermum* 'Pink Whirls', with their spoon-tipped petals.

Veronica austriaca subsp. teucrium

This mat-forming perennial has long-lasting racemes of rich blue flowers that from a distance look like a cloud of intense blue. Hybrids include gentian-blue 'Kapitän' and rich, deep 'Crater Lake Blue' ♀, both 30cm (12in) tall, and vivid sky-blue 'Shirley Blue' ♀, just 6–10cm (2–4in). All harmonize with white, pink, and pale blue flowers, such as violas and osteospermums, and contrast with the glaucous foliage of Tardiana Group hostas, sea kale, eryngiums, and many grasses. Although shade-tolerant, they need full sun to produce a solid sheet of blue. *V. prostrata* ♀, 15cm (6in) tall, and *V.p.* 'Loddon Blue', 20cm (8in), have similar uses, while *V.p.* 'Trehane' has yellow-green leaves that are useful for combining with other yellow-green foliage plants of bolder

◑ *Crambe maritima*, *Eryngium* × *tripartitum*, *Euonymus fortunei* 'Emerald 'n' Gold', *Salvia* × *sylvestris* 'Mainacht', *Sisyrinchium striatum* p.287 **A** ❏ p.224 **B**

H: 10–50cm (4–20in) S: 15–45cm (6–18in)
❀ **Late spring to mid-summer**

 ◊◊ ▢-■ **Z5 pH5.5–7.5**

Viola 'Huntercombe Purple' ♀

The flowers of this mat-forming perennial viola are intense purple-blue and produced profusely throughout much of spring. In areas where late spring and summer are cool, intermittent blooms continue appearing until late summer, when there is a second flush of blue flowers. The plant is particularly effective as a contrast with yellow flowers, and yellow-green flowers or foliage, and blends harmoniously with cool colors such as pink, mauve, and blue, or with glaucous and silver foliage plants. It can be used beneath widely spaced roses with an open branch structure – some of the China roses, for example – and may be combined with short-growing purple foliage plants, arranged as a dusky carpet against which to display the paler viola flowers. 'Martin' ♀ is similar, with flowers perhaps a little darker. Plants are vulnerable to aphid attack, which can curtail flowering, particularly in hot, dry spells.

◐ *Ajuga reptans* 'Atropurpurea', *Humulus lupulus* 'Aureus' p.122 **C**, *Rosa* × *odorata* 'Mutabilis', *Stachys byzantina* 'Primrose Heron'

H: 15cm (6in) S: 30cm (12in)
❀ **Mid-spring to late summer**

◊◊ ▢-■ **Z4 pH5.5–7.5**

B

The rich flowers of *Viola* 'Huntercombe Purple' contrast effectively with the yellow flowers of golden garlic (*Allium moly*) and the yellow-green foliage of golden creeping Jenny (*Lysimachia nummularia* 'Aurea').

C

In this softly pretty planting arrangement, the dusky pink flowers of *Viola* 'Nellie Britton' match exactly those of the speedwell *Veronica spicata* 'Erika', whose foliage is lightly silvered, harmonizing with the white-edged leaves of *Ajania pacifica*.

Viola 'Nellie Britton' ♀

This viola (syn. 'Haslemere') is one of the most successful hybrids and certainly one of the loveliest, with its small, dainty flowers in an uncommon shade of dusky mauve-pink (pink is a relatively rare color among viola cultivars). It works well with cool shades such as cream, lilac, blue, and palest sulfur-yellow, but the color is so delicate that it can easily be overwhelmed by crude contrasts such as magenta-pink, gold, and pure white. It makes a pleasant association at the front of a border with silver, purple, or glaucous foliage, especially blue fescues or some of the smaller Tardiana Group hostas – 'Blue Blush', 'Blue Moon', or 'Hadspen Blue', for example. 'Vita' is similar, although the flowers are a little larger and a slightly purer shade of pink.

◐ *Epimedium* × *versicolor* 'Sulphureum', *Hebe pinguifolia* 'Pagei', *Helichrysum petiolatum*, *Heuchera* 'Plum Pudding', *Myosotis sylvatica*, *Nemophila menziesii*

H: 15cm (6in) S: 30cm (12in)
❀ **Late spring to mid-summer**

 ◊◊ ▢-■ **Z4 pH5.5–7.5**

Yucca flaccida 'Golden Sword' ♛

Yuccas are architectural plants, valuable as focal points, emphatically so in the case of stiff-leaved, stem-forming species such as *Y. aloifolia*, *Y. elephantipes* ♛, and *Y. gloriosa* ♛. Clump-forming species are less strident in their effect, particularly if the leaves tend to flop, as they do in *Y. filifera* and *Y. flaccida* and its cultivars 'Ivory' ♛ and 'Golden Sword' ♛, so these can be used for gentler impact. The almost stemless 'Golden Sword' is grown for its foliage, which has bright gold central variegation, most colorful from autumn until spring. Best planted near the front of a sunny border or gravel garden, it makes greater impact when set in front of plants of similar size and surrounded by lower ones. It harmonizes with glaucous grasses, bronze or strap-shaped foliage, and hot colors, and contrasts well with blue flowers such as agapanthus. Other cultivars such as 'Ivory' flower far more freely.

● *Agapanthus* 'Loch Hope', *Crocosmia* × *crocosmiiflora* 'Lady Hamilton', *C.* 'Lucifer', *Helictotrichon sempervirens*, *Hemerocallis* red-flowered cultivars, *Kniphofia* 'Bees' Sunset', *Phormium* 'Bronze Baby', *Phygelius* × *rectus* 'African Queen', *Watsonia fourcadei*

H: 1.8m (6ft)   **S: 1.2m** (4ft)   ❀ **Mid- to late summer**
◊-◊◊   ▣-▦   **Z7   pH5.5–7.5**

In this combination for foliage effect that would work equally well with the plants more widely spaced through a low ground cover, *Yucca flaccida* 'Golden Sword' is joined by the grass *Stipa arundinacea* and the shrubby honeysuckle *Lonicera nitida* 'Baggesen's Gold'.

BULBS

❦

*BULBS HAVE A ROLE to play in
both formal and informal plantings,
looking good as part of a neat bedding
arrangement or naturalized in drifts
on banks or in lawns. They are ideal
for grouping with each other for early
color or for combining with
herbaceous and evergreen perennials as
part of an evolving long-term display.*

I N GARDENING, the word bulb is used very loosely to refer to any plant with a more-or-less swollen, underground storage organ that can be dried and sold as a conveniently packaged object: bulb catalogues offer true bulbs (daffodils, lilies, muscaris, tulips), corms (crocosmias, crocuses, gladioli), and assorted tubers, tuberous roots, and rhizomes (dahlias, anemones, aconitums). Strictly speaking, however, a bulb is a compressed shoot with fleshy leaves packed with food, arranged around a flattened "stem", the basal plate.

The vast majority of these "bulbous" plants share a common lifestyle as perennials, returning annually to their underground resting state. They come from a range of natural habitats, including desert margins, alpine pastures, and deciduous woodlands, most requiring them to grow, flower, and die down in the short space of time that the conditions are favorable. Bulbs also usually have short-lived brightly colored blooms, a quality needed to attract pollinating insects, and many have fairly uninteresting, often strap-shaped foliage. In other respects, such as height and flower presentation and form, they are very varied.

Gardening with bulbs

In reasonably sheltered gardens, there can be bulbs in flower all the year round – from the earliest snowdrops, crocuses, and scillas, through phalanxes of narcissi, tulips, and fritillaries, to imposing lilies and gladioli, irises and zantedeschias, then bright amaryllis, nerines, and sternbergias, before finally the autumn and winter flowering crocuses and colchicums. The spring-bloomers are perhaps the most magical of bulbs, pushing up through near-frozen ground to produce seemingly fragile blooms of beautiful proportions, but all bulbous plants have a contribution to make, and most are perfect for a wide range of companion planting.

Bulbs are inexpensive when bought in bulk, and some suppliers are willing to sell even quite small quantities fairly cheaply. While crocuses, daffodils, and tulips are among the most popular, other good value bulbs include chionodoxas, scillas, and checker lilies. Alliums, lilies, and tigridias, although slightly more costly, are well worth the outlay for their statuesque growth habit or exotic flowers.

Many bulbs are easy to grow. If they are chosen to suit the situation, they will spread and flower with increasing abundance each year with no effort required on the part of the gardener. In fact, the majority of bulbous plants benefit from being left undisturbed year after year. Because they are essentially pre-packed plants with their own supply of food, they are almost guaranteed

Tulip cultivars are among the brightest and most reliable bulbs for providing color in spring. Here, their large solid blooms on stout stems make brilliant highlights above a carpet of traditional bedding plants that includes wallflowers and forget-me-nots.

to produce a flower in the first year they are planted. This is especially the case with tulips, where the flower is already formed inside the bulb before it begins to grow.

Bedding and borders

Bulbs are very useful for creating early bedding displays. Tulips, especially, are effective planted alone or through a carpet of forget-me-nots, pansies, polyanthus, or wallflowers to produce a colorful carpet of flowers in mid- to late spring. Hyacinths are also ideal for short-term color, although they must be combined with similarly low-growing companions. In some gardens, the bulbs and their partners are removed to make way for summer bedding.

An underplanting of bulbs can be as gorgeous, or as naturalistic and subdued as befits the setting, using them to cover all available bare ground, woven in loose drifts among the emerging plants. The biggest, boldest and brightest sorts should be used with conviction

but be restricted to more sophisticated and showy planting, perhaps near the house. The leaves of perennials and deciduous shrubs will cover the dying bulb foliage after they have flowered. (Bulbs are best mixed with other plants when used for edging, otherwise there will be a gap when they retreat below ground.)

Summer flowering bulbs can be integrated into borders and used in much the same way as herbaceous plants. Lilies are perfect for pairing with tall delphiniums or placing in front of Shrub or Climbing roses, both combinations being popular in cottage gardens, while gladioli and irises will provide strong focal points among cranesbills and other plants with lax or rounded forms, or punctuation for those with soft foliage, such as fennel and artemisias.

Bulbs in pots

Most bulbs are ideal for pot culture and many will enjoy the special conditions that can be created; for example, lime-hating lilies can

As well as being indispensable for bedding displays and drifts of early color in mixed borders, bulbs are also very effective when massed in a dedicated bulb border such as this, in which tulips, narcissi, and crown imperials provide height behind leucojums, erythroniums, muscaris, and checker lilies.

be grown in containers of acidic compost in areas of alkaline soil. Pots of early bulbs can be forced to make them flower even earlier, providing long-lasting delight in late winter and early spring. Window boxes bring the flowers closer to eye level, where their delicate markings and, with some, wonderful scent can be more fully appreciated. As the weather gets warmer, containers of pale tulips with forget-me-nots or bright hyacinths with polyanthus can decorate terraces and patios. Lilies, planted with annuals beneath, make ideal subjects for large pots later in the summer, while many even later-flowering bulbs – nerines and sternbergias – also benefit from being in containers. Growing them in this way allows for the provision of free drainage and winter protection. If the bulbs are left undisturbed, they will respond with ever greater freedom of flowering year after year.

Naturalizing bulbs

Many spring flowering bulbs are perfect for naturalizing in grass or under trees. Where they are in grass, it can be left uncut until mid-summer, meaning less work for the gardener; an attendant benefit is that the grass will gradually be colonized by wild flowers, which prefer the meadow-like maintenance routine. Delicate drifts of cowslips and checker lilies or, in more shaded sites, carpets of cyclamens, anemones, and primroses are the rewards for such relaxed gardening.

Facing page: In this border in England, ribbons of hot-colored tulips create vivacious contrasts with the more demure coloring of forget-me-nots, ornamental cherries, and euphorbias.

Below: Colonies of dwarf bulbs such as muscaris, smaller narcissi, and fritillaries will become denser and more lavish if they are left undisturbed to multiply and spread. Larger tulips and narcissi in pots can be lifted after flowering to make way for summer bedding.

Allium carinatum subsp. *pulchellum* ♕

The slightly diffuse flower heads of this slender, grassy plant are made up of dainty amethyst florets that droop until pollinated, after which they turn upwards. The plants form loose drifts rather than solid clumps, ideal for interweaving with shorter ground-cover plants, and effective when combined with cranesbills, catmints, shorter artemisias, or eryngiums. Their coloring works well with silver, glaucous, or purple foliage, and cool flower colors such as crimson, lavender, pale pink, pale mauve, and white, and is strong enough to contrast successfully with yellow-green foliage and flowers or pale sulfur-yellow flowers. A white-flowered variant is *A.c.* subsp. *pulchellum* f. *album*, the best selections of which are very pretty plants. All these ornamental onions readily self-seed and can be difficult to control.

◉ *Artemisia stelleriana* 'Boughton Silver', *Heuchera* 'Amethyst Myst', *Populus alba* 'Richardii' p.77 **A**

H: 45cm (18in)   **S: 5cm** (2in)
✿ **Mid- to late summer**

◊-◊◊   ▢-▦   ■ **Z6 pH5–7.5**

The delicate, amethyst flowers of *Allium carinatum* subsp. *pulchellum* are intimately mixed with the taller, starry flower heads of *Eryngium × oliverianum*, to striking effect. This combination would perhaps work even better with an eryngium that grows to the same height as the allium – for example *E. bourgatii* 'Picos Blue'.

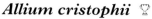

Allium cristophii ♕

This ornamental onion produces stout stems topped with bold globes of mauve, starry flowers that mature to spheres of beige-colored seedheads, almost as eye-catching as the flowers themselves. Its broad leaves start to die back at flowering time and are best hidden by neighbors such as late-leafing herbaceous plants whose foliage can form a foil beneath the allium flower heads, or a feathery annual such as nigella. It can be interplanted with bush roses and old shrub roses, although these need to be pruned fairly hard to allow sunlight to reach the allium leaves early in the year and to match the height of its flower heads. The color of these, varying between pale silvery greyish mauve and rich amethyst, combines attractively with cool shades, while the most richly colored forms can be contrasted with pale yellow flowers or yellow-green foliage and flowers. Good companions include Bearded irises, catmints, and shorter, silver-leaved artemisias. Although this allium prefers a well drained site, even gravel, it will grow in any good soil, where it self-seeds readily, allowing a particular color to be selected and saved.

Above left: *Allium cristophii* flowers at exactly the same height as *Nigella damascena* 'Miss Jekyll', the leaves of the nigella hiding the allium's messy dying foliage.

Above: The same combination is attractive in seed, the silvery seedheads of the ornamental onion contrasting effectively with the nigella's brown pods.

◉ *Allium sphaerocephalon* p.303 **C**, *Anemone × hybrida* 'Honorine Jobert' p.185 **A**, *Geranium* 'Ann Folkard' p.225 **B**, *Lavandula stoechas* subsp. *pedunculata* p.64 **C**, *Rosa* 'Prince Charles' p.149 **C**, *Spiraea japonica* (yellow-green leaved) p.93 **C** ⊔ pp.153 **B**, 178 **C**, 284 **B**

H: 45cm (18in)   **S: 30cm** (12in)
✿ **Early to mid-summer**

◊-◊◊   ▢-▦   ■ **Z4 pH5–8**

Allium hollandicum ♛

This is perhaps the easiest and most useful ornamental onion for general garden use, with bold heads of mauve flowers growing on slender stems. The spherical flower heads, often confused with those of the taller lilac *A. aflatunense*, form an effective pattern when repeated through a border, especially with late-flowering tulips and other late spring bulbs, early roses, and bedding plants such as wallflowers. Other suitable companions include Bearded irises, columbines, and later-flowering deciduous azaleas. It looks effective with cool colors, white flowers, and silver or purple foliage, in either a gravel garden or a reasonably well-drained border. 'Purple Sensation' ♛ is a mixture of three, more richly colored clones, perhaps the best of which is 'Purple Surprise'. Their color is sufficiently intense to contrast with yellow-green foliage and flowers, and with fairly strong yellow flowers. All variants of this species and the closely related *A. aflatunense* self-seed readily and must be kept separate if they are to remain distinct. Their seedheads are an attractive feature as they change from green to a beige color by late summer.

Aquilegia vulgaris var. *stellata* p.187 **A**, *Clematis montana* var. *rubens* p.114 **B**, *Crambe maritima* p.206 **B**, *Galactites tomentosa* p.380 **C**, *Laburnum × watereri* 'Vossii' p.63 **A**, *Tellima grandiflora* p.290 **A**, *Tulipa* 'Red Shine' p.353 **B** ❏ pp.125 **B**, 154 **C**

H: 90cm (36in) S: 30cm (12in) ❀ **Late spring**
◊-◊◊ ▢-▨ ■ **Z4 pH5–7.5**

Right: The amethyst *Allium hollandicum* and *A.h.* 'Purple Sensation', together with the royal blue *Anchusa azurea* 'Loddon Loyalist' and purplish blue *Geranium* 'Johnson's Blue', make a striking contrast against the background of yellow-green foliage of *Robinia pseudoacacia* 'Frisia' and *Philadelphus coronarius* 'Aureus'.

Below: Used as late spring bedding in harmonious colors, the spherical *Allium hollandicum* contrasts with the initially cup-shaped then flat *Tulipa* 'Blue Parrot'. Here, both are set in a carpet of blue wood forget-me-nots (*Myosotis sylvatica*).

Allium karataviense ♛

This short, relatively early-flowering
ornamental onion bears globes of mauve-
flushed flowers at the same time as its broad
greyish green leaves, which are variably
flushed with purple. The seedheads remain
attractive after flowering and dry to a
pleasant beige color by mid- to late summer,
by which time the leaves have disappeared.
Although appealing in flower, it is valued
more for its handsome architectural form,
the plants making a bold statement that can
be enhanced by companions with small
leaves and flowers to provide a filigree foil.
It is a good plant for a rock garden or gravel
garden, or for growing in a sink or shallow
trough, and also for the front of a border,
where it can be grown through a low carpet
of ground-cover plants such as acaenas,
bugleweeds, or smaller cranesbills. Attractive
companions include silver, purple, or
glaucous foliage plants, and flowers in cool
colors, particularly mauve, purple, pink, or
crimson, and white. Plants self-seed freely.

◖ *Acaena saccaticupula* 'Blue Haze', *Ajuga reptans*
'Arctic Fox', *Festuca glauca* 'Blaufuchs', *Geranium*
× *riversleaianum* 'Mavis Simpson', *Sedum* 'Red Rum'

H: 20cm (8in) S: 30cm (12in) ❅ **Late spring**
▬▭▬ ◊ ▢-▨ ■ **Z3 pH5–7.5**

The delicately colored, spherical flower heads and
bold, strap-shaped leaves of *Allium karataviense* contrast
effectively in form with the succulent *Sedum* 'Herbstfreude'.

Allium moly ♛

A bright display can be guaranteed from
this clump-forming ornamental onion, which
is well suited to a position at the front of a
border, or in a gravel or rock garden. It has
shapely glaucous foliage and showy, sharp
yellow flowers that harmonize with hot colors
and contrast effectively with blue or purple.
Plants also combine well with glaucous or
silver foliage, violas, euphorbias, and late
spring bloomers such as shorter, richer blue
alpine forget-me-nots, late-flowering
wallflowers, and shorter late-flowering tulips.
'Jeannine' ♛ is an improved form that has
broad glaucous foliage and bolder flowers,
sometimes with two flower stems per bulb.
They flower most profusely in full sun,
although this may scorch the leaf tips.

◖ *Artemisia schmidtiana* 'Nana', *Carex comans* (bronze),
Euphorbia cyparissias 'Fens Ruby', *Heuchera* 'Can-can',
Rumex flexuosus, *Viola* 'Huntercombe Purple' p.292 **B**

H: 20cm (8in) S: 5cm (2in)
❅ **Late spring to early summer**
▬▭▬ ◊-◊◊ ▢-▨ ■ **Z7 pH5–7.5**

Above: Planted beneath a clump of woolly lamb's ears
(*Stachys byzantina*), *Allium moly* spangles the silvery grey
stems with its bright umbels of yellow flowers.

Below: The bold yellow flowers of *Allium moly* 'Jeannine'
are scattered randomly among the smaller-flowered purple
Viola 'Gustav Wermig' to form a striking color contrast.

Tall white flower heads of *Allium nigrum*, born aloft on parallel ramrod stems, are here contrasted with the shorter, rich purple-leaved *Euphorbia dulcis* 'Chameleon'.

Allium nigrum

The starry flowers of this undemanding, tall ornamental onion grow in domed umbels on extremely straight stalks. Their color is usually creamy white with a green vein at the center of each petal, but sometimes they are flushed with mauve, while the nectaries in the middle of each floret are either green or black. The most common cultivated variants lack the mauve flush and can therefore be used to good effect with almost any other color, although they are perhaps most arresting when combined with white flowers or contrasting dark foliage. The stiff upright stems look impressive planted as a bold group in a gravel garden, and can make a striking accent for repeating at intervals along a sunny border. To achieve the best effect, it is advisable to grow the plants among later-leafing herbaceous perennials so that the allium foliage receives adequate light during its active growth, but is hidden from view as it dies back.

⬤ *Actaea simplex* Atropurpurea Group, *Aster lateriflorus* 'Lady in Black', *Berberis thunbergii* 'Helmond Pillar', *Geranium phaeum*, *Lysimachia ciliata* 'Firecracker'

H: 60cm (24in) **S: 20cm** (8in)
❁ Late spring to early summer

 Z4 pH5–7.5

Allium sphaerocephalon
ROUND-HEADED LEEK

This is an easy bulb for a gravel garden or sunny border, where it is useful as a unifying theme if repeated at intervals in loose, informal drifts. Its magenta-purple flower heads are an attractive and valuable accessory in a late summer border, although it needs to be grown in generous quantities to be really effective. The flower color combines well with cool shades, particularly pink, lilac, and lavender, and can be contrasted with pale yellow flowers or with yellow-green foliage and flowers such as late-flowering euphorbias. Its slender growth allows it to weave prettily through groups of other plants, although the flower stems often lean at divergent angles, producing a confusing impression that may be avoided by growing the plants through an airy, branching perennial neighbor such as an eryngium or gypsophila.

⬤ *Bupleurum rotundifolium*, *Eryngium planum* 'Blaukappe', *Euphorbia palustris*, *Gaura lindheimeri* 'Whirling Butterflies', *Gypsophila paniculata* 'Flamingo'

H: 60cm (24in) **S: 8cm** (3½in)
❁ Early to late summer

Z6 pH5–7.5

Above: Save for a ruff of narrow bracts, the egg-shaped flower heads of *Eryngium × tripartitum* match the smaller ones of *Allium sphaerocephalon* and harmonize in color.

Below: In this equally harmonious scheme, *Knautia macedonica* matches *Allium sphaerocephalon* perfectly in color, along with lilac *Viola cornuta*, blue cornflowers (*Centaurea cyanus*), and bold seedheads of *Allium cristophii*.

Anemone apennina ♀

This is not a true bulb but a rhizome, sold dry by bulb merchants and often requiring a full season after planting to establish and produce reliable results. Its many "petals" are in fact strap-shaped sepals, which are typically bright lavender-blue and very appealing in combinations with cool colors such as pink, crimson, mauve, and lilac, or with glaucous or yellow-green foliage. A valuable plant for naturalizing, it can be used to create a carpet through which to grow larger spring flowers and bulbs, such as narcissi, smaller tulips, primroses, polyanthus, cowslips, erythroniums, epimediums, and (in sunnier sites) smaller fritillaries. It is also attractive with early-leafing perennials, early-flowering euphorbias, lesser celandine and its variants, particularly those in soft yellow or white, and with spring bedding. Other uses include planting underneath herbaceous and mixed borders, even beneath bush roses, and combining with late-leafing hostas and other herbaceous plants that unfurl their leaves when the anemone's foliage starts to die back. It enjoys humus-rich soils and a sunny site in cool climates, although in warmer areas it can tolerate a considerable amount of shade, such as that of deciduous

◗ *Epimedium × youngianum* 'Niveum', *Euphorbia polychroma* 'Major', *Hosta* 'Blue Arrow', *Primula* 'Guinevere', *Ranunculus ficaria* 'Salmon's White', *Tulipa praestans* 'Unicum', *Valeriana phu* 'Aurea' ❏ p.349 **B**

H: 15cm (6in) S: 20cm (8in) ❀ **Early to mid-spring**
◊◊ ☐-◼ ◼ **Z6 pH5–7.5**

In spring, when the dagger-like leaves of Bearded irises (here, *Iris pallida* 'Variegata') are too small to hide the bare earth between each shoot, the addition of a small plant such as the pretty, bright lavender-blue *Anemone apennina* can complete the picture perfectly.

Anemone blanda has a loose growth habit that makes it suitable for naturalistic plantings, as well as for beds and borders. In informal situations it contrasts well with soft yellow flowers such as primroses (*Primula vulgaris*).

Anemone blanda ♀

Although similar in appearance, cultivation, and uses to *Anemone apennina* (left), and differing only in minor botanical details such as the nodding habit of its mature seedheads, this is an outstandingly versatile species for garden use because of its large number of color variants. These include 'Ingramii' ♀, in rich lavender-blue with a purple reverse to the sepals, and 'Violet Star', which has amethyst-violet flowers. 'Charmer' is rich mauve-pink, while 'Radar' ♀ has striking magenta flowers with a white center. One of the most useful variants is 'White Splendour' ♀, which is white with a mauve-flushed reverse, and is capable of blending with almost any other color; it is perhaps most effective with blue flowers such as muscaris, forget-me-nots, blue hyacinths, and omphalodes. Although in its Mediterranean homeland this anemone grows in full or partial shade, in cooler gardens the flowers require full sun to open completely.

◗ *Hyacinthus orientalis*, *Muscari armeniacum* 'Valerie Finnis', *Omphalodes cappadocica*, *Primula veris*, *Scilla siberica* p.341 **B**, *Tulipa clusiana* p.346 **B**

H: 20cm (8in) S: 30cm (12in)
❀ **Early to mid-spring**
◊◊ ☐-◼ ◼ **Z6 pH5–7.5**

Anemone coronaria
Saint Bridgid Group

This group of showy tuberous herbaceous perennials includes scarlet, crimson, purple, or lavender-blue selections, with all shades between these and white. They are easily raised from seed, or may be bought as a mixture or as single-colored cultivars. Mixtures can be used for naturalizing, to create a millefleurs tapestry effect, and blend well with bluebells, cowslips, and primroses, producing an attractive carpet in a fairly sunny glade, perhaps under a specimen tree such as a magnolia or a dogwood. The single colors are useful for planned color schemes – the semi-double, deep lavender-blue 'Lord Lieutenant', for example, blends with pale lilac, white, or sulfur-yellow, while the semi-double white 'Mount Everest' combines with almost any other color, especially blue.

🌑 *Allium neapolitanum, Amelanchier × grandiflora* 'Ballerina', *Cornus florida, Iris pallida, Magnolia* 'Susan', *Narcissus poeticus* var. *recurvus, Tulipa* 'Maywonder'

H: 40cm (16in) S: 15cm (6in)
❋ **Mid- to late spring**
▬▬▬ 🔲 ◌-◌◌ ⬜ Z8 pH5–7

A limited color range of *Anemone coronaria* Saint Bridgid Group and single anemones combine with bluebells (*Hyacinthoides non-scripta*) in this semi-natural, delightfully simple planting. The bluebells provide contrast in floral form in a harmonious but distinct color.

Anemone nemorosa 🏆
EUROPEAN WOOD ANEMONE

This rhizomatous species is excellent for naturalizing in woodland, and for planting among late-leafing perennials and taller bulbs in borders. There are many double or single cultivars with green, lavender, pink, or white flowers, a few with a green ruff. Good whites include the tall, large-flowered 'Lychette', 'Leeds' Variety' 🏆, and 'Wilks' Giant', and the doubles 'Alba Plena' (also known as 'Flore Pleno') and 'Vestal' 🏆. 'Lismore Pink' is a delicate pale pink, effective with deep pink flowers. Pale lavender-blue cultivars such as the large-flowered 'Blue Beauty'

and 'Robinsoniana' 🏆 are too softly colored for contrasts, but blend effectively with deeper lavender-blue and white. Richer lavender-blue cultivars, including 'Allenii' 🏆, 'Atrocaerulea', 'Blue Bonnet', and 'Royal Blue', harmonize with other lavender-blue flowers and contrast with pale sulfur-yellow or yellow-green foliage and flowers.

🌑 *Anemone × lipsiensis, Arum italicum* 'Marmoratum', *Corydalis solida, Dryopteris erythrosora, Hosta undulata* var. *albomarginata* p.247 **C**, *Lathyrus vernus, Muscari armeniacum* p.330 **A**, *Primula denticulata* 'Snowball', *Scilla bifolia* p.340 **A**, *Trillium grandiflorum*

H: 8–20cm (3½–8in) S: 30cm (12in)
❋ **Early to late spring**
▬▬▬ ◌◌ ⬜-▦ ⬛ Z4 pH4.5–7.5

This charmingly natural and informal mix of mainly woodland flowers would brighten any lightly shaded area. With no pretensions to color scheming yet no clashes, *Anemone nemorosa* is joined by *Muscari armeniacum*, primroses (*Primula vulgaris*), *Cyclamen repandum*, and Siberian squill (*Scilla siberica*).

Anemone pavonina
PEACOCK ANEMONE

This tuberous-rooted herbaceous perennial is similar in appearance, color range, and cultivation requirements to *A. coronaria*, differing mainly in the shape of its leaves, which are deeply cut and lobed, but not divided into separate leaflets. Its garden uses match those of *A. coronaria* Saint Bridgid Group (left), but it is easier to grow and longer-lived, with a more elegant, slender-stemmed appearance that is especially appealing when the plants are naturalized. Attractive companions include early-flowering ceanothus, daphnes, exochordas, magnolias, shrubby, spring-flowering ornamental cherries, white flowering currants, spiraeas, viburnums, and dwarf lilacs.

🌑 *Cytisus × kewensis, Exochorda × macrantha* 'The Bride', *Prunus tenella* 'Fire Hill', *Ribes sanguineum* White Icicle, *Spiraea × vanhouttei, Syringa meyeri* var. *spontanea* 'Palibin', *Viburnum × burkwoodii*

H: 25cm (10in) S: 15cm (6in)
❋ **Mid- to late spring**
▬▬▬ ◌ ⬜ Z8 pH5–7

A pleasant carpet of *Anemone pavonina* in a range of colors, some with white eyes, is shown here growing through grass on a sunny bank together with the smaller-flowered English daisies (*Bellis perennis*).

The upright flowers of *Arisaema erubescens* look to left and right, like a family of rabbits peering anxiously over the undergrowth. Seen here above the fronds of the shield fern *Polystichum setiferum* (Divisilobum Group) 'Herrenhausen', their extravagantly striped and blotched stems and their backing of radiating leaflets are as attractive as their hooded spathes.

The sculptural yellow spathes and bright yellow spadices of *Arum creticum* combine perfectly with the yellow-green inflorescences and purple-flushed leaves of Mrs Robb's bonnet (*Euphorbia amygdaloides* var. *robbiae*).

Arisaema erubescens

Arisaemas are tuberous or rhizomatous perennials with palmate leaves on blotched and spotted stalks, and slightly sinister-looking hooded flowers, usually in subdued colors and often pleasantly striped and veined. Those of the tuberous *A. erubescens* are brownish pink, red, or purple, and covered with a whitish bloom. Their curious beauty is best appreciated at close range, perhaps growing through a carpet of ground cover, preferably of a significantly different color and low enough to reveal the attractive leaves and flower stalks. This is a plant for quiet color schemes, and blends well with warm shades such as brick-red, soft orange, peach, or apricot. It is an appealing subject for a woodland garden and looks good with hostas, ferns, ivies, and epimediums, but it is possibly most effective surrounded by small, finely textured foliage so that the arisaema's distinctive leaf shape is clearly seen.

● *Adiantum pedatum, Epimedium × warleyense* 'Orangekönigin', *Geum* 'Georgenburg', *Heuchera* 'Green Ivory', *Polygonatum falcatum*

H & S: 30cm (12in)
❀ **Late spring to early summer**

 ◊◊ ▫-▪ ▪ Z6 pH4.5–6.5

Arisaema triphyllum

JACK-IN-THE-PULPIT

A familiar native wild flower of the north-eastern United States, this is a tuberous perennial with a hooded white, purple, and green spathe surrounding the central purple or green spadix. In early summer the leaves die back and the spathe shrivels, to be followed in autumn by showy orange-red berries, which combine well with autumn-coloring plants. The muted flowers are effective above a fine-textured ground-cover plant of fairly different leaf color, such as a pale or deep shade of green or yellow-green. The purple flush on the inside of the spathe, and also on the leaf and flower stalks, suits combinations with shades of red or purple, especially crimson and dusky maroon flowers.

● *Aquilegia canadensis, Dicentra* 'Pearl Drops', *Euphorbia polychroma, Geranium × oxonianum* 'Lace Time', *Hosta* 'August Moon', *Iris × fulvala*

H: 45cm (18in) **S: 30cm** (12in)
❀ **Late spring to early summer**

 ◊◊ ▫-▪ ▪ Z4 pH4.5–6.5

The handsome leaves and elegant striped spathe of *Arisaema triphyllum* stand clear and uncluttered above the grey-green filigree foliage and racemes of wine-colored flowers of *Dicentra* 'Bacchanal'.

Arum creticum

This striking tuberous perennial bears glossy, rich green, arrow-shaped leaves and elegantly curved, soft pale yellow spathes surrounding a bright yellow spadix – a coloring that combines effectively with other late spring flowers in blue, yellow, white, or yellow-green, and with yellow-green or glaucous foliage. Attractive companions include muscaris, omphalodes, blue corydalis, euphorbias, yellow-green grasses and sedges, smaller anthemis, smaller narcissi, and late-flowering species tulips. It can be propagated by separating the offsets that form around the main tuber, but established tubers may pull themselves well into the ground, and care should be taken not to sever the main one. Although tender, given a sheltered sunny site this species can survive over winter in cold areas. In hot areas it requires some shade.

● *Anthemis punctata* subsp. *cupaniana, Corydalis flexuosa, Euphorbia amygdaloides* 'Purpurea', *Milium effusum* 'Aureum', *Narcissus* 'Hawera', *Tulipa sprengeri*

H: 45cm (18in) **S: 30cm** (12in) ❀ **Late spring**
▪▪▪▪ ◊◊ ▫-▪ ▪ Z7 pH5–7.5

Arum italicum 'Marmoratum' ♛

In areas where its striking, white-veined leaves are not injured by cold weather, this cultivar of the tuberous Italian or painted arum is very useful for combining with winter-flowering bulbs such as winter aconites, early crocuses, snowdrops, and *Cyclamen coum* variants, as well as winter heaths, bergenias, and small evergreen shrubs such as *Euonymus fortunei* cultivars. In spring it blends well with sedges and evergreen ferns, narcissi, smaller species tulips, bugleweeds, primroses, polyanthus, cowslips, evergreen epimediums, and smaller mahonias. It is happy in sun or partial shade, although its leaf markings are stronger in sun, and it can be grown in a woodland garden or toward the front of a border, where its pale green flower spikes are good with late-leafing perennials. There is a second season of interest in autumn, when showy orange-red berries develop on the spikes – these are enhanced by a low ground cover such as an unvariegated, plain green or yellow-green ivy.

◉ *Ajuga reptans* 'Catlin's Giant', *Erica carnea*, *Narcissus* 'Tête-à-tête', *Skimmia japonica* 'Rubella' p.92 **B**, *Vinca minor* 'Illumination' ❑ pp.53 **C**, 221 **C**

H: 30cm (12in) S: 20cm (8in)
❀ **Late spring to early summer**
 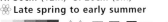 ◊◊ ⬜-▧ ◼ **Z7 pH5–7.5**

Above: In late spring, the eye-catching white-veined leaves of *Arum italicum* 'Marmoratum' combine effectively with foliage of contrasting form, including that of snowdrops, lady's mantle (*Alchemilla mollis*), ostrich fern (*Matteuccia struthiopteris*), and a mahonia, to create an intricate pattern for close-range viewing.

Below: In autumn, the glossy evergreen foliage of *Sarcococca confusa* provides a pleasant foil for the glistening vermilion berries of *Arum italicum* 'Marmoratum'.

The creamy white, star-shaped flowers of *Camassia leichtlinii* 'Semiplena' grow on stiffly upright stems above a planting of vibrantly colored, magenta and yellow columbines beneath. The very dark background, which is provided by *Berberis thunbergii* f. *atropurpurea* above and *Ligularia dentata* 'Desdemona' below, sets off the creamy camassia flowers to dramatic effect.

Camassia leichtlinii 'Semiplena'

This elegant bulbous perennial blooms after most spring bulbs, but before the main flush of summer flowers. Its double florets give the flower spike extra substance, prolonging flowering and enhancing the display. Their soft, creamy color blends with many others, especially warm shades such as peach, apricot, soft orange, and scarlet; it is also good with soft powder blues and deep blues, but is overpowered by very strong mid-blues. The leaves can be unkempt at flowering time, but biennials or hardy annuals, such as nigellas, can be planted in front to screen the foliage as it dies back and the flowers appear. The plants look most effective in loose groups or drifts, blended with yellow or red columbines, geums, ceanothus, late-flowering deciduous azaleas, early yellow roses, and glaucous, yellow-green, or yellow-variegated foliage. Good contrasts can be made with purple or red-flushed foliage.

◉ *Ceanothus* 'Concha', *Eupatorium rugosum* 'Chocolate', *Geranium* × *oxonianum*, *Lunaria annua* 'Variegata', *Rosa* 'Helen Knight'

H: 80cm (31in) S: 23cm (9in)
❀ **Late spring to early summer**
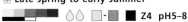 ◊◊ ⬜-▧ ◼ **Z4 pH5–8**

Chionodoxa forbesii

This spring-flowering bulb has star-shaped, soft lavender flowers, with pale centers. An easy bulb for sunny sites, it is useful for planting under mixed or herbaceous borders, where it may be combined with low carpeting plants such as bugleweeds or acaenas. The color blends well with cream, pale yellow, bluish pink, mauve, purple, blue, and white, and with purple, glaucous, or silver foliage. It contrasts reasonably well with yellow-green, but cannot hold its own against strong yellow. The species is often confused with *C. luciliae*; however, it bears 4–12 florets per stem (*C. luciliae* has only one or two).

◔ *Acorus gramineus* 'Ôgon', *Ajuga reptans* 'Arctic Fox', *Dianthus gratianopolitanus*, *Erica carnea* 'Springwood White', *Festuca glauca*, *Narcissus* 'Geranium' p.334 **A**, *Ranunculus ficaria* 'Coffee Cream' ⌐ p.336 **A**

H: 15cm (6in) S: 10cm (4in) ❀ **Early to mid-spring**
◖ △-△△ ▢-◼ **Z4 pH5–8**

Tulips and a carpet of *Chionodoxa forbesii* surround the dark shoots of a *Paeonia lactiflora* cultivar. The bulbs will have finished flowering before the peony casts them into shade, making them useful for planting beneath herbaceous plants.

Chionodoxa forbesii 'Pink Giant'

The soft mauve-pink of this chionodoxa mixes with many of the same colors as *C. forbesii* (above) – white, cream, mauves, blues, and purples – although it is too delicate to contrast satisfactorily with yellow-green, and is not at all successful with yellow. It is a sport of *C.f.* 'Rosea', which differs from the species only in color, but 'Pink Giant' is larger in all respects, enabling it to grow over more neighbors, including wood anemones, and to grow through taller carpeting plants. 'Blue Giant' is equally large and has the lavender flowers of the species, while pure white 'Alba' resembles the species in size and is suitable for lightening any color scheme; it is particularly pretty in plantings with silver foliage, intended to be seen at close range.

◔ *Acaena caesiiglauca*, *Aubrieta* 'Gloriosa', *Dianthus* 'Dewdrop', *Lathyrus vernus*, *Narcissus bulbocodium* p.331 **B**, *Ophiopogon planiscapus* 'Nigrescens'

H: 15cm (6in) S: 10cm (4in) ❀ **Early to mid-spring**
◖ △-△△ ▢-◼ **Z4 pH5–8**

A carpet of neat, dark-leaved bugleweed (*Ajuga reptans* 'Atropurpurea') provides an effective foil for the mauve-pink flowers of *Chionodoxa forbesii* 'Pink Giant'.

The starry, checkered pink flowers of *Colchicum agrippinum* stand out dramatically against the foil of a dark-leaved cultivar of *Ajuga reptans*. This bugleweed is a useful companion for both early and late bulbs.

Colchicum agrippinum ♔

Colchicums (sometimes erroneously called autumn crocuses) are versatile bulbs that flower from late summer until mid-autumn, before their leaves appear. They are supremely effective naturalized in grass or flowering through a carpet of low ground cover – although they are ungainly and readily mud-spattered if grown in bare earth.

C. agrippinum has obscure origins but is probably a hybrid of *C. variegatum*, the species with the most strongly checkered flowers but a difficult plant to grow, whereas *C. agrippinum* is robust and increases well, and withstands being naturalized. It blooms in the middle of the colchicum season, and combines well with flowers in mauve, blue, purple, white, and pink shades on the blue side of primary pink, and also with purple foliage – for example, a carpet of purple-leaved violets. Perhaps the most markedly checkered of the easier garden colchicums, it mixes well with true autumn crocuses such as *Crocus speciosus* ♔ and its cultivars.

🌑 *Achillea clavennae*, *Ajania pacifica*, *Cyclamen hederifolium* 'Silver Cloud', *Haloragis erecta* 'Wellington Bronze', *Scabiosa* Butterfly Blue, *Zephyranthes candida*

H & S: 8cm (3½in)
🌸 **Late summer to early autumn**
◌◌ ▢-▣ **Z5 pH5–7.5**

Colchicum autumnale

AUTUMN CROCUS, MEADOW SAFFRON

This an easy, mid-season colchicum and one of the best for naturalizing in grass, which may be mown until the flowers emerge in early autumn. It can also be grown in beds or borders through a carpet of ground cover, although it lacks the refined flower shape and rich color of some other colchicums and is not perhaps the choicest kind for this purpose. The most useful cultivar for general planting is 'Nancy Lindsay' ♔, which is exceptionally prolific with flowers of rich glowing pink. Double forms that are occasionally grown include 'Pleniflorum', whose star-shaped flowers in the typical mauve-pink color of the species are not so profuse or richly colored as *C.* 'Waterlily' ♔, a prodigious hybrid cultivar whose only fault is a tendency to flop under the weight of its blooms. *C.a.* 'Alboplenum' has starry, double white flowers that are very charming but not absolutely pure white.

Cutting back a carpet of *Lamium maculatum* after its first flush of flowers provides fresh new foliage and some late bloom to flatter meadow saffron (*Colchicum autumnale*).

🌑 *Aster thomsonii* 'Nanus', *Convolvulus sabatius*, *Diascia* 'Lilac Belle', *Geranium* 'Pink Spice', *Hebe pimeleoides* 'Quicksilver', *Hosta* 'Blue Blush', *Origanum laevigatum* 'Herrenhausen', *Verbena* 'Silver Anne'

H: 10cm (4in) **S: 8cm** (3½in)
🌸 **Late summer to early autumn**
◌◌ ▢-▣ **Z5 pH5–7.5**

Colchicum speciosum 'Album' ♔

The colchicum *C. speciosum* ♔ is notable for its late flowering time and the remarkable beauty of its rich magenta-pink flowers, which have broad petals and an immaculate goblet shape. The cultivar 'Atrorubens' has large purple-pink flowers with glowing red stalks. The species is perhaps surpassed in loveliness by the pure white cultivar, 'Album', whose superlative blooms have a touch of yellow towards the base of their petals and are carried on yellow-green stems. This combines agreeably with any color, but it looks particularly effective when grown through a carpet of silver foliage or if starkly contrasted against the leaves of a dusky plant such as a purple-leaved bugleweed or violet.

🌑 *Anthemis punctata* subsp. *cupaniana*, *Ceratostigma willmottianum* Forest Blue, *Fuchsia* 'Tom West', *Liriope muscari*, *Nerine bowdenii*, *Penstemon digitalis* 'Husker Red', *Petunia* 'Purple Wave'

H: 18cm (7in) **S: 10cm** (4in)
🌸 **Early to mid-autumn**
◌◌ ▢-▣ **Z6 pH5–7.5**

Tender carpeting plants such as shrubby *Helichrysum petiolare* 'Variegatum' can be used to furnish the naked flowers of *Colchicum speciosum* 'Album', the yellow tints in the colchicum's blooms harmonizing perfectly with the

The dark, ferny, basal leaves of *Anthriscus sylvestris* 'Ravenswing' make an effective background for the blooms of *Crocus* 'Ladykiller', a cultivar derived principally from *C. biflorus*, although the closely related *C. chrysanthus* is also thought to be involved in its parentage.

Crocus chrysanthus hybrids

These cormous plants are cultivars of *Crocus chrysanthus* (which is yellow), *C. biflorus* (white, purple, or blue), and of hybrids between the two. They vary in color, often with bold markings, and many multiply even when naturalized in grass, especially if clumps are divided in late spring. They grow well in gravel, rock, and pebble gardens, and the front of borders. Generalizations about color combinations are difficult, except to point out that golden or orange cultivars do not mix well with lavender-blue or purple. Attractive cultivars include 'Blue Pearl' ♟, white with pale lavender-blue outer petals; 'Cream Beauty' ♟; 'E.A. Bowles' ♟, rich yellow with purple feathering; 'Ladykiller' ♟, white with deep purple markings; and 'Zwanenburg Bronze' ♟, yellow with broad maroon bands.

Carex morrowii 'Variegata', *Erica carnea* 'Vivellii', *Lamium maculatum*, *Narcissus* 'Eystettensis', *Viola* 'Magnifico', *V. riviniana* Purpurea Group

H: 8cm (3½in) **S: 5cm** (2in)
❀ **Late winter to early spring**

◐ ○-○○ ▢-▧ **Z4 pH5.5–8**

Crocus goulimyi ♟

This fairly easy autumn-flowering crocus, with sweetly scented lilac flowers, is suitable for growing in gravel or rock gardens and at the front of sunny beds or borders. It looks especially fine with white or deep violet variants of *Crocus speciosus*, dark bugleweeds, contrasting forms of *Cyclamen hederifolium*, or a dusky background of purple heucheras.

Other easy autumn crocuses include lilac *C. cartwrightianus* ♟, and its pure white cultivar 'Albus' ♟. *C. pulchellus* ♟ has pretty, dark-veined lavender flowers and is a good choice for naturalizing; its hybrid, 'Zephyr' ♟, is pale lilac. Perhaps most useful of all is *C. speciosus* ♟, which naturalizes and self-seeds readily, and its excellent selections the pure white 'Albus' ♟, the deep lavender-blue 'Conqueror', and the violet 'Oxonian'.

◐ *Acaena microphylla* 'Kupferteppich', *Ajuga reptans* 'Braunherz', *Festuca glauca*, *Geranium* 'Chocolate Candy', *Hebe* 'Mrs Winder', *Verbena* 'Silver Anne'

H: 10cm (4in) **S: 5cm** (2in) ❀ **Mid-autumn**
○-○○ ▢-▧ **Z6 pH5.5–8**

The naked lilac flowers of *Crocus goulimyi* have a backdrop provided by the handsome evergreen *Heuchera* 'Plum Pudding', its purple leaves overlaid (except on its veins) with a metallic sheen. The heuchera should be divided and replanted every two years or so in mid-spring rather than the usual early autumn to avoid impairing its foliage when the crocus comes into bloom.

The goblets of *Crocus* × *luteus* 'Golden Yellow' are set off beautifully by a surrounding carpet of naturalized *Cyclamen coum* in shades of magenta. The cyclamen provides both attractive foliage and contrasting blooms – paler pink variants would form a less effective combination with the orange-yellow crocus. Snowdrops could be added for extra sparkle.

Crocus × *luteus* 'Golden Yellow'
DUTCH YELLOW CROCUS

One of the oldest of all garden hybrids, probably arising in the late sixteenth century, the golden yellow crocus is derived from *C. angustifolius* ♟, from which it inherits the dark stripes at the base of its petals, and *C. flavus*. It is easily grown, and vigorous enough to naturalize successfully in grass, and it multiplies freely into expanding clumps, although as a hybrid its flowers are sterile and cannot produce seeds. It looks effective at the front of beds or borders, especially growing through a low ground cover, alone or in association with other early spring bulbs such as smaller narcissi and snowdrops, and *Crocus chrysanthus* hybrids in white, cream, or pale yellow. It makes pleasant combinations with muscaris or scillas in white or pale to mid-blue shades, but not those inclining towards lavender.

◐ *Ajuga reptans* 'Catlin's Giant', *Carex comans* (bronze), *Euphorbia myrsinites*, *Galanthus nivalis*, *Heuchera* 'Blackbird', *Lysimachia nummularia* 'Aurea', *Narcissus* 'Tête-à-tête', *Scilla siberica* 'Spring Beauty'

H: 8cm (3½in) **S: 5cm** (2in)
❀ **Late winter to early spring**

○-○○ ▢-▧ **Z4 pH5–8**

Crocus tommasinianus ♔

A superlative crocus for growing through a low ground cover or grass, this species has pale lilac to reddish violet flowers, often with silver markings. It is excellent with snowdrops, *Cyclamen coum*, or *Crocus chrysanthus* hybrids in white, pale blue, or lilac, and with pale yellow flowers such as earlier, smaller narcissi. It is also good with winter heaths or beneath yellow witch hazel. This crocus self-seeds freely and thinning may be needed to maintain a balance with companion plants. Various forms bloom from mid-winter to mid-spring: 'Eric Smith' has purple-speckled buds opening to pure white flowers in mid- and late winter; f. *albus* is pure white and flowers in late winter to early spring; and 'Ruby Giant' and 'Whitewell Purple' are larger and slightly later, flowering from late winter to mid-spring.

 Daphne bholua 'Darjeeling', *Eranthis hyemalis* p.312 **B**, *Galanthus elwesii* var. *monostictus* p.316 **A**, *Helleborus* × *hybridus*, *Prunus* × *subhirtella* 'Autumnalis', *Viburnum* × *bodnantense* 'Dawn' ⌐ pp.317 **A**, 321 **B**

H: 8cm (3½in) S: 5cm (2in)
✿ **Mid-winter to mid-spring**
◊-◊◊ ▨-▨ Z5 pH5–8

The heart-shaped leaves and pale flowers of *Cyclamen coum* f. *pallidum*, enlivened by a burgundy blotch at the base of each petal, blend attractively with the violet blooms of *Crocus tommasinianus*. Both plants will self-seed readily, making them ideal for naturalizing.

Crocus vernus cultivars

The flowers of *Crocus vernus* cultivars vary from white and lilac to lavender or deep purple, and first appear in late winter or early spring, a week or two after *C. tommasinianus* (left) and *C. chrysanthus* hybrids (facing page) start to flower. Robust plants that multiply freely, they look effective with winter heaths, *Cyclamen coum* variants, chionodoxas, and snowdrops, or with purple or silver foliage. The deepest purples show up less well from a distance and are not so useful for naturalizing, whereas striped varieties provide a lighter, paler tone for growing in grass. Attractive cultivars include the light mauve-purple 'Enchantress' and the light violet 'Flower Record'; 'Graecus', in soft lavender; 'Jeanne d'Arc', in pure white with a hint of purple; the mid-lavender 'Queen of the

The small, white-lined foliage of *Crocus vernus* 'Jeanne d'Arc' is echoed exactly by the much larger, handsome evergreen leaves of *Iris foetidissima* 'Variegata'. Woolly lamb's ears (*Stachys byzantina*), planted throughout to give a later ground cover, could be replaced with a more evergreen carpeting plant such as a small-leaved ivy.

Blues', and 'Vanguard', in pale lilac with deeper lilac-grey outer petals. Good purples include 'Paulus Potter' and 'Remembrance', while 'Pickwick' and 'Striped Beauty' are striped. For the most pleasant results when naturalizing, choose closely related colors and plant in uneven, overlapping drifts.

 Chionodoxa forbesii, *Heuchera* 'Purple Petticoats', *Lamium maculatum* 'Beedham's White', *Primula vulgaris* subsp. *sibthorpii*, *Vinca minor* 'Argenteovariegata'

H: 10–13cm (4–5in) S: 5cm (2in)
✿ **Late winter to late spring**
◊-◊◊◊ ▨-▨ Z4 pH5–8

Cyclamen hederifolium 🏆

Although fairly tolerant of sun in areas with cool summers, this easy autumn cyclamen revels in dappled shade, in beds or at the front of borders, in a woodland garden, or beneath deciduous trees and shrubs in bare ground (it will not compete with grass). The flower color ranges from white to magenta-red, and the variable leaf shape resembles a narrow ivy leaf, often with silver markings. A tuberous plant appearing first in late summer, usually without leaves, it mixes well with colchicums and autumn crocuses. Purple foliage contrasts well with the white forms or harmonizes with pink to magenta-red ones; white f. *albiflorum* is particularly striking with near-black foliage. Useful selections include 'Rosenteppich', deep magenta-pink to magenta-red, and 'Ruby Glow', even deeper magenta or magenta-purple, sometimes paling at the margins. Bowles' Apollo Group comprises white- or pink-flowered plants with shield-shaped, silver leaf markings, flushed red when young, while 'Silver Cloud' has fully silver leaves and pink flowers.

🌐 *Arum italicum* 'Marmoratum', *Buddleja davidii* 'Dartmoor', *Caryopteris* × *clandonensis*, *Ceratostigma willmottianum*, *Colchicum agrippinum*, *Crocus speciosus*, *Hedera helix* 'Glacier', *Nerine bowdenii*, *Salvia officinalis* 'Purpurascens' ❏ pp.237 **C**, 321 **A**

H: 10–13cm (4–5in) **S: 15cm** (6in)
✽ **Late summer to mid-autumn**
⬛⬜ 🌑🌑 ⬛ **Z5 pH5–8**

The white flowers of *Cyclamen hederifolium* f. *albiflorum* stand out dramatically against mondo grass (*Ophiopogon planiscapus* 'Nigrescens'). The leaves of the cyclamen will overlap those of the ophiopogon in spring.

Eranthis hyemalis, each bloom surrounded by a decorative ruff of leaves, creates a striking color contrast with the early-flowering *Crocus tommasinianus* 'Whitewell Purple'.

Eranthis hyemalis 🏆
WINTER ACONITE

This tuberous plant may be naturalized beneath deciduous trees or shrubs, where it looks charming when flowering with the first spring bulbs, such as early snowdrops, pure white *Cyclamen coum* f. *albissimum*, and light to mid-blue early scillas. Here it will seed itself readily on bare ground, but it cannot compete with dense grass. All winter aconites are also useful for borders, planted in positions where they are later covered by deciduous foliage. Cilicica Group (syn. *E. cilicica*) has larger flowers of a more golden yellow, and bronze-flushed foliage. The hybrid between this and Tubergenii Group, the typical species, has extra vigor, and bears outstanding golden flowers and bronze-flushed foliage, particularly noteworthy in the cultivar 'Guinea Gold' 🏆. Despite being so vigorous, this cultivar does not self-seed.

🌐 *Carex buchananii*, *Euphorbia amygdaloides* 'Purpurea', *Galanthus nivalis*, *Hamamelis* × *intermedia*, *Leucothoe* Scarletta, *Vinca minor* ❏ pp.317 **A**, 331 **B**

H & S: 5cm (2in) ✽ **Late winter to early spring**
⬛⬜ 🌑🌑 ⬛ **Z5 pH5.5–7.5**

Erythronium californicum 'White Beauty' ♛

Erythroniums are among the most graceful of all spring bulbs. The European dog's-tooth violet (*E. dens-canis* ♛), with white, pink, or purple flowers and dappled leaves, is well-known, but some North American species and hybrids are more vigorous. *E. californicum* 'White Beauty' has creamy white flowers and bold foliage, attractively veined and shaded silvery green and bronze. It looks good in a woodland site or beneath a border where it is exposed to sun while in leaf. Its delicate color mixes with almost any other, but it looks best with blue or rich yellow. The foliage contrasts well with ferns, corydalis, grasses, and sedges, particularly in bronze or yellow-green. The pure white *E.* 'Minnehaha' ♛ is taller and very elegant.

🌣 *Athyrium filix-femina, Carex flagellifera, Corydalis flexuosa, Dicentra spectabilis* 'Alba', *Epimedium* × *perralchicum, Hepatica nobilis, Muscari latifolium, Myosotis sylvatica, Primula bulleyana*

H: 25cm (10in) **S: 15cm** (6in)
❀ **Mid- to late spring**

 ◊◊ ▨ ■ Z5 pH5–7.5

The boldly shaped cream and yellow flowers of *Erythronium californicum* 'White Beauty' contrast in size and color with the tiny blue florets of *Brunnera macrophylla*.

Erythronium 'Pagoda' ♛

This vigorous hybrid produces slender stems of sulfur-yellow flowers, above a clump of bold, fresh green leaves, which – unlike those of its parent *E. californicum* 'White Beauty' (left) – lack any significant markings. Its other parent is *E. tuolumnense* ♛, from which it inherits its very free production of offsets. 'Kondo' is another yellow-flowered hybrid with the same parentage, closely related to two other excellent cultivars: 'Citronella', slightly later with clear yellow flowers and dark anthers, and 'Sundisc', with yellow horizontal petals and a red throat. All may be used in the same situations as 'White Beauty', combined with blue, cream, white, or orange flowers, and with bronze or yellow-green foliage, including grasses, sedges, and ferns.

🌣 *Dryopteris affinis, Geranium* × *oxonianum* 'Walter's Gift', *Geum* 'Lemon Drops', *Hosta* 'Golden Tiara', *Lathyrus aureus, Milium effusum* 'Aureum', *Omphalodes cappadocica, Ranunculus bulbosus* 'F.M. Burton'

H: 30cm (12in) **S: 15cm** (6in)
❀ **Mid- to late spring**

 ◊◊ ▨ ■ Z5 pH5–7.5

The elegant blooms of *Erythronium* 'Pagoda', born above handsome, unmarked green leaves, harmonize with a carpet of the much smaller *Anemone ranunculoides*, a rhizomatous species useful for a spring ground cover.

Erythronium revolutum provides attractive blooms and ground cover between emerging fronds of the ostrich fern (*Matteuccia struthiopteris*), its rich rose-pink flowers contrasting with the fern's bright green leaves. The fern foliage will splay out to cover most of the ground as the erythronium dies back.

Erythronium revolutum ♛

The leaves of this species, perhaps the most handsomely marked in the whole genus, are heavily marbled with silvery green and bronze. Each stem bears up to four rose-pink flowers. 'Pink Beauty', in mauve-pink, and 'Rose Beauty', in deep pink with leaves strongly marked with bronze, are two fine cultivars; 'Joanna' is a hybrid with an unusual floral mix of pink and yellow. Johnsonii Group covers some outstanding pink-flowered variants; the pretty, soft pink hybrid 'Rosalind' is a seedling of this group. All these erythroniums thrive in the same situations as *E. californicum* 'White Beauty' (left) and combine with mauve, lilac, white, purple, cream, or crimson flowers, and with purple, silver, or glaucous foliage. They work well with small rhododendrons and, for foliage contrast, with ferns, grasses, or sedges.

🌣 *Camellia* × *williamsii* 'Donation', *Cardamine pentaphylla, Primula denticulata, Pulmonaria* 'Lewis Palmer', *Vinca minor* 'Gertrude Jekyll'

H: 20–30cm (10–12in) **S: 15cm** (6in)
❀ **Mid- to late spring**

◊◊ ▨ ■ Z5 pH5–7.5

The erect, pale apple-green racemes of *Eucomis pallidiflora* contrast with the elegant, pink, scented flowers of *Lilium speciosum* in a sheltered site at the foot of a wall.

Eucomis pallidiflora

In favored climates and sunny positions, this is an exceedingly handsome bulb, its pale apple-green flowers and bold strap-shaped leaves making a strong architectural accent. It suits the second rank of a border, together with agapanthus, white Japanese anemones, or late lilies, and combines well with blue, white, and yellow-green, and warm colors such as peach and apricot, as well as contrasting with rich pink. Other species commonly grown include *E. bicolor*, with pale green flowers edged maroon, maroon anthers, and a topknot of bracts that gives the genus its common name of pineapple lily. *E. comosa* has a shorter topknot and taller spike of whitish flowers, with narrow maroon edges and maroon ovaries; some of its selections have purple-flushed foliage and flowers. The tallest species is *E. pole-evansii*, at 1.8m (6ft), with soft green, cream-centered flowers.

○ *Agapanthus* 'Loch Hope', *Clematis durandii*, *Dahlia* 'David Howard', *Fuchsia* 'Genii', *Melianthus major*, *Plectranthus argentatus*, *Ricinus communis* 'Carmencita', *Salpiglossis* 'Royale Chocolate'

H: 60cm (24in)   S: 30cm (12in)
❋ **Late summer to early autumn**

○○ ■-■ **Z8   pH5–7.5**

Fritillaria imperialis
CROWN IMPERIAL

This is an imposing, architectural spring bulb, creating bold focal points when planted in groups, and tall enough to interact with white lilacs, kerrias, physocarpus, and other shrubs of medium height, or with deciduous azaleas if the soil is not too acid or too wet. Yellow cultivars work well with cream or blue flowers, yellow-green foliage and flowers, and glaucous foliage. Orange cultivars are good with cream, warm colors such as peach or apricot, and bronze foliage. The red cultivars combine with orange or scarlet, yellow-green foliage and flowers, and bronze foliage; they are outstanding planted with late tulips, late narcissi, and early-leafing hostas. Among the best are 'Maxima Lutea' ♥, which is slightly shorter than the species; 'Sulpherino', in tangerine-orange with purplish veins; 'The Premier' is orange and flowers early; and 'Rubra Maxima' has large florets. The red 'Argenteovariegata', with white-edged leaves, is shorter-growing and good for jazzy effects.

○ *Chaenomeles speciosa* 'Geisha Girl', *Euphorbia characias* subsp. *wulfenii*, *Kerria japonica* 'Picta', *Philadelphus coronarius* 'Aureus' ❑ p.343 **C**

H: 75–120cm (30–48in)   S: 25cm (10in)
❋ **Mid- to late spring**

 ○○ ■-■ **Z5   pH5–7.5**

A statuesque group of burnt orange crown imperials (*Fritillaria imperialis*), among the tallest of spring bulbs, harmonizes with warm-colored tulips including the Single Early Group *Tulipa* 'Apricot Beauty'.

The nodding bells of checker lily (*Fritillaria meleagris*), with checkered markings in burgundy and dusky pink, are especially fine seen at close range. Here, they are daintily poised above Siberian squill (*Scilla siberica*).

Fritillaria meleagris ♈

GUINEA-HEN FLOWER

Moist springs and cool, dryish summers best suit this subtly colored water-meadow plant, with distinctive nodding flowers in checkered shades of dusky pinkish purple. It can be grown with plants that like similar conditions, such as *Saxifraga granulata* and *Cardamine pratensis* cultivars, and with bergenias, muscaris, primulas, purple-leaved heucheras, and cream or white narcissi, especially the smaller kinds. Its subdued colors are effective with pink, mauve, and white flowers, and with purple foliage. The white variant, var. *unicolor* subvar. *alba* ♈, has faint white and pale greenish cream checkering; 'Aphrodite' is a large, fine selection of this, effective with almost any color, especially blue flowers. Other cultivars include 'Jupiter', a richer, deeper and more reddish shade than the species, and 'Mars', in deep purple. The subtle markings of all these benefit from being seen at close range.

◉ *Bergenia cordifolia* 'Purpurea', *Brunnera macrophylla* 'Dawson's White', *Heuchera* 'Plum Pudding', *Lathyrus vernus* 'Alboroseus', *Muscari armeniacum*, *Narcissus* 'Thalia', *Ornithogalum nutans* p.338 **C**, *Primula elatior* p.277 **A**, *Tulipa linifolia* Batalinii Group p.349 **B**

H: 15–30cm (6–12in) S: 15cm (6in)
✿ Mid- to late spring
 ◊◊-◊◊◊ ▢-▢ Z4 pH5–7.5

Fritillaria persica

This fritillary is a highly variable species with bell-shaped, pendant flowers, born on sturdy stems, and lance-shaped leaves. Its most reliable cultivar is 'Adiyaman' ♈, 1m (40in) high and best grown among shorter plants so that its impressive glaucous foliage and brooding, plum-purple flowers are clearly seen from all sides. It harmonizes well with blue, purple, crimson, and pink flowers on the blue side of primary pink, and with glaucous, silver, or purple foliage. It makes effective contrasts with soft yellow and cream, and its dusky appearance can be enlivened by combinations with reds, deep pinks, and red foliage on the orange side of primary red. Good companions include late tulips, cream or pale yellow late narcissi, polyanthus, and some *Ranunculus asiaticus* cultivars.

◉ *Erysimum* 'Bowles' Mauve', *Lunaria annua* 'Variegata', *Pittosporum tenuifolium* 'Nigricans', *Ruta graveolens* 'Jackman's Blue'

H: 60–120cm (24–48in) S: 30cm (12in)
✿ Mid- to late spring
▬▬▬ ◊-◊◊ ▢-▢ Z6 pH5–8

In this display of rich reds and purples, the bold spikes of dusky bells of *Fritillaria persica* 'Adiyaman' harmonize with blood-red tulips and a Japanese maple (*Acer palmatum* f. *atropurpureum*), while the fritillary's glaucous foliage provides a pleasant contrast.

Fritillaria pyrenaica ♈

This easy, vigorous fritillary will grace any sunny border, rock garden, or gravel garden – especially if it is planted where its elegant, nodding flowers can be seen at close range since their brown-purple coloring does not show up well from a distance. It is perhaps most effective combined with soft oranges, apricots, creams, or soft yellows, or with yellow-green foliage and flowers such as early-flowering euphorbias. Similar associations suit other easy, subtly colored fritillaries, such as *F. acmopetala* ♈, with pale green flowers stained purple-brown on the

The bright yellow-green flower heads of *Euphorbia polychroma* 'Major' provide an effective foil for the dusky maroon bells of *Fritillaria pyrenaica*.

inner petals; *F. graeca* subsp. *thessala*, which is pale greenish brown and lightly checkered; and *F. messanensis*, which has green flowers checkered brown-purple towards the edges.

◉ *Dicentra* 'Pearl Drops', *Plantago lanceolata* 'Golden Spears', *Salvia officinalis* 'Icterina', *Stachys byzantina* 'Primrose Heron', *Thymus vulgaris* 'Silver Posie'

H: 45cm (18in) S: 20cm (8in)
✿ Mid- to late spring
 ◊-◊◊ ▢-▢ Z6 pH5–8

Galanthus elwesii var. *monostictus*

This broad-leaved snowdrop, formerly called *G. caucasicus* hort., is an easy, handsome bulb, useful for naturalizing or planting on a large scale, perhaps combined with early crocuses, winter aconites, winter heaths, early-flowering hellebores, *Iris unguicularis* cultivars and Reticulata hybrids, *Cyclamen coum*, and evergreens such as bergenias, *Euonymus fortunei* cultivars, asarums, and heucheras. The cultivar 'Hiemalis' is useful as it flowers in mid-winter, while 'Washfield Colesbourne' a variety of *G. elwesii*, makes a tall, handsome plant with flowers with deep emerald-green inner petals. All can be grown through short ground-covering plants like bugleweeds or smaller ivies, and are happy in both deciduous woodland or at the front of a sunny border.

Bergenia 'Eric Smith', *Crocus sieberi*, *Hedera helix* 'Glymii', *Helleborus foetidus*, *Iris unguicularis* p.253 C

H: 12–23cm (5–9in) **S: 15cm** (6in)
Late winter to mid-spring
Z5 pH5–7.5

The bold foliage and relatively large flowers of the snowdrop *Galanthus elwesii* var. *monostictus* make a showy early display with mauve *Crocus tommasinianus*. Both are vigorous, widely available, and suited to naturalizing on a large scale in the open or under deciduous trees and shrubs.

A

Galanthus nivalis ♀

COMMON SNOWDROP

This undemanding species resembles *G. elwesii* var. *monostictus* (facing page) in its uses, cultivation, and combinations, although its smaller size is more suited to intimate planting schemes and tiny gardens. Many dozens of variants are cultivated, a few readily available from nurseries. Perhaps the most useful is 'Flore Pleno' ♀, the double common snowdrop. Although this lacks the simplicity of the species, its longer-lasting flowers appear larger and showier, making more impact when naturalized. Other attractive cultivars include 'Lady Elphinstone', a double

Above: The showy flowers of the double snowdrop *Galanthus nivalis* 'Flore Pleno' sit prettily among other early flowers such as *Crocus tommasinianus*, winter aconites (*Eranthis hyemalis*), and *Cyclamen coum*. All are suited to naturalizing and all but the snowdrop will self-seed freely.

Left: The elegant single flowers of the common snowdrop (*Galanthus nivalis*) combine well with evergreen perennials and small shrubs such as the brightly variegated *Euonymus fortunei* 'Emerald 'n' Gold'.

that has yellow markings on the inner petals, and 'Pusey Green Tip', also double, with outer petals flushed green. The leaf-like spathes of Sharlockii Group are split into two and overlap the flowers, while 'Viridapicis' has a long spathe, sometimes split into two, and green markings on the outer petals. Like all snowdrops, these are best transplanted when in green leaf or during the two or three months afterwards, when plants are dormant – bulbs bought from a store may be dried up and therefore difficult to establish.

◉ *Arum italicum* 'Marmoratum', *Bergenia cordifolia* 'Purpurea' p.197 **B**, *Eranthis hyemalis*, *Hedera helix* 'Manda's Crested', *Heuchera micrantha* var. *diversifolia* 'Palace Purple', *Vinca minor* ❏ p.321 **C**

H: 8–13cm (3–5in) S: 10cm (4in)
❀ **Late winter to mid-spring**
░░░░ ◊◊ ▢-▪ ■ **Z4 pH4.5–8**

Galtonia candicans

This useful bulb, flowering in late summer, has pendant bell-shaped flowers, white with a light green basal tint, and long, strap-shaped leaves that tend to kink untidily. Its subtle hues combine successfully with any color, but it looks particularly effective in a white garden, planted together with blue or green flowers such as nicotianas, or weaving through a carpet of shorter bedding plants. Other good companions include agapanthus, dahlias, *Aster amellus* cultivars, sun-tolerant hostas, and tender, late summer perennials – cannas, argyranthemums, and late-flowering lilies, for example – while shorter fuchsias can be used to hide its foliage from sight. It is an excellent choice for taking the place of earlier flowers, such as Oriental poppies, after they have died back. *G. viridiflora* ♀, a slightly less hardy species, is similar, but with elegant green bell-like flowers that do not show up well against the green foliage unless seen at close range.

◉ *Agapanthus* 'Loch Hope', *Agastache* 'Firebird', *Artemisia lactiflora* Guizhou Group, *Dahlia* 'Bednall Beauty', *Filipendula rubra* 'Venusta', *Lilium* 'Black Beauty', *Nicotiana langsdorffii*, *Papaver orientale* 'Sultana'

H: 1.2m (4ft) S: 30cm (12in) ❀ Late summer
░░░░ ◊◊ ▢-▪ ■ **Z7 pH5.5–7.5**

The white bells of *Galtonia candicans* bloom above the old Dwarf Bedding Group dahlia *D.* 'Hatton Castle' in a striking late summer display. The dahlia disguises the galtonia's foliage, which tends to become unkempt as flowering time nears. Other good companions for the galtonia are the dahlias 'Gallery Art Deco' and 'Orange Nugget'.

Gladiolus communis subsp. *byzantinus* ♚

The deep magenta, funnel-shaped flowers of this gladiolus species have a grace and elegance that is lacking in some of the large-flowered gladiolus hybrids. The vibrant color blends well with soft shades such as mauves, pinks, and blues, and with silver or purple foliage, and makes a striking contrast with flowers or foliage in soft yellow or yellow-green. Vigorous and very easy to grow, and spreading readily from cormlets, it is an excellent choice for sunny sites with well drained soil. It combines authentically with other Mediterranean plants such as cistus, rosemaries, sages, lavenders, and lavender cotton, especially if these are positioned where they can mask the sparse, fairly unattractive base of the gladiolus clumps.

◑ *Cistus* × *purpureus*, *Cytisus* × *praecox* 'Warminster', *Iris pallida*, *Lavandula stoechas* subsp. *pedunculata*, *Phormium* 'Bronze Baby', *Rosmarinus officinalis*

H: 90cm (36in) **S: 30cm** (12in) ✿ **Early summer**
◌-◌◌◌ ▢-▇ **Z7 pH5.5–7**

Magenta-flowered *Gladiolus communis* subsp. *byzantinus* and *Geranium psilostemon* have contrasting flower shapes that combine well. Their rich color is brightened by the silver leaves of rose campion (*Lychnis coronaria*), which will add its own magenta blooms before the gladiolus fades.

A

B

A drift of showy *Gladiolus* 'Dancing Doll' (there is also a Butterfly Group cultivar of this name) is combined with other plants with vertical inflorescences, including pure blue *Salvia patens* and *Penstemon* 'Mother of Pearl'. These form an effective contrast with the rounded flower heads of *Phlox paniculata* cultivars. *Gladiolus* 'Windsong' would look equally good in such a planting.

Gladiolus Grandiflorus Group

Hybrid gladioli of the Grandiflorus Group are available in every color except pure blue, black, and blue-green. The Giant-, Large-, and Medium-flowered hybrids have great impact and an almost tropical exuberance that suits large-scale plantings. Their spikily emphatic growth habit makes bold accents, and any stiffness can be masked by planting shorter, mound-forming plants in front. Staking is often necessary to anchor the bottom half of their stems. They are excellent with dark-leaved dahlias or when echoing the growth of *Crocosmia paniculata* and *C. masoniorum* cultivars and hybrids. The Small- and Miniature-flowered Grandiflorus gladioli are more graceful and suitable for smaller gardens, but their dramatic potential is less.

◑ *Cleome hassleriana*, *Dahlia* 'Arabian Night', *Lavatera* 'Barnsley', *Miscanthus sinensis* 'Kleine Silberspinne', *Penstemon* 'King George V', *Phygelius* × *rectus*

H: 1.5–1.8m (5–6ft) **S: 20cm** (8in)
✿ **Early to late summer**
◌-◌◌◌ ▢-▇ **Z9 pH5.5–7**

Gladiolus small-flowered hybrids

There are several groups of small-flowered gladioli, with more graceful stems than those in the Grandiflorus Group (above), usually with fewer, smaller, more widely spaced flowers, and less disfigured by fading blooms. Most have slender, often kinked foliage, and benefit from carpeting plants in front. Nanus Group produces two or three slender spikes of loosely arranged blooms in early summer. Primulinus Group has one thin stem, with up to 23 buds in a stepladder arrangement, in early to mid-summer. Tubergenii Group cultivars have slender flower spikes in early summer. All are effective near the front of a sunny border, with smaller philadelphus and Shrub roses, larger pinks, and diascias.

◑ *Erysimum* 'Bowles' Mauve', *Euphorbia palustris*, *Philadelphus* 'Manteau d'Hermine', *Phlomis purpurea*, *Rosa* Sweet Dream, *Spiraea japonica* 'Bullata'

H: 1–1.2m (3¼–4ft) **S: 15cm** (6in)
✿ **Early to late summer**
◌-◌◌◌ ▢-▇ **Z9 pH5.5–7**

C

The sumptuous red blooms of *Gladiolus* 'Georgette', one of several of this name, harmonize in color but contrast in form with the dainty hanging bells of *Fuchsia magellanica* 'Versicolor', contrasting well with the fuchsia's pale leaves.

Hyacinthoides hispanica
SPANISH BLUEBELL

This vigorous bulbous perennial is a native of shady places but tolerates full sun and naturalizes well – although its flower heads, with florets arranged round the stem, lack the informality of the common bluebell, which has one-sided spikes. It is also effective when used underneath borders or for a woodland garden, where nearby herbaceous plants and deciduous shrubs can hide its dying foliage. The campanula-blue florets, enlivened by a deeper, purer blue mid-rib, combine happily with white or soft yellow flowers, yellow-green foliage and flowers, and glaucous foliage. They work well with late narcissi, tulips, and primroses, and are also acceptable with saxifrages and other pink or mauve flowers. Cultivars include blue 'Excelsior', 'La Grandesse', which is white, and mauve-pink 'Rosabella' and 'Rose'.

● *Euonymus fortunei* 'Silver Queen' p.49 **B**, *Euphorbia characias* subsp. *wulfenii*, *Lamium galeobdolon* 'Hermann's Pride', *Narcissus* 'Spellbinder', *Primula vulgaris*, *Saxifraga umbrosa*, *Symphytum* 'Goldsmith', *Tanacetum vulgare* 'Isla Gold', *Valeriana phu* 'Aurea'

H: 40cm (16in) **S: 15cm** (6in) ❀ **Late spring**
◌-◌◌ ☐-■ **Z4 pH4–8**

The soft flowers of the bluebell *Hyacinthoides hispanica* harmonize with the emerging glaucous leaves of the plume poppy (*Macleaya cordata*). The latter's leaves will expand to cover the fading flowers and foliage of the bluebell.

Gladiolus tristis var. *concolor*

Gladiolus tristis is a variable species with creamy white flowers, tinged yellowish green and flushed or dotted with mauve, red, brown, or purple. In var. *concolor*, the creamy white grades to yellowish green at the center of each petal and towards the base of the flower. A lovely plant, worthy of a precious warm position in cooler gardens, it has elegant blooms with an exquisite fragrance, especially in the evening. Its color blends with almost any other, especially with blue, pure yellow, and crimson flowers, yellow-green foliage and flowers, and glaucous foliage. The grassy foliage tends to kink, so it is best masked by growing it through other short, loosely cushioning plants. Superlative

The cream flowers of *Gladiolus tristis* var. *concolor*, with their greenish yellow centers and buds, create a gentle contrast with the lilac-mauve flowers of Single Late Group *Tulipa* 'Bleu Aimable' and the perfectly matching variegated moneyplant (*Lunaria annua* 'Variegata'), together with blue alpine forget-me-nots (*Myosotis alpestris*).

companions include forget-me-nots, dark sweet Williams and hyacinths, and also tulips (except the most brilliantly colored kinds, which tend to upstage the gladiolus).

● *Brunnera macrophylla*, *Dianthus barbatus* Nigrescens Group, *Euphorbia* × *martini*, *Melissa officinalis* 'Aurea', *Prunus glandulosa* 'Alba Plena', *Spiraea japonica* 'Goldflame', *Tanacetum parthenium* 'Aureum'

H: 45cm (18in) **S: 15cm** (6in)
❀ **Late spring to early summer**
◌-◌◌ ☐-■ **Z9 pH5.5–7**

Hyacinthus orientalis

The common hyacinth is popular as a fragrant indoor plant, but its potential outdoors is neglected by many gardeners. Full-size bulbs produce coarse, rather heavy flower spikes when grown as individual plants or in small gardens, but permanent outdoor plantings form small clumps with slender flower spikes that seem more graceful and natural. The single or double flowers are available in most colors, except strong yellow and rich orange, and look extremely attractive mixed in loose drifts of different shades of the same color – three or four irregularly blended shades of blue, for example, can look very pleasant interplanted with taller, softer yellow narcissi. White, yellow, or orange narcissi are ideal planting companions for hyacinths, as are tulips, wallflowers, silver-leaved pulmonarias, polyanthus, *Prunus tenella* cultivars, exochordas, daphnes (especially variants of *Daphne mezereum*), rock cress, aubrietas, and bluebell cultivars in a distinctly different color. For a daintier effect, *H.o.* var. *albulus*, the white-flowered Roman hyacinth, has numerous, more slender spikes of flowers; and the blue-flowered var. *provincialis* has a similar habit. Among the best hyacinth cultivars are the pale pink 'Anna Marie' ♀; 'Blue Jacket' ♀ in deep blue; 'City of Haarlem' ♀ in soft primrose-yellow; 'Delft Blue' ♀ in soft blue; 'Gipsy Queen' ♀ in peach; the purplish blue 'Ostara' ♀; 'Pink Pearl' ♀ in deep pink; 'L'Innocence' ♀ in white; and 'Borah' ♀, which has numerous, very slender lavender-blue spikes.

◗ *Arabis blepharophylla* 'Frühlingszauber', *Daphne mezereum* f. *alba*, *Erysimum cheiri* Prince Series, *Euphorbia polychroma* 'Major', *Lamium maculatum*, *Myosotis sylvatica*, *Narcissus* 'February Gold' p.332 **B**, *N.* 'Jetfire', *Nonea lutea*, *Primula* Cowichan Venetian Group, *Pulmonaria* Opal, *Viola* Ultima Series

H: 20–30cm (8–12in) S: 15cm (6in)
❀ **Early to mid-spring**
◊-◊◊ ▢-▮ **Z5 pH4.5–7.5**

Above right: The dainty flower spikes of the Dutch hyacinth (*Hyacinthus orientalis* var. *albulus*) are ideal for a smaller scale of planting such as a window box. Here, they drape themselves gracefully over the box's edge, elegantly decorating the brightly bicolored blooms of the relatively short Single Early Group *Tulipa* 'Keizerskroon'.

Right: This mixture of hyacinths is saved from dullness by the uneven grouping of three cultivars, white *Hyacinthus orientalis* 'L'Innocence', purplish-blue 'Ostara', and the slightly deeper 'Blue Jacket'. Adding a fourth plant, perhaps a soft yellow narcissus or a yellow-green euphorbia such as *E. polychroma* 'Major', would also be effective.

The bright, early blooms of *Iris danfordiae* shine against
the dark, attractively zoned foliage of *Cyclamen hederifolium*.
A white-flowered variant of an early-blooming cyclamen,
for example *C. coum*, could also be used.

Iris danfordiae

This winter-flowering Reticulata iris, with
bright chrome-yellow flowers enlivened by
greenish markings at the base of the falls, is
a good subject for a rock or gravel garden,
and for the front of a border, perhaps through
a carpet of very low-growing ground cover.
It can be combined with snowdrops, white
Cyclamen coum, stinking hellebores, and blue
Reticulata irises, and makes a dramatic
contrast with black mondo grass. Deep
planting to a depth of about 20cm (8in) can
prevent bulbs disintegrating after flowering
into tiny bulblets, the size of rice grains,
which take many years to reach flowering size
again. Like other Reticulata irises, the leaves
become long and grassy after flowering; they
must have full sun to guarantee blooms the
following year, and plants need careful siting,
to ensure the foliage will not be intrusive.

◐ *Euphorbia myrsinites*, *Galanthus* 'S. Arnott',
Heuchera 'Chocolate Veil', *Sedum spathulifolium*
'Purpureum', *Trifolium repens* 'Purpurascens'

H: 10cm (4in) S: 5cm (2in)
❊ **Late winter to early spring**

 Z5 pH6–7.5

Iris 'George'

Slightly easier to grow than *Iris danfordiae*
(left), this winter-flowering Reticulata iris is
less liable to divide into small, non-flowering
bulblets and requires less (although still
good) drainage. Its plum-colored flowers,
enlivened by a gold splash on the falls, mix
well with the same plants as *I. danfordiae*,
especially with pink and carmine variants of
Cyclamen coum and early crocuses such as *C.
tommasinianus* variants. It can be combined
with winter heaths, although care is needed to
ensure that these do not overwhelm the irises
for successful interaction. It is also excellent
in pots or window boxes, especially with
variegated ivies.

◐ *Ajuga reptans* 'Burgundy Glow', *Chionodoxa forbesii*
'Pink Giant', *Cyclamen hederifolium*, *Erica carnea*,
Primula vulgaris subsp. *sibthorpii*

H: 13cm (5in) S: 5cm (2in)
❊ **Late winter to early spring**

 Z4 pH5–7.5

Black mondo grass (*Ophiopogon planiscapus* 'Nigrescens')
provides a dusky background for the sumptuous purple
blooms of *Iris* 'George'. Mauve *Crocus tommasinianus* will
lighten the combination before the iris fades.

Pure blue *Iris* 'Joyce'
harmonizes perfectly with
the glaucous foliage of
the rue *Ruta graveolens*
'Jackman's Blue', the
variegated leaves of the
periwinkle *Vinca major*
'Variegata', and common
snowdrops (*Galanthus
nivalis*). This display
would work equally well
on a larger scale, with the
iris clumped less solidly
and more intermingled
with its partners.

Iris 'Joyce'

This is another Reticulata iris, which
resembles 'George' (above) in being fairly
easy to grow. It thrives in gravel and rock
gardens and at the front of a border, in a
carpet of low-growing ground cover or in
combination with plants such as snowdrops,
early scillas, Lenten roses and other early-
flowering hellebores, winter heaths (especially
white-flowered cultivars), and early-flowering
crocuses, for example *Crocus biflorus* variants
and hybrids with *C. chrysanthus*. Its blue
flowers are suitable for contrasts with low-
growing, yellow-green leaved evergreens such
as *Euonymus fortunei* cultivars. Other good
blue Reticulata cultivars include the rich blue
'Gordon' and 'Cantab', very pale blue with
darker falls.

◐ *Helianthemum* 'Rhodanthe Carneum', *Helleborus*
× *sternii*, *Heuchera* 'Raspberry Regal', *Thymus*
× *citriodorus* 'Silver Queen', *Vinca minor* 'Illumination'

H: 13cm (5in) S: 5cm (2in)
❊ **Late winter to early spring**

 Z4 pH5–7.5

A

Iris 'Symphony'

Dutch irises are hybrids between variants of the Spanish iris, *I. xiphium*, and the frost-tender *I. tingitana*. Their flowering season extends beyond spring bulbs such as tulips and narcissi, bridging the gap between these and many summer flowers. 'Symphony' is an excellent cultivar, as is 'Apollo', both of them white and yellow bicolors. Other yellowish Dutch irises include 'Golden Harvest' and 'Royal Yellow', with golden yellow falls and paler standards; and 'Yellow Queen', in golden yellow, with an orange blotch on the falls. With their upright, narrow growth habit, they are all useful for planting among slightly shorter herbaceous or biennial plants with simpler shapes or significantly different colors, above which the irises' elegant flowers can be seen clearly, or with small to medium-sized shrubs such as spiraeas, smaller ceanothus, and shrub roses. They are best in loose drifts, associated with late spring and early summer bedding, forget-me-nots, wallflowers, and early poppies. Their yellow tones combine well with soft-colored flowers in apricot, peach, or orange, and yellow-green or glaucous foliage, and contrast with blue flowers.

Facing page: The bright colors of Dutch Group *Iris* 'Symphony' shine among the orange flowers of *Geum* 'Prinses Juliana' and an Oriental poppy (*Papaver orientale*). Adding more of the iris and poppy, perhaps with some bronze foliage, would also be effective.

 Aquilegia chrysantha 'Yellow Queen', *Ceanothus* 'Puget Blue', *Erysimum* × *allionii*, *Papaver nudicaule*, *Potentilla fruticosa* 'Hopleys Orange', *Rosa xanthina* 'Canary Bird', *Spiraea japonica* Golden Princess

H: 65cm (26in) S: 10cm (4in)
❀ **Late spring to early summer**
 Z7 pH5.5–7.5

The white, bell-shaped flowers of *Leucojum aestivum* 'Gravetye Giant' combine attractively with dainty blue *Corydalis flexuosa*. Adding a plant of intermediate height, perhaps with glaucous or yellow-green foliage, would help bridge the difference in height between the two.

Leucojum aestivum 'Gravetye Giant' ♛

This is a vigorous cultivar of the summer snowflake, *L. aestivum*, a misleading name since its flowers are usually over by early summer. Unlike other *Leucojum* species, it grows well in moist borders and beside water, and in more natural situations where its simplicity is not upstaged by brasher plants. This is a rather leafy bulbous perennial, best fronted by shorter neighbors to disguise the imbalance between foliage and flowers. Its charming blooms, white with green tips, mix well with blue, soft yellow, or yellow-green flowers, and with yellow-green or glaucous leaves. It associates prettily with Jonquilla narcissi, trollius, early-flowering Candelabra primulas, and fritillaries, and with the contrasting foliage of early-leafing ferns, corydalis, brunneras, and symphytums.

 Doronicum 'Miss Mason', *Dryopteris erythrosora*, *Epimedium* × *perralchicum* 'Frohnleiten', *Meconopsis cambrica*, *Nonea lutea*, *Primula denticulata*, *Trollius* × *cultorum* 'Alabaster', *Vinca major* 'Variegata' ❏ p.79 **C**

H: 60cm (24in) S: 25cm (10in)
❀ **Mid- to late spring**
 Z4 pH5.5–7

Floating above a sea of azure wood forget-me-nots (*Myosotis sylvatica*), the bold shape of *Iris* 'Wedgwood' and the contrasting yellow flare on its falls prevent its soft blue flowers from being camouflaged among its neighbors. This subtle, hazy effect could be made brighter by adding white flowers, or more piquant by adding yellow-green.

Iris 'Wedgwood'

This is one of several fine purplish blue Dutch irises, with yellow markings on the falls. Others include 'H.C. van Vliet', in dark violet-blue, with an orange blotch on its grey-blue falls; 'Imperator', in indigo-blue with an orange blotch on the falls; and 'Professor Blaauw', in violet-blue with a golden yellow blotch on the falls. All succeed in the same combinations as 'Symphony' (above), but especially with white or pale blue flowers, and in contrasts with soft yellow or yellow-green flowers, and yellow-green or glaucous foliage. There are also several excellent white Dutch irises, such as 'White Bridge', 'White van Vliet', 'White Excelsior', 'White Superior', and 'White Wedgwood', all of which are effective with yellow, blue, mauve, and pink.

 *Cerinthe major* 'Purpurascens', *Dicentra spectabilis* 'Alba', *Euphorbia characias*, *Lunaria annua* var. *albiflora* 'Alba Variegata', *Smyrnium perfoliatum*, *Tulipa* 'Spring Green'

H: 65cm (26in) S: 10cm (4in)
❀ **Late spring to early summer**
 Z7 pH5.5–7.5

Lilium African Queen Group

These lilies form a group of Aurelian hybrids derived from *L. henryi* ♀, *L. leucanthum*, and *L. sargentiae*, and typically have large, trumpet-shaped flowers in shades of rich yellow and apricot-orange. 'African Queen' was selected as the best seedling of the group and has flowers in more intense colors: the petals are warm deep tangerine-apricot inside and warm mahogany brown suffused with yellow outside. Its bold shape and beautiful lines, also characteristic of other lilies in this group, make a strong architectural impact and add a striking note of superlative quality wherever it is used. The dark stems contribute to the effect, making this an excellent plant to associate with bronze foliage and warm colors such as peach, apricot, and soft orange. It is also strongly fragrant.

The African Queen Group are outstanding combined with yellow-green foliage such as that of some larger hostas, and are tall enough to interact with medium-sized shrubs including Shrub roses, for instance some of David Austin's English roses. Like many other lilies, they can be very impressive mixed with other plants in large, deep containers, although pots should be turned frequently to prevent the lilies from leaning towards the light.

With their tall, narrow habit, most lilies look good weaving through shorter plants to create extended groups or drifts. If they are to thrive and increase, or at least maintain their size from year to year, they should not be crowded by companion plants of comparable size. Individual stems may need to be supported with stakes about one-third or half the ultimate height of the flowering stem, especially if the bulbs are grown where uneven lighting causes them to lean in the direction of the sun.

Like all lilies, these are very attractive to slugs and snails, and should be given some protection; they are also susceptible to viral diseases, the best precaution against which is to purchase the very largest size of bulb.

◑ *Canna* 'Durban', *Foeniculum vulgare* 'Purpureum', *Hosta* 'Sum and Substance', *Physocarpus opulifolius* Diabolo, *Rosa* Graham Thomas, *Weigela* Briant Rubidor

H: 1.8m (6ft) S: 20cm (8in)
✿ **Mid- to late summer**

 ◊◊ ☐-■ ■ Z5 pH5.5–7.5

This is a dramatic combination of warm colors consisting of *Lilium* African Queen Group, *Crocosmia* 'Lucifer', and the double daylily *Hemerocallis fulva* 'Flore Pleno'.

A

The warm orange *Lilium* Bellingham Group forms a striking contrast with sumptuous indigo *Delphinium* King Arthur Group, its blooms enlivened by their white eyes.

Lilium Bellingham Group ♛

This is a strong-growing hybrid group derived from crosses between the tall, brilliantly colored turkscap lily *L. humboldtii*, the leopard lily (*L. pardalinum*), and the beautiful yellow *L. parryi*. Clones are vigorous and persistent, and can tolerate some shade. The unscented flowers range from clear yellow to bright orange-red, most of them spotted with rusty brown. The most common clones are a rich, hot orange, with exquisite markings that are best appreciated at close range.

With their imposing stature and elegant growth habit, free from any tendency to flop or lean towards the sun, these lilies are ideal for large-scale plantings in sunny or partially shaded borders, and in open glades in a woodland garden. They all harmonize with hot colors and bronze foliage, and contrast impressively with blue, blue-purple, or yellow-green flowers, and with yellow-green foliage. Suitable companions include yellow-green hostas, delphiniums, and late azaleas.

Anchusa azurea, Euphorbia palustris, Meconopsis × sheldonii, Osmanthus heterophyllus 'Purpureus', *Rhododendron* 'Delicatissimum'

H: 2m (6½ft) S: 20cm (8in)
❀ **Early to mid-summer**

 ◊◊ ▢-▦ ▮ **Z5 pH5–7.5**

Lilium 'Black Beauty'

Robust and aristocratic in form, this scented Oriental Hybrid lily combines the deep crimson coloring and large flower size of one of its parents, *L. speciosum* var. *rubrum*, with the recurved flower shape, easy culture, and vigor of its other parent, *L. henryi* ♛. With good cultivation in a humus-rich soil, it is capable of producing a prodigious candelabra of blooms, each stem bearing dozens of individual flowers – as many as 150 have been reported on one stem.

This summer combination of flowers in similar shades of rose-pink and crimson includes the blooms of the Oriental Hybrid lily *Lilium* 'Black Beauty', upward-facing Texensis Group *Clematis* 'Duchess of Albany', and *Anisodontea capensis*. They form a close harmony that is charming and intricate at close range – although from a distance it would be hard to distinguish the individual blooms.

The complex architecture and geometry of a well-grown flower spike, with its remarkable secondary and tertiary branching, has a pleasing symmetry that can be destroyed if any limbs of the candelabra are lost through overcrowding by each other or companion plants, or by damage from slugs.

'Black Beauty' blends well with pink, crimson, or white flowers, and can make a major impact in combination with glaucous foliage or grown against a background of deep purple leaves. It also looks attractive contrasted with pale apple-green.

Anemone × hybrida 'September Charm', *Atriplex hortensis* var. *rubra, Buddleja davidii* 'Nanho Petite Indigo', *Fuchsia magellanica, Phlox paniculata* 'Harlequin', *Phygelius aequalis* Sensation, *Weigela florida* 'Foliis Purpureis'

H: 1.8m (6ft) S: 20cm (8in) ❀ **Mid-summer**
◊◊ ▢-▦ ▮ **Z6 pH5–6.5**

Careful planting of the hybrid lavender *Lavandula × intermedia*, both in front of and behind *Lilium candidum*, has hidden the Madonna lily's untidy basal foliage.

Lilium candidum ♕

MADONNA LILY

Cultivated forms of this traditional cottage garden plant have broad petals that give the trumpet-shaped flowers superlative substance and elegance. Because their leaves die as the flowers open, these powerfully scented lilies are best planted in a broad, shallowly sloped border, behind a taller plant that will hide the foliage without overcrowding it. Alternatively, annuals such as nigellas or *Silene coeli-rosa*, and annual or perennial gypsophilas, can screen the dying foliage. Jazzy or contrasting color schemes detract from this lily's simple beauty, but it mixes well with most other colors, especially blue, pink, mauve, apricot, or peach flowers, and glaucous or silver foliage. It looks charming in large groups at the foot of a sunny wall, or combined with old roses, lavenders, catmints, or pinks. These lilies thrive in lime-rich soil, and need plenty of sun and air around them to avoid botrytis.

Ⓒ *Artemisia* 'Powis Castle', *Dianthus* 'Mrs Sinkins', *Lavandula* 'Sawyers', *Nepeta* 'Six Hills Giant', *Nigella damascena* 'Oxford Blue', *Rosa* 'De Rescht', *R. glauca*

H: 1.5m (5ft) S: 30cm (12in)
❀ **Early to mid-summer**

◖◖ ▢-▨ ▉ **Z6 pH5.5–8**

In this combination, *Lilium* 'Enchantment' contrasts boldly with *Lavandula × intermedia* Old English Group. Yearly mid-spring pruning of the lavender will be needed, in order to let in enough light for the lily to survive.

Lilium 'Enchantment' ♕

Perhaps the best known of all the lily hybrids, this early-flowering Asiatic Hybrid has rich orange, unscented blooms, gathered in compact, egg-shaped flower heads topped by a radiating crown of buds. The flowers have a strong shape that can provide a gentle focal point or, if plants are repeated along a border, will create an attractive pattern. Their color is very striking and vibrant, especially in full sun, and can be difficult to combine with other plants, although they do associate well with hot colors, cream flowers, and bronze foliage, and make effective contrasts with blue or yellow-green.

Older cultivars such as this can suffer from an accumulation of viral disease, although choosing the largest bulbs helps to guarantee relative freedom from the disease and confer continued health and vigor.

Ⓒ *Acanthus mollis* 'Hollard's Gold', *Achillea* 'Moonshine', *Alchemilla mollis*, *Campanula glomerata* 'Superba', *Canna indica* 'Purpurea', *Centaurea cyanus*, *Corokia × virgata* 'Bronze King', *Hemerocallis* 'Corky', *Lysimachia ciliata* 'Firecracker', *Phygelius × rectus* 'Sunshine', *Rosa* Amber Queen

H: 90cm (36in) S: 20cm (8in) ❀ **Early summer**
◖◖ ▢-▨ ▉ **Z5 pH5.5–7.5**

Lilium 'Connecticut King'

This early-flowering Asiatic Hybrid lily is very vigorous and easy to grow, with upright stems bearing dark green, glossy foliage and unscented, sharp yellow star-shaped flowers that face upward. Although the flowers are not as elegant as those of other cultivars, their color makes a powerful impact and combines dramatically with hot oranges and reds. They also look impressive with cream or bright blue flowers, and with glaucous foliage. Effective companions include yellow-variegated grasses, such as transversely banded miscanthus cultivars, and yellow-green hostas. Other similar yellow-flowered cultivars include 'Destiny', 'Sun Ray', and the considerably shorter Golden Pixie ('Ceb Golden').

Ⓒ *Achillea* 'Inca Gold', *Coreopsis* 'Sunray', *Delphinium grandiflorum*, *Lychnis chalcedonica*, *Miscanthus sinensis* 'Zebrinus', *Tagetes patula* Favourite Series (mixed)

H: 1m (3¼ft) S: 20cm (8in)
❀ **Early to mid-summer**

◖◖ ▢-▨ ▉ **Z5 pH5.5–7.5**

Bright yellow *Lilium* 'Connecticut King' provides the focal point in this hot mixture of orange day lilies (*Hemerocallis fulva* 'Flore Pleno') and red *Crocosmia* 'Lucifer'.

Lilium 'Joy'

Often sold under the synonym 'Le Rêve', this Oriental Hybrid lily is distinguished by its bowl-shaped, soft pink flowers, enlivened by a light scattering of maroon spots on the lower half of the petals and contrasting yellow-green nectaries and rust-colored anthers. The delicately ruffled margins and slightly reflexed tips of the petals give an elegant shape to the unscented flowers, which grow on stalks long enough to allow each floret a separate,

uncluttered identity. Although a slightly bluish pink, the flower color is close enough to primary pink to mix successfully with rose-pink, salmon, peach, magenta, crimson, and white, and to combine well with glaucous or purple foliage. Plants are good in small groups in the middle row of borders, among soft pink achilleas, cranesbills, and shrubs such as *Deutzia* × *elegantissima*, or they can be massed with lavenders, brachyglottis, and roses, perhaps mingled with white *Campanula latifolia* to echo their flower form.

◐ *Achillea millefolium* 'Lilac Beauty', *Astrantia major* 'Roma', *Berberis thunbergii* 'Pink Queen', *Campanula* 'Burghaltii', *Geranium pratense* Midnight Reiter strain, *Gypsophila paniculata* 'Flamingo', *Heuchera* 'Raspberry Regal', *Hosta* 'Krossa Regal', *Rosa glauca*, *Salvia officinalis* 'Purpurascens', *Stachys byzantina*

H: 75cm (30in) S: 20cm (8in) ❀ **Mid-summer**
◌◌ ▨-▨ ■ **Z6 pH5–6.5**

Lilium 'Joy' harmonizes with the blooms of *Geranium* 'Ann Folkard', joined by gently contrasting bluish bracts of *Cerinthe major* 'Purpurascens', *Salvia patens* 'Cambridge Blue', and the sharp yellow-green leaves of the cranesbill.

A

Lilium lancifolium var. *splendens*

These handsome plants, which are vigorous selections of the tiger lily (*L. lancifolium*, syn. *L. tigrinum*), are grown for their large, soft orange-red, attractively spotted, turkscap flowers. They blend well with cream flowers and warm colors such as apricot, peach, and coral, and with bronze or purple foliage. Lilac or purple flowers make striking contrasts, and yellow-greens are also effective. Since they are late-flowering, tiger lilies are useful partners for chrysanthemums, except those in the hottest colors or the kinds that form solid mounds of flowers, which can overwhelm the lilies and detract from their airy grace.

◐ *Chrysanthemum* 'Mary Stoker', *Dahlia* 'Bishop of Llandaff', *Hydrangea arborescens* 'Annabelle', *Phygelius* × *rectus* 'Winchester Fanfare', *Verbena bonariensis*

H: 1.5m (5ft) S: 20cm (8in)
❀ **Late summer to early autumn**
◌◌ ☐-☐ ■ Z4 pH5–6.5

In this pleasant contrast of color and form, *Lilium lancifolium* var. *splendens* mingles with *Lobelia* 'Kompliment Blau'. Although the lobelia is fairly hardy and will often survive the winter without protection, it grows most vigorously if raised from seed each year.

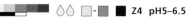

The orange flowers and airy growth habit of *Lilium leichtlinii* var. *maximowiczii* here contrast effectively with the bold glaucous foliage of *Hosta sieboldiana* var. *elegans*.

Lilium leichtlinii var. *maximowiczii*

Two forms of this soft orange-red variant of yellow *L. leichtlinii* are grown: one has stoloniferous roots like the species, but is hard to grow, while the other resembles the tiger lily (*L. lancifolium*, above) but does not have bulbils on its stems. Both are smaller, slimmer, and more graceful than the tiger lily, bearing pendant, wide turkscap flowers, on green rather than dark colored stems. The tops of the plants benefit from being in sun, while their bases should be kept cool and shaded by growing among shorter neighbors. They are used in the same way as *L. lancifolium* var. *splendens* (above), although they are more useful wherever a smaller or daintier plant is required, as in smaller beds or for viewing at close range.

◐ *Alchemilla mollis*, *Dryopteris affinis*, *Euphorbia schillingii*, *Geranium sylvaticum* 'Album', *Hypericum androsaemum* 'Albury Purple', *Lysimachia ciliata* 'Firecracker', *Tanacetum parthenium* 'Aureum'

H: 1.2m (4ft) S: 20cm (8in)
❀ **Late summer to early autumn**
◌◌ ☐-☐ ■ Z4 pH5–6.5

Lilium pyrenaicum var. *pyrenaicum*

Very easy and early-flowering, this lily is suitable for naturalizing in grass and for growing in a bed, border, or wild garden. With its yellow or greenish yellow turkscap flowers, it is most successful combined with cream or palest yellow flowers or contrasted with blue, although it is also effective with yellow-green flowers and foliage, with soft orange or apricot flowers, and with glaucous foliage. It blends well with blue cranesbills, early-flowering Shrub roses, and silver foliage, provided this has a slight yellow flush or is accompanied by yellow flowers such as some phlomis or brachyglottis species.

The other *L. pyrenaicum* variety, var. *rubrum*, tends to be a stronger plant, with orange-red to blood-red flowers. Because of this greater vigor, it is usually var. *rubrum* that nurseries offer as *L. pyrenaicum*. As a result, it is not safe to assume that purchases will produce yellow flowers unless *L. pyrenaicum* var. *pyrenaicum* is specified.

◐ *Aquilegia* 'Roman Bronze', *Brachyglottis monroi*, *Euphorbia griffithii*, *Geranium pyrenaicum* 'Bill Wallis', *Phlomis fruticosa*, *Rosa* English Garden

H: 75cm (30in) S: 20cm (8in) ❀ **Early summer**
◌◌ ☐-☐ ■ Z3 pH5.5–7.5

At the foot of a sunny wall, the bright yellow flowers of *Lilium pyrenaicum* var. *pyrenaicum* harmonize with yellow *Fremontodendron* 'California Glory' and contrast with the early-flowering cranesbill, *Geranium* 'Johnson's Blue'.

Lilium speciosum ♔

Light shade and an acid soil are essential for this superlative, late-flowering lily, which revels in openings in woodland gardens, in partially shaded beds and borders, and in mixed containers. Its sweetly scented turkscap flowers are white or pink, shading through deeper carmine to a center spotted with deepest crimson. It associates well with purple or glaucous foliage, and purple, pink, crimson, white, or pale green flowers. Plants may be combined with colchicums, late-flowering tricyrtis, actaeas, Japanese anemones, and numerous airy asters such as variants of *A. cordifolius* and *A. ericoides*. Late-flowering shrubs such as *Itea ilicifolia* and hydrangeas, especially *H. paniculata* cultivars, are also good companions.

Among the best cultivated selections are var. *album*, in pure white with contrasting purplish brown stems, and the vigorous var. *rubrum*, with deep purplish stems and carmine flowers. All may need some staking.

◐ *Anemone* × *hybrida* 'Lady Gilmour', *Aster ericoides* 'Pink Cloud', *Eucomis pallidiflora* p.314 **A**, *Hydrangea aspera*, *H. paniculata*, *Tricyrtis formosana*

H: 1–1.5m (3¼–5ft) **S: 20cm** (8in)
❀ **Late summer to early autumn**
◌◌ ▢-▣ ■ Z5 pH5–6.5

In this group of pinks and reds, *Lilium speciosum* is given space to arch gracefully over its neighbors, including the pink cranesbill *Geranium* × *riversleaianum* 'Mavis Simpson'. It is backed by the hips and glaucous leaves of *Rosa glauca*.

Lilium regale ♔

Possibly the most popular of all lily species, this is vigorous and easy to grow, with superbly shaped and very sweetly scented white trumpets, shaded pink and brownish red on the reverse. Since it is inexpensive to buy, it is a good choice for ambitious displays involving extended drifts or bold, repeated groups. It mixes well with most colors, in particular warm pinks, pale yellow-green or pale green flowers, and reddish foliage. 'Album', without the pinkish reverse to the petals, combines with almost any color, and is an invaluable ingredient of white or silver color schemes. Plants have a slight tendency

In this white-flowered display, which would be equally effective with larger groups of each plant, *Lilium regale* is joined by *Hydrangea arborescens* 'Grandiflora', feverfew (*Tanacetum parthenium*), Miss Willmott's ghost (*Eryngium giganteum*), and the seedheads of *Allium aflatunense*.

to lean towards the light, and may require staking. They start growing very early and their young shoots benefit from the shelter of evergreen shrubs such as skimmias, cistus, olearias, osmanthus, and larger berberis.

◐ *Astilbe* × *arendsii* 'Cattleya', *Cryptotaenia japonica* f. *atropurpurea*, *Nicotiana langsdorffii*, *Oenothera fruticosa* 'Fyrverkeri', *Ruta graveolens*, *Weigela* 'Victoria'

H: 1.8m (6ft) **S: 20cm** (8in) ❀ **Mid-summer**
◌◌ ▢-▣ ■ Z5 pH5–7.5

The large blue spikes of *Muscari armeniacum* provide a strong foreground for the pale lavender-blue wood anemone *A. nemorosa* 'Robinsoniana' and the soft white *Narcissus* 'Thalia'. Because the muscari can spread fairly rapidly, this grouping may be best in a semi-wild area.

Muscari armeniacum ♕

Perhaps the easiest of several bulbous species commonly called grape hyacinths, this is a very free-flowering muscari with relatively large flower spikes. It is a good plant for the front of a border and for gravel or rock gardens, and excellent underneath late-leafing herbaceous plants and deciduous shrubs. Its foliage appears in autumn, but by flowering time the leaves have flopped into an unkempt mat, an affliction not shared to the same extent by the neater, smaller-flowered *M. azureum* ♕ and *M. botryoides*. Planting among erythroniums, wood anemones, pulmonarias, or euphorbias helps disguise this fault. Plants mix well with white, cream, and soft yellow flowers, such as smaller narcissi, and with yellow-green foliage and flowers. 'Argaei Album' is white; 'Blue Spike' has larger, longer-lasting double flowers; and 'Saffier' is a paler campanula-blue.

Euphorbia dulcis 'Chameleon', *Mahonia aquifolium* 'Apollo' p.67 **C**, *Puschkinia scilloides* p.339 **B**, *Tulipa linifolia* Batalinii Group p.349 **B** ❑ p.305 **B**

H: 20cm (8in) **S: 15cm** (6in) **Mid- to late spring**
Z4 pH5–7.5

Muscari latifolium

This beautiful, robust species is one of the largest muscaris, with dusky deep purple-blue fertile florets, topped by paler sterile florets and born in racemes above broad leaves. The dark coloring is not very conspicuous from a distance, but at close range it provides an effective contrast for soft yellow and yellow-green foliage and flowers, and also blends well with mauve, lighter purple, blue, and cream. It is useful for combining with euphorbias, erythroniums, wood anemones, and smaller narcissi at the front of a border or in a rock garden, and for underneath late-leafing herbaceous perennials. *M. neglectum* has narrower, grassy leaves and a similar dusky color that is valuable for the same combinations and close-range viewing.

Cardamine pentaphylla, *Primula* 'Lady Greer', *Spiraea* × *vanhouttei* Pink Ice, *Valeriana phu* 'Aurea', *Vinca minor* 'Argenteovariegata', *Viola* 'Dawn'

H: 20cm (8in) **S: 15cm** (6in) **Mid- to late spring**
Z4 pH5–7.5

The dusky and recessive purple and royal-blue flowers of *Muscari latifolium*, most visible at close range, are here contrasted with the yellow-green flower heads of the glaucous-leaved donkeytail spurge (*Euphorbia myrsinites*).

Narcissus 'Actaea' ♕

A vigorous and easy late-flowering Poeticus narcissus, this has pure white petals surrounding a golden yellow cup edged with deep red. It can be contrasted with red foliage or mixed with hot colors, but its whiteness can seem rather stark in such combinations and it is more effective with warm colors such as peach, apricot, soft yellow, and soft orange, and with gently bronze-flushed foliage. Because white predominates in the flower coloring, it is unnecessary to harmonize with the yellow and orange of the cup. This bulb is suitable for beds and borders, for naturalizing in grass, and for underneath deciduous shrubs, and looks very effective with azaleas, hardy hybrid rhododendrons, trollius, geums, primulas, and kerrias. The flowers are larger and more solid in outline than those of *N. poeticus* and its variants, suiting it to extravagant effects, but *N. poeticus* has a more graceful, natural appearance ideal for use in wilder parts of the garden. 'Actaea' needs regular dividing to prevent it from becoming too congested.

Epimedium × *warleyense* 'Orangekönigin', *Erythronium* 'Pagoda', *Geum rivale* 'Leonard's Variety', *Kerria japonica* 'Picta', *Rhododendron* 'Surrey Heath'

H: 45cm (18in) **S: 20cm** (8in) **Late spring**
Z4 pH5–7.5

Beneath a young birch, the russet young leaves of evergreen, mauve-flowered *Epimedium acuminatum* bridge the gap between the flowers of *Narcissus* 'Actaea' and those of the wood forget-me-not (*Myosotis sylvatica*).

A

Narcissus bulbocodium 🏆

HOOP-PETTICOAT DAFFODIL

With a preference for moist but well-drained conditions when in active growth and drier conditions in summer, this is a good choice for naturalizing in unfertilized grass, such as an old meadow or grassland that has been regularly mown, with the clippings habitually removed for some years; it cannot compete with vigorously growing grass, however. It may also be grown in a rock garden, provided moisture is adequate, but it is not so easy to grow in beds and borders, where its small stature makes it liable to be overwhelmed by other plants. It looks most seductive mingling with pale blues, light pinks, and similar softer colors, as well as white. Suitable neighbors include meadow flowers such as cardamines, guinea-hen flowers, snowdrops, *Leucojum aestivum*, spring-flowering cyclamens, and violets. When naturalized in ideal conditions it will self-seed prolifically, provided the grass is not cut before the seeds have had time to fall – here, mass planting will produce spectacular large-scale effects. However, the fascinating flaring, almost trumpet-shaped, deep yellow flowers, with their usually ruffled margins and ring of rudimentary outer petals, also merit closer examination. Of the numerous variants, the most attractive and useful for gardens is probably the pale yellow var. *citrinus*.

Acaena microphylla 'Kupferteppich', *Ajuga reptans* 'Jungle Beauty', *Cyclamen coum*, *Geranium sessiliflorum* subsp. *novae-zelandiae* 'Nigricans', *Ipheion uniflorum*, *Pulmonaria* Opal, *Ranunculus ficaria* var. *aurantiacus*, *Stachys byzantina* 'Primrose Heron', *Viola* 'Huntercombe Purple'

H: 10–15cm (4–6in) **S: 5cm** (2in) **Mid-spring**
Z6 pH5–6.5

Above: *Narcissus bulbocodium* and paler *N.b.* var. *citrinus* are naturalized with mixed shades of the dog's-tooth violet (*Erythronium dens-canis*). Both flower at the same height.

Below: Deep yellow *Narcissus bulbocodium* is here grown at the front of a bed with *Chionodoxa forbesii* 'Pink Giant' and, now out of flower, winter aconites (*Eranthis hyemalis*).

B

Narcissus 'February Gold' 🏆

While lacking the elegantly swept-back petals of its parent *N. cyclamineus*, this Cyclamineus cultivar is early, vigorous, and free-flowering, and one of the best for general garden use and for naturalizing. Its name is slightly misleading because it usually flowers in early spring rather than late winter. With smaller blooms than Trumpet daffodils, it is ideal for small gardens, and its early season makes it suitable for mixing with plants such as crocuses, snowdrops, Reticulata irises, and white-flowered winter heaths. Palest yellow, cream, white, blue, and yellow-green are good color combinations. Other notable Cyclamineus cultivars include 'Bartley', which has a long, narrow trumpet and slender, reflexed petals, and 'Charity May' 🏆, with greenish yellow petals and a yellow cup fading to white. All Cyclamineus cultivars bear one flower per stem.

🔘 *Crocus chrysanthus* 'Cream Beauty', *Erica carnea* 'Springwood White', *Euphorbia characias*, *Helleborus* × *hybridus*, *Spiraea japonica* 'Gold Mound', *Trachystemon orientalis*

H: 30cm (12in) S: 10cm (4in) ❀ **Early spring**
▮▮▮▮▯ ◊◊ ▯-▮ ▮ **Z5 pH5–7.5**

The cheerful yellow blooms of *Narcissus* 'February Gold' are here contrasted with fragrant, dark-stemmed *Hyacinthus orientalis* 'Delft Blue', a combination that could equally be used in large containers or flower beds.

Narcissus 'Eystettensis'
QUEE ANNE'S DOUBLE DAFFODIL

Narcissus cultivars with slightly muddled or untidy flowers, such as doubles or those with split coronas, are sometimes considered inferior to the classic trumpet-flowered varieties, but they have their own unique beauty. 'Eystettensis' has charming blooms, each with six ranks of petals, decreasing in size towards the center of the flower. It is an attractive plant for beds and borders, especially at close range, but its vigor is not quite strong enough for naturalizing (although adequate for most other garden uses). Its soft pale yellow combines very

Sulfur-flowered *Narcissus* 'Eystettensis' grows through a carpet of glistening yellow blooms and near-black leaves of the celandine *Ranunculus ficaria* 'Brazen Hussy'.

successfully with blue flowers such as hyacinths, with rich gold, cream, and white flowers, and with yellow foliage and flowers. It also contrasts effectively with dark foliage, such as purple-leaved bugleweeds or the young crimson foliage of herbaceous peonies.

🔘 *Doronicum* 'Little Leo', *Heuchera* 'Purple Petticoats', *Hyacinthus orientalis* 'Blue Magic', *Plantago lanceolata* 'Golden Spears', *Symphytum ibericum* 'All Gold'

H: 20cm (8in) S: 8cm (3in) ❀ **Mid-spring**
▮▮▮▮▯ ◊◊ ▯-▮ ▮ **Z4 pH5–7**

Narcissus 'February Silver'

This is a Cyclamineus narcissus, with slightly reflexed white petals and large yellow trumpets. It is similar to 'Jack Snipe' (p.335) but a little larger and the trumpet is more flared and fluted. It flowers in early spring rather than in winter, a week or two after 'February Gold' (facing page) has started to bloom. It is a good choice for general use, for planting underneath herbaceous plants or deciduous shrubs, and for naturalizing in grass. Its pale coloring associates well with most other hues, especially blue or gold flowers and yellow-green foliage or flowers,

and it also makes an excellent foil for dusky purple blooms. Many other desirable hybrids have been created by crossing Trumpet daffodils with *N. cyclamineus*, itself one of the most beautiful of all narcissus species. Among the best bicolored hybrids are 'Dove Wings' ♀, with creamy white petals surrounding a long, primrose-yellow trumpet that fades gently with age; 'Foundling' ♀, white with a rosy pink cup; and 'Jenny' ♀, similar to 'Dove Wings', but with narrower, more pointed petals. 'Tracey' has white petals surrounding a soft lemon-yellow trumpet.

All these bicolors are effective massed in flower beds, with bare soil or dark plants to

provide a contrasting background. 'February Silver' is particularly satisfying in generous drifts through a leafy carpet of heathers or the basketry of bare stems of climbers such as *Hydrangea anomala* subsp. *petiolaris* and *Clematis* ×*jouiniana* planted as a ground cover.

◖ *Centaurea montana* 'Gold Bullion', *Helleborus foetidus*, *Paeonia lactiflora* 'Crimson Glory', *Prunus* 'Shirotae' p.78 **B**, *Pulmonaria angustifolia* subsp. *azurea*

H: 30cm (12in) **S: 10cm** (4in) ✿ **Early spring**
◌◌ ☐-■ ■ **Z5 pH5–7.5**

The pale *Narcissus* 'February Silver' and *Pulmonaria officinalis* 'Blue Mist' work well against the dusky maroon blooms of *Trillium sessile* and *Fritillaria persica*.

Grown through a carpet of *Chionodoxa forbesii*, a generous clump of *Narcissus* 'Geranium' contrasts in flower color and makes an imposing focal point.

Narcissus 'Geranium' ♔

This narcissus is one of the Tazetta cultivars, which produce as many as 20 small flowers per stem. They have broad petals and small cups and are usually sweetly scented. Some inherit the tenderness of their parents, which might be any of the Section *Tazetti*, including *N. tazetta* itself, *N. papyraceus* (the paper white narcissus), or *N. aureus*. The stout stems and broad leaves of most cultivars give them a slightly coarse appearance, but make them excellent for cutting. 'Geranium' has white petals and small orange cups. Scarcely big enough to clash with any color, these add piquancy to combinations with blue, purple, or yellow-green, and harmonize with warm colors such as peach, yellow, apricot, and soft orange. This is an excellent narcissus for beds and borders, for planting under herbaceous plants and deciduous shrubs (including roses), and for naturalizing. It is also popular for forcing under glass, and for growing in containers, both indoors and out.

◑ *Carex comans* (bronze), *Epimedium × versicolor* 'Cupreum', *Hyacinthus orientalis* 'Gypsy Queen', *Nonea lutea*, *Sambucus nigra* Black Beauty, *Spiraea japonica* 'Goldflame'

H: 35cm (14in) S: 15cm (6in)
✿ Mid- to late spring

 ◌◌ ▢-▮ ▮ Z4 pH5–7.5

Narcissus 'Hawera' ♔

'Hawera' is a Triandrus daffodil, with the graceful growth habit and bunched flowers of its parent *N. triandrus*, together with its slightly reflexed petals and fairly rounded cup. The soft yellow coloring is excellent with golden yellow or cream, and contrasts well with mid- or pale blue flowers such as forget-me-nots, although it is not a strong enough shade to work successfully against the rich or deep blue of plants such as brunneras or bluebells. Its charming shape and deportment merit close inspection and make it a good choice for small gardens.

Many Triandrus hybrids have been produced by crossing *N. triandrus* with the jonquil, *N. jonquilla*, combining the grace and delicate shape of the former with the jonquil's vigor and good constitution. They include 'April Tears' ♔, with which 'Hawera' is often confused. The two are similar in height and shape, but the flowers of 'April Tears' are a slightly deeper buttercup-yellow that is strong enough to contrast with rich blue flowers. 'Frosty Morn' is pure white and about 15cm (6in) high, while the white 'Ice Wings' is taller at 35cm (14in).

◑ *Hakonechloa macra* 'Aureola', *Ilex crenata* 'Golden Gem', *Luzula sylvatica* 'Taggart's Cream', *Omphalodes cappadocica*, *Ribes sanguineum* 'Brocklebankii', *Veronica peduncularis* 'Georgia Blue' ❏ p.71 **C**

H: 23cm (9in) S: 8cm (3½in) ✿ Late spring
◌◌ ▢-▮ ▮ Z4 pH5–7

The dainty, nodding, sulfur-yellow flowers of *Narcissus* 'Hawera' stand out well above a dense blue covering of wood forget-me-nots (*Myosotis sylvatica*).

Narcissus 'Jack Snipe' harmonizes perfectly at the foot of a bush of evergreen *Elaeagnus pungens* 'Frederici', although viewed from a distance the narcissus may be camouflaged.

Narcissus 'Jack Snipe' ♈

This vigorous and easy Cyclamineus narcissus, with long-lasting, bicolored flowers in white and lemon-yellow, looks like a smaller version of 'February Silver' (p.333), and is valuable for smaller gardens or intimate combinations, such as in window boxes and other containers. It is an excellent choice for the front of beds and borders or underneath later-leafing perennials, especially if planted in generous colonies and left to multiply. It flowers early enough to be useful with white winter-flowering heaths, and looks very attractive with gold flowers and yellow-green flowers or foliage. It also makes outstanding contrasts with blue flowers such as scillas and muscaris.

◐ *Erica* × *darleyensis* 'Jenny Porter', *Helleborus argutifolius* 'Pacific Frost', *Ipheion uniflorum*, *Muscari armeniacum* 'Valerie Finnis', *M. botryoides* 'Superstar'

H: 20cm (8in) S: 8cm (3½in)
❀ **Early to mid-spring**

◊◊ ▨-▨ ■ Z5 pH5–7

Grown beneath *Narcissus poeticus* var. *recurvus*, alpine forget-me-nots (*Myosotis alpestris*) provide an attractive foil for the elegant flowers of the narcissus.

Narcissus poeticus var. *recurvus* ♈
PHEASANT'S EYE NARCISSUS

This fragrant, late-blooming narcissus is valuable for extending the flowering season towards early summer. It is vigorous and easily grown in beds and borders, planted in loose drifts where late-leafing shrubs can cover up its dying foliage. It is equally successful naturalized in grass, where it can be used with late spring flowering bulbs, such as camassias, and wild flowers such as cow parsley that match its simplicity. The small, red-rimmed yellow cup, giving an attractive focus to each dainty white recurved bloom, barely provides enough color to influence combinations. As a result, this narcissus may be grown successfully with almost any color, although blue and warm shades such as soft orange, sulfur-yellow, peach, and apricot are possibly the most charming partners. The double *N.p.* 'Plenus' is even more fragrant and flowers very late, sometimes lasting into early summer.

◐ *Camassia quamash*, *Carex testacea*, *Cornus alba* 'Spaethii', *Diervilla* × *splendens*, *Hosta* 'Fire and Ice', *Mahonia aquifolium* 'Apollo', *Ranunculus aconitifolius* 'Flore Pleno', *Ribes* × *gordonianum*, *Viburnum carlesii*

H: 35cm (14in) S: 15cm (6in) ❀ **Late spring**

◊◊ ▨-▨ ■ Z4 pH5–7.5

Narcissus 'Jetfire' ♈

For a Cyclamineus narcissus, this has fairly large flowers that are richly colored in gold and strong orange, although the orange becomes paler with age in full sun. 'Jetfire' is a superb subject for bold flower beds, for grouping at the front of beds and borders, and for planting under late-leafing perennials. Effective with flowers in reds, oranges, and bright yellows, it also looks good with yellow-green foliage or flowers and in contrasts with cream or strong blue. Primroses, polyanthus, muscaris, and Greigii or Kaufmanniana tulips make fine companions. Narcissus hybrids like 'Jetfire', with small but conspicuous orange or

This large-scale combination of a white *Arabis alpina* cultivar with *Narcissus* 'Jetfire' could equally be repeated in smaller groups for ground cover in borders.

red cups, are also useful for adding sparks of early warm color to shady corners. They include 'Beryl', yellow with an orange cup; 'Scarlet Gem', yellow and light red; and 'Foundling' ♈, white and rose-pink.

◐ *Erysimum* 'John Codrington', *Luzula sylvatica* 'Aurea', *Primula* Cowichan Blue Group, *Pulmonaria angustifolia*, *Tulipa* 'Orange Emperor'

H: 20cm (8in) S: 8cm (3½in)
❀ **Early to mid-spring**

◊◊ ▨-▨ ■ Z5 pH5–7

In this informal planting *Narcissus pseudonarcissus* is scattered unevenly and naturalistically through a carpet of contrasting lavender-blue *Chionodoxa forbesii*.

Narcissus pseudonarcissus

COMMON DAFFODIL

The flowers of this vigorous, easily grown species have slightly twisted, sulfur-yellow petals surrounding a golden yellow trumpet. With their natural grace, they look very much at home in wilder parts of the garden or naturalized in grass, although the plant is sufficiently showy to succeed almost anywhere, especially in beds and borders and underneath later-leafing herbaceous perennials and deciduous shrubs. It may be naturalized in drifts and groups in more open woodland areas, and makes a charming display with primroses, cowslips, and blue flowers such as bluebells. Its comparatively small scale also qualifies it for use in smaller gardens and close-range plantings, where it is often more appropriate than some of the larger hybrid Trumpet daffodils.

The Tenby daffodil, *N. obvallaris*, once classed as a subspecies of the daffodil, is slightly shorter, equally vigorous, and similar in appearance, but the flowers are more upright and a deeper shade of golden yellow.

○ *Acorus gramineus* 'Ôgon', *Glechoma hederacea* 'Variegata', *Hyacinthoides hispanica*, *Hyacinthus orientalis* 'Delft Blue', *Primula veris*, *P. vulgaris*, *Pulmonaria* 'Apple Frost', *Vinca minor* 'La Grave'

H: 25cm (10in) S: 10cm (4in) ❀ Early spring
Z4 pH5–7.5

Narcissus 'Spellbinder' ♔

This daffodil has gorgeous flowers with broad, overlapping mid-yellow petals, tinged yellowish green and paler at the base, and a flared, ruffled trumpet, aging almost to white. While vigorous enough for naturalizing in grass, its bold flowers are best used for extravagant, large-scale plantings. Its slight greenish tinge suits greenish yellow, cream, or white, and contrasts with blue. Other large Trumpet daffodils include 'Dutch Master' ♔ and 'Golden Harvest', both rich golden yellow. Large-cupped narcissi such as golden yellow 'Carlton' ♔ and the flamboyant double 'Golden Ducat' are equally useful for bold displays. All associate well with hyacinths, Darwinhybrid tulips, and crown imperials.

○ *Anemone blanda*, *Carex flagellifera*, *Chamaecyparis obtusa* 'Fernspray Gold', *Euonymus fortunei* 'Silver Queen', *Fritillaria imperialis* 'Aureomarginata'

H: 50cm (20in) S: 20cm (8in) ❀ Mid-spring
Z4 pH5–7.5

The newly opened blooms of *Narcissus* 'Spellbinder', which will become paler as the flowers age, are here prettily partnered by alpine forget-me-nots (*Myosotis alpestris*).

The charming round flowers of *Narcissus* 'Sun Disc', born with elegance above grassy foliage, combine happily with the nodding azure flowers of Virginia bluebells (*Mertensia virginica*) at the front of a border.

Narcissus 'Sun Disc' ♔

This miniature narcissus, one of the Jonquilla and Apodanthus cultivars, is a hybrid between *N. rupicola* and *N. poeticus*. It is an easy and undemanding cultivar for general use in most parts of the garden, although its Alpine pedigree as a relative of *N. rupicola* especially qualifies it for growing in rock gardens and gravel gardens. (Other cultivars in this group derived from the water-loving *N. jonquilla* tolerate high winter water tables and are better suited to waterside planting.) Its flowers are among the most perfectly circular of the genus, pale yellow with a deep yellow cup, and particularly effective when contrasted with blue flowers or harmonized with white or golden yellow. 'Sundial' has the same parentage and is similar, flowering a little earlier and bearing smaller flowers with slightly darker mid-yellow petals and cup.

○ *Arabis alpina* 'Flore Pleno', *Chrysosplenium davidianum*, *Hepatica nobilis*, *Ophiopogon jaburan* 'Vittatus', *Santolina pinnata* 'Edward Bowles', *Viola sororia* 'Freckles'

H: 18cm (7in) S: 8cm (3½in) ❀ Mid-spring
Z4 pH5.5–7.5

Narcissus 'Tête-à-tête' ♛

Officially classed as a Miscellaneous daffodil, this dainty dwarf narcissus displays characteristics from both its parents, *N. cyclamineus* and *N. tazetta*. It flowers very early in the year, typically bearing two or three blooms per stem, in a strong yellow that looks spectacular when contrasted with other flowers in blue or purple, or harmonized with those in cream, pale yellow, yellowish green, orange, or white, including white kinds of winter heaths and Darley Dale heaths. 'Tête-à-tête' is an excellent subject for rock gardens and for the front of beds or borders, especially where it will be viewed at close range, and in smaller gardens; it looks particularly pretty when combined with other early spring flowers such as snowdrops, scillas, muscaris, and pulmonarias.

● *Crocus vernus* 'Purpureus Grandiflorus', *Scilla mischtschenkoana* p.341 **A**, *Thuja occidentalis* 'Rheingold', *Uncinia egmontiana* ⬚ pp.47 **A**, 237 **C**

H: 15cm (6in) **S: 8cm** (3in) ❈ **Early spring**
◊◊ ▢-▮ ▮ **Z4 pH5–7**

Grown among a group of bright blue lungwort (*Pulmonaria* 'Lewis Palmer'), the strong yellow blooms of *Narcissus* 'Tête-à-tête' are displayed at the same height, creating an effective contrast of color and form.

A

In this striking mixture of *Nerine bowdenii* with *Aster amellus* 'Veilchenkönigin', the aster grows between the slightly taller nerine bulbs, producing an almost solid carpet of bloom. In late autumn, the aster covers the nerine's leaves, but not until they start to die back.

Nerine bowdenii ♔

One of the hardiest nerines, this superlative autumn-flowering bulb has elegant, vibrant pink blooms, born without the leaves and therefore benefiting from close association with other plants that can provide a foil to the flowers. Dark purple or silver foliage plants are excellent, together with markedly paler or darker flowers, perhaps white or palest pink, crimson, ruby, lavender, or deep purple. It is especially effective with shorter *Aster amellus*, *A. × frikartii*, and *A. novi-belgii* cultivars, dark-leaved coleus, shorter artemisias, and Charm chrysanthemums. However, these must not obscure the nerine leaves from winter and spring sunlight, essential to help it store reserves for good flower production. 'Mark Fenwick' and 'Pink Triumph' are superior pink cultivars, 'Mollie Cowie' has variegated leaves, and 'Alba' is off-white.

🌼 *Artemisia stelleriana*, *Chrysanthemum yezoense*, *Convolvulus cneorum*, *Helichrysum petiolare*, *Pelargonium* 'Lady Plymouth', *Solenostemon* 'Palisandra'

H: 45cm (18in) S: 8cm (3½in)
❀ **Early to late autumn**
 ◊-◊◊ ⬜-⬛ **Z8 pH5.5–7.5**

Nerine 'Zeal Giant'

This showy and relatively hardy large-flowered hybrid of *N. bowdenii* (above) is suitable for a sheltered, sunny spot, especially at the foot of a warm wall, where it makes a charming, slightly exotic fringe of color. With its large size and bright coloring, it is a better choice for grander, more dramatic displays than *N. bowdenii*. It can be used in similar plant associations, and looks excellent with tender salvias, dark-leaved iresines, and schizostylis lilies, while its stronger coloring – close to primary pink – is a good match for brighter, more dazzling plantings, perhaps with a slightly tropical theme. It is good with red and purple foliage; combinations with magenta or vermilion can seem exciting or disconcerting, depending on personal taste. The bulbs are best left undisturbed, and clumps divided only when flowering declines.

This combination of *Nerine* 'Zeal Giant' with coleus (*Solenostemon scutellarioides*) is highly effective: the coleus provides a solid background for the nerine flowers and covers the nerine foliage only as the leaves start to die.

🌼 *Heliotropium* 'Marine', *Ipomoea batatas* 'Blackie', *Iresine herbstii* 'Brilliantissima', *Plectranthus argentatus*

H: 53cm (21in) S: 10cm (4in)
❀ **Early to late autumn**
 ◊-◊◊ ⬜-⬛ **Z8 pH5.5–7.5**

In a subdued but charming scheme, the silvery green flowers of *Ornithogalum nutans* are joined by white guinea-hen flowers (*Fritillaria meleagris* var. *unicolor* subvar. *alba*) and the smaller cream bells of *Symphytum ibericum*.

Ornithogalum nutans ♔

The exquisite flowers of this bulbous species have white petals, each with a central silvery grey-green stripe, producing a subtle color scheme that merits close inspection and is especially good in combinations with silver or green foliage and white flowers. It is a shade-tolerant plant, with slightly unkempt foliage, and benefits from being hidden at flowering time by other plants so only the flowers are seen. Good companions include blue flowers such as omphalodes, corydalis, meconopsis, brunneras, and *Hyacinthus orientalis* cultivars, while the green-striped petals of Viridiflora tulips subtly echo those of the ornithogalum. A similar effect can be achieved using a variety of *Hosta undulata*. *En masse* the ornithogalum flowers resemble filigree, so are best offset by bold foliage and flowers, such as those of pulmonarias, aspidistras, tulips, and larger late narcissi.

🌼 *Asplenium scolopendrium*, *Brunnera macrophylla* 'Dawson's White', *Geranium renardii*, *Helleborus foetidus*, *Hosta* 'Night before Christmas', *Omphalodes verna*, *Pulmonaria* 'Excalibur', *Tulipa* 'Spring Green'

H: 30cm (12in) S: 25cm (10in) ❀ **Late spring**
◊-◊◊ ⬜-⬛ **Z6 pH5.5–7.5**

Ornithogalum pyramidale

Distinguished by its attractive, neatly conical heads of starry white flowers, this bulbous perennial has slightly unkempt grassy foliage that is perhaps best masked by a companion plant, preferably one of contrasting floral form that does not obstruct the sun from reaching the ornithogalum's leaves until it is just about to flower. Many annuals are ideal for this, provided they are early flowering and feathery leaved – as are nigellas, for example – with plenty of small blooms that are not too strongly colored. Some biennials, such as a single-colored cultivar of *Silene coeli-rosa*, are suitable, as are white flowers for viewing at close range – from a distance, they might camouflage the ornithogalum blooms. Annuals or biennials in mixed colors are not recommended because they would add an intrusive note of visual confusion.

O. narbonense is similar, but only 45cm (18in) high, with slimmer heads of smaller flowers that appear from late spring onwards.

◉ *Cerinthe major* 'Purpurascens', *Echinops ritro* 'Veitch's Blue', *Eucalyptus gunnii*, *Eupatorium rugosum* 'Chocolate', *Nigella damascena* 'Miss Jekyll', *Osmanthus heterophyllus* 'Purpureus', *Phormium* 'Bronze Baby'

H: 1m (40in) **S: 20cm** (8in) ❀ **Early summer**
◇-◇◇ ▢-▩ **Z7 pH5.5–7.5**

This combination uses the feathery silver leaves of tender shrubby *Artemisia arborescens* to hide the dying foliage of *Ornithogalum pyramidale* and to fill in between the bulb's spindly flower stems. The artemisia can be grown from cuttings taken in late summer or early autumn, overwintered indoors, and planted out as soon as the danger of frost has passed.

In this pleasant partnership for a rock garden or the front of a bed or border, the harmonious colors and matching height and growth habit of *Muscari armeniacum* and *Puschkinia scilloides* are balanced by a contrast of form.

Puschkinia scilloides

This pretty spring-flowering bulb is similar in appearance to a squill. It bears delicate blue flowers, which are very attractive with richer blues and white flowers, and with silver foliage. However, the blooms are a little too pale to stand up to contrasts with strong yellows. It is a useful plant for combining with muscaris, smaller white narcissi, ipheions, and wood anemones, and contrasts effectively with very dark-leaved ground-cover plants such as black mondo grass or purple bugleweed. The flowers of *P.s.* var. *libanotica* are usually white and capable of blending with almost any other color; occasionally they are striped with blue, an attractive variation for isolated groups and drifts. *P.s.* var. *l.* 'Alba' is similar, but generally cleaner in color. Neither white form is as eye-catching as the species unless massed in bold patches among a contrasting dark ground-cover plant.

◉ *Ajuga reptans* 'Atropurpurea', *Festuca glauca*, *Fragaria* Pink Panda, *Ipheion* 'Rolf Fiedler', *Muscari armeniacum*, *Ophiopogon planiscapus* 'Nigrescens'

H: 20cm (8in) **S: 8cm** (3½in) ❀ **Early spring**
◇-◇◇ ▢-▩ **Z5 pH5.5–7.5**

Scilla bifolia 🏆

A mountain species most at home in relatively cool climates, this is an easy bulbous plant, which is suitable for growing in a border or rock garden, or for naturalizing. The tiny, star-like lavender-blue florets make an effective contrast of scale with larger-flowered bulbs and spring plants, and benefit from close-range viewing. It is most attractive combined with white and deep blue flowers, and has a strong enough color to contrast with soft yellow flowers, such as those of smaller narcissi. It associates well with epimediums,

anemones, celandines, wood anemones, and low ground covers such as bugleweeds, and may be contrasted with yellow-green foliage and flowers, such as early-flowering euphorbias and hellebores. 'Alba' is a white-flowered variant, although there are several forms of it, not all of them pure in color; the same caveat applies to 'Rosea', which is available in various shades of mauve to pink – the best selections of both, however, deserve a place in the garden. All variants associate well with smaller species tulips, smaller crocuses, ipheions, small-flowered winter violas, fritillaries, and erythroniums.

◐ *Anemone nemorosa*, *Crocus chrysanthus* 'Cream Beauty', *Epimedium* × *youngianum* 'Niveum', *Euphorbia dulcis* 'Chameleon', *Helleborus* × *hybridus* (primrose), *Ipheion uniflorum*, *Milium effusum* 'Aureum', *Narcissus* 'Jack Snipe', *Ranunculus ficaria*, *Valeriana phu* 'Aurea'

H: 13cm (5in) S: 5cm (2in) ❀ **Early spring**
◌-◌◌ ▢-■ **Z6 pH5.5–7.5**

The dainty lavender-blue flowers of *Scilla bifolia* (squill), with their matching floret stems, and wood anemones (*Anemone nemorosa*) make a charming and informal combination, suitable for a sunny space in a woodland garden or for planting beneath herbaceous plants or deciduous trees and shrubs. Squills grow happily through the crowns of other plants such as the Bearded irises here.

A

Scilla mischtschenkoana 'Tubergeniana' is the most richly colored variant of the species and is especially well-suited to contrasts with yellow. Here, it is perfectly matched in height with the dwarf *Narcissus* 'Tête-à-tête', attractively and neatly filling a narrow border between a path and a wall.

Scilla mischtschenkoana

A pretty squill, suitable for edging, for the front of a border, or for a rock garden, this species has silvery blue flowers, marked with a darker stripe down the center of each petal and opening flatter than the more familiar *S. siberica* (below). The best-known cultivar is 'Tubergeniana' ♀, whose flowers are a strong enough blue to contrast successfully with the soft yellow of, for example, smaller narcissi and crocuses, *Anemone* × *lipsiensis*, and *A. ranunculoides* cultivars. Other good companions include early-flowering

Reticulata irises, winter-flowering hellebores, snowdrops, and white variants of *Cyclamen coum*. Like most squills, it looks charming beneath late-leafing perennials such as hostas and, as one of the first spring bulbs to flower, is worth planting liberally for early color.

◉ *Crocus chrysanthus* 'Blue Pearl', *C. sieberi* 'Albus', *Cyclamen coum* f. *pallidum* 'Album', *Galanthus plicatus*, *Helleborus* × *nigercors*, *Hosta* 'Blue Angel', *Iris* 'Cantab', *Primula vulgaris*, *Saxifraga* × *urbium* 'Aureopunctata'

H: 13cm (5in) **S: 5cm** (2in)
❀ **Late winter to early spring**

◐◐◐ ▨-▨ **Z4 pH5.5–7.5**

This carmine selection of *Tigridia pavonia*, flopping obligingly to place itself among the matching, sprawling *Verbena* 'Sissinghurst', creates a fascinating picture to be viewed at close range at the front of a border.

Scilla siberica ♀
SIBERIAN SQUILL

This is perhaps the best-known squill, deservedly so because of its easy culture and rich color which make it useful as an edging plant; it is also good naturalized in lawns, being robust enough to compete successfully with grass. Its flowers combine greenish blue and purplish blue, two gently clashing tones that add extra richness and vibrancy to the blooms, and produce dramatic contrasts with white, yellow, or yellow-green flowers, such as early-flowering euphorbias, narcissi, smaller tulips, crocuses, and snowdrops. *S.s.* 'Spring Beauty', a nursery selection, is almost identical to the species, while subsp. *armena* has larger flowers born singly on their stems. There is also a white cultivar, 'Alba', which blends prettily with almost any other color.

◉ *Adiantum aleuticum* 'Japonicum' p.180 **C**, *Ajuga reptans* 'Arctic Fox', *Corydalis solida* 'Snowstorm', *Euphorbia myrsinites*, *E. polychroma* 'Candy', *Fritillaria meleagris* p.315 **A**, *Hyacinthus orientalis* 'Gypsy Queen', *Lamium maculatum* 'Roseum', *Plantago lanceolata* 'Golden Spears', *Tulipa kaufmanniana* ▭ p305 **B**

H: 15cm (6in) **S: 5cm** (2in) ❀ **Early to late spring**
◐-◐◐ ▨-▨ **Z5 pH5–7.5**

White and blue flowers with rich green foliage invariably create a pleasant combination, as seen here in this small but charming group consisting of *Scilla siberica*, *Anemone blanda* 'White Splendour', with yellow eyes, and *Pulmonaria* 'Sissinghurst White'. This mix would be equally successful on a greater scale, with large, intermingling groups of each.

Tigridia pavonia
TIGER FLOWER

This exotic-looking tender bulb has grassy foliage, and flowers in a wide range of colors, namely white, yellow, orange, pink, red, and purplish red, marked and mottled dramatically with yellow and red. Each flower lasts only for a day, and although they appear in succession it is seldom in sufficient profusion to make an impact through color alone. They associate most effectively with yellow-green foliage and flowers, and dark foliage, especially neater plants with more attractive or shapely leaves. Examples of good companions include dark-leaved dahlias, cannas, coleus, *Hibiscus acetosella*, and flowers in warm colors such as peach or apricot. Tiger flowers require warmth and sun. In cold areas, they need to be taken inside for winter, like gladioli.

◉ *Argyranthemum* 'Jamaica Primrose', *Canna* 'Champigny', *Dahlia* 'Roxy', *Phormium* 'Yellow Wave', *Salvia greggii* 'Peach', *Solenostemon* 'Walter Turner'

H: 45cm (18in) **S: 23cm** (9in)
❀ **Mid-summer to early autumn**
◐◐ ▨ **Z9 pH5–7**

Tulips

TULIPS ARE AVAILABLE in a wide range of colors, including bicolors, making them particularly welcome after the more limited shades of the other key spring bulb, the daffodil. There are 15 groups or divisions of tulips, categorized mainly according to flower type or season, and they offer endless possibilities for effective associations, including combinations that are subtle in both color and form, and more adventurous contrasts between hot and cool colors, or strong elegant shapes blooming above massed smaller flowers. There are tulips suitable for formal bedding displays as well as those that are ideal for wilder areas of the garden.

Of the 15 categories, the most widely grown is the stately Single Late Group, formerly subdivided into the Darwin Group, the aristocrats of spring bedding, and the Cottage Group. As the name suggests, tulips in this group have single flowers that appear late in the season. They are also relatively tall. Single Early tulips are much shorter and a month or so earlier to flower but equally colorful. The Triumph Group is intermediate in height and season and was derived by crossing Single Early tulips with other cultivars. Large, single flowers produced on sturdy stems over a long season are typical of the Darwinhybrids, created by crossing *T. fosteriana* with the Darwin Group. Tulips from all these divisions are excellent for formal beds or less formal mixed borders. Some of the Darwinhybrids are suitable for naturalizing in grass.

The Double Early and Double Late Groups have peony-like blooms, often in subtle color blends. The flowers are susceptible to weather damage, but are good in pots and for sheltered bedding.

Tulips in the Parrot, Fringed, and Lily-flowered Groups have flowers quite unlike the egg-shaped blooms of most of the other groups. Those of Parrot tulips are dissected and twisted, while the petals of

Fringed tulips have ragged edges. Lily-flowered tulips have an elegant tapering form. All these can be used for exotic effects in combination with other tulips or with a wide variety of foliage and early-flowering plants. For interesting color schemes, Viridiflora tulips have an attractive green stripe down the center of each petal, and the petals of Rembrandt tulips are "feathered" with darker colors.

Tulip bulbs should be planted about 10–15cm (4–6in) deep in fertile soil in a

The earliest tulips bloom before their traditional spring-bedding partners, so pansies and violas are ideal alternative companions. Here, Forerunner Series makes a cool contrast to the bright pink Single Early tulip 'Christmas Cheer'.

sunny site in autumn. In cool or wet climates some need to be lifted annually after flowering, otherwise the number of blooms will diminish; however, species tulips and those from the Greigii, Kaufmanniana, and Fosteriana Groups can remain in the soil. These small-flowered tulips are ideal for rock gardens, pots, or near border edges.

Tulipa 'Abu Hassan'

This Triumph Group tulip has gold-edged, rich mahogany-red flowers, a very striking combination that emphasizes the flower shape and harmonizes especially well in hot color schemes. It is effective planted in drifts in a border, where it can partner sulfur-yellow or orange wallflowers, and plants with yellow-green leaves such as perfoliate alexanders, early-flowering euphorbias, and shrubs with yellow-green foliage. It is also good with bronze foliage, soft yellow or cream hyacinths and narcissi, doronicums, kerrias, fritillaries, soft yellow erythroniums, epimediums, and early-leafing ferns. Triumph Group tulips are particularly useful for their mid-season flowering and their height, which allows them to be grown through shorter plants.

⊙ *Epimedium* × *perralchicum*, *Erythronium oregonum*, *Foeniculum vulgare* 'Purpureum', *Hyacinthus orientalis* 'City of Haarlem', *Narcissus* 'Binkie'

H: 50cm (20in) **S: 15cm** (6in) ✿ **Late spring**
◊ ▢-▢ ■ **Z4 pH5–7.5**

Pale petal edges of *Tulipa* 'Abu Hassan' emphasize its flower shape, helping it to be seen distinctly against the orange-red and yellow wallflowers (*Erysimum cheiri*) beneath.

Tall scarlet *Tulipa* 'Apeldoorn', standing evenly spaced above a carpet of wallflowers (*Erysimum cheiri*), is topped by statuesque crown imperials (*Fritillaria imperialis*) in a mixture of harmonious colors.

Tulipa 'Apeldoorn' ♔

'Apeldoorn' is one of the most popular red-flowered Darwinhybrid Group tulips. Blooming in mid-season, it is useful both for bedding and for permanent planting in herbaceous and mixed borders, and is effective with hot-colored flowers or in contrasts with white and yellow-green foliage and flowers. The intense color of its large scarlet blooms can overwhelm warm tints, but it is very attractive grown through orange wallflowers or with early-flowering euphorbias, yellow-green hellebores, white or orange narcissi, leucojums, Candelabra primulas and polyanthus in hot colors, and plants with bronze or red-flushed foliage.

Like all the Darwinhybrids, 'Apeldoorn' is remarkable for its vigor and persistence, even in cool wet climates. While the color range of this group is more restricted than other tulip categories, there is enough choice to make wonderful sequences and blends – for example, from ivory through cream and soft yellow to apricot and orange.

⊙ *Cornus alba* 'Elegantissima', *Erysimum* 'Apricot Twist', *Euphorbia* Redwing, *Kerria japonica* 'Golden Guinea', *Spiraea japonica* 'Goldflame'

H: 55cm (22in) **S: 15cm** (6in) ✿ **Mid-spring**
◊-◊◊ ▢-▢ ■ **Z4 pH4.5–7.5**

Tulipa 'Angélique' ♔

The small flowers of this Double Late Group tulip open pale pink and deepen a little with age; its petals are edged and streaked with a lighter color, and the outer ones are flushed with green. This soft coloring allows it to mingle with cool-colored flowers in blue, mauve, purple, or crimson, and with purple or silver foliage. As a bedding plant, it can be grown through forget-me-nots in white, pink, or blue, or with a tulip of contrasting form – for example, a Lily-flowered Group cultivar blooming at the same time. It combines well with rock cress and aubrietas, herbaceous plants such as dicentras, pulmonarias, and the earliest cranesbills, and hyacinths and the latest narcissi such as Poeticus cultivars.

⊙ *Arabis blepharophylla* 'Frühlingszauber', *Aubrieta* 'Bressingham Pink', *Brunnera macrophylla*, *Convolvulus cneorum*, *Dicentra spectabilis*, *Heuchera* 'Can-can', *Narcissus* 'Actaea', *Pulmonaria* 'Lewis Palmer'

The attractively edged blooms of *Tulipa* 'Angélique' stand clear of short alpine forget-me-nots (*Myosotis alpestris*) in front of the mauve wallflowers *Erysimum* 'Bowles' Mauve'.

H: 45cm (18in) **S: 15cm** (6in) ✿ **Late spring**

◊ ▢-▢ ■ **Z4 pH5–7.5**

Tulipa 'Apricot Beauty' ♡

This is a Single Early Group tulip with pale apricot flowers tinged with salmon. While most of the group is fairly short, 'Apricot Beauty' is relatively tall, allowing it to be planted through a carpet of lower plants. It is superlative with warm-colored flowers, but is also sufficiently strong in color to be contrasted with blue – early forget-me-nots, for example – as well as with yellow-green foliage or flowers and bronze foliage. It mixes well with dark-leaved heucheras, soft orange celandines, soft yellow rhizomatous anemones, and epimediums (particularly those with copper-flushed foliage), and makes charming associations with white rock cress, early euphorbias, white narcissi, primroses, and polyanthus. Blooming at the same time as the majority of narcissi, all Single Early tulips are immensely useful for early display. However, their flowering season comes before some of the more traditional tulip companions, such as wallflowers.

● *Anemone* × *lipsiensis*, *Arabis alpina* subsp. *caucasica*, *Epimedium* × *versicolor* 'Sulphureum', *Fritillaria imperialis* p.314 **B**, *Ranunculus ficaria* var. *aurantiacus*

H: 45cm (18in) **S: 15cm** (6in) ❀ **Mid-spring**
◇ ☐-◼ ◼ **Z4 pH5–7.5**

Tulipa 'Apricot Beauty', towards the front of a permanently planted bed, blends perfectly with the bronze-flushed foliage of *Photinia* × *fraseri* 'Red Robin'. Yellow-green foliage or scarlet flowers would also be effective here.

Tulipa 'Ballerina' ♡

'Ballerina' is a fairly tall, fragrant tulip belonging to the Lily-flowered Group. All Lily-flowered tulips have blooms with elongated petals tips and usually elegant waists, although some cultivars have blooms that open to a flat star, which, while exposing a greater area of colored petal, can diminish the graceful shape of the bloom. 'Ballerina' has the characteristic tapering petals, blood-red in the center, grading to vermilion, with a narrow lemon-yellow edge (lighter cultivars are sometimes sold under this name). It may be used for the same combinations as 'Abu Hassan' (p.343), although its subtly graded hues produce a distinctly more restful effect. Varying between 45 and 60cm (18–24in)

Growing through the daisy-like *Anthemis punctata* subsp. *cupaniana* at the edge of a border, shapely *Tulipa* 'Ballerina' adds pizzazz in front of brightly variegated ribbon grass (*Phalaris arundinacea* var. *picta*).

high, Lily-flowered tulips bloom from mid- to late season. Their flowering overlaps with all but the Double Early, Single Early, Greigii, and Kaufmanniana groups, so they can be used with other cultivars with different flower shapes to create a more varied effect.

● *Erysimum* Walberton's Fragrant Sunshine, *Euphorbia* × *martini*, *Heuchera* 'Amber Waves', *Kerria japonica* 'Picta', *Narcissus* 'Cassata', *Ribes alpinum* 'Aureum', *Spiraea japonica* 'Fire Light'

H: 55cm (22in) **S: 15cm** (6in) ❀ **Late spring**
◼ ◇ ☐-◼ **Z4 pH5–7.5**

Tulipa 'Blenda'

Belonging to the Triumph Group, 'Blenda' has deep rose flowers with a white or creamy white base. It blends well with cool colors such as blue, paler pink, crimson, and purple, yet is rich enough to contrast strikingly with white or yellow-green flowers. It can look sumptuous partnered by crimson or purple flowers and dark foliage such as that of dusky heucheras, ornamental cherries, or berberis. It associates well with hyacinths, bergenias, perfoliate alexanders, white narcissi, and euphorbias (including bronze- or purple-leaved cultivars), and among flowering shrubs such as viburnums, rhododendrons, spiraeas, exochordas, and camellias.

🔴 *Berberis* × *ottawensis* 'Silver Miles', *Bergenia* 'Brahms', *Camellia* × *williamsii* 'Garden Glory', *Exochorda* × *macrantha* 'The Bride', *Heuchera* 'Regina'

H: 45cm (18in) **S: 15cm** (6in)
✿ **Mid- to late spring**
⬛⬛⬜ ◌ ⬜-⬛ ⬛ **Z4 pH5–7.5**

Drifts of rose-pink *Tulipa* 'Blenda' and black-purple *T.* 'Queen of Night' alternate along a spacious and naturalistically planted border in light shade under a tree.

In an unusual but effective color scheme at the front of a border, dusky purple *Tulipa* 'Burgundy' is combined with soft blue wood forget-me-nots (*Myosotis sylvatica*), yellow wallflowers (*Erysimum cheiri* 'Primrose Bedder'), and the yellow-green flower heads of *Euphorbia polychroma*. Each plant plays a part, and omitting any one would impair the ensemble.

Tulipa 'Burgundy'

This Lily-flowered tulip has elegant and slender petals grading from dusky purple in the center to a lighter magenta-purple towards the edge. It is useful for opulent combinations with other purple and crimson flowers and with dark or glaucous foliage and purple-leaved shrubs, or it can provide a base note in plantings with paler cool colors such as mauve, pink, and blue, as well as contrasting soft yellow, cream, or yellow-green. As it is a late bloomer, it can be used with early-leafing hostas, columbines, moneyplant, and forget-me-nots. It looks outstanding growing through harmonizing plants such as moricandias or contrasting ones such as pale yellow wallflowers, and also associates well with bergenias, pink rock cress, dark-leaved heucheras, and contrasting grasses such as golden millet grass.

🔴 *Aquilegia* 'Hensol Harebell', *Bergenia* 'Ballawley', *Dicentra* 'Bountiful', *Erysimum* 'Bowles' Mauve', *Euphorbia amygdaloides* 'Purpurea', *Heuchera* 'Raspberry Regal', *Hosta* 'True Blue', *Milium effusum* 'Aureum', *Moricandia moricandioides*, *Viola* 'Martin'

H: 50cm (20in) **S: 15cm** (6in) ✿ **Late spring**
⬛⬛⬜ ◌ ⬜-⬛ ⬛ **Z4 pH5–7.5**

Tulipa 'China Pink' ♛

One of the longest-lasting Lily-flowered tulips, 'China Pink' often remains in bloom throughout the whole of late spring, its rich pink flowers opening out into a star and gradually becoming paler as they age. It combines well with cool colors such as blue, mauve, purple, and crimson, and with purple foliage such as that of berberis, as well as contrasting effectively with yellow-green foliage and flowers. It is particularly good with bergenias, heucheras, rock cress, forget-me-nots, primroses, polyanthus, and violas, with other bulbs such as hyacinths or later-flowering white narcissi, and with flowering shrubs such as exochordas, daphnes, and smaller magnolias. Like most Lily-flowered cultivars, its graceful flower form makes it a popular alternative to the Darwinhybrids, whose flowering period is very similar, and it is a good choice both for massed spring bedding and for planting in containers.

🔴 *Berberis* × *ottawensis* f. *purpurea* 'Superba', *Heracleum minimum* 'Roseum', × *Heucherella alba* 'Rosalie', *Magnolia* × *loebneri* 'Leonard Messel', *Narcissus* 'Thalia', *Viola cornuta*

H: 45cm (18in) **S: 15cm** (6in) ✿ **Late spring**
⬛⬛⬜ ◌ ⬜-⬛ ⬛ **Z4 pH5–7.5**

In moist ground and light shade, the ornamental rhubarb *Rheum palmatum* 'Atrosanguineum' makes an imposing focal point behind *Tulipa* 'China Pink', growing through a carpet of wood forget-me-nots (*Myosotis sylvatica*).

Tulipa clusiana

This elegant species is an old-fashioned plant, grown in gardens since the seventeenth century. Relatively early to appear, its flowers have white petals with a deep purple-black blotch at the base and the outer three petals stained crimson. It is a pretty tulip for rock gardens, for the front of a border – where it can be grown through a mat of shorter plants – and for more intimate plantings. It mixes well with silver or purple foliage including heucheras, acaenas, smaller

winter violas, bergenias, corydalis, smaller daphnes, and other bulbs such as chionodoxas, muscaris, rhizomatous anemones, later-flowering snowdrops, spring-flowering cyclamens, and pink or white erythroniums. Useful variants include var. *chrysantha*, with mainly yellow petals, good for blending with flowers in hot colors, and with bronze or yellow-green foliage; 'Tubergen's Gem' is a selection of var. *chrysantha*. In *T.c.* 'Cynthia' ♀ the flowers are creamy yellow, flushed red on the outer petals and with a green edge.

◓ *Acaena microphylla* 'Kupferteppich', *Anaphalis triplinervis* 'Sommerschnee', *Anthemis punctata* subsp. *cupaniana*, *Chionodoxa forbesii* 'Pink Giant', *Convolvulus cneorum*, *Daphne cneorum* 'Eximia', *Heuchera* 'Quilter's Joy', *Lavandula* 'Sawyers', *Stachys byzantina* 'Big Ears'

H: 25cm (10in) **S: 10cm** (4in)
❀ **Early to mid-spring**
▮▮▮▮▮ ⬤ ▢-▨ ◼ **Z5 pH5.5–7.5**

Left: The vibrant *Tulipa clusiana* var. *chrysantha* combines with bugleweed (*Ajuga reptans* 'Atropurpurea'), wallflowers (*Erysimum × allionii*), and magenta aubrietas.

Below: More gently colored *Tulipa clusiana* in a semi-wild display mingles with bluebells (*Hyacinthoides non-scripta*) and anemones (*Anemone blanda* 'White Splendor').

Exuberantly splashed and streaked, carmine-red *Tulipa* 'Cordell Hull' makes a dramatic display above a carpet of pale blue wood forget-me-nots (*Myosotis sylvatica*).

Tulipa 'Cordell Hull'

A Single Late Group tulip of Cottage Group origin, 'Cordell Hull' is rich carmine-red, splashed and blotched with white. It is close enough to primary red to favor combinations with both hot or cool colors, while its two-tone effect, although slightly obscuring the elegant shape of the blooms, adds sparkle to the overall impression. It combines well with red or purple foliage, and contrasts effectively with yellow-green foliage and flowers, including euphorbias. As with most members of the Single Late Group, it is relatively tall, and its height makes it suitable for growing through plants such as wallflowers as high as 30–40cm (12–16in), and permits exciting partnerships with taller shrubs like deciduous azaleas, dark-leaved berberis, exochordas, kolkwitzias, camellias, and smaller magnolias.

◓ *Berberis thunbergii* 'Red Chief', *Camellia × williamsii* 'Mirage', *Dianthus barbatus* 'Sooty', *Erysimum* 'Sweet Sorbet', *Hebe* 'Mrs Winder', *Magnolia stellata* 'Waterlily', *Penstemon digitalis* 'Husker Red'

H: 55cm (22in) **S: 15cm** (6in) ❀ **Late spring**
▮▮▮▮▮ ◊ ▢-▨ ◼ **Z4 pH5–7.5**

Tulipa 'Fantasy' ♛

All Parrot Group tulips, of which 'Fantasy' is one, have extravagantly ruffled and fringed petals that are often broader than those of the cultivars from which they have sported, and appear larger and showier. 'Fantasy', a relatively late-blooming member of the group, has flowers in deep rose, paler towards the edges and on the outside, with a satin sheen and some green cresting near the tips of the petals. It is close enough to primary red to be combined with cool colors and purple foliage, silver or glaucous leaves, and white flowers, or with warm tints such as peach, coral, and bronze; contrasts with yellow-green foliage or flowers are also excellent. It can be grown through a wide variety of spring bedding plants such as wallflowers, forget-me-nots, or moricandias, and also combines effectively with dark-leaved heucheras, berberis, and smaller ornamental cherries.

◉ *Astrantia major* 'Sunningdale Variegated', *Cerinthe major* 'Purpurascens', *Cryptotaenia japonica* f. *atropurpurea*, *Prunus* × *cistena*, *Weigela* 'Victoria'

H: 55cm (22in) S: 15cm (6in) ✿ **Late spring**
▨ ◊ ▢-▨ ■ **Z4 pH5–7.5**

Here, *Tulipa* 'Fantasy' is grown as bedding through *Anthemis punctata* subsp. *cupaniana*, a combination that could equally be used on a smaller scale in a border.

Tulipa 'Elegant Lady'

This fairly tall Lily-flowered Group tulip bears creamy yellow blooms that fade a little as they age, with streaks and flecks of deep magenta-pink, particularly at the edges of the petals, although this is scarcely visible from a distance. Its predominately yellow coloring suits contrasts with blue flowers, including forget-me-nots, and harmonizes with white, rich golden yellow, or warm tints such as peach and apricot, and with yellow-green foliage or flowers. It is tall enough to be grown through a carpet of wallflowers and similar plants, and to be combined with flowering shrubs such as brooms, deciduous

Tulipa 'Elegant Lady' contrasts gently with wood forget-me-nots (*Myosotis sylvatica*), the blue flowers of *Centaurea montana*, and variegated moneyplant (*Lunaria annua* 'Alba Variegata') in a permanently planted border.

azaleas, berberis, mahonias, ceanothus, and kerrias. Other good partners are euphorbias, later-flowering narcissi, fritillaries (including crown imperials), and hyacinths.

◉ *Berberis thunbergii* Bonanza Gold, *Heuchera* 'Purple Petticoats', *Coronilla valentina* subsp. *glauca* 'Citrina', *Corydalis lutea*, *Cytisus* × *praecox* 'Warminster', *Erysimum* 'Bredon', *Euphorbia characias* Silver Swan, *Kerria japonica* 'Picta', *Lathyrus aureus*

H: 60cm (24in) S: 15cm (6in) ✿ **Late spring**
▨ ◊ ▢-▨ ■ **Z4 pH5–7.5**

A

Tulipa 'Greuze'

The blooms of this Single Late Group tulip are a rich deep magenta-purple, a color found in only very few cultivars. It can be used in combinations with cool colors – either rich and sumptuous, like crimson, strong blue, or purple and purple foliage, or delicate, paler tints such as mauve, pink, and pale blue – and it also contrasts effectively with soft yellow, yellow-green foliage and flowers, and (for those who dare) orange flowers. As is typical in this group, it is fairly tall, making it useful for growing above shorter plants such as hyacinths, moricandias, wallflowers, and forget-me-nots, and it also combines well with dark-leaved heucheras, dicentras, columbines, euphorbias, and bergenias, and with shrubs such as deciduous azaleas, brooms, and early yellow roses.

◐ *Aquilegia vulgaris* var. *stellata* 'Royal Purple', *Bellis perennis* 'Tasso Strawberries and Cream', *Cytisus* 'Hollandia', *Dicentra* 'Bountiful', *Erysimum* 'Sweet Sorbet', *Heuchera* 'Magic Wand', *Iris pallida* 'Variegata', *Rosa* 'Frühlingsgold', *Rubus microphyllus* 'Variegatus'

H: 55cm (22in) S: 15cm (6in) ✿ **Late spring**
◊ ▨-▨ ■ **Z4 pH5–7.5**

Although the camera sees them differently, to the naked eye *Tulipa* 'Greuze' and the wallflower *Erysimum cheiri* 'Purple Queen' are closely matched in color.

B

Tulipa 'Golden Oxford'

This is a fragrant tulip of the Darwinhybrid Group, and is golden yellow with a narrow red edge to the petals. Although comparable in many respects to 'Jewel of Spring' (facing page), it is slightly shorter, with deeper yellow flowers that have a less distinct edge to the petals; however, these differences are so slight that they are scarcely noticeable at a distance and hardly affect the choice of companion plants. It combines well with hot colors and with bronze, red, or yellow-green foliage, and contrasts effectively with white or blue flowers. Good companions include forget-me-nots, wallflowers, brunneras, later-flowering cream or white narcissi, hyacinths, bronze-leaved heucheras, and yellow- or cream-variegated shrubs such as elaeagnus or holly

Tulipa 'Golden Oxford', planted permanently in a border and contrasted with blue *Brunnera macrophylla*, only just overlaps the white Triandrus Group *Narcissus* 'Thalia' at the start of its flowering, although it will grow another 10cm (4in) taller before its petals are shed.

cultivars. Like most Darwinhybrid Group tulips, it is relatively vigorous, and well-suited to being planted permanently, without any need for annual lifting.

◐ *Brunnera macrophylla*, *Ceanothus* Zanzibar, *Elaeagnus* × *ebbingei* 'Limelight', *Erysimum cheiri* 'Cloth of Gold', *Euonymus fortunei* 'Emerald 'n' Gold', *Euphorbia griffithii* 'Fireglow', *Heuchera micrantha* var. *diversifolia* 'Palace Purple', *Ilex aquifolium* 'Golden Milkboy', *Thuja occidentalis* 'Rheingold'

H: 55cm (22in) S: 15cm (6in)
✿ **Mid- to late spring**
◊-◊◊ ▨-▨ ■ **Z4 pH4.5–7.5**

Tulipa 'Jewel of Spring' ♔

This Darwinhybrid Group tulip is very similar in appearance to 'Golden Oxford' (facing page), although its flowers are a slightly paler yellow, with petals edged in a stronger red. Its paler coloring is still strong enough to contrast with blue flowers and to combine with hot or rich colors, while the extra red around the petal margins provides a link with orange or red flowers, warm colors such as peach and apricot, and red-flushed foliage. Its greater height – it is 5–10cm (2–4in) taller than 'Golden Oxford' – makes it suitable for combinations with medium-sized shrubs such as elaeagnus and holly, while its typical Darwinhybrid Group tolerance of a little shade allows permanent planting under the fairly light canopy of deciduous trees or in a semi-shaded border.

In this permanent planting of *Tulipa* 'Jewel of Spring', the yellow petals and their narrow red edging harmonize with the red-flushed, yellow-green young foliage of *Spiraea japonica* 'Goldflame'.

◐ *Carex comans* (bronze), *Euphorbia dulcis* 'Chameleon', *Lychnis* × *arkwrightii* 'Vesuvius', *Meconopsis cambrica* 'Muriel Brown', *Narcissus* 'Cheerfulness', *Nonea lutea*, *Paeonia lactiflora* 'Crimson Glory', *Symphytum* 'Goldsmith'

H: 60cm (24in) S: 15cm (6in)
✿ **Mid- to late spring**

◊-◊◊ ▨-▨ ■ Z4 pH4.5–7.5

Tulipa linifolia Batalinii Group ♔

Tulips of the Batalinii Group are rather variable, with pronounced blue-grey foliage and dainty flowers ranging from pale or bright yellow, flushed to a greater or lesser extent with bronze, through apricot to vermilion, colors that are particularly suited to combinations with other warm hues and bronze foliage, or to contrasts with blue. They are very easy to grow in rock or gravel gardens, and near the front of a border, where they can be planted through a mat of low carpeting plants such as acaenas or bugleweeds. They succeed in small-scale plantings with the tiniest shrubs, including small glaucous-leaved hebes, and combine well with spring bulbs such as erythroniums, muscaris, smaller narcissi, white checker lilies, ipheions, and rhizomatous anemones. Useful selections include 'Apricot Jewel', apricot with an orange flush; 'Bright Gem' ♔, sulfur-yellow with an orange flush; 'Bronze Charm', yellow feathered with bronze; the vermilion 'Red Gem'; and 'Yellow Jewel', soft yellow tinged with pink.

◐ *Acaena microphylla* 'Pewter Carpet', *Chamaecyparis thyoides* 'Ericoides', *Festuca glauca* 'Elijah Blue', *Hebe pimeleoides* 'Quicksilver', *Ipheion uniflorum* 'Wisley Blue', *Pittosporum tenuifolium* 'Tom Thumb', *Salix* 'Boydii', *Saxifraga exarata* subsp. *moschata*, 'Cloth of Gold', *Thymus* × *citriodorus* 'Silver Queen', *Uncinia egmontiana*, *Veronica peduncularis* 'Georgia Blue'

H: 15cm (6in) S: 10cm (4in)
✿ **Early to mid-spring**

◊ ▨-▨ ■ Z5 pH4.5–7.5

Apricot *Tulipa linifolia* Batalinii Group mingle with blue *Muscari armeniacum, Anemone apennina,* and white checker lily (*Fritillaria meleagris* var. *unicolor* subvar. *alba*).

In this combination *Tulipa* 'Mariette' is planted through a carpet of alpine forget-me-nots (*Myosotis alpestris*) around the apothecary's rose (*Rosa gallica* var. *officinalis*). Harder pruning of the rose would allow the display to continue uninterrupted through the area it occupies.

Tulipa 'Mariette'

This Lily-flowered Group cultivar has rich rose-pink flowers with a white base, and markedly reflexed petals that give it a notably elegant outline. It is a little deeper in color than 'China Pink' (p.345), and slightly taller, but is otherwise so similar in appearance that the two tulips can be combined to provide subtle variations in color and height, and also a slightly extended flowering season, because 'Mariette' flowers a few days later. Its deeper coloring is a useful element in more luxuriant, darker-hued schemes with, for instance, purple foliage. It mixes well with bergenias, heucheras, and forget-me-nots, violas, primroses, and polyanthus, and with other bulbs such as hyacinths and white narcissi. Exochordas, daphnes, and smaller magnolias are suitable shrubby partners.

◐ *Cordyline australis* 'Purple Tower', *Magnolia* × *loebneri* 'Leonard Messel', *Tulipa* 'Marjolein' p.350 **B**, *Viola* (Sorbet Series) 'Yesterday, Today and Tomorrow'

H: 55cm (22in) S: 15cm (6in) ☼ Late spring
�water drop ☐-■ ■ **Z4 pH5–7.5**

Tulipa 'Mariette' and its sport *T.* 'Marjolein' clash gently above a carpet of alpine forget-me-nots (*Myosotis alpestris*), while matching perfectly in form and growth habit.

Tulipa 'Marjolein' ♛

A sport of 'Mariette' (left), this Lily-flowered Group cultivar has flame-colored flowers with a soft yellow base, but is otherwise identical. Its warm color is rich enough to be combined with scarlet or strong orange, but also blends well with soft or burnt orange, peach, and apricot, as well as clashing agreeably with pink tulips such as 'Mariette' itself. It combines effectively with wallflowers, euphorbias, primroses, polyanthus, and geums, yellow-green foliage and flowers, and bronze foliage such as that of heucheras.

◐ *Chaenomeles* × *superba* 'Knap Hill Scarlet', *Erysimum* × *allionii*, *Euphorbia characias*, *Filipendula ulmaria* 'Aurea', *Phormium* 'Bronze Baby'

H: 55cm (22in) S: 15cm (6in) ☼ Late spring
◐ water drop ☐-■ ■ **Z4 pH5–7.5**

Tulipa 'Negrita'

This is a sumptuous Triumph Group tulip, with rich royal purple flowers veined with darker purple. Although its coloring may not be easily visible from a distance and is perhaps best appreciated at close range, it is superlative for combinations with cool colors and contrasts with orange or yellow-green. It is a valuable cultivar for providing a base note in plantings of brighter flowers in, for example, magenta or carmine. Eye-catching combinations can be made with

Sumptuous purple *Tulipa* 'Negrita' is planted here through a gently contrasting orange wallflower (*Erysimum cheiri*) in a rich blend that shows up best at close range.

lightly purple-flushed foliage, such as purple sage, with mauve flowers like moricandias, and with euphorbias and wallflowers.

◐ *Ruta graveolens*, *Salvia officinalis* 'Tricolor', *Silene dioica* 'Graham's Delight'

H: 45cm (18in) S: 15cm (6in)
☼ Mid- to late spring
■ water drop ☐-■ ■ **Z4 pH5–7.5**

Tulipa 'Orange Favorite'

The complex and very fragrant, vermilion flowers of this Parrot Group tulip are shaded with coral and lighter orange, and have yellow at the base and occasional flecks of green at the tips. The cut edges to the petals and subtle shadings within each bloom give the cultivar great appeal, and it is especially attractive when viewed at close range. Like many Parrot Group and double tulips, the extra weight of the flower may cause it to flop,

but in a container this can be an advantage – the stems tend to sprawl over the edge and arch back in an elegant curve. It suits hot-color schemes and contrasts with glaucous foliage, yellow-green leaves or flowers, and blue flowers; further dramatic contrasts can be made with white flowers such as rock cress or climbing purple wallflowers. A relatively late tulip, it combines well with forget-me-nots, brunneras, omphalodes, deciduous azaleas, shorter ceanothus, and bronze- or purple-leaved shrubs such as berberis.

◐ *Anthriscus sylvestris* 'Ravenswing', *Berberis thunbergii* 'Golden Ring', *Euphorbia amygdaloides* 'Purpurea', *Omphalodes cappadocica*, *Rhododendron* 'Glowing Embers', *Rubus cockburnianus* 'Goldenvale', *Salvia officinalis* 'Icterina', *Thalictrum flavum* 'Illuminator'

H: 50cm (20in) **S: 15cm** (6in) ❀ **Late spring**
◊ ▢-▢ ■ **Z4 pH5–7.5**

Tulipa 'Orange Favorite' and deep black-purple *T.* 'Queen of Night' are here closely planted and thoroughly mixed together at the front of a bed. This rich and exuberant combination depends on the identical flowering season of the two cultivars for its extraordinary effect.

A

Tulipa 'Orange Wonder'

Although similar in coloring to 'Orange Favorite' (p.351), this is a Triumph Group tulip, so it has a more regular and classically shaped flower, and a tendency to be more upright, which makes it more suitable for formal displays and for bedding through a ground cover of lower plants. It has attractive vermilion blooms, shaded with bronze and a paler orange towards the edge of the petals. It harmonizes with bronze foliage and hot colors, and contrasts very effectively with yellow-green foliage and flowers; its bright coloring is more inclined towards red than that of 'Orange Favorite', so contrasts with blue are not so dramatic. White rock cress and purple wallflowers make exciting companions, as does purple foliage.

◐ *Foeniculum vulgare* 'Purpureum', *Chaenomeles speciosa* 'Geisha Girl', *Salvia officinalis* 'Icterina', *Trollius × cultorum* 'Orange Princess'

H: 45cm (18in) S: 15cm (6in)
❀ Mid- to late spring
◼◼◻ ◊ ◻-◼ ◼ Z4 pH5–7.5

In this informal planting, which is filled in front by variegated stinking iris (*Iris foetidissima* 'Variegata'), the vibrant blooms of *Tulipa* 'Orange Wonder' are effectively contrasted against a background of yellow-green perfoliate alexanders (*Smyrnium perfoliatum*).

Tulipa 'Prinses Irene' ♛

This relatively short Triumph Group tulip has soft orange blooms, flamed with reddish purple and green down the center of the petals, a color combination that is rather more subdued than some of the other orange tulips. In this respect it is less suitable for very hot or dramatically contrasting color schemes, but is excellent with soft colors such as peach, apricot, and coral, or with bronze, glaucous, or purple foliage, and contrasts well with blue flowers and yellow-green foliage or flowers. Its own foliage is attractively glaucous and contrasts pleasantly with its flowers. It is most appealing with geums, heucheras, wallflowers, forget-me-nots, and euphorbias, and makes a good plant for containers.

◐ *Euphorbia cyparissias*, *Geranium* 'Ann Folkard', *Geum* 'Georgenburg', *Hebe ochracea*, *Lonicera nitida* 'Baggesen's Gold', *Myosotis alpestris* 'Royal Blue'

H: 35cm (14in) S: 15cm (6in)
❀ Mid- to late spring
◼◼◻ ◊ ◻-◼ ◼ Z4 pH5–7.5

The curiously striped, soft orange tones of *Tulipa* 'Prinses Irene' combine perfectly with *Geum* 'Beech House Apricot' in a display to which rich bronze foliage and/or yellow-green, blood-red, or cream flowers could be added.

Tulipa 'Palestrina'

A tulip belonging to the Triumph Group, 'Palestrina' has large, rich deep salmon flowers that are flushed with green on the outside. It combines well with warm colors, white flowers, and bronze, red, and silver foliage plants, such as artemisias, and makes fine contrasts with yellow-green foliage and flowers. It blooms relatively late, and so makes good partnerships with euphorbias, wallflowers, heucheras, and geums, and can be particularly effective with strong green foliage such as that of parsley.

The warm salmon blooms of *Tulipa* 'Palestrina' glow against the silver foliage of woolly lamb's ears (*Stachys byzantina*) and *Artemisia ludoviciana*, with a sprinkling of wood forget-me-nots (*Myosotis sylvatica*). 'Palestrina' is a sturdy cultivar that is ideally suited to temporary spring displays, as well as making a strong impact in containers.

◐ *Anaphalis triplinervis*, *Astelia chathamica*, *Choisya ternata* Sundance, *Coronilla valentina* subsp. *glauca*, *Erysimum cheiri* 'Cloth of Gold', *Geum* 'Fire Opal', *Leymus arenarius*, *Lotus hirsutus*, *Lunaria annua* var. *albiflora* 'Alba Variegata', *Physocarpus opulifolius* 'Diabolo', *Ruta graveolens*, *Yucca filamentosa*

H: 40cm (16in) S: 15cm (6in) ❀ Late spring
◼◼◻ ◊ ◻-◼ ◼ Z4 pH5–7.5

The pale flowers of a carpet of beige-pink wallflower (*Erysimum cheiri* 'Eastern Queen') help to show up the rich, dark blooms of *Tulipa* 'Queen of Night'. The wallflower looks identical to one often sold (incorrectly) as *Erysimum* 'Ellen Willmott'.

Tulipa 'Queen of Night'

This magnificent Single Late Group tulip is even darker than 'Negrita' (p.350), with black-purple flowers, shaded rich plum-purple. Although suitable for the same kinds of combinations – with cool colors and softly purple-flushed foliage, for example – the deep coloring makes it even less visible from a distance, and it needs to be planted where it can be seen clearly, perhaps against a contrast of orange or yellow-green. Taller and later than 'Negrita', it is especially useful for providing the base notes in a combination with another, brighter tulip, and possibly one of contrasting shape. It is outstanding planted through a carpet of wallflowers, heucheras, moricandias, or similar shorter plants, and combines well with euphorbias, columbines, moneyplant, bergenias, dicentras, and the earliest cranesbills.

◐ *Berberis thunbergii* 'Atropurpurea Nana' p.32 **B**, *Cynara cardunculus*, *Euphorbia polychroma* 'Major' *Erysimum* 'Butterscotch', *Heuchera* 'Plum Pudding' p.241 **A**, *Tulipa* 'Orange Favorite' p.351 **A** ❑ p.345 **A**

H: 60cm (24in) **S: 15cm** (6in) ❀ **Late spring**
▬▬▭▭ ◊ ▭▬ ■ **Z4 pH5–7.5**

Tulipa 'Red Shine' ♈

The exceptionally long-lasting flowers of this Lily-flowered Group tulip are a deep primary red, with petals that are blunter than in most others of the group and only slightly reflexed at the tip. The blooms open slowly over a couple of weeks from their initial cup shape to form a spreading star. 'Red Shine' works well with both hot and cool colors, and makes an effective contrast with yellow-green foliage and flowers like euphorbias. It is very handsome planted with purple foliage such as that of heucheras, purple sage, and purple smoke bush, and also associates well with moneyplant, columbines, and bulbs such as crown imperials and early-flowering alliums.

◐ *Cornus alba* 'Elegantissima', *Cotinus coggygria* 'Royal Purple', *Miscanthus sinensis* 'Zebrinus', *Phlox paniculata* 'Norah Leigh', *Salvia officinalis* 'Purpurascens', *Scrophularia auriculata* 'Variegata'

H: 60cm (24in) **S: 15cm** (6in) ❀ **Late spring**
▬▬▭▭ ◊ ▭▬ ■ **Z4 pH5–7.5**

When *Tulipa* 'Red Shine' is in full bloom, the ornamental onion *Allium hollandicum* 'Purple Sensation' passes it on its way upward as its own rich amethyst blooms begin to open. Both are vigorous and persistent enough to be used as permanent planting among herbaceous perennials that can hide their dying leaves.

Tulipa 'Spring Green' ♈

This is a Viridiflora Group tulip of medium height. The typical green stripe down the center of the petals shades through yellowish cream to white towards the edges and tips; each petal is slightly twisted and reflexed, with a pointed tip, rather like a Lily-flowered tulip. This subtle color scheme suits combinations with white, yellow, yellow-green, or green flowers, and yellow-green foliage. 'Spring Green' can be planted or naturalized in wilder areas, where it looks handsome with flowers of contrasting floral form, such as early-flowering umbellifers. It associates well with blue flowers – forget-me-nots, pulmonarias, omphalodes, and brunneras, for example – and early white-flowered shrubs such as exochordas and spiraeas. Other good partners include hostas, and early-flowering peonies and yellow roses.

◐ *Brunnera macrophylla* 'Dawson's White', *Exochorda serratifolia* 'Snow White', *Hosta* 'Fire and Ice', *Paeonia mlokosewitschii*, *Pulmonaria* 'White Wings', *Spiraea thunbergii* 'Mount Fuji', *Viburnum carlesii*

H: 50cm (20in) **S: 15cm** (6in) ❀ **Late spring**
▬▬▭▭ ◊ ▭▬ ■ **Z4 pH5–7.5**

This is a subtle combination consisting of *Tulipa* 'Spring Green', its blooms shaded from green through yellow-green and cream to white, and yellow-green *Euphorbia polychroma*.

A

Tulipa 'Sweet Harmony' 🏆

The gentle overall effect of this Single Late Group tulip, with its lemon-yellow blooms grading softly to ivory-white at the petal edges, qualifies it for use in combinations with warm colors such as apricot, and with yellow-green flowers or foliage, rather than for lively arrangements with hot colors, where a stronger yellow might be more successful. It is an outstanding partner for white flowers, especially late narcissi, umbellifers, white moneyplant, and white forget-me-nots, and it is also good associated with early-leafing, glaucous or yellow-green hostas and yellow-green euphorbias. Other suitable companions include brooms, genistas, kerrias, and deep gold or ivory wallflowers.

🌸 *Aquilegia vulgaris* var. *stellata* 'Greenapples', *Cytisus* × *kewensis*, *Euonymus fortunei* 'Silver Queen', *Genista lydia*, *Griselinia littoralis* 'Dixon's Cream', *Milium effusum* 'Aureum', *Ranunculus bulbosus* 'F.M. Burton', *Sambucus nigra* 'Madonna', *Sisyrinchium striatum* 'Aunt May', *Smyrnium perfoliatum*

H: 55cm (22in) **S: 15cm** (6in) ❈ **Late spring**
◖ ⬤ ▢-▦ ■ **Z4 pH5–7.5**

Facing page: *Tulipa* 'Sweet Harmony' and the similarly colored *T.* 'Maja' of the Fringed Group are here planted through the emerging yellowish green fronds of the ostrich fern (*Matteuccia struthiopteris*) beside a pond. Although the relatively damp, semi-shaded conditions are not ideal for tulips, which generally prefer a reasonably dry and sunny site, it is a stunningly successful combination, and helps to light up an otherwise fairly dark corner. Sadly, the tulips may be short-lived in such conditions.

Tulipa 'West Point' 🏆

As the sweetly scented flowers of this Lily-flowered Group tulip age, they open from a slender, narrowly tapered and reflexed form into a less elegant star shape. The bright yellow coloring works well with other hot colors, such as orange and red, with bronze or purple foliage, with yellow-green foliage and flowers, or with white flowers, and contrasts effectively with blue forget-me-nots. 'West Point' can be combined with other tulips flowering at the same time, preferably with a different floral form, but also looks good on its own in large containers. White moneyplant, early-flowering shrubs such as

The classic combination of yellow tulips with rich blue alpine forget-me-nots (*Myosotis alpestris*) perhaps works best with the elegantly shaped *T.* 'West Point'.

brooms, and dark-leaved shrubs like berberis are suitable companions, as are hot-colored wallflowers, white or cream late-flowering narcissi, euphorbias, dark-leaved heucheras, crown imperials, and geums.

🌸 *Berberis thunbergii* 'Red Chief', *Fritillaria imperialis*, *Lysimachia ciliata* 'Firecracker' p.262 **B**, *Narcissus* 'Thalia', *Pentaglottis sempervirens*, *Tulipa* 'White Triumphator' p.355 **B**, *Viburnum sargentii* 'Onondaga'

H: 50cm (20in) **S: 15cm** (6in) ❈ **Late spring**
◖ ⬤ ▢-▦ ■ **Z4 pH5–7.5**

Tulipa 'White Triumphator' 🏆

This is a tall and elegant Lily-flowered Group tulip, with blooms maturing pure white from greenish ivory buds. The petals are less exaggeratedly tapered and reflexed than those of 'West Point' (above right), giving a flower form that is less extreme but equally graceful. Its color mixes with any other, but looks outstanding in white flower displays, with silver foliage, or with yellow-green, yellow, or blue flowers and glaucous or yellow-green foliage. It combines well with flowers of contrasting floral form (umbellifers, for example), smaller late-flowering narcissi, star of Bethlehem, and shrubs such as spiraeas, brooms, genistas, and exochordas. Striking contrasts can be made by planting it against dark foliage – through a carpet of purple-leaved plants such as heucheras, for example, against a background of dark evergreens

such as yew, or intermingled with a dark-leaved cow parsley. With its elegant shape and subdued coloring, it is suitable for naturalizing in wilder parts of the garden and also for growing in larger containers.

🌸 *Anthriscus sylvestris* 'Ravenswing', *Atriplex halimus*, *Brunnera macrophylla* 'Betty Bowring', *Crambe maritima*, *Eupatorium rugosum* 'Chocolate', *Euphorbia characias* 'Portuguese Velvet', *Farfugium japonicum* 'Argenteum', *Foeniculum vulgare* 'Purpureum', *Geranium pratense* Midnight Reiter strain, *Melianthus major*, *Ornithogalum nutans*, *Potentilla fruticosa* 'Abbotswood', *Rosa glauca*, *Sambucus nigra* Black Beauty

H: 60cm (24in) **S: 15cm** (6in) ❈ **Late spring**
◖ ⬤ ▢-▦ ■ **Z4 pH5–7.5**

A sunny mix of three bulbs in graduated heights, white *Narcissus* 'Thalia', 35cm (14in), yellow *Tulipa* 'West Point', 50cm (20in), and the slightly taller *T.* 'White Triumphator', is here planted around *Helleborus foetidus*. Through replanting, the flowering of the narcissus has been slightly delayed to coincide with the tulips.

Above: The rich coral-red flowers and sword-like foliage of *Watsonia* 'Stanford Scarlet' and spiky *Cordyline australis* 'Torbay Dazzler' create a bold, almost tropical effect.

Below: A clump of coral-red *Watsonia fourcadei* is here given ample room to display its imposing growth habit. Its blooms contrast with large *Agapanthus praecox* subsp. *orientalis* and a smaller agapanthus. White Japanese anemones (*Anemone × hybrida*) brighten the rich colors.

Watsonia species and cultivars

Watsonias are rather tender South African relatives of the gladiolus, growing from corms and requiring good drainage, but with ample moisture when in full growth. They are therefore good plants for stream banks, combined with other waterside plants like phormiums, zantedeschias, and agapanthus, and tender perennials such as cannas and dahlias. The flowers of *Watsonia fourcadei* are pink, red, vermilion or, more rarely, purple, born above the foliage in two-ranked spikes of elegant long-tubed florets. Its colors associate well with warm and hot tints, and with bronze or red-flushed foliage. In frost-prone areas, spring-flowering watsonias can be lifted in autumn and stored as dried corms for planting as tender perennials, but summer-flowering species such as *W. fourcadei* are best not disturbed: spring transplanting diminishes flowering, while autumn or winter disturbance can lead to rotting; transplanting immediately after flowering, however, is a possibility.

◐ *Agapanthus* 'Loch Hope', *Agastache* 'Firebird', *Beschornia yuccoides*, *Canna* 'Cleopatra', *Dahlia* 'Bednall Beauty', *Hedychium gardnerianum*, *Hemerocallis* 'Frans Hals', *Kniphofia* 'Timothy', *Leonotis leonurus*, *Lobelia tupa*, *Nandina domestica*, *Phormium* 'Yellow Wave', *Phygelius × rectus* 'Sunshine', *Yucca gloriosa*

H: 45–150cm (18–60in) S: 40cm (16in)
※ **Early spring to early autumn**
  ◊◊ ☐ **Z9 pH5–7**

In hot climates, the calla lily (*Zantedeschia aethiopica*) will flower happily in partial shade, where it can be combined with other shade-loving plants such as the dainty *Begonia* 'Ricinifolia', with its elegant sprays of pink flowers.

Zantedeschia aethiopica
CALLA LILY

This beautiful rhizomatous perennial is happiest in moist soils and pond margins, where reflections can double its impact, but it does tolerate ordinary border soils if not too dry. The arrow-shaped, glossy deep green leaves are overtopped by the flowers, which consist of an elegantly shaped white spathe surrounding a yellow spadix. Calla lilies provide a bold, tropical effect that combines well with astilbes, Siberian irises, moisture-loving euphorbias, filipendulas, veratrums, and larger ferns. Even after flowering, its foliage is a handsome companion for water cannas, hedychiums, hostas, and rodgersias. It is slightly tender and in cold climates benefits from a thick mulch for protection. Useful cultivars include the relatively hardy 'Crowborough' ♀; 'Green Goddess' ♀, with charming green spathes; and 'Little Gem' and 'Childsiana', both about 60cm (24in) tall.

◐ *Astilbe* 'Deutschland', *Canna* 'Erebus', *Dryopteris filix-mas*, *Filipendula rubra* 'Venusta', *Iris* 'Butter and Sugar', *Rodgersia aesculifolia*

H: 90cm (36in) S: 60cm (24in)
※ **Late spring to mid-summer**
 ◊◊-◊◊◊ ☐-■ ■ **Z8 pH5–7.5**

The atamasco lily (*Zephyranthes atamasca*) does not need full sun to flower in hot climates but benefits from a sunny position in colder climates. Here, it fills a border by a path beneath evergreen oaks (*Quercus ilex*).

Zephyranthes species
ZEPHYR LILY

The zephyr lilies are rather tender bulbs, relatives of narcissi, with showy flowers in white, pink, or yellow. The most widely grown species is *Z. candida*, 10–20cm (4–8in) high and flowering in early to mid-autumn. It is useful for the front of a border, growing through a low ground cover, perhaps with New York asters, Charm chrysanthemums, nerines, colchicums, and autumn crocuses. The atamasco lily (*Z. atamasca*) is 20–30cm (8–12in) tall and has very large flowers, usually white but occasionally pale pink. It combines well with other spring bulbs, grown through compact ivy, bugleweeds, or arisaemas. The autumn-flowering *Z. rosea*, 15–20cm (6–8in), bears rose-pink flowers with a greenish base, while *Z. grandiflora*, 10–20cm (4–8in) has rose-pink flowers from mid-summer to early autumn – both may be used in similar ways to *Z. candida*.

◐ *Aster thomsonii* 'Nanus', *Colchicum speciosum, Crocus speciosus, Cyclamen hederifolium, Hedera helix* 'Kolibri', *Nerine undulata, Sternbergia lutea*

H: 10–30cm (4–12in) **S: 5–10cm** (2–4in)
❀ **Late spring to mid-autumn**
◊◊ ☐-■ **Z8–10 pH5.5–7.5**

Zigadenus elegans

This very hardy bulb, with airy spikes of charming creamy green flowers, is a sun-loving species for the front of a warm border, although it will tolerate some shade in areas with hotter summers and may then be grown in a light woodland setting. It resents prolonged drought, but needs very good drainage, making it a good candidate for a gravel garden. It looks attractive growing through low ground-cover plants, against a background of dark foliage or where it can be appreciated at close range without much competition. The quiet color of its flowers combines well with glaucous foliage, and with other flowers in white, soft yellow, pure blue, very deep blue or purple, and yellow-green such as summer-flowering euphorbias.

◐ *Agapanthus* 'Bressingham Blue', *Agastache rugosa, Eryngium alpinum* 'Blue Star', *Phygelius aequalis* 'Yellow Trumpet', *Verbena rigida, Veronica spicata*

H: 70cm (27in) **S: 8cm** (3½in)
❀ **Mid- to late summer**
◊-◊◊ ☐-■ **Z5 pH5.5–7.5**

An airy veil of green and cream flowers of *Zigadenus elegans* is enlivened by the brilliant magenta, dark-veined blooms of the sprawling, long-flowering cranesbill *Geranium wallichianum* 'Syabru' in front of a carpet of *G. macrorrhizum*.

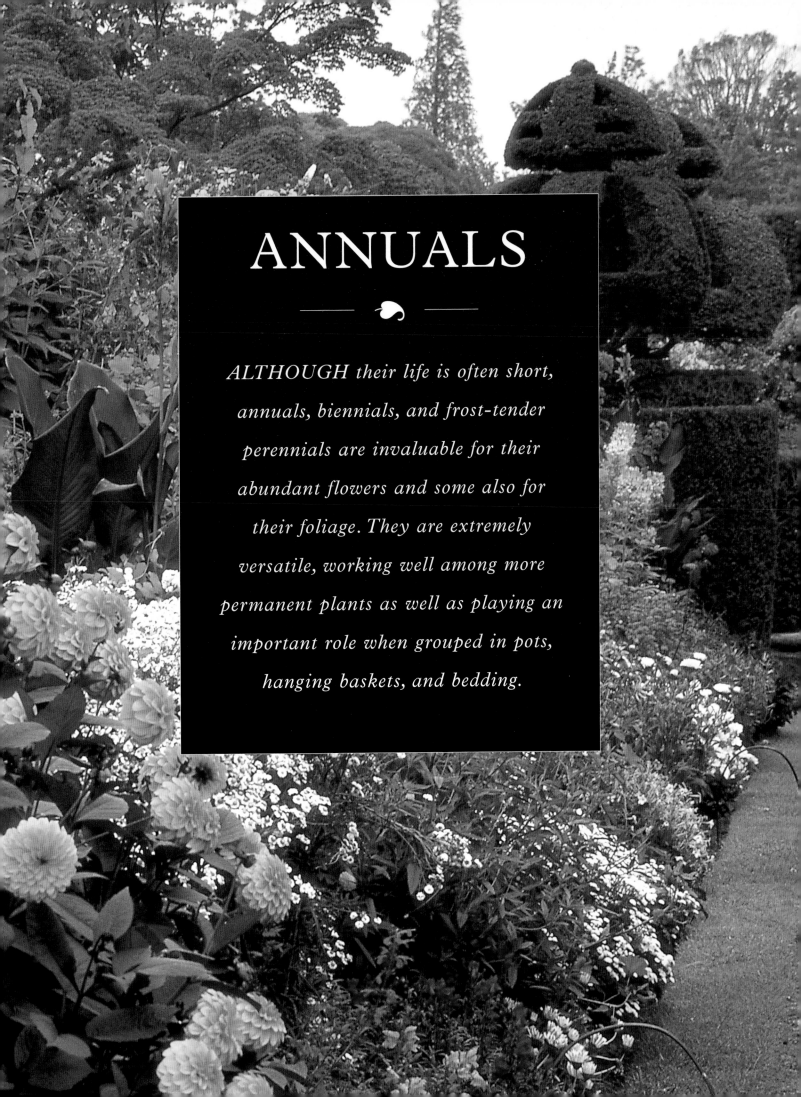

ANNUALS

❦

ALTHOUGH their life is often short, annuals, biennials, and frost-tender perennials are invaluable for their abundant flowers and some also for their foliage. They are extremely versatile, working well among more permanent plants as well as playing an important role when grouped in pots, hanging baskets, and bedding.

Often the brightest flowers and most spectacular foliage in gardens are provided by the shortest-lived plants – the annuals and biennials, and tender perennials that are used for summer display (those not reliably hardy in Zone 8 are included here). True annuals and biennials are plants that invest all their energy into one season of flower and seed production before dying. Tender perennials are from climates without cold winters; this means they evolved to flower freely over a very long period. The result in all cases is maximum flower power, a feature that plant breeders have often intensified by producing astonishing color ranges on compact and uniform plants.

The downside is that all such plants are temporary visitors, contributing nothing to the permanent structure of the garden. Most are costly in time and money to raise or buy, to plant and remove each year, and, in the case of tender perennials, perhaps to overwinter. However, most gardeners would consider the outlay well worth it as the impact of these plants begins instantly and increases rapidly as summer progresses. By selecting some of the taller-growing and larger annuals – cosmos, tithonias, cleomes, ricinus, *Nicotiana sylvestris* – an astonishing, albeit temporary, sense of maturity can be achieved in a new garden, especially if these are supplemented by climbing annuals such as sweet peas and morning glories on obelisks, teepees, or trellises.

Seed-raised plants

Hardy annuals are easy to sow where they are to flower, and thinned out to final spacings when they are established. One delightful way of using them is in a mixture: many seed companies offer packets of mixed tall or short annuals, while more adventurous gardeners may like to concoct their own mixes for a particular range of colors or heights. The seeds can be sown sparsely in straight rows and thinned to small clumps of seedlings, 15–20cm (6–8in) apart. The fast-

Among the most popular and dependable of tender perennials, dahlias provide bold colors and strong shapes in borders from mid-summer until the autumn frosts. Here, single-, double-, and cactus-flowered cultivars in a range of sumptuous reds make a vibrant partnership, the effect enhanced by a background of deep purple foliage.

growing plants then disguise the straight rows and produce a colorful, ever-changing display of early bloomers succeeded by later ones.

Biennials need to be sown the year before they are required in flower and then put in their flowering positions the following autumn or spring. Some hardy annuals can be treated in the same way. Being sown the previous late summer or autumn means they flower earlier on larger plants, thus widening the possible flowering combinations. Sweet peas are ideal for this treatment in suitable climates.

Half-hardy annuals and many tender perennials are also easy to raise from seed. In cold areas, these should be sown in pots or trays somewhere bright and warm, such as on a window sill or in a greenhouse, and the seedlings must not be planted out into the garden until no further frosts are expected.

Formal and informal bedding

Annuals and tender perennials are very popular for bedding. Plants used in spring displays are usually low-growing biennials, such as daisies and wallflowers, and bulbs are often included. The choice of plants for summer bedding is much wider and a huge range of effects can be achieved. Plants may be arranged in patterns or mixed loosely together to create a tapestry of mingled colors and varied forms. Careful selection of colors, forms, and textures can produce gentle, romantic moods or bright, vibrant ones. For example, the vivid red salvia, once so popular for formal beds in public parks, is now available in a variety of softer colors which produce a much more delicate display. Where there is more space, taller-growing tender perennials with bold foliage can be used to produce exciting sub-tropical or jungle-like areas in the garden: bananas, cannas, ricinus, and eucalyptus are all excellent.

Although some gardeners devote entire beds to these comparatively short-lived displays, most prefer the informality that can be achieved with less concentrated planting – mixing groups of summer annuals among plants in a herbaceous or mixed border, for example. This can be done to fill gaps where permanent plants have not yet covered their allotted space, or planned as a regular part of the border's changing display. It is easy to find annuals in colors and forms that match the character of the border as a whole. Drifts of quiet color – pale antirrhinums, cosmos, lavateras, and nigellas – will enrich a subtle bed, while cannas, dahlias, ricinus, and many salvias, will bring a border of hot-colored roses, kniphofias, and purple-leaved shrubs to a fiery climax.

Imaginative compositions of annuals and tender perennials can supply an exciting patchwork of summer color, especially if balanced with complementary shades. For example, these vivid scarlet salvias and pelargoniums are toned down by integrating them with softer-colored flowers such as the nicotianas, impatiens, and phlox.

A well-branched plant of *Aeonium* 'Zwartkop' contrasts dramatically against the near-white stems of *Leucophyta brownii*. Both benefit from a sunny site with good drainage and relatively low nitrogen availability.

Aeonium 'Zwartkop' ♈

Aeoniums are tender perennial succulents with rosettes of leaves that are fascinating for their geometrical perfection. 'Zwartkop' is the most extraordinary, its leaves aging from bronze through deep chocolate to lustrous black. Single young rosettes are used in formal carpet bedding, while more mature branching plants combine well in pots with a contrasting foliage plant – a glaucous-leaved lotus, for example. They are most effective with silver foliage but also excel in sumptuous dark color schemes, such as red borders, or with hot colors and bronze foliage. In rich soil, 'Zwartkop' tends to flop and its stems may break; here, a better choice is *A. arboreum* 'Atropurpureum' ♈, which is more erect and slightly lighter in color.

ⓘ *Cordyline australis* Purpurea Group, *Dahlia* 'Bishop of Llandaff', *Fuchsia* 'Thalia', *Lotus berthelotii*, *Plectranthus argentatus*, *Ricinus communis* 'Carmencita', *Senecio cineraria* 'Silver Dust'

H: 45cm (18in) **S: 35cm** (14in) ❉ **Late spring**
 ◊ ▢-▨ ■ **Z10 pH5.5–7**

A veil of shining scarlet florets of *Alonsoa warscewiczii* (mask flower) shows up brightly against the dusky, reddish purple foliage of a smoke bush (*Cotinus coggygria*) cultivar in a steeply sloped detail at the front of a border.

Ageratum houstonianum 'Old Grey'

'Old Grey' is one of the taller *A. houstonianum* cultivars, annuals that are distinguished by a loose growth habit that allows them to intermingle successfully with other annual and herbaceous plants toward the front of a border. The name is misleading because its flower color is really a soft lavender-blue, which mixes well with other lavender flowers and with blue, purple, mauve, or white, as well as purple, glaucous, or silver foliage. Its numerous tiny, fuzzy flower heads provide an ideal foil for larger, bolder flowers such as marguerites, petunias, and osteospermums, while its slightly diffuse flowering habit combines well with heliotropes, an equally valuable foil for larger-flowered plants. Shorter ageratum cultivars have a stockier, more solid outline, which is excellent for formal carpet bedding but less satisfactory for interaction with neighboring plants.

ⓘ *Argyranthemum gracile* 'Chelsea Girl', *Brachyscome iberidifolia* 'Summer Skies', *Helichrysum petiolare*, *Heliotropium arborescens* 'Princess Marina', *Osteospermum* 'White Pim', *Senecio cineraria* 'Cirrus'

H: 45cm (18in) **S: 30cm** (12in)
❉ **Early summer to early autumn**
 ◊◊ ▢-▨ ■ **Z10 pH5.5–7.5**

At the front of a border, the small flower heads of *Ageratum houstonianum* 'Old Grey' and bicolored florets of *Nemesia* 'KLM' contrast in size with the larger, more solid flowers of *Petunia* (Pearl Series) 'Pearl Azure Blue' and *Salpiglossis* 'Kew Blue', all of them in harmonious shades.

Alonsoa warscewiczii ♈

This is a sub-shrubby perennial with broadly oval, serrated leaves that are evergreen where it survives the winter. Elsewhere, it is usually raised from seed as an annual, bearing clouds of tiny scarlet flowers on harmonizing red stems. The miniature size of its florets and their diffuseness can diminish their impact at a distance, but it is a most useful flower for providing a contrast with larger, bolder blooms. It combines well with hot colors, peach and apricot shades, and bronze foliage, and looks effective with yellow-green foliage and flowers. Such tiny, evenly spaced blooms also produce an attractive shimmering effect if mixed with flowers of similar size in a clashing color, such as magenta or rich carmine-pink. The cultivar 'Peachy-keen' has charming salmon-pink flowers.

ⓘ *Calceolaria* 'Camden Hero', *Canna indica* 'Purpurea', *Cordyline australis* Purpurea Group, *Dahlia* 'Bednall Beauty', *D.* 'Yelno Harmony', *Fuchsia* 'Thalia', *Lobelia* 'Fan Orchidrosa', *Lysimachia nummularia* 'Aurea', *Nicotiana* 'Domino Red', *N.* 'Lime Green', *Pelargonium* 'Paul Crampel', *Salvia splendens* p.400 **C**

H: 45cm (18in) **S: 30cm** (12in)
❉ **Early summer to mid-autumn**
 ◊◊ ▢-▨ ■ **Z9 pH5–7.5**

The flattish, lacy heads of *Ammi majus* contrast in form and color with the blue columns of the larkspur *Consolida ajacis* 'Blue Spire', both exactly the same height.

Ammi majus

The white flower heads of this hardy annual umbellifer have a distinctly lacy, ethereal beauty that makes an excellent foil for flowers of bolder floral form and color. Other annuals, such as larkspurs, biennials, herbaceous perennials, or shrubs (including Shrub roses) are all suitable for this kind of partnership. *A. majus* (bishop's flower) may be used to contrast with strong colors or to form gentle harmonies with pastel shades, and it is an indispensable ingredient of a white garden. Large, well-branched plants are essential for maximum impact and prolonged flowering, so it is important to thin young stock to
give them the generous space they need
to develop fully, and to avoid crowding

◑ *Briza maxima*, *Lunaria annua* 'Variegata', *Paeonia lactiflora* 'Albert Crousse', *Rosa × francofurtana* 'Empress Josephine', *Weigela florida* Lucifer

H: 60–90cm (24–36in) S: 30cm (12in)
✿ **Early to mid-summer**

⬛⬜⬜⬛ ◊◊ ⬜-⬛ ⬛ Z6 pH5.5–7.5

The white petals and contrasting golden discs of *Argyranthemum foeniculaceum* hort., along with its feathery glaucous foliage, lift the recessive tints of lavender, lilac, and indigo supplied by sea lavender (*Limonium latifolium*), the cranesbill *Geranium himalayense*, horned violets (*Viola cornuta*), and the annual clary, *Salvia viridis* 'Claryssa Blue'.

Antirrhinum majus

SNAPDRAGON

Snapdragons are short-lived perennials usually grown as hardy annuals. They are available in a wide range of sizes, and in colors from yellow through orange to scarlet, crimson, pink, and white. Tall kinds are elegant, their tapering spires echoing the form of delphiniums, verbascums, and lupines, and supplying a shape and color unavailable from other species, especially in late summer. White is the most versatile, yellow is excellent as a contrast for blue, while the hotter shades work well with red, bronze, and purple foliage. The Rocket Series, at 90cm (36in), is a popular tall form. Intermediates such as the fairly rust-resistant Monarch Series, 45cm (18in), and the Coronet and Sonnet Series, 40cm (16in), are very useful in the second row of a border. The shorter spikes of dwarf varieties are valuable for providing contrasts with flat-headed flowers such as achilleas.

◑ *Atriplex hortensis* var. *rubra*, *Cosmos bipinnatus* 'Sonata White', *Cotinus coggygria* 'Royal Purple', *Ricinus communis* 'Carmencita', *Verbena rigida*

H: 15–120cm (6–48in) S: 15–30cm (6–12in)
✿ **Early summer to early autumn**

 ◊◊ ⬜-⬛ ⬛ Z6 pH5.5–7.5

Spikes of *Antirrhinum majus* 'Black Prince' and the rounded flower heads of sweet William (*Dianthus barbatus* Nigrescens Group) match perfectly in flower and foliage color.

Argyranthemum foeniculaceum hort.

The true *A. foeniculaceum*, a dainty foliage plant that has filamentous blue-green leaves, flowers shyly from mid-autumn to early mid-summer. The plant known as *A. foeniculaceum* hort. (a tender evergreen sub-shrub, like the true species) is more free-flowering, with incessant white daisies and attractive feathery, glaucous foliage that associates well with blue flowers, silver foliage, and soft shades generally, while contrasting with soft yellow or rich flower colors. With its bright flowers and even growth habit, it is an excellent candidate for bedding or for the front of a mixed or herbaceous border, the plants developing into symmetrical domes that are useful for gentle punctuation along its length. They are also effective in containers combined with a trailing petunia or verbena. Plants may be disbudded and trained over two seasons to produce handsome standards.

◑ *Allium hollandicum* 'Purple Sensation', *Brachyscome iberidifolia* 'Summer Skies', *Heliotropium arborescens* 'Princess Marina', *Pelargonium* 'Paul Crampel', *Petunia* 'Frenzy Buttercup', *Phygelius aequalis* 'Yellow Trumpet', *Salvia farinacea* 'Victoria', *Senecio cineraria* 'Silver Dust', *Verbena* 'Silver Anne'

H: 75cm (30in) S: 60cm (24in) ✿ **All year**

⬛⬜⬜⬛ ◊◊ ⬜-⬛ ⬛ Z9 pH5–7.5

Argyranthemum 'Jamaica Primrose' ♀

This tender shrub, with dark green leaves and abundant soft yellow, single daisy flowers born incessantly throughout the year, is one of the more sizable cultivars of argyranthemum. With its large, bulky form, it is suitable for containers and for the second rank of herbaceous or mixed borders, where it is best placed in front of other plants of the same height to give it space to achieve its full potential. Excellent in combinations with hot colors such as red and orange, the yellow is also a soft enough shade for use with warm apricot or peach. Good contrasts can be made with blue flowers such as agapanthus or perovskias, variegated foliage, and glaucous or yellow-green foliage, for example that of some grasses. Annuals make good partners for 'Jamaica Primrose', including osteospermums, ageratums, nigellas, tropaeolums, petunias, rudbeckias, zinnias, ursinias, salvias such as *S. farinacea* cultivars, and yellow-green or green flowers like nicotianas, together with tender perennials such as *Helichrysum petiolare* cultivars, cannas, cupheas, calceolarias, heliotropes, coleus, and bidens. Where a smaller cultivar is needed, there are numerous alternatives, such as 'Cornish Gold' ♀, with green leaves, or *A. maderense* ♀, only 40cm (16in) high, with dramatic blue-green foliage and soft yellow flowers that are particularly good with blue.

◉ *Agapanthus* 'Loch Hope', *Arundo donax* var. *versicolor*, *Dahlia* 'David Howard', *Helichrysum petiolare* 'Variegatum', *Nicotiana* 'Lime Green', *Nigella damascena* 'Miss Jekyll', *Perovskia* 'Blue Spire', *Salvia farinacea* 'Strata'

H & S: 1m (40in) ❀ **Late spring to mid-autumn**
◊◊ ☐-■ **Z9 pH5–7.5**

Left: Yellow-flowered *Potentilla aurea* and *P.* 'Gibson's Scarlet' scramble through *Argyranthemum* 'Jamaica Primrose', providing a contrast of flower size and foliage form at the front of a border in early summer.

Below: In late summer and early autumn, *Argyranthemum* 'Jamaica Primrose' remains in full bloom, combining beautifully with warm, bronze-orange *Rudbeckia hirta* 'Rustic Dwarfs' and the sprawling yellow *Bidens ferulifolia*, which fills in the space in front of both, spilling onto the adjoining path. Foliage of contrasting form, either grassy or bold, in bronze, yellow-green, or variegated with gold, could be added to the three daisies.

The distinctive, upright stems of the grass *Arundo donax* var. *versicolor* provide a striking accent among the harmonious flowers of yellow *Xanthophthalmum segetum*, white Japanese anemones (*Anemone* × *hybrida* 'Honorine Jobert') and, behind, the shrubby *Bupleurum fruticosum*.

Arundo donax var. *versicolor*

With its tall, upright habit and eye-catching variegation, this tender perennial grass is an ideal choice for bold accents in mixed borders or semi-tropical bedding areas; it also thrives in bog gardens and containers. The variegation usually emerges whitish, becoming cream with age, but there are clones that start cream and turn yellow by late summer. It makes a useful filler plant for summer plantings, and may also be planted in drifts for foliar contrast, especially if grown between slightly shorter plants. It combines successfully with many tender perennials such as cannas or dahlias, and *Nicotiana sylvestris*, castor oil plant, and other larger plants grown as annuals. In mixed or herbaceous borders, it works well with hardy plants as a temporary accent and in restrained color schemes with silver foliage and white or blue flowers.

◉ *Canna indica*, *Cleome hassleriana* Colour Fountain Series, *Dahlia coccinea*, *Melianthus major*, *Musa basjoo*, *Ricinus communis* 'Carmencita', *Verbena bonariensis*

H: 1.8m (6ft) S: 60cm (24in)
❀ **(Mid- to late autumn)**

◊◊-◊◊◊ ☐-■ **Z9 pH4.5–7.5**

Atriplex hortensis var. *rubra*
RED GARDEN ORACH

This is an easy, slim annual with leaves flushed red or purple, and insignificant flowers followed by plume-like seedheads that turn to parchment colors in autumn. Cultivars such as 'Purpurea', 'Cupreata', 'Rosea', 'Atrosanguinea', 'Superba', and the Plumes Series vary in leaf color from pink-flushed to crimson, copper, or rich purple-black. Magenta, crimson, and purple forms blend well with cool colors and purple foliage, while purple and bronze kinds combine with hot colors. In borders, they are effective sown in drifts, repeated at intervals, or allowed to weave through other plants. Red garden orach is invaluable in red borders, excellent with dahlias and contrasting lime green or yellow-green flowers, and also mixed with the yellow-green variant (golden orach) and daylilies.

◉ *Cotinus coggygria* 'Royal Purple', *Dahlia* 'Bishop of Llandaff', *Echinops bannaticus* 'Taplow Blue', *Eryngium giganteum*, *Hemerocallis* 'Stafford', *Nicotiana* 'Lime Green', *Plectranthus argentatus*

H: 1.2m (4ft) **S: 30cm** (12in)
✿ (Early to mid-summer)
 ◊◊ ▢-▣ Z7 pH5–7.5

The large, dusky purple-red leaves of *Atriplex hortensis* var. *rubra* fill in the gaps between and unify the cool colors of various perennials – *Allium giganteum*, with spherical flower heads, pale blue *Campanula lactiflora*, and *Salvia verticillata* 'Purple Rain'. In the foreground is a mound of contrasting yellow-green lady's mantle (*Alchemilla mollis*).

In this combination entirely of daisies, *Bidens ferulifolia* (center) scrambles between the annual *Rudbeckia fulgida* var. *sullivantii* 'Goldsturm' (left), tender *Osteospermum* 'Buttermilk' (bottom), and hardy perennial *Anthemis tinctoria* 'E.C. Buxton' (right), unifying the ensemble. The varied flower sizes and contrasting dark centers of the rudbeckias and osteospermums add interest.

Brachyscome iberidifolia
SWAN RIVER DAISY

This attractive annual has single daisy flowers in white, mauve, purple or, perhaps most dramatically, electric lavender-blue with a yellow or black central disc. It flowers profusely and can sprawl gracefully in baskets and containers, or at the front of a border. It is effective with cool colors, white flowers, and plants of more definite structure, mainly silver or glaucous foliage plants such as sea kale. Good companions include alyssums, petunias, verbenas, heliotropes, lavender, sage, catmint, and pinks. For contrast, it can be grown with smaller yellow California poppies, yellow-green grasses, and shorter euphorbias. Useful cultivars include the Splendour Series, with black or yellow discs; the Bravo Series, available in various colors; compact 'Brachy Blue', good for edging; and 'Summer Skies', in pastels and deeper tones.

◉ *Crambe maritima*, *Eschscholzia caespitosa* 'Sundew', *Heliotropium arborescens* 'Princess Marina', *Petunia* 'Frenzy Buttercup', *Verbena peruviana* 'Alba'

H: 30–45cm (12–18in) **S: 30cm** (12in)
✿ Early to late summer
 ◊◊ ▢-▣ Z9 pH5.5–7.5

Bidens ferulifolia ♛

This drought-resistant perennial, usually grown as an annual bedding plant, has divided, feathery leaves and golden yellow daisy flowers. If grown from seed, it is upright until pinched out, which causes it to sprawl, a valuable quality that allows it to weave charmingly through other plants and tumble over the edge of a container or hanging basket, especially with other trailers such as *Helichrysum petiolare* or *Anagallis monellii* cultivars. At the front of a border, it can be grown with hot-colored flowers and foliage, including coleus, with contrasting hardy herbaceous plants such as achilleas or salvias, or between or through small to medium-sized shrubs such as Patio and Ground Cover roses or caryopteris. 'Shining Star' is a lighter yellow cultivar.

◉ *Argyranthemum* 'Jamaica Primrose' p.364 **B**, *Caryopteris* × *clandonensis*, *Dahlia* 'Moonfire' p.374 **B**, *Solenostemon* 'Glory of Luxembourg'

H: 20–60cm (8–24in) **S: 30–100cm** (12–40in)
✿ Late spring to late autumn
▬▬▬ ◊◊ ▢-▣ Z8 pH5–7.5

This charming incident with dark-eyed, vivid lavender *Brachyscome iberidifolia* set in a carpet of sweet alyssum (*Lobularia maritima*) could be repeated on a larger scale, perhaps with contrasting soft yellow or yellow-green foliage and flowers for greater impact.

The radiating purple-flushed leaves and magenta midribs of *Brassica oleracea* (Acephala Group) 'Red Peacock' make a focal point in this container planting, harmonizing with *Osteospermum* 'Pink Whirls', *Verbena* 'Hidcote Purple' (top), and sprawling *V. tenuisecta* (bottom). The bizarre form and eccentric charm of both the kale and the osteospermum add considerably to the effect.

Brassica oleracea Acephala Group
ORNAMENTAL KALE

The most familiar ornamental kales (all of which are biennials) have feathery glaucous leaves that develop white, pink, or magenta variegation at the onset of autumn, and make excellent winter bedding plants with, for example, winter pansies. Varieties include the Peacock Series, 20–30cm (8–12in), in red or white; the Feather Series, also red or white and, at 35cm (14in), tall enough to stand clear of lower planting; the slightly shorter Kamone Series, with fringed red or white heads; and the Northern Lights Series, with large rosettes in white, pink, or magenta. Several culinary kales are extremely ornamental: black kales such as 'Nero di Toscana' and 'Laciniato', with slim, arching, and puckered blue-green leaves, resemble miniature palms and make striking foliage plants among shorter summer bedding.

⬤ **Colored kales:** *Chrysanthemum* 'Anastasia', *Skimmia japonica* 'Rubella', *Viola* Universal Series
Black kales: *Crambe maritima*, *Petunia* Surfinia Blue, *Solenostemon* 'Lord Falmouth'

H & S: 30–45cm (12–18in)
❄ **(Late spring to mid-summer)**

 ◌◌ ▢-▣ **Z5–6 pH6–8**

Briza maxima
QUAKING GRASS

This curious grass can be spring-sown as a summer-flowering annual or autumn-sown as a biennial to flower in late spring and early summer. Plants remain attractive after flowering as their seedheads dry, but if autumn-sown these disintegrate by mid-summer and plants are then best replaced with summer bedding. Although showing little form or texture at a distance, they are most attractive at close range, especially if sowings are thinned to produce erect, bushy plants 15–20cm (6–8in) apart. This grass is charming near the front of a border, loosely mixed with other overwintering biennials such as nigellas and Shirley poppies. It may also be grown in gravel, and looks particularly effective when allowed to seed itself.

⬤ *Calendula officinalis* Pacific Beauty Series, *Centaurea cyanus*, *Nigella damascena* 'Miss Jekyll', *Papaver rhoeas* (Shirley Group) 'Angels' Choir'

H: 45–60cm (18–24in) **S: 25cm** (10in)
❄ **Late spring to late summer**

◌-◌◌ ▢-▣ **Z6 pH5.5–7.5**

Sown beneath a mature, sprawling plant of *Helianthemum* 'Ben Hope', the flower heads of quaking grass (*Briza maxima*) mix thoroughly with the helianthemum to offer an intriguing pattern of contrasting shapes and colors.

Floriferous orange *Calceolaria* 'Camden Hero' (bottom) is combined with other flowers that are rich but slightly muted in color, giving a warm but not searingly brilliant effect. Included are salmon *Stachys coccinea*, red *Mimulus aurantiacus* var. *puniceus*, and a dark-leaved dahlia, all of them colorful from late spring, when they are planted out, until the first frosts.

Calceolaria 'Camden Hero'

A tender perennial overwintered indoors from late summer cuttings, this is a short sub-shrub with a profuse display of striking flowers in a rare, rich shade of burnt orange. It is an ideal plant for combining with hot colors and bronze foliage in a conspicuous position toward the front of a border. The bushy plants are very brittle, the weight of a shower of rain often causing stems to snap off unless stakes are worked between them for support. If grown in the same site for a number of seasons, plants may become prone to fungal disease that can kill the entire group, so they should ideally be grown in a different place each year. 'Kentish Hero' is similar, slightly lighter in color and more free-flowering, but with even more brittle stems. Like 'Camden Hero', it flowers from late spring until the first frosts.

⬤ *Calendula officinalis* Fiesta Gitana Series, *Canna* 'Durban', *Cordyline australis* Purpurea Group, *Dahlia* 'Moonfire', *Fuchsia* 'Genii', *Perilla frutescens* var. *crispa*, *Tagetes patula* 'Striped Marvel'

H & S: 30cm (12in) ❄ **Late spring to mid-autumn**

◌◌ ▢-▣ **Z8 pH5–7**

Calendula officinalis

POT MARIGOLD

This cottage garden flower is a hardy annual that may be sown in autumn for blooms in early summer, or in spring for flowers from mid- or late summer. Shorter kinds such as the double Fiesta Gitana Series ♀, at 20cm (8in), are best at the front of a border or in gravel. Intermediate varieties include 'Lemon Queen' and 'Orange King', both 45cm (18in) with double flowers; orange 'Radio', 45cm (18in), with quilled petals; and 'Touch of Red', 40cm (16in), in deep orange with bronze-red reverse. Taller kinds include Kablouna Series, 60cm (24in), with anemone-centered blooms; the double Pacific Beauty Series, 60cm (24in), in colors such as pale yellow and apricot; and The Prince Series,

double, to 75cm (30in), including 'Indian Prince', in deep orange with reddish brown reverse. All blend well with other hot colors, and with yellow-green foliage, flowers and bronze leaves. They go well with nasturtiums, parsley, and lettuces in vegetable gardens.

⊙ *Briza maxima, Centaurea cyanus, Euphorbia schillingii, Nigella damascena* 'Miss Jekyll', *Papaver rhoeas* Shirley Group (double mixed) p.392 **B**, *Stipa tenuissima*

H: 30–70cm (12–27in) **S: 30–45cm** (12–18in)
✳ **Early summer to mid-autumn**

◻◻ ◻-◼ **Z6 pH5.5–7.5**

The bright flowers of the pot marigold *Calendula officinalis* (Fiesta Gitana Series) 'Gitana Orange' create a vibrant combination at the front of a border with a magenta-centered, purple-leaved ornamental cultivar of cabbage (*Brassica oleracea* Capitata Group) and a compact, variegated nasturtium (*Tropaeolum majus* Alaska Series).

B

This exotic combination, mainly of tender plants, includes salmon-pink *Canna* 'Erebus', scarlet *Lobelia* 'Queen Victoria', the ray-like umbels of papyrus (*Cyperus papyrus*), a dark-leaved canna, and the cider gum (*Eucalyptus gunnii*). The canna's flowers act as the focal point of the group, harmonizing with the red blooms and contrasting gently with the glaucous foliage of the gum.

Canna 'Erebus'

Cannas are tender, rhizomatous perennials used mainly for bedding and for summer display. They have bold foliage, which is sometimes dramatically colored or striped, and exotic-looking flowers in bright, brassy, hot colors that can introduce a hint of the tropics even to cooler gardens. 'Erebus' is less extrovert than most, with elegant glaucous foliage and salmon-pink flowers. With this restrained coloring, it is an excellent choice for less jazzy displays together with cream, white, peach, or apricot flowers and glaucous foliage, although it also looks good in brighter partnerships with scarlet or coral flowers, and with bronze or deep red foliage. Planting this canna behind or through a sprawling or spreading plant about 20–30cm (8–12in) high will conceal the unsightly bases. Its height can vary from 90cm (3ft) in climates with cool summers to 3m (10ft) in warmer areas.

⊙ *Cordyline australis* Purpurea Group, *Dahlia* 'Alva's Doris', *Diascia rigescens, Fuchsia* 'Thalia', *Ricinus communis* 'Carmencita', *Verbena bonariensis*

H: 1.2m (4ft) **S: 50cm** (20in)
✳ **Mid-summer to early autumn**

◻◻-◻◻◻ ◻-◼ **Z9 pH5.5–7.5**

A

Cerinthe major 'Purpurascens'

This annual, sometimes grown as a biennial in warmer climates, has glaucous foliage and rather subdued purple or brown flowers covered by spectacular bracts that vary from intense blue to deep purple. At close range, the luminosity of that area of the flower stem where the color changes through glaucous green to blue and purple is most remarkable, particularly at dusk. This is enhanced by neighbors with glaucous or silver foliage, soft yellow, white flowers, or blue flowers, yellow-green foliage and flowers, and contrasting foliage, such as grasses, irises, or cardoons. Plants grown as biennials flower from late spring onwards, combining well with Bearded irises, and may self-seed a late summer generation. Spring-sown plants flower in summer and look good with grasses such as small miscanthus cultivars and agapanthus.

🌐 *Eschscholzia caespitosa* 'Sundew', *Euphorbia characias* 'Blue Hills', *Iris* 'Jane Phillips', *Lilium* 'Joy' p.327 **A**, *Miscanthus sinensis* 'Kleine Fontäne'

H: 45cm (18in) **S:** 30cm (12in)
✺ **Early to late summer**

◊◊ ▢-▦ **Z7 pH5.5–7.5**

This cool-colored combination consists of *Cerinthe major* 'Purpurascens' and lavender (*Lavandula angustifolia*) – both favorite food plants of bees – behind a clipped edging of dwarf boxwood (*Buxus sempervirens* 'Suffruticosa').

Cleome hassleriana
SPIDER FLOWER

The relatively tall height of this handsome half-hardy annual makes it a useful plant for growing at the back of an annual border or in drifts through a herbaceous or mixed border. Good cultivars include 'Violet Queen', 'Cherry Queen', 'Pink Queen', pure white 'Helen Campbell', and Color Fountain Series, a mixture sometimes available as separate colors, including a fine amaranth-purple. These cultivars mix well with cool pink, crimson, lilac, purple, or white, and with glaucous, purple, and white-variegated foliage, such as some larger miscanthus cultivars, for example. They are excellent with dahlias, asters such as *A.* × *frikartii* cultivars, and larger China asters, while for a tropical effect they can be mixed with cannas, melianthus, and larger-flowering tender solanums. Spider flowers require warm summers to thrive.

White and purplish crimson spider flowers (*Cleome hassleriana*) are ideally matched in height to *Verbena bonariensis*, whose small purple flower heads produce a soft haze of contrasting blooms. In front, *Cosmos bipinnatus* closely corresponds with the colors of the spider flowers but provides a contrast of floral form.

🌐 *Aster frikartii* 'Wunder von Stäfa', *Crambe maritima*, *Dahlia* 'Gerrie Hoek', *Lathyrus rotundifolius* p.125 **C**, *Populus alba* 'Richardii' (pruned) p.77 **A**

H: 1.2m (4ft) **S:** 45cm (18in)
✺ **Mid- to late summer**

◊◊ ▢-▦ **Z9 pH5.5–7**

Consolida species and cultivars
LARKSPUR

Garden larkspurs are annuals mainly derived from *Consolida ajacis* and *C. orientalis*, both with flowers in tightly packed spikes, and the airy *C. regalis*. Spike-forming cultivars usually make a single stiff flower stem, useful for repeated bold vertical accents; among the best are the blue and white 'Frosted Skies' and the dusky pink 'Early Grey', both 75cm (30in) high. Attractive *C. regalis* cultivars include 'Snow Cloud', 75cm (30in), with single creamy white florets on branching plants that flop and intermingle charmingly; and members of the Exquisite Strain, such as rich royal-blue 'Blue Cloud', 90cm (36in), and 'Salmon Beauty', also 90cm (36in), with a central flower spike followed by graceful lateral spikes of semi-double blooms.

◉ *Ammi majus* p.363 **A**, *Antirrhinum majus* 'White Wonder', *Clarkia unguiculata* Royal Bouquet Series, *Lychnis coronaria* 'Alba', *Plecostachys serpyllifolia*

H: 30–120cm (12–48in) **S:** 23–30cm (9–12in)
✿ **Early to late summer**

◊◊ ▣-▣ **Z7 pH5.5–7.5**

The columnar racemes of this attractive rich blue cultivar of *Consolida ajacis* are tall enough to appear among and just above the contrasting white flowers of an annual mallow (*Lavatera trimestris* 'Mont Blanc').

In its third year, *Cordyline australis* Purpurea Group will just rise over the matching dark foliage and scarlet flowers of *Dahlia* 'Bishop of Llandaff', making a strong focal point in a border. Cordylines in their second year could be used effectively with shorter dahlias, such as *D.* 'Bednall Beauty', 'Preston Park', or 'Moonfire'.

Cosmos bipinnatus

This versatile annual daisy has feathery foliage and single or semi-double flowers in all shades from white to wine red, and a height range that varies considerably. The Sensation Series, 90cm (36in), has single flowers in pink, carmine, and white; white 'Purity' is 90cm (36in); while the Sonata Series ♀, in white, carmine, and pink, is only 60cm (24in). All variants have a fairly bare base and are best planted behind shorter cushion-forming plants. The taller cultivars belong in the second or third rank of a border. They make excellent bedding, and mingle easily with annuals such as cleomes, *Verbena bonariensis*, and larkspurs. The Sonata Series and other shorter kinds work well with plants of contrasting floral form, including spiky plants such as salvias and pennisetums.

◉ *Cleome hassleriana* p.368 **B**, *Consolida regalis* 'Snow Cloud', *Dianthus barbatus* p.376 **A**, *Pennisetum villosum*, *Salvia farinacea* 'White Victory'

H: 60–120cm (24–48in) **S:** 45–60cm (18–24in)
✿ **Mid-summer to mid-autumn**

◊◊ ▣-▣ **Z7–8 pH5–8**

Cordyline australis
Purpurea Group

The cabbage tree (*Cordyline australis* ♀) is a small tree, usually single-stemmed and branching only after flowering. It is immensely useful for temporary summer display because of its emphatic effect and tropical appearance. The leaves of Purpurea Group vary from reddish bronze to purple, and from 1 to 5cm (½ to 2in) in width (as a general rule, deeper color and broader foliage indicate reduced hardiness). The group as a whole is effective with hot colors such as scarlet and orange, warm shades like peach and apricot, and in contrasts with lime green and yellow-green. Good companions include pelargoniums, dahlias, nicotianas, cannas, reddish-leaved castor oil plants, and true palms. There are also many variegated cultivars of *C. australis* that can make striking accents in a border, including 'Albertii' ♀, in green with broad creamy yellow stripes.

◉ *Canna* 'Wyoming', *Chamaerops humilis* 'Vulcano', *Dahlia* 'Alva's Doris' p.370 **A**, *Nicotiana* 'Lime Green', *Pelargonium* 'Orangesonne', *Ricinus communis* 'Impala'

H: 6m (20ft) **S:** 3m (10ft) ✿ **Early to late summer**
◊◊ ▣-▣ **Z9 pH5.5–7.5**

A relatively short cosmos such as *Cosmos bipinnatus* (Sonata Series) 'Sonata White' interplanted with a relatively tall scarlet salvia such as *Salvia splendens* 'Rambo' together provide a striking, dramatic contrast of color and form.

Dahlias

DAHLIAS, especially the dinner-plate dahlias beloved of exhibitors, are among the boldest of garden flowers. Their color range is unequaled by any other plant except perhaps the tulip, lacking only clear blue, geen and black. Unlike the tulip, they flower continuously and increasingly freely from early summer until the first frosts. In height they range from miniatures of 25cm (10in) to 2.5m (8ft) giants, and flower head size varies from 10cm (4in) to a massive 25cm (10in) or more.

The other main source of variation in the dahlia is flower form. Those classified as Decorative dahlias have fully double blooms with broad, generally flat petals (strictly, ray florets). In Waterlily dahlias the petals are fewer and broader, while in the elegant Cactus or Semi-cactus cultivars they are rolled back into narrow quills. At the other end of the spectrum the Ball and Pompon dahlias have petals rolled into cones arranged in tight spheres. Single-flowered and Collerette dahlias have a single ring of petals around a yellow eye or an inner ruff of shorter petals.

The one weak point of the dahlia is its coarse, potato-like foliage. In 'Bishop of Llandaff' and a few of its modern offspring the foliage is more dissected and an attractive deep bronze-maroon. Some of the species are also more refined, but the majority of dahlias are best surrounded by other plants, in a herbaceous border for example where they will reinforce color schemes with their abundance of flower.

Dahlias are tender tuberous perennials, but in light soil and warm sites most will overwinter successfully in the ground, especially if protected with a thick straw mulch. It is safer, however, to lift the tubers in late autumn, overwinter them in frost-free conditions, and replant in spring. Many of the smaller dahlias are easily raised from seed. They make excellent bedding or front-of-border plants and are ideal for pots and other containers.

Dahlia 'Alva's Doris' ♧

This is a small Semi-cactus Group dahlia, with blood-red flowers, fully double and with petals rolled back to form a quill, so presenting an exotic outline in a border. Its rich coloring suits combinations with orange, gold, and other red flowers, and dark red or purple foliage, and it is a traditional component of red borders, with its spiky shape echoed by a dark-leaved cordyline and its color emphasized by a background of dark-leaved shrubs. In hot color schemes, it combines well with late-flowering crocosmias, heleniums, rudbeckias, zinnias, daylilies, euphorbias, Mexican sunflowers, and common sunflowers. It contrasts particularly well with yellow-green, magenta, pure blue, and green flowers such as nicotianas.

◔ *Cotinus coggygria* 'Royal Purple', *Crocosmia* 'Late Lucifer', *Helianthus annuus* 'Velvet Queen', *Nicotiana langsdorffii*, *Tithonia rotundifolia* 'Goldfinger'

H: 1.2m (4ft) S: 60cm (24in)
❀ **Mid-summer to mid-autumn**

░░░░ ◊◊ ▢-▨ ▉ Z8 pH5–7.5

Top: In a border of red flowers and both green and dark foliage, *Dahlia* 'Alva's Doris' and *Lobelia* 'Queen Victoria' match perfectly in color, while the grass *Miscanthus sinensis* 'Gracillimus' and spiky *Cordyline australis* Purpurea Group are backlit dramatically by the sun.

Above: *Dahlia* 'Alva's Doris' is here joined by the exotic foliage of *Canna indica* 'Purpurea' and contrasting glaucous-leaved cider gum (*Eucalyptus gunnii*), grown from seed sown indoors and used as a bedding plant.

The rounded, sumptuous blood-red blooms and dark foliage of *Dahlia* 'Arabian Night' contrast strikingly in form with those of its neighbor, the sword-leaved, vermilion-flowered *Crocosmia* 'Lucifer'.

Dahlia 'Arabian Night'

This dahlia has exceptionally deep blood-red flowers, fully double with broad flat petals and the rounded outline typical of the Small Decorative Group. Although similar in color to 'Alva's Doris' (facing page), its darker center produces a more subdued effect, better suited to mellow, sumptuous arrangements than to bright or vivacious plantings, and the flowers are a little less visible from a distance. However, it combines with many of the partners suggested for 'Alva's Doris', as well as with purple orach, cannas, amaranthus, pelargoniums, and tender salvias, and can look opulent with dark-leaved shrubs such as purple smoke bush, berberis, or ornamental cherries. It also interacts well with yellow-green to enliven its deeper tones.

◑ *Amaranthus caudatus* 'Viridis', *Atriplex hortensis* var. *rubra*, *Berberis* × *ottawensis* f. *purpurea* 'Superba', *Canna* 'Roi Humbert', *Choisya ternata* Sundance

H: 1m (40in) S: 45cm (18in)
❀ **Mid-summer to mid-autumn**
■■□□ ◊◊ □-■ ■ Z8 pH5–7.5

Dahlia 'Bednall Beauty'

A typical example of a Dwarf Bedding Group dahlia, 'Bednall Beauty' is suitable for bedding or positions towards the front of a mixed or herbaceous border. The colors of its dainty dark leaves and semi-double, rich scarlet flowers suit the same kinds of combinations as 'Alva's Doris' (facing page) and 'Arabian Night' (left), but its shorter stature allows it also to partner smaller companions such as iresines, nasturtiums, scarlet verbenas, orange or rusty red French marigolds, and dark-leaved antirrhinums, heucheras, sedums, and beets. As a bedding plant, it may be grown among Patio and Ground Cover roses, and looks effective edged with a yellow-green or variegated grass. It is also an excellent plant for containers.

◑ *Antirrhinum majus* 'Black Prince', *Hakonechloa macra* 'Alboaurea', *Iresine lindenii*, *Rosa* 'Europeana', *Tagetes patula* 'Spanish Brocade', *Verbena* Temari Scarlet

H & S: 40cm (16in)
❀ **Mid-summer to mid-autumn**
■■□□ ◊◊ □-■ ■ Z8 pH5–7.5

In this border consisting of a variety of red flowers, and with a warm-colored brick wall behind, *Dahlia* 'Bednall Beauty' is echoed further back by *D.* 'Bishop of Llandaff', with *Rosa* 'Frensham' beyond. The dark blue-green leaved nasturtium *Tropaeolum majus* 'Empress of India' and *Geum* 'Mrs J. Bradshaw' complete the border's edge.

Dahlia 'Bishop of Llandaff' ♛

Although classed as a Miscellaneous dahlia, this is in effect a tall version of 'Bednall Beauty' (above), with similar finely divided dark foliage and semi-double, rich scarlet flowers. It can be used to echo 'Bednall Beauty' further back in a border, and succeeds in the same groupings, as well as in those of 'Alva's Doris' (facing page) and 'Arabian Night' (left). It blends particularly well with castor oil plant and contrasting green-flowered nicotianas, and is tall enough to combine with shrubs with dark and yellow-green leaves. Several clones are in cultivation, so it is worth selecting growing plants for good dark foliage color and floral form.

Red flowers and dusky foliage are backed by a dark yew hedge and castor oil plant (*Ricinus communis*) to dramatic effect. *Dahlia* 'Bishop of Llandaff' grows between Small Decorative Group dahlias 'Blaisdon Red' and 'Anchorite', behind the large-leaved *Beta vulgaris* 'Rhubarb Chard', *B.v.* 'Mr McGregor's Favorite', and verbenas. In the second row are nicotianas, beefsteak plants (*Iresine herbstii* 'Brilliantissima'), and the pink-flowered *Sedum telephium* subsp. *maximum* 'Atropurpureum'.

◑ *Cordyline australis* Purpurea Group p.369 **B**, *Dahlia* 'Bednall Beauty' p.371 **B**, *Lobelia* 'Queen Victoria' p.259 **C**, *Nicotiana* 'Domino Red' p.389 **A**, *N.* 'Lime Green' p.390 **A**, *Pelargonium* 'Paul Crampel' p.394 **A**

H: 1.2m (4ft) S: 60cm (24in)
❀ **Mid-summer to mid-autumn**
■■□□ ◊◊ □-■ ■ Z8 pH5–7.5

Dahlia 'David Howard' ♛

The bronze foliage and soft orange flowers, deeper at the center, of this Miniature Decorative Group dahlia are indispensable for richly colored arrangements and autumn combinations with plants such as agastaches, hedychiums, and kirengeshomas. It looks very attractive with hot colors such as gold and scarlet, with soft yellow, peach, and apricot, with yellow-green (particularly later-flowering euphorbias), and with contrasting purple and blue. Crocosmias, chrysanthemums, yellow daisies (heleniums, sunflowers, and rudbeckias), and fruiting roses such as *Rosa moyesii* cultivars and hybrids are all good autumn companions. Earlier in the season it is effective with cannas, red kniphofias, large American marigolds, achilleas, plume poppies, perennial lobelias, daylilies, tiger lilies and recurrent-flowering Shrub roses.

◑ *Cautleya spicata* 'Robusta' p.201 **B**, *Euphorbia schillingii*, *Hedychium coccineum*, *Kniphofia uvaria* 'Nobilis', *Rosa* 'Geranium', *Spartium junceum* p.93 **B**

H: 1.5m (5ft) S: 75cm (30in)
❀ **Mid-summer to mid-autumn**

▬▬▭ ◊◊ ▢-◼ ◼ **Z8 pH5–7.5**

Verbena bonariensis is able to thread itself through the heart of a large *Dahlia* 'David Howard', its lavender florets, emerging from purple calyces, forming a gentle contrast with the warm orange, formal blooms of the dahlia. *Canna* 'Wyoming', with dark leaves and orange blooms that perfectly match the dahlia, just rises above the ensemble, which by autumn has reached almost 1.8m (6ft).

Dahlia 'Gerrie Hoek'

This is a Small Waterlily Group dahlia, very free-flowering with fairly informal, fully double, silvery pink blooms. It is suitable for positions in the middle rows of a border, where it blends particularly well with purple, glaucous, and dark foliage plants, such as red garden orach, dark-leaved castor oil plants, and purple-leaved shrubs. It is also a good companion for cool-colored flowers, including cosmos and Japanese anemones, or for plants with contrasting floral forms, such as salvias, aconitums, actaeas, and later-flowering achilleas. Other partners include

The superlative blooms of *Dahlia* 'Gerrie Hoek' form the focal point of this arrangement. In the front, *Lobelia × gerardii* 'Vedrariensis' provides contrast in form with the taller *Lavatera* 'Barnsley' and *Onopordum nervosum* behind.

campanulas, asters, agapanthus, taller verbenas and grasses, such as miscanthus cultivars, recurrent-flowering roses, *Phlox paniculata* cultivars, and monardas.

◑ *Anemone × hybrida* 'Honorine Jobert', *Cosmos bipinnatus* 'Sonata White', *Phlox paniculata* 'Mount Fuji', *Pittosporum tenuifolium* 'Purpureum'

H: 1.2m (4ft) S: 60cm (24in)
❀ **Mid-summer to mid-autumn**

▬▬▭ ◊◊ ▢-◼ ◼ **Z8 pH5–7.5**

The luminous blooms of *Dahlia* 'Glorie van Heemstede' shine beneath a cloud of beige-colored florets of a plume poppy (*Macleaya microcarpa*), beside the lacy yellow-green flowers of fennel (*Foeniculum vulgare*).

Dahlia 'Glorie van Heemstede' 🏆

Flowering prolifically over a long season, this Small Waterlily Group dahlia can be relied on to provide an eye-catching display of soft yellow blooms on strong stems. Its clear shade of yellow is definite enough to be combined with hot colors, yet not too harsh to complement warm tints such as apricot, and it makes effective contrasts with blue flowers such as agapanthus, perovskias, and caryopteris. It is attractive with glaucous or gold-variegated shrubs, yellow-green foliage, and larger grasses such as miscanthus cultivars, and green or yellow-green flowers, including nicotianas and later-flowering euphorbias. Pleasant combinations are also possible with chrysanthemums, larger tender salvias, hedychiums, cannas, and recurrent-flowering Shrub roses in warmer tints.

◐ *Agapanthus* 'Blue Moon', *Elaeagnus pungens* 'Maculata', *Melianthus major*, *Miscanthus sinensis* 'Zebrinus', *Nicotiana langsdorffii*, *Rosa* 'Buff Beauty'

H: 1.4m (4½ft) **S: 60cm** (24in)
✿ **Mid-summer to mid-autumn**

 Z8 pH5–7.5

Dahlia 'Grenadier'

This is a Small Waterlily Group dahlia, typical of the group in having fully double blooms, more than twice as wide as they are deep and with fewer petals than other double dahlias, so offering a slightly less formal and complex appearance. 'Grenadier' is a rich red cultivar, traditionally used in a similar way to 'Arabian Night' (p.371) as a key component of red or hot-colored borders. Although differing in flower shape from 'Arabian Night', it succeeds with the same partners, especially in groups with yellow-green flowers and foliage, and dark or purple foliage plants such as smoke bush, berberis, and ornamental cherries. It also combines well with cannas, crocosmias, later-flowering daylilies, and roses grown for their fruits, especially *R. moyesii* cultivars and hybrids.

◐ *Hemerocallis fulva* 'Flore Pleno', *Prunus × cistena*, *Ricinus communis* 'Impala', *Rosa rugosa*, *Verbena bonariensis* p.404 **A**, *Zinnia elegans* 'Envy' ⌐p.259 **B**

H: 1m (40in) **S: 45cm** (18in)
✿ **Mid-summer to mid-autumn**

 Z8 pH5–7.5

Dark-leaved, shining scarlet *Dahlia* 'Grenadier' makes a dramatic contrast with the cream-edged leaves of the variegated dogwood *Cornus alba* 'Elegantissima'. This relatively steeply sloped grouping could be used in a comparatively narrow border.

Dahlia 'Laciniata Atropurpurea'

Probably the parent of modern dark-leaved cultivars such as 'Bishop of Llandaff', this is a single-flowered dahlia with attractive, doubly pinnate leaves that bear tiny, deep purple leaflets. It has charming open-centered blooms with one or two complete outer rows of petals that vary in color according to climate and situation – generally, the flowers are a deep and resonant plum purple, although in some positions they can appear deep purplish red, even occasionally zoned with blood-red. It is an admirable cultivar for blending into hot color schemes, where it will provide an intense background for brighter flowers, and can also be used in sumptuous combinations with deep purplish blue flowers such as aconitums. Steeply sloped borders are ideal for this dahlia, allowing its intricate foliage to be appreciated at close range.

🔵 *Aconitum napellus*, *A.* 'Spark's Variety', *Aster amellus* 'Veilchenkönigin', *A. novae-angliae* 'Barr's Violet', *Fuchsia* 'Thalia', *Helianthus annuus* 'Prado Red'

H: 75cm (30in) **S: 45cm** (18in)
✲ **Mid-summer to mid-autumn**
◻◻ 🌢🌢 ◻-▨ ■ **Z8 pH5–7.5**

A neat plant suited to the second row of a border, the dark-leaved *Dahlia* 'Laciniata Atropurpurea' here creates an attractive combination with gentian-blue *Salvia patens* behind a dwarf boxwood hedge.

A

B

The shape of the soft yellow blooms of *Dahlia* 'Moonfire' is emphasized by the striking scarlet zone, while the dark purple foliage acts as a perfect foil to the flowers. Its warm-colored companions include a carpet of feathery-leaved *Bidens ferulifolia*, which decorate the stems, and a background of yellow-green *Euphorbia sikkimensis*.

Dahlia 'Moonfire'

This is a fairly compact Dwarf Bedding Group dahlia, with dark foliage and single blooms of amber-yellow with a clear red zone in the center. Its size and growth habit make it suitable for summer containers, bedding, and positions towards the front of a border, where it can be blended successfully with hot or warm colors. It associates well with purple or bronze foliage plants, including bronze sedges, dark-leaved heucheras, cannas, coleus, and dark-leaved begonias, and with yellow-green or yellow-variegated foliage or flowers, such as euphorbias and larger grasses. It can be combined with bedding plants such as bidens, zinnias, arctotis, and gazanias, as well as with perennials such as crocosmias, smaller kniphofias, and larger scarlet lobelias.

🔵 *Begonia semperflorens* Cocktail Series, *Heuchera micrantha* var. *diversifolia* 'Palace Purple', *Solenostemon* 'Crimson Ruffles'

H & S: 40cm (16in)
✲ **Mid-summer to mid-autumn**
◻◻ 🌢🌢 ◻-▨ ■ **Z8 pH5–7.5**

Dahlia 'Pink Michigan'

A Dwarf Bedding Group dahlia, 'Pink Michigan' has magenta blooms, shading to light carmine-pink. Although a little larger than average for the group, and too tall for most bedding purposes, it is well suited to the second or third rank of a border, where it blends with cool colors and glaucous or silver foliage, including argyranthemums, artemisias, and osteospermums in white or pink, seedling or pruned eucalyptus, and white-variegated or glaucous grasses. It goes with purple or dark foliage plants, such as red garden orach, purple smoke bush, and black or purple curly kale. Companion flowers include cosmos, asters, verbenas, nicotianas, salvias, clarkias, lavateras, larkspurs, Japanese anemones, aconites, phlox, thalictrums, caryopteris, perovskias, and indigoferas.

🔵 *Argyranthemum foeniculaceum* hort., *Brassica oleracea* (Acephala Group) 'Nero di Toscana', *Helictotrichon sempervirens*, *Osteospermum* 'White Pim'

H: 70cm (27in) **S: 45cm** (18in)
✲ **Mid-summer to mid-autumn**
◻◻ 🌢🌢 ◻-▨ ■ **Z8 pH5–7.5**

C

Dahlia 'Pink Michigan' is grown here towards the front of a purple border behind the rich purple *Aster novi-belgii* 'Cliff Lewis'. By mid-autumn it has reached a substantial size, just topped by the magenta *D.* 'Requiem' and pale violet *Aster turbinellus* hort. (beyond). The distant scarlet hips of *Rosa* 'Geranium' provide a touch of contrast and save the arrangement from blandness.

Dahlia 'Requiem'

This is a Small Decorative Group dahlia with magenta flowers that become a little paler at the tips of the petals as blooms age. Although taller than 'Pink Michigan' (facing page), its similar coloring suits the same kinds of combinations in the second or third row of a border. It is particularly successful with perennials such as silver artemisias, pruned or seedling eucalyptus, Japanese anemones, and later-flowering thalictrums, while its slightly greater height allows it to be combined with taller plants, for example taller asters, aconitums, and even buddleias. The richer shade of magenta also permits its use in dusky and sumptuous groups with crimsons and purple or dark foliage, such as red garden orach, purple smoke bush, and red or purple ornamental cabbage or kale. In beddings it can partner amaranthus, coleus cultivars, and – perhaps above all – cleomes.

🌑 *Amaranthus caudatus, Anemone* × *hybrida* 'Max Vogel', *Buddleja davidii* 'Royal Red', *Cleome hassleriana* Colour Fountain Series, *Cordyline australis* Purpurea Group, *Dahlia* 'Pink Michigan' p.374 **C**, *Eucalyptus gunnii* (pruned), *Sambucus nigra* 'Guincho Purple', *Thalictrum delavayi* 'Hewitt's Double'

H: 80cm (31in) **S: 45cm** (18in)
❀ **Mid-summer to mid-autumn**

▨▨▨ ◌◌ ▢-▨ ■ Z8 pH5–7.5

Asters are often suited in height and color to autumn combinations with dahlias, providing a significant contrast of flower shape and size. Here, *Aster turbinellus* hort. makes a perfect foil for the richly colored blooms of *D*. 'Requiem' behind the glaucous-leaved *Baptisia australis*. The herbaceous baptisia starts this display in early summer with airy spikes of lavender-blue flowers.

Dahlia 'Yelno Harmony' 🏆

Classed as both a Small Decorative and a Dwarf Bedding cultivar, this is a relatively small-growing dahlia, with soft orange petals, deeper at the center of the bloom. Although similar to 'David Howard' (p.372), the flowers are paler in color and less double. 'Yelno Harmony' harmonizes with warm-colored flowers and bronze foliage, and makes effective contrasts with yellow-green leaves and flowers and with purple or blue. It can be used towards the front of a border, where it combines well with plants such as nicotianas, crocosmias, smaller grasses, and smaller later-flowering euphorbias, and is especially useful for bedding with verbenas, pelargoniums, salvias, perillas, and zinnias. Foliage plants such as purple-leaved beets or curly kales also make good companions, as do plants with glaucous foliage.

In this bedding combination, the squirrel tail grass (*Hordeum jubatum*) has been planted in and among *Dahlia* 'Yelno Harmony'. When the grass (45cm/18in high) starts to flower and set seed in early to mid-summer, its silky seedheads just rise above the dahlia, creating a subtly charming mix.

🌑 *Beta vulgaris* 'Bull's Blood', *B.v.* 'Mr McGregor's Favourite', *Cerinthe major* 'Purpurascens', *Festuca glauca* 'Blaufuchs', *Lysimachia congestiflora* 'Outback Sunset', *Nicotiana* 'Domino Red', *Pelargonium* 'Paul Crampel', *Perilla frutescens* var. *crispa*, *Salvia coccinea* 'Lady in Red', *Zinnia* 'Chippendale'

H: 60cm (24in) **S: 45cm** (18in)
❀ **Mid-summer to mid-autumn**

 ◌◌ ▢-▨ ■ Z8 pH5–7.5

Dianthus barbatus

SWEET WILLIAM

These traditional cottage garden biennials provide valuable color after most spring flowers and before many summer ones open. Some kinds have dark leaves and flowers – Nigrescens Group ♀ and 'Sooty', for example – while others, such as Auricula-eyed mixtures, have attractive markings. A few are available as single colors, including Beauty Series, Hollandia Series, and Standard Series. Dwarf types can be grown as annuals from a spring sowing indoors, but many have a dumpy, inelegant growth habit and a fairly short flowering season. 'Roundabout', (15cm/6in), is perhaps the most useful, with

A restful effect is achieved by combining harmonious, cool-colored flowers with glaucous and grey-green foliage in this grouping consisting of mixed *Dianthus barbatus*, opium poppies (*Papaver somniferum*), a mixture of short *Cosmos bipinnatus*, and shrubby *Artemisia* 'Powis Castle'.

spreading plants flowering from early summer to early autumn. All associate well with early summer flowers such as shorter foxgloves, columbines, lupines, and early roses.

◖ *Antirrhinum majus* 'Black Prince' p.363 **B**, *Aquilegia vulgaris* (mixed), *Digitalis purpurea* Foxy Group, *Lupinus* 'Gallery White', *Rosa* 'Fantin-Latour'

H: 10–70cm (4–27in) **S: 20–30cm** (8–12in)
✳ **Late spring to early summer**
◖▬▬▭▭ ◌◌ ▭-▪ Z4 pH5.5–8

Diascia 'Dark Eyes' ♀

This diascia is a tender perennial, popular for its long and lavish flowering, and normally grown as an annual from cuttings rooted in late summer and overwintered indoors. Its fairly loose, sprawling growth habit makes it useful for interweaving with other lax plants such as verbena cultivars, *Helichrysum petiolare* cultivars, and trailing lobelias. It is a good plant for the front of a border, and for containers and hanging baskets, its coral-pink color harmonizing with peach, apricot, scarlet, and cream, and with bronze or red foliage. Pleasant contrasts can be made with purple or mid-blue flowers, and with yellow-green foliage and flowers. If trimmed back after the first flush of flowers, it will bloom again in late summer and autumn.

◖ *Alonsoa warscewiczii*, *Isotoma axillaris*, *Lobelia erinus* 'Sapphire', *Petunia* 'Frenzy Buttercup', *P.* Million Bells Blue, *Scaevola* Purple Fan

H: 23cm (9in) **S: 50cm** (20in)
✳ **Early summer to mid-autumn**
◖▬▬▭▭ ◌◌ ▭-▪ Z8 pH5.5–7.5

In this piquant color combination of contrasting plants in a container, *Diascia* 'Dark Eyes', *Verbena* Tapien Violet, and *Helichrysum petiolare* 'Limelight' intermingle and trail gracefully over the edge. An alternative in harmonious cool colors would be to use a mauve diascia such as *D.* 'Lilac Belle' with the same verbena and the grey-green leaved *Helichrysum petiolare* itself.

Diascia rigescens ♧

The salmon-pink flowers of this diascia are carried on dense, clearly defined spikes. It is a good plant at the front of a border, and a very useful ingredient of hanging baskets and containers, mixed with other sprawling plants such as trailing verbenas and *Helichrysum petiolare* cultivars. Its coloring suits the same combinations as *D.* 'Dark Eyes' (facing page), but it is a slightly beefier plant and so mixes more successfully with other sprawlers that have larger blooms and leaves. In frost-prone areas, this diascia is not reliably hardy, but even where plants will survive winters outdoors, it performs best if grown from young plants raised each year from cuttings taken in late summer. It is also intolerant of very dry conditions in summer.

🌑 *Convolvulus cneorum* (foliage), *Helianthemum* 'Wisley White', *Petunia* 'Scarlet Ice', *Rehmannia elata* p.280 **A**, *Verbena* Temari Blue, *V.* Temari Scarlet

H: 30cm (12in) S: 50cm (20in)
❀ **Early summer to early autumn**
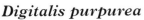 ◊◊ ▢-▩ **Z8 pH5.5–7.5**

The rich pink blooms of *Diascia rigescens* harmonize with the red centers of their companion pinks and provide contrast of floral form. Both are ideal for the front of a sunny border, backed by mound-forming plants such as catmints.

Digitalis purpurea

COMMON FOXGLOVE

The typical foxglove (a biennial or short-lived perennial plant) has magenta or white flowers in a slim, elegant, one-sided spike. 'Sutton's Apricot' ♧ is a superlative cultivar, its soft pale peach color combining attractively with bronze foliage and white or pure blue flowers, for example blue poppies. However, the florets always hang towards the sun, unlike showier selections such as Excelsior Group ♧ and Foxy Group, which bear their flowers all around the stem, making the spike seem more substantial from every side. All foxgloves are excellent in a sunny or partially shaded border, or in a lightly shaded woodland garden as drifts of sentinel spikes standing above other plants. Late-flowering azaleas and rhododendrons, as well as elderberries, make perfect woodland partners. The slightly shorter Foxy Group is also very successful with Shrub roses such as some of the smaller Gallicas. Most foxgloves blend well with pink, mauve, crimson, and purple, and contrast with yellow-green.

Above: The narrow, one-sided spikes of *Digitalis purpurea* f. *albiflora* provide bold vertical accents in this relatively informal grouping with old roses, *Thalictrum aquilegiifolium*, and *Hesperis matronalis* var. *albiflora*.

Left: The spikes of *Digitalis purpurea* 'Sutton's Apricot', perhaps more accurately described as flesh-pink, match the flat flower heads of an elderberry (*Sambucus nigra* 'Guincho Purple') behind, while offering an intriguing contrast in form; the white foxgloves (*D.p.* f. *albiflora*) serve to leaven the effect. The large foxglove plants are later replaced by summer bedding as their flowering passes its peak.

🌑 *Abutilon vitifolium* var. *album* p.28 **C**, *Euphorbia polychroma* 'Major' p.220 **B**, *Heuchera micrantha* var. *diversifolia* 'Palace Purple', *Meconopsis betonicifolia* p.264 **A**, *Rosa* 'Complicata' p.154 **A**, *R.* 'Fantin-Latour' p.147 **B**, *R.* 'Gruss an Aachen' p.165 **A**, *R. multiflora* p.142 **C**, *R.* 'Penelope' p.159 **B**,

H: 1.2–2m (4–6½ft) S: 50cm (20in)
❀ **Early summer**
 ◊◊ ▢-▩ **Z5 pH4.5–8**

The handsome flower heads of giant eryngo (*Eryngium giganteum*), their striking silvery bracts with a hint of blue, benefit from the plain background of contrasting foliage provided by *Berberis thunbergii* 'Aurea'.

Eryngium giganteum 🏆

MISS WILLMOTT'S GHOST

In its usual cultivated form, this easy-to-grow biennial bears heads of flowers surrounded by jagged, pale silvery grey-green bracts, sometimes containing a hint of blue. Each plant makes an imposing candelabra of stems and is particularly effective when surrounded by lower plants and repeated as loosely scattered drifts to give unity to a border. The ripening seedheads assume attractive parchment tints, although dead and dying leaves can mar the effect unless screened by shorter plants. The coloring blends with almost any other, but looks outstanding in a white garden or with silver or glaucous foliage; it is worth seeking out strains with more blue in the flowers to combine with cream, soft yellow, or blue flowers. The whiter, frillier cultivar 'Silver Ghost' 🏆 is an excellent garden plant but should be kept apart from the more usual form if either is to breed true from seed.

◕ *Campanula* 'Burghaltii' p.199 **B**, *Eschscholzia californica* Thai Silk Series, *Glaucium corniculatum*, *Helianthemum* cultivars p.57 **B**, *Helictotrichon sempervirens*, *Lilium regale* p.329 **A**, *Salvia sclarea* 'Vatican White', *Stachys byzantina* p.288 **A**

H: 90cm (36in) **S:** 30cm (12in)
✻ **Early to mid-summer**

▰▰▱▱▱ ◊-◊◊◊ ▨-▰ **Z6 pH5–8**

Erysimum × *allionii*

SIBERIAN WALLFLOWER

Later-flowering than the 'Cheiri' wallflower (below), and with a neater habit, this biennial wallflower forms a spreading mound of flowers in a very vibrant shade of orange, even richer in 'Orange Queen'; cultivars in other colors such as light orange, golden yellow, and pale yellow are occasionally available. The flowers have a delicious scent, making it a good choice near sitting areas; since plants prefer good drainage and full sun, they are also suitable for gravel gardens. They blend with peach, apricot, pale yellow, scarlet, yellow-green, and bronze, and contrast with blue, purple, and magenta. Good companions include forget-me-nots, euphorbias, late tulips, and many fritillaries.

◕ *Euphorbia polychroma* 'Major', *Iris* 'Curlew' p.249 **B**, *Muscari armeniacum*, *Tulipa* 'Elegant Lady', *T.* 'Queen of Night', *T.* 'Sweet Harmony' ⌐ p.346 **A**

H: 50–60cm (20–24in) **S:** 30cm (12in)
✻ **Late spring**

▰▰▱▱▱ ◊-◊◊◊ ▨-▰ **Z3 pH5.5–8**

The rich orange flowers and mahogany buds of the wallflower (*Erysimum* × *allionii*) contrast effectively with blue alpine forget-me-nots (*Myosotis alpestris*). Bulbs could be planted through both of these, for example fritillaries, or tulips in cream, soft yellow, or purple-black.

Erysimum cheiri

COMMON WALLFLOWER

This biennial is indispensable for spring bedding in beds and borders, and for planting beneath tulips or crown imperials. Single colors are the most useful, since mixtures run the risk of uneven heights and disparate shades, although purple-black or the yellow-green of euphorbias flatter any wallflower color. The tallest kinds, about 40cm (16in) high, are useful with taller tulips and come in a wide range of colors, including 'Blood Red', 'Cloth of Gold', vermilion 'Fire King',

'Purple Queen', and 'Vulcan', in deep crimson. Compact varieties are more limited. The most useful of these is the Bedder Series, 25–30cm (10–12in) high, in gold, golden orange, primrose, and scarlet.

A mixture of the common wallflower (*Erysimum cheiri*) in warm colors combines beautifully with the bronze foliage of *Euphorbia dulcis* 'Chameleon'. This grouping could be used on a larger scale, perhaps together with bulbs such as crown imperials or cream or red tulips, with a backing of bronze-leaved shrubs such as *Berberis thunbergii* f. *atropurpurea* or *Acer palmatum* cultivars.

◕ *Brunnera macrophylla*, *Erysimum* 'Bowles' Mauve' p.48 **A**, *Euphorbia griffithii* 'Dixter' p.219 **B**, *Heuchera* 'Plum Pudding' p.241 **A**, *Rosa* 'Helen Knight' p.157 **A**, *Tulipa* 'Abu Hassan' p.343 **A**, *T.* 'Apeldoorn' p.343 **C**, *T.* 'Burgundy' p.345 **B**, *T.* 'Greuze' p.348 **B**, *T.* 'Negrita' p.350 **C**, *T.* 'Queen of Night' p.353 **A**

H: 25–80cm (10–31in) **S:** 30cm (12in)
✻ **Mid- to late spring**

▰▰▱▱▱ ◊-◊◊◊ ▨-▰ **Z7 pH5.5–8**

Eschscholzia californica ♔

CALIFORNIA POPPY

This colorful hardy annual, easily grown as a biennial in sheltered, warmer areas, ranges widely in size. Tall cultivars, about 45cm (18in) high, include 'Milky White', 'Purple Gleam', and 'Red Chief', while shorter kinds (30cm/12in) include the Thai Silk Series, with fluted flowers in mixed or single colors. Double cultivars such as 'Ballerina Mixed' are charming but lack the elegance of single-flowered kinds. Single-colored cultivars with good silver foliage include 'Apricot Chiffon' and 'Rose Chiffon', and there are several fine orange and yellow kinds, such as 'Orange King'. All revel in a well-drained border or gravel garden, combined with scarlet poppies, sprawling anthemis, and glaucous, yellow-green, or bronze foliage. Shorter types are useful for covering the unattractive bases of Dwarf or Intermediate Bearded irises.

◐ *Anthemis punctata* subsp. *cupaniana*, *Cerinthe major* 'Purpurascens', *Glaucium corniculatum*, *Hordeum jubatum*, *Papaver somniferum* 'Danebrog'

H: 30–45cm (12–18in) S: 30cm (12in)
❅ **Early to late summer**
 ◊◊ ▢-◼ **Z7 pH5.5–7.5**

In California, *Eschscholzia californica* grows as a biennial and flowers in spring, providing a decorative filler between young plants of the chaparral prickly pear cactus *Opuntia oricola*, which requires the same climatic conditions.

Felicia petiolata

Although often grown as an annual for summer display, this plant is actually a sub-shrubby perennial. If given a sheltered microclimate such as within the skirts of a prostrate shrub (a cistus or ceanothus, for example), it can overwinter, even in some frost-prone areas, without protection and will scramble through the supporting shrub. Its flower color varies from a dingy blush-white to a good rose-pink, therefore if combining it with a cistus it is best to choose one in a contrasting color, either in pure white or rich magenta. This felicia is a pretty plant for the front of a border, but its growth can be unruly if the soil is too moist or rich.

◐ *Argyranthemum foeniculaceum* hort., *Cistus monspeliensis*, *C.* × *purpureus*, *Lavandula stoechas* subsp. *pedunculata*, *Osteospermum* 'Whirlygig'

H: 45cm (18in) S: 1m (40in)
❅ **Late spring to late summer**
 ◊◊ ▢-◼ **Z9 pH5.5–7.5**

This attractive combination of the scrambling *Felicia petiolata* with the slightly hardier *Ceanothus thyrsiflorus* var. *repens* in a frost-prone area is made possible by a sunny microclimate and the protection given by the ceanothus to the felicia. Both plants flower profusely in late spring.

Fuchsia 'Genii' ♔

An upright perennial of borderline hardiness, often grown for summer display, this fuchsia has yellow-green leaves that contrast brightly with the red stems, and cherry-red flowers with a violet corolla that ages to purple-red. It is much more successful outdoors than indoors, where it often drops both buds and flowers, and the bushy growth may be difficult to control. Full sun is needed for maximum flowering, but it may be grown in moderate shade as a foliage plant. It is very effective with hot colors such as yellow, orange and, above all, scarlet, and is useful in containers with companions such as scarlet trailing verbenas. Like all fuchsias, it is prone to pest damage. Yellow-green 'Cloth of Gold', and 'Tom West', with cream and pale green variegated leaves, are other good foliage cultivars for similar use, although they are slightly less hardy (Zone 9–10).

◐ *Canna* 'Striata', *Dahlia* 'Arabian Night', *Impatiens walleriana* 'Mega Orange Star', *Pelargonium* 'Orangesonne', *Petunia* Million Bells Lemon, *Salvia coccinea* 'Lady in Red', *Verbena* Temari Scarlet

H & S: 80cm (31in)
❅ **Early summer to late autumn**
 ◊◊ ▢-◼ **Z8–9 pH4.5–7**

In autumn, the contrasting flower and foliage colors of *Fuchsia* 'Genii' combine beautifully with other autumn-coloring foliage and fruits, such as those of the dwarf cranberry tree (*Viburnum opulus* 'Compactum'). A backing of taller autumn-coloring shrubs could be added, with shorter flowers such as Charm chrysanthemums in front.

The upright *Fuchsia* 'Thalia' adds height to this bold container planting, in which silver-leaved *Senecio viravira* is used to contrast with the fuchsia's dark foliage and bright flowers, as well as filling in around its stalky base. The Ivy-leaved, red-flowered *Pelargonium* 'Yale' scrambles through the senecio and tumbles over the side of the pot.

Fuchsia 'Thalia' ♀

This vigorous tender perennial is typical of Triphylla fuchsias, which have a more erect growth habit and definite form than most fuchsia hybrids, useful for adding height to container plantings and as filler in bedding or in the second row of a border. It bears red-flushed leaves with a purple-red underside, and bunches of coral-red hanging flowers, often confused with those of the very similar 'Gartenmeister Bonstedt' ♀, in which the flowers have a more bulging tube. Although it works with hot shades, 'Thalia' is more suited to subtle color schemes in salmon-pink, peach, apricot, and deep blood-red. It harmonizes with deep-red foliage and contrasts well with silver, glaucous, or yellow-green foliage, and also lime green flowers such as nicotianas. Other excellent Triphylla fuchsias include 'Coralle' ♀, in salmon-pink, and 'Mary' ♀, in cherry-red.

◐ *Beta vulgaris* 'Bull's Blood', *B.v.* 'Mr McGregor's Favourite', *Canna* 'Erebus', *Dahlia* 'Bishop of Llandaff', *Diascia rigescens*, *Nicotiana* 'Lime Green'

H: 80cm (31in) S: 45cm (18in)
❀ **Early summer to late autumn**
 ◌◌ ☐-■ Z10 pH5–7

By late spring, the winter rosettes of *Galactites tomentosa* have produced elongating shoots clad with elegant, pale and spiky leaves. Here, they conceal the dying foliage of *Allium hollandicum* and provide a filler between its flower stems in front of the contrasting yellow-green inflorescences of *Euphorbia characias* subsp. *wulfenii*.

Gaillardia pulchella 'Red Plume'

The Plume Series, perhaps the most reliable and uniform of the annual gaillardias includes 'Red Plume' and 'Yellow Plume', whose even color, upright growth habit, and fully double flowers make them valuable for mixing with other annuals of similar growth habit and flowering season. 'Red Plume' has a distinct richness that adds depth to jazzier shades of scarlet and orange, and also contrasts effectively with mid-blue or yellow-green. It combines well with osteospermums and dimorphothecas, and also with California poppies. *G.p.* var. *lorenziana*, with petals turned into elegant long trumpets, is usually offered in a double mixture, as is *G.p.* 'Lollipops', which blends bicolors with cream, yellow, and blood-red.

◐ *Dimorphotheca pluvialis*, *Eschscholzia californica* 'Orange King', *Nicotiana langsdorffii*, *Osteospermum* 'White Pim', *Scabiosa atropurpurea* 'Blue Cockade'

H: 35cm (14in) S: 15cm (6in)
❀ **Mid- to late summer**
 ◌◌ ☐-■ Z8 pH5.5–7.5

The warm, rich color of *Gaillardia pulchella* 'Red Plume' (blanket flower) is here contrasted with the cool delicacy of blue lace flower (*Trachymene coerulea*), which was started in a greenhouse from a spring sowing. The domed flower heads of both match perfectly in shape and size.

Galactites tomentosa

The main attraction of this ornamental thistle is its spiky filigree leaves, heavily veined and netted with white. They are followed by light-mauve flowers, although these are not profuse enough to create an impact, and plants become a little untidy soon after blooming starts. It is perhaps most useful grown as a biennial from a late summer or early autumn sowing, for planting between spring bulbs to help hide their dying leaves with the fresh rosettes of thistle foliage. The delicate leaf markings look best at close range, but the plant's outline is distinctive and can be emphasized by a dark background such as purple bugleweed or other low ground cover. It is an excellent subject for a white or silver garden, and can tolerate some drought.

◐ *Acaena microphylla* 'Kupferteppich', *Ajuga reptans* 'Atropurpurea', *Muscari latifolium*, *Narcissus* 'February Silver', *Tulipa* 'Ballerina', *T.* 'Elegant Lady'

H: 1m (40in) S: 40cm (16in)
❀ **(Early to mid-summer)**
 ◌◌ ☐-■ Z8 pH5.5–7.5

Glaucium corniculatum
RED HORNED POPPY

This sprawling, short-lived perennial, often grown as an annual or biennial, is a native of sea shores and so thrives in gravel gardens, although it also succeeds at the front of a dry, sunny border, in groups close to contrasting plants such as nasturtiums, teucriums, and corydalis species. Its chief glory is its lobed, curled, and sculptured glaucous foliage; its flowers are also attractive, but are usually born rather sparsely, especially in moist or rich soils. Its relative *Glaucium flavum*, the orange-flowered *G.f.* f. *fulvum*, and *G. leiocarpum*, with deep-yellow to apricot flowers, are all used in the same way. Their growth habit, colorings, and planting companions are similar to those of the shorter California poppy cultivars, with which they harmonize well.

Atriplex hortensis var. *rubra*, *Crambe maritima*, *Eryngium giganteum*, *Eschscholzia californica* Thai Silk Series, *Limnanthes douglasii*, *Papaver somniferum*

H: 30cm (12in) **S: 40cm** (16in)
✿ **Early summer to early autumn**
◊–◊◊ **Z7 pH5.5–7.5**

The horned poppy (*Glaucium corniculatum*) provides contrasting glaucous foliage and harmonious red flowers in front of *Helenium* 'Moerheim Beauty', whose rusty red blooms grow just above the poppy.

A

Helianthus annuus
COMMON SUNFLOWER

Tall annual sunflowers scarcely interact with other plants, but the less ungainly, branching types produce bold effects in sunny borders. 'Velvet Queen', 1.8m (6ft), is a sumptuous mahogany-red and a good foil for warm and hot colors; 'Prado Red' (syn. 'Ruby Sunset') is more uniform. Hybrids with pale creamy yellow flowers and a dark disc include 'Moonwalker', 'Valentine', and 'Vanilla Ice', all 1.5m (5ft). Short types – such as gold 'Teddy Bear', 60cm (24in), and clear yellow 'Pacino', 35cm (14in) – look striking at the front of a border. Yellow and light orange sunflowers contrast well with blue or purple, and with bold glaucous foliage such as arundos or plume poppies. They also can be used in hot color schemes with cannas, dahlias, or larger salvias, and with golden, variegated, yellow-green, bronze, or red foliage. The more subdued colors are good in autumnal schemes with buffs, bronzes, and burnt oranges. All combine dramatically with larger miscanthus, heleniums, and heliopsis.

Yellow/light orange: *Arundo donax*, *Echinops bannaticus* 'Taplow Blue', *Macleaya cordata*
Bright colours: *Berberis* × *ottawensis* f. *purpurea* 'Superba', *Canna* 'Roi Humbert', *Dahlia* 'Alva's Doris'
Subdued colours: *Achillea filipendulina* 'Gold Plate' p.179 **A**, *Tithonia rotundifolia* 'Goldfinger' p.402 **C**

H: 60cm–5m (2–16ft) **S: 30–120cm** (1–4ft)
✿ **Mid-summer to early autumn**
◊◊ **Z4 pH5–7**

The sunflower *Helianthus* 'Moonwalker', a 1.5m (5ft) tall hybrid derived from *H. annuus* and *H. debilis* subsp. *cucumerifolius*, branches to provide a succession of flowers, contrasting here with *Verbena hastata* and the spring-sown, short-growing sweet pea *Lathyrus odoratus* 'Chatsworth'.

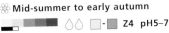

B

The small-leaved *Helichrysum petiolare* 'Roundabout', its white-felted foliage edged with cream, intermingles with the sprawling tender perennial *Verbena* 'Kemerton', contrasting well with its magenta-purple flowers. This is a combination that could be used equally successfully in a container or at the front of a border.

Helichrysum petiolare ♀

Grown for its grey-woolly leaves, this tender, sprawling shrub is very useful for containers, hanging baskets, and the front of borders, where it can weave between other plants. It is highly vigorous and comfortable only in the largest containers, but the pale yellow-green 'Limelight' ♀ and 'Variegatum' ♀ have more restrained growth. All combine well with other sprawling plants of comparable vigor such as trailing petunias, verbenas, and Ivy-leaved pelargoniums, and all scramble freely into and over small shrubs; their graceful shoots are ideal for breaking up areas of intense flower color or dull foliage. The species and its variegated sports combine with any colors. 'Limelight' contrasts well with blue flowers and glaucous foliage.

◉ *Agapanthus* 'Loch Hope' p.181 **A**, *Colchicum speciosum* 'Album' p.309 **C**, *Diascia* 'Dark Eyes' p.376 **B**, *Impatiens walleriana* p.382 **C**, *Lysimachia nummularia* 'Aurea', *Pelargonium* 'Hederinum', *Petunia* 'Buttercream' p.396 **B**, *P.* Million Bells Pink, *Rosa* 'American Pillar' p.139 **A**, *Scaevola aemula* p.401 **A**

H: 50cm (20in) S: 2m (6½ft)
❀ **Late summer to mid-autumn**

 ◊◊ ▣-▩ **Z9 pH5–7.5**

Heliotropium arborescens 'Princess Marina' ♀

The rich purple flowers and dark foliage of this compact, tender sub-shrub provide an excellent base accompaniment for brighter flowers and bolder shapes; its seductive and pervasive scent is an added bonus, making it a popular choice near a deck. Harmonies with pale to mid-lavender blue, mauve, or magenta flowers are effective, as are contrasts with soft orange, apricot, pale yellow, and lime green; stark contrasts are possible with silver-leaved plants such as *Helichrysum petiolare* cultivars, and with white-flowered, glaucous-leaved argyranthemums. This heliotrope combines successfully with taller ageratums, mauve or carmine impatiens, and sprawling and more upright verbenas.

◉ *Ageratum houstonianum* 'Old Grey', *Argyranthemum foeniculaceum* hort., *Dahlia* 'Yelno Harmony', *Impatiens walleriana* 'Mosaic Lilac', *Verbena* Temari Scarlet

H & S: 30cm (12in)
❀ **Early summer to mid-autumn**

▭▬▬ ◊◊ ▣-▩ **Z9 pH5.5–8**

The rich dark leaves and purple blooms of *Heliotropium arborescens* 'Princess Marina' tend to be recessive, not showing up well from a distance unless lifted by paler flowers or foliage, such as the brightly edged *Plectranthus madagascariensis* 'Variegated Mintleaf'. Both of these plants are suited to bedding, the front of borders, or containers.

Impatiens (*Impatiens walleriana*), seen here in a mixture, can be solid in outline, especially in the case of some compact modern cultivars, and almost too densely covered in bloom. Here, the mass of flowers on rounded plants is broken up by trails of silvery *Helichrysum petiolare*.

Impatiens walleriana
BUSY LIZZIE

Unlike most bedding plants, this tender sub-shrubby perennial thrives in shade, with its flowers facing in all directions, so it is very useful for window boxes and other plantings to be viewed from the shady side. The colors range from white through salmon-pink, mauve-pink, vermilion, and red to magenta-purple; Starbright Mixed and some of the Accent Series have white-striped petals, and there are also picotee cultivars such as the Swirl Series. Modern cultivars tend to be short, typically 10–15cm (4–6in) high, and make useful carpets for other flowers to grow through, but taller kinds, such as the Blitz Series (45cm/18in), are more generally garden-worthy. All are effective with bronze, silver, or yellow-green foliage plants, and associate easily with antirrhinums, diascias, pelargoniums, and sprawling verbenas. Many impatiens colors contrast well with lime green flowers such as nicotianas.

◉ *Antirrhinum majus* Coronet Series, *Begonia* (Semperflorens Cultorum Group), *Fuchsia* 'Genii', *Lobelia* 'Fan Orchidrosa' p.385 **A**, *Scaevola aemula* p.401 **A**

H: 10–60cm (4–24in) S: 20–60cm (8–24in)
❀ **Early summer to mid-autumn**

 ◊◊ ▣-▩ **Z9 pH5–7**

Ipomoea tricolor 'Mini Sky-blue'

This superb, restrained morning glory (a tender perennial usually grown as an annual) is too short to be used as a climber, but is excellent in the second row of a sunny border or in containers in a sunlit spot. Here it will scramble over neighboring plants, introducing an informality and natural grace that other annuals and bedding plants often lack. Its flowers, which tend to close at about midday, are sky-blue, in some cases with a hint of mauve, and very effective with yellow-green or glaucous foliage, or with blue, white, or cream flowers, and in contrasts with yellow flowers. Companion plants need to be sturdy enough to support its meandering stems, so small to medium-sized shrubs or sub-shrubs make the best hosts. Berberis, ceanothus, argyranthemums, and some smaller deutzias are suitable partners, as are forsythias, fuchsias, hypericums, philadelphus, rosemaries, shrubby salvias, and weigelas.

⬤ *Argyranthemum* 'Jamaica Primrose', *Berberis thunbergii* 'Aurea', *Ceanothus* × *delileanus* 'Gloire de Versailles', *Coronilla valentina* subsp. *glauca*, *Fuchsia magellanica* var. *gracilis*, *Salvia guaranitica*

H: 1.2m (4ft) **S: 25–45cm** (10–18in)
✲ **Mid-summer to early autumn**
◊◊ ▦ **Z8 pH6–8**

Ipomoea tricolor 'Mini Sky-blue' here weaves over and through two tender sub-shrubby perennials used as summer bedding plants: harmonious rich lavender *Salvia farinacea* 'Blue Victory' and gently contrasting creamy yellow variegated, white-flowered *Osteospermum* 'Silver Sparkler'.

A

A carpet of *Lantana camara* 'Orange Beauty' provides a foil for the spectacular and extravagant purple-flushed, variegated foliage of *Canna* 'Durban'. The canna will soon bear orange flowers matching those of the lantana.

Lantana camara 'Orange Beauty'

A tender scrambling sub-shrub, 'Orange Beauty' is an adaptable plant that may be used in summer containers and in bedding arrangements, or as a temporary ground cover. The florets open golden yellow from orange buds and age to vermilion, giving attractive gradations of color within the same flower head, blending well with hot colors, yellow-green, and bronze or red foliage, and contrasting with blue flowers. When used as bedding, it can be massed beneath architectural plants, including cannas, bronze cordylines, and dark-leaved castor oil plant. In a border it can be used similarly with rich blue or white agapanthus, coreopsis, heleniums, crocosmias, larger gold-variegated grasses, and bronze sedges or bronze-flowered pennisetums.

◉ *Agapanthus* 'Lilliput', *Carex comans* (bronze), *Cordyline australis* Purpurea Group, *Miscanthus sinensis* 'Strictus', *Ricinus communis* 'Impala'

H: **30cm** (12in) S: **1.5m** (5ft)
❀ **Late spring to late autumn**
◐◐ ▫- ▨ **Z9 pH5.5–7**

If grown as a biennial, the poached egg flower (*Limnanthes douglasii*) blooms in late spring, when the foliage of purple sage (*Salvia officinalis* 'Purpurascens') is most colorful. It will flower again, in autumn, from self-sown seedlings.

Lavatera trimestris

This loosely informal hardy annual suits mixed or herbaceous borders and cottage garden arrangements. It has rounded flowers in white to deep pink, the latter often with pretty veining and deeper centers. It mixes well with cool colors and purple or silver foliage, including artemisias and heucheras, while the richer, deeper pinks contrast with yellow-green or lime green. Flowers of contrasting form are good foils, especially the tiny blooms of gypsophilas or clarkias and spiky panicles of salvias or veronicas; further back in the border hollyhocks can echo its shape. Other partners include opium poppies, argyranthemums, osteospermums, verbenas, nicotianas, larkspurs, antirrhinums, and asters. Plants sown in autumn flower in early to late summer; those sown in spring bloom in mid-summer to early autumn.

◉ *Alcea rosea* Chater's Double Group, *Consolida ajacis* (blue) p.369 **A**, *Gypsophila paniculata* 'Bristol Fairy', *Nicotiana* 'Lime Green', *Veronica spicata*

H: **50–120cm** (20–48in) S: **30–45cm** (12–18in)
❀ **Early summer to early autumn**
◐◐ ▨ **Z7 pH5.5–7.5**

Pairing *Lavatera trimestris* 'Rose Beauty', its flowers just to the blue side of primary pink, with scarlet *Salvia coccinea* 'Lady in Red' gives the frisson of a near clash and a contrast of form. The salvia covers the lavatera's bare base.

Limnanthes douglasii ♛
POACHED EGG FLOWER

The five-petalled flowers of the poached egg flower are almost round in outline, each petal usually having a yellow base and a white tip; all-white and all-yellow variants are also available. It is useful for the front of a border, for rock gardens and walls, and beside paths where it can sprawl over the edge of the bed. It combines well with warm or hot colors, blue, and yellow-green, and looks good with silver carpeting plants such as blue or orange nemesias, shorter artemisias, shorter glaucous or yellow-green grasses, sea kale, and some delphinium cultivars. Other partners include nigellas, anthemis, nemophilas, alchemillas, echiums, marigolds, and nasturtiums. The poached egg flower is an annual, but in sheltered and warmer areas it can be grown as a biennial from autumn sowings.

◉ *Crambe maritima*, *Echium vulgare* 'Blue Bedder', *Festuca glauca* 'Blaufuchs', *Iris* 'Nightfall' p.248 **B**, *Nemesia strumosa* 'Blue Gem', *Nigella damascena* 'Miss Jekyll', *Tagetes tenuifolia* 'Tangerine Gem'

H & S: **15cm** (6in) ❀ **Late spring to late autumn**
◐◐ ▨ **Z8 pH5.5–7.5**

In this semi-formal bedding arrangement, magenta *Lobelia* 'Fan Orchidrosa' is planted close to the edge of the bed, its bold vertical spikes emphasizing the bed's sweeping curve. Gently clashing busy Lizzies (*Impatiens walleriana* 'Accent Salmon'), on the opposite side of primary deep pink to the lobelia, grow below and between.

Lobelia 'Fan Orchidrosa' ♀

This is a short-lived hardy herbaceous perennial with a narrow growth habit, useful for bedding in drifts or as an accent, for waterside planting, and for massing in moist mixed or herbaceous borders. Its magenta flowers, born in erect spikes, combine effectively with dark foliage such as red garden orach and purple-leaved heucheras, and cool-colored flowers and yellow-green or gold variegated grasses. It contrasts gently with sulfur-yellow flowers and yellow-green foliage and flowers, or, more vibrantly, with orange or vermilion flowers. In bedding arrangements, it can combine with lavateras, taller verbenas, cleomes, and nicotianas, and in borders with phlox, late astilbes, Japanese anemones, eryngiums, asters, and monardas.

● *Atriplex hortensis* var. *rubra*, *Euphorbia schillingii*, *Hakonechloa macra* 'Aureola', *Nicotiana* 'Lime Green', *Tithonia rotundifolia* 'Sundance', *Verbena rigida*

H: 70cm (27in) **S: 30cm** (12in)
☼ **Mid-summer to mid-autumn**

 ◊◊-◊◊◊ ▮ Z6 pH5.5–7.5

Lobelia richardsonii ♀

Usually raised as an annual from cuttings, this is a tender evergreen perennial, similar to *Lobelia erinus* cultivars, from which it differs mainly in its larger size. It is a good container and hanging basket plant that can also be used in bedding and at the front of a border. Its pale sky-blue flowers blend attractively with cool colors, silver and glaucous foliage, particularly argyranthemums and smaller fescues, and contrast well with yellow-green foliage or flowers and soft yellow blooms. It looks very effective with bidens, French marigolds, *Helichrysum petiolare* cultivars, petunias, especially smaller-flowered cultivars, and achimenes. When grown on its own, it has a prostrate growth habit, but it will scramble between and through a companion of modest height, embellishing it with a diffuse haze of tiny flowers, an effect that is charming with a smaller, sparsely branched shrub such as *Hebe* 'Quicksilver'.

● *Argyranthemum foeniculaceum* hort., *Bidens ferulifolia* 'Shining Star', *Festuca glauca* 'Blaufuchs', *Petunia* Million Bells Lemon, *Tagetes tenuifolia* 'Lemon Gem'

H: 10cm (4in) **S: 30cm** (12in)
☼ **Early summer to mid-autumn**

◊◊ ▮ Z9–10 pH5.5–7.5

In a partially shaded bed beneath trees, there is sufficient light for *Lobelia richardsonii* to flower freely and for Bowles' golden sedge (*Carex elata* 'Aurea') to color well. This site also suits the handsome hart's tongue fern (*Asplenium scolopendrium* 'Crispum Bolton's Nobile'), which thrives in shade and becomes scorched by the sun.

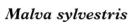

Lunaria annua 'Variegata' contrasts effectively with tulips in this spring border. The variegated moneyplant makes a suitable companion for many other late-flowering bulbs, including blue Dutch irises such as 'Wedgewood'.

Lunaria annua 'Variegata'
VARIEGATED ANNUAL HONESTY

An easy biennial with white, lilac, or reddish purple flowers, this is noted for its variegated leaves, entirely green at first but developing a creamy marginal mottling that matures to a pure, creamy white edge as plants flower. At this time, it combines well with other late spring flowers such as bluebells, camassias, comfreys, and columbines, together with most cool-colored flowers and purple foliage plants. It can be contrasted with orange and soft yellow or yellow-green. Because it grows mainly when deciduous shrubs and most herbaceous plants are out of leaf, it can be used between these, towards the back of a mixed border, together with pale yellow, cream, or pink brooms, early peonies, roses, and cranesbills, and bulbs such as Poeticus narcissi, late-flowering tulips, and irises.

🌑 *Camassia cusickii* 'Zwanenburg', *Gladiolus tristis* var. *concolor* p.319 **A**, *Hyacinthoides non-scripta*, *Iris* 'Grapesicle', *Narcissus* 'Actaea'

H: 90cm (36in) S: 30cm (12in)
� **Late spring to early summer**
 ◊◊ ☐-■ **Z6 pH5.5–8**

Malva sylvestris
HIGH MALLOW

This highly variable species is a short-lived perennial but variants often behave as biennials, and all forms may be grown as annuals. The typical species is pretty and floriferous, blooming mainly in early to mid-summer, and is suitable for a wild garden. Forms include white *M.s.* f. *alba*; lavender-blue 'Primley Blue'; 'Brave Heart', which is magenta with purple-black veins and base; and *M.s.* subsp. *mauritanica*, a handsome plant for the back of a border, with magenta flowers marked in deep purple-black with a purple base ('Bibor Fehlo' is similar but has larger, ruffled blooms). Mauve 'Zebrina', vigorous lavender Marina ('Dema'), and lilac 'Highnam' are all good with cool colors; the more richly hued variants can be contrasted with soft yellow, yellow-green, or orange.

🌑 *Achillea* 'Moonshine', *Briza maxima*, *Calendula officinalis* 'Orange King', *Crocosmia* 'Lucifer' p.207 **C**, *Euphorbia cyparissias*, *Nicotiana* 'Lime Green'

H: 20–120cm (8–48in) S: 30–60cm (12–24in)
✾ **Late spring to mid-autumn**
 ◊◊ ☐-■ **Z5 pH5.5–8**

In this harmony of crimson flowers of similar outline, *Malva sylvestris* 'Brave Heart' mingles with *Knautia macedonica* and *Lychnis coronaria* Atrosanguinea Group, whose grey-green stems and foliage lighten the grouping.

After being cut to the ground by winter cold, *Melianthus major* makes an imposing mound of magnificent foliage by the following autumn, matching the exact color of the blue lyme grass (*Leymus arenarius*) in front, although contrasting markedly in form. Beside it, the tiny leaflets of a double white form of the Scotch rose (*Rosa pimpinellifolia*) take on fiery tints before being shed.

Melianthus major

One of the most handsome of all foliage plants, this tender shrub has vast glaucous, pinnate leaves and spike-like racemes of mahogany flowers that are perhaps more fascinating than beautiful. It is excellent for helping to create a tropical arrangement and provide a unifying theme with flowers or foliage of similar color in borders and big containers. Its leaves blend very well with white, blue, or yellow-green flowers, silver or glaucous foliage, and white-variegated plants. It is especially effective with foliage of contrasting form, including grasses such as variegated arundo and miscanthus cultivars, and eucalyptus that has been pruned or grown from seed as a bedding plant. Other suitable partners include tetrapanax, wigandias, white cosmos, argyranthemums, agapanthus, eryngiums, glaucous cannas, and palms (either young plants or those that are naturally low-growing and suckering).

🌑 *Canna* 'Erebus', *Chamaerops humilis*, *Cosmos bipinnatus* 'Sonata White', *Eucalyptus gunnii* (stooled), *Miscanthus sinensis* 'Variegatus', *Tetrapanax papyrifer*

H: 2–3m (6½–10ft) S: 1–2m (3¼–6½ft)
✾ **Late spring to mid-summer**
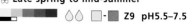 ◊◊ ☐-■ **Z9 pH5.5–7.5**

Musa basjoo

JAPANESE BANANA

Despite being regarded widely as a tree, this is a tender herbaceous perennial with stems that can survive for several years, especially if wrapped up with insulation to protect it from frost in cool areas. As an alternative in cold gardens, it can be overwintered under cover and planted out as a bedding plant, to create a tropical impact or contribute to the boldest, large-scale foliage effects. Its impressive bright green leaves arch out languidly from a stem composed of the furled leaf bases, and can reach 3m (10ft) long in humid positions and moist, fertile soils, although 1.8m (6ft) is more usual. These stems and their leaves die after flowering, and are replaced by suckers from the surviving rootstock.

Good large-leaved partners include pruned catalpas or paulownias, tetrapanax, cannas, gunneras, rheums, and large grasses such as arundos and bamboos, together with palms, colocasias, wigandias, and castor oil plants. In favored areas, plants can produce dramatic brown inflorescences, in large, pendent spikes with the buds enclosed in conspicuous bracts, followed by small greenish banana fruits. Although usually used for planting on a grand scale, it is valuable for smaller gardens where a dramatically over-scale effect is wanted. It benefits from a sheltered situation because strong winds can shred the leaves, making them look unsightly.

Other bananas for the same conditions and uses include *M. velutina*, a more compact species, only 1.8m (6ft) high, with leaves 90–120cm (3–4ft) long and upright spikes of yellow flowers enclosed in red bracts. 'Dwarf Cavendish' is a hardier, more compact cultivar of *M. acuminata*, the main parent of most edible bananas, and in a warm summer can ripen hands of sweet fruits on plants that grow to 3m (10ft) high. Most other banana species are too tender for outdoor cultivation in climates cooler than Zone 10.

⬤ *Arundo donax, Canna indica* 'Purpurea', *Catalpa bignonioides* (stooled), *Rheum palmatum*, *Ricinus communis* 'Carmencita' p.397 **B**

H: 2.7m (9ft) S: 2m (6½ft) ❋ **Mid- to late summer**
◼◻ ◊◊ ◻-◼ ◼ **Z9 pH5.5–7**

Even where summers are barely warm, *Musa basjoo* can supply luxuriant tropical effect, provided its growing point and rootstock do not freeze in winter. In this grouping of green foliage, it makes a bold focus behind the curious *Amicia zygomeris*, with its maroon-shaded stipules, and the handsome palmate African hemp, *Sparrmannia africana*.

Myosotis sylvatica
WOOD FORGET-ME-NOT

Often grown as a biennial, this short-lived perennial, with saucer-shaped, yellow-eyed, blue or white flowers, has a loose, airy growth habit suitable for informal parts of the garden. It harmonizes well with ipheions, muscaris, narcissi, tulips, primroses, yellow or cream wallflowers, white rock cress, and *Aurinia saxatilis* cultivars. Shorter, richer blue variants of *M. alpestris* include 'Blue Ball' ♀, 'Bouquet' ♀, and 'Ultramarine' ♀. Their stronger color contrasts boldly with yellow, orange, or gold, and their more even growth habit suits carpet bedding and other formal arrangements.

○ *Allium hollandicum* p.301 **B**, *Artemisia ludoviciana* p.189 **B**, *Geranium albanum* p.225 **A**, *Gymnocarpium dryopteris* p.233 **A**, *Iris* 'Grapesicle' p.249 **C**, *I.* 'Wedgwood' p.323 **A**, *Narcissus* 'Actaea' p.330 **C**, *N.* 'Hawera' p.334 **B**, *Polemonium caeruleum* p.275 **B**, *Primula veris* p.279 **A**, *Stachys byzantina* p.288 **A**, *Tulipa* 'Burgundy' p.345 **B**, *T.* 'China Pink' p.345 **C**, *T.* 'Cordell Hull' p.346 **C**, *T.* 'Elegant Lady' p.347, **A** *T.* 'Palestrina' p.352 **B** ⌐ p.114 **B**

H: 20–30cm (8–12in) S: 15cm (6in)
❀ **Mid-spring to early summer**
 ◌◌-◌◌◌ ▢-▨ ■ Z5 pH4.5–7.5

The self-sown sky-blue *Myosotis sylvatica* forms a striking contrast with the sword-like foliage of *Libertia peregrinans*, which adopts an orange-brown hue, especially bright along the midribs of the leaves, in winter through to late spring.

Nemesia 'Innocence' ♀

The yellow-lipped white flowers of this tender sub-shrub are charming at close range, but its rather amorphous growth habit suits it to a supporting role with plants of more definite structure. It is attractive in containers and hanging baskets, and for the front of a border, where it combines successfully with silver foliage and most flower colors, especially blue. Like all nemesias, it resents prolonged drought and enjoys similar conditions to diascias, with which it can be grown to produce a froth of pale colors as a flattering background for plants that have a more solid shape. Deadheading can help to increase and prolong flowering, and prevent the appearance of inferior seedlings. Cuttings may be taken and rooted in late summer for overwintering indoors.

○ *Alonsoa warscewiczii*, *Antirrhinum majus* 'Black Prince', *Artemisia schmidtiana*, *Diascia rigescens*, *Pericallis × hybrida* 'Royalty Sky Blue', *Salvia farinacea* 'Strata', *Verbena* 'Lawrence Johnston'

H: 45cm (18in) S: 60cm (24in)
❀ **Late spring to mid-autumn**
 ◌◌ ▢-▨ ■ Z9 pH5–7

Sparkling white, yellow-lipped blooms of *Nemesia* 'Innocence' contrast dramatically against the mahogany-red flowers and foliage of *Sedum telephium* 'Arthur Branch'.

Nemophila menziesii
BABY-BLUE-EYES

This is a pretty annual for positions at the front of a border, where it can sprawl over the edge of adjacent paving or scramble into neighboring plants. The bright blue flowers, with lighter blue centers often stained white or yellow, are particularly effective combined with white, cream, or yellow flowers, and yellow-green, glaucous, and white- or gold-variegated foliage. Attractive color variants are sometimes available, including one with pure white flowers (var. *atomaria*) and another that is purple-black, edged with white (var. *discoidalis*, sometimes sold as 'Penny Black'). All may be grown as annuals if sown in early to late spring, or as biennials from sowings in late summer or early autumn; the seeds should always be sown *in situ*. This plant cannot survive drought but will tolerate a little shade, especially in sunnier climates.

○ *Argyranthemum* 'Jamaica Primrose', *Euphorbia rigida* (foliage), *Hakonechloa macra* 'Alboaurea', *Limnanthes douglasii*, *Spiraea japonica* 'Goldflame'

H: 20cm (8in) S: 30cm (12in)
❀ **Early to late summer**
 ◌◌ ▢-▨ ■ Z7 pH5.5–7.5

In early summer, the blue flowers of baby-blue-eyes (*Nemophila menziesii*) are joined in this flat area of planting by the white flowers of *Osteospermum* 'Gold Sparkler', with their slaty reverses, contrasting yellow *Viola aetolica*, and the five-spot (*Nemophila maculata*), to produce a charming millefleurs tapestry of flowers.

Nicotiana langsdorffii 🏆

This charming annual nicotiana has elegant, nodding, rich apple-green flowers, which are rounded at the mouth and carried on slender stems. The flowers are best viewed at close range or, if planted some distance away, they benefit from a background of very dark foliage. Plants combine well with yellow-green, silver, purple, or reddish foliage, and with white or pure blue flowers; satisfying contrasts can be made with scarlet, salmon-pink, or rich deep pink. Other nicotianas such as *N.* 'Lime Green' and 'Domino Lime Green' also make excellent partners.

While *N. langsdorffii* can reach 1.5m (5ft), it is often much shorter. It is fairly resistant to tobacco blue mold, a problem with many other flowering nicotianas.

◐ *Consolida* 'Frosted Skies', *Cotinus coggygria* 'Royal Purple', *Delphinium* 'Sungleam', *Hydrangea paniculata* 'Greenspire' p.60 **B**, *Onopordum nervosum*

H: 1.2m (4ft) **S: 40cm** (16in)
❁ **Early summer to mid-autumn**
◻◻◻◻◻◻ ◌◌ ◻-◼ ◼ **Z9 pH5–7.5**

In this blend of flowers and foliage in subdued colorings, two species tobaccos are used, not for their "flower power", but for their elegant form. In the foreground, *Nicotiana langsdorffii* casts a veil of nodding apple-green bells in front of the handsome foliage of *N. sylvestris*, whose extraordinary, long-tubed flowers cascade in front of a backdrop of the feathery cut-leaved elderberry, *Sambucus racemosa* 'Plumosa Aurea'.

Nicotiana Domino Series 🏆

Showy, upturned, brightly colored flowers adorn these popular plants, which are perennials usually grown as annuals. Being among the taller bedding nicotianas, they can be used toward the front of a herbaceous or mixed border, grading into the rest of the planting. About a dozen single colors are available, in crimson, red, purple, white, and salmon-pink; some have white eyes or petals edged with a different color. There is also a lime green variant ('Domino Lime Green'), which is paler and less acid than *N.* 'Lime Green' (p.390) and is very effective mixed with white or salmon-pink. 'Domino Red' combines well with hot colors and purple, bronze, or red foliage. Unlike with some nicotianas, the florets of all Domino Series stay open during the day, but lack fragrance.

In recent years, many flowering nicotianas in some places have been killed by tobacco blue mold, making them unreliable for garden use on a large scale. The risks are decreased by growing a few widely spaced plants, with good aeration all round, and spraying with fungicide. Old plants should be removed at the end of the flowering season.

Top: In this richly colored scheme, *Nicotiana* 'Domino Red' is joined by the flat yellow flower heads of *Achillea filipendulina* 'Gold Plate', the yellow daisy flowers of *Rudbeckia* 'Herbstsonne', bright red *Dahlia* 'Bishop of Llandaff', the orange spikes of *Kniphofia uvaria* 'Nobilis', orange *Crocosmia paniculata* and *C.* 'Vulcan', the puckered leaves of the beets *Beta vulgaris* 'Mr McGregor's Favorite' and *B.v.* 'Rhubarb Chard', pelargoniums, and verbenas.

Above: This is a charming combination of two gently contrasting tobacco plants, *Nicotiana* 'Domino Salmon Pink' and 'Domino Lime Green'.

◐ *Canna indica* 'Purpurea', *Cosmos bipinnatus*, *Helichrysum petiolare*, *Heuchera* 'Plum Pudding', *Perilla frutescens* var. *crispa*, *Plectranthus argentatus*, *Rosa* 'Frensham', *R.* Iceberg, *Salvia farinacea* 'Cirrus', *Verbena* 'Lawrence Johnston'

H: 40cm (16in) **S: 20cm** (8in)
❁ **Early summer to mid-autumn**
◻◻◻◻◻◻ ◌◌ ◻-◼ ◼ **Z8 pH5–7.5**

The elegant, slightly nodding flowers of *Nicotiana* 'Lime Green' are never more effectively contrasted than when combined with scarlet flowers and dark foliage, as here with *Dahlia* 'Bishop of Llandaff', a good partnership for containers or toward the front of a border.

Nicotiana 'Lime Green' ♔

The striking yellowish green of this annual nicotiana's flowers is a sharper, more definite color than that of 'Domino Lime Green' (p.389), and better suited to creating contrasts with scarlet, coral, and pure blue flowers, as well as with reddish, purple, or bronze foliage. Like the yellow-green of *Alchemilla mollis*, it is a color that blends easily with most others, whether in gentle contrasts, or to make pleasant harmonies such as may be achieved with yellow, white, or cream flowers, and glaucous or yellow-variegated foliage. The slightly airy, open growth habit helps plants withstand cool, wet weather; it also enables them to resist tobacco blue mold more successfully than some of the more congested modern cultivars, although it is still more susceptible than species such as *N. langsdorffii* or *N. sylvestris*.

❀ *Alstroemeria psittacina* p.184 **C**, *Ipomoea tricolor* 'Mini Sky-blue', *Lobelia richardsonii*, *Pelargonium* 'Paul Crampel' p.394 **A**, *Penstemon* 'Chester Scarlet'

H: 60cm (24in) S: 25cm (10in)
❀ **Early summer to mid-autumn**
 ◊◊ ☐-■ ■ **Z9 pH5–7.5**

Nigella damascena
LOVE-IN-A-MIST

Cultivars of this annual are usually blue, but may be white or pink. The most popular is 'Miss Jekyll', 45cm (18in), with double sky-blue flowers, together with 'Miss Jekyll Dark Blue', 'Miss Jekyll Rose', and 'Miss Jekyll Alba'. 'Oxford Blue', 75cm (30in), is similar in color to 'Miss Jekyll Dark Blue'; the Persian Jewel Series, 40cm (16in), is usually sold as a mixture of blues, pinks, and white. All thrive in any good soil but look especially fine in gravel. They bear distinctive, inflated seedpods and feathery foliage that is a useful filigree filler between more solid plants such as Bearded irises, and helps hide the dying foliage of bulbs. Blue cultivars are most effective with soft yellow or amber flowers.

❀ *Achillea* 'Moonshine', *Allium cristophii* p.300 **B**, *Geranium* × *oxonianum* f. 'Thurstonianum' p.227 **B**, *Rosa gallica* 'Versicolor' p.148 **B**, *R.* 'Raubritter' p.169 **A**, *R.* 'Tuscany Superb' p.150 **B**

H: 20–75cm (8–30in) S: 15–23cm (6–9in)
❀ **Early to late summer**
■■□□ ◊◊ ☐-■ ■ **Z6 pH5–7.5**

This charmingly simple, single variant of love-in-a mist (*Nigella damascena*) exactly matches exotic-looking *Rehmannia elata* in height, mingling attractively with it.

Oenothera biennis
COMMON EVENING PRIMROSE

The large, sweetly scented lemon-yellow flowers of this biennial open in the evening and close the following morning. The plant is not particularly showy during the day, so its relatively undistinguished foliage and growth habit are best screened by shorter plants such as lavenders, catmints, and white-flowered cistus or halimiocistus growing in front. It revels in well drained soils, even those low in nutrients, and self-seeds freely. Other

comparable species include *O. stricta* and its more attractive pale cultivar 'Sulphurea', 80cm (31in) tall, and *O. glazioviana* (syns *O. erythrosepala*, *O. lamarckiana*), about 2m (6½ft) high and bearing soft yellow flowers set off by mahogany-colored sepals.

❀ *Buphthalmum salicifolium* p.198 **C**, *Deschampsia cespitosa* 'Bronzeschleier', *Lavandula angustifolia* 'Hidcote', *Nepeta* 'Six Hills Giant'

H: 1.5m (5ft) S: 60cm (24in)
❀ **Early summer to early autumn**
 ◊◊ ☐-■ ■ **Z4 pH5–7.5**

Watsonia meriana, a tender corm whose flowers range from pink to red or purple, is an unusual companion for the fully hardy evening primrose (*Oenothera biennis*). Both need the same conditions of well-drained soil in a sunny position. Here, the combination is enhanced by bold clumps of ornamental grasses.

Onopordum nervosum 🏆

Plenty of space is essential for this dramatic biennial cotton thistle to develop its huge candelabra of silvery stems with jagged leaves. It is an imposing architectural plant, especially effective against a dark background or in planting groups based on white flowers and silver foliage. The mauve thistle flowers add little to the impact of what is primarily a foliage plant, valuable for use as bold punctuation or as a unifying theme if planted at intervals along a border. It prefers well drained soils, but low fertility may lead the plant to produce fewer branches and die back earlier than in richer soils. Young leaf rosettes should not be crowded by neighbors, and larger specimens may need discreet support with a stake or rod to prevent the whole plant from keeling over prematurely.

🌼 *Acanthus spinosus*, *Artemisia ludoviciana* 'Silver Queen', *Cotinus coggygria* 'Royal Purple', *Crambe cordifolia*, *Lavatera* 'Barnsley', *Miscanthus sacchariflorus*, *M. sinensis* 'Variegatus', *Rosa* 'Highdownensis', *R.* 'Pink Perpétué' p.144 **A**, *Salix exigua*, *Sambucus nigra* 'Guincho Purple' ⌐ p.372 **B**

H: 3m (10ft) **S: 1m** (3¼ft) 🌼 **Mid- to late summer**
◻◼◼◼ ◊◊ ◻-◼ ◼ **Z6 pH5.5–7.5**

The dramatic pale leaves of *Onopordum nervosum* (cotton thistle) transform this subtly colored scheme, which blends pink blooms of *Pimpinella major* 'Rosea' and *Rosa glauca* with glaucous foliage from the rose and *Thalictrum flavum* subsp. *glaucum*, which also contributes yellow-green buds.

Orlaya grandiflora

This charming annual umbellifer, with lacy white flowers set off by rich green, feathery leaves, may be used in the same way as *Nigella damascena* (facing page), as a filigree foil to plants of more definite architectural form. It blends well with other annuals, such as common poppies, cornflowers, and daisies, to produce a tapestry of color. A sunny position is essential, together with a soil that is rich enough to encourage the plant to develop a well-branched structure and so continue longer in flower. The Queen-Anne's-lace (*Daucus carota*) has less showy outer florets, but can be used in a similar way; superlative white or, more rarely, pink strains are sometimes available.

🌼 *Allium hollandicum* 'Purple Sensation', *Aquilegia vulgaris* (mixed), *Centaurea cyanus* 'Blue Diadem', *C. montana*, *Iris sibirica* 'Cambridge', *Paeonia officinalis*, *Papaver rhoeas* (Shirley Group) 'Cedric Morris', *Rosa* Avalanche p.163 **A**, *Tulipa* 'Ballerina', *T.* 'Elegant Lady', *Xanthophthalmum segetum* 'Prado'

H: 60cm (24in) **S: 45cm** (18in)
🌼 **Late spring to mid-summer**
◻◼◼◼ ◊◊ ◻-◼ ◼ **Z6 pH5.5–7.5**

The filigree foliage and lacy flowers of *Orlaya grandiflora* decorate the base of *Phormium* 'Maori Sunrise', softening the plant's rather bold form and strong coloring.

The carpeting growth habit of *Osteospermum* 'White Pim' allows it to be used at the front of a slightly sloped border, in a bed of fairly flat planting, or in a large rock garden, with other plants that are low growing and spreading, such as *Veronica austriaca* subsp. *teucrium* 'Kapitän', seen here.

Osteospermum 'White Pim' 🏆

A tender evergreen sub-shrub usually grown, like many osteospermums, as a half-hardy annual, the outstanding 'White Pim' has shining white ray petals, often slightly mauve-flushed, arranged around a glistening center. It is an excellent mat-forming plant for the front of beds and borders, and for containers, especially combined with cool colors and glaucous, silver, or purple foliage. Other more shrubby, upright osteospermums are ideal for adding height to bedding and container planting. There are long-flowering varieties in colors from rich yellow to white, mauve-pink, and purple; some, such as 'Whirlygig' 🏆 and the Nasinga Series, have spoon-shaped petals. Similar in many ways to argyranthemums, they generally have less appealing foliage and cannot tolerate long periods of drought, but their range includes useful prostrate varieties, and unrivaled rich purple shades.

🌼 *Aeonium* 'Zwartkop', *Argyranthemum* 'Jamaica Primrose', *Brachyscome iberidifolia*, *Felicia petiolata*, *Nemophila menziesii*, *Plectranthus argentatus*

H: 15cm (6in) **S: 60cm** (24in)
🌼 **Late spring to mid-autumn**
◻◼◼◼ ◊◊ ◻-◼ ◼ **Z9 pH5.5–7.5**

Papaver rhoeas

SHIRLEY POPPY

Sometimes called Flanders poppy or field poppy, this annual can be used in its wild, scarlet-flowered state or as cultivars to produce flowery meads on sunny sites with well-drained, even rather poor soil. In this role they may be combined with other annuals or biennials such as agrostemma, *Ammi majus*, cornflowers, opium poppies, and *Phacelia tanacetifolia*. The most famous of the many variants are Shirley poppies, which include white and pink shades and varied picotees. The painter Sir Cedric Morris developed selections from these, excluding the red tints and favoring smoky mauves and lilacs – these are sold under various names including 'Cedric Morris', 'Fairy Wings', and 'Mother of Pearl'. The double 'Angels' Choir' mixture is longer-flowering. Selections in which scarlet and salmon predominate may be used for harmonies with peach, apricot, and white, or for contrasts with pure blue, and also blend well with glaucous, bronze, or reddish foliage. Those with smoky tints work well with carmine, lilac, mauve, and magenta flowers, and purple or silver foliage.

Above left: If given space to make large, vigorous plants, double *Papaver rhoeas* (Shirley Group) 'Angels' Choir' will bloom into late summer, the red flowers it contains harmonizing with *Crocosmia masoniorum* 'Dixter Flame'.

Above: Although once containing only pastel colors, *Papaver rhoeas* Shirley Group double mixed now often comprises mostly richer tints, allowing warm-colored combinations with *Calendula officinalis* Fiesta Gitana Series.

◉ *Agrostemma githago, Briza maxima, Centaurea cyanus, Leucanthemum vulgare, Malva sylvestris, Papaver somniferum, Rosa* 'De Rescht' p.147 **A**

H: 25–40cm (10–16in) **S: 30cm** (12in)
❊ **Early to late summer**

  ◌◌ ▨-▨ ■ **Z5 pH5.5–7.5**

Papaver somniferum ♈

OPIUM POPPY

The color range of this annual poppy is extensive – white, pink, mauve, scarlet, and crimson, to nearly black – and there are both single and double selections. Very double ones ("peony-flowered") include 'Pink Chiffon' and 'White Cloud', while 'Crimson Feathers', 'Fluffy Ruffles', and 'Rose Feathers' all have cut petals. 'Danebrog' (syn. 'Danish Flag') is a remarkable single, with frilled scarlet petals marked at the base with a white blotch. All the colors except salmon and scarlet blend with cool shades, and make attractive loose groups or drifts in a border. The glaucous foliage is striking, as are the seedpods; these are best removed if self-seeding is unwelcome, although they look good as a repeated accent in borders, perhaps echoed by the round flower heads of alliums.

◉ *Allium sphaerocephalon, Aquilegia vulgaris* (mixed), *Artemisia ludoviciana* 'Silver Queen', *Briza maxima, Dianthus barbatus* p.376 **A**, *Helictotrichon sempervirens, Iris* 'Kent Pride', *Lavatera trimestris, Nigella damascena* 'Miss Jekyll', *Rosa glauca* ⌐ p.167 **A**

H: 60–120cm (24–48in) **S: 30cm** (12in)
❊ **Early to late summer**

 ◌◌ ▨-▨ ■ **Z7 pH5–7.5**

Above left: The scarlet flowers of this *Papaver somniferum* selection contrast with its glaucous pods and harmonize with *Lychnis chalcedonica* and *Rosa* Westerland.

Above: After flowering, the glaucous pods of opium poppy (*Papaver somniferum*) remain attractive, combined here with *Salvia sclarea* var. *turkestanica, Phlox paniculata*, and alliums.

Pelargonium 'Hederinum'

Also known as 'Balcon Rose' or 'Ville de Paris', this is the oldest Ivy-leaved pelargonium cultivar, dating back to 1786. Its numerous sports include 'Hederinum Variegatum' (syn. 'Duke of Edinburgh', 'Madame Margot'), with white variegation; red-flowered 'Roi des Balcons Impérial' (syn. 'Balcon Rouge'); and mauve-pink 'Roi des Balcons Lilas' (syn. 'Balcon Lilas'). These make spectacular cascades from hanging baskets and window boxes, combined with trailing plants of similar vigor such as black-eyed Susans, helichrysums, lophospermums, morning glories, and plectranthus. Plants in the shorter-jointed Mini-cascade Series are also useful for containers, mixed with less energetic sprawlers – ivies and shorter *Helichrysum petiolare* cultivars, for example. The Decora Series are pale-stemmed sports.

Helichrysum petiolare, *Ipomoea tricolor* 'Mini Sky-blue', *Lobelia erinus* 'Sapphire', *Lophospermum erubescens*, *Plectranthus argentatus*, *Thunbergia alata*

H: 30cm (12in) S: 1.5m (5ft)
Late spring to mid-autumn
Z9 pH5–7.5

The long-jointed stems of pink-flowered *Pelargonium* 'Hederinum' and red *P.* 'Roi des Balcons Impérial' look glorious cascading from balconies and window boxes, lacking the congestion of more compact sorts.

A

B

Pelargonium Multibloom Series

This is one of the most successful series of F1 hybrid pelargoniums that can be raised from seed. Tender perennials usually grown as half-hardy annuals, they are compact and flower very early, having up to 15 flower heads at one time, each 8–10cm (3½–4in) wide. The series is available as a mixture or in separate shades of red, scarlet, salmon, bright rose, pink, lavender, white, and scarlet with a white eye. Plants have a high tolerance of cool, wet summers, and are excellent for flower beds and window boxes, although large, older specimens raised from cuttings are better for groups in borders, where they need to blend into the rest of the planting.

Seed-raised pelargoniums are one of the most important advances in bedding plant breeding in recent decades. Because of their low and even habit of growth, they are well suited to extended plantings, mixed with flowers of a contrasting shape such as *Verbena rigida*, which can be used to cast a haze of purple above pelargoniums in carmine or contrasting bright or rich salmon.

'Cherie', one of the earliest cultivars of this type, has delicately shaded, pale salmon-pink flowers and an attractive dark leaf zone. The very early flowering Orbit Series has large heads, about 13cm (5in) across, in a range of 16 colors; the Pulsar (syn. Pinto) Series has strongly zoned leaves and brilliantly colored heads in 11 shades that shine in massed bedding.

Varieties raised specifically for strong performance in cool, wet summers include the dark-leaved Video Series; the strongly branching, free-flowering Sensation Series, in a range of colors that includes blush-pink, coral-pink, rose, cherry-red, and scarlet; and the rather spreading Breakaway Series, which has strong semi-trailing branches that make it a particularly good candidate for window boxes and hanging baskets.

Pelargonium 'Multibloom Salmon' and *Zinnia* 'Dreamland Coral' make good companions, with flowers of harmonious colors but contrasting form on plants of the same height.

Abutilon pictum 'Thompsonii', *Canna* 'Lucifer', *Cordyline australis* Purpurea Group, *Heliotropium arborescens* 'Princess Marina', *Lobularia maritima* 'Snow Crystals', *Nicotiana langsdorffii*, *Petunia* Surfinia Blue, *Phormium* 'Bronze Baby', *Senecio cineraria* 'Silver Dust', *Verbena* Tapien Violet

H & S: 30cm (12in) Late spring to mid-autumn
Z9 pH5–7.5

Pelargonium 'Paul Crampel'

This is regarded as the archetypal Victorian scarlet pelargonium. A tender perennial propagated only by cuttings, it is much less compact than seed-raised varieties and bears fewer flower heads than modern kinds, although each contains hundreds of florets so that an individual head can remain in flower for several months. The intense scarlet color combines well with bronze, red, yellow-green, silver, and gold-variegated foliage, harmonizes with salmon and hot colors such as golden yellow and orange, and makes good contrasts with lime green or yellow-green. Plants are tall enough to blend into a border effectively, and look impressive in large containers; they can also be trained on a cool greenhouse wall, mixed with other climbers such as morning glory, and with *Helichrysum petiolare* cultivars, which are easily trained upwards.

◉ *Abutilon* 'Savitzii', *Canna* 'Erebus', *Iresine herbstii* 'Aureoreticulata', *Lobelia richardsonii*, *Perilla frutescens* var. *crispa*, *Thunbergia alata*, *Zinnia elegans* 'Envy'

H: 45cm (18in) **S:** 38cm (15in)
✿ **Late spring to mid-autumn**

◌-◌◌ ▢-◼ **Z9 pH5–7.5**

This steeply sloped planting at the foot of a sunny wall is based on rich scarlet and contrasting pale green flowers with dark foliage. It comprises *Pelargonium* 'Paul Crampel', *Dahlia* 'Bishop of Llandaff', *Nicotiana* 'Lime Green', and *Heuchera micrantha* var. *diversifolia* 'Palace Purple', with the castor oil plant *Ricinus communis* 'Carmencita' behind, and *Cordyline australis* providing a spiky focal point.

Penstemon 'Andenken an Friedrich Hahn' ♔

Although one of the hardiest hybrid penstemons, this perennial sub-shrub is best treated as a bedding plant by raising it from cuttings taken in late summer and overwintered indoors, a method that ensures vigorous, uniform, and free-flowering young plants. Also known as 'Garnet', it has flowers that are slightly on the blue side of primary red, grown in fairly loose spikes. It benefits from association with plants of more substance, such as grasses and phormiums, or may be grown in the second row of a herbaceous or mixed border, behind smaller plants such as lavenders, pinks, or catmints; it is also very appealing planted in front of old roses. Its color combines well with purple, harmonizes pleasantly with pink, and contrasts with lime green flowers and silver, yellow-green, and gold-variegated foliage.

◉ *Alstroemeria ligtu* hybrids p.184 **B**, *Dianthus* 'Doris', *Lavandula angustifolia* 'Hidcote', *Miscanthus sinensis* 'Variegatus', *Nicotiana* 'Lime Green', *Rosa* 'Geranium' p.155 **A**, *Verbena* 'Silver Anne' p.405 **C**

H: 60cm (24in) **S:** 45cm (18in)
✿ **Mid-summer to mid-autumn**

◌◌ ▢ **Z7 pH5–7.5**

Penstemon 'Andenken an Friedrich Hahn' covers the base of the gold-variegated *Phormium tenax* 'Veitchianum', supplying rich color to complement the phormium's long, dramatic leaves.

Penstemon 'Chester Scarlet' ♔

In spite of its name, the flowers of this excellent cultivar are a rich cherry-red, rather than a pure scarlet. It is a perennial sub-shrub, like 'Andenken an Friedrich Hahn' (above) but not as hardy, and it tends to produce rather taller plants. It belongs in the second rank of a border, although its higher, longer flower stems qualify it admirably for more steeply sloped planting arrangements. Its sumptuous color mixes well with purple, rose-pink, coral-pink, and salmon, and with hot colors such as scarlet and vermilion. Like 'Andenken an Friedrich Hahn', the red flowers form dramatic contrasts with lime green flowers and silver, yellow-green, and gold-variegated foliage.

◉ *Pelargonium* 'Paul Crampel', *Perilla frutescens* var. *crispa*, *Phygelius* × *rectus* 'Pink Elf', *Verbena* Tapien Violet, *Zinnia elegans* 'Envy'

H: 65cm (26in) **S:** 40cm (16in)
✿ **Mid-summer to mid-autumn**

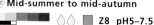 ◌◌ ◼ **Z8 pH5–7.5**

The relatively upright stems of *Penstemon* 'Chester Scarlet', overlapped along most of their length with flowers, are ideal for a sloping border behind mound-forming plants, such as with lady's mantle (*Alchemilla mollis*) and contrasting silver-leaved *Artemisia ludoviciana*.

The sheer gorgeousness of the blooms of *Penstemon* 'King George V' lends it to richly colored arrangements, as seen here with orange kniphofias and the dark-leaved *Actaea simplex* Atropurpurea Group.

Penstemon 'King George V'

This eye-catching, sub-shrubby penstemon is one of the more tender, large-flowered × *gloxinioides* types, with individual florets that are large enough to create an impression of a fairly solid spike of flowers, making it appear more substantial than many other penstemons. Each floret also has a conspicuous white eye, giving the flowering plant a distinct sparkle. It is a showy, almost flashy cultivar, more so than either 'Chester Scarlet' or 'Andenken an Friedrich Hahn' (both facing page), and is well suited to use with hot colors, bronze or purple foliage, and yellow-green or gold-variegated leaves. It fits comfortably into the second rank of a bed or border, combined with more exotic-looking plants such as cannas, cordylines, phormiums, and dark-leaved dahlias.

◑ *Canna indica* 'Purpurea', *Cordyline australis* Purpurea Group, *Dahlia* 'Bishop of Llandaff', *Diascia rigescens*, *Phormium tenax* Purpureum Group

H: 65cm (26in) S: 45cm (18in)
❋ **Mid-summer to mid-autumn**
◊◊ ▨ Z8–9 pH5–7.5

Pericallis × hybrida
CINERARA

Cineraras are tender sub-shrubs, grown from cuttings or sown as biennials, in white, pink, crimson, blue, or purple. Modern cultivars such as 'Brilliant Mixed', Jester Series, and 'Star Wars Mixed' are squat and difficult to combine well, while older clones and species usually have a looser growth habit, with greyish leaves and almost continuous flowers. The most common are 'Purple Picotee', often mistaken for *P. heritieri*, with crimson discs and magenta-tipped white ray petals, and electric violet-blue 'Webberiana'. Both grow 40cm (16in) tall and are remarkable for their brilliance. They shine in containers or at the front of a border in areas with warm summers. They go well with purple and silver foliage plants.

◑ *Helichrysum petiolare*, *Heuchera micrantha* var. *diversifolia* 'Palace Purple', *Salvia farinacea* 'Victoria', *Senecio cineraria* 'Silver Dust'

H: 15–45cm (6–18in) S: 20–40cm (8–16in)
❋ **Mid-summer to late autumn**
◊◊ ▨ Z9 pH5.5–7.5

From sowing indoors in late winter to early spring, cinerareas can be used for mid-summer to autumn display outdoors. Here, *Pericallis* 'Royalty Sky Blue' forms a striking contrast with the striped grass *Hakonechloa macra* 'Aureola'.

This is a sumptuous combination with *Perilla frutescens* var. *crispa* and *Salvia coccinea* 'Lady in Red' in mid-summer. The perilla will grow taller as the season advances and will rise over the salvia, allowing it to be used as a formal accent or filler plant.

Perilla frutescens var. crispa ♛

A tender perennial usually grown as a half-hardy annual, this perilla (also known as var. *nankinensis*) is used in flower beds as a traditional filler plant with a rich, appealing color. The frilliness of its leaves masks the form of the plant, however, and it is only at close range that their intricacy and iridescent metallic sheen can be appreciated. It is a valuable container plant, blending equally with hot and cool colors, and may also be used towards the front of a summer border.

In Japan, it is used as a herb and as a garnish. The beefsteak plant (var. *purpurascens*) has leaves that are not indented or curled, and can be used in a similar way, although not all selections have the same deep coloring and metallic quality as var. *crispa*.

◑ *Begonia semperflorens* Cocktail Series, *Dahlia* 'Bednall Beauty', *Pelargonium* Multibloom Series, *Salvia splendens* 'Vanguard', *Verbena* 'Kemerton'

H: 1m (40in) S: 30cm (12in)
❋ **(Mid-summer to mid-autumn)**
◊◊ ▨ Z8 pH5.5–7.5

Above: In a planting that would be equally effective in a hanging basket or window box, the soft lavender-blue *Petunia* (Frenzy Series) 'Frenzy Light Blue' is contrasted with sulfur-yellow *P.* 'Buttercream'. *Helichrysum petiolare* 'Limelight', which is able to drape itself gracefully over the edges of any container, adds a contrast of form.

Left: Petunias, lobelias, and pelargoniums can be combined to provide cheerful color with a variety of floral form. In this window box, the shape of *Petunia* (Ice Series) 'Scarlet Ice' is emphasized by its white edging; it is joined by other petunias in white, pink, and purple, *Pelargonium* 'Decora Rouge', and *Lobelia erinus* 'Sapphire'.

Petunia seed-raised cultivars

Tender perennials usually grown as annuals, petunias have showy, saucer- or trumpet-shaped flowers in colors including pink, red, yellow, violet, and white. Grandiflora petunias are sprawling plants with very wide, shallow flowers that are often vulnerable to rain damage. The blooms of Multiflora petunias are generally veined, and are smaller but more numerous than those of Grandifloras, as well as being more weather resistant. The many series of Multiflora cultivars include Carpet Series ♀, short, spreading plants in strong colors; Mirage Series ♀, with delicately veined blooms; and Primetime Series, in 24 colors, some with contrasting veins, picotee edges, and star-shaped centers. Frenzy Series has one of the largest color ranges, including an exceptional soft yellow, 'Frenzy Buttercup'. It is good at the front of a border, where it mixes well with smaller agapanthus, glaucous fescues, and parsley, and with many other summer bedding plants.

With their flamboyant but barely weather-proof flowers, Grandiflora cultivars are best reserved for hanging baskets, containers, and sunny sheltered corners. The Celebrity Series is compact, with a wide range of bright shades as well as pastels; Picotee Series has ruffled, white-edged blooms; and the Ice Series comprises five outstanding cultivars – 'Blue Ice', in which the ground color is deep purplish blue, 'Burgundy Ice', 'Rose Ice' with a cherry-red ground, deep purple 'Velvet Ice', and 'Scarlet Ice', whose flowers are edged in white. With this coloring, 'Scarlet Ice' is effective even when used, for example, in an all-red arrangement, combined perhaps with red or bronze foliage, pelargoniums, impatiens, and small-flowered petunias.

⬤ **Mixed:** *Helichrysum petiolare* 'Roundabout', *Perilla frutescens* var. *crispa*, *Senecio cineraria* 'Silver Dust'
Yellow: *Agapanthus* 'Lilliput', *Ageratum houstonianum* 'Old Grey' p.362 **B**, *Brachyscome iberidifolia*

H: 10–40cm (4–16in) **S: 10cm–1.2m** (4in–4ft)
❀ Early summer to mid-autumn

◊◊ ☐-☐ Z9–10 pH5–7.5

Plectranthus argentatus ♔

This tender sub-shrub, usually grown as an annual from cuttings, is valued most for its silvery grey-green, silky foliage, although it also has purplish stems and pale lilac flowers emerging from purple calyces. It is useful for a white garden, for beds and borders, and for large containers, and by the end of the season can make an imposing and well-balanced plant, especially if grown in relative isolation as an accent plant. It is excellent with silver foliage plants of contrasting form, including senecios and glaucous or white-variegated grasses, and with purple- or red-leaved plants such as perillas, red garden orach, sedums, coleus, ornamental and red or purple ornamental cabbages. Although effective with cool colors, it is perhaps most imposing combined with China asters, salvias such as *S. farinacea* cultivars, *Cosmos bipinnatus* cultivars, and pruned or seedling eucalyptus. Other good partners include taller verbenas, argyranthemums, heliotropes, brachycomes, eryngiums, and purple-leaved heucheras.

◉ *Callistephus chinensis* Milady Series, *Fuchsia* 'Thalia', *Helictotrichon sempervirens*, *Senecio cineraria* 'Silver Dust', *Solenostemon* 'Crimson Ruffles'

H & S: 1m (40in) ❀ **Mid-summer to mid-autumn**
◊◊ ▢-▨ **Z10 pH5–7.5**

In a planting that combines varied leaf textures and shapes as well as different flower colors and forms, the silvers, greys, and steely lavenders of *Plectranthus argentatus*, *Anaphalis margaritacea* var. *yedoensis*, and *Aster* 'Little Carlow' are enlivened by the brilliant, black-centered, yellow daisy-like flower heads of *Rudbeckia fulgida* var. *deamii*, with coral *Agastache* 'Firebird' and grasses in front.

Just two plants of exotic appearance, *Ricinus communis* 'Carmencita' and the Japanese banana (*Musa basjoo*), contrasting in leaf color and shape, are sufficient to suggest an almost tropical environment.

Ricinus communis 'Carmencita' ♔

This castor oil plant is a tender shrub, usually grown as an annual from cuttings, with handsome red-flushed palmate leaves and insignificant flowers that later produce showy, bright red seedpods. Although useful as a dot plant or focal point in the middle of a border, set in front of other plants of its own height, it is grown mainly for the bold impact of its foliage in tropical bedding displays. Here, it can be combined with other fine foliage plants such as bananas, palms, cannas, melianthus, wigandias, fatsias, tetrapanax, and large brugmansias. Further back in the border, it can be echoed by a larger castor bean such as *R.c.* var. *zanzibarensis*, at 2.5m (8ft), with green white-veined leaves, or *R.c.* 'Red Spire', also 2.5m (8ft), with bronze-flushed leaves and red stems; 'Impala', at 1.2m (4ft), with reddish purple leaves, is good for planting in front. Elsewhere it is effective with dark plants such as purple smoke bush and dark-flowered sunflowers, together with tithonias, cleomes, and *Nicotiana sylvestris*.

◉ *Brugmansia* × *candida* 'Grand Marnier', *Dahlia* 'Bishop of Llandaff', *Melianthus major*, *Nicotiana* 'Lime Green', *Pelargonium* 'Paul Crampel' p.394 **A**

H: 1.8m (6ft) **S: 90cm** (3ft)
❀ **Mid-summer to early autumn**
 ◊◊ ▢-▨ ■ **Z9 pH5.5–7.5**

Rudbeckia hirta

These daisies may be treated as biennials from summer sowings planted out in autumn, or as annuals from a late winter sowing indoors. There are many cultivars and mixtures, among the best of which are 'Rustic Dwarfs' 45cm (18in), in shades of gold, bronze, and mahogany including bicolors; 'Goldilocks' 40cm (16in), in golden yellow with a double row of petals; and 'Kelvedon Glory' (syn. 'Sonora'), also 40cm (16in), which is yellow with an almost black disc and yellow-veined black bases to the petals. Taller

kinds include 'Irish Eyes', about 70cm (27in), golden yellow with a green eye, and 'Aslan', 60cm (24in), which has fully double, shaggy golden yellow blooms with a green center ages chocolate-brown. They all combine well with bronze, purple, yellow-green, and gold-variegated foliage, while cultivars that are closest to pure yellow make good contrasts with pure blue. Early-flowering Charm chrysanthemums (particularly those with small yellow flowers), smaller-flowered French marigolds, yellow or cream argyranthemums, yellow-variegated grasses, and coleus cultivars are all superlative companions.

Above left: Rich golden-yellow *Rudbeckia hirta* 'Marmalade', 50cm (20in) high but here flopping forward to the front of the border, mingles and contrasts with the violet-blue variant of annual clary (*Salvia viridis*).

Above: *Rudbeckia hirta* 'Rustic Dwarfs', 45cm (18in) tall, supplies richness and varied flower size to its fellow daisies, *Bidens ferulifolia* and *Argyranthemum* 'Jamaica Primrose'.

◑ *Berberis thunbergii* f. *atropurpurea*, *Cortaderia selloana* 'Aureolineata', *Solenostemon* 'Lemon Dash', *Tagetes patula* 'Striped Marvel'

H: 30–90cm (12–36in) S: 30–45cm (12–18in)
❋ **Mid-summer to mid-autumn**
◊-◊◊ ☐-■ ■ Z3 pH5.5–7.5

Salpiglossis Royale Series

Salpiglossis flowers deserve to be planted in containers or towards the front of a border, where their unique, deeply embossed texture and intricate veining and lacing can be enjoyed at close range. They are annuals or short-lived perennials, and most resent cool, wet summers, but the Royale Series has been raised specifically to tolerate such climates. Although Royale Series mixed has shades that do not flatter each other, good combinations can be created from individual colors, such as the striking 'Royale Orange Bicolour' and 'Royale Yellow'. 'Royale Chocolate' is valuable for supplying the base note in opulent planting combinations, with its velvety blooms echoing deepest bronze foliage or acting as a foil for bright colors, hot shades, and acid yellow-green. 'Kew Blue' is also sumptuous – as rich and velvety as 'Royale Chocolate', but with deep purplish blue flowers.

◑ *Aeonium* 'Zwartkop', *Cosmos atrosanguineus*, *Dahlia* 'Bishop of Llandaff', *Perilla frutescens* var. *crispa*, *Plectranthus argentatus*, *Salvia farinacea* 'Victoria'

H: 30–45cm (12–18in) S: 23cm (9in)
❋ **Mid-summer to early autumn**
◊◊ ☐-■ ■ Z8 pH5.5–7.5

The rich mahogany, black-veined flowers of *Salpiglossis* 'Royale Chocolate' have a perfect background provided by the dusky foliage of *Heuchera* 'Stormy Seas', with its patchwork of pewter netted with bronzed green veins and its clouds of tiny whitish blooms. The piquant bright yellow-green, red-splashed leaves of the coleus *Solenostemon* 'Pineapplette' lift the combination.

Salvia coccinea 'Lady in Red' ♈

This shrubby tender perennial, usually grown as an annual, is altogether daintier and more elegant in appearance than the familiar *S. splendens* varieties that are used widely in summer bedding arrangements. Even though it is bred to be a little shorter and more prolific than other bedding salvias, its scarlet flower spikes retain an airy, open arrangement that has great impact when plants are grown in generous groups and can be seen from a distance. Its brilliant coloring mixes well with hot colors or warm shades such as coral, peach, and rich salmon, and with bronze or red foliage. It contrasts dramatically with lime green and yellow-green. Other attractive *S. coccinea* cultivars include 'Coral Nymph', a mid- and pale salmon bicolor, and the pure white 'Snow Nymph'.

◕ *Lavatera trimestris* p.384 **B**, *Nicotiana* 'Lime Green', *Pelargonium* 'Queen of Denmark', *Perilla frutescens* var. *crispa* p.395 **C**, *Salvia splendens* p.400 **C**

H: 40cm (16in) **S: 25cm** (10in)
❋ **Mid-summer to mid-autumn**

◼◼◻ ◊◊ ◻-◼ ◼ **Z8 pH5–7.5**

In a sumptuous combination for early autumn, the scarlet spikes of *Salvia coccinea* 'Lady in Red' clash gently with the purple blooms of interplanted *Verbena rigida* and, behind, skillfully staked with lilac *Aster sedifolius*.

A *Salvia coccinea* 'Lady in Red'

The vertical racemes of *Salvia farinacea* 'Victoria' emphasize the swirling lines of this semi-formal bedding, backed by *Ageratum houstonianum* 'Blue Horizon', interplanted with pale lilac *Verbena rigida* 'Polaris', and topped by a cloud of purple *V. bonariensis*. In the foreground, the gently discordant kingfisher-blue *Felicia amoena*, with its contrasting yellow centers, saves the display from blandness.

Salvia farinacea

MEALY-CUP SAGE

This slightly tender perennial is usually grown from seed as an annual. 'Victoria' ♀, once the best lavender-blue cultivar, now lacks uniformity, making it more useful as a border plant than for bedding. Other, slightly shorter cultivars, 35cm (14in) high, include 'Blue Victory' ♀ and 'Rhea', both in lavender-blue, and 'White Victory' ♀ and 'Cirrus' in white. 'Strata', 45cm (18in), is pleasantly bicolored with lavender-blue flowers emerging from white calyces. All are good in larger groups, seen from a distance, with their vertical spikes contrasted with flowers of a different shape, such as horizontal plates or airy clouds. The blue kinds combine well with mauve, lilac, purple, and silver, and contrast with pale sulfur-yellow or yellow-green.

◐ *Argyranthemum* 'Jamaica Primrose', *Brachyscome iberidifolia*, *Ipomoea tricolor* 'Mini Sky-blue' p.383 **A**, *Papaver rhoeas* (Shirley Group) 'Cedric Morris', *Pelargonium* 'Galilee', *Petunia* 'Frenzy Buttercup'

H: 45cm (18in) S: 30cm (12in)
※ **Mid-summer to mid-autumn**

 ◊◊ ▢-▢ ■ **Z8 pH5–7.5**

In this hot-colored border, *Salvia splendens* forms a vibrant foreground in front of *S. coccinea* 'Lady in Red', the lax racemes of *Alonsoa warscewiczii*, the daisy *Helenium* 'Moerheim Beauty', African marigolds (*Tagetes erecta*), dahlias, and the arching spikes of *Crocosmia* 'Lucifer'.

Salvia sclarea 'Vatican White'

The biennial clary, *S. sclarea*, is a variable species, with mauve to lavender-blue flowers (more rarely, white) and, within the flower spike, bracts that are flushed pink or lilac. 'Vatican White' has pure white florets, born on upright flowering stems like a densely branched candelabra; these create soft vertical accents, while the green calyces and flower stems produce an overall impression of pale greenish white rather than pure white, making plants highly effective in contrasts with yellow and blue. It is an excellent subject for white gardens or for weaving through an early summer border, and looks attractive with old Shrub roses or flowers of contrasting form, such as achilleas. After flowering, plants may be removed or left to self-seed.

◐ *Achillea* 'Coronation Gold', *Campanula persicifolia* 'Telham Beauty', *Delphinium* 'Alice Artindale', *Hemerocallis* 'Corky', *Iris* 'Curlew', *Papaver orientale* 'Black and White', *Rosa* 'Tuscany Superb'

H: 90cm (36in) S: 45cm (18in)
※ **Early to mid-summer**

 ◊◊ ▢-▢ ■ **Z6 pH5–7.5**

The white candelabra of *Salvia sclarea* 'Vatican White' form a backdrop for the bright blooms of an early yellow kniphofia and the contrasting blue flowers of viper's bugloss (*Echium vulgare*), in early summer.

Salvia splendens

This archetypal scarlet bedding plant, a tender perennial usually grown as a half-hardy annual, has a number of fine cultivars, including 'Red Riches' ♀, 'Red River', and 'Scarlet King' ♀, 28cm (11in) high, and 'Vanguard' ♀, 25cm (10in). All are suitable for carpet bedding, window boxes, and the front of borders. Vista Series, 28cm (11in), and Salsa Series, 25cm (10in), include lilac, purple, salmon, and white – colors that do not flatter each other, so it is best to mix separate shades as needed. These shorter cultivars work well with bold, red or bronze foliage or contrasting textures such as grasses and phormiums. 'Van-Houttei' ♀, with scarlet flowers and maroon calyces, up to 1.5m (5ft), is an elegant plant for late display, and hot color schemes or contrasts with lime green.

◐ *Abutilon* 'Savitzii', *Briza maxima*, *Canna* 'Black Knight', *Cosmos bipinnatus* 'Sonata White' p.369 **C**, *Senecio cineraria* 'Silver Dust'

H: 20–150cm (8–60in) S: 20–45cm (8–18in)
※ **Mid-summer to mid-autumn**

 ◊◊ ▢-▢ ■ **Z9 pH5–7.5**

Scaevola aemula

A tender perennial usually grown as an
annual, this fan flower is an immensely useful
and vigorous sprawling plant for containers
and hanging baskets, or the front of a border,
weaving among neighbors of comparable
vigor; it also looks impressive cascading from
a basket or retaining wall. It combines well
with silver foliage and white-variegated
plectranthus or Ivy-leaved pelargoniums,
and with flowers in pink, mauve, purple,
blue, magenta, or crimson; pale sulfur-yellow
makes a satisfying contrast. 'Blue Wonder',
perhaps the oldest cultivar, is large and
relatively late but shy-flowering. More
compact and floriferous blue kinds include
'Saphira', 'Petite Wonder', 'New Wonder',
'Blue Fandango', Blaue Fächer, and 'Sunfan'.
'White Champ' and 'Moon White' are white,
and 'Burgundi Gemini' is purple.

◉ *Diascia* 'Lilac Belle', *Leucophyta brownii, Lobelia
erinus* Cascade Series, *Lysimachia congestiflora* 'Outback
Sunset', *Osteospermum* 'White Pim', *Pelargonium* Rose
Evka, *Petunia* Million Bells Lemon, *Plectranthus forsteri*
'Marginatus', *Torenia* Pink Moon

H: 20–30cm (8–12in) S: 30–60cm (12–24in)
❀ **Early summer to mid-autumn**
△△ ■-■ ■ Z9 pH5.5–7.5

In this cool-colored carpet of plants, a compact, rich
lavender cultivar of the fan flower *Scaevola aemula* is
combined with magenta busy Lizzies (*Impatiens walleriana*
'Accent Violet') and a short *Ageratum houstonianum* cultivar,
leavened by the silvery trails of *Helichrysum petiolare*.

Smyrnium perfoliatum
PERFOLIATE ALEXANDERS

This upright biennial can be used to great
effect to echo the bright yellow-green of
many euphorbias. Because it is slim and
tolerates some shade, it may also be
successfully woven among other plants,
leaving only a small gap after dying back.
Its greenish yellow umbels are particularly
effective with contrasting blue plants such as
brunneras, larger forget-me-nots, pentaglottis,
or blue poppies, and in harmonies with pale
sulfur-yellow, apple-green, or cream flowers,

In late spring, the yellow
flowers and yellow-green
bracts of perfoliate
alexanders (*Smyrnium
perfoliatum*) mingle with
the emerging bronze-
tinged fronds of the
sensitive fern (*Onoclea
sensibilis*) to create an
intricate and pleasing
pattern. The Alexanders
turn green after flowering
and are removed, leaving
one or two plants to shed
seed for the following
year's display.

and with yellow-green spring foliage.
Dramatic combinations can be made with hot
colors such as orange and scarlet, and with
bronze leaves. Late-flowering tulips or crown
imperials, and columbines in contrasting
colors are all excellent partners. Plants can
be raised from fresh seed or left to self-seed.

◉ *Aquilegia* 'Hensol Harebell', *Brunnera macrophylla,
Euphorbia amygdaloides* var. *robbiae, Pentaglottis
sempervirens, Tulipa* 'Orange Wonder' p.352 **A**

H: 1.2m (4ft) S: 45cm (18in)
❀ **Late spring to early summer**
△△ ■-■ ■ Z6 pH5.5–7.5

Solenostemon
COLEUS, PAINTED NETTLE

Coleus are popular for their colorful foliage,
varying from yellow-green through orange to
scarlet and purple; in many the leaves are
attractively margined, veined, ruffled, or
divided. Tender sub-shrubs grown from
cuttings or as half-hardy annuals from seed,
they are shade-tolerant plants, useful for
bedding or for the front of a border (larger,
overwintered plants in the second row). Here
they combine well with French marigolds,
scarlet or soft yellow petunias, scarlet or
vermilion impatiens, or contrasting foliage
such as cannas and grasses. Among the best
cultivars are 'Crimson Ruffles' ♥, in beetroot-
red with a frilled, faint green edge; 'Glory of
Luxembourg' ♥, velvety red edged in yellow;
and gold and maroon 'Pineapple Beauty' ♥.

◉ *Canna* 'Erebus', *Impatiens walleriana* 'Impact
Scarlet', *Nerine* 'Zeal Giant' p.338 **B**, *Petunia* 'Frenzy
Buttercup', *Salpiglossis* Royale Series p.398 **C**

H & S: 30–60cm (12–24in)
❀ **(Mid-summer to mid-autumn)**
△△ ■ ■ Z10 pH5.5–7.5

Coleus (*Solenostemon scutellarioides*) form a rich tapestry
at the front of a narrow border. Feathery *Eupatorium
capillifolium* 'Elegant Feather' acts as a foil and separates the
coleus visually from the ivy (*Hedera helix* 'Buttercup') behind.

The pretty striped flowers of *Tagetes patula* 'Dwarf Harlequin' form an excellent edging to this predominantly orange-flowered border. Its companions include the larger blooms of the dwarf triploid marigold *Tagetes* 'Seven Star Red', the bronze-green foliage of *Haloragis erecta* 'Wellington Bronze', and the mixed nasturtiums *Tropaeolum majus* Alaska Series.

Tagetes patula
FRENCH MARIGOLD

This half-hardy annual varies greatly in height, and is available in a color range from lemon-yellow through gold to orange and mahogany-red; there are striped variants and picotees with blotched petals, and single, double, and anemone-centered cultivars. Most recent cultivars are dwarf, useful as carpet bedding or at the front of a border. Medium-sized varieties include 'Spanish Brocade', with double mahogany-red flowers with a gold edge, and 'Naughty Marietta', with single gold flowers and a maroon blotch; both are 30cm (12in) high. Their colors blend with hot shades, bronze or purple foliage, and yellow-green flowers and foliage and their small flowers and fine texture contrast well with grasses and bolder-leaved plants.

◐ *Aira elegantissima*, *Canna indica* 'Purpurea', *Nicotiana* 'Lime Green', *Solenostemon* 'Glory of Luxembourg', *Zinnia elegans* 'Envy'

H: 15–50cm (6–20in) S: 15–30cm (6–12in)
✳ **Early summer to mid-autumn**

 ◌◌ ▢-▢ **Z9 pH5.5–7.5**

Tagetes patula 'Striped Marvel'

Although not quite as floriferous as most modern cultivars of *T. patula*, this half-hardy annual derived from the Victorian 'Legion of Honour' grows high enough to be blended into tall planting in beds and borders. Its flowers combine particularly well with orange, vermilion, scarlet, or mahogany, with bronze or yellow-variegated foliage, and with yellow-green foliage and flowers. The foliage of cannas, coleus, and bolder grasses make effective contrasts. Among other taller French marigolds, at about 60cm (24in) high, are the Favorite Series and the Mischief Series, the latter including single-colored cultivars such as 'Mischief Gold' ♥, 'Mischief Mahogany' ♥, and 'Mischief Orange/Red' ♥. These are all excellent for larger containers.

◐ *Argyranthemum* 'Jamaica Primrose', *Rudbeckia hirta* 'Rustic Dwarfs', *Salvia splendens* 'Vanguard', *Tithonia rotundifolia* 'Sundance', *Zinnia* 'Chippendale'

H: 45cm (18in) S: 30cm (12in)
✳ **Early summer to mid-autumn**

▬▬▢▢ ◌◌ ▢-▢ **Z9 pH5.5–7.5**

The relatively tall, elegant French marigold *Tagetes patula* 'Striped Marvel' is a charming plant for close inspection and is effective in the second rank of a border. Here, it is seen behind the rich rusty red 'Cinnabar', whose dwarf growth habit makes it useful as an edging plant.

Tithonia rotundifolia 'Goldfinger' is a valuable and imposing plant for the second or third rank of a bed or border. Here, it combines easily with the taller reddish brown sunflower *Helianthus annuus* 'Velvet Queen', gently clashing mauve *Lavatera thuringiaca*, and osteospermums.

Tithonia rotundifolia
MEXICAN SUNFLOWER

Cultivars of the Mexican sunflower, a slightly tender annual, range in height from 30cm to 1.8m (1–6ft). Perhaps the most useful are the taller kinds, from 90cm (3ft) high, with intense orange flowers born stiffly above handsome foliage. These include 'Goldfinger' and the orange-vermilion 'Sundance', both 90cm (3ft) high, and the bright reddish orange 'Torch', at about 1.5m (5ft). 'Sunset', 'Aztec Gold', and 'Yellow Torch' are all yellow-flowered cultivars also growing to about 1.5m (5ft). 'Fiesta del Sol' is a dwarf cultivar, at only 30cm (12in), in rich vivid orange. All Mexican sunflowers combine well with hot colors and bronze foliage, and contrast effectively with yellow-green foliage and flowers. They can be used with scarlet lobelias, sunflowers, kniphofias, larger crocosmias, dahlias, and the taller, spikier salvias. They may also be combined with climbers such as the morning glory *Ipomoea lobata* growing on other supports nearby.

◐ *Crocosmia* 'Late Lucifer', *Haloragis erecta* 'Wellington Bronze', *Kniphofia uvaria* 'Nobilis', *Lobelia* 'Fan Scharlach', *Nicotiana* 'Lime Green'

H: 30cm–1.8m (1–6ft) S: 30–60cm (1–2ft)
✳ **Late summer to mid-autumn**

 ◌◌ ▢-▢ **Z8 pH5.5–7.5**

Tolpis barbata, here flopping gracefully across the gravel in which it has seeded itself, might seem thin-textured and insubstantial if grown alone, but it can mingle well with the foliage or flowers of another plant – as here with the golden hop (*Humulus lupulus* 'Aureus').

Tolpis barbata

The flowers of this showy, hardy annual daisy are bright lemon-yellow, set off by a dark central disc. They look very effective planted with cream, gold, orange, or mahogany, and with coleus, perillas, and similar bronze-leaved plants to echo the chocolate-brown of the flower center. Plants relate well to gold- or cream-variegated foliage, and also to the yellow-green foliage of a *Helichrysum petiolare* cultivar such as 'Limelight', especially if this is allowed to sprawl between the plants. Good contrasts include blue flowers and blue-green foliage. For best results, tolpis should be grown in a sunny position toward the front of a border (perhaps with one low-growing plant in front of it). As a native of Mediterranean regions, it thrives in well-drained sites such as gravel beds and paths.

◉ *Cerinthe major* 'Purpurascens', *Felicia amelloides* (variegated), *Molinia caerulea* 'Variegata', *Perilla frutescens* var. *crispa*, *Pilosella aurantiaca*, *Solenostemon scutellarioides* Wizard Series

H: 50cm (20in) **S: 30cm** (12in)
☼ **Early to late summer**
△△ ▢-▨ **Z8 pH5.5–7.5**

Blue *Tweedia caerulea* harmonizes perfectly with this weathered copper tub. Large plants of the tweedia are used in their second season after being raised from spring-sown seed, producing vigorous stems that can mingle with other flowers (here, the profuse daisies of *Argyranthemum* 'Petite Pink'), trail forward, or be trained to the wall behind.

Tweedia caerulea ♕

This attractive twining plant is a sub-shrub that flowers best in areas with warm summers. However, it can also be grown from seed as an annual, producing in its first year flowers of an extraordinary shade of blue, slightly greener than primary blue, but not quite turquoise. The oldest flowers assume lavender tints before they fade, creating a curious but pleasant contrast. Its height suits container planting, but it can look charming scrambling over low-growing shrubs, perhaps with a dwarf morning glory or another fairly short twining plant of contrasting floral form. This tweedia is very effective with felicias and other deeper blue flowers, and with pink, white, yellow-green, or lime green flowers, such as nicotianas, and glaucous, silver, or yellow-green foliage. It also makes an arresting contrast with pale lemon-yellow. Marguerites and pelargoniums make good companions in containers.

◉ *Argyranthemum* 'Jamaica Primrose', *Felicia bergeriana*, *Ipomoea tricolor* 'Mini Sky-blue', *Nicotiana* 'Lime Green', *Pelargonium* Rose Evka, *Thunbergia alata*

H & S: 90cm (36in)
☼ **Mid-summer to early autumn**
△△ ▢-▨ **Z9 pH5.5–7.5**

Tropaeolum majus
Alaska Series ♕

This bushy, hardy annual is usually available in a mixture of yellow, orange, mahogany, scarlet, peach, coral, and salmon, single color forms that are rarely available singly. The leaf variegation is striking at close range, but from a distance it may camouflage the distinctive leaf shape, adding an element of visual confusion. It tends to flop slightly, and so will sprawl informally over the sides of containers or edge of a border. Plants combine well with yellow-green *Helichrysum petiolare* cultivars and coleus, *Nicotiana* 'Lime Green', and some of the larger French marigolds. For greatest impact it is best with bold, contrasting foliage such as cannas, bronze castor beans, or cordylines. To flower prolifically it needs full sun and soil that is neither too rich nor too damp.

◉ *Calendula officinalis* p.367 **A**, *Cordyline australis* Purpurea Group, *Solenostemon* 'Lemon Dash', *Tagetes patula* 'Dwarf Harlequin' p.402 **A**

H: 30cm (12in) **S: 45cm** (18in)
☼ **Mid-summer to mid-autumn**
△△ ▢-▨ **Z8 pH5–7.5**

The striking variegated foliage of the nasturtium *Tropaeolum majus* Alaska Series here provides a unifying theme with the boldly striped leaves of *Iris japonica* 'Variegata'. The warm-colored nasturtium flowers grow well above the leaves.

Verbena bonariensis

This upright, wiry herbaceous perennial, with heads of tiny lavender florets emerging from reddish purple calyces, is often grown as an annual in areas where it is not hardy. Its slender habit and tall height make it a useful plant for weaving through other plants in a border or gravel garden, and its flower color blends agreeably with other cool colors, yet is strong enough to contrast with hot colors such as yellow or orange and with acid yellow-green. Plants that combine effectively include dahlias, repeat-flowering Shrub roses, taller bush roses, cosmos, cleomes, taller nicotianas, tithonias, annual sunflowers, seedling eucalyptus, larkspurs, and *Phlox paniculata* and *P. maculata* cultivars. Taller plants such as Japanese anemones, echinops, daylilies, crocosmias, and

Ceanothus × *delileanus* and *C.* × *pallidus* cultivars are also successful partners. Companions with similar small, subdivided inflorescences and close color harmonies are best avoided, since they can be visually confusing and flatter neither plant.

◐ *Cleome hassleriana* p.368 **B**, *Dahlia* 'David Howard' p.372 **A**, *Echinacea purpurea* 'Magnus' p.213 **C**, *Patrinia scabiosifolia* p.271 **C**, *Phlox paniculata* 'Orange Perfection', *Salvia farinacea* 'Victoria' p.400 **A**

H: 1.8m (6ft) S: 45cm (18in)
❀ Mid-summer to mid-autumn

◌◌ ▨-▨ Z7 pH5.5–7.5

The thin, upright habit of lavender-colored and reddish purple *Verbena bonariensis* allows it to mingle thoroughly with its neighboring plants. Here, the verbena contrasts gently with a rich red Single Waterlily Group dahlia (*D.* 'Grenadier') and a small pale peach Hybrid Tea rose (*R.* 'Mrs Oakley Fisher').

In this low, gently undulating flower bed, the magenta blooms of *Verbena* 'Kemerton' perfectly match the vertical inflorescences of purple-leaved lobelia, brightened by silvery *Plecostachys serpyllifolia* (foreground) and *Artemisia arborescens* (behind), as well as *Osteospermum* 'White Pim'.

Verbena 'Kemerton'

A good performer in damp climates and areas with cool summers, this sub-shrubby perennial, grown as an annual from cuttings, is a useful, sprawling plant for the front of a border and for containers and hanging baskets. Its rich burgundy flowers combine well with cool colors and purple foliage and contrast effectively with silver foliage, orange, soft yellow, or yellow-green. Suitable partners include annuals such as mauve or purple alyssums and impatiens, perennials like shorter orange and soft yellow crocosmias and shorter *Aster amellus* cultivars, and later bulbs including earlier colchicums, late alliums, and purple-leaved eucomis. It may also be interplanted with smaller agapanthus, cordylines, silver-leaved centaureas, and other plants of definite and contrasting form.

◐ *Agapanthus* 'Lilliput', *Crocosmia* × *crocosmiiflora* 'Lady Hamilton', *Helichrysum petiolare* 'Roundabout' p.382 **A**, *Lobularia maritima* 'Oriental Night'

H: 35cm (14in) S: 60cm (24in)
❀ Mid-summer to early autumn

 ◌◌ ▨-▨ ■ Z9 pH5.5–7.5

Verbena 'Lawrence Johnston' ♛

Unlike many verbenas, this lax, tender perennial, usually grown from overwintered cuttings, is relatively weather-resistant and tolerant of cool, damp summers. The scarlet flowers blend well with hot colors and red or bronze foliage – begonias, coleus, salvias, zinnias, scarlet pelargoniums, and red curly kales, for example – and contrast memorably with yellow-green or variegated foliage, as well as with yellow-green flowers. Especially good partners include bidens, amaranthus, coreopsis, California poppies, African daisies, gazanias, and coral or apricot diascias. It also suits the combinations suggested for *V*. 'Kemerton' (facing page), together with annuals such as ageratums, antirrhinums, brachycomes, lobelias, clarkias, nicotianas, lavateras, petunias, and orange French marigolds, as well as perennials such as penstemons and shorter cranesbills.

⊙ *Begonia semperflorens* Cocktail Series, *Brassica oleracea* (Acephala Group) 'Redbor', *Diascia barberae* 'Blackthorn Apricot', *Hakonechloa macra* 'Alboaurea'

H: 30cm (12in) **S: 60cm** (24in)
❀ **Mid-summer to early autumn**
▱▱▱▱▱ ◊◊ ▱-▰ ▰ **Z9 pH5.5–7.5**

The scarlet *Verbena* 'Lawrence Johnston', an ideal carpeting plant for the front of beds and borders, is seen here with the purplish pink flower heads of *Sedum telephium* subsp. *maximum* 'Atropurpureum' and the crimson-leaved tender perennial beefsteak plant (*Iresine herbstii* 'Brilliantissima').

The fragrant *Verbena rigida* is used here to produce bold swaths of color in a relatively low planting across a broad bed. The bright purple color of its flowers is juxtaposed with the vibrant scarlet of a dwarf cultivar of *Salvia splendens* to create a dazzling effect.

Verbena rigida ♛

Although strictly perennial, this upright verbena (syn. *V. venosa*) is usually grown as an annual. Its purple flowers are carried on wiry stems, the central ones grow stiffly upright while the outer ones force their way diagonally through neighboring plants, so that by late summer its companions are decorated with a haze of purple flower heads. This phenomenon, which Victorian gardeners called the "shot silk effect", was commonly used with pelargoniums in bright scarlet, but it is equally effective with other contrasting colors such as soft yellow, yellow-green, or orange. *V. rigida* combines well with cool colors, especially if its companions have markedly larger flower heads, and with purple or red-leaved plants and glaucous grasses.

⊙ *Festuca glauca*, *Pelargonium* 'Orangesonne', *Perilla frutescens* var. *crispa*, *Petunia* 'Frenzy Buttercup', *Salvia coccinea* 'Lady in Red' p.399 **A**

H: 50cm (20in) **S: 40cm** (16in)
❀ **Mid-summer to mid-autumn**
▱▱▱▱▱ ◊◊ ▱-▰ ▰ **Z8 pH5.5–7.5**

Verbena 'Silver Anne' ♛

This tender perennial, usually grown as an annual, makes an upright plant at first, later sprawling outwards, and has strongly fragrant flowers that open carmine-pink and become paler with age, giving an attractive two-toned effect. It is useful for weaving among other plants, especially in containers around sitting areas, where its scent can be best enjoyed, and also at the front of a border, where it can sprawl onto an adjoining path. Although not really strong enough to be used for contrasts, its color works well with purple or silver foliage and cool-colored flowers – purple-leaved sedums and heucheras, silver plants such as helichrysums and shorter artemisias, senecios, centaureas, pinks, and glaucous grasses such as fescues. Most of the combinations for *V*. 'Kemerton' (facing page) are equally suitable for 'Silver Anne'.

⊙ *Helichrysum petiolare*, *Salvia farinacea* 'Strata', *Sedum telephium* 'Arthur Branch', *Senecio cineraria* 'Silver Dust', *Silene coeli-rosa* Angel Series

H: 30cm (12in) **S: 60cm** (24in)
❀ **Mid-summer to mid-autumn**
▱▱▱▱▱ ◊◊ ▱-▰ ▰ **Z9 pH5.5–7.5**

Harmonious colors and contrasting floral form are seen in this striking combination of *Verbena* 'Silver Anne' and *Penstemon* 'Andenken an Friedrich Hahn'.

Verbena 'Sissinghurst' ♔

This tender sub-shrubby perennial, usually grown as an annual in cooler climates, has deep carmine flowers, and a sprawling growth habit that suits it to containers or the front of a border, where it can weave freely among other plants. It is really effective threading through fairly short, silver-leaved sub-shrubs. This verbena works well with silver, purple, or yellow-green foliage, and pink, lime green, yellow-green, or deep crimson flowers. Free-flowering 'Sissinghurst White' is a good companion to the deep pink form, with clear white blooms and a similar growth habit.

Several recent verbena series combine long flowering, frilly foliage, and horizontal growth, suiting them for the same uses as 'Sissinghurst'. Among them are the Tapien Series, 20cm (8in) high and spreading to 45cm (18in), which includes ivory-white, salmon-pink, rich violet, and clear pink cultivars, and the Temari Series, of similar size, in shades that include rich blue, coral-pink, lilac, scarlet, violet-purple, and white.

🌑 *Antirrhinum majus* 'Black Prince', *Leucophyta brownii*, *Osteospermum* 'Pink Whirls', *Salvia officinalis* 'Purpurascens', *Tigridia pavonia* p.341 **C**

H: 15–20cm (6–8in) **S: 90cm** (36in)
❀ **Early summer to early autumn**

◐◐ ▢-▨ ■ **Z9 pH5.5–7.5**

Right: Deep carmine *Verbena* 'Sissinghurst' and clear pink *Diascia vigilis*, seen here with the tubular-flowered *Penstemon* 'Evelyn', are both sprawling plants that can interweave and mix with each other and their neighbors to make delightful harmonies in beds, borders, or containers.

Below: Threading through the stems of the compact, grey-green leaved sub-shrub *Argyranthemum* 'Vancouver' are *Verbena* 'Sissinghurst', *Diascia vigilis*, and lavender *Nemesia caerulea*, all of which are useful plants that mingle together easily, providing an abundant display of flowers.

Viola tricolor

JOHNNY-JUMP-UP

Best grown as a biennial for late spring and early summer display, *V. tricolor* is a charming perennial with very variable flowers, usually in a combination of lavender-blue, yellow, and white. From this, several more distinct cultivars have been developed. They include *V.* 'Bowles' Black', nearly black with a tiny yellow eye; 'Helen Mount' (syn. 'Johnny Jump Up'), in lavender and yellow; 'Prince Henry', in rich purple; and 'Prince John', in golden yellow.

Although *V. tricolor* is more heat-tolerant than many hybrid violas, hot, dry summers curtail flowering, so plants behave as late spring bedding; but where summers are cool and moist, plants will flower until mid-summer and, if then cut back, again in autumn.

ⓘ *Aquilegia vulgaris* (mixed), *Erysimum* 'Bowles' Mauve', *Muscari armeniacum*, *Rosa elegantula* 'Persetosa', *Tulipa* 'Queen of Night', *T.* 'Spring Green'

H: 8–13cm (3–5in) **S: 10–15cm** (4–6in)
❀ **Mid-spring to mid-autumn**
 ◊◊ ▨-▨ ■ **Z4 pH5.5–7.5**

In a charming cottage garden mix that has no pretensions to color mixing, compact *Viola tricolor* 'Helen Mount', the pink *Dianthus deltoides* 'Leuchtfunk', and the low-growing cransbill *Geranium cinereum* 'Ballerina' fill a narrow border at the foot of a garden wall.

Zinnia elegans cultivars

Zinnias are showy half-hardy annuals that perform best in countries with warm or hot summers. They can be difficult to grow well in regions with cool summers, so in these areas they should be sown no earlier than mid-spring for planting out in late spring or early summer. Sumptuous double or dahlia-flowered kinds such as 'Dasher', 'Parasol', and 'Peppermint Stick' are perhaps the most familiar, but there are some very attractive single-flowered cultivars, including the easy-to-grow 'Chippendale', bushy plants bearing bicolored flowers in deep brownish red with a yellow margin. All suit positions in the front rows of a border, where they combine with hot colors and bronze foliage, or with yellow-green foliage and flowers. Good plants for contrast include bronze sedges, coleus, and purple beets.

ⓘ *Beta vulgaris* 'Bull's Blood', *Carex comans* (bronze), *Nicotiana* 'Lime Green', *Rudbeckia hirta* 'Marmalade', *Solenostemon scutellarioides* Wizard Series

H: 30–90cm (12–36in) **S: 15–40cm** (6–16in)
❀ **Mid-summer to mid-autumn**
 ◊◊ ▨-▨ ■ **Z8 pH5.5–7.5**

Zinnia 'Chippendale' decorates the front of a border, backed by *Z.* Giant Double Mixed, the dogwood *Cornus alba* 'Elegantissima', and the shrubby *Bupleurum fruticosum*.

The intricate blooms of *Zinnia* 'Persian Carpet Mixed' here provide richness to a warm-colored combination with the single-flowered Signet marigold *Tagetes tenuifolia* 'Lulu' and button-flowered *Lonas annua*.

Zinnia 'Persian Carpet Mixed'

This compact half-hardy annual is suitable for the front of a border or for growing behind a short carpeting plant. The mixture includes a range of colors from deep scarlet to darkest mahogany, with the petals tipped in yellow or cream. The colors are more muted than in some exuberant varieties available, and are well suited to mixing with cream, rich peach, and the richest blood-red or mahogany flowers. It makes good combinations with chrysanthemums, lime green nicotianas, and red-leaved beets, and with the contrasting foliage of coleus, perillas, dark-leaved dahlias, and grasses or sedges.

Other compact cultivars for similar use include the graceful 'Starbright Mixed', 35cm (14in), with loose and informal single blooms in clear yellows and white; and the Profusion Series, 30cm (12in), with small, shapely, white, orange, and cherry-red single blooms that have a fresh, clean appearance all season.

ⓘ *Carex buchananii*, *Chrysanthemum* Charm Group, *Dahlia* 'Bednall Beauty', *Perilla frutescens* var. *crispa*, *Rudbeckia hirta* 'Rustic Dwarfs'

H: 40cm (16in) **S: 20cm** (8in)
❀ **Mid-summer to mid-autumn**
 ◊◊ ▨-▨ ■ **Z8 pH5.5–7.5**

COMMON PLANT NAMES

The following list comprises the common plant names used in this book.

African daisy – *Arctotis*
African hemp – *Sparrmannia africana*
Algerian iris – *Iris unguicularis*
Alpine forget-me-not – *Myosotis alpestris*
American marigolds – *Tagetes erecta* cultivars
Annual clary – *Salvia viridis*
Añu – *Tropaeolum tuberosum*
Apothecary's rose – *Rosa gallica* var. *officinalis*
Apple mint – *Menta suaveolens*
Atamasco lily – *Zephyrantes atamasca*
Autumn crocus – *Colchicum autumnale*
Azalea – part of *Rhododendron*
Baby's breath – *Gypsophila paniculata*
Baby-blue-eyes – *Nemophila menziesii*
Banana – *Musa*
Bay – *Laurus*
Beech – *Fagus*
Beefsteak plant – *Iresine herbstii, Perilla frutescens* var. *purpurascens*
Beet – *Beta*
Bellflower – *Campanula*
Bergamot – *Monarda*
Bethlehem sage – *Pulmonaria saccharata*
Bigleaf goldenray – *Ligularia dentate*
Birch – *Betula*
Black locust – *Robinia pseudoacacia*
Black-eyed Susan vine – *Thunbergia alata*
Black mondo grass – *Ophiopogon planiscapus* 'Nigrescens'
Bleeding heart – *Dicentra spectabilis*
Blue fescue – *Festuca glauca*
Blue lace flower – *Trachymene coerulea*
Blue lyme grass – *Leymus arenarius*
Blue oat grass – *Helictotrichon sempervirens*
Blue wheatgrass – *Elymus hispidus*
Bluebell – *Hyacinthoides*
Borage – *Borago officinalis*
Boston ivy – *Parthenocissus tricuspidata*
Bowles' golden sedge – *Carex elata* 'Aurea'
Boxwood – *Buxus*
Bronze fennel – *Foeniculum vulgare* 'Purpureum'
Broom – *Genista*
Buddleja – *Buddleja*
Busy Lizzie – *Impatiens walleriana*
Butterfly bush – *Buddleja davidii*
Butterfly weed – *Asclepias tuberosa*
Cabbage tree – *Cordyline australis*
California poppy – *Eschscholzia californica*
Calla lily – *Zantedeschia aethiopica*
Campion – *Lychnis*
Canary creeper – *Tropaeolum peregrinum*
Candytuft – *Iberis*
Canterbury bells – *Campanula medium*
Cardoon – *Cynara cardunculus*
Carnation – *Dianthus*
Castor oil plant – *Ricinus communis*
Catmint – *Nepeta*
Cedar – *Cedrus*
Celandine – *Ranunculus ficaria*
Chamomile – *Anthemis*

Chaparral prickly pear cactus – *Opuntia oricola*
Checker lily – *Fritillaria meleagris*
Cherry plum – *Prunus cerasifera* 'Pissardii'
Chilean bellflower – *Lapageria rosea*
China aster – *Callistephus*
Chinese foxglove – *Rehmannia elata*
Chinese lantern – *Physalis alkekengi*
Chinese pink – *Dianthus chinensis*
Chinese wisteria – *Wisteria sinensis*
Chives – *Allium schoenoprasum*
Cider gum – *Eucalyptus gunnii*
Cinerarea – *Pericallis × hybrida*
Cinquefoil – *Potentilla*
Coleus – *Solenostemon*
Columbine – *Aquilegia, Aquilegia vulgaris*
Comfrey – *Symphytum*
Common boxwood – *Buxus sempervirens*
Common bugleweed – *Ajuga reptans*
Common camellia – *Camellia japonica*
Common daffodil – *Narcissus pseudonarcissus*
Common evening primrose – *Oenothera biennis*
Common fennel – *Foeniculum vulgare*
Common foxglove – *Digitalis purpurea*
Common garden peony – *Paeonia lactiflora*
Common lilac – *Syringa vulgaris*
Common primrose – *Primula vulgaris*
Common sage – *Salvia officinalis*
Common snowdrop – *Galanthus nivalis*
Common sunflower – *Helianthus annuus*
Common wallflower – *Erysimum cheiri*
Corn cockle – *Agrostemma*
Cornflower – *Centaurea cyanus*
Cow parsley – *Anthriscus sylvestris*
Cowslip – *Primula veris*
Crab apple – *Malus*
Cranberry tree – *Viburnum opulus*
Cranesbill – *Geranium, G. pratense*
Crimson glory vine – *Vitis coignetiae*
Crown imperial – *Fritillaria imperialis*
Curry plant – *Helichrysum italicum*
Cypress – *Chamaecyparis*
Cypress spurge – *Euphorbia cyparissias*
Daisy – *Xanthophthalmum segetum*
Darley Dale heath – *Erica × darleyensis*
Day lily – *Hemerocallis*
Deadnettle – *Lamium*
Dickson's elm – *Ulmus minor* 'Dicksonii'
Dill – *Anethum graveolens*
Dog's-tooth violet – *Erythronium dens-canis*
Dogwood – *Cornus*
Dutch yellow crocus – *Crocus × luteus* 'Golden Yellow'
Eastern red cedar – *Juniperus virginiana*
Eglantine rose – *Rosa eglanteria*
Elderberry – *Sambucus*
Elecampane – *Inula helenium*
Elm – *Ulmus*
English daisy – *Bellis perennis*
Eryngo – *Eryngium*
European elderberry – *Sambucus nigra*
European ivy *Hedera helix*
European spindle – *Euonymus europaeus*
European wood anemone – *Anemone nemorosa*

European yew – *Taxus baccata*
False spikenard – *Smilacina racemosa*
Fan flower – *Scaevola aemula*
Feather reed grass – *Calamagrostis × acutiflora*
February daphne – *Daphne mezereum*
Fescue – *Festuca*
Feverfew – *Tanacetum parthenium*
Five-spot – *Nemophila maculata*
Flame nasturtium – *Tropaeolum speciosum*
Flax – *Linum*
Fleabane – *Erigeron*
Flowering currant – *Ribes sanguineum*
Flowering dogwood – *Cornus florida*
Flowering quince – *Chaenomeles*
Foamflower – *Tiarella cordifolia*
French lavender – *Lavandula stoechas*
French marigold – *Tagetes patula* cultivars
Fringe cups – *Tellima grandiflora*
Fritillary – *Fritillaria*
Giant bellflower – *Campanula latifolia*
Giant dracaena – *Cordyline australis*
Giant feather grass – *Stipa gigantea*
Giant fennel – *Ferula, Ferula. communis*
Giant reed – *Arundo donax*
Giant scabious – *Cephalaria gigantea*
Giant wake robin – *Trillium chloropetalum*
Ginger lily – *Hedychium coccineum*
Globe thistle – *Echinops*
Glory flower – *Eccremocarpus scaber*
Glory rose – *Rosa* 'Gloire de Dijon'
Glory tree – *Clerodendrum bungeii*
Goat's rue – *Galega*
Goatsbeard – *Aruncus dioicus*
Gold-banded pampas grass – *Cortaderia selloana* 'Aureolineata'
Golden California privet – *Ligustrum ovalifolium* 'Aureum'
Golden chamomile – *Anthemis tinctoria*
Golden creeping Jenny – *Lysimachia nummularia* 'Aurea'
Golden creeping oregano – *Origanum vulgare* 'Aureum'
Golden feverfew – *Tanacetum parthenium* 'Aureum'
Golden garlic – *Allium moly*
Golden hop – *Humulus lupulus* 'Aureus'
Golden millet grass – *Milium effusum* 'Aureum'
Golden mock orange – *Philadelphus coronarius* 'Aureus'
Golden queen-of-the-meadow – *Filipendula ulmaria* 'Aurea'
Golden rain – *Laburnum*
Goldenrod – *Solidago*
Golden willow – *Salix alba* var. *vitellina*
Gorse – *Ulex*
Grape hyacinth – *Muscari armeniacum*
Grape vine – *Vitis*
Greater celandine – *Chelidonium majus*
Guinea-hen flower – *Buxus sempervirens* 'Suffruticosa'
Hart's tongue fern – *Asplenium scolopendrium*
Hawthorn – *Crataegus*
Hazel – *Corylus*
Heath – *Erica*

Heavenly bamboo – *Nandina domestica*
Heliotrope – *Heliotropium*
Hickory – *Carya*
Holly – *Ilex aquifolium*
Hollyhock – *Alcea*
Honey locust – *Gleditsia triacanthos*
Honeysuckle – *Lonicera*
Hoop-petticoat daffodil – *Narcissus bulbocodium*
Hop – *Humulus lupulus*
Hornbeam – *Carpinus*
Horned violet – *Viola cornuta*
Horse chestnut – *Aesculus*
Hyacinth – *Hyacinthus*
Hybrid crack willow – *Salix × rubens*
Hyssop – *Hyssopus officinalis*
Irish yew – *Taxus baccata* 'Fastigiata'
Italian woodbine – *Lonicera caprifolium*
Ivy – *Hedera*
Jack-in-the-pulpit – *Arisaema triphyllum*
Jacob's ladder – *Polemonium caeruleum*
Japanese anemone – *Anemone × hybrida*
Japanese banana – *Musa basjoo*
Japanese irises – *Iris ensata* and cultivars
Japanese maples – *Acer japonicum* and cultivars, *A. palmatum* and cultivars
Japanese shield fern – *Dryopteris erythrosora*
Jasmine – *Jasminum*
Jerusalem cherry – *Solanum pseudocapsicum*
Jerusalem cross – *Lychnis chalcedonica*
Jerusalem sage – *Phlomis fruticosa*
Johnny-jump-up – *Viola tricolor*
Juniper – *Juniperus*
Kale – *Brassica oleracea* Acephala Group
Lady fern – *Athyrium filix-femina*
Lady's mantle – *Alchemilla mollis*
Lady's smock – *Cardamine pratensis*
Lamarck serviceberry – *Amelanchier lamarckii*
Larch – *Larix*
Larkspur – *Consolida, C. ajacis*
Lavender – *Lavandula*
Lavender cotton – *Santolina chamaecyparissus*
Lawson cypress – *Chamaecyparis lawsoniana*
Lenten rose – *Helleborus hybridus*
Leopard lily – *Lilium pardalinum*
Lesser celandine – *Ranunculus ficaria*
Lilac – *Syringa*
Lily – *Lilium*
Lily-of-the-valley – *Convallaria majalis*
Lilyturf – *Liriope, Ophiogon*
Lime – *Tilia*
Live-forever – *Sedum telephium*
London pride – *Saxifraga × urbium*
Loosestrife – *Lysimachia*
Love-in-a-mist – *Nigella damascena*
Lupine – *Lupinus*
Madonna lily – *Lilium candidum*
Maiden grass – *Miscanthus sinensis* 'Gracillimus'
Maidenhair fern – *Adiantum*
Mallow – *Lavatera trimestris, Malva*
Maple – *Acer*
Marguerite – *Argyranthemum frutescens*
Marjoram – *Origanum*
Marsh marigold – *Caltha palustris*

Meadow buttercup – *Ranunculus acris*

Meadow clary – *Salvia pratensis*

Meadow rue – *Thalictrum*

Meadow saffron – *Colchicum autumnale*

Mealy-cup sage – *Salvia farinacea*

Mexican orange – *Choisya ternata*

Mexican sunflower – *Tithonia rotundifolia*

Miss Willmott's ghost – *Eryngium giganteum*

Molly the witch – *Paeonia mlokosewitschii*

Monkshood – *Aconitum napellus*

Montbretia – *Crocosmia × crocosmiiflora*

Mountain bluet – *Centaurea montana*

Mourning widow – *Geranium phaeum*

Mrs Robb's bonnet – *Euphorbia amygdaloides* var. *robbiae*

Mugo pine – *Pinus mugo*

Musk mallow – *Malva moschata*

Myrtle spurge – *Euphorbia myrsinites*

Nasturtium – *Tropaeolum majus*

New York aster – *Aster novi-belgii*

New Zealand flax – *Phormium tenax*

New Zealand hair grass – *Cortaderia richardii*

Oak – *Quercus*

Oak fern – *Gymnocarpium dryopteris*

Opium poppy – *Papaver somniferum*

Oregon grape – *Mahonia aquifolium*

Oriental poppy – *Papaver orientale*

Ornamental cabbage – *Brassica oleracea* Capitata Group

Ornamental cherry – *Prunus*

Ornamental onion – *Allium*

Orpine – *Sedum telephium*

Ostrich fern – *Matteuccia struthiopteris*

Oxeye daisy – *Leucanthemum vulgare*

Oxlip – *Primula elatior*

Painted nettle – *Solenostemon*

Palm lily – *Cordyline australis*

Pampas grass – *Cortaderia selloana*

Pansy – *Viola*

Paper white narcissus – *Narcissus papyraceus*

Paperbark maple – *Acer griseum*

Papyrus – *Cyperus papyrus*

Parsley – *Petroselinum crispum*

Pasque flower – *Pulsatilla vulgaris*

Peach-leaved bellflower – *Campanula persicifolia*

Peacock anemone – *Anemone pavonina*

Pear – *Pyrus*

Peegee hydrangea – *Hydrangea paniculata* 'Grandiflora'

Peony – *Paeonia*

Perennial candytuft – *Iberis sempervirens*

Perennial cornflower – *Centaurea montana*

Perennial pea – *Lathyrus grandiflorus*

Perfoliate Alexanders – *Smyrnium perfoliatum*

Periwinkle – *Vinca major, V. minor*

Persian ivy – *Hedera colchica*

Peruvian lily – *Alstroemeria*

Pheasant's-eye narcissus – *Narcissus poeticus* var. *recurvus*

Pimpernel – *Anagalis*

Pine – *Pinus*

Pineapple broom – *Cytisus battandieri*

Pineapple flower – *Eucomis bicolor*

Pink – *Dianthus*

Pink purslane – *Claytonia sibirica*

Plantain lily – *Hosta, H. fortunei*

Plume poppy – *Macleaya microcarpa*

Poached egg flower – *Limnanthes douglasii*

Poplar – *Populus*

Poppy – *Papaver*

Porcupine grass – *Miscanthus sinensis* 'Strictus'

Pot marigold – *Calendula officinalis*

Potato vine – *Solanum crispum*

Primrose – *Primula vulgaris*

Privet – *Ligustrum*

Prostrate speedwell – *Veronica prostrata*

Purple cone flower – *Echinacea purpurea*

Purple filbert – *Corylus maxima* 'Purpurea'

Purple sage – *Salvia officinalis* 'Purpurascens'

Purple sloe – *Prunus spinosa* 'Purpurea'

Purple toadflax – *Linaria purpurea*

Quaking grass – *Briza maxima*

Queen Anne's double daffodil – *Narcissus* 'Eystettensis'

Queen-Anne's-lace – *Daucus carota*

Red garden orach – *Atriplex hortensis* var. *rubra*

Red ginger lily – *Hedychium coccineum*

Red horned poppy – *Glaucium corniculatum*

Red hot poker – *Kniphofia*

Red osier dogwood – *Cornus stolonifera*

Red valerian – *Centranthus ruber*

Rhubarb – *Rheum*

Ribbon grass – *Phalaris arundinacea* var. *picta*

Rock cress – *Arabis*

Rock rose – *Cistus*

Rosa mundi – *Rosa gallica* 'Versicolor'

Rose – *Rosa*

Rose campion – *Lychnis coronaria*

Rosemary – *Rosmarinus, R. officinalis*

Roseroot – *Rhodiola rosea*

Round-headed leek – *Allium sphaerocephalon*

Rowan – *Sorbus aucuparia*

Rue – *Ruta*

Sage – *Salvia*

Saxifrage – *Saxifraga*

Scotch heather – *Calluna vulgaris*

Scotch rose – *Rosa pimpinellifolia*

Sea buckthorn – *Hippophae rhamnoides*

Sea holly – *Eryngium maritimum*

Sea kale – *Crambe maritima*

Sea lavender – *Limonium latifolium*

Sedge – *Carex*

Sensitive fern – *Onoclea sensibilis*

Shasta daisy – *Leucanthemum × superbum*

Shield fern – *Polystichum*

Shirley poppy – *Papaver rhoeas*

Shrubby cinquefoil – *Potentilla fruticosa*

Siberian iris – *Iris sibirica*

Siberian squill – *Scilla siberica*

Siberian wallflower – *Erysimum × allionii*

Silver willow – *Salix alba* var. *sericea*

Silverweed – *Potentilla anserina*

Singleseed juniper – *Juniperus squamata*

Small yellow foxglove – *Digitalis lutea*

Smoke bush – *Cotinus coggygria*

Snapdragon – *Antirrhinum majus*

Sneezeweed – *Helenium*

Snowball bush – *Viburnum opulus* 'Roseum'

Snowberry – *Symphoricarpos*

Snowdrop – *Galanthus*

Snowgum – *Eucalyptus pauciflora* subsp. *niphophila*

Snow-in-summer – *Cerastium tomentosum*

Soft shield fern – *Polystichum setiferum*

Solomon's seal – *Polygonatum*

Spanish bluebell – *Hyacinthoides hispanica*

Spanish broom – *Genista hispanica, Spartium junceum*

Spanish dagger – *Yucca gloriosa*

Spanish flag – *Ipomoea labata*

Speedwell – *Veronica*

Spider flower – *Cleome hassleriana*

Spotted deadnettle – *Lamium maculatum*

Spruce – *Picea*

Squirrel tail grass – *Hordeum jubatum*

Squirting cucumber – *Ecballium elaterium*

Star of Bethlehem – *Ornithogalum*

Stinking hellebore – *Helleborus foetidus*

Stinking iris – *Iris foetidissima*

Stock – *Matthiola*

Sumac – *Rhus*

Summer snowflake – *Leucojum aestivum*

Sun rose – *Helianthemum*

Swan river daisy – *Brachycome iberidifolia*

Sweet alyssum – *Lobularia maritima*

Sweet pea – *Lathyrus odoratus*

Sweet rocket – *Hesperis nationalis*

Sweet William – *Dianthus barbatus*

Sycamore – *Acer pseudoplatanus*

Tamarisk – *Tamarix*

Teasel – *Dipsacus*

Thistle – *Onopordum*

Threepenny bit rose – *Rosa elegantula* 'Persetosa'

Thrift – *Armeria*

Tibetan blue poppy – *Meconopsis betonicifolia*

Tiger flower – *Tigridia pavonia*

Tiger lily – *Lilium lancifolium*

Toadflax – *Linaria*

Toetoe grass – *Cortaderia richardii*

Tree lupine – *Lupinus arboreus*

Tree mallow – *Malva sylvestris*

Tree of heaven – *Ailanthus altissima*

Tree poppy – *Romneya*

Trumpet creeper – *Campsis radicans*

Tufted hair grass – *Deschampsia cespitosa*

Tulip – *Tulipa*

Variegated annual honesty – *Lunaria annua*

Variegated moor grass – *Molinia caerulea* 'Variegata'

Variegated tall oat grass – *Arrhenatherum elatius* subsp. *bulbosum* 'Variegatum'

Variegated yellow flag – *Iris pseudacorus* 'Variegata'

Violet – *Viola*

Viper's bugloss – *Echium vulgare*

Virginia bluebell – *Mertensia pulmonarioides*

Virginia creeper – *Parthenocissus quinquefolia*

Walnut – *Juglans*

Warminster broom – *Cytisus × praecox* 'Warminster'

Weeping blue spruce – *Picea pungens* Pendula Group

Weeping willow-leaf pear – *Pyrus salicifolia* 'Pendula'

Welsh poppy – *Meconopsis cambrica*

Whitebeam – *Sorbus aria*

White wake-robin – *Trillium grandiflorum*

Wild columbine – *Aquilegia canadensis*

Wild strawberry – *Fragaria × ananassa*

Wild sweet William – *Phlox maculata*

Willow – *Salix*

Willow gentian – *Gentiana asclepiadea*

Wine grape – *Vitis vinifera* 'Purpurea'

Winter aconite – *Eranthis hyemalis*

Winter heath – *Erica carnea*

Winter jasmine – *Jasminum nudiflorum*

Witch hazel – *Hamamelis × intermedia*

Wood cranesbill – *Geranium sylvaticum*

Wood fern – *Dryopteris affinis*

Wood forget-me-not – *Myosotis, M. sylvatica*

Wood spurge – *Euphorbia amygdaloides*

Woodbine – *Lonicera periclymenum*

Woodrush – *Luzula*

Woolly lamb's ear – *Stachys byzantina*

Wormwood – *Artemisia*

Yarrow – *Achillea*

Yellow archangel – *Lamium galeobdolon*

Yellow asphodel – *Asphodeline lutea*

Yellow foxglove – *Digitalis grandiflora*

Yellow Lady Banks rose – *Rosa banksiae* 'Lutea'

Yellow skunk cabbage – *Lysichiton americanus*

Yew – *Taxus*

Zephyr lily – *Zephyranthes* species

INDEX

All plants featured in this book are fully indexed below. Other cultivars referred to may not be listed by name, but are indexed by page number. Page numbers in **bold** indicate a main plant entry. Page numbers in *italic* indicate pictures.

A

Abelia × *grandiflora* 'Francis Mason' **28**
Abies
concolor Violacea Group 37
koreana 'Silberlocke' **28**, 35, 62
Abutilon & cultivars 24, 394, 400
pictum 'Thompsonii' 393
× *suntense* 'Jermyns' 141
vitifolium & cultivars 28, 123
var. *album* **28**, 377
Acacia
baileyana 'Purpurea' 139
dealbata 139
Acaena 248
caesiiglauca 57, 308
microphylla & cultivars 220, 262, 288, 310, 331, 346, 349, 380
saccaticupula 'Blue Haze' 262, 276, 302
Acanthus 174
mollis & cultivars 145, 178, 326
spinosus 131, **178**, 391
Acer
griseum **29**, 205
palmatum & cultivars **29**, 43, *81*, 84, 130, 243
f. *atropurpureum* 29, 49, 52, 69, 79, *81*, *82*, 85, 86, 194, 243, 280, *315*
var. *dissectum* & cultivars 29, *29*, *53*, *69*, 195, 281, 244, *244*, 268
pensylvanicum 'Erythrocladum' **30**
platanoides 'Crimson King' 141
shirasawanum 'Aureum' **30**, 91, 104, 246
Achillea & cultivars *13*, 14, *18*, *19*, 65, 66, *93*, 108, 109, 140, 149, 153, 159, 163, 169, 170, 175, 178, 184, 186, 198, 201, 208, 213, 214, 216, 217, 229, 235, *255*, 259, 266, 273, 275, 286, 326, 386, 390
clavennae 309
clypeolata *291*
'Coronation Gold' *156*, **178**, *205*, 223, *239*, *254*, 258, 282, 400
credo 111
'Fanal' 155, **178**, 232, 289
filipendulina & cultivars 179, 265
'Gold Plate' **179**, 217, *239*, 257, *258*, 266, *283*, 381, *389*
'Lachsschönheit' 73, 125, **179**, 191, 240, 272
× *lewisii* 'King Edward' 222
millefolium & cultivars 228, 327
'Cerise Queen' 99, **179**, 192, 254, 283
Aconitum & cultivars 46, 57, 58, 66, *184*, 232
× *cammarum* & cultivars 59, 65, 180
hemsleyanum 46, 66, **104**, 122
lycoctonum subsp. *vulparia* 200
napellus & cultivars 36, 44, 58, 118, 149, *164*, **180**, 183, 186, 195, 205, 218, 271, 374
Acorus
calamus 180
gramineus & cultivars 180, 308, 336
'Variegatus' **180**
Actaea
cordifolia **108**
racemosa 60
simplex & cultivars 77, 256, *266*, 303, *395*
Actinidia kolomikta **104**, 106, *110*, 119
Adiantum
aleuticum 'Japonicum' **180**, 246, 341
pedatum 306
Aeonium
arboreum 'Atropurpureum' 362
'Zwartkop' **362**, 391, 398
Agapanthus & cultivars *31*, 61, 77, *123*, *179*, 239, 357, 373, 384, 396, 404
caulescens subsp. *caulescens* 59
inapertus 76
'Loch Hope' 31, 57, 74, **181**, 205, 255, 267, 293, 314, 317, 356, 362, 382
praecox subsp. *orientalis* 356
Agastache
'Firebird' 32, 42, 140, **181**, 317, 356, *397*
rugosa 357
Ageratum houstonianum & cultivars *400*, *401*
'Old Grey' **362**, 382, 392
Agrostemma githago 392
Ailanthus altissima 247
Aira elegantissima 402
Ajania pacifica *292*, 309
Ajuga
genevensis 74
reptans & cultivars *86*, 89, **182**, 201, 210, 212, 215, 237, 246, *252*, 262, 264, *268*, 274, 276, 287, 288, 290, 292, 302, 307, 308, *309*, 310, 321, 331, *339*, 341, *346*, 380
Alcea rosea Chater's Double Group 384
Alchemilla mollis 40, *43*, *66*, *89*, *122*, 147, 153, 163, *178*, **182**, 210, 273, 283, 290, *307*, 326, 328, *365*, *394*
Allium & cultivars 15, *25*, 33, 39, *64*, *149*, *392*
aflatunense *80*, 83, *269*, 301, *329*
caeruleum *274*
carinatum subsp. *pulchellum* 77, **300**
cristophii *64*, *93*, *149*, *153*, 178, *178*, *185*, 188, 221, *225*, 230, 241, 260, 275, 284, **300**, *303*, 390
flavum 248
giganteum *269*, *365*
hollandicum & cultivars *33*, *48*, *63*, 71, 81, 87, *114*, 125, 131, 141, 146, *154*, *187*, 206, 218, 227, *290*, 300, **301**, *353*, 363, *380*, 388, 391
karataviense 285, **302**
moly & cultivars 183, 288, *292*, **302**
neapolitanum 305
nigrum 219, **303**
schoenoprasum 33, *64*, **183**, 187, 250
senescens *267*, *285*
sphaerocephalon & cultivars 183, 217, 254, 260, 300, **303**, 392
Alonsoa
warscewiczii & cultivars 42, 184, 186, 234, 254, **362**, 376, 399, *400*
Alstroemeria *209*
'Apollo' **183**, 269
aurea & cultivars *149*, *167*, **184**, 263
haemantha 184
ligtu hybrids *38*, **184**, *263*, 271, 394
psittacina **184**, 390
Amaranthus & cultivars 153
caudatus & cultivars 371, 375
Amelanchier 24
× *grandiflora* & cultivars 78, 305
laevis 79
lamarckii **31**, 43, 67, 75, 92, 95, 107, 113, 130, 256
Amicia zygomeris *387*
Ammi majus 71, 91, *163*, **363**, 369
Ampelopsis
glandulosa var. *brevipedunculata* 69
'Elegans' **105**, 130
megalophylla 141
Anagallis monellii 274
Anaphalis
margaritacea var. yedoensis *397*
triplinervis & cultivars 346, 352
Anchusa *24*, *25*
azurea & cultivars 66, 86, 87, *93*, 271, *301*, 325
Anemone *174*, 298
apennina 252, **304**, *349*
blanda & cultivars 122, **304**, 336, *341*, *346*
coronaria & cultivars 305
Saint Bridgid Group **305**
hupehensis 'Bowles' Pink' 171
× *hybrida* & cultivars 26, 39, 53, 57, 180, **185**, 192, 193, 203, 205, 218, 223, 265, 285, 300, 325, 329, *356*, 364, 372, 375
× *lipsiensis* & cultivars 18, 305, 344
nemorosa & cultivars *18*, 82, 204, 244, *247*, 277, 279, 290, **305**, 330, 340, *340*
pavonina **305**
ranunculoides 215, *313*
sylvestris 218
Anethum graveolens *189*
Angelica
archangelica *223*
gigas 51
Anisodontea capensis *325*
Anthemis & cultivars 57, 64, 186
punctata subsp. *cupaniana* 64, **185**, 218, 222, *255*, 268, 285, 306, 309, 344, 346, *347*, 379
sancti-johannis **186**
tinctoria & cultivars 64, *109*, 165, *176*, **186**, 225, 229, *255*, 257, *365*
Anthriscus sylvestris & cultivars 31, 71, 81, 83, 94, 95, *99*, 168, 187, 200, 230, 257, 283, 291, *310*, 351, 355
Antirrhinum *174*
majus & cultivars **363**, *369*, 371, 376, 382, 388, 406
Aquilegia & cultivars 50, 146, *187*, 232, *270*, 328, 345, 401
canadensis 44, 66, 81, **186**, 249, 252, 270, 273, 306
chrysantha & cultivars 139, *153*, 252, 323
formosa 44, 186
vulgaris & cultivars 71, 150, 156, 168, *183*, **187**, *201*, 223, 228, 230, 241, 249, 257, 269, 283, 301, 348, 355, 376, 391, 392, *407*
Arabis
alpina & cultivars 45, 196, 335, 336, 344
blepharophylla 'Frühlingszauber' 320, 343
Aralia
elata & cultivars 31, 69
'Aureovariegata' 28, **31**, 207, 239, 240
racemosa 247
Arctostaphylos uva-ursi 72
Arctotis × *hybridus* 'Flame' 191, 254
Arenaria montana *195*
Argyranthemum & cultivars 56, 73, 175, 364, *403*, *406*
foeniculaceum hort. **363**, 374, 379, 382, 385
gracile 'Chelsea Girl' 362
'Jamaica Primrose' 123, 181, 341, **364**, 365, 383, 388, 391, *398*, 400, 402, 403
maderense 73, 364
Arisaema
erubescens 276, **306**
triphyllum **306**
Armeria pseudarmeria 257
Aronia arbutifolia *43*
Arrhenatherum elatius subsp. *bulbosum* 'Variegatum' **188**, 205, 209
Artemisa 136, *174*
abrotanum *86*
absinthium 'Lambrook Silver' *59*
alba 'Canescens' 48, 53, **188**, 215, 227, 228, 230, 285
arborescens *157*, *339*, *404*
caucasica 48
lactiflora & cultivars *218*, *265*, 317
ludoviciana & cultivars 56, *56*, 111, 123, 124, 178, **189**, 197, 199, *231*, *239*, *250*, 260, 276, 284, 291, 352, 388, 391, 392, *394*
pontica *199*
'Powis Castle' **31**, 55, 163, *171*, 181, *196*, *219*, *267*, 283, 286, 326, *376*
schmidtiana & cultivars 64, 179, **189**, 201, 210, 222, 263, 275, 284, 302, 388
stelleriana 338
'Boughton Silver' 72, 188, **190**, 225, 300
Arum 14
creticum 218, **306**
italicum 'Marmoratum' *53*, *92*, 204, 211, *221*, 263, 290, 305, **307**, 312, 317
Aruncus
dioicus & cultivars 34, 71, 72, **191**, 193, 200, 247
Arundo
donax *59*, 381, 387
var. *versicolor* 185, **364**
Asarum
europaeum 256
shuttleworthii 191
Asclepias
curassavica 149
tuberosa **191**, 221
Asparagus densiflorus Springeri Group 124
Asphodeline lutea *51*
Asplenium scolopendrium & cultivars **191**, 195, *204*, 211, 233, 246, 338, *385*
Astelia chathamica *107*, 352
Aster & cultivars 57, 397
amellus & cultivars 53, *281*, 287, *338*. 374
divaricatus **192**, 266
ericoides 'Pink Cloud' 329
× *frikartii* & cultivars *213*, *281*, 368
'Mönch' 180, **192**, *236*, 265, 266, 285, 289
lateriflorus & cultivars *265*, 303
macrophyllus 192
novae-angliae 'Harrington's Pink' *192*
novi-belgii & cultivars 185, **193**, 203, 205, 213, 256, 281, 374, *374*
sedifolius *399*
thomsonii 'Nanus' 309, 357
turbinellus hort. 57, 256, *374*, *375*
Astilbe & cultivars *33*, 253, 356
× *arendsii* hybrids **193**, 201, 264, 266, 278, 329
chinensis & cultivars 194
var. *taquetii* 59
'Superba' **194**, 243
× *crispa* 'Perkeo' 180
'Red Sentinel' 40, 191, **194**, 247, 249, 258
Astrantia
major & cultivars 150, *180*, *186*, 194, 327
'Hadspen Blood' **194**
'Sunningdale Variegated' *56*, *93*, **195**, *210*, 212, 268, 347
maxima 159, 170, 263
Athyrium filix-femina & cultivars **195**, 313
Atriplex
halimus 108, 355
hortensis & cultivars 365
var. *rubra* 123, 153, 160, 273, 325, 363, **365**, 371, 381, 385
Aubrieta & cultivars 48, 195, **196**, *218*, 220, 308, 343, *346*
'Argenteovariegata' **195**, 220
Aucuba japonica & cultivars 34, 52, 68
Aurinia saxatilis & cultivars **196**, 220
Azalea see *Rhododendron*

B

Ballota pseudodictamnus 31, **196**, 215, 257
Baptisia australis **197**, 209, 255, 375
Begonia & cultivars *356*
semperflorens Cocktail Series 374, 382, 395, 405
Bellis perennis & cultivars *305*, 348
Berberis
× *carminea* 'Pirate King' 93
darwinii **32**, 52, 63
julianae 46
× *ottawensis* f. *purpurea* & cultivars *51*, 91, *124*, 126, 130, 235, *275*, *286*, 345, 371, 381
× *stenophylla* 'Lemon Queen' 63
temolaica 28, 108, 149
thunbergii & cultivars 28, 29, **32**, *46*, 53, *58*, 71, *73*, 86, 93, 94, 99, 107, 113, *117*, 123, 125, 144, *149*, 159, *164*, 179, *181*, *184*, 189, *193*, *194*, *216*, 218, 219, 220, 230, 243, 250, 252, 260, 270, *272*, 276, 303, *307*, 327, 346, 347, 351, 353, 355, *378*, 383, *398*
wilsoniae 29, 49, 52, 79
Bergenia & cultivars 14, 15, 43, 83, 85, 110, *110*, 175, *192*, 225, 316, 345
ciliata 47
cordifolia 'Purpurea' 45, 89, 90, 92, 96, 121, **197**, 233, 275, 279, 315, 317
'Morgenröte' 98, **198**, 285, 290
stracheyi 47
Beschornia yuccoides 356
Beta vulgaris & cultivars *371*, 375, 380, *389*, 407
Betula 24
utilis var. *jacquemontii* & cultivars **33**
Bidens ferulifolia & cultivars *19*, 186, 281, 364, **365**, 374, 385, *398*
Billardiera longiflora fructu-albo 105
Bougainvillea 102
Brachyglottis
monroi 328
'Sunshine' *43*, *54*, 63, 103, 109, *123*, 219, *254*
Brachyscome iberidifolia & cultivars 284, 362, 363, **365**, 391, 396, 400
Bracteantha bracteata 'Dargan Hill Monarch' *219*
Brassica oleracea & cultivars 53, *356*, 366, *367*, 374, 405
Acephala Group **366**
Briza maxima 57, 363, **366**, 367, 386, 392, 400
Brugmansia × *candida* 'Grand Marnier' 397
Brunnera macrophylla & cultivars 30, 42, 44, 49, *62*, 82, **198**, 199, 211, 215, 223, 244, 262, 270, 279, 287, *313*, 315, 319, 338, 343, 348, *348*, 353, 355, 378, 401
Buddleja & cultivars 55, 60, 77, 107, *109*, 111, 117, *156*, 325
alternifolia & cultivars 28, **33**, 90, 183
davidii & cultivars 33, 56, 65, 325, 375
'Dartmoor' **33**, 110, 112, 312
fallowiana & cultivars 131, 145
× *weyeriana* 79
Buphthalmum salicifolium **198**, 390
Bupleurum
fruticosum *109*, 153, *364*, *407*
rotundifolium 303
Buxus & cultivars 34, *69*, 136
sempervirens & cultivars **34**, *51*, *72*, *122*, *147*, *191*, *216*, 237, *368*
sinica var. *insularis* cultivars 34

C

Calamagrostis × *acutiflora* 'Karl Foerster' *268*, *284*
Calceolaria
angustifolia *93*, *201*
'Camden Hero' 362, **366**
Calendula officinalis & cultivars 182, 186, 366, **367**, 386, *392*, 403
Callistephus chinensis Milady Series 397
Calluna vulgaris & cultivars 25, 28, **35**, 47, 62, 74, 84, 108, 109, 110, *110*, 122, 209
Caltha
leptosepala 262
palustris & cultivars 180, **199**, 252, 262, *262*
polypetala 199
Camassia
cusickii 'Zwanenburg' 38, 254, 386
leichtlinii 36, 50, 81
'Semiplena' 86, 258, 283, **307**
quamash & cultivars 18, 84, 335
Camellia & cultivars 35, 67, 75
'Cornish Snow' **35**, 54, 96
japonica & cultivars 30, 34, **35**, 75, 78
× *williamsii* & cultivars *30*, 67, 75, 78, 96, 313, 345, 346
Campanula & cultivars 56, 199
'Burghaltii' 188, **199**, 261, 271, 327, 378
glomerata & cultivars 186, 326
'Kent Belle' 200, **200**, 247, 274
lactiflora & cultivars 33, 45, 71, 145, 149, 161, *284*, *365*
latifolia & cultivars 71, 122, 145, **200**, *255*, 263, 273
latiloba & cultivars 148, 153, *153*, *186*
pallida 200
persicifolia & cultivars *171*, 183, **200**, *284*, 287, 400
poscharskyana 75
punctata & cultivars 157, 165, 200
takesimana **201**
Campsis 102, 123
radicans & cultivars **105**, 117
Canna & cultivars *15*, 136, 149, 155, 175, 234, 238, 255, 324, 341, 356, 366, *367*, 369, *372*, 379, 384, 393, 400
'Erebus' 201, 232, 259, 356, **367**, 371, 380, 381, 386, 394, 401
indica & cultivars *179*, 191, 326, 362, 364, *370*, 387, 389, 395, 402
Cardamine
pentaphylla 313, 330
pratensis 277
trifolia 215
Carex
brunnea 85
buchananii 312, 407
comans (bronze) 57, 159, 197, 220, 270, 278, 302, 310, 334, 349, 384, 407
elata 'Aurea' 218, *243*, 267, 270, 277, 279, *385*
flagellifera *189*, 313, 336
grayi 194, 195, 222
morrowii 'Variegata' 310
muskingumensis 'Ice Fountains' 167
oshimensis 'Evergold' 40, 74, 199, 243, 249, 268
pendula 258, 259
siderosticha 'Variegata' 233, 281
testacea 153, 335
Carpentaria californica *211*
Caryopteris × *clandonensis* & cultivars *28*, 77, 93, 112, 267, 312, 365

Cassiope 'Edinburgh' 28
Catalpa bignonioides 232, 387
Catanache caerulea 145
Cautleya spicata 'Robusta' *19*, **201**, 372
Ceanothus & cultivars 37, 38, 39, *64*, 76, *94*, *98*, *102*, 105, 131, *139*, 141, 142, 307, 323, 348
arboreus & cultivars 46, 114, 139
'Cascade' **36**, 50, 63, 86, 94, 116, 122
× *delileanus* 'Gloire de Versailles' **36**, 42, 44, 60, 107, 110, 113, 117, 120, 127, 236, 383
foliosus **36**
impressus **37**, *116*
× *pallidus* & cultivars 109, 111, 113
thyrsiflorus & cultivars *39*, *379*
Celastrus orbiculatus & cultivars 49, 69, 128, 131
Celmisia
semicordata 56, 76, 131
spectabilis 227
Centaurea
cyanus & cultivars *303*, 326, 366, 367, 391, 392
hypoleuca 'John Coutts' 147
macrocephala 186, 214
montana & cultivars 149, 187, **201**, *202*, *212*, 270, 333, *347*, 391
Centranthus ruber & cultivars *45*, *141*, 143, *165*, 201, **202**, *220*, 227, 235
Cephalaria gigantea 209
Cerastium tomentosum *154*, 196
Ceratostigma
plumbaginoides 29, 93
willmottianum & cultivars 122, *280*, 288, 309, 312
Cercidiphyllum
japonicum 69
magnificum 291
Cercis canadensis 'Forest Pansy' 113, 118
Cerinthe major 'Purpurascens' 92, 210, 221, 323, *327*, 339, 347, **368**, 375, 379, 403
Chaenomeles & cultivars 32
speciosa 'Geisha Girl' 314, 352
× *superba* & cultivars 107, 113
'Knap Hill Scarlet' **37**, 350
Chaerophyllum hirsutum 'Roseum' 70, 71, 83, 95, **202**, 228, 257
Chamaecyparis
lawsoniana & cultivars 37, 96, 140
'Winston Churchill' **37**
obtusa 'Fernspray Gold' 336
thyoides 'Ericoides' 349
Chamaerops humilis & cultivars 369, 386
Chelidonium majus 204, 244
Chionodoxa
forbesii & cultivars 67, 90, 269, **308**, 311, *334*, *336*
'Pink Giant' 182, **308**, 321, *331*, 346
luciliae 308
Choisya & cultivars 42, 76
ternata & cultivars 36, **38**, 44, *89*, 99, *109*, 114, 180, 247, 260, 352, 371
Chrysanthemum cultivars 53, 157, 185, 192, 193, **203**, 205, 265, 285, 288, 328, 366, 407
segetum 'Prado' 391
yezoense 338
Chrysosplenium davidianum 336
Cirsium rivulare 'Atropurpureum' 150
Cissus rhombifolia 124
Cistus & cultivars 25, 31, 39, 64, 92
× *argenteus* 'Blushing Peggy Sammons' 65
× *argenteus* 'Silver Pink' 31, 250, 267
× *cyprius* **38**, 89, 93, 184, 225, 259
× *hybridus* 38, 54, 66, 95
monspeliensis 379
× *purpureus* **39**, 189, 196, 318, 379
× *skanbergii* 252
Cladrastis kentukea 92
Clarkia
amoena Satin Series *284*
unguiculata Royal Bouquet Series 369
Claytonia sibirica *268*
Clematis **106–19**
'Abundance' 49
'Alba Luxurians' *58*, **107**, 117, 141, 185
alpina & cultivars *38*, 106, **107**
'Columella' 107
'Frances Rivis' 74
'Propertius' 107
'Ruby' *68*, 79, *107*
subsp. *sibirica*
'Riga' 107
'White Moth' 107
'White Columbine' 107
'White Swan' 86
'Arabella' *149*
armandii *52*
'Bees' Jubilee' 28
'Bill MacKenzie' *120*
'Blekitny Aniol' 58
'Blue Bird' 113, *113*
× *bonstedtii* 106
× *cartmanii* 'Avalanche' 62
'Comtesse de Bouchaud' *106*, **108**, 111, *118*, *140*
'Duchess of Albany' 105, 144, *325*
× *durandii* 66, 71, 106, **108**, *142*, 153, 161, 254, 314
'Edward Prichard' 62
× *eriostemon* 111
'Blue Boy' **109**, 186
'Etoile Rose' **109**
'Etoile Violette' *55*, *87*, **110**, *116*, 123, 126, *243*
flammula 103, 123
'Floralia' 113
florida
var. *flore-pleno* 110
var. *sieboldii* 104, **110**
'Gravetye Beauty' *106*, **110**, *146*
'Hagley Hybrid' 109, 118, 119, *144*, *258*
'Helios' 142
heracleifolia 89, 106
'Huldine' 36, 46, *106*, 110, 118
integrifolia **111**
'Pastel Blue' 291
'Jackmanii' 103, 106, *108*, **111**, *119*, 121
'Jackmanii Superba' *106*, *111*, *118*
× *jouiniana* 'Praecox' *33*, 106, **112**, 118, *279*, 333
'Kermesina' 12, 105, **112**, *118*, 122, 125, 126, 127
'Little Nell' 119, 149
macropetala 65, 107, **113**, *125*
'Ballet Skirt' 113
'Jan Lindmark' 113
'Lagoon' 113
'Maidwell Hall' 113
'Markham's Pink' 68, 113, *113*
'Pauline' 113
'Purple Spider' 113
'Snowbird' 113
'Madame Julia Correvon' 58, 104, 113, *150*, *272*
'Margot Koster' **113**
'Minuet' 39, 117, 118
montana 106, **114–15**, 126, *131*
'Gothenburg' 31
f. *grandiflora* 63
var. *rubens* *38*, *67*, 94, 106, 114, 301
'Tetrarose' *114*
var. *wilsonii* 71, 114, *126*
'Moonlight' 37, **116**, 127
'Niobe' 127, 141
'Perle d'Azur' *65*, *106*, 110, **116**, 117, *117*, 118, *119*, 120, *131*, 144, *239*
'Polish Spirit' 110, *127*
potaninii 61
'Prince Charles' 32, 46, 58, 104, 107, 109, 113, **117**, 118, 119, *239*
'Princess Diana' 140, 160
recta 106
'Velvet Night' 160
rehderiana 49
'Rhapsody' 77
'Rosie O'Grady' 113
'Rouge Cardinal' 142
'Silver Denny' *250*
'Silver Moon' 145
Tangutica Group 106, 109
tibetana subsp. *vernayi* 'Orange Peel' 116, **117**
× *triternata* 'Rubromarginata' 106, 108, 117, 118
'Venosa Violacea' 66, **117**, 118, 124, 140, *142*, *145*
'Victoria' 110, 112, *112*, **118**, 119
'Ville de Lyon' *106*, 111, 116, **118**
viticella & cultivars 96, 106, 107, 108, 109
'Mary Rose' 96, 108, 119
'Purpurea Plena Elegans' 111, 116, 117, **119**, 149
'Viticella Rubra' 112
'White Swan' 113
Cleome hassleriana & cultivars *77*, *125*, 147, 318, 364, **368**, 369, 375, 404
Clerodendrum bungei **39**, 131
Codonopsis
grey-wilsonii 43
ovata 197
Colchicum
agrippinum 182, **309**, 312
autumnale & cultivars 256, 288, **309**
speciosum & cultivars 262, 309, 357
'Album' 93, 262, 284, **309**, 382
Colutea arborescens 93
Consolida species & cultivars **369**
ajacis & cultivars 71, 161, *363*, 369, 384, 389
orientalis 369
regalis & cultivars 369
Convallaria majalis & cultivars 191, **204**, 276
Convolvulus
althaeoides 103
cneorum 31, **39**, 48, 54, 64, 225, 233, 338, 343, 346, 377
sabatius 54, *263*, 309
tricolor 'Royal Ensign' 161
Cordyline australis & cultivars 350, *358*, 369, *394*
Purpurea Group 362, 366, 367, **369**, *370*, 371, 375, 384, 393, 395, 403
Coreopsis 178
lanceolata 'Sterntaler' **205**
verticillata & cultivars *18*, *19*, 161, 165
Cornus
alba & cultivars *18*, *19*, 35, **40**, *45*, 47, *47*, 69, 89, 141, *182*, *188*, 193, *194*, 197, *216*, *235*, 236, 253, 262, 272, 277, 282, 291, 335, 343, 353, *373*, *407*
alternifolia 'Argentea' 41
controversa 'Variegata' 14, *26*, **41**, *255*
florida & cultivars **41**, 273, 305
mas 67
sanguinea & cultivars 30, *62*, 89, *209*
sericea & cultivars **40**, 47, *47*, 90, 121
Corokia × *virgata* & cultivars 76, 142, 326
Coronilla valentina subsp. *glauca* & cultivars 123, 234, 347, 352, 383
'Variegata' **42**, 93, 122
Cortaderia
richardii *18*, *19*, 58, *93*, 205
selloana & cultivars 49, *49*, 86, *181*, *188*, 193, 203, **205**, 218, 271, *285*, 398
Corydalis
flexuosa & cultivars 76, 180, 204, **206**, 211, 212, 233, 246, 264, 269, *277*, 279, *280*, 287, 289, 306, 313, *323*
lutea 347
ochroleuca 75
solida & cultivars *75*, 83, 305, 341
Corylopsis pauciflora 52, 253
Corylus maxima 'Purpurea' *74*, 126, 150, 235, 239, 259, 274
Cosmos *174*
atrosanguineus *19*, *201*, 398
bipinnatus & cultivars 31, 79, 152, 363, 368, **369**, 372, *376*, 386, 389, 400
sulphureus 'Polidor' 164
Cotinus
coggygria & cultivars 39, 42, 49, 66, 79, *105*, *120*, 141, 159, 193, 194, 203, 205, *214*, 233, 235, 238, 263, *266*, *362*
'Royal Purple' 33, **42**, *72*, 74, 86, *95*, 109, 120, 125, 126, *126*, 139, 144, 145, 150, 184, 202, 213, 216, 227, 228, *230*, *239*, *254*, *258*, 283, 353, 363, 365, 370, 389, 391
obovatus 105
Cotoneaster 96
conspicuus 'Decorus' **43**
frigidus 'Cornubia' *33*, **43**, 79
horizontalis **43**, 182, *284*
lacteus 142
salicifolius 'Rothschildianus' 68, 128
simonsii *140*
Crambe 174
cordifolia 64, 79, *149*, *153*, *159*, 391
maritima *79*, 125, 198, **206**, 209, 292, 301, 355, 365, 366, 368, 381, 384
Crataegus
laevigata 'Rosea Flore Pleno' 98
monogyna 'Biflora' 78
Crinodendron hookerianum 75
Crocosmia & cultivars *15*, 16, *17*, 31, 44, 109, 160, *164*, 174, *184*, *194*, *259*, 370, *389*, 402
× *crocosmiiflora* & cultivars *33*, 61, *61*, 155, *155*, 157, 181, 201, **207**, 271, 272, *272*, 281, 286, 293, 404
'Lucifer' *29*, 123, 155, *165*, *178*, 179, 188, **207**, 221, *234*, *238*, 265, 266, 287, 293, *324*, *326*, *371*, 386, *400*
masoniorum 'Dixter Flame' *284*, *392*
paniculata *162*, *389*
Crocus *78*, *90*
biflorus 310
cartwrightianus 310
chrysanthus hybrids 47, 253, **310**, 332, 340
goulimyi 240, **310**
× *luteus* 'Golden Yellow' **310**
pulchellus 310
sieberi & cultivars 47, 316, 341
speciosus & cultivars 284, 310, 312, 357
tommasinianus & cultivars 89, 197, **311**, *312*, *316*, *317*, 321
vernus & cultivars 288, 310, **311**, 337
Cryptomeria japonica Elegans Group 75, 79
Cryptotaenia japonica f. *atropurpurea* 329, 347
Cyclamen 14, 298
coum & cultivars 47, 92, 191, *310*, *311*, *317*, 321, *321*, 331, 341
hederifolium & cultivars *237*, 268, 309, **312**, 321, *321*, 357
repandum *305*
Cynara cardunculus 145, 175, **208**, 214, *224*, *239*, 272, 288, 353
Cyperus papyrus *367*
Cytisus hybrid cultivars 26, 36, 37, **44**, 150, 348
battandieri 142, *209*
× *kewensis* 44, 88, 272, 305, 355
multiflorus 92
nigricans *36*, **44**, 225
× *praecox* & cultivars *24*, 38, 44, 46, 95
'Warminster' 36, 37, **44**, 71, 219, 252, 270, 318, 347

D

Daboecia cantabrica f. *alba* 62
Dahlia *15*, 136, *162*, 175, *366*, **370–5**, *400*
'Alva's Doris' 259, 367, 369, **370**, 381
'Anchorite' *371*
'Arabian Night' 207, 318, **371**, 379
'Autumn Lustre' 31
'Bednall Beauty' 164, 233, 317, 356, 362, *369*, **371**, 395, 407
'Bishop of Llandaff' 123, 178, 181, *259*, 286, 328, 362, 365, *369*, 370, **371**, 380, *389*, *390*, *394*, 395, 397, 398
'Blaisdon Red' *179*, *371*
coccinea 364
'Comet' *155*
'David Howard' *19*, 42, *93*, *201*, 314, 364, **372**, 404
'Gallery Art Deco' *317*
'Gerrie Hoek' 65, 368, **372**
'Glorie van Heemstede' 31, 223, 263, **373**
'Grenadier' 40, *259*, 287, **373**, *404*
'Hatton Castle' *317*
'Klankstad Kerkrade' 46
'Laciniata Atropurpurea' **374**
'Moonfire' 44, 76, 238, 365, 366, *369*, **374**
'Orange Nugget' *317*
'Pink Michigan' 192, 193, **374**, 375
'Preston Park' *369*
'Requiem' 197, 203, *374*, **375**
'Roxy' 341
'Tally Ho' 163
'Yelno Harmony' 362, **375**, 382
Daphne 14
bholua 'Darjeeling' 311
cneorum 'Eximia' **45**, 346
mezereum & cultivars **45**, 47, 52, 320
Darmera peltata *232*
Daucus carota 391
Delphinium & cultivars 16 17, *19*, 28, 33, 46, 65, 66, 77, 79, 103, 145, *156*, 163, 174, 175, 198, 205, 209, *224*, 250, 270, 283, *325*
'Alice Artindale' 96, 122, 179, 200, **208**, 271, 400
grandiflorum 'Blue Butterfly' 266
'Sabrina' 178, 183, 197, **209**, 250
'Sungleam' 163, 179, 208, **209**, 250, 258, 282, 389
Deschampsia cespitosa & cultivars 40, 192, 205, **209**, 225, 239, 258, 266, 280, 282, 390
Deutzia
× *elegantissima* 'Rosealind' 140
× *hybrida* 'Mont Rose' 143
longifolia & cultivars 45
'Vilmoriniae' **45**, 202, 220
scabra 124
setchuenensis var. *corymbiflora* 60
Dianthus & cultivars 38, 39, 48, 64, 73, 99, 136, 148, 154, 165, 188, 217, *228*, 229, 308, 326, 394
Allwoodii Alpinus Group 182, 189, 190, **210**, 216
barbatus & cultivars 231, 319, 346, *363*, 369, **376**, 392
chinensis, 'Princess Salmon' *233*
deltoides & cultivars *284*, *407*
gratianopolitanus 308
'Haytor White' 39, 64, 92, **210**
Diascia & cultivars *169*, 178, 309, *376*, 401
barberae
'Blackthorn Apricot' 73, 167, 169, 179, 195, **210**, 276, 405
'Ruby Field' 76, *167*, 181, 210, **211**
'Dark Eyes' 274, **376**, 382
rigescens 233, *280*, 367, **377**, 380, 388, 395
viligis *406*
Dicentra & cultivars 41, 45, 82, 199, *306*, 345, 348
eximia 93, **211**, *215*, 227, 256, 270, 279, 290
formosa 211
'Pearl Drops' 33, *206*, **211**, 221, 306, 315
peregrina 250
scandens *104*
spectabilis & cultivars 83, **212**, 220, 241, 313, 323, 343
Dictamnus albus var. *purpureus* 230, 270
Diervilla × *splendens* 335
Digitalis 14, 17
lutea 201, 208, **212**
× *mertonensis* *200*
purpurea & cultivars 51, 91, *91*, 141, 147, *147*, *154*, *159*, *165*, 376, **377**
f. *albiflora* *28*, 79, *91*, *142*, 180, 228, *264*, 272, *377*
Dimorphotheca pluvialis 380
Dipelta floribunda 99
Dipsacus fullonum 273
Dodonaea viscosa 'Purpurea' 76
Doronicum & cultivars 323, 332
Dryopteris
affinis *53*, 212, **213**, 225, 246, 262, 278, 280, 281, 313, 328
erythrosora *33*, 75, 84, *85*, *195*, 244, 305, 323
filix-mas & cultivars *211*, *356*
wallichiana 85

E

Ecballium elaterium *227*
Eccremocarpus scaber & cultivars 102, 103, 112, 117, **120**, 126, 149
Echinacea
purpurea & cultivars 192, **213**, 240, 261, 265, 273, 283, 404
tennesseensis *191*
Echinops *174*
bannaticus 'Taplow Blue' 200, **214**, 236, 282, 365, 381
ritro & cultivars 214, 289, 339
sphaerocephalus 'Arctic Glow' 165
Echium vulgare & cultivars 384, *400*
Elaeagnus 17
commutata 33, *260*
× *ebbingei* 348
'Gilt Edge' **46**, 89
pungens & cultivars 46, *335*
'Maculata' **46**, 373
'Quicksilver' 33, 36, **46**, *51*, 57, *79*, 104, *105*, 123, 124, 140, 145, 181, *265*
Elymus
hispidus 214
magellanicus 178, 182, **214**, 229
Embothrium coccineum 75
Epimedium 175, *211*
acuminatum *330*
× *perralchicum* & cultivars 313, 323, 343
× *versicolor* & cultivars 33, 72, 180, 211, **215**, 244, 247, 268, 269, 290, 292, 334, 344
× *warleyense* & cultivars 85, 306, 330
× *youngianum* & cultivars 215
'Niveum' 51, **215**, *244*, 304, 340
Eranthis & cultivars 312
hyemalis 54, 89, 197, 237, 311, **312**, 317, *317*, *331*
Eremurus robustus 28, 142, 147
Erica *110*
arborea 'Albert's Gold' 62
carnea & cultivars *28*, *40*, **47**, 62, 74, 89, 90, 96, 110, 197, *279*, 307, 308, 310, 321, 332
cinerea 'Pentreath' 110
× *darleyensis* & cultivars *35*, *40*, *45*, **47**, 54, *74*, 75, *90*, 98, *121*, 335
erigena 'Irish Dusk' 85
Erigeron & cultivars 150, **215**, 261
Erodium
glandulosum 233
pelargoniiflorum 250

trifolium **216**, 220, 250
Eryngium & cultivars *174*
alpinum & cultivars *73*, **216**, 283, 357
bourgatii 'Picos Blue' 39, 40, 214, **216**, 284, *300*
giganteum & cultivars 32, *57*, 150, 171, *199*, 210, *288*, *329*, 365, **378**, 381
maritimum **217**, 222
× *oliverianum* 145, *300*
planum 'Blaukappe' *289*, 303
× *tripartitum* 71, 77, 179, 215, **217**, 229, 280, 283, 292, *303*
variifolium *289*
Erysimum & cultivars 16, *37*, 195, *296*, 297, 335, 343, 344, 346, 347, 348, 353
× *allionii* & cultivars 157, 186, *249*, 323, *346*, 350, **378**
'Bowles' Mauve' *39*, **48**, 92, *125*, 225, 241, *260*, 315, 318, *343*, 345, 378, 407
cheiri & cultivars *18*, 29, *48*, 50, *157*, 219, *219*, *241*, 320, *343*, *345*, 348, *348*, *350*, 352, *353*, **378**
hieraciifolium 182
linifolium 'Variegatum' 196
mutabile 48
'Wenlock Beauty' **48**, 249
Erythronium & cultivars 297, 313
californicum 'White Beauty' 96, 198, 279, **313**
dens-canis 297, 313, *331*
oregonum 343
'Pagoda' 204, 237, 287, **313**, 330
revolutum & cultivars 198, 263, **313**
tuolumnense 313
Eschscholzia
caespitosa 'Sundew' 214, 365, 368
californica & cultivars 156, 163, 378, **379**, 380, 381
Eucalyptus
gunnii 158, 339, *367*, *370*, 375, 386
kybeanensis 139
pauciflora subsp. *niphophila* *67*
Eucomis
bicolor 314
comosa *260*, 314
pallidiflora **314**, 329
pole-evansii 314
Euonymus *26*, 92, *96*
alatus & cultivars 43, 48, 49, 155
var. *apterus* **49**, 92, 256
europaeus & cultivars *68*, 79
fortunei & cultivars *40*, *47*, 49, *55*, 68, 72, 74, 98, *171*, 182, *210*, 292, 317, 348
'Silver Queen' 36, **49**, 124, 197, 319, 336, 355
hamiltonianus subsp. *sieboldianus* **49**, 205
japonicus 'Ovatus Aureus' 34
Eupatorium
capillifolium 154, 164, *401*
c. 'Elegant Feather' 154, 164
purpureum 118, 218, 232, 265
subsp. *maculatum* 'Atropurpureum' 217, **218**, *285*
rugosum 'Chocolate' 153, 307, 339, 355
Euphorbia & cultivars 24, *26*, *37*, *88*, *298*, 343
amygdaloides & cultivars 29, 81, *88*, 215, 306, 312, 345, 351
var. *robbiae* 81, 83, 186, 194, 196, **218**, *228*, *306*, 401
characias & cultivars 37, 44, 46, 48, *189*, *259*, *276*, 323, 332, 347, 350, 355, 368
subsp. *wulfenii* & cultivars 36, *48*, **50**, 95, 138, 220, *260*, 272, 275, 287, 314, 319, *380*
cyparissias & cultivars *57*, *185*, **218**, *228*, 302, 352, 386
dulcis 'Chameleon' 31, 34, **219**, 303, 330, 349, *378*
griffithii & cultivars 75, 219, 277, 328, 348
'Dixter' 32, 44, 50, 73, 76, 84, 131, 139, 141, **219**, 249, 290, 378
× *martini* **51**, 99, *215*, 319, 344
myrsinites 32, 89, 92, **220**, *285*, 310, 321, *330*, 341
palustris 75, 147, *243*, *270*, 303, 318, 325
polychroma & cultivars *45*, 157, *212*, 220, 306, 341, *345*
'Major' 44, 48, *50*, 83, 195, *196*, 198, 202, **220**, 235, 249, 277, 304, *315*, 320, *320*, 353, *353*, 377, 378
rigida 56, **220**, 235, 388
schillingii 33, 36, 113, 181, 184, 194, 201, *211*, **221**, 230, 243, 246, 260, 271, 272, 280, 328, 367, 372, 385
seguieriana subsp. *niciciana* 38, 57, 73, 210, 215, **221**, 282
sikkimensis 46, 77, 139, 158, 234, *374*
Exochorda
giraldii var. *wilsonii* 31
× *macrantha* 'The Bride' 36, 44, 94, 107, 113, 305, 345
serratifolia 'Snow White' 353

F
Fagus sylvatica 141, *191*
'Purpurea Pendula' **51**
Farfugium japonicum 'Argenteum' 355
Fargesia
murielae & cultivars 28, 35, 195, *232*
nitida 58
× *Fatshedera lizei* 236
Fatsia japonica 33, 34, 35, 41, **51**, 69, *123*, 246
Felicia
amelloides & cultivars 73, 403
amoena *400*
bergeriana 403
petiolata **379**, 391
Ferula communis **221**
Festuca glauca & cultivars 39, 53, 55, 72, 75, 92, 182, 185, 210, 215, 216, 221, **222**, 225, 229, 233, 241, 243, 285, 302, 308, 310, 339, 349, 375, 384, 385, 405
Filipendula
camtschatica 194
'Kahome' **222**
rubra & cultivars *58*, 118, 154, *176*, 317, 356
ulmaria 'Aurea' 157, **223**, 227, 350
Foeniculum vulgare 118, **223**, 228, *234*, *247*, *373*
'Purpureum' *140*, 153, 178, *178*, 179, 181, 194, 223, *223*, *227*, 324, 343, 352, 355
Forsythia
× *intermedia* & cultivars *32*, **52**, 86, 289
ovata 'Tetragold' 46, 67
suspensa 'Nymans' 61
Fothergilla
gardenii *82*
major 79
Monticola Group 29, **52**, *84*
Fragaria Pink Panda 339
Fraxinus 15
angustifolia Raywood 141
excelsior 'Jaspidea' 128
Fremontodendron & cultivars 127, 142, *328*
californicum 123
Fritillaria *298*
acmopetala 315
graeca subsp. *thessala* 315
imperialis & cultivars 18, 37, 50, 73, 85, 131, 157, 198, **314**, 336, *343*, 344, 355
meleagris & cultivars 277, *277*, 297, 298, **315**, *338*, 341, *349*
messanensis 315
persica & cultivars **315**, *333*
pyrenaica 220, **315**
verticillata 85
Fuchsia & cultivars 39, 58, 309, 379, 380
'Checkerboard' 29, **53**
'Genii' 314, 366, **379**, 382
magellanica 325
var. *gracilis* & cultivars *31*, **53**, 60, 110, 120, 149, *159*, 284, *318*, 383
'Thalia' 238, 362, 367, 374, **380**, 397
'Tom Thumb' **53**, 285

G
Gaillardia 17
pulchella & cultivars 380
'Red Plume' **380**
Galactites tomentosa & cultivars 150, 301, **380**
Galanthus & cultivars 54, 68, *124*, *237*, *307*, *310*
elwesii & cultivars 35, 47, 316
var. *monostictus* 90, 122, *253*, 311, **316**
nivalis & cultivars 89, 124, 191, *197*, 236, 253, 310, 312, **317**, *321*
plicatus & cultivars 35, 45, 47, 321, 341
Galax urceolata 236
Galega
'His Majesty' 148
orientalis 150, 208
Galtonia
candicans 154, **317**
viridiflora 317
Garrya elliptica 'James Roof' 124
Gaultheria 96
mucronata *30*, 35
Gaura lindheimeri & cultivars 241, 303
Genista 24
aetnensis *18*, *19*
hispanica **54**, 88, 93
lydia 355
sagittalis *259*
tenera 'Golden Showers' 116
Gentiana asclepiadea 89, **223**, 243, 247
Geranium 14, *25*, 136, *187*, **224–31**
albanum 99, **225**, 388
'Ann Folkard' *44*, 73, *77*, *86*, 182, *186*, *190*, *209*, 217, **225**, *230*, *240*, 268, 300, 327, 352
'Brookside' 56, 161
× *cantabrigiense* 224, **225**
'Biokovo' 225
'Cambridge' 225, *225*
'Karmina' 225
'Chocolate Candy' 53, 99, 216, *226*, **227**, 228, 310
cinereum
'Ballerina' *407*
var. *subcaulescens* 'Splendens' *220*
clarkei 'Kashmir Purple' *159*, 199
'Dusky Crûg' *227*
'Emily' 170
himalayense 158, *363*
'Plenum' *218*
ibericum *224*
'Johnson's Blue' 66, 72, 87, *93*, *165*, 178, 184, *202*, 205, 212, *223*, **227**, 232, 235, 246, *249*, *256*, 264, *301*, *328*
'Kashmir Blue' *283*
kishtvariense 43
'Lydia' 159
macrorrhizum 224, 357
maderense 224
× *magnificum* *40*, *93*, *224*
nodosum *246*
× *oxonianum* 56, *211*, 223, 224, **227**, *242*, 244, *254*, 307
'A.T. Johnston' 227, 267, 283
'Claridge Druce' *42*, *70*, *71*, 227, *247*, 274
'Julie Brennan' 147
'Lace Time' 306
'Phoebe Noble' 227
'Prestbury Blush' 227, 284
'Rose Clair' 227
f. *thurstonianum* *224*, *227*, 390
'Walter's Gift' 313
'Wargrave Pink' 197, 200, 227, 235
'Winscombe' 145
palmatum 224
phaeum 147, *187*, *202*, 218, **228**, 257, 303
'Album' 44, *187*, 228
'Blue Shadow' 228
'Joan Baker' 228
'Lily Lovell' 228
'Rose Air' 153
'Pink Spice' 309
pratense 224, **228**
f. *albiflorum* 228
'Galactic' 228
Midnight Reiter strain 327, 355
'Mrs Kendall Clark' 208, *224*, 228, *228*
'Plenum Violaceum' 216, 228
subsp. *stewartianum* 'Elizabeth Yeo' 228
Victor Reiter 228
procurrens 224
psilostemon 33, *73*, *148*, 205, *224*, **228**, *318*
'Bressingham Flair' *125*, *227*, 228
pyrenaicum 'Bill Wallis' 153, *231*, 328
renardii 184, **229**, 338
'Tcschelda' 229
'Whiteknights' 229
'Zetterlund' 229
× *riversleaianum* & cultivars 43, 90, **229**
'Mavis Simpson' 94, 165, 178, 214, 229, *229*, 233, 302, *329*
'Russell Prichard' *217*, 229, *229*, *240*, 241
Rozanne 75
sanguineum
'Cedric Morris' 149
var. *striatum* 188, **230**, 272, *282*, 285
sessiliflorum subsp. *novae-zelandiae*
'Nigricans' *268*, 331
'Sirak' 150
'Sue Crûg' 199
sylvaticum 148, *187*, **230**
f. *albiflorum* 219, 230, *230*
'Album' 328
'Baker's Pink' 71
'Mayflower' 44, 225, 230, *230*
var. *wanneri* 83
tuberosum 189, **231**, 249, 250
wallichianum 'Syabru' *357*
Geum & cultivars *37*, 51, 73, *76*, 85, 186, 210, 232, *232*, 270, 306, 313, *323*, 352, *352*, *371*
chiloense 73
'Lady Stratheden' 161, 186, **232**, 264, 278
rivale 'Leonard's Variety' 213, *229*, 241, 330
Gladiolus & cultivars 297, *318*
communis subsp. *byzantinus* & cultivars 228, 254, 261, **318**
Grandiflorus Group **318**
small-flowered hybrids **318**
tristis 319
var. *concolor* **319**, 386
Glaucium
corniculatum 257, 378, 379, **381**
flavum & cultivars 381
leiocarpum 381
Glechoma hederacea 'Variegata' 336
Gleditsia triacanthos 'Sunburst' 87, *234*
Griselinia littoralis 'Dixon's Cream' 355
Gunnera
magellanica 212
manicata 14, **232**, *246*, 247, 258, 262
tinctoria 232
Gymnocarpium dryopteris **233**, 388
Gypsophila 39, *64*, 174, 176, 233, 280
elegans 'Giant White' *165*
paniculata & cultivars 125, 233, 303, 327, 384
'Compacta Plena' **233**, 284

H
Hakonechloa macra & cultivars 72, 74, 77, 171, 233, *260*, 334, 385, *395*
'Alboaurea' 163, 205, 232, **233**, 243, 259, 278, 371, 388, 405
× *Halimiocistus wintonensis* & cultivars 50, 54, 88, 93, 255, 272
Halimium 64
lasianthum *216*
ocymoides **54**, 89
Haloragis erecta 'Wellington Bronze' 309, 402, *402*
Hamamelis × *intermedia* & cultivars 24, 30, **54**, 68, 92, 96, 312
Hebe & cultivars 14, 55, *96*, 157, 169, 276, 310, 346
albicans *160*
cupressoides 93
× *franciscana* 'Variegata' 92
'Midsummer Beauty' 45, **55**, 65, 110
'Nicola's Blush' **55**
ochracea & cultivars **56**, 90, 195, 227, 352
pimeleoides 'Quicksilver' 309, 349
pinguifolia 'Pagei' 55, *182*, 190, 229, 262, 292
speciosa 'La Séduisante' 76
stenophylla **56**, 227
'Watson's Pink' **56**, 189
Hedera 102, 103
canariensis & cultivars 195, 246
'Gloire de Marengo' *53*, 79, 92, **120**, *122*, 130, 290
colchica & cultivars 34, 41, 47, 54, 79, 90, *111*, 117, **121**, 124, *127*, *128*, 139, *142*, 197
helix & cultivars *36*, 68, 98, 105, 120, **122**, 123, 124, *126*, 127, *128*, 130, 191, 223, 276, 312, 316, 317, 357, *401*
Hedychium
coccineum 'Tara' 51, 191, 201, 223, **234**, 372
densiflorum 'Assam Orange' 234
gardnerianum 356
Helenium & cultivars *15*, 155, *179*, 213, 234, *234*, *259*, *266*, 271, *283*, *381*, *400*
'Wyndley' 207, **234**, 283, 287
Helianthemum & cultivars 54, 56, **57**, 64, 92, 196, 218, *221*, 233, 252, 267, 321, *366*, 377, 378
lunulatum 88
Helianthus & cultivars 234, 235, 381, *381*
annuus & cultivars *179*, 370, 374, **381**, *402*
debilis subsp. *cucumerifolius* 'Italian White' 117
decapetalus 'Soleil d'Or' 96, **234**, 265
'Monarch' 40, 86, 93, 155, **235**, 256
salicifolius *33*
Helichrysum
italicum *34*
petiolare & cultivars *139*, *181*, 210, 292, *309*, 338, 362, 364, *376*, **382**, 389, 393, 395, 396, *396*, *401*, 404, 405
Helictotrichon sempervirens 56, 77, 201, 205, 217, 219, 221, **235**, 239, 293, 374, 378, 392, 397
Heliophila coronopifolia 266
Heliopsis helianthoides & cultivars 19, *201*, 236, *282*
'Patula' 192, **236**
Heliotropium & cultivars 17, *287*, 338
arborescens 'Princess Marina' 362, 363, 365, **382**, 393
Helleborus 17, *124*, 175, 236
argutifolius & cultivars 49, 51, 75, 82, 83, 335
atrorubens 89
× *ericsmithii* 236
foetidus & cultivars *40*, 67, 76, 83, 86, 90, 185, **236**, 237, *253*, 316, 333, 338, 340, *355*
× *hybridus* 34, *34*, 49, 51, 52, 75, 78, 82, 83, *83*, 85, 124, *182*, 215, **237**, 253, *256*, 264, 311
niger 67, 236
× *nigercors* 45, 236, 341
× *sternii* 37, 45, 48, 81, 82, 83, 85, 321
Hemerocallis & cultivars 26, 42, 44, 58, 77, 140, 153, 157, 158, 159, 164, 165, 167, 171, 174, 175, 178, 179, 188, *194*, 208, *222*, **239**, *258*, *261*, 262, *273*, 326, 356, 365, 400
fulva 272
'Flore Pleno' 207, 234, **238**, 259, 281, *324*, *326*, 373
'Golden Chimes' 65, 123, 156, 165, 186, 217, **238**, 240, 254, 260, 274, 283
'Hyperion' 116, **239**
Hepatica nobilis 313, 336
Heracleum
mantagazzianum 257
minimum 'Roseum' 345
Hesperis matronalis & cultivars 41, 71, 153, *158*, 208, 233, *253*, *271*, 283, *291*, *377*
Heuchera & cultivars 45, 47, 48, 53, 56, 73, 81, 83, 154, 171, 175, 191, 199, *201*, 212, *248*, 300, 302, 306, 310, 311, 321, 327, 332, 343, 344, 345, 346, 348, *398*
cylindrica 'Greenfinch' 225
micrantha var. *diversifolia*
Bressingham Bronze 240
'Palace Purple' *169*, *179*, 184, 186, 194, *213*, 225, 229, 231, *238*, 239, **240**, 241, 246, 249, 268, 276, 277, 317, 348, 374, *394*, 395
'Plum Pudding' 184, 201, 211, 221, 227, 228, 236, **241**, 250, 273, 274, 292, *310*, 315, 353, 378, 389
'Purple Petticoats' 347
'Rachel' **241**, *248*, 263
× *Heucherella* & cultivars 169
alba 'Rosalie' 225, **241**, 345
Hibiscus syriacus & cultivars 31, 39, **57**, 109
Hippophae rhamnoides & cultivars **58**, 95, 107, 123
Holodiscus discolor 61
Hordeum jubatum *375*, 379
Hosta 15, 17, 20, 175, **242–7**
'Aspen Gold' 243
'August Moon' 61, 110, 180, 234, **243**, 306
'Big Daddy' 77, 246
'Big Mama' 246
'Birchwood Parky's Gold' 243
'Blue Angel' 153, 246, 341
'Blue Arrow' 304
'Blue Blush' 309
'Blue Seer' 246
'Blue Umbrellas' 246
'Blue Vision' 30
'Buckshaw Blue' 43, 169, 180, **243**, 280
crispula *175*
'Fire and Ice' 335, 353
fortunei 200, **244–5**
'Albomarginata' 215, 244, *244*
var. *albopicta* 199, 244, 268
f. *aurea* 200, 244,*244*, 264, 269, 279
'Antioch' 244
'Aoki' 244
var. *aureomarginata* 66, 244, *244*, *278*
'Crowned Imperial' *81*, 244
'Francee' 202, 222, 244, *244*, 256
'Gold Standard' 213
var. *hyacinthina* 29, 244, *244*
'Spinners' *242*
'Ginko Craig' 242, 281
'Gold Edger' 243
'Golden Prayers' 243
'Golden Scepter' (*nakaiana*) 243

'Golden Tiara' 313
'Halcyon' 76, 99, 147, 168, 180, 187, 211, 221, 222, 228, *242*, **247**, 264, 266
'Honeybells' 272
'Hydon Sunset' **246**, 273
'June' 74, *218*, 355
'Krossa Regal' *30*, 167, 327
'Night Before Christmas' 338
plantaginea 242
'Shade Fanfare' 194, **246**
sieboldiana 242
var. *elegans* 81, 89, 140, 193, 221, 228, 232, *242*, 243, **246**, 247, 250, 252, 259, *328*
'Frances Williams' *242*
'Sum and Substance' 51, 60, 81, 84, 163, 181, 223, 227, **247**, 259, 324
'Sun Power' *246*
'Sunset' 246
'Tall Boy' *194*
tardiflora *233*
tokudama 'Golden Medallion' 243
'True Blue' 345
undulata
var. *albomarginata* **247**, 305
var. *erromena* 247
var. *undulata* *83*, 247
var. *univittata* *59*, 247
ventricosa 41
venusta 242
'Yellow Splash' *246*
'Zounds' 198
Humulus lupulus 'Aureus' *42*, 112, 118, **122**, 123, *126*, 130, 145, *208*, 292, *403*
Hyacinthoides & cultivars *32*, 83
hispanica & cultivars 41, *49*, 211, 223, 279, 290, **319**, 336
non-scripta 81, *83*, *84*, 94, 244, *244*, *305*, *346*, 386
Hyacinthus 17, 297, 298
orientalis & cultivars *18*, 304, **320**, 332, *332*, 334, 336, 341, 343
Hydrangea *15*, 24
anomala subsp. *petiolaris* 333
arborescens & cultivars **58**, 76, 111, *183*, 252, 263, 328, *329*
aspera & cultivars *258*, 329
Villosa Group **58**, 117, 119
macrophylla & cultivars 36, 39, 58, **59**, 60, 76, 246, 247, 267
paniculata & cultivars **59**, 329
'Grandiflora' 36, **60**, 183
'Greenspire' **60**, 389
quercifolia *36*, *175*
serrata 'Rosalba' 59, **60**, 130
Hypericum & cultivars 61
androsaemum 'Albury Purple' 159, 160, 167, 328
cerastioides 56
forrestii **61**, 207, 236
frondosum 165, 171
kouytchense *18*, *19*, *201*
Hyssop officinalis 'Roseus' 147

I
Iberis sempervirens & cultivars *45*, *88*, *196*
Ilex *96*
× *altaclerensis* & cultivars 34, 60, 95, 128
aquifolium & cultivars 30, 33, 52, **61**, *67*, 68, 93, 96, 124, 130, *140*, 348
crenata 'Golden Gem' 98, 334
verticillata 'Winter Red' 49
Impatiens walleriana & cultivars *361*, 379, **382**, *385*, 401, *401*
Indigofera amblyantha 167
Ipheion & cultivars 339
uniflorum & cultivars 47, 195, 196, 249, 331, 335, 340, 349
Ipomoea
batatas 'Blackie' 108, 338
lobata & cultivars 42, 105, 117, **123**
purpurea 119
tricolor & cultivars 66, 102, 103, *122*
'Crimson Rambler' 119, **123**
'Heavenly Blue' 31, 46, 58, 59, 71, 74, 77, 104, 112, **123**
'Mini Sky-blue' **383**, 390, 393, 400, 403
Iresine
herbstii & cultivars 338, *371*, 394, *405*
lindenii 371
Iris *124*, **248–53**, *270*, 297
'Apollo' 323
'Banbury Beauty' 168
'Blenheim Royal' 158
'Braithwaite' 228
'Cambridge Blue' 250
'Cantab' 321, 341
'Champagne Elegance' 159
chrysographes 227, 248, **249**, 262
chrysophylla 248
'Clarke Cosgrove' 250
crocea 248
'Curlew' 88, 185, 186, **249**, 378, 400
danfordiae **321**
delavayi 248
douglasiana 248
'Dreaming Spires' 169, 253
'Elixir' 153
ensata 194, 248
ensata cultivars 262, 278
foetidissima 248
'Variegata' *311*, *352*
forrestii 249
× *fulvala* 306
'George' 268, **321**
'Golden Harvest' 323
'Golden Muffin' 270
'Gordon' 321
'Grapesicle' 188, **249**, 386, 388
'H.C. van Vliet' 323
'Imperator' 323
innominata 248
'Jane Phillips' 72, 111, 154, 221, 269, 368
japonica 248
'Variegata' *403*
'Joyce' 89, **321**
'Kent Pride' *248*, 392
'Lavinia' **250**
'Lydia Jane' 250
monnieri 248
Monspur Group 250
'Nightfall' 189, *248*, **250**, 283, 384
orientalis 45, 163, 198, 248, **250–1**, 260, 277
'Pa Mist' 169
pallida 238, **252**, 305, 318
'Argentea Variegata' 182, 252, *304*
subsp. *cengialtii* 252
subsp. *pallida* 352
'Variegata' 179, 181, 221, 252, *252*, 254, 348
'Professor Blaauw' 323
pseudacorus 'Variegata' *58*, 193, *199*, 222, *246*, **252**, 258, 259, *262*
pumila subsp. *atroviolacea* 249
'Rocket' 186, **252**
'Royal Yellow' 323
'Saltwood' 157
sanguinea 248
'Shelford Giant' 250
sibirica *158*, 248, **253**
'Butter and Sugar' 158, 356
'Cambridge' 30, 45, 46, 94, 163, 186, 193,202, 223, 253, 278, 391
'Crème Chantilly' 253
'Harpswell Happiness' 216, 246, 253
'Oban' 253
'Ruffled Velvet' 253
'Shirley Pope' 253
'White Swirl' 210, 253
'Wisley White' 253
'Sierra Nevada' 250
spuria 250
'Sunny Day' 250
'Supreme Sultan' 252
'Symphony' 210, 271, **322–3**
tenax 250
tingitana 323
unguicularis *124*, *130*, 236, 248, **253**, 316
'Alba' 253
'Mary Barnard' 253, *253*
'Walter Butt' 253
'Victoria Falls' 141
'Wedgwood' *18*, **323**, *386*, 388
'White Bridge' 323
'White Excelsior' 323
'White Superior' 323
'White van Vliet' 323
'White Wedgwood' 323
xiphium 323
'Yellow Queen' 323
Isotoma axillaris 376

J
Jasminum 102, 103
beesianum 105
nudiflorum **124**, 253
officinale & cultivars 119, 138, 142, 145
× *stephanense* 104
Juncus effusus f. *spiralis* 209
Juniperus
chinensis 'Plumosa Aurea' *120*
communis 'Depressa Aurea' 56, *57*
horizontalis & cultivars 35, 74, 89, 110, 196
× *pfitzeriana* & cultivars 79, 128, *222*
recurva var. *coxii* *74*
sabina var. *tamariscifolia* 110
squamata & cultivars **62**, 93, 128, 198
virginiana 62
'Grey Owl' 40, **62**

K
Kerria japonica & cultivars 46, 116, 139, 270, 314, 330, 343, 344, 347
Kirengeshoma palmata *50*, *244*, 280
Knautia macedonica 42, *108*, 139, 146, *152*, *179*, **254**, *303*, *386*
Kniphofia & cultivars 15, 65, *77*, 123, 155, 157, 164, 185, 191, *194*, 209, 234, 238, 239, **255**, 289, 293, 356, *400*
'Atlanta' 201, 227, **254**
caulescens 234
'David' 73, 95, 178, 184, 239, **254**, 287
rooperi 160, 193, 234
uvaria 'Nobilis' 372, *389*, 402
Kolkwitzia amabilis & cultivars 71, 98, 165

L
Laburnum *25*, 131
alpinum *95*
anagyroides *37*, *95*
× *watereri* 'Vossii' 36, *37*, **63**, 94, *95*, 301
Lamium
galeobdolon & cultivars *290*, 319
maculatum & cultivars 154, 171, 200, 227, *244*, **256**, *309*, 310, 311, 320, 341
Lantana camara 'Orange Beauty' **384**
Lapageria rosea & cultivars **124**
Lathyrus
aureus 313, 347
chloranthus 165
grandiflorus 118, 160
latifolius & cultivars 59, 89, 94, 110, 118, 124
'Albus' 62, **124**
odoratus & cultivars 102, 103, 110, 112, *112*, 113, 118, **125**, 228, *381*
rotundifolius & cultivars 108, **125**, 368
sativus 66
vernus & cultivars 305, 308, 315
Lavandula 25, 103, 136, 169, 267, 326, 346
angustifolia & cultivars 54, 56, 64, *145*, 154, 165, 171, *217*, *368*
'Hidcote' *13*, 31, 55, **64**, 77, *176*, 185, 186, 190, 196, 210, 287, 390, 394
× *intermedia* & cultivars 56, *326*
lanata **64**, 124, 189, 210, 225
stoechas 39, 64. 167
subsp. *pedunculata* & cultivars 38, 55, **64**, 88, 183, 300, 318, 379
Lavatera & cultivars 26, 169
'Barnsley' 55, 58, **65**, 116, 117, *178*, 318, *372*, 391
maritima & cultivars 65, 149, 159
thuringiaca *402*
trimestris & cultivars *369*, **384**, 392, 399
Leonitis leonurus 234, 356
Leptospermum scoparium *39*
Leucanthemella serotina **256**
Leucanthemum
× *superbum* & cultivars *58*, 154
vulgare & cultivars **257**, 392
Leucojum *297*
aestivum *79*
'Gravetye Giant' 206, **323**
Leucophyta brownii *362*, 401, 406
Leucothoe & cultivars 25, 84, 312
Leuzea centauroides 154
Leycesteria formosa Golden Lantern 159
Leymus arenarius 171, *174*, 221, **257**, *267*, 352, 386
Liatris spicata 145
Libertia peregrinans *388*
Ligularia
dentata & cultivars 42, *164*, *178*, 191, 193, 239, **258**, 259, 272, 278, *307*
przewalskii 258
stenocephala & cultivars *209*, 232, **258**, 262
Ligustrum
lucidum 'Excelsum Superbum' 145
ovalifolium & cultivars *272*
'Aureum' **65**, *113*
quihoui *69*
sinense 'Variegatum' *72*
Lilium & cultivars 26, 33, 36, 42, 44, 46, 51, 58, 59, 60, *127*, 142, 200, 232, *238*, 291, 297–8
African Queen Group 238, 267, **324**
auratum 51
Bellingham Group **325**
'Black Beauty' *274*, 317, **325**
candidum 148, 201, **326**
'Connecticut King' 238, **326**
'Enchantment' **326**
henryi 167, 325
humboldtii 325
'Joy' 225, **327**, 368
lancifolium & cultivars 142
var. splendens 223, **328**
leichtlinii var. *maximowiczii* 246, **328**
martagon & cultivars 30, 41, *127*, *175*, 213, 291
pardalinum *111*, 325
parryi 325
pyrenaicum var. *pyrenaicum* 94, 227, **328**
regale & cultivars 58, 60, 281, **329**, 378
speciosum & cultivars 155, 229, 280, *314*, 325, **329**
Limnanthes douglasii 90, *248*, 249, 381, **384**, 388
Limonium latifolium *363*
Linaria purpurea & cultivars *147*, 149, *149*, *150*, *186*, *257*
Lindera
benzoin 92
obtusiloba 30, 52, 128
Linum narbonense & cultivars **259**
Liriodendron tulipifera 128
Liriope 14
muscari 309
Lithodora diffusa & cultivars *24*, *75*, *191*
Lobelia & cultivars 165, 266, *328*, 402
'Cherry Ripe' 155, 238, 258, **259**
erinus & cultivars 376, 393, *396*, 401
'Fan Orchidrosa' 362, 382, **385**
× *gerardii* 'La Fresco' 165,
'Vedrariensis' *372*
'Queen Victoria' 193, 201, **259**, 280, *367*, *370*, 371
richardsonii 191, 262, **385**, 390, 394
siphilitica 89, 221, 246
tupa 356
Lobularia maritima & cultivars *365*, 393, 404
Lonas annua *407*
Lonicera 102, 103
× *americana* *110*, 114, **126**
caprifolium & cultivars 42, 122, 123, **126**
fragrantissima 96
× *heckrottii* & cultivars 122, **126**
× *italica* & cultivars *104*, 126, 138
japonica var. *repens* 140
nitida & cultivars 147
'Baggesen's Gold' 15, *43*, *46*, **66**, 91, *93*, *108*, 117, *293*, 352
periclymenum & cultivars 72, 108, **127**, 141, 143, 144, 145, 154
× *purpusii* 35, 253
sempervirens & cultivars 51, 116
tatarica 'Hack's Red' 154
× *tellmanniana* 116, 121, **127**
tragophylla *117*, 127
Lophospermum erubescens 110, 119, 125, 393
Lotus
berthelotii 362
hirsutus *54*, 352
Luma apiculata 'Variegata' *111*
Lunaria
annua & cultivars 41, 81, *114*, 233, *249*, 323, *347*, 352
'Variegata' 283, 307, 315, *319*, 363, **386**
rediviva 142
Lupinus & cultivars 50, 150, *156*, 158, 164, 165, 167, 174, 175, 208, *224*, 250, 252, **260**, 267, 270, 271, 273, 376
arboreus & cultivars 45, **66**, 145, 158, 160, 182
Luzula sylvatica & cultivars 84, 215, 334, 335
Lychnis & cultivars 17, 260
× *arkwrightii* 'Vesuvius' 163, 184, 186, 233, **260**, 349
chalcedonica *167*, *178*, *221*, *392*
coronaria & cultivars 123, *146*, 147, *147*, *148*, *150*, 153, *199*, *213*, *215*, **261**, *318*, 369, *386*
× *haageana* & cultivars 260
Lysichiton
americanus 199, 252, **262**
camtschatcensis 262
Lysimachia
ciliata *258*
'Firecracker' 160, *164*, 259, **262**, 303, 326, 328, 355
clethroides *107*, 194, 247
congestiflora 'Outback Sunset' 375, 401
ephemerum 167
nummularia 262
'Aurea' 216, **262**, 274, *292*, 310, 362, 382
punctata 247, *270*
Lythrum *108*
salicaria & cultivars 154, 222, *266*
virgatum & cultivars 216, 249, 266

M
Macleaya
cordata 273, *319*, 381
× *kewensis* *291*
microcarpa & cultivars 184, **263**, 276, *373*
Magnolia 24, 305
grandiflora 126
kobus 75, 78
× *loebneri* & cultivars 31, 35, 67
'Leonard Messel' **67**, 345, 350
× *soulangeana* & cultivars **67**, 237
stellata 'Waterlily' 346
Mahonia 24–5, *307*
aquifolium & cultivars *61*, **67**, 236, 330, 335
japonica 54
× *media* & cultivars 46, **68**
napaulensis *52*
pinnata 69
repens 69
Malus & cultivars *49*, *68*, *96*, 98
× *atrosanguinea* 67
floribunda 78
hupehensis 31
× *zumi* 'Golden Hornet' **68**, 107, 114, 128
Malva
moschata 149, *214*
f. *alba* 159, *171*, *241*, **263**, 265
sylvestris & cultivars *207*, 254, 261, **386**, 392
Matteuccia struthiopteris *79*, 223, 243, 262, **263**, 264, 268, 277, *307*, *313*, *355*
Maurandya barclayana 76, 105, 108, 118
Meconopsis
betonicifolia & cultivars 81, 206, 212, 243, **264**, 281, 291, 377
cambrica & cultivars *270*, 323, 349
grandis 30, 49, 76, *158*, 264
integrifolia 81
napaulensis *215*
× *sheldonii* 264, 325
Melianthus major 314, 355, 364, 373, **386**, 397
Melissa officinalis 'Aurea' 319
Mentha suaveolens 'Variegata' *225*
Mertensia
simplicissima *284*
virginica 81, 204, 336
Milium effusum 'Aureum' 49, 67, 81, 82, 195, 212, 215, 230, 233, *237*, 243, **264**, 277, 279, 306, 313, 340, 345, 355
Mimulus
aurantiacus & cultivars 194, 259, *366*
cardinalis 186, 280
Miscanthus 175
sacchariflorus 232, 247, 391
sinensis & cultivars 30, 31, 36, 40, 43, 44, 46, 49, 58, 59, 61, 65, 66, 69, 74, 79, 84, 145, 153, 155, 160, 163, 167, 180, *185*, 192, 193, 202, 213, 214, 216, 217, 221, 228, 234, 239, 246, *263*, **265**, *291*, 318, 353, 366, *370*, 373, 384
'Variegatus' 181, 221, 228, **265**, *280*, 386, 391, 394
Molinia caerulea 'Variegata' 35, 216, 225, 259, **266**, 278, 281, 403
Monarda & cultivars *20*, *116*, 147, 157, 171, 178, 213, 221, 249
'Adam' 207, **266**
'Beauty of Cobham' 59, 112, **266**, 280
Moricandia moricandioides 249, 345
Morus alba 'Pendula' **69**
Musa *15*, 387
acuminata 387
basjoo & cultivars 51, 364, **387**, *397*
velutina 387
Muscari 17, *297*, *298*
armeniacum & cultivars *18*, 49, *67*, 196, 262, 304, 305, *305*, 315, **330**, 335, 339, *339*, *349*, 378, 407
azureum 330
botryoides & cultivars 330, 335
latifolium 86, 89, 220, 268, 313, **330**, 380
neglectum 330
Mutisia oligodon 119
Myosotis *114*, *296*, 297, 298, *298*

alpestris 185, *319*, *335*, *336*, *343*, *350*, 352, 353, *378*
sylvatica & cultivars *18*, 81, 96, *189*, 210, 215, 223, *225*, *233*, 244, 246, *249*, 262, *275*, *279*, *288*, 289, 290, 292, *301*, 313, 320, *323*, *330*, *334*, *345*, *346*, **388**

N
Nandina domestica & cultivars 29, 43, 51, **69**, 356
Narcissus & cultivars 28, 31, 32, 35, *35*, 37, 42, 45, 47, *48*, 49, 52, 67, 75, 78, 82, 83, 85, 86, 90, 96, 163, 237, *290*, *298*, 315, *330*, 332, 334, 335, 336, 343, 344, 345, *346*, 349, 355, *355*, 380
'Actaea' 33, 89, 196, 262, 290, **330**, 343, 386, 388
bulbocodium & cultivars 195, 308, **331**
cyclamineus 332, 333
'Eystettensis' *18*, 310, **332**
'February Gold' 320, **332**
'February Silver' **333**
'Geranium' 85, 308, **334**
'Hawera' *18*, 48, *71*, 196, 198, 290, 306, **334**, 388
'Jack Snipe' **335**, 340
'Jetfire' 320, **335**
jonquilla 334, 336
obvallaris 336
poeticus & cultivars 44, 330, 335
var. *recurvus* 31, 95, 305, **335**, 388
pseudonarcissus **336**
rupicola 336
'Spellbinder' 319, **336**
'Sun Disc' 277, **336**
'Tête-à-tête' *47*, *237*, 279, 307, 310, **337**, *341*
triandrus 334
Nectaroscordum siculum *158*
Neillia thibetica **70**
Nemesia & cultivars *362*
caerulea *406*
'Innocence' 286, **388**
strumosa 'Blue Gem' 384
Nemophila
maculata *388*
menziesii & cultivars 188, 266, 292, **388**, 391
Nepeta
× *faassenii* & cultivars 77, 88, 92, 199, 229, 284, 285
govaniana 160, **267**
grandiflora 'Dawn to Dusk' 154
sibirica & cultivars 31, *108*, 111, 272
'Six Hills Giant' 72, 89, 152, *163*, 171, 200, 221, 255, 257, *260*, **267**, 326, 390
Nerine 298
bowdenii & cultivars 53, 284, 309, 312, **338**
undulata 357
'Zeal Giant' 53, **338**, 401
Nicotiana *15*, *361*, *371*
Domino Series 53, 231, 282, 362, 371, 375, **389**
'Lime Green' 44, 59, 73, 76, 123, 163, *184*, 362, 364, 365, 369, 371, 380, 384, 385, 386, 389, *389*, **390**, 394, *394*, 397, 399, 402, 403, 407
langsdorffii & cultivars *60*, 164, 169, 281, 317, 329, 370, 373, 380, **389**, 390, 393
sylvestris 151, *389*, 390
Nigella damascena & cultivars 39, 66, *148*, *150*, 156, 163, *169*, 188, *227*, 266, 280, 284, *300*, 326, 339, 364, 366, 367, 384, **390**, 392
Nonea lutea 320, 323, 334, 349
Nosta plantaginea 58

O
Oenothera
biennis *19*, *284*, **390**
fruticosa 'Fyrverkeri' 329
glazioviana 390
speciosa 'Siskiyou' **267**
stricta & cultivars 390
Olearia × *haastii* 93
Omphalodes
cappadocica & cultivars 45, 49, 74, 75, 211, 223, 244, *263*, **268**, 277, 279, 289, 290, 304, 313, 334, 351
verna 338
Onoclea sensibilis *401*
Onopordum nervosum 28, 79, *144*, 155, 178, 208, 214, 221, *372*, 389, **391**
Ophiopogon
jaburan 'Vittatus' 336
planiscapus 'Nigrescens' *29*, 76, 188, 214, 227, **268**, 308, *312*, *321*, 339
Opuntia oricola *205*, *379*
Origanum & cultivars 267
laevigatum 'Herrenhausen' 309
vulgare 'Aureum' 182, 183, 190, *195*, *225*, **268**
Orlaya grandiflora *163*, **391**
Ornithogalum
narbonense 339
nutans 45, 233, 315, **338**, 355
pyramidale **339**
Osmanthus
delavayi 35, 259
heterophyllus 'Purpureus' 325, 339
Osmunda regalis 262
Osteospermum & cultivars *292*, *365*, *366*, 379, *383*, *388*, 391, *402*, 406
'White Pim' 362, 374, 380, **391**, 401, *404*
Ozothamnus ledifolius *26*, 93

P
Pachysandra terminalis 196
Paeonia 26, 103
delavayi 75, *116*, 141
emodi **269**
lactiflora & cultivars 66, 71, 124, 142, 186, 250, 260, 267, **269**, *270*, 283, *308*, 333, 349, 363
'August Dessert' **270**
mlokosewitschii *157*, 249, **270**, 353
officinalis 391
rockii 141
Papaver
commutatum 'Ladybird' *284*
'Fireball' **270**
nudicaule 323
orientale & cultivars 66, 71, *199*, 208, 210, 228, 260, 269, **271**, 287, 317, *323*, 391, 400
rhoeas & cultivars *147*, 254, 366, 367, **392**, 400
somniferum & cultivars *167*, *249*, *376*, 379, 381, **392**
Parthenocissus
henryana 121, **128**, 131, 144
himalayana var. *rubrifolia* 92
quinquefolia *62*, 120, 121, 122, **128–9**, 141
tricuspidata & cultivars 43, 61, 120, 122, 123, **128**
Passiflora caerulea 110
Patrinia
scabiosifolia **271**, 404
triloba var. *palmata* 281
Paulownia tomentosa 247
Pelargonium & cultivars *274*, 338, 369, 379, 380, *389*, 393, *393*, *396*, 399, 400, 401, 403, 405
'Hederinum' 382, **393**
Multibloom Series **393**, 395
'Paul Crampel' 240, 362, 363, 371, 375, 390, **394**, 397
Pennisetum
setaceum 'Rubrum' 53
villosum 369
Penstemon & cultivars 55, 56, 152, 171, 175, 211, *211*, *252*, *318*, *406*
'Andenken an Friedrich Hahn' *155*, *184*, 275, **394**, *405*
barbatus 149
'Chester Scarlet' 182, 189, 390, **394**
digitalis 'Husker Red' 309, 346
'King George V' 318, **395**
Pentaglottis sempervirens 353, 401
Pericallis
heritieri 395
× *hybrida* & cultivars 388, **395**
Perilla frutescens var. *crispa* 366, 375, 389, 394, **395**, 396, 398, 399, 403, 405, 407
Perovskia & cultivars 55, 60, 77, *174*, 190, *200*, 267, 285, 364
Persicaria *20*
amplexicaulis & cultivars 153, 207, *213*, **272**, 280
bistorta & cultivars 143, 150
microcephala 'Red Dragon' 164, 169
virginiana Compton's form 159
Petunia & cultivars 73, 309, *362*, 363, 365, 366, 376, 377, 379, 382, 385, 393, **396**, 400, 401, 405
Phalaris arundinacea var. *picta* & cultivars *208*, 216, 222, 272, *344*
'Picta' 32, **272**
Philadelphus & cultivars 24, *25*, 43, 141, 145
'Beauclerk' **71**, 227
'Belle Etoile' 33, 70, **71**, *143*, 231
coronarius & cultivars 99, 142, *250*
'Aureus' 24, 31, *32*, *41*, *44*, **71**, 107, 108, 113, 123, 126, 127, 178, 209, 216, 246, *279*, *301*, 314
intectus & cultivars **72**, 140, 191, 318
Phillyrea latifolia **72**
Phlomis
chrysophylla 50, 54, 64
fruticosa 54, **72**, 92, 196, 227, 252, 259, *267*, 328
italica 72
purpurea 318
russeliana 65, **272**
Phlox *174*, 175, *361*
divaricata 41, *41*, *186*, *278*
subsp. *laphamii* 'Chattahoochee' *246*, **273**, *289*
maculata & cultivars 58, 159, *213*, **273**
paniculata & cultivars *58*, *123*, 142, 150, 152, *266*, 274, *318*, 325, 372, *392*, 404
'Norah Leigh' *77*, **274**, 353
Phormium & cultivars 76, 160, *169*, 216, 341, 356, *391*
'Bronze Baby' 194, 216, 232, 260, **274**, 293, 318, 339, 350, 393
cookianum subsp. *hookeri* 'Tricolor' *69*
'Duet' 239, **274**, 289
tenax & cultivars 51, *51*, *99*, 122, *207*, 274, 275, *280*, 395
tenax 'Veitchianum' 122, 221, **275**, *394*
Photinia
beauverdiana 79
× *fraseri* & cultivars **73**, 84, 99, 138, 219, *344*
Phuopsis stylosa 149
Phygelius
aequalis & cultivars 56, 144, *254*, 325
'Yellow Trumpet' **73**, 211, 228, 238, 357, 363
capensis 155
× *rectus* & cultivars 32, **73**, 142, 149, 160, 184, 210, 216, 234, 274, 276, 293, 318, 326, 328, 356, 394
Phyllostachys nigra & cultivars *33*, 40, 194, 247
Physalis alkekengi 52, 69
Physocarpus opulifolius & cultivars *50*, 74, 81, 138, 324, 352
'Dart's Gold' 46, **74**, 95
Physostegia virginiana & cultivars 167, 169, 285
Picea pungens & cultivars 37, 74, 95, 205
'Globosa' **74**
Pendula Group 47, **74**
Pieris & cultivars 31
formosa & cultivars **75**, *84*
japonica & cultivars **75**
Pilosella aurantiaca 403
Pimpinella major 'Rosea' *391*
Pinus mugo & cultivars 35
'Winter Gold' *24*, **75**
Piptanthus nepalensis 142
Pittosporum & cultivars 24, 58
tenuifolium & cultivars 76, 275, 315, 372
'Irene Paterson' **76**
'Tom Thumb' **76**, *349*
Plantago
lanceolata 'Golden Spears' 315, 332, 341
major 'Rubrifolia' *244*
Plecostachys serphyllifolia 369, *404*
Plectranthus
argentatus 210, 281, 314, 338, 362, 365, 389, 391, 393, **397**, 398
forsteri 'Marginatus' 401
madagascariensis 'Variegated Mintleaf' *382*
Pleioblastus auricomus 30, 51, 69, **76**, 246
Plumbago auriculata *123*
Polemonium
archibaldiae 275
caeruleum & cultivars 93, 157, 230, **275**, 388
foliosissimum 77
Polygonatum *175*
fucatum 306
× *hybridum* *81*
Polystichum setiferum & cultivars 33, 34, 43, *204*, *263*, 275, **276**, 287, *306*
Populus alba 'Richardii' 77, 225, 282, 368
Potentilla & cultivars 24, *61*, 164, *165*, *364*
anserina *264*
aurea *364*
'Etna' **276**
fruticosa & cultivars 45, 54, 59, 60, 77, 94, 99, 141, 158, *161*, 200, 209, 216, 270, 274, *285*, 323, 355
nepalensis & cultivars *163*, *176*
'Miss Willmott' 154, **276**
recta 157
Primula & cultivars 67, 241, 277
bulleyana 313
Candelabra *180*, 278
Inshriach hybrids 194, 219, 223, **277**
'Rowallane Rose' 244, **278**
capitata 249
denticulata & cultivars 305, 313, 323
elatior **277**, 315
florindae 246, 252, 264
japonica & cultivars 82, 180, 243, 273, **278**, 330
polyanthus *18*, 51, *51*, 163, 198, 241, 279, 297, 298, 320, 335
'Guinevere' 82, 196, 206, **277**, 279, 304
rosea 262
sikkimensis 277
veris 71, 182, 198, **279**, 298, 304, 336, 388
vialii *246*
vulgaris & cultivars 17, 204, 237, 279, 298, *304*, *305*, 311, 319, 321, 336, 341
Prunus & cultivars 31, 35, 78, *78*, 114, 333
cerasifera & cultivars 95, 108, 114, 118, 126, 140, *141*, *165*, *214*
× *cistena* *65*, 83, 347, 373
glandulosa 'Alba Plena' 107, 113, 319
mume 'Omoi-no-mama' 35
padus 'Watereri' 63
pendula & cultivars 35
'Pendula Rosea' 35, **78**
Sato-zakura Group **78**
spinosa 'Purpurea 81, 91, 107, 109, 116, 117, 118
× *subhirtella* & cultivars 78, 311
tenella 'Fire Hill' 305
Pseudopanax lessonii 'Purpureus' 76
Pulmonaria & cultivars 67, 83, *89*, *195*, *198*, 320, 331, 336, 338, *341*
angustifolia & cultivars *90*, 279, 333, 335
'Lewis Palmer' 47, *82*, **279**, 313, *337*, 343
officinalis & cultivars *333*, 353
rubra 'David Ward' *273*
saccharata & cultivars 82, 112, 180, 246, 277, **279**, 290
Pulsatilla vulgaris 277
Puschkinia scilloides & cultivars 330, **339**
Pyracantha & cultivars 28, 38, 68, 79, *96*, *120*, 128
angustifolia **79**
atalantioides 'Aurea' 128
coccinea & cultivars **79**, 124
rogersiana f. *flava* 128
Pyrus
communis 'Beech Hill' 31
elaeagnifolia 79
salicifolia 'Pendula' **79**, 96, *107*, 123, 140, *157*, 219, 263

Q
Quercus ilex *357*

R
Ranunculus
aconitifolius 'Flore Pleno' 335
acris *257*
bulbosus 'F.M. Burton' 313, 355
ficaria & cultivars *18*, 89, 199, 244, 304, 308, 331, *332*, 340, 344
repens var. *pleniflorus* 257
Rehmannia elata *167*, *217*, 244, **280**, 377, *390*
Rhamnus alaternus 'Argenteovariegata' 145, 158, *182*
Rheum palmatum & cultivars *345*, 387
Rhodiola rosea *195*
Rhodochiton atrosanguineus *124*
Rhododendron (including *Azalea*) 17, 24, 25, *25*, 75, **80–5**, 248
'Albatross Townhill White' 37
'Amethyst' 81, **81**
'Amoenum' *269*
arboreum 75
augustinii 35, 76
auriculatum 80
austrinum 41
Blinklicht Group 29, **81**, 250
'Blue Diamond' 62
'Blue Peter' **81**, 244
calendulaceum 79
campylocarpum **82**
'Chanticleer' *85*
'Christmas Cheer' 35
Cilpinense Group *35*, **82**, 279
'Coccineum Speciosum' 73, 76
dauricum 78
'Delicatissimum' 325
'Dora Amateis' 34
'Elizabeth Lockhart' 81, 82
Exbury *26*
'Fabia' 81, 84
'Fandango' 29, **82**, 83
fastigiatum 81
'Gloria Mundi' 75
'Glowing Embers' 351
'Golden Torch' 75
hippophaeoides **83**, 237
'Habashan' 83
impeditum 81
'Irene Koster' 99
'Kirin' **83**, 247
'Klondyke' 84
'Linda' **83**
lutescens 'Bagshot Sands' 35
luteum 52, 79, **84**, 92, 130, 244, 280
macabeanum 37, 80
'May Day' 52, **84**
× *mucronatum* 96
mucronulatum 78, 96
'Narcissiflorum' 76, 230, 253, 278
orbiculare **85**
'Palestrina' 241
'Persil' 30, 63
'Polar Bear' 80, 264
'Praecox' 47
pseudochrysanthum **85**
quinquefolium 49
'Rex' 80
russatum 81
'Sarled' 28, 74
schlippenbachii 35, 67, 78
Shilsonii Group 80
'Spek's Brilliant' **85**
'Surrey Heath' 330
viscosum 70
williamsianum 67, *83*
'Yellow Hammer' 62
Rhus
× *pulvinata* & cultivars 86, 205
Autumn Lace Group **86**, 90, 192, 203, 213, 225, 265
typhina & cultivars 49, 52, 69, 79
Ribes
alpinum 'Aureum' 344
× *gordonianum* 139, 335
sanguineum & cultivars 52, **86**, 107, 113, 124, *236*, 305
'Brocklebankii' **86**, 334
Ricinus communis & cultivars 266, 369, *371*, 373, 384, 397
'Carmencita' 314, 362, 363, 364, 367, 387, *394*, **397**
Robinia pseudoacacia 'Frisia' 25, **87**, 110, 128, *286*, *301*
Rodgersia 15, *29*
aesculifolia 356
pinnata & cultivars 201, 213, 243, *243*, 258, 262, 264, 272, 277, **280**
podophylla *213*, *258*, 265, **280**
Romneya californica 65
Rosa 15, 16, 17, 96, 102, 103, **132–71**, *224*
Climbing and Rambler roses **138–45**
Ground Cover roses **170–1**
Hybrid Teas & Floribundas **162–7**
larger species & larger modern Shrub roses **152–61**
old Shrub roses **146–51**
smaller species & smaller modern Shrub roses **168–9**
'Albertine' 131, **138**, *139*, 183
'Alchymist' 79
'Aloha' *197*
Altissimo 105
Amber Queen 326
'American Pillar' 138, **139**, 382
Anne Harkness *162*
'Arthur de Sansal' 147
Avalanche **163**, 391
'Ballerina' 60
banksiae
var. *banksiae* 139
'Lutea' 36, 94, 114, **139**
'Lutescens' 139
var. *normalis* 139
Benjamin Britten 239
'Blairii Number Two' *145*
'Blanche Double de Coubert' 79
'Bleu Magenta' *136*
Bonica 60, **152**, 254
'Botany Bay' *136*
'Brenda Colvin' 108, **140**
'Buff Beauty' 99, 125, 126, **153**, 186, 228, 232, 283, 373
'Carmenetta' 99, 124, **153**, 189
'Cécile Brunner' 168, 210

'Cerise Bouquet' 33, 72, 124, 127, **153**
'Charles de Mills' **146**, 188, 194, 250, 261, 269, 273
'Chinatown' 46, 162, **163**, 254, 267
'Climbing Iceberg' 36, 117, 126, 127
'Climbing Madame Caroline Testout' 112
'Climbing Paul Lédé' 61, **140**, 223, 291
'Climbing Pompon de Paris' 110
'Complicata' 98, 377, **154**, 270
'Constance Spry' 124, **140**, 144
'Cooperi' 114
'Cornelia' *243*
'Crown Princess Margareta' 267
'De Rescht' **147**, 225, 274, 326, 392
'Doctor W. Van Fleet' 143
'Easlea's Golden Rambler' **141**, 202
elegantula 'Persetosa' 43, 71, **168**, 407
Elina 46, 61
English Garden 328
'Europeana' **163**, 276, 371
Evelyn Fison 32, **164**, 258
'Excellenz von Schubert' **154**
'Eyepaint' *135*
'Fantin-Latour' 28, 45, *147*, **147**, 188, 208, 376, 377
'Felicia' 33, *77*, **154**, 183, 196, 214
'Félicité Perpétue' 140
filipes 138
'Kiftsgate' **141**
× *fortuneana* 36, 63, 95, **141**, 231
× *francofurtana* 'Empress Josephine' **147**, 261, 363
'François Juranville' 126, 127
'Frensham' 96, 122, 123, 162, **164**, 183, 210, 247, 262, *371*, 389
'Frühlingsgold' 66, 348
gallica
var. *officinalis 111*, *350*
'Versicolor' **148**, 150, 228, 261, 390
'Geranium' 130, **155**, *235*, *259*, 265, 372, *374*, 394
Gertrude Jekyll *269*
glauca 33, 70, 117, 152, 153, **155**, 178, 197, 207, 225, 241, 246, *255*, 326, 327, *329*, 355, *391*, 392
'Gloire de Dijon' *113*
'Golden Wings' 54, 77, 79
'Goldfinch' 126
Grace 236, 239
Graham Thomas 61, 65, **156**, 182, 186, 209, 234, 260, 324
'Grevillei' 142
'Gruss an Aachen' **165**, 377
× *harisonii* 'Harison's Yellow' 36
'Helen Knight' 32, **157**, 249, 269, 270, 307, 378
helenae 68
Heritage *228*
'Hermosa' *210*
'Highdownensis' **157**, 191, 391
Iceberg 55, 60, 65, 79, 109, 162, **165**, 202, 210, 227, 389
Immensee 110
'Indigo' 147
'Karlsruhe' 117, **142**
'Kathleen Harrop' 150
× *kordesii* 142
'La Vie de Bruxelles' *149*
'Lavender Lassie' 79, 111, **157**
'Leverkusen' 108, 110, 127
Lilli Marleen **165**, *238*
'Madame Alfred Carrière' 36, 126
'Madame Grégoire Staechelin' 104
'Madame Knorr' 147
'Madame Pierre Oger' 32, **149**
'Maigold' 38, 126, **158**, 252, 253, 254, 283
'Manning's Blush' 43
'Marchesa Boccella' 147
Mary Rose *165*
'Mermaid' 36, 112, 121, **142**
'Mevrouw Nathalie Nypels' 53
Molineux 167
moyesii 152
'Mrs Oakley Fisher' *404*
multiflora 108, 138, **142**, 152, 377
'Narrow Water' 144
'Nevada' 71, **158**
'New Dawn' 71, **143**
News *108*
'Nozomi' **170**, 200, 225
nutkana 'Plena' 71
× *odorata*
'Mutabilis' **149**, 292
'Pseudindica' 116
Pat Austin 167
'Paul Noël' 126
'Pax' 69
Peach Blossom **159**, 263, 288
'Penelope' **159**, 185, 377
pimpinellifolia 168, *386*
'Grandiflora' 37, 50, 198
Pink Bells **171**, 189, 241, 263, 284
Flower Carpet 64
'Pink Perpétué 124, **144**, 391
Pink Symphony *135*
primula 44, 63, 107, 113
'Prince Charles' **149**, 184, 300
'Prosperity' 58
'Rambling Rector' *140*, **144**
'Raubritter' **169**, 390
'Reine des Centifeuilles' **150**, 243
'Reine Victoria' 110, 149
'Robin Hood' **159**
'Rosemary Rose' *32*
'Roseriae de l'Haÿ' 44, **160**, 262
rugosa 131, **160**, 285, 373
'Alba' 160
'Rubra' 160
'Sally Holmes' 77, **161**
'Sander's White Rambler' 46, 87, 116, **145**
'Seagull' 140, **145**, *200*
'Sophie's Perpetual' 117, **145**
'Splendens' 140
Suffolk **171**
Super Dorothy 109, 111, 112, 118, 119
Super Excelsa 118
Surrey 31, **171**
Sweet Dream 125, **169**, 240, 318
'The Fairy **166–7**, 225
'Tuscany Superb' 99, *148*, **150**, 250, 261, 390, 400
'Vanity' *154*
'Wedding Day' *136*
Westerland **167**, 238, *392*
wichurana 138
xanthina 107, 113
'Canary Bird' 323
f. *hugonis* 36, 37
'Yesterday' 60, 162, **167**, 210, 280
'Zéphirine Drouhin' **150–1**
Roscoea cautleyoides & cultivars 206, **281**
Rosmarinus officinalis & cultivars 25, 42, 54, **88**, 89, 90, 189, 196, 218, 250, 252, 259, *289*, 318
Rubus & cultivars 63
cockburnianus 33
'Goldenvale' *46*, 69, **89**, 182, *223*, 351
microphyllus 'Variegatus' 348
thibetanus 30, 40, **89**, 90
Rudbeckia & cultivars 77, 86, 157, 192, 289, *365*
fulgida
var. *deamii 193*, *207*, 266, **281**, 282, 283, *397*
'Herbstsonne' 40, 160, 236, 281, **282**, *389*
hirta & cultivars *15*, 209, *362*, **398**, 402, 407
maxima 282
Rumex flexuosus 302
Ruta graveolens & cultivars 89, 145, 169, 329, 350, 352
'Jackman's Blue' **89**, 179, 221, 259, 315, *321*

S
Salix
aegyptiaca 52
alba & cultivars 96, 109, 111, 119, 349
var. *vitellina* & cultivars **90**, 121
daphnoides 'Aglaia' 35
elaeagnos subsp. *angustifolia* 104, 107, 117, 119
exigua 253, 391
hastata 'Wehrhahnii' *288*
× *rubens* & cultivars **90**
Salpiglossis & cultivars *362*
Royale Series 314, **398**, 401
Salvia 26, 136, 174, *174*
aethiopis 145
chamaedryoides 64
coccinea & cultivars 266, 399
'Lady in Red' 234, 375, 379, *384*, *395*, **399**, *400*, 405
farinacea & cultivars 363, 364, 369, *383*, 388, 389, 395, 398, **400**, 404, 405
greggii & cultivars 73, 341
guaranitica 155, 383
lavandulifolia 38, 72, *223*
lyrata 'Burgundy Bliss' 168
nemorosa & cultivars 146, 165, 170, 178, 209, 221, *221*, 230, 280, **282**
officinalis & cultivars *34*, 54, *54*, 56, *64*, 89, 183, 190, *229*, 315, 327, 350, 351, 352
'Purpurascens' *24*, *33*, *34*, *55*, 56, 64, *86*, *88*, **90**, 146, 170, 189, 196, 229, 268, 312, 353, *384*, 406
patens & cultivars 73, 155, *318*, *327*, *374*
pratensis & cultivars 179, **283**
sclarea 147, 400
var. *turkestanica 392*
'Vatican White' 378, **400**
splendens & cultivars 362, *369*, 395, 399, **400**, 402, *405*
× *superba* & cultivars 179, 192, *217*, 255, **283**, 284
× *sylvestris* & cultivars 283
'Mainacht' **283**, 292
tenuissima 185
verticillata 'Purple Rain' 150, 171, *365*
viridis & cultivars *363*, *398*
Sambucus
nigra & cultivars 29, 37, **91**, 130, 146, 181, 209, 234, 282, 287, 334, 355, 375, 377, *377*, 391
racemosa 'Plumosa Aurea' *389*
Sanguisorba tenuifolia 'Alba' **284**
Santolina
chamaecyparissus & cultivars 88, **92**, 124
pinnata & cultivars *13*, *176*, 336
rosmarinifolia 92
Saponaria officinalis 'Rosea Plena' 157, 159
Sarcococca
confusa 34, 67, 96, *307*
hookeriana var. *humilis* 236
Sasa veitchii 194
Saxifraga & cultivars *20*, 229
exarata subsp. *moschata* 349
fortunei 256, 291
granulata 212
umbrosa 319
× *urbium* 136, 341
Scabiosa & cultivars 167
atropurpurea 'Blue Cockade' 380
Butterfly Blue 200, **284**, 309
Scaevola aemula & cultivars 376, 382, **401**
Schizophragma hydrangeoides 130, 246
'Roseum' 122, **130**
Schizostylis & cultivars 53
coccinea 'Major' 43, 203, **284**
Scilla 297
bifolia & cultivars 305, **340**
mischtschenkoana & cultivars 337, **341**
siberica & cultivars 28, 42, 47, *180*, 262, 277, 304, *305*, 310, *315*, **341**
Scrophularia
auriculata 'Variegata' 353
buergeriana 'Lemon and Lime' 158
Sedum & cultivars 175, *288*, 302
'Bertram Anderson' 53, 220, **285**
'Herbstfreude' 77, *160*, *188*, *198*, 205, 218, *228*, 284, **285**, *302*
spathulifolium 'Purpureum' 321
spectabile & cultivars 190, *203*, *235*, **285**
telephium & cultivars 55, 64, 87, 171, *207*, **286**, *371*, *388*, 405, *405*
Selinum wallichianum 142
Senecio
cineraria & cultivars 167, *189*, *210*, 362, 363, 393, 395, 396, 397, 400, 405
viravira 55, *73*, 139, *185*, *380*
Sequoia sempervirens 'Cantab' 37
Seriphidium nutans 187
Shibataea kumasasa 72
Sidalcea & cultivars 157, 159
candida 165, 171
Silene
coeli-rosa Angel Series 405
dioica & cultivars *135*, *157*, *241*, 257, 350
Silybum marianum 150
Sisyrinchium striatum & cultivars *13*, *176*, 181, 216, 238, **287**, 292, 355
Skimmia japonica 'Rubella' *48*, 75, **92**, 274, 307, 366
Smilacena racemosa 50, 206, **287**
Smilax aspera 124
Smyrnium perfoliatum 81, 82, 323, 352, 355, **401**
Solanum
crispum 'Glasnevin' 120, *144*
laxum 123
Solenostemon & cultivars 338, 365, 366, 375, 397, 398, *398*, 401, 402, 403
scutellarioides & cultivars 122, *338*, 341, **401**, 403, 407
Solidago & cultivars 17, *162*, *188*
'Crown of Rays' **287**
× *Solidaster luteus* 157
Sorbaria sorbifolia 193
Sorbus & cultivars 49, 92, *96*
'Joseph Rock' 68, **92**
vilmorinii 69, **93**
Sparrmannia africana 387
Spartium junceum 18, *19*, 54, **93**, 372
Spiraea & cultivars 36, 86, *114*, *158*
canescens 71
cantoniensis 70
japonica & cultivars 37, **93**, 193, 195, *211*, 227, *275*, 300, 318, 319, 323, 332, 334, 343, 344, *349*, 388
nipponica & cultivars 94
'Snowmound' **94**, 197
thunbergii 'Mount Fuji' 353
× *vanhouttei* & cultivars 305, 330
Stachys 136, *174*
byzantina & cultivars *159*, 170, *208*, 241, 275, **288**, 292, *302*, *311*, 315, 327, 331, 346, *352*, 378, 388
citrina 54
coccinea 167, *366*
macrantha & cultivars *108*, 111, *116*, 147, *186*, *276*
Stephanandra
incisa 72
tanakae 29, 33, 41
Sternbergia 298
lutea 357
Stipa
arundinacea 140, *293*
calamagrostis 205, 207, **288**, 291
capillata 178, 180, 287, **289**
gigantea 260, 267
tenuissima 88, 192, 283, 284, *289*, 367
Stokesia laevis & cultivars 157, 159, 169
Strobilanthes attenuata 157
Styrax japonicus 'Pink Chimes' 72
Symphytum
caucasicum 46, 84
'Goldsmith' *52*, 273, **289**, 319, 349
ibericum & cultivars *182*, 332, *338*
× *uplandicum* 'Variegatum' 89
Syringa 24
× *josiflexa* 'Bellicent' 72
meyeri var. *spontanea* 'Palibin' 43, 305
oblata 78
× *persica* 'Alba' 44
× *prestoniae* 'Elinor' 71
vulgaris & cultivars 32, 36, 46, 63, **94**, 95, 98, 99, 114, *114*, 124
'Charles Joly' **95**, 131, *141*

T
Tagetes
erecta 400
patula & cultivars 164, 326, 371, **402**, 403
'Striped Marvel' 191, 234, 254, 366, 398, **402**
tenuifolia & cultivars *198*, 384, 385, *407*
Tamarix
ramorissima 'Pink Cascade' 217
tetrandra **95**
Tanacetum
macrophyllum 156
parthenium & cultivars *178*, 186, *200*, *219*, *249*, *255*, *270*, 319, 328, *329*
vulgare 'Isla Gold' 157, 319
Taxus baccata & cultivars 15, *18*, *19*, 34, 68, *94*, **95**, *130*, *157*, *254*
Tellima grandiflora & cultivars 212, 228, **290**, 301
Tetrapanax papyrifer 232, 386
Teucrium
fruticans 42, 267
hircanicum 147
Thalictrum 174
aquilegiifolium 71, *377*
delavayi & cultivars 65, 157, 200, 266, 283, 375
flavum & cultivars 66, *108*, *164*, 283, 351, 391
Thuja
occidentalis 'Rheingold' 337, 348
plicata 'Atrovirens' 37
Thunbergia alata 393, 394, 403
Thymus
× *citriodorus* 'Silver Queen' 321, 349
vulgaris 'Silver Posie' 315
Tiarella
cordifolia 81, 256, *290*
trifoliata 212
wherryi & cultivars 41, 246
Tigridia pavonia **341**, 406
Tithonia rotundifolia & cultivars 65, 77, 117, 164, 370, 381, 385, **402**
Tolpis barbata 122, **403**
Torenia Pink Moon 401
Trachelospermum jasminoides 130
Trachymene coerulea 380
Trachystemon orientalis 332
Tradescantia Andersoniana Group 'Purple Dome' 249
Tricyrtis formosana 329
Trifolium repens 'Purpurascens' 321
Trillium
chloropetalum **290**
grandiflorum **290**, 305
sessile 333
Trollius
× *cultorum* & cultivars 85, 213, 253, 323, 352
europaeus 257
Tropaeolum
majus & cultivars 117, *167*, *371*
Alaska Series *367*, *402*, **403**
peregrinum 103, 123, *123*
speciosum 60, 95, 123, **130**
tricolor 105
tuberosum & cultivars **130**
Tulipa 16, *96*, *219*, *296*, 297, *297*, 298, *298*, **342–55**
'Abu Hassan' **343**, 378
'Angélique' 48, **343**
'Apeldoorn' **343**, 378
'Apricot Beauty' 85, *314*, **344**
'Ballerina' 185, 272, **344**, 380, 391
'Black Swan' *13*
'Blenda' **345**
'Bleu Aimable' *319*
'Blue Parrot' *301*
'Burgundy' 86, 241, **345**, 378, 388
'China Pink' **345**, 388
'Christmas Cheer' *342*
clusiana 196, 304, **346**
var. *chrysantha* 182, 346, *346*
'Tubergen's Gem' 346
'Cynthia' 346
'Cordell Hull' **346**, 388
'Couleur Cardinal' 163
'Elegant Lady' 99, 201, **347**, 378, 380, 391
'Fantasy' 185, **347**
Forerunner Series *342*
Fosteriana Group 52
'Gold Medal' *13*
'Golden Artist' 44, 157
'Golden Oxford' *18*, 86, 198, **348**
'Greuze' **348**, 378
'Jewel of Spring' 18, 93, **349**
kaufmanniana 341
'Keizerskroon' *320*
linifolia Batalinii Group 315, 330, **349**
'Apricot Jewel' 349
'Bright Gem' 349
'Bronze Charm' 349
'Red Gem' 349
'Yellow Jewel' 349
'Maja' 37
'Mariette' *350*, **350**
'Marjolein' 350, **350**
'Maywonder' 305
'Monte Carlo' 49
'Negrita' **350**, 352, 378
'Orange Emperor' 335
'Orange Favourite' 37, 219, **351**, 352, 353
'Orange Wonder' **352**, 401
'Palestrina' 189, 262, 288, **352**, 388
praestans 'Unicum' 304
'Prinses Irene' 73, 198, **352**
'Queen of Night' *32*, 95, *241*, *345*, *351*, **353**, 378, 407
'Queen of Sheba' 44, *44*
'Red Shine' 241, 301, **353**
saxatilis 45
sprengeri 306
'Spring Green' 36, 44, 75, 212, 220, 323, 338, **353**, 407
'Sweet Harmony' 37, 263, **354–5**, 378
turkestanica 47
'West Point' *18*, *262*, **355**
'White Triumphator' *18*, 36, 202,236, **355**
Tweedia caerulea **403**

U
Ulmus minor 'Dicksonii' **96**
Uncinia egmontiana 159, 337, 349

V
Vaccinium vitis-idaea 'Koralle' 28, 35
Valeriana 17
phu 'Aurea' 249, 304, 319, 330, 340
Veratrum nigrum 277, **291**
Verbascum & cultivars 108, 142, 149, 163, *164*, 174, *178*, 198, 283
'Helen Johnson' *140*, 265, **291**
Verbena & cultivars 274, *274*, 275, *366*, 371, *376*, 377, 379, 382, *389*, 393, 394
bonariensis 15, 125, 152, 192, *213*, *271*,

328, 364, 367, *368, 372*, 373, *400*, **404**
hastata 381
'Kemerton' *382*, 395, **404**
'Lawrence Johnston' 274, 286, 388, 389, 405
noveboracensis 152
peruviana 'Alba' 365
rigida & cultivars 357, 363, 385, *399*, *400*, **405**
'Silver Anne' 309, 310, 363, 394, **405**
'Sissinghurst' *341*, **406**
tenuisecta 366
Veronica & cultivars 170
austriaca subsp. *teucrium* & cultivars 224, 233, *287*, **292**, 391
peduncularis 'Georgia Blue' 334, 349
prostrata & cultivars 292
spicata & cultivars 147, *292*, 357, 384
Veronicastrum virginicum album 263

Viburnum
× *bodnantense* & cultivars 78, **96**, 311
× *burkwoodii* & cultivars 78, **96–7**, 305
carlesii 335, 353
davidii 72, **98**
opulus & cultivars *379*
'Roseum' 36, *44*, 70, **98**, 107, 117
plicatum 'Mariesii' *54*, 244
rhytidophyllum **99**, 142
sargentii 'Onondaga' 143, 147, 355
tinus 'Eve Price' 89, 90
Vinca 175
major & cultivars *77*, *90*, *107*, *321*, 323
minor & cultivars 67, 225, 307, 311, 312, 313, 317, 321, 330, 336
Viola & cultivars *18*, *71*, *77*, 136, *168*, *179*, *220*, *228*, *276*, 289, 292, *302*, 310, 320, 330, 345,350, 407

aetolica 388
cornuta & cultivars 148, *167*, 178, 182, *230*, *303*, 345, 350, *363*
'Huntercombe Purple' *122*, 218, 262, **292**, 302, 331
'Nellie Britton' **292**
riviniana Purpurea Group 310
sororia 'Freckles' *233*, *244*, 336
tricolor & cultivars 196, **407**
× *wittrockiana* Universal Series 366
Vitis & cultivars 69, 105, 128
coignetiae 102, 131, 141, 193
vinifera & cultivars 111
'Purpurea' *39*, 104, 105, 116, 118, 119, 120, 130, **131**, *138*, 140, 141, 144, *160*

W
Watsonia & cultivars 53, **356**

fourcadei 293, 356, *356*
meriania 390
Weigela & cultivars 99, 145, *153*, 324, 329, 347
florida & cultivars 99
'Foliis purpureis' **99**, 142, 153, 325, 363
'Florida Variegata' **99**, 225
Wisteria 63, 102, 103, 114
floribunda & cultivars 63, *102*, 114, 141
sinensis & cultivars 95, 114, **131**, 139

X
Xanthophthalmum segetum 364
Xanthorhiza simplicissima 49, 69

Y
Yucca 14

aloifolia 293
elephantipes 293
filamentosa 352
filifera 292
flaccida & cultivars 292, 293
'Golden Sword' 66, 239, **293**
gloriosa & cultivars *205*, *221*, 293, 356

Z
Zantedeschia aethiopica & cultivars **356**
Zephyranthes **357**
atamasca 357, *357*
candida 309, 357
grandiflora 357
rosea 357
Zigadenus elegans 357
Zinnia & cultivars 40, 281, 375, *393*, 402, 407, *407*
elegans & cultivars 373, 394, 402
'Persian Carpet Mixed' **407**

PHOTOGRAPHIC ACKNOWLEDGMENTS

All photographs have been taken by Andrew Lawson, with the exception of the following.

Key: a above, b below, l left, r right

Adrian Bloom 95br, 209br, 222bl, 234ar; Jonathan Buckley 29r, 33ar, 46al, 53b, 218a, 56b, 190, 223br, 243r, 265b, 271b, 278a, 279br, 288b, 293, 309a & br, 335bl, 344r, 373br, 397bl, 401br; Eric Crichton 135b, 236bl, 330al, 386al; John Fielding 33al, 35b, 36al, 40a, 44al & r, 47a, 48l & r, 49ar, 52b, 53al, 54b, 57al, 59b, 64al, 71al, 72 al & r, 76ar, 86a, 90bl, 99 a l, 99 al & r, 106b, 115, 123b, 124a, 125b, 126b, 127al, 130 al, 138, 142b, 149a, 159al, 165ar, 170, 175, 178a & bl, 180b, 181l, 182b, 185b, 188a & b, 195ar, 200ar, 201br, 205a & b, 207bl, 214b, 215a & bl, 219a, 220bl, 228b, 233al, 237b, 239l, 240, 241al, 243l, 245, 250a, 252a, 253br, 260b, 267br, 269br, 272ar, 273l, 274al & r, 280b, 281bl, 289b, 296, 306ar, 307b, 309bl, 310al & r, 312b, 318bl & r, 319b, 320a, 321al & r, 325r, 328a, 329r, 330br, 332a, 334r, 335ar, 337, 338ar & b, 340, 344l, 345a, 356al, 365br, 398 b, 296, 306ar, 307bl, 362b, 370b, 376br, 378b, 380al & r, 382ar & b, 383, 389a, 395al & r, 396r, 398b, 401br, 402al &b, 403al; Garden Picture Library photo David Askham 161, 171ar, Lynne Brotchie 270al, Brian Carter 58br, 157al, Christi Carter 154ar, 379bl, 384b, Eric Crichton 37br, Ron Evans 322, John Glover 210ar, 120b, 210ar, 241b, Sunniva Harte 1789ar, 291a, Clive Nichols 136, Joanne Pavia 223bl, Howard Rice 142al, 206r, J S Sira 14, 31b, 140a, 187a, 382al, Juliette Wade 394br, Mel Watson 377ar, Didier Willery 44b, 379br; John Glover 145al, 287ar; Harpur Garden Library photo Jerry Harpur 176, Marcus Harpur 270 bl; Holt Studios International photo Rosemary Mayer 12a & b; W Anthony Lord 13b, 15a & b, 16a & b, 17, 20, 28ar, 37bl, 38r, 39ar, 42l, 46b, 50a & b, 56 ar, 58a, 59al & r, 60ar, 64b, 72b, 77ar, 79 ar, 80l, 86bl & r, 91b, 93 ar, 94a, 96r, 98a, 102, 105r, 108br, 109a & b, 110l & br, 112a, 116a & br, 118l, 119a, 123al, 130 ar, 131l, 132-133, 134, 137, 150b, 154b, 155b, 158l, 168, 174, 180ar, 182ar, 184b, 185al, 189b, 191al, 193al, 194al &b, 195al & b, 198a, 199r, 200al & b, 201a & bl, 208b, 209bl, 216a, b & bl, 217bl, 218bl & r, 219br, 220br, 221ar, 224a & b, 225a & br, 226ar, 227br, 229br, 230al &b, 234al, 235l, 242, 244bl, 248b, 249b, 252 bl &r, 254bl & r, 255ar, 256a &bl, 257b, 259al & r, 260ar, 262ar, 263al & b, 266ar & b, 268a, 270ar, 271ar, 272b, 273r, 282a & b, 283br, 284al, 287b, 288l, 290l, 297, 298, 299, 307ar, 314l

& r, 315b, 317br, 319a, 328r, 339b, 349b, 350a l, 352a, bl & r, 354, 355a, 357a, 358-9, 361, 363al, 364b, ar & l, 365 bl, 366b, 367r, 368r, 370a, 372bl, 374br, 375, 377bl, 378al, 379a, 380b, 381a, 385l & r, 386ar, 389bl & r, 391bl & r, 392al &r, 393l & r, 396l, 398ar, 399, 400 al & b, 401a & bl, 402ar, 403ar, 405a & br, 407ar & b; Clive Nichols Garden Pictures 26, 49al, Glaisher, Kent 142ar, Wollerton Old Hall, Shropshire 151, Hadspen Garden, Somerset 167a, designer Helen Dillon 177, Copton Ash, Kent 196 al, Wollerton Old Hall, Shropshire 209a, designer Elisabeth Woodhouse 248a, the Prior, Kemerton 372br; Jerry Pavia 30r, 92bl, 191b, 356bl, Photos Horticultural 33ar, 65l & r, 120a, 140b, 144b, 145b, 171b, 210b, 233b; Howard Rice 36ar & b, 45al, 51br, 53ar, 54al, 55r, 62al & b, 70, 71b, 74bl, 77b, 81R, 89ar, 94b, 128b, 159ar, 172-3, 198bl, 231, 235r, 251l, 256ar, 265b, 268br, 269a, 283a, 285al & b, 290ar, 328bl, 335al, 336al &r, 341al; Harry Smith Collection 25b, 39b, 52ar, 305br.

PUBLISHER'S ACKNOWLEDGMENTS

The publishers would like to thank the following for their specialist advice and contributions to the text: Richard Bisgrove, Andi Clevely, Geoff Stebbins, and Alan Toogood. Also, Mary Loebig Giles for her editorial work on this edition.